W9-ABN-272

The Age of Maturity, 1929-1941

Concise Dictionary of American Literary Biography

The Age of Maturity, 1929-1941

A Bruccoli Clark Layman Book
Gale Research Inc. • Book Tower • Detroit, Michigan 48226

Advisory Board for
CONCISE DICTIONARY
OF AMERICAN LITERARY BIOGRAPHY

Matthew J. Bruccoli and Richard Layman, *Editorial Directors*
C. E. Frazer Clark, Jr., *Managing Editor*

Copyright © 1989
GALE RESEARCH INC.
ISBN 0-8103-1820-2

Printed in the United States of America

Published simultaneously in the United Kingdom
by Gale Research International Limited
(An affiliated company of Gale Research Inc.)

Contents

Plan of the Work

The six-volume *Concise Dictionary of American Literary Biography* was developed in response to requests from high school and junior college teachers and librarians, and from small- to medium-sized public libraries, for a compilation of entries from the standard *Dictionary of Literary Biography* chosen to meet their needs and their budgets. The *DLB*, which comprises over ninety volumes as of the end of 1987, is moving steadily toward its goal of providing a history of literature in all languages developed through the biographies of writers. Basic as the *DLB* is, many librarians have expressed the need for a less comprehensive reference work which in other respects retains the merits of *DLB*. The *Concise DALB* provides this resource.

This series was planned by a seven-member advisory board, consisting primarily of secondary school educators, who developed a method of organization and presentation for selected *DLB* entries suitable for high school and beginning college students. Their preliminary plan was circulated to some five thousand school librarians and English teachers, who were asked to respond to the organization of the series and the table of contents. Those responses were incorporated into the plan described here.

Uses for the Concise DALB

Students are the primary audience for the *Concise DALB*. The stated purpose of the standard *DLB* is to make our literary heritage more accessible. *Concise DALB* has the same goal and seeks a wider audience. What the author wrote; what the facts of his life are; a description of his literary works; a discussion of the critical response to his works; and a bibliography of critical works to be consulted for further information: These are the elements of a *Concise DALB* entry.

The first step in the planning process for this series, after identifying the audience, was to contemplate its uses. The advisory board acknowledged that the integrity of *Concise DALB* as a reference book is crucial to its utility. The *Concise DALB* adheres to the scholarly standards established by the parent series. Thus, within the scope of major American literary figures, the *Concise DALB* is a ready reference source of established value, providing reliable biographical and bibliographical information.

It is anticipated that this series will not be confined to uses within the library. Just as *DLB* has been a tool for stimulating students' literary interests in the college classroom—for comparative studies of authors, for example, and, through its ample illustrations, as a means of invigorating literary study—the *Concise DALB* is a primary resource for high school and junior college educators. The series is organized to facilitate lesson planning, and the contextual diagrams (explained below) that introduce each entry are a source of topics for classroom discussion and writing assignments.

Organization

The advisory board further determined that entries from the standard *DLB* should be presented complete—without abridgment. Their feeling was that the utility of the *DLB* format has been proven, and that only minimal changes should be made.

The advisory board further decided that the organization of the *Concise DALB* should be chronological to emphasize the historical development of American literature. Each volume is devoted to a single historical period and includes the most significant literary figures from all genres who were active during that time. Thus, the volume that includes modern mainstream novelists Saul Bellow, Bernard Malamud, and John Cheever will also include poets who were active at the same time—such as Allen Ginsberg, Lawrence Ferlinghetti, and John Berryman—and dramatists who were their contemporaries—such as Tennessee Williams, Arthur Miller, and William Inge. It should be noted that the volume of the *Concise DALB* that includes these authors comprises thirty-six entries, while the volumes in the standard *DLB* covering the same period include some four hundred author biographies. The *Concise DALB* limits itself to major figures, but it provides the same coverage of those figures as the *DLB* does.

The six period volumes of the *Concise DALB* are *Colonization to the American Renaissance, 1640-1865; Realism, Naturalism, and Local Color, 1865-*

1917; The Twenties, 1917-1929; The Age of Maturity, 1929-1941; The New Consciousness, 1941-1968; Broadening Views, 1968-1987. The sixth volume will also contain a comprehensive index by subjects and proper names to the entire *Concise DALB.* (As in the standard *DLB* series, there is a cumulative index to author entries in each *Concise DALB* volume.)

Form of Entry

The form of entry in the *Concise DALB* is substantially the same as in the standard series, with the following alterations:

1) Each entry has been updated to include a discussion of works published since the standard entry appeared and to reflect recent criticism and research of interest to the high school audience.

2) The secondary bibliography for each entry has been selected to include those books and articles of particular interest and usefulness to high school and junior college students. In addition, the secondary bibliography has been annotated to assist students in assessing whether a reference will meet their needs.

3) Each entry is preceded by a "contextual diagram"–a graphic presentation of the places, literary influences, personal relationships, literary movements, major themes, cultural and artistic influences, and social and economic forces associated with the author. This chart allows students– and teachers–to place the author in his literary and social context at a glance.

It bears repeating that the *Concise DALB* is restricted to major American literary figures. It is anticipated that users of this series will find it advantageous to consult the standard *DLB* for information about those writers omitted from the *Concise DALB* whose significance to contemporary readers may have faded but whose contribution to our cultural heritage remains meaningful.

Comments about the series and suggestions about how to improve it are earnestly invited.

A Note to Students

The purpose of the *Concise DALB* is to enrich the study of literature. In their various ways, writers react in their works to the circumstances of their lives, the events of their time, and the culture that envelops them (which are represented on the contextual diagrams that precede each *Concise DALB* entry). Writers provide a way to see and understand what they have observed and experienced. Besides being inherently interesting, biographies of writers provide a basic perspective on literature.

Concise DALB entries start with the most important facts about writers: What they wrote. We strongly recommend that you also start there. The chronological listing of an author's works is an outline for the examination of his or her career achievement. The biographies that follow set the stage for the presentation of the works. Each of the author's important works and the most respected critical evaluations of them are discussed in *Concise DALB*. If you require more information about the author or fuller critical studies of the author's works, the annotated references section at the end of the entry will guide you.

Illustrations are an integral element of *Concise DALB* entries. Photographs of the author are reminders that literature is the product of a writer's imagination; facsimiles of the author's working drafts are the best evidence available for understanding the act of composition–the author in the process of refining his work and acting as self-editor; dust jacket and advertisements demonstrate how literature comes to us through the marketplace, which sometimes serves to alter our perceptions of the works.

Literary study is a complex and immensely rewarding endeavor. Our goal is to provide you with the information you need to make that experience as rich as possible.

Acknowledgments

This book was produced by Bruccoli Clark Layman, Inc. Karen L. Rood is senior editor for the *Dictionary of Literary Biography* series. Laura Ingram was the in-house editor.

System manager is Robert A. Folts. Art supervisor is Susan Todd. Penney L. Haughton is responsible for layout and graphics. Copyediting supervisor is Joan M. Prince. Typesetting supervisor is Kathleen M. Flanagan. William Adams and Michael D. Senecal are editorial associates. The production staff includes Rowena Betts, Charles D. Brower, Joseph M. Bruccoli, Amanda Caulley, Teresa Chaney, Patricia Coate, Mary Colborn, Sarah A. Estes, Brian A. Glassman, Cynthia Hallman, James W. Hipp, Kathy S. Merlette, Laura Garren Moore, Sheri Beckett Neal, and Virginia Smith. Jean W. Ross is permissions editor.

Walter W. Ross and Jennifer Toth did the library research with the assistance of the reference staff at the Thomas Cooper Library of the University of South Carolina: Daniel Boice, Cathy Eckman, Gary Geer, Cathie Gottlieb, David L. Haggard, Jens Holley, Dennis Isbell, Jackie Kinder, Marcia Martin, Jean Rhyne, Beverly Steele, Ellen Tillett, Carol Tobin, and Virginia Weathers.

The Age of Maturity, 1929-1941

Concise Dictionary of American Literary Biography

Conrad Aiken

This entry was updated by Michael D. Senecal from the entry by Stephen Cummings (University of Western Ontario) in DLB 45, American Poets, 1880-1945.

Places	London Savannah	Boston	Cape Cod
Influences and Relationships	T. S. Eliot George Santayana Harriet Monroe Malcolm Cowley	John Gould Fletcher John Masefield	William Carlos Williams Malcolm Lowry
Literary Movements and Forms	Lyrical Poetry	Literary Criticism	The Novel
Major Themes	The Supernatural Death Greek, Roman, and Egyptian Myth	Human Potential vs. Determinism The Voyage Erotic Love	The Individual vs. the Collective Mind The Quest for Identity
Cultural and Artistic Influences	Freudian Psychology Vaudeville	Classical Symphonies Modern Art	Metaphysical Philosophy
Social and Economic Influences	Censorship	Pacifism	

See also the Aiken entry in DLB 9, American Novelists, 1910-1945.

BIRTH: Savannah, Georgia, 5 August 1889, to William Ford and Anna Potter Aiken.

EDUCATION: A.B., Harvard, 1912.

MARRIAGES: 25 August 1912 to Jessie McDonald (divorced); children: John Kempton, Jane Kempton, Joan Delano. 27 February 1930 to Clarissa Lorenz (divorced). 7 August 1937 to Mary Hoover.

AWARDS: Pulitzer Prize for *Selected Poems*, 1930; Shelley Memorial Award, 1930; Guggenheim Fellowship, 1934; Bryher Award, 1950; National Book Award for *Collected Poems*, 1954; Bollingen Prize in Poetry, 1956; Academy of American Poets Fellowship, 1957; National Institute of Arts and Letters Gold Medal, 1958; Huntington Hartford Foundation Award, 1960; St. Botolph Award, 1965; Brandeis University Creative Arts Medal, 1967; National Medal for Literature, 1969; Poet Laureate of Georgia, 1973.

DEATH: Savannah, Georgia, 17 August 1973.

BOOKS: *Earth Triumphant and Other Tales in Verse* (New York: Macmillan, 1914; London: Macmillan, 1914);
Turns and Movies and Other Tales in Verse (Boston & New York: Houghton Mifflin, 1916; London: Constable/Boston & New York: Houghton Mifflin, 1916);
The Jig of Forslin: A Symphony (Boston: Four Seas, 1916; London: Secker, 1922);
Nocturne of Remembered Spring and Other Poems (Boston: Four Seas, 1917; London: Secker, 1922);
The Charnel Rose, Senlin: A Biography, and Other Poems (Boston: Four Seas, 1918);
Scepticisms: Notes on Contemporary Poetry (New York: Knopf, 1919);
The House of Dust: A Symphony (Boston: Four Seas, 1920);
Punch: The Immortal Liar, Documents in His History (New York: Knopf, 1921; London: Secker, 1921);
Priapus and the Pool (Cambridge, Mass.: Dunster House, 1922);
The Pilgrimage of Festus (New York: Knopf, 1923; London: Secker, 1924);

Conrad Aiken, 1914

Bring! Bring! (London: Secker, 1925); republished as *Bring! Bring! and Other Stories* (New York: Boni & Liveright, 1925);
Senlin: A Biography (London: Leonard & Virginia Woolf at the Hogarth Press, 1925);
Priapus and the Pool and Other Poems (New York: Boni & Liveright, 1925);
Blue Voyage (London: Howe, 1927; New York: Scribners, 1927);
Conrad Aiken, The Pamphlet Poets, edited by Louis Untermeyer (New York: Simon & Schuster, 1928);
Costumes by Eros (New York: Scribners, 1928; London: Cape, 1929);
Prelude, The Poetry Quartos (New York: Random House, 1929);
Selected Poems (New York & London: Scribners, 1929);
John Deth: A Metaphysical Legend, and Other Poems (New York: Scribners, 1930);
Gehenna (New York: Random House, 1930);
The Coming Forth by Day of Osiris Jones (New York: Scribners, 1931);
Preludes for Memnon: or, Preludes to Attitude (New York & London: Scribners, 1931);

And in the Hanging Gardens (Baltimore: Linweave Limited Editions, 1933);

Great Circle (New York: Scribners, 1933; London: Wishart, 1933);

Among the Lost People (New York: Scribners, 1934);

Landscape West of Eden (London: Dent, 1934; New York: Scribners, 1935);

King Coffin (London: Dent, 1935; New York: Scribners, 1935);

Time in the Rock: Preludes to Definition (New York: Scribners, 1936);

A Heart for the Gods of Mexico (London: Secker, 1939);

Conversation: or Pilgrims' Progress (New York: Duell, Sloan & Pearce, 1940); republished as *The Conversation: or Pilgrims' Progress* (London: Phillips & Green, 1940);

And In The Human Heart (New York: Duell, Sloan & Pearce, 1940; London: Staples, 1949);

Brownstone Eclogues and Other Poems (New York: Duell, Sloan & Pearce, 1942);

The Soldier (Norfolk, Conn.: New Directions, 1944; London: Editions Poetry, 1946);

The Kid (New York: Duell, Sloan & Pearce, 1947; London: Lehmann, 1947);

Skylight One: Fifteen Poems (New York: Oxford University Press, 1949; London: Lehmann, 1951);

The Divine Pilgrim (Athens: University of Georgia Press, 1949);

The Short Stories of Conrad Aiken (New York: Duell, Sloan & Pearce, 1950);

Ushant: An Essay (New York: Duell, Sloan & Pearce/ Boston: Little, Brown, 1952; London: Allen, 1963);

Collected Poems (New York: Oxford University Press, 1953; augmented, 1970);

A Letter from Li Po and Other Poems (New York: Oxford University Press, 1955);

Mr. Arcularis: A Play (Cambridge: Harvard University Press, 1957; London: Oxford University Press, 1958);

Sheepfold Hill: Fifteen Poems (New York: Sagamore, 1958);

A Reviewer's ABC: Collected Criticism of Conrad Aiken from 1916 to the Present, edited by Rufus A. Blanshard (New York: Greenwich/ Meridian, 1958; London: Allen, 1961); republished as *Collected Criticism* (London, Oxford & New York: Oxford University Press, 1968);

The Collected Short Stories of Conrad Aiken (Cleveland & New York: World, 1960; London: Heinemann, 1966);

Selected Poems (New York: Oxford University Press, 1961; London, Oxford & New York: Oxford University Press, 1969);

The Morning Song of Lord Zero: Poems Old and New (New York: Oxford University Press, 1963; London: Oxford University Press, 1963);

The Collected Novels of Conrad Aiken: Blue Voyage, Great Circle, King Coffin, A Heart for the Gods of Mexico, Conversation (New York, Chicago & San Francisco: Holt, Rinehart & Winston, 1964);

A Seizure of Limericks (New York, Chicago & San Francisco: Holt, Rinehart & Winston, 1964; London: Allen, 1965);

3 Novels: Blue Voyage/Great Circle/King Coffin (New York, Toronto & San Francisco: McGraw-Hill, 1965; London: Allen, 1965);

Cats and Bats and Things with Wings (New York: Atheneum, 1965);

Preludes: Preludes for Memnon/Time in the Rock (New York: Oxford University Press, 1966; London: Oxford University Press, 1966);

Tom, Sue and the Clock (New York: Collier/ London: Collier-Macmillan, 1966);

Thee: a Poem (New York: Braziller, 1967; London: Inca, 1973);

The Clerk's Journal: Being the Diary of a Queer Man (New York: Eakins Press, 1971);

A Little Who's Zoo of Mild Animals (London: Cape, 1977; New York: Cape/Atheneum, 1977).

OTHER: Thomas Hardy, *Two Wessex Tales*, foreword by Aiken (Boston: Four Seas, 1919);

Modern American Poets, selected, with a preface, by Aiken (London: Secker, 1922); revised contents, with a new preface, by Aiken (New York: Modern Library, 1927); enlarged as *Twentieth Century American Poetry*, with an augmented preface by Aiken (New York: Modern Library, 1945; revised, 1963);

Selected Poems of Emily Dickinson, edited, with a preface, by Aiken (London: Cape, 1924);

American Poetry, 1671-1928: A Comprehensive Anthology, edited, with a preface, by Aiken (New York: Modern Library, 1929); revised and enlarged as *A Comprehensive Anthology of American Poetry* (New York: Modern Library, 1944);

An Anthology of Famous English and American Poetry, edited, with introductions, by Aiken and William Rose Benét (New York: Modern Library, 1945).

Conrad Aiken's long and productive literary career has prompted such descriptions of him as "the buried giant of twentieth-century American writing" (Malcolm Cowley), "the best known unread poet of the twentieth century" (Louis Untermeyer), and appreciations such as "When the tide of aesthetic sterility which is slowly engulfing us has withdrawn, our first great poet will be left. Perhaps he [Aiken] is the man" (William Faulkner). Hayden Carruth has suggested that Aiken's influence had significant impact "in determining, almost while no one was aware of it, the look and sound of the poetry written in our age." While no consensus has been reached, Aiken's thirty volumes of poetry, five novels, dozens of short stories, hundreds of critical articles and reviews, and his autobiography, plus collected and selected editions of poetry, short stories, novels, and criticism, constitute a major and imposing body of work. Translations have appeared in fifteen languages, and adaptations or readings of his work have been presented on radio or television on seventy different occasions between 1936 and 1971, in the United States, Canada, England, and Germany. The argument concerning its value has extended through hundreds of journal articles and reviews of his work and in four full-length treatments by Houston Peterson (1931), Jay Martin (1962), Frederick J. Hoffman (1962), and Reuel Denney (1964); in two Aiken "numbers" of literary journals (*Wake 11*, 1952; *Studies in the Literary Imagination*, 1980); in sixteen Ph.D. dissertations since 1961; and, by implication, in an edition of his letters (1978) and in a recent "confession" by his second wife (1983).

The body of work posed—and poses—a reading problem to critics, which perhaps arose from both the bulk and the nature of its content. In a bibliographical review of Aiken criticism Catherine Harris points out that "Scholars and critics of the nineteen-seventies re-emphasized that Aiken's poetry deserved to be, indeed benefitted from being, considered as a whole," and "Many critics found Aiken's fiction to be a prose version of the poetry." This remarkable sense of integration among both poetry and prose seems to center upon Aiken's notion of the autobiographical. Freud and the apparatus of psychoanalysis are essential to his method, and his theme, as R. P. Blackmur describes it, "is the struggle of the mind which has become permanently aware of itself to

rediscover and unite itself with the world in which it is lodged." The object of Aiken's autobiographical analysis is, then, not merely Aiken-the-man, but Aiken-the-consciousness, by which his work rises above the personal and becomes the record of a pilgrimage in which the reader may share. Such a pilgrimage must be, of necessity, circular in form, for the arrival at one's goal is marked only by an enlargement of consciousness in an ever-changing and at the same time alienating present. That Aiken's life reflects an astonishing symmetry attests, perhaps, to a relentless honesty and to a will to fuse the realms of art and life.

Although Conrad Potter Aiken was born in Savannah, Georgia, in 1889, lived there with his two brothers and one sister until 1901, and died there at the age of eighty-four in 1973, he was not a southerner. Both of his parents were descendants of John Akin, a Scottish Quaker who arrived in America in 1680 and settled in New England. His mother's maiden name was Anna Aiken Potter. Thus her marriage to Dr. William Ford Aiken meant that her married name was a transposition of her maiden name: Anna Aiken Potter became Anna Potter Aiken. "It was just an accident my father came to Savannah. Physician's jobs were hard to find in the North and there was a scarcity of doctors in the South," Conrad Aiken explained in an interview. His maternal grandfather, William James Potter (1829-1893), proved a lifelong influence. Potter was a radical Unitarian minister, who with Ralph Waldo Emerson and a "Colonel Higginson" (probably Thomas Wentworth Higginson) founded the Free Religious Association in 1867. Conrad Aiken later said that he always had with him a copy of his grandfather's collected sermons. He has also said that summer trips to New England were useful to him, as "Shock treatment . . . the milieu so wholly different," but simple transplantation was not to be so shocking as what happened in 1901 when he was eleven.

In his edition of Aiken's *Selected Letters* (1978) Joseph Killorin reports a conversation with Aiken: "On the morning of February 27, 1901, he awoke about seven to hear his father and mother, in their bedroom, quarreling: 'And I heard my father's voice counting: "One, two, three." And a pistol shot, and then another shot. I got out of my bed and walked through the children's bedroom, next to my parents' and where Elizabeth and Kempton and Robert were in their cribs, and opened the folding doors to my parents' room. I had to step over my father's body to go to my mother. But she was dead, her mouth wide open in the act of screaming. I came out, closed the folding doors, told the children to stay in their beds and that the nurse would come to them. I dressed myself, went downstairs and told the cook there had been an accident and to give the children breakfast downstairs, and to keep them in the dining room. Then I walked to the police station a block away and told them my father had shot my mother and himself, and they said: "Who is your father?" And I said: "Dr. Aiken." So they came with me and took command.'" The murder-suicide of his parents dramatically ended his childhood, dissolved completely his life in a family–his brothers and sister were adopted by Frederick Winslow Taylor in Philadelphia, while he was moved to Cambridge to live with his Uncle William Tillinghast where, as he says, "I more or less lost touch with them"– and opened a psychological door through which his pilgrimage in search of self began.

Aiken committed himself early on to writing, producing a handwritten and later typed magazine called the *Story Teller* at the age of thirteen, and writing for and editing the Middlesex School (Concord, Massachusetts) magazine, *Anvil*, between 1904 and his entrance to Harvard in 1907. He was part of the illustrious Harvard classes of 1910-1911, which included Heywood Broun, Stuart Chase, E. E. Cummings, Walter Lippmann, and John Reed, but perhaps his most important friendship was with T. S. Eliot, who had entered in 1906. At the end of his freshman year Aiken was elected to the Harvard *Advocate* and began to write for it. In his junior year he was elected its president. During his senior year he took advantage of his place on the dean's list to cut classes to translate Théophile Gautier's *La Morte Amoureuse* but was placed on probation (the translation was never published; Aiken acknowledged *La Morte Amoureuse* as the source of the vampire narrative in *The Jig of Forslin*). He felt his probation to be unfair treatment, but his resignation from Harvard was perhaps also prompted by shyness: he had been chosen class poet and would have had to perform the public duties of that office. Among the teachers who influenced his thinking were Charles T. Copeland, Dean Le Baron Russell Briggs, and George Santayana. Robert Hunter Wilbur has pointed out in his 1965 dissertation (Columbia University) that "Santayana's ideas on poetry had a lasting importance upon Aiken. . . . Santayana's insistence that the greatest

Aiken, circa 1895 (courtesy of Mary Aiken)

poetry was 'philosophical poetry,' said Aiken . . . 'fixed my view of what poetry would ultimately be . . . that it really had to begin by *understanding*, or trying to understand.'" After resigning from Harvard he traveled in Europe, visiting Eliot in Paris, but he returned to Harvard in autumn 1911 to complete his degree (1912).

As Aiken describes it in his autobiography, *Ushant* (1952), this interlude in Europe was formative: "He had himself a hand in the shaping of that magical spring and summer, which had, for him, the effect of finally opening doors, everywhere. It was his decision that his life must be lived *off-stage*, behind the scenes, out of view, and that only thus could he excel, . . . that had now established for the first time his freedom to maneuver as he wished to, and as he knew best he could. And this freedom, for him, must be inviolable." Aiken would, all of his life, maintain his distance from subjugating group identities, even stating this distance to be a necessity in a *New Republic* essay (18 September 1935) titled "A Plea for Anonymity": "Our writers must learn once more in the best sense how to *stand clear*, in order that they may preserve that sort of impersonal anonymity, and that deep and pure provincialism, in which the terms approach universals, and in which alone they will find, perhaps, the freedom for the greatest work."

Upon his return to Cambridge, Aiken fell into regular meetings with Eliot (who had returned in the fall of 1911 from the Sorbonne). Much has been argued concerning the influence of the two young poets on each other; Aiken says, "the juices went both ways." The general opinion of Aiken as imitator, preferred in the 1920s and still echoed by Frederick J. Hoffman in 1962, has perhaps reversed. An anonymous *Times Literary Supplement* review in 1963 suggested that "the test of time had revealed Aiken as an innovator rather than a copier, a lender rather than a borrower." It was, however, Aiken who advanced Eliot when he carried typescripts of "The Love Song of J. Alfred Prufrock" and "La Figlia che Piange" to England on a trip in 1914 and showed these poems to Ezra Pound. In 1922 Aiken confirmed that their relationship was a two-way street when he wrote to Robert Linscott about Eliot's *The Waste Land* (1922): "Am I cuckoo in fancying that it cancels the debt I owed him? I seem to detect echoes or parodies of *Senlin, House, Forslin*: in the evening at the violet hour etc, Madame Sosostris etc, and in general the 'symphonic' nature, the references to music (Wagner, Strawinsky [*sic*]) and the repetition of motifs, and the 'crowd' stuff beginning 'Unreal city.' "

Aiken's earliest verse was unimpressive, at best. The lyrics published in the *Advocate*, and even the long narrative *The Clerk's Journal*–which, although written in 1910-1911, was not published until 1971–are often clumsy and labored with heavy-breathing sentiment. *The Clerk's Journal* is important, however, because it shows Aiken already at work on the problems of adapting musical structure to poetry and his use of ordinary citizens as central characters. A two-part narrative, of more than four hundred lines, it relates the aspirations and general moodiness of a clerk whose love affair with a waitress has gone sour. In his preface Aiken himself described the poem as "unmistakably the work of a very young man," and noted that it was often "very funny when it didn't quite mean to be."

Three years after he completed *The Clerk's Journal*, in September 1914, Aiken's first volume

of poetry was published by Macmillan. The poems in *Earth Triumphant and Other Tales in Verse* represent continuing experiment and should be viewed as products of the discipline of a poet-in-training. Many were written during a year in Europe with his wife Jessie McDonald, whom he had married in Canada in August 1912. Others were written in Cambridge, to which they had returned in preparation for the birth of the first of their three children, John Kempton, in October 1913 (all of his three children were to publish novels, although the youngest, Joan Aiken, is best known). None of the poems in *Earth Triumphant* has been included in any subsequent selected or collected edition of his poetry, for none was considered to be, as he says in the preface to the *Collected Poems* (1953), "even remotely salvageable." The book shows no sign of experimental or original verse. Traditional and romantic in their rhythm and rhyme schemes, the poems owe much to John Masefield. The title poem, a narrative written in octosyllabics, describes a young man's disillusion with life and asserts the solid realities of earth and love over the abstractions of art and intellection.

Aiken had begun to produce, and by 1920 he would publish another five books of poetry. His next, *Turns and Movies and Other Tales in Verse* (1916), contains his first explicit experiments with musical form. "Turns and Movies," a collection of fifteen vignettes concerned with the lives of vaudeville actors, takes its title from the *Boston Transcript*, which published an entertainment column under that name. These poems are dramatic where "Earth Triumphant" was narrative and exhibit a surer hand than those of the earlier volume; as Hoffman says, "We have a sense of genuine, legitimate feeling in these statements by vaudevillians and circus-men." According to Jay Martin, Aiken produced a second series of vaudeville poems, "The Tinsel Circuit," in the fall of 1915. Although three poems from this sequence appeared in the December 1935 issue of *Esquire* and seven poems from it appeared in the Fall issue of *Carolina Quarterly*, the whole sequence, much revised from earlier appearances, was first published in *The Morning Song of Lord Zero* (1963). The full sequence reappears in the 1970 edition of his collected poems, where it is dated "1916-1961." Martin suggests that "The Tinsel Circuit" contains elements of both *Turns and Movies* and of the later symphonies and is thus transitional in nature.

Of the other four poems in *Turns and Movies* two are love lyrics ("Discordants" and "Evensong"), one, "Disenchantment," is a narrative concerning disillusionment in a marriage, and the last, "This Dance of Life," is a second installment of the long title narrative of *Earth Triumphant*. The first section of "Discordants" became so popular with anthologists—who seemed to prefer it to more current work—that eventually Aiken refused to allow it to be reprinted. "Disenchantment: A Tone Poem" is perhaps Aiken's first explicit experiment with musical variation as a poetic method: he uses variations rather than simple repetitions of phrase, and juxtaposes cacophony and harmony, stanza by stanza and section by section. It is dedicated to Lucien Crist, an American composer Aiken met in England during his absence from Harvard.

Nocturne of Remembered Spring (1917) contains ten poems, largely concerned with themes which had become familiar to Aiken's small group of readers: disillusionment, guilt, nostalgia, anxiety, and melancholy. They may still be considered experimental, and at least half are attempts at adapting ideas of musical structure to poetry (an analogy Aiken was developing on a larger scale in his symphonies, which include *The Jig of Forslin*, published in 1916). Aiken called "Episode in Grey," to be included in his *Collected Poems*, "a sufficient example of the lengths to which an obsession with the 'musical' analogies of poetry could be carried." The book also contains the third and final installment of "Earth Triumphant." In an anonymous review of his own work, published in the *Chicago News* (January 1917), Aiken disinflated himself: "In *Turns and Movies* he willfully sacrificed his ability to write in smoothly involute curves for a dubious gain in matter-of-fact forcefulness. In *The Jig of Forslin* he recanted, and, with occasional sops to downright and rigid realism, abandoned himself to a luxuriation of romantic virtuosity. And now, in *Nocturne of Remembered Spring*, he is more clearly than ever a schizophrenic."

Among other reviewers of his early work, the names of William Faulkner (*Mississippian*, February 1921), John Gould Fletcher (*Poetry Journal*, July 1916), H. L. Mencken (*Smart Set*, February 1917), William Dean Howells (*Harper's Monthly Magazine*, September 1915), and Harriet Monroe (*Poetry*, November 1918) indicate an awareness of Aiken's poetry in some of the most widely read writers of the time. In general, critics both well known and little known commented upon the in-

Conrad Aiken

fluence of John Masefield on the poems of *Earth Triumphant* but noted Aiken's originality; poems in *Turns and Movies* and *The Jig of Forslin* were variously praised for their vivid imagery but faulted for psychological or sensational themes; those of *Nocturne of Remembered Spring* revealed to several critics a growing mastery of technique but were called too intellectually slight. Critical reaction was, if mixed, at least constant.

By 1917 Aiken had begun to establish himself as a critic. Of the 238 articles and reviews listed in Rufus Blanshard's "Checklist of Conrad Aiken's Critical Writings," in *A Reviewer's ABC* (1958), some sixty-two appeared between 1915 and 1919 (the publication date of Aiken's first collection of criticism, *Scepticisms*). He had distinguished himself by attacks on imagism—or "Amygism," with reference to Amy Lowell—in the *New Republic* and *Poetry Journal* and had addressed himself to recent poetry of many of his contemporaries in newspapers, the *Dial*, and *Poetry* (Chicago). That Aiken's acute, candid, and occasionally cutting observations were sometimes directed toward poets who would later review his work has been suggested as one source of the generally unfavorable reviews his work received, as book by book it emerged. Whatever the political wisdom of his reviewing, Marianne Moore was later to say of him, in *Wake 11* (1952), that "he was the perfect reviewer, Diogenes' one honest man, fearing only to displease himself. . . ." General reaction to the collected criticism in *A Reviewer's ABC* was very favorable. And Blanshard, in his introduction to the volume, suggests that Aiken's criticism was "everywhere informed with that natural but unassertive authority of the dedicated and engaged writer to whom the extra reputation he might win as critic is not so important as the self-rewards of the critical experience."

During this period Aiken launched what was to be the major work of his early career, the six "symphonies." He and Jessie Aiken continued to live in Boston, where their second child, Jane Kempton, was born in December 1917. His encounter with army conscription in 1917 brought about a change in the law: he successfully argued that his profession as a writer was an "essential profession" and became the first American poet to be deferred because he was a poet. They lived on a small income, supplemented by earnings from reviewing. But neither the necessities of daily life nor the relative contentment of his domestic environment distracted him from a feverish production of poetry.

In a letter to Houston Peterson in 1928 Aiken traces the source of the symphonies back to 1912-1914 and a "passing passion for Richard Strauss," and provides this account of their writing: "In 1915, then, I began the first out-and-out symphony, on the theme of nympholepsy: *The Charnel Rose*. And it was as I was bringing this to a close, in November of that year, that I first thought of a series of symphonies which might project a kind of rough and ready 'general view.' I think Santayana's preface to *Three Philosophical Poets,* and the book itself, were deeply influencing me at this time. . . . Anyway, I began *The Jig of Forslin* on the same day that I finished *The Charnel Rose*, and had it done early in 1916. And here again the new poem led on to the next one: I saw the *House of Dust* as I was finishing *Forslin,* saw it as a corollary." After writing *The House of Dust* in winter 1916-1917, Aiken wrote the first half of his long narrative poem *Punch: The Immortal Liar* (1921), but he put it aside in early 1918 to write another symphony, *Senlin*. Returning to and finishing *Punch* later in 1918, Aiken began *The Pilgrimage of Festus* in fall 1919 and took "(with intermissions) two years" to complete it.

The symphonies were published in a slightly different order: *The Jig of Forslin* (1916),

The Charnel Rose, Senlin (1918) in a single volume, *The House of Dust* (1920), *The Pilgrimage of Festus* (1923). When they were gathered in *The Divine Pilgrim* (1949), they were arranged in their order of composition and a sixth poem, *Changing Mind* (written in 1924-1925), was added as a coda to the whole series.

In the symphonies Aiken's interest in the long poem, pursued since the early experiment *The Clerk's Journal,* comes to fruition on a grand scale. Musical analogy in Aiken's "symphonic form" refers to patterns of narrative repetition and variation: words and in some cases whole lines are repeated (as in the opening and closing sections of *The House of Dust*); situations are varied (as in the morning, noon, and evening songs of *Senlin*); and words and phrases are repeated or echoed in repeated or varied situations (as in the opening passages of parts 1 and 2 of *The House of Dust* and in such lines as "Beautiful darkener of hearts, weaver of silence," "Beautiful pale-lipped visionary," and "Beautiful woman! golden woman whose heart is silence!" in part 2, section 1 of *The Pilgrimage of Festus*). In abandoning smooth, chronological narrative structure which might be likened to the classical symphonies of Mozart, Beethoven, and Haydn, Aiken is working in a more contemporary tradition of the symphony, derived from such composers as Anton Bruckner, Gustav Mahler, Arnold Schoenberg, Anton von Webern, and Igor Stravinsky. The juxtapositions, abrupt transitions, repetitions, and variations of his narrative structures are also analogous to the work of such artists as Cézanne, Picasso, and, for occasional cacophony, Duchamp.

The Charnel Rose is the least effective of the symphonies, as Aiken himself said in a review of his own work, published in *Poetry* in 1919 at the invitation of Harriet Monroe. Concerned with the pursuit of, possession by, and disillusionment in, love, it contains dreamlike visions of lamias and death–for which, as Steven Eric Olson says in his 1981 dissertation (Stanford University), "Aiken has often been regarded as a latter-day decadent with Freudian proclivities." In his prefaces and in the 1919 review Aiken established for each symphony a precise though lengthy statement of theme, but Olson suggests that these statements have led critics to read them "as over-structured works hopelessly burdened with musical analogies and intellectual themes verging on the didactic. Aiken so lucidly described his technique and 'themes' that he led critics down a garden-path of

First page of the manuscript for The Clerk's Journal *(by permission of Mary Aiken, courtesy of Eakins Press)*

false scents to an architecturally impressive but ultimately empty gazebo."

The Jig of Forslin presents a sort of Everyman in reverie:

> That he was oldish, and that his name was Forslin,
> And that he sat in a small bare gaslit room.
>
> In the mute evening, as the music sounded,
> Each voice of it, weaving gold or silver,
> Seemed to open a separate door for him. . . .

But this Everyman's fantastic inventions are peopled with prostitutes, vampires, and demons and include murders and a religious debauch, in manner not unlike Berlioz's *Symphonie Fantastique:* Aiken views the modern world as confused, rapacious, and selfish, alienating, and hostile. In some of its details it is a vision not unlike the cities of Rimbaud and Baudelaire or the hallucinations of Flaubert's *The Temptation of Saint Antony.*

The very long and complex *House of Dust* explores an analogy between the city and the human body, playing individual against crowd and poet against collective mind. In a letter to John Freeman, Aiken said there is "a roughly orderly progression from the crowd to the individual, and again from the individual superficially seen (as a mere atom in the crowd) to the individual seen intimately, subjectively, at a moment when his consciousness is sharply focussed by an emotional crisis." Parts 1 and 2 are chronological and present events of the city and activities of individuals between sundown one day to the following night. Parts 3 and 4 are comprised mainly of vignettes of individuals, in part fulfilling the Poet's quest: "I will ask them all, I will ask them all their dreams,/I will hold my light above and seek their faces./I will hear them whisper, invisible in their veins. . . ." The quest is for quintessential identity, and the poem explores the dimensions of identity on the levels of the crowd, the individual as extension of the crowd, and the solitary individual. *The House of Dust* is a virtuoso performance, in which technique and theme seem perfectly matched. Aiken's control of variation, repetition, and tonal modulation seem more finely tuned than in the preceding symphonies.

Senlin: A Biography (1925) is generally considered to be the most successful of the symphonies. Senlin represents a fluid consciousness, seeking its own form. He incorporates the particulars of his own world—in such physical manifestations as a forest, a desert, a city, and a house—and at the same time he exists self-consciously independent of them. Senlin is whatever he imagines himself to be; and he is also the expression of very human imperatives. The poet's quest is to identify the city with the consciousness of it:

> It is morning, Senlin says, and in the morning
> When the light drips through the shutters like the dew,
> I arise, I face the sunrise,
> And do the things my fathers learned to do.
>
> Stars in the purple dusk above the rooftops
> Pale in a saffron mist and seem to die,
> And I myself on a swiftly tilting planet
> Stand before a glass and tie my tie.

Who and what am I, the poem asks; how can I move in my own way, with my own balance, when the planet moves on its? How can one be firm and upright and independent, while "on a star unstable?" The theme runs through much of Aiken's poetry.

The Pilgrimage of Festus returns to a more concrete conception of personality. Festus, searching for truth and knowledge, observes and reports his own fantasies. Nightmarish scenes such as the vivisection of the princess are counterbalanced by specific and alternate points of view, encountered in imaginary conversations with the Buddha, Confucius, Jesus, and Mephistopheles. Festus searches for wisdom, but Mephistopheles suggests that self-exploration pleases.

In *Changing Mind* (1925), added to the sequence when Aiken reorganized the symphonies as *The Divine Pilgrim,* the artist directly confronts the problems of identity and reality in a shifting and indeterminate world; the self seeking its identity is the "I" of the artist looking at Forslin, Festus, Senlin, and himself; the self looks not only at the shifting external universe but also—through the offices of Doctor Wundt—at the shifting indeterminacies of the internal world of the psyche:

> "Laugh if you like," she said, whose golden hair
> Fell round me fine as water-sifted sunlight.
> "Whistle derision from Rome to Jericho;
> Sell him to Doctor Wundt the psycho-analyst
> Whose sex-ray eyes will separate him out
> Into a handful of blank syllables,—
> Like a grammarian, whose beak can parse
> A sentence till its gaudy words mean nothing."

The five symphonies up to and including *The Pilgrimage of Festus* deal with humanity's experience; the "I" is generic, not specific. *Changing*

Mind is the pilgrimage of the artist at a particular moment of his history and hence experience: Jay Martin suggests that in this coda to *The Divine Pilgrim* Aiken is "recreating, in order to understand, the whole process of his development." The protagonist of *Changing Mind* confronts and attempts to understand his "constituent particles" (Aiken's phrase), the elements that created him. Between the completion of *The Pilgrimage of Festus* and *Changing Mind*, Aiken had turned to the writing of short stories. He incorporates prose in *Changing Mind*, an experiment which would recur in *The Coming Forth by Day of Osiris Jones* (1931).

The 261 pages devoted to the symphonies in Aiken's *Collected Poems* contain a major achievement. Critics were quick to dismiss them as they appeared. John Middleton Murry (*Athenaeum*, September 1919) said, "We are far from saying that Mr. Aiken's poetry is merely a chemical compound of the 'nineties, Freud, and introspective Imperialism; but we do think it is liable to resolve at the most inopportune moments into those elements, and that such moments occur with distressing frequency." Allen Tate (*Nation*, January 1926) noted that repetition and diffuseness result in failures in such long poems as *Senlin*. Hoffman, too, has dismissed them as both transitional and representing "an almost wasteful brilliance." The symphonies do represent an advance in technique, from misty conception to sure execution–which is itself a statement of enlarging consciousness. Aiken would write other long poems, but in the symphonies he had completed his most literal attempts to adapt musical structure to poetry.

Punch: The Immortal Liar, Documents in His History and *Senlin*, both composed in 1917-1918, were perhaps Aiken's best-received works of this period, and it is interesting to note that, whereas *Senlin* is the most lyrical of the symphonies, *Punch* is almost purely narrative. Reviews of *Senlin* were qualified by regret that the poems were overly dependent upon psychological ideas, but they generally concluded that "*Senlin . . . is the profoundest and most unified of his allegories in this kind*" (unsigned review, *Times Literary Supplement*, August 1925). *Punch* fared better with the critics; Maxwell Anderson (*Measure*, May 1921) called the second part of *Punch* "one of the most poignant lyrics ever written." Amy Lowell (*New Republic*, September 1921) said that *Punch* was "one of the most significant books of the poetry renaissance." Aiken's Punch, the archetypal figure of the Punch and Judy puppet shows, has

later literary predecessors in the Pierrots of Jules Laforgue, Aubrey Beardsley, and Picasso; in the Harlequins of Cézanne; in Richard Strauss's Tyl Ulenspiegel; in Stravinsky's *Petrouchka* (1911) and *Pulcinella* (1920); in Schoenberg's *Pierrot Lunaire* (1912); and in Ferruccio Busoni's *Arlecchino* (1917). In Aiken's version, which is devoid of authorial comment, Punch is presented from several points of view: the testimony by two old men, Punch's own story (as "the immortal liar") and its refutation by Polly Prim; an account of Punch's death. In the second part Punch is seen from Mountebank's point of view as a misshapen hunchback trapped in a marriage to Judy but driven by lust toward Polly, who will not have him. In an epilogue Mountebank, who both carved the puppet and determined his fate, muses on Punch's story and says, "I too am a puppet." Punch's story presents life as mysterious, luxurious; Polly's presents it ironically; Mountebank sees it mechanistically. The poem is dominated by Punch's fertile imagination–yet he is a puppet. Essentially, the poem is a balancing act between a view of man as limitless potential and resourceful imagination and of man as limited, deterministically controlled. The language of Punch is, on the whole, analytical where that of the symphonies had been emotive, evocative. *Punch* is narrative; *Senlin* is lyrical. Insofar as the symphonies other than *Senlin* had attempted a fusion of the lyrical and the narrative, they had failed to produce the new poetic form Aiken had sought and had not, in Aiken's view, adequately expressed or increased man's consciousness.

Following a scouting trip to London in 1920, Aiken decided to move his family to England in the fall of 1921. When Amy Lowell wrote to him in August of 1921, offering to review *Punch*, he replied, "I should, in any case, value your praise very highly, but I value it all the more in *this* case, first because we have so often, professionally, been at swords' points, and second because my own judgment of *Punch* has been, as it happens, and still is, singularly uncertain and wavering." Lowell's review in *New Republic* (September 1921) is an indication that Aiken was, if not well received, then clearly established as an American poet. The move to England, however, presaged another frustration: another climb from obscurity. A few months later, in December 1921, he would write to Robert Linscott that the English edition of *Punch* "is sharing the ostracism of his author. It's been out over a month, with no sale and no reviews, save a tiny 'note' in the

Conrad Aiken, 1937; portrait by his third wife, Mary (courtesy of Mary Aiken)

he quarreled with Bennet Cerf and Saxe Commins of Random House over their exclusion of Ezra Pound, whom Commins had called a "fascist and traitor").

Priapus and the Pool (1922), which later appeared in *Priapus and the Pool and Other Poems* (1925), is in Martin's opinion Aiken's first successful use of the serial form, a musical form that is neither wholly lyrical nor wholly narrative but which permits an exploration of theme by increment and variation. The mythical Priapus, god of fertility, gardens, and herds, is here used as a grotesque and deformed phallic symbol; as Douglas Robillard points out in his 1965 dissertation (Wayne State University), the fifteen poems of the series have a double theme, Priapus and Narcissus: "Priapic love is intensely phallic, entirely sexual," and the pool is the one in which Narcissus looked and fell in love with his own image. The poems play up "the themes of intense feeling and of meditation, of action and thought, transience and permanence, desire and memory." The prefatory poem (a dialogue) asks what the ego can remember. Is it merely a reflective surface like a pool, or has it its own (priapic?) identity and autonomy? The succeeding fourteen poems answer these questions and, although (as Robillard noted) not a sonnet sequence, *Priapus and the Pool* "follows the typical sonnet plot of love and loss, and the sublimation of feeling into art."

John Deth: A Metaphysical Legend (1930) was completed in 1924, shortly after Aiken moved to Rye, in England. The felicitous names of his characters–John Deth, Millicent Piggistaile, and Juliana Goatibed–were the names of the first three landowners of Winchelsea, near Rye: the materials of the poem have both historical and personal bases. "Here was the dance of death, localized," Aiken wrote Houston Peterson in October 1928, "and my Deth would have two complementary figures, one of whom would symbolize . . . consciousness, while the other would symbolize the unconscious or the merely physical." The narrative derives from the Dance of Death allegory and may have been prompted by Aiken's seeing, in Lucerne in 1911, Hans Holbein's series of paintings *Dance of Death*. It is a difficult and at times obscure poem (Aiken confessed to Peterson that "my meaning was, and has largely remained, obscure to me"), but if the poem (following Aiken's own lead) is read as "possibly a direct reproduction of racial consciousness," it is remarkably strong. Yet it has frequently been neglected.

Times which appeared day before yesterday."

Aiken lived for a year in London, renewing his friendship with John Gould Fletcher (whom he had lived near in Boston). In October 1919 he had begun a series of commentaries and reviews of contemporary poetry, "Letters from America," for the London *Athenaeum;* just before his move to England in the autumn of 1921, he began contributing similar material under the same title to the London *Mercury* and continued to do so in England. He moved from London to a cottage in Winchelsea, Sussex, and then to Rye. Between 1920 and 1927–when he began his great work, the Preludes–he produced only two volumes of poetry and a relatively few shorter poems. Instead, he turned to writing short stories and a novel, *Blue Voyage* (1927). In 1922 he edited the first of several anthologies, most notable of which are the *Selected Poems of Emily Dickinson* (1924) and *An Anthology of Famous English and American Poetry* (1945), the product of what he called a "shotgun alliance" with William Rose Benét (during which

Part 1 is a fairly straightforward account of how De[a]th dances his victims away from life, willing or not; part 2 (which Robillard correctly calls the most difficult of the poem) joins in marriage the negative and the positive: weary, sterile Deth; sexual, carnal, fertile, and above all, lively Millicent Piggistaile–and from their union comes Juliana Goatibed, "joint consciousness." This section of the poem is remarkable for the grotesqueness of its dream world: "Aiken has a penchant for the weird," says Robillard, "but in strangeness and eeriness this part of *John Deth* far outdoes all the vampires, lamias, dissections and Witches' Sabbaths of the symphonies."

The poem is a discussion/exploration of the Freudian notion (as expressed, perhaps, in Freud's *Civilization and Its Discontents*) that the allegorical Everyman figures Deth, Piggistaile, and Goatibed are, in Aiken's words, "doomed to an infinite and wearisome repetition of their ritual." Robillard calls part 3 of the poem "another *Parlement of Foules*": the birds seek in their discussion "the principle behind beauty, mortality, pain and life," and learn (from the bat) that the principle is Venus, the goddess of love. To break the endless cycle of death-birth-love, Venus must be killed. Part 4 (the weakest in the poem) asserts that the love principle cannot be killed even by Death, and in part 5 the poem ends inconclusively: Juliana Goatibed buries John Deth and Millicent Piggistaile, but he is sleeping, not dead, and the process will go on. That the poem received lukewarm reception is perhaps a result–despite Aiken's own misgivings of its persuasiveness–more of habit among his critics than of a careful reading of the poem. Critics such as Babette Deutsch (*New York Herald Tribune Books*, 25 January 1931) and Louise Bogan (*New Yorker*, March 1931) echoed the qualified praise Aiken had so often received before. Percy Hutchinson (*New York Times Book Review*, October 1930) said, "So gifted is [Aiken] with poetic accomplishments and power that his work can never be less than distinguished, however unsatisfactory it may be in point of content."

Aiken began work on his first novel, *Blue Voyage*, in 1922 but turned away to short stories in order to refine his craft and–he hoped–to increase his income. (His third child, Joan Delano, was born in 1924.) His first volume of short stories, *Bring! Bring! and Other Stories*, appeared in 1925, but his fiction did not produce the financial security for which he hoped; this led to a period of intense suffering, resulting first in divorce

in 1929 and then in a suicide attempt in 1932. Yet his emotional decline did not reduce his output significantly. It was during this period that Aiken began, in 1927, the work for which he has since become best known as a poet, the Preludes. Aiken returned to Boston several times; there, in 1926, he met Clarissa Lorenz, whom he married in 1930 at William Carlos Williams's house in Rutherford, New Jersey. In September of 1927 he was appointed tutor at Harvard, but after graduates complained that "the author of *Blue Voyage* was not a fit teacher of the young" (though the book is innocuous enough), he was fired for "moral turpitude." One of Aiken's pupils at the time was Nathan Pusey, who later served as president of Harvard from 1953 to 1971, and it was likely with some satisfaction that Aiken refused, in 1961, the offer of an honorary degree from Harvard. In 1929 he began his long and often complex relationship with Malcolm Lowry, during which he became Lowry's guardian for a time. In 1930 his fortunes seemed to turn for he received both the Pulitzer Prize for his *Selected Poems* and the Shelley Memorial Award, and in that same year he returned to Rye with Clarissa Aiken and Lowry. Although 1931 saw the publication of two new books of poetry, *Preludes for Memnon* and *The Coming Forth by Day of Osiris Jones*, and Houston Peterson's full-length study of his work, *The Melody of Chaos*, Aiken's frustrations mounted. In September 1932 he attempted suicide. Ironically, the next month he set in motion a series of events which led to the release of John Gould Fletcher from Bethlehem Hospital, to which Fletcher's wife secretly committed him following Fletcher's own suicide attempt.

The Coming Forth by Day of Osiris Jones is perhaps more poetic in attempt than in execution, though Jay Martin (and indeed Aiken himself) views it as central to his career. A funerary book, it is a report, a document, a letter, a parable, even a myth. It is rich in resource, incorporating several voices in colloquy, choral response, dialogue. Aiken's note to the poem quotes E. A. Wallis Budge to the effect that in Egyptian funerary books the deceased (whose life is recorded there) is called Osiris (the ruler and judge of the underworld), "true of voice." The deceased must fully report the facts of his life so that he may be judged true of voice–and thereby step from darkness into light: the judgment is based on the completeness of the account, not on the deeds of the life itself. The aim at completeness, then, accounts for the resourcefulness (and difficulty) of the writing–parts of the poem are simply verba-tim quotations from *The Book of the Dead* ar-ranged as verse. As a funerary book it is a fitting complement to *John Deth;* in it the *things* of life, both physical and psychical, have their say. Their speech is often fragmentary and prosaic, as Mari-anne Moore commented (in *Wake 11*), "as on a late dynastic roll . . . there were sometimes illustra-tions, there arise here–not consecutively–favorite thoughts or might one say vignettes, and certain sensations prominent to the consciousness of Osi-ris Jones." As Jay Martin comments in his excel-lent analysis of the poem, "Jones is wholly under-stood as he wholly understands, completely accepted as he completely accepts."

In a preface to his 1961 *Selected Poems*, Aiken says that *The Coming Forth by Day of Osiris Jones* "was actually written after *Preludes for Mem-non*, and before *Time in the Rock;* but I have now placed it ahead of those poems, and for two rea-sons. For one thing, it helps, I think, to explain those two sequences; and for another, it enables me to put them together, as they were meant to be–to all intents, they are one poem." The frag-mentary, quasi-narrative *The Coming Forth by Day of Osiris Jones* is, in fact, a prologue to the 159 medi-tations of the two books of Preludes. Jay Martin calls the three books, and *Landscape West of Eden* (1934), "the central poem in Aiken's career," to-ward which all the earlier poems build and from which the later poems derive. (It is curious, in light of Aiken's careful shaping and reshaping of all his poems and works, that the four poems have never–except in the *Selected Poems*–appeared together: in the second edition of the *Collected Poems* (1970) Aiken preserved the arrangement of the 1953 collection.)

Preludes for Memnon: or, Preludes to Attitude (1931) are "for" the colossal statue of Memnon at Luxor which, split, sang at dawn, as the rising sun struck it, and reminded the Greeks of the Memnon who was killed at Troy, waiting for his mother Aurora (Dawn), who fought the dark. The title reasserts, then, a focus on the concerns of *The Coming Forth by Day of Osiris Jones.* The poems are preludes because they record mo-ments of consciousness, of awareness; preserve memories against oblivion; consciousness tran-scends vicissitude and flux. They address the prob-lems encountered in a search for a meaningful or consistent view of a fluid consciousness rang-ing between knowledge and desire, memory and sensation, matter and transcendence. There is, therefore, both a consciousness-in-flux and a

Mary and Conrad Aiken, 1941 (courtesy of Mary Aiken)

consciousness-which-views the consciousness-in-flux: the epistemological mirror which is the es-sence of Aiken's autobiographical method. De-spair and love are polar conditions of the consciousness-which-views; despair arises from the inability of the consciousness-which-views to af-fect or control the consciousness-in-flux, and love arises from a simple acceptance of the gulf which separates the two consciousnesses. Hope, if there is to be hope, lies in self-knowledge, in the great-est possible scope for the consciousness-which-views. The serial form of the Preludes allows Aiken to come at his theme again and again, often with great lyrical power, as in the central lines of "Prelude XXIX":

There is no doubt that we shall do, as always,
Just what the crocus does. There is no doubt
Your Helen of Troy is all that she has seen,–
All filth, all beauty, all honor and deceit.
The spider's web will hang in her bright mind,–
The dead fly die there doubly; and the rat
Find sewers to his liking. She will walk
In such a world as this alone could give–
This of the moment, this mad world of mirrors
And of corrosive memory. She will know
The lecheries of the cockroach and the worm,
The chemistry of the sunset, the foul seeds

15

Laid by the intellect in the simple heart . . .
And knowing all these things, she will be she.

In *Time in the Rock: Preludes to Definition*
(1936), Aiken explores the paradox of innocence–
that those who recognize innocence in others are
not themselves innocent–as a possible bridge between knowing and being. His conclusion is that innocence is transient, as transient as youth, and is
lost as a mode of being to that old world-weary
consciousness-which-views. Nevertheless, that
same old consciousness is free to choose its attitude toward innocence, whether to despair its
own loss of innocence or to celebrate the presence of innocence in others or in memory with
joy. Even the "posing mind"–the mind which pretends to be other than it is, that poses "like an acrobat" and "like an actor" in "Prelude IX" of *Time
in the Rock,* that *performs* rather than *is*–is capable
of the bright moment, "the bright the brief the
brave, the seeming certain,"

> upon the stage of his own making
> there in the dirty wings on dirty sawdust
> against the trumpets of a vivid world.

What redeems the moment, bright or dark,
from futility and pathos, is love, a transcendent
angel, as in these lines from "Prelude LXXV"
where, viewing unfaithful love and "a change
of heart," caught in bravado and self-con-
gratulation, knowing one's own failure to be
ashamed at one's own dereliction and betrayal of
others, grinning, brazening it out, grinning "at
your own grin":

> Yes, and you have noted
> how the chemistry of the soul at midnight
> secretes particular virtue from such poisons:
> you have been pleased: rubbed metaphoric
>   hands
> saying to yourself that the suffering, the
>   shame,
> the pity, and the self-pity, and the horror,
> that all these things refine love's angel,
> filth in flame made perfect.

The higher awareness of the consciousness-
which-views is neither limited to, nor does it exclude, the ironic or the pathetic. It is inclusive, luminous, and capable of liberation. One breaks
out of the darkness by accepting it: knowledge is
transcendence. In the words of "Prelude LXXV,"
"you [hold] the candle nearer that you might see/
the essential horror." *Thence,* bright moments.

In *Landscape West of Eden* Aiken pursues
these ideas in an allegorical geography, in which
not an omnipotent God, not a fixity, but a god in
the process of development proceeds west from
Eden, followed by Adam, and learns that knowledge is a complex state of mind, compounded by
aging and dying. With these four poems, Aiken arrives at his final philosophical position and concludes his experiments with musical form (although his poems will speak of music again, they
cease to be based upon musical analogies). The
clear narrative line of *Landscape West of Eden* also
points to a decision as to how best he may explore the implications of his philosophical position: narrative is the means to revelatory autobiography, and lyrics are the means to record songs
along the way. "Prelude XLV," of *Preludes for Memnon,* supplies the titles of two subsequent books,
Time in the Rock (1936) and *And In The Human
Heart* (1940), as well as the narrative theme of
Landscape West of Eden:

> I have read
> Time in the rock and in the human heart,
> ....
> He moved the universe from east to west,
> Slowly, disastrously,–but with such splendor
> As god, the supreme poet of delight, might envy,–
> To the magnificent sepulchre of sleep.

Landscape West of Eden, perhaps Aiken's most complex poem, weighs the alternatives: move west, toward risk, with Adam (and develop), or resist
that, seek fixity, with Eve (and stagnate).

And In The Human Heart is a sequence of
forty-three sonnets, twenty-two of which were contained in letters written to his third wife, Mary
Hoover, whom he married in 1937 after his divorce from Clarissa Lorenz. The book was conceived as a more formal continuance of the serial
structure of the Preludes, but here the poems celebrate love more optimistically: the sequence ends
with the line, "Rejoice, my love, our histories
begin!"

The complex relationships among Aiken's
works of this period reveal that the "central
poem" is located, in fact, in a net of many works
of this period and may or may not be limited to
the four titles which Jay Martin identified. This
complexity drew from R. P. Blackmur the comment that "more than any other American poet,
Mr. Aiken has exhibited organic growth, has matured in sensibility, and has developed a form capable of expressing or enacting his material at
the most significant level appropriate to his pecu-

liar, and profound, talent" (*New Republic,* 13 January 1937). The "organic growth" between 1925 and 1940 most resembles an explosion, for during these fifteen years he published eight books of poetry, three collections of short stories, all five of his novels, one hundred and fifteen articles and reviews, and edited two anthologies of poetry–all of this roughly equal to half his total production, excluding selected, collected, or revised work–and in his personal life he concluded his first marriage, entered into and concluded a second, and entered into his third. During these years, in which he reached the emotional depths of attempted suicide and the heights of new love, he also conducted a summer school for artists and writers in Rye and maintained often difficult relationships with artists and writers such as Edward Burra and Malcolm Lowry. In 1934-1936 he was also London correspondent for the *New Yorker,* under the pseudonym Samuel Jeake, Jr. (His house in Rye had been built in 1689 by Samuel Jeake.)

In 1939 Aiken returned to his cottage at Cape Cod and the next year bought an old farmhouse in Brewster, Massachusetts, which he called 41 Doors. Aiken's many trips across the Atlantic by boat provided him with an image central to his work, the voyage (especially in *Blue Voyage, Great Circle,* and *Ushant*), but his return to New England signaled a change of focus, away from the voyage of self-discovery set in the immediate past and present and toward ancestral roots. His reputation among critics continued to be a source of considerable frustration. He wrote to Malcolm Cowley in 1941, "It makes me a little sad that after all this time I still can't be given to a critic who is both intelligent and not wholly unsympathetic," noting that Vincent McHugh's description of *King Coffin* as "a little masterpiece" had been cut from McHugh's review when it was published in the *New Republic.* He went on to say that "of the reviews all the way from *John Deth* and *Blue Voyage* through *Osiris Jones, Preludes for Memnon, Landscape West of Eden, Great Circle,* and the book of short stories to *Conversation,* not one but was tepid and pejorative, not one that admitted or suggested that my work as a whole was of any importance, or added up to anything. Frankly, this has been a poisoned thorn in my side. . . ." Such reviews he concluded were in direct contrast to "the views of Graham Greene, for example, who thought *Great Circle* and *King Coffin* amongst the best novels of their decade, with a kind of Elizabethan power, or Freud, who

said *Great Circle* was a masterpiece, or the *Times Literary Supplement,* which two years ago devoted half a leading article to *Festus, Senlin* and *Punch,* under the title 'Virtues of Abundance.' "

In one sense the four volumes of poetry published during the 1940s concern the American–or more often, the New England–experience within a larger historical framework. *Brownstone Eclogues* (1942)–a series of thirty-eight lyrics, in various stanzaic, rhythmic, and rhyme patterns–addresses the problems of life in the city but without a controlling, central metaphor such as he had used in *The House of Dust.* The book also contains two longer elegies, "Blues for Ruby Matrix," in jazzy cadence with occasional playful syncopation, and the elegant "The Poet in Granada," for García Lorca. *The Soldier* (1944) can be compared to *The Coming Forth by Day of Osiris Jones* for its use of several voices in colloquy, choral response, and dialogue. War is conceived not only in terms of its simple brutalities but as a necessary societal phase which brings forth culture as well as death. *The Kid* (1947) brings together a number of historical personages, most notably William Blackstone, John James Audubon, Kit Carson, Billy the Kid, Paul Revere, Willard Gibbs, Henry Adams, Walt Whitman, Herman Melville, and Emily Dickinson, to create a composite American figure who explores the immense regions of American geography and spirit. *Skylight One* (1949) is a mixed collection of poems containing a four-poem sequence on the seasons, an elegy for Franklin D. Roosevelt ("Crepe Myrtle"), a poem in celebration of Quaker and Puritan backgrounds ("Mayflower"), and an attack on the commercialization of Halloween in which the dead retaliate.

Aiken's literary fortunes began a slow turn for the better in 1947 with his election as a Fellow in American Letters of the Library of Congress. In 1950 he became Poetry Consultant at the Library of Congress, holding the position for two years. During his tenure there he completed work begun some twenty years earlier on his important autobiography, *Ushant.* Also in 1952 *Wake 11* devoted a special number to Aiken, and its contributors included Malcolm Cowley, Allen Tate, Marianne Moore, Mark Schorer, Malcolm Lowry, and Julian Symons, among others. Aiken's completion of *Ushant,* at the age of sixty-three, closes a cycle of productivity. *The Kid* was his last long poem and *Ushant,* his last prose narrative. He continued, however, to write articles and to comment on literary matters in letters to editors; his last appeared in the *Times Literary Supplement* in

April 1971. Between 1950 and his death in 1973 he received nine major literary awards, including a National Book Award, the Bollingen Prize in Poetry, and the National Institute of Arts and Letters Gold Medal, and became the fifth winner of the National Medal for Literature.

Aiken's poetry of the 1950s and 1960s appeared in four volumes, *A Letter from Li Po and Other Poems* (1955), *Sheepfold Hill: Fifteen Poems* (1958), *The Morning Song of Lord Zero: Poems Old and New* (1963), and *Thee: A Poem* (1967). In the best of these poems, such as "A Letter from Li Po," "Overture to Today," and "The Cicada," Aiken's craft is sure, sustained, and graceful. While many of the poems are serial in form, they are generally medium length rather than book length. They pursue the themes of "world and life as word." The language of art, says Aiken, is capable of surviving the ravages of time, transforming the world into "immortal text," as in "A Letter from Li Po":

> Chang Hsu, calligrapher of great renown,
> needed to put but his three cupfuls down
> to tip his brush with lightning. On the scroll,
> wreaths of cloud rolled left and right, the sky
> opened upon Forever. Which is which?
> The poem? Or the peachtree in the ditch?
> Or is all one? Yes, all is text, the immortal text,
> Sheepfold Hill the poem, the poem Sheepfold Hill,
> and we, Li Po, the man who sings, sings as he
>   climbs,
> transposing rhymes to rocks and rocks to rhymes.

One senses here an affirmation and a reconciliation with the world which is not present in Aiken's early work. Perhaps it was this changed perspective which provided the groundwork for the extraordinary closing chapter in Aiken's life.

According to Joseph Killorin, Aiken had "revisited Savannah twice since 'the day of the long drive between the two black-plumed hearses' and found that 'everything had waited for him.'" In 1960 Hy Sobiloff, a businessman, poet, and friend of Aiken's, visited Savannah and bought the house next door to Aiken's old home. After restoring it, Sobiloff gave Aiken the right to live in it for the rest of his life. The Aikens moved into the house in February 1962, at first living there only during the winter months. Later in his life Aiken's illness made it impossible to return to Brewster during the summer. *A Seizure of Limericks* (1964), *Cats and Bats and Things with Wings* (1965; a book of children's verse), and *Thee*

(1967)—a sort of hymn, dedicated to his wife Mary—were among the last things Aiken wrote.

A recent revival of interest in Aiken, measured in numbers of doctoral dissertations and the publication of such scholarly tools as Catherine Harris's *Conrad Aiken: Critical Recognition, 1914-1981* (1983) and the Bonnells' *Conrad Aiken: A Bibliography (1902-1978)* (1982), suggests that Aiken is no longer the neglected or buried giant of American letters; yet the absence of Aiken's work from recent popular anthologies and textbooks also suggests that he remains unread except by specialists. The power and grace of his craftsmanship, the daring of his experiments with poetic form, the complex interrelationships of his total output, and the intelligence of his literary mind remain a rich resource to students of American literature in particular and of the human spirit in general.

A reading of Aiken would be incomplete without a sense of the man in his last years. By the time he qualified as a "senior citizen," the emotional turbulence of his youth and middle years, so painfully explored in his writing, had dropped from his life. Late interviews with Aiken record a memorable smile and his laughter. In a statement to the President's Council on Aging in 1965, at the age of seventy-five, he wrote, "It's extraordinary how little I can now remember of Cicero's famous essay on Old Age, which I had to read in Latin at school—but perhaps natural, for what does the boy want to know of old age, or what can he feel about it? All he does know is that grandfather and grandmother are old, and that this is a preliminary to death, that other mystery. He is still himself completely enthralled in what Santayana called animal faith, and of course is not in the least aware that the very act of being born is to be embarked on a process that leads to death: we live our lives, but in a sense we die them too. I find it profoundly reassuring to consider this inexplicable wonder, as I myself grow older: it has the perfection of a work of art. . . . Ignore the changed face that looks at you from the mirror, it is really the boy who still looks at you there, *he* has not changed; or if he has, it is only in the fact that he has all his life been gathering an inestimable treasure of memory: his own great poem to the universe. Encourage him to go on with it, and every morning, for this is *you*, the one and only never-to-be-replaced *you*, with its own private, but also cosmic, view of the world. Go along with him, and on crutches, if you have to, but let him enjoy it. And he will."

Letters:

Joseph Killorin, ed., *Selected Letters of Conrad Aiken* (New Haven: Yale University Press, 1978).

Letters to family and friends concentrating on the relationship of Aiken's life to his art.

Bibliographies:

F. W. Bonnell and F. C. Bonnell, *Conrad Aiken: A Bibliography (1902-1978)* (San Marino, Cal.: Huntington Library, 1982).

Descriptive bibliography of published and unpublished works by Aiken.

Catherine Harris, *Conrad Aiken: Critical Recognition, 1914-1981. A Bibliographic Guide* (New York & London: Garland, 1983).

Lists secondary materials such as reviews, critical articles, and book sections on Aiken's writings.

Biographies:

Clarissa Lorenz, *Lorelei Two: My Life with Conrad Aiken* (Athens: University of Georgia Press, 1983).

A memoir by Aiken's second wife describing "the delights and disasters of life with a genius."

Edward Butscher, *Conrad Aiken: Poet of White Horse Vale* (Athens: University of Georgia Press, 1988).

The first of two volumes, this biography chronicles the poet's first thirty-six years, including his traumatic childhood, his relationship with T. S. Eliot, and his confessional poetry.

References:

Reuel Denney, *Conrad Aiken,* University of Minnesota Pamphlets on American Writers, No. 38 (Minneapolis: University of Minnesota Press, 1964).

Chapter-length summary of Aiken's career, in part from a psychoanalytic point of view.

Frederick J. Hoffman, *Conrad Aiken* (New York: Twayne, 1962).

Brief critical and biographical overview emphasizing Aiken's development as a poet.

Harry Marten, *The Art of Knowing: The Poetry and Prose of Conrad Aiken* (Columbia: University of Missouri Press, 1988).

Thematic and technical study of Aiken's novels and narrative poems.

Jay Martin, *Conrad Aiken: A Life of His Art* (Princeton: Princeton University Press, 1962).

Critical biography concentrating on Aiken's "investigation, exploration, and definition of his own developing consciousness."

Houston Peterson, *The Melody of Chaos* (New York: Longmans, Green, 1931).

Early critical study of Aiken focusing upon his eclectic vision and his attempt to find sense in disorder; superceded by Hoffman, Marten, Martin, and Spivey.

Ted Ray Spivey, *The Writer as Shaman: The Pilgrimages of Conrad Aiken and Walker Percy* (Macon, Ga.: Mercer University Press, 1986).

Asserts that childhood traumas and the resultant alienation motivated both writers to undertake quests for spiritual affirmation through art.

Wake 11, special Aiken issue, edited by Seymour Lawrence (1952).

Contains selections by Aiken as well as appraisals of his life and career by writers and critics such as Malcolm Cowley, Malcolm Lowry, Allen Tate, and Marianne Moore.

Papers:

The major collections of Aiken's papers are located at the Huntington Library in San Marino, California, and the Houghton Library, at Harvard University.

Raymond Chandler

Paul Skenazy

Places	Southern California	London	
Influences and Relationships	Dashiell Hammett Ernest Hemingway	Alfred Knopf Hamish Hamilton	Capt. Joseph Shaw
Literary Movements and Forms	Hardboiled Detective Fiction	Realism	Film Noir

Major Themes	Misogyny
	Moral Degeneration
	The Detective as a
	    Redemptive Figure
		The Influence of
		    the Past on the
		    Present
		The Underworld
			Identity and Disguise
			Political and Institu-
			    tional Corruption

Cultural and Artistic Influences	The Chivalric
	    Tradition
		English Educational
		    System
			Film Industry

Social and Economic Influences	World War I	The Great Depression	

See also the Chandler entry in *DLB: Documentary Series 6.*

BIRTH: Chicago, Illinois, 23 July 1888, to Maurice Benjamin and Florence Dart Thornton Chandler.

MARRIAGE: 6 February 1924 to Pearl Eugenie Hurlburt ("Cissy") Pascal (deceased 1954).

AWARDS AND HONORS: Mystery Writers of America Edgar Award for *The Blue Dahlia,* 1946; Mystery Writers of America Edgar Award for *The Long Goodbye,* 1955; elected president, Mystery Writers of America, 1959.

DEATH: La Jolla, California, 26 March 1959.

BOOKS: *The Big Sleep* (New York: Knopf, 1939; London: Hamish Hamilton, 1939);
Farewell, My Lovely (New York & London: Knopf, 1940; London: Hamish Hamilton, 1940);
The High Window (New York: Knopf, 1942; London: Hamish Hamilton, 1943);
The Lady in the Lake (New York: Knopf, 1943; London: Hamish Hamilton, 1944);
Five Murderers (New York: Avon, 1944);
Five Sinister Characters (New York: Avon, 1945);
Finger Man and Other Stories (New York: Avon, 1947);
The Little Sister (London: Hamish Hamilton, 1949; Boston: Houghton Mifflin, 1949);
The Simple Art of Murder (Boston: Houghton Mifflin, 1950; London: Hamish Hamilton, 1950);
The Long Goodbye (London: Hamish Hamilton, 1953; Boston: Houghton Mifflin, 1954);
Playback (London: Hamish Hamilton, 1958; Boston: Houghton Mifflin, 1958);
Killer in the Rain (London: Hamish Hamilton, 1964; Boston: Houghton Mifflin, 1964);
Chandler Before Marlowe: Raymond Chandler's Early Prose and Poetry, 1908-1912, edited by Matthew J. Bruccoli (Columbia: University of South Carolina Press, 1973);
The Blue Dahlia: A Screenplay, edited, with an afterword, by Bruccoli (Carbondale & Edwardsville: Southern Illinois University Press, 1976; London: Hamish Hamilton, 1976);
The Notebooks of Raymond Chandler, and English Summer: A Gothic Romance, edited by Frank MacShane (New York: The Ecco Press,

Raymond Chandler

1976; London: Weidenfeld & Nicolson, 1977);
Raymond Chandler's Unknown Thriller: The Screenplay of "Playback," edited by James Pepper (New York: The Mysterious Press, 1985).

MOTION PICTURES: *Double Indemnity,* screenplay by Chandler and Billy Wilder from the novel by James M. Cain, Paramount, 1944;
And Now Tomorrow, screenplay by Chandler and Frank Partos from the novel by Rachel Field, Paramount, 1944;
The Unseen, screenplay by Chandler and Hagar Wilde; adapted by Wilde and Ken Englund from *Her Heart in Her Throat* by Ethel Lina White, Paramount, 1945;
The Blue Dahlia, original screenplay by Chandler, Paramount, 1946;
Strangers on a Train, screenplay by Chandler and Czenzi Ormonde; adapted by Whitfield

Cook from the novel by Patricia Highsmith, Warner Brothers, 1951.

OTHER: *Double Indemnity*, screenplay by Chandler and Billy Wilder, in *Best Film Plays, 1945*, edited by John Gassner and Dudley Nichols (New York: Garland, 1977).

Born in Chicago and educated in England, a failed poet and a successful businessman, Raymond Chandler did not publish his first full-length fiction until he was fifty years old. Yet his seven novels were instrumental in the development of the American murder mystery from the straightforward crime puzzle to a stylistically complex narrative form. In the figure of Philip Marlowe, a "shop-soiled Galahad," Chandler developed the characteristics of the series detective. And, through Marlowe's observations of Los Angeles during the 1930s, 1940s, and 1950s, Chandler offers a sometimes bemused, frequently bitter, always penetrating portrait of Southern California that has helped shape popular myths about the region. Chandler's mixture of irony, stark realism, and scarred but dogged idealism—expressed in Marlowe's wise, and frequently wisecracking, voice—remains a model for writers.

Late in his life, Raymond Thornton Chandler said that if he ever wrote a nonfiction book, "it would probably turn out to be the autobiography of a split personality." Chandler's values and ideals were formed in another country and even a different century than the one he gained fame for chronicling. Though he was born in Chicago 23 July 1888 and spent his early childhood in that city and with his mother's family in Nebraska, he lived in England and Europe from 1895 until 1912. His father, Maurice Chandler, was an alcoholic who worked for the railroads. Chandler later dismissed him as an "utter swine." The boy developed a strong emotional attachment to his mother, Florence Dart Thornton Chandler, and never saw his father again after his parents divorced when he was seven. He and his mother settled with her sister and mother in Upper Norwood, a London suburb, where they were, in the words of Chandler's friend Natasha Spender, "made to feel like disgraced poor relations." An uncle supported Chandler while he attended Dulwich English public school in Upper Norwood but living with his mother's family seems to have increased the boy's feelings of exclusion and isolation.

Chandler studied both classical and modern subjects at Dulwich and hoped to study for the law after graduation. Because the family resisted the idea of supporting him for this length of time, he instead traveled in France and Germany, studying languages in preparation for a civil service career.

When Chandler returned to England in 1907, he was naturalized as a British subject. He obtained a position as assistant store officer under the Controller of the Navy but became bored and resigned the post within six months. For the next four years Chandler tried, mostly unsuccessfully, to support himself as a writer. Finally, in 1912, frustrated by his limited achievements as a writer and anxious to test his talents away from family disapproval, he borrowed five hundred pounds from his uncle and sailed back to America.

On the voyage, Chandler met Warren and Alma Lloyd, who invited him to join them in Los Angeles and helped him acquire a position as a bookkeeper for the Los Angeles Creamery. They introduced him to their friends, including Julian Pascal and his wife, Pearl Eugenie Hurlburt ("Cissy") Pascal, and by 1916 Chandler felt established enough to have his mother join him; he was to live with her and support her until her death in 1923.

In 1917, prompted by America's entrance into World War I, Chandler enlisted in the Canadian Army, which offered a dependent allowance for his mother. He served on the front lines in France and was the sole survivor of a German attack on his unit. He wrote very little about his war experiences, but this encounter seems to have left an indelible mark on him.

After his discharge from the army in February 1919, Chandler returned to Los Angeles. He renewed his friendships with the Lloyds and the Pascals and soon became intimate with Cissy, with whom he had been corresponding. Cissy was forty-eight and Chandler thirty, but she left her husband to be with him. Between 1920 and 1924 the couple maintained a semblance of separate residences out of deference to Chandler's mother's strenuous objections to the relationship, but they eventually married in 1924.

The relationship between Chandler's marriage and his work has been the source of immense controversy among his critics. Frank MacShane, Chandler's biographer, stresses Chandler's devotion and emphasizes Cissy's beauty, youthfulness, and sophistication at the time they became involved. Other commentators stress the age gap, the initial conflict between mother and lover for Chandler's affection, and Chandler's later alternating periods of philandering and loyalty to suggest that the marriage implies everything from unacknowledged homosexuality on Chandler's part, to unresolved Oedipal feelings, to a misogyny that emerges less in real life than in fiction. They note the absence of happy family relationships or close marital ties in his work and how the few portraits of older women depict dominating, evil figures who demean and belittle those around them. But Cissy's death at eighty-four in 1954 left Chandler at the edge of suicide and immersed him in a period of drinking and self-pity from which he never entirely recovered.

The early 1920s produced a dramatic change in Chandler's finances. With the help of the Lloyds, Chandler found a job with the Dabney Oil Syndicate, a firm involved in the massive oil boom in the Los Angeles area. A sequence of unexpected events resulted in Chandler's promotion to auditor and, quickly thereafter, to vice-president, but eventually affairs with company employees and prolonged absences from work prompted by heavy drinking forced the company to fire him in 1932.

Unemployed at age forty-four, Chandler renewed his writing ambitions, directing his attention this time to the pulp literature which was being published in magazines like *Black Mask*. He taught himself the tough-guy form by rewriting plots that appeared in the magazines, and in 1933 he submitted his first story to *Black Mask*, "Blackmailers Don't Shoot." In the next five years Chandler published sixteen short stories, mostly in *Black Mask*. His work still stands out for its energy, intelligence, range, characterization, and pacing. According to rumor, Joseph T. Shaw, the editor of *Black Mask*, challenged other writers to revise or edit Chandler's manuscripts, claiming that they were crafted with unerring precision.

Today many of the stories seem dated and superficial, and as Chandler himself noted, the tales get by "on an idea or a character or a twist without any real dramatic development." But a feeling of "life lived on the edge" survives the occasional technical lapses, gratuitous violence, and frequent melodrama. In his introduction to *The Simple Art of Murder* (1950), a selection of early stories, Chandler pointed out that the pulps demanded constant action: "When in doubt have a man come through the door with a gun in his hand. This could get to be pretty silly, but somehow it didn't seem to matter." For despite the fact that such fiction was overly violent and formulaic, Chandler praised this early work for "the smell of fear which these stories managed to generate" and for their portrayal of "a world gone wrong, a world in which ... civilization had created the machinery for its own destruction," a world in which "the streets were dark with something more than night."

In these early tales–the best of which is probably "Goldfish," the story of a thief whose ancient crime comes back to haunt him–one sees Chandler gaining control of his form: learning how to balance action, dialogue, scene, and characterization; understanding how to structure social observation into narrative, locale, and thematic development; and, most important, writing his way into the voice and viewpoint of his detective figure. Early prototypes of Philip Marlowe are sometimes rich men living off the spoils of corrupt families and playing detective as a hobby, sometimes cops, sometimes poor detectives scraping by and trying to find a way to matter a little bit in an unkind world. Their cases leave them with a mixture of frustrated zeal and world-weary self-pity that would become Marlowe's (and Chandler's) trademark: "I felt tired and old and not much use to anybody," says the hero of "Killer in the Rain."

By 1938 Chandler was working on *The Big Sleep*. He created the plot for his first novel through "cannibalizing," a grafting process in which he reworked several previously published short fictions into a sustained story. Chandler's genius involved not so much the creation of new plot schemes or new character types; he revealed his individuality through designing variations on preexistent themes. Chandler's cannibalizing technique allowed him to create novels featuring multiple dramatic climaxes, though it also tended to make his plots episodic.

The Big Sleep (1939) is notable for the opening bravura by which Chandler sets the stage for his later works. Through the narrative voice of Philip Marlowe, Chandler develops a charged and suggestive atmosphere for *The Big Sleep*, introducing his detective below a stained-glass panel with a "knight in dark armor rescuing a lady who was tied to a tree." The plot that follows moves erratically, but convincingly, to the shocking conclusion. Hired by General Sternwood to deal with blackmail arising from his younger daughter Carmen's gambling debt, Marlowe quickly becomes aware of other crimes, criminals, and threats radiating from the family: Carmen's link to a murdered blackmailer/pornographer; the older sister Vivian's ties to gambler Eddie Mars; and the relationship of Vivian's missing husband, Rusty Regan, both to the General and to Mars's wife. As Marlowe assembles seemingly disconnected events into a coherent narrative, he reveals how the wealthy depend on the underworld to satisfy their cravings for illicit excitement. The plot emphasizes three related issues: the degeneration of a family over time, represented by apathy and amorality in the children and culminating in a secret crime (Carmen's killing of Regan); the disappearance of a family member (Regan), whose absence exemplifies that degeneration; and the family's resulting vulnerability to blackmail.

Fredric Jameson has noted how all of Chandler's novels "are first and foremost descriptions of searches" which take shape from someone's desperate need to recover a missing person or object. Marlowe becomes Rusty Regan's double: he too possesses what the General calls a "soldier's eye" and briefly assumes Regan's place as the General's drinking companion and as Vivian's potential sexual partner. He eventually reveals Carmen as the murderer by reenacting the moment when she killed Regan.

The Big Sleep has its weaknesses. The reader occasionally loses touch with the story in a jumble of new situations, fresh revelations, and sudden bursts of violence. Character is often sacrificed to melodramatic effect, scenes seem to take precedence over the overall plot structure, and bouts of sentimentality mix uneasily with the harsh and extravagant energy of the similes.

Most of these problems are linked to Chandler's deliberate defiance of traditional categories and generic assumptions rather than his blindnesses or literary incapacities. He freely confessed to being a "poor plotter" and argued against the importance of the buildup of suspense to a dramatic climax. As he wrote to Joseph Sistrom in 1947, "the really good mystery is one you would read even if you knew somebody had torn out the last chapter."

The uneasy mixture of pulp, burlesque, and tragedy has caused critics to read *The Big Sleep* as "a comedy of human frailty" (in MacShane's words), an "antiromance" (William Ruehlmann's judgment), and an anti-detective novel which produces "a pervasive sense of individual despair, social chaos, and the triumph of evil" (Peter Rabinowitz). It is hard to dismiss (or accept) any of these judgments; none quite encompasses the playfulness, grotesque humor, wit, dogged heroism, and melancholic pain that the novel evokes.

The ending in particular lends itself to much speculation. Although the reader learns who killed Regan, this revelation resolves little. Marlowe kills the blackmailer and removes this threat from the Sternwoods, but Eddie Mars remains unpunished. Marlowe's only unalloyed achievement, in fact, is his ability to reconstruct the crime and its consequences, and even this aesthetic satisfaction must be balanced against his despondency at the novel's end as he looks down from the Sternwood mansion onto the abandoned oil field and meditates on death, the "big sleep," as a grim equalizer.

Whatever its other merits, *The Big Sleep* will remain significant as the novel that introduced Marlowe. And because he is introduced beneath the knightly figure struggling fruitlessly, if eternally, to free a maiden, critics have argued about whether one can rightly define him as a knight, or should instead see Chandler's novels as parodies of the chivalric tradition. Philip Marlowe's name has variously been interpreted as an allusion to Sir Philip Sidney, playwright Christopher Marlowe, and Joseph Conrad's storytelling Captain Marlow. In his comments on the detective as a redemptive figure in "The Simple Art of Murder" in 1944, Chandler seems to idealize him: "down these mean streets a man must go who is not himself mean, who is neither tarnished nor afraid."

Only rarely does Marlowe fit this heroic image; instead, he stands as a modern revision of male sentimentality, a restatement of traditional principles in contemporary California dialect. When Marlowe plays chess in *The Big Sleep,* for example, he compares the rules that govern the game with the more human, less functional, laws governing his own moves: "Knights had no meaning in this game. It wasn't a game for knights." But while mocking the parallels between his own situation and that of the knight-errant, Marlowe never quite disavows his interest in, and even loyalty to, that tradition. *The Big Sleep*–and Chandler's later work–suggests that the novelist wanted his detective to inherit the knightly mission and at the same time display the impossibility of its achievement.

The reader knows little about Marlowe. He ages from thirty-three in *The Big Sleep* to forty-two in *The Long Goodbye.* Near the beginning of *The Big Sleep* Marlowe reports that he "went to col-

Chandler as a student at Dulwich College

lege once and can still speak English if there's any demand for it," worked for the district attorney until fired for "insubordination," and lives in a small apartment. He conducts business out of an unimpressive two-room office on Hollywood Boulevard, spends much of his time in his car, drinks and smokes, and relaxes when he can over his chess board, playing out classic games. The end of a case leaves him moody and pensive, his sense of hope and renewal removed with the absence of mystery, uncertainty, and action.

In a letter written in 1951, Chandler admitted that Marlowe is less a character in his own right than a voice: "Marlowe is not a real person. He is a creature of fantasy. He is in a false position because I put him there." Marlowe's assertive presence as narrator and his curious ghostliness as a realistic figure of action are part of

Chandler's effort to create what he calls the "objective method." The term "objective" has led to much confusion; since one always remains inside Marlowe's consciousness, true objectivity is impossible. What the term does suggest is the seemingly contradictory role the detective-narrator must play in first-person accounts like Chandler's: at once a naive observer who can be held accountable for accuracy and an implicated character whose involvement is betrayed by his comments and curiosities. The fullest way to understand his shrouded personality is to understand through as well as with the aid of his voice.

The Big Sleep sold well for a first novel (more than ten thousand copies in the United States), but Chandler did not see himself as primarily a detective novelist. Instead, he hoped to use his detective fiction to get "two years' money ahead" so he might write "dramatic" and "fantastic" stories.

In 1940, instead of working on these new fictional ideas, Chandler moved first from La Jolla to Big Bear Lake (later the setting for *The Lady in the Lake*), then to Santa Monica (model for the Bay City of several novels), and Pacific Palisades. He was worried about the impending war, fighting off occasional bouts of ill health, tending to Cissy's physical ailments, and attempting to rework his short fiction into *Farewell, My Lovely* and *The Lady in the Lake*. He would stop work on one novel in frustration, only to return to it when his energy flagged on the other. In 1940 he was able to complete *Farewell, My Lovely*, which appeared that year, then worked on and off on *The High Window* (1942) and *The Lady in the Lake* (1943). The books have much in common. Both *Farewell, My Lovely* and *The Lady in the Lake* were at one time entitled "Law Is Where You Find It," and all three novels explore the gap between the presumed and actual control of public life in America.

In a 1949 letter, Chandler recognized that he would "never again equal *The Big Sleep* for pace nor *Farewell, My Lovely* for plot complication." *Farewell, My Lovely* moves more slowly than *The Big Sleep*, and the language is both denser and darker. The similes are more extravagant, but the mood is grimmer. Marlowe and those he serves pay dearly for his determined efforts to make sense of the world.

Two seemingly disparate plots converge in *Farewell, My Lovely*. In the black section of Los Angeles, Marlowe discovers Moose Malloy, newly released from prison, who has returned to his old haunts to find his "little Velma," a redhead "cute as lace pants." After Malloy kills a black man Marlowe makes some inquiries about Velma, and he returns to his office the next morning to meet Lindsay Marriott, who wants Marlowe to accompany him to exchange money for a stolen jade necklace. That exchange results in the murder of Marriott, for which Marlowe is framed. Marlowe sorts through a complicated series of deceptions before he discovers how his meetings with Malloy and Marriott are related. He is befriended by Anne Riordan, the daughter of a former police chief, and tempted by Helen Grayle, the young wife of an elderly man of wealth and power.

Chandler manipulates a seemingly disjointed series of confrontations into a curiously moving and grotesquely symbolic version of the romantic quest. Moose's singlemindedness accords him a comic human dignity, however wrongheaded and destructive his passion proves to be. Marlowe balances descriptions of his power with the "shine close to tears" in his eyes and a recognition of his love, which transcends the bounds of self-protection. As Moose's name describes his personality, that of Helen Grayle (in reality the beloved Velma) provides an ironic comment upon her character. Her selfishness and ambition affect the fate of everyone who knows her. Her refusal to confront Moose's recognition and love is a denial of the person she once was, and so at least partially remains.

This equation between love denied and selfhood denied gives shape and a curious redemptive substance to the tawdry and violent world of the novel. Commenting on the novel in a letter, Chandler felt that it was his best work: "I shall never again achieve quite the same combination of ingredients. The bony structure was much more solid, the invention less forced and more fluent." Though most critics have agreed with this assessment, Stephen Knight finds the tale implausible and awkward, and Peter Wolfe berates it as a "hodgepodge of false starts, loose ends and melodramatic gleams." Such judgments depend on the assumption that Chandler is a realistic novelist attempting to present a clear vision of the actual world, a notion which comes from Chandler's comments on detective fiction in "The Simple Art of Murder," his brilliant defense of the American hard-boiled tale. Arguing against the artificial British version of the mystery story with its stilted vocabulary, upper-class environment and aristocratic characters, and puzzle-like arbitrariness of plot and solution, Chandler dismisses it as unrealistic, "too little aware of what goes on in the world." In contrast, he offers the work of Dashiell Hammett, who wrote about "something he had firsthand information about." Hammett, Chandler claims, "took murder out of the Venetian vase and dropped it into the alley."

The irony of these remarks is that Chandler is himself as much the child of that Venetian vase as of dark alleys. Condemning the British detective novel and defending Hammett for giving "murder back to the kind of people that commit it for reasons, . . . and with the means at hand," he acknowledged his own Americanism. Chandler's great gift was his complex mix of Victorian strictures and American vulgarity.

That mixture has its negative aspects as well. Many critics focus on Chandler's portrayal of Marlowe's relationships with women, particularly in *Farewell, My Lovely.* Marlowe almost succumbs to Helen Grayle's beauty and inadvertently uses Moose as a sacrificial substitute for himself when Grayle threatens him with a gun in the climactic scene of the novel. At the same time, he resists Anne Riordan's more sincere gestures of love, prompting Stephen Knight and others to suggest that Marlowe is incapable of emotional intimacy. This terror of involvement seems part of Marlowe's loneliness; he uses his privacy as his shield. Thus some recent critical commentary suggests that Marlowe's sense of manhood is defensive, based on keeping himself and his world free from intrusion.

The High Window, Chandler's first "original" novel (that is, not cannibalized from previous stories), concerns abuse of authority. Again, the plot uses the search to explore deeper issues of subterfuge and moral absence. Marlowe is hired by Mrs. Elizabeth Bright Murdock, who wants him to obtain and return the Brasher Doubloon, a rare gold coin. Mrs. Murdock suspects Linda Conquest, her son Leslie's wife, of stealing the coin. Mrs. Murdock has held both her son and her secretary, Merle Davis, in emotional bondage for years. Leslie has made feeble attempts to free himself by gambling away the family fortune and by his marriage to Conquest (a singer) over his mother's protests. Davis, on the other hand, is passionately devoted to her employer. She is securely enchained by the illusion that Mrs. Murdock is protecting her by preserving a secret: that eight years before, Merle killed Mrs. Murdock's first husband, Horace Bright, by throwing him from a window when he tried to sexually abuse her. But it was Leslie, not Linda, who stole the coin, and it was Mrs. Murdock herself, not Merle, who threw

Chandler as a member of the Canadian Gordon Highlanders during World War I

ridden world of Los Angeles's Beacon Hill with its worn tenements, drunken apartment managers, and desperate, defeated citizens. But in *The High Window,* he at times too blithely stereotypes people. Mrs. Murdock is portrayed as ruthless and manipulative, and Merle Davis is cast as an innocent victim. Other characters are similarly frozen into static relations. In his discussion of *Farewell, My Lovely,* Walter Wells says that "In Marlowe's world, innocence does not exist at the beginning; hence there is none to restore." Merle Davis is an exception to this rule, the closest Chandler ever came to creating a picture of guiltlessness, and Marlowe's interactions with her place him in a heroic role that is unequalled in the other novels.

But by and large, *The High Window* is a limited success with structural weaknesses and conventional characters. Among its redeeming features are descriptions of the city viewed as it alters personality with the hour and season: "It was getting dark outside now. The rushing sound of the traffic had died a little and the air . . . had that tired end-of-day smell of dust, automobile exhaust, sunlight rising from hot walls and sidewalks, the remote smell of food in a thousand restaurants, and perhaps . . . a touch of that peculiar tomcat smell that eucalyptus trees give off in hot weather."

The third product of the early 1940s was *The Lady in the Lake,* which Chandler began before *Farewell, My Lovely* but put aside in frustration. It is cannibalized from short stories, though the plot is more integrated and the tone more consistent than the earlier works. A tale of mistaken identity and selfish ambition, the novel is notable less for its wit or language than for the intricate sexual misalliances that reflect a pervasive dissatisfaction throughout the society. *The Lady in the Lake* is a study of defeat and the desperate, self-destructive ways people try to avoid recognition of their frustrated dreams.

The story begins with the disappearance of Crystal Kingsley, who has supposedly run off to obtain a divorce from her husband Derace to marry her lover, Chris Lavery. But she is already dead, her body discovered in a lake and mistaken for the remains of Muriel Chess, wife to the caretaker of the Kingsley mountain cabin at Little Fawn Lake. Muriel killed Crystal and impersonated her to escape her own marriage. This is not her first deception, nor her first killing. By the time Mildred/Muriel is done with her greedy escapade, she has killed three people.

Bright from the "high window," later convincing the terrified girl that she was to blame. When a coin dealer, a naive detective, and a blackmailer turn up dead, Marlowe reveals the intricate dependency that implicates the whole society.

As usual, Chandler has provided brilliant small portraits, from his quick sketches of the main characters to his glimpses into the poverty-

With its ironic title, mock-aristocratic names, and playful bits of dialogue spoofing detective fiction, *The Lady in the Lake* is sardonically anti-romantic. It overturns the heroic forms to which it alludes, from the bloated body of the dead lady in the lake and a "silver slipper" that proves damning evidence to film props that deface the lakeshore.

Central to the interconnections of the characters is the near-faceless interchangeability of people. Images of acting and role-playing abound, and at the center of the plot is a grand illusion. In many ways, *The Lady in the Lake* parallels and concludes the projection of evil onto female figures that occurs in the three previous novels. Peter Wolfe interprets the novel as Chandler's "warning about the danger of loving a woman." Like Velma and Mrs. Murdock, Mildred kills for ambition; however, there is also a desperate, self-protective quality to her attacks. With each killing, Mildred disappears briefly and becomes someone new. Both of the women she kills have acquired the social position she longs for and have shared men with her. If Marlowe condemns Mildred, he also recognizes, even sympathizes with, her misguided efforts to alter her condition.

The Lady in the Lake is carefully controlled but often flat. Except for Mildred and Patton, the main characters are too drab to sustain the reader's interest. Mildred's cunning does not remain at center stage, and so her unmasking has less intensity than the discoveries in earlier novels. Marlowe's partnership with Sheriff Patton of Little Fawn Lake, a father figure whose laconic speech belies his intelligence, is comically intriguing but diminishes the active role of Marlowe and thus makes the book less focused.

Chandler's growing reputation led to his being hired as a screenwriter in 1943 by Paramount, originally to work with Billy Wilder on the adaptation of James M. Cain's *Double Indemnity*. Wilder remembered Chandler as "bad-tempered–kind of acid, sour, grouchy," but the two men got on well enough to produce an exciting, though flawed, screenplay which was nominated for an Oscar in 1944. Chandler worked in Hollywood off and on during the 1940s but remained uneasy with the film medium. In the articles on Hollywood he wrote for the *Atlantic Monthly* during this period, Chandler attacked the studios for destroying "the link between a writer and his subconscious." At the same time, he freely admitted that he thought movies had

the possibility of becoming "the only art at which we of this generation have any possible chance to greatly excel." MacShane argues that Chandler enjoyed many of the personal contacts he made during these years and took pride in much of the writing he did for the studios. But his work in films also forced Chandler to confront his own limitations: his tendency toward isolation, his inability to work with others in a sustained way, and his paradoxical attitudes toward popular forms.

Chandler's characteristic wit and melancholic romanticism mark *Double Indemnity* (1944) and *Strangers on a Train* (1951), two films he helped adapt from others' novels, as well as *The Blue Dahlia* (1946), his original screenplay. He objected to the way Hollywood undermined his intentions–the way it altered *The Blue Dahlia*, for example, from a psychological study of a man who partially forgets his crime into a "routine whodunit." But he received his second Oscar nomination for the screenplay of *The Blue Dahlia* and also won an Edgar from the Mystery Writers of America for the script. By 1947 he was able to obtain a contract which guaranteed him complete artistic independence and final approval of the shooting script for his work. (The story which resulted from this contract, *Playback*, never was filmed; Chandler later rewrote it as a Marlowe novel.) But perhaps Chandler's most important contribution to films were the 1940s adaptations, by other writers, of two of his novels: the second film production of *Farewell, My Lovely* (as *Murder, My Sweet*, starring Dick Powell, in 1945), and the now-classic version of *The Big Sleep* (starring Humphrey Bogart and Lauren Bacall, in 1946). Chandler disapproved of some films based on his fiction (he disliked the camera-eye-as-detective technique of Robert Montgomery's *The Lady in the Lake*, for example), but he recognized that Bogart brought to his portrayal of Marlowe "a sense of humor that contains a grating undertone of contempt."

Shortly after completing the screenplay of *Double Indemnity*, Chandler wrote Alfred Knopf about plans for "a first-person story about Philip Marlowe" involving murder which would not be a mystery. But partly as a result of his continuing Hollywood work, Chandler was unable to complete novels from the publication of *The Lady in the Lake* in 1943 to 1949, when he published *The Little Sister*. During these studio years he made more money than he ever had before. Dissatisfied with life in Hollywood and Los Angeles, he moved to La Jolla and became more retiring in his habits as well as more distant from the film world. He acquired a long list of correspondents; as he wrote in one of his more self-dramatizing moments: "all of my best friends I have never met."

He was nearly sixty as he began work on *The Little Sister*, and, as he wrote in 1948: "Five years of fighting Hollywood has not left me with many reserves of energy." His Hollywood experiences made him bitter; his time away from the detective form made him increasingly resistant to the constrictions and formulaic patterns of the mystery structure. In other letters he admits that he finds himself "spoofing more and more," finds the attitude demanded by Marlowe's voice and presence "more and more artificial," and realizes that the quality of his writing "creates a schism between the melodramatic exaggeration of [the] story and the way [one] writes about it."

Chandler's disillusion in the late 1940s helps explain the confusing and disharmonious elements of *The Little Sister*. In the novel, Chandler draws upon his Hollywood years to tell the story of Mavis Weld (née Leila Quest), an actress on the edge of greatness who, as Marlowe puts it, "finds herself in one of those Hollywood jams that really mean curtains." The threatened revelation of her ties to a gambler links her to murder; she, in the meantime, is willing to sacrifice herself to aid her unscrupulous brother and sister, who are anxious to prey upon her vulnerability.

As usual, Chandler's story moves from a missing-person investigation to blackmail and murder. As the "Quest" family name suggests, Chandler is again using the romantic narrative tradition while noting its perversion in the contemporary world. Hollywood provides a backdrop for his tale of false promise. Aliases, mistaken identities, and misleading evidence take on heightened significance in the world of films, where it is sometimes hard to distinguish public performance from private reality. Chandler's ambiguous attribution of crimes and distribution of guilt become even more complex and confusing; Marlowe finally admits that he has lost control of the whole experience: "it gets too complicated. The whole damn case was that way. There was never a point where I could do the natural obvious thing without stopping to rack my head dizzy with figuring how it would affect somebody I owed something to."

Unfortunately, the same awkward and premeditated quality is apparent in Chandler's arrangement of the novel. Though Chandler at

Chandler's first crime story appeared in Black Mask *in 1933; he became a star contributor (courtesy of Otto Penzler)*

times looked back to the novel with some pride, he wrote James Sandoe that it was "the only book of mine I have actively disliked." The novel is cunning, absorbing, and witty, but more a daring performance than a fully imagined narrative. There is a gratuitous misanthropy that distinguishes it from Chandler's earlier work. It is filled with biting satiric portraits but, as critics have noted, the elements of the story are not entirely cohesive and do not display the range of social reference characteristic of Chandler.

MacShane describes *The Little Sister* as an "overripe" novel that remained too long on the artistic vine. The story is upstaged by the intensity of the language, the excessively clever similes, the harsh character sketches, and the bitter descriptions of Southern California. A sense of life gone to disrepair permeates the smallest descriptive details as well as Marlowe's thoughts on Los Angeles, from the old days when it was "a big dry sunny place with ugly homes and no style, but goodhearted and peaceful," to the present, when it resembles a "neon-lighted slum, . . . a big hard-boiled city with no more personality than a paper cup."

The Little Sister was followed in 1950 by the publication of *The Simple Art of Murder,* a collection of twelve of Chandler's early detective stories. (Chandler excluded those he had cannibalized for his novels, which were not published until 1964, as *Killer in the Rain.*) The two books signaled a significant shift in Chandler's attitude toward his work. In 1950 he wrote a friend that he had begun to feel that he was "filling orders"; from then on, he contended, he was "going to write what I want to write as I want to write it."

In *The Long Goodbye* (1953), his most ambitious, self-conscious, and lengthy fiction, Chandler attempts to expand the boundaries of the mystery genre by limiting the physical violence, deemphasizing the crime, depending less on spurts of verbal brilliance, and instead developing character and theme.

The novel describes Marlowe's relationship to Terry Lennox, a gentleman drunk. Marlowe develops what he calls an "accidental friendship" with Lennox and helps him escape to Mexico the night Lennox's wife is found dead. When Lennox's body turns up in a small Mexican town along with a confession of guilt, Marlowe investigates the circle of lovers and companions who surrounded him: Harlan Potter, Lennox's wealthy and aggressive father-in-law; Linda Loring, Potter's other daughter; and Roger and Eileen Wade, a successful but self-destructive popular novelist and his unhappy wife. Before Marlowe is able to make peace with his friend's memory, Roger Wade dies, a supposed suicide. Marlowe has all but succumbed to Eileen Wade's seductive charms, and he has confronted Potter's threats and power.

The Long Goodbye is at once summative and suggestive, a realignment of issues and ideas that had haunted Chandler from his first stories. Through Marlowe's relationship to Lennox, Chandler explores the implications of friendship, personal loyalty, and ethics in a world ruled by violence and greed. As is characteristic of Chandler's plots, the detective hired to keep the lid on a secret attempts to heal the wounds by disclosing deeds which have been carefully suppressed. The frustrated yearning that had turned rancid in *The Little Sister* is here a more complex effort to come to terms with old age and the altered conditions of the world. In *The Long Goodbye,* the characters are living lives determined by an unresolved trauma in the past; they try to account for their actions by referring to a bygone era and a lost self.

As Spender points out, Chandler has created three complex self-portraits in the figures of Marlowe, Lennox, and Wade. Roger Wade is a popular novelist whose sense of artistic failure has nearly destroyed him. Lennox's army experiences are the closest Chandler ever came to revealing his own battle scars. And, like Rusty Regan in *The Big Sleep,* Lennox is at times a double for Marlowe. The last scenes, in which Marlowe condemns Lennox, reveal a "road not taken" by both author and detective, an alternative life in which morality has been sacrificed in self-protective manners and grace.

The Long Goodbye is a daring book in which the aging Chandler tested himself and his form by probing deeply into the central issues of his life. He challenges the detective's supposed emotional invulnerability and convincingly presents the psychological contradictions of his characters while muting their self-protective wit.

Critics have been divided about the merits of *The Long Goodbye.* They note the slow pace and the absence of the vitality and cunning revelations that account for the success of *The Big Sleep* and *Farewell, My Lovely.* Even so, the imaginative intensity with which Chandler created this mirror of his self-questioning soul is impressive. Here he managed to combine his voice with Marlowe's, enriching rather than obscuring the detective's personality in the process. He projected his tensions onto the landscape and characters, augmenting rather than discrediting his insight into the actual Southern California world. If the very solemnity of *The Long Goodbye* makes it less satisfying than some of the early works, it remains one of Chandler's more enduring and complex fictions.

The titles of Chandler's last novels–*The Long Goodbye* and *Playback* (1958)–provide an apt summary of the last decade of Chandler's life. In 1952 he and Cissy traveled to England; though he found himself heralded as a writer of importance in his second "native" country, he also felt uncomfortable there, a discomfort exacerbated by Cissy's age and failing health. She grew quite ill on the return trip home, and for the next two years Chandler spent much of his time nursing her. She died on 12 December 1954, at the age of eighty-four. Soon after, he wrote a friend: "For thirty years, ten months and four days, she was the light of my life, my whole ambition. Anything else I did was just the fire for her to warm her hands at." Her death left him without focus or purpose.

Chandler began to drink again during Cissy's last illness, and his drinking increased in the next years. Frequent threats of suicide became a form of emotional blackmail to gain the devotion of friends. He was institutionalized in 1955 for firing a revolver in a supposed suicide attempt. His melancholy and depression were only temporarily interrupted by trips to England, the attention of an admiring group of young women, and brief periods of work. He completed *Playback*, a novel, and a story, "Marlowe Takes on the Syndicate"; returned to the manuscript of "English Summer" begun in the late 1930s; started "The Poodle Springs Story" (an uncompleted Marlowe adventure set in Palm Springs); and made preliminary plans to write a drama for the English stage. He even hoped for a time to move to England permanently.

The fiction of these years is often marred by the problems with which Chandler was struggling; what is remarkable is that they were written at all, or that they emerge with the energy and clarity they contain. Chandler first attempted to convert the *Playback* screenplay into a novel in 1953, before he began work on *The Long Goodbye*. He altered his screenplay about a woman who attempts to escape her past in Vancouver, Canada, into a tale of blackmail and pretense in Southern California. He inserted Marlowe as his central consciousness (the screenplay featured a different detective figure), eliminated most of the mob and syndicate suggestions of the screenplay, and concentrated instead on the multiple, contradictory identities and deceptions created by Betty Mayfield, the central character. Marlowe is hired by an unknown client to follow her, but his job soon involves him in a case of blackmail.

Here once again, a character's denial of her past leaves her vulnerable as Betty Mayfield's aliases and her rapid shifts of loyalty lead to murder charges. The novel manages to develop an ambiguous tension, but, as critics have been quick to point out, *Playback* lacks the dark, suggestive undercurrent of implication that sustains Chandler's other novels. The dialogue depends too frequently on artificial muscle flexing reminiscent of the most commonplace and cliché-ridden examples of the tough-guy tale. The writing is professional but toneless, and the structure is too linear, too predictable, and too schematic.

The main problems, however, come from Chandler's failure to vitalize Betty Mayfield or to develop a convincing portrait of Marlowe. Mayfield emerges as an unbelievable mixture of hard-edged talk, shameless cynicism, and naive vulnerability. The Marlowe of *Playback* depends on posturing and overstatement that are out of character, as when he explains himself to Mayfield: "If I wasn't hard, I wouldn't be alive. If I couldn't ever be gentle, I wouldn't deserve to be alive." This might be an apt summary of Marlowe's personality, but Chandler has never made him mouth such quotable aphorisms before. And Chandler's attempt to provide a brief and unusual bit of happiness for Marlowe in the last pages by evoking the memory of Linda Loring of *The Long Goodbye* is more sentimental than credible. What is missing is the tension that Ross Macdonald noted between author and detective, the educated creator and his streetwise alter ego.

That tendency seems destined to continue in "The Poodle Springs Story," a fragment of a novel, which was excerpted in *Raymond Chandler Speaking* (1962). Marlowe and Loring are married and about to establish residence outside a barely fictional version of Palm Springs in a comedy of manners portraying Marlowe in a contest of will, love, and wealth with his new wife. The unfinished novel is lighthearted fun as it stands, but the insolence that makes for much of Marlowe's tactless warmth and hard-edged humor is absent.

In the loneliness and alcoholism of his last years, Chandler was susceptible to the attentions of younger women and twice proposed marriage, though both proposals were eventually retracted. By the late 1950s, he seemed to have found some contentment with Helga Greene, his agent in England. He accepted the presidency of the Mystery Writers of America in 1959, but on his return to La Jolla for the induction ceremony he became ill and died 26 March 1959, at the age of seventy.

When his wife died, Chandler wrote a friend that "It was my great and now useless regret that I never wrote anything really worth her attention, no book that I could dedicate to her. . . . Perhaps I couldn't have written it." Whatever the comment suggests about Chandler's relationship to Cissy, it also reveals his lifelong ambivalence about the value of his work and suggests that he at times thought he had written nothing worthy of himself.

His readers have been more generous. English critic Dilys Powell noted the "quality of shady poetry" in Chandler's work. W. H. Auden

*Pearl Eugenie Hurlburt (Cissy), whom Chandler
married in 1924*

praised Chandler's artistry and his "powerful and extremely depressing" depictions of "a criminal milieu, the Great Wrong Place." Edmund Wilson added his voice in the late 1940s, praising Chandler's stylistic skill and the way books like *Farewell, My Lovely* conveyed the "horror of a hidden conspiracy" to readers. More recently, MacShane has called Chandler "a prophet of modern America, . . . one of the most important writers of his time." Critics have also argued that Chandler never entirely escaped the ideological boundaries of the detective story. His intense homophobia mars *The Big Sleep* and *Farewell, My Lovely,* for example, and he frequently displays a deep-rooted terror of female power, as well as a cynicism toward emotional involvement. In Philip Marlowe, Chandler created the quintessential American detective hero. Chandler once wrote that "to me Mar-

lowe is the American mind; a heavy portion of rugged realism, a dash of good hard vulgarity, a strong overtone of strident wit, an equally strong undertone of pure sentimentalism, an ocean of slang, and an utterly unexpected range of sensitivity." While praising Marlowe's extraordinary depth, several critics (Knight in particular) argue that in Marlowe, Chandler provided a picture of the male as redeemer whose every alliance saps his strength, and whose very invulnerability is allied to his loneliness.

Chandler at his best worked from a simple feeling about the inequity of life–the unfairness of reward and punishment, happiness and misery, and success and failure, be they social, economic, or divine. Marlowe says in *The High Window* that he is seeking "the justice we dream of but don't find." As J. B. Priestley explains: "[Chandler] reduces the bright California scene to an empty despair, dead bottles and a heap of cigarette butts under the meaningless neon lights, . . . and suggests, to my mind, almost better than anybody else the failure of a life that is somehow short of a dimension." But Chandler provided more than glimpses of the rancid wastes of the culture; his theme, Ross Macdonald suggested, "is big-city loneliness, and the wry pain of a sensitive man coping with the roughest elements of a corrupt society." Chandler lacks Hammett's social clarity and his insistence that any detective must be nearly as duplicitous as the characters and world that surround him. To quote Macdonald again, Chandler is without Hammett's "tragic unity," but he possesses a compensatory "hallucinated brilliance of detail." Chandler has a taste for words and a flair for imagery that provide an excitement and color that Hammett resists in his tight-lipped, monochromatic stories.

Chandler's stature has risen immensely in recent years as the prejudice against popular culture has diminished among critics and as readers have developed more sophisticated ways to approach popular forms. Yet Jameson recognizes that if Chandler is to be praised as "a painter of American life" it is not so much for the "large-scale model" of experience he provides but for the "fragmentary pictures of setting and place, fragmentary perceptions which are by some formal paradox somehow inaccessible to serious literature." Chandler's social criticism comes not so much through the implications he builds into the solutions of crimes or the structures of his plots as the way the mystery form itself isolates, highlights, and gives potential significance to the random incidents, unobserved oddities, and mundane and casual interactions of contemporary life.

MacShane opens his biography of Chandler by quoting from a letter: "I have lived my life at the edge of nothing." The other side of his despair was Chandler's dreamy idealism; as R. W. Lid noted, "In the end Chandler's romantic sensibility recoiled from the vision of evil which his art insisted upon." Chandler's dark hope is apparent in all that he wrote; his particular mixture of despair and stoicism, yearning and idealism, chivalry and cynicism mark each page of his fiction as they did the events of his life.

It was Chandler's habit and curse throughout his life to be divided against himself: to be both proud and self-effacing, a snob and a democrat, a Californian and an Englishman, a sentimentalist and realist, a native and an exile. His attitude toward detective fiction and his own place as a mystery writer were similarly contradictory, but it was just this mixture of dedication and resistance to the strictures of the hard-boiled detective form that creates so much of the artistic tension in his work. More than is true of most writers, Chandler's achievement is a process of self-discovery through reaction and resistance. His career is a paradox: his romantic sensibility took form in the hard-boiled mystery, and his idealism acquired power in the unreflective accents of a tough private eye. Chandler managed to straitjacket his pretensions and sentimentality, and so released them as a meaningful and necessary counterpoint to the violent and corrupt world he portrayed. He remains America's foremost authority on a city he lived in but always remained suspicious of, able to convert his own exile into a feeling for the disaffection and fear that haunted a population.

Letters:

Raymond Chandler Speaking, edited by Dorothy Gardiner and Kathrine Sorley Walker (London: Hamish Hamilton, 1962; Boston: Houghton Mifflin, 1962).
   Includes excerpts from letters and notebooks, articles, a story ("A Couple of Writers"), and a section from "The Poodle Springs Story," a novel left unfinished at Chandler's death.

Letters: Raymond Chandler and James M. Fox, edited by James Pepper (Santa Barbara: Neville-Yellin, 1978).

Chandler's correspondence from late in life with a Dutch-born adventure writer.

Selected Letters of Raymond Chandler, edited by Frank MacShane (New York: Columbia University Press, 1981; London: Cape, 1981).
   A revealing and carefully edited volume covering correspondence from 1937 to Chandler's death; as MacShane notes, the letters are as much a "writer's notebook" as notes to friends.

Bibliography:

Matthew J. Bruccoli, *Raymond Chandler: A Descriptive Bibliography* (Pittsburgh: University of Pittsburgh Press, 1979).
   In addition to books, lists first periodical publications, including interviews; produced and unproduced screenplays; and a selection of secondary materials.

Biography:

Frank MacShane, *The Life of Raymond Chandler* (New York: Dutton, 1976).
   A superb critical yet sympathetic discussion of Chandler's life, beliefs, and writings; the one essential text for any Chandler student.

References:

Leon Arden, "A Knock at the Backdoor of Art: The Entrance of Raymond Chandler," in *Art in Crime Writing: Essays on Detective Fiction*, edited by Bernard Benstock (New York: St. Martin's Press, 1983), pp. 73-96.
   A discussion of all of Chandler's novels, demonstrating their ability to reveal character and landscape through subjective and detailed descriptions of people and places.

Liahna K. Babener, "Raymond Chandler's City of Lies," in *Los Angeles in Fiction*, edited by David Fine (Albuquerque: University of New Mexico Press, 1984), pp. 109-131.
   Shows how issues of deception and false constructions dominate all aspects of Chandler's regional vision, from references to Hollywood, city architecture, and views of nature to the double-dealing of the characters.

E. M. Beekman, "Raymond Chandler and an American Genre," *Massachusetts Review* (Winter 1973): 149-173.

Surveys Chandler's entire career against the English detective tradition and the work of Dashiell Hammett, arguing for Chandler's literary skills; particularly useful on the stylistic and narrative recasting of story material into the novels.

Philip Durham, *Down These Mean Streets A Man Must Go* (Chapel Hill: University of North Carolina Press, 1963).
The first book-length study of Chandler, alternating chapters of biography and critical commentary on Chandler's vision of Los Angeles, his development of Marlowe as a hero, and his technical strategies; although somewhat superseded by MacShane, remains a helpful introduction.

Miriam Gross, ed., *The World of Raymond Chandler* (New York: A & W Publishers, 1978).
Fifteen essays by Chandler's friends, critics, and writers which cover his early writings, his film work and movie versions of his books, his characterization of women, and his last years; the personal, often poignant, observations of intimates and acquaintances are particularly interesting.

Fredric Jameson, "On Raymond Chandler," in *The Poetics of Murder: Detective Fiction and Literary Theory,* edited by Glenn W. Most and William W. Stowe (New York: Harcourt Brace Jovanovich, 1983), pp. 122-148.
A wide-ranging, suggestive, speculative study that discusses how Chandler reveals aspects of American culture unavailable in the "high" art of his time through the narration of Marlowe and by his descriptions of Southern California.

Stephen Knight, *Form and Ideology in Crime Fiction* (Bloomington: Indiana University Press, 1980).
Argues that Chandler's social views emerge from his class biases and that his detective self-protectively distances himself from the threats posed by crime and its victims; one of the more critical readings of Chandler as a social analyst.

Gavin Lambert, *The Dangerous Edge* (London: Barrie & Jenkins, 1975), pp. 210-234.
A series of biographical/critical portraits of crime artists, including Chandler, which em-

phasizes how Chandler writes of people "who desperately needed protection ... from 'a world gone wrong.'"

R. W. Lid, "Philip Marlowe Speaking," *Kenyon Review,* 31 (Spring 1969): 153-178.
An appreciative overview of Chandler's skills as a writer and social critic, which also notes how sentimental inconsistencies in Marlowe's viewpoint allow Chandler to overlook some of the implications of his own insights.

William Luhr, *Raymond Chandler and Film* (New York: Ungar, 1982).
Examines Chandler as a film writer and as a writer influenced by films.

K. A. MacDermott, "Ideology and Narrative Stereotyping: The Case of Raymond Chandler," *Clues: A Journal of Detection,* 2 (1981): 77-90.
A challenging study of the ideological implications of Chandler's nostalgia and patterns of stereotyping.

Edward Margolies, *Which Way Did He Go?: The Private Eye in Dashiell Hammett, Raymond Chandler, Chester Himes, and Ross Macdonald* (New York: Holmes & Meier, 1982).
A study of the detective as he changes from the 1920s to the 1970s; discusses Marlowe's role in perceiving alternatives amid the seemingly blank and futureless California landscape.

William Marling, *Raymond Chandler* (Boston: Twayne, 1986).
A careful, extensive discussion of Chandler's life and work that emphasizes the ways he attempted to reconceive the detective genre, particularly through his stylistic skills.

Geoffrey O'Brien, *Hardboiled America* (New York: Van Nostrand Reinhold, 1981).
A fine study of the relationship between hardboiled fiction, changing popular tastes, social realities, and the publishing industry through an examination of paperback fiction and how it was written and sold; contains a brief but excellent section on Chandler in the context of other hardboiled artists.

Stephen Pendo, *Raymond Chandler: His Novels Into Film* (Metuchen, N.J.: Scarecrow Press, 1976).

> Comparative study that argues the relative merits of several film versions of Chandler's novels; contains useful plot summaries that point to the distinctions among the versions, but says little about the way meaning is conveyed in novels versus films.

Peter J. Rabinowitz, " 'Rats Behind the Wainscoting': Politics, Convention, and Chandler's *The Big Sleep*," *Texas Studies in Literature and Language*, 22 (Summer 1980): 222-245.

> Demonstrates that Chandler's subversion of the conventions of traditional detective fiction have political implications and reveal a dark and unredeemable world.

T. S. Reck, "Raymond Chandler's Los Angeles," *Nation* (20 December 1975): 661-663.

> Suggests that Chandler's portrait of Los Angeles in his novels partakes both of realism and nightmarish hallucination; is both objective and personally driven.

Herbert Ruhm, "Raymond Chandler: From Bloomsbury to the Jungle–and Beyond," in *Tough Guy Writers of the Thirties*, edited by David Madden (Carbondale: Southern Illinois University Press, 1968), pp. 171-185.

> Discusses the way Chandler's attempts to move beyond the detective genre revealed contradictions in the form itself, particularly the problem of seeing his detective as a character and a plot catalyst.

Paul Skenazy, "Behind the Territory Ahead," in *Los Angeles in Fiction*, edited by David Fine (Albuquerque: University of New Mexico Press, 1984), pp. 85-107.

> Examines how the California detective novels of Hammett, Chandler, and Macdonald suggest the power of the past–particularly the lives lived before migration to California–to determine the present.

Skenazy, *The New Wild West: The Urban Mysteries of Dashiell Hammett and Raymond Chandler*

(Boise, Idaho: Boise State University Press, 1982).

> An overview of Hammett's and Chandler's writings, emphasizing how plot and idea relate to and helped develop our mythologies of California.

Jerry Speir, *Raymond Chandler* (New York: Ungar, 1981).

> An examination of Chandler's career, stressing his skills with language and character creation and focusing on the role of Marlowe's voice as a determining element in the fiction.

Julian Symons, *Mortal Consequences* (New York: Harper & Row, 1972); revised as *Bloody Murder* (New York: Viking, 1985).

> The best history of the detective story to date; praises Chandler for his dialogue, developing skills with plot, and ability to describe environments, but suggests the limitations of his achievement.

Peter Wolfe, *Something More Than Night: The Case of Raymond Chandler* (Bowling Green, Ohio: Bowling Green State University Popular Press, 1985).

> A study of Chandler's fiction which develops the idea of deep-seated cultural and personal ambivalences and divisions at the heart of Chandler's artistry; thorough and helpful if also at times excessive in its readings.

Papers:

The largest private collection of Chandler's work, amassed from his private files and including manuscripts of published and unpublished writings, screenplays, photographs, notebooks, and correspondence, is at Bodleian Library, Oxford University. Chandler himself helped establish the largest major public repository of his work as the Chandler collection in the Department of Special Collections at the library of the University of California at Los Angeles. The collection includes books and manuscripts, letters, and other papers.

E. E. Cummings

This entry was updated by Jenny Penberthy (Simon Frazer University) from her entry in DLB 48, American Poets, 1880-1945, Second Series.

Places	Cambridge, Mass. France	Greenwich Village	Russia
Influences and Relationships	Marianne Moore John Dos Passos Ezra Pound	Elaine and Schofield Thayer	William Carlos Williams
Literary Movements and Forms	Typographical Eccentricity Dadaism	Surrealism Fairy Tales Satire	The Sonnet Free Verse Romanticism
Major Themes	The Idyll of Childhood Erotic Love Superiority of Process over Product	The Individual vs. "Mostpeople" The True Nature of Heroism	Criticism of American Culture Futility of War Death-in-Life
Cultural and Artistic Influences	Bohemianism Freudian Psychology	Theater (Mime and the Circus)	Cubism
Social and Economic Influences	World War I The Great Depression	Fascism	Pacifism

See also the Cummings entry in DLB 4, American Writers in Paris, 1920-1939.

BIRTH: Cambridge, Massachusetts, 14 October 1894, to Edward and Rebecca Haswell Clarke Cummings.

EDUCATION: A.B., 1915; A.M., 1916; Harvard University.

MARRIAGES: 19 March 1924 to Elaine Orr Thayer (divorced); child: Nancy. 1 May 1929 to Anne Minnerly Barton (divorced). 1934 (common-law) to Marion Morehouse.

AWARDS AND HONORS: *Dial* award, 1925; Guggenheim Fellowships, 1933, 1951; Levinson Prize (*Poetry* magazine), 1939; Shelley Memorial Award, 1945; Academy of American Poets Fellowship, 1950; Harriet Monroe Poetry Award, 1950; Eunice Teitjens Memorial Prize (*Poetry* magazine), 1952; Charles Eliot Norton Professor of Poetry (Harvard University), 1952-1953; National Book Award Special Citation for *Poems 1923-1954*, 1955; Bollingen Prize in Poetry, 1958; Oscar Blumenthal Prize (*Poetry* magazine), 1962.

DEATH: Madison, New Hampshire, 3 September 1962.

BOOKS: *Eight Harvard Poets,* by Cummings and others (New York: Gomme, 1917);
The Enormous Room (New York: Boni & Liveright, 1922; London: Cape, 1928);
Tulips and Chimneys (New York: Seltzer, 1923; enlarged edition, Mount Vernon, N.Y.: Golden Eagle Press, 1937);
& (New York: Privately printed, 1925);
XLI Poems (New York: Dial Press, 1925);
Is 5 (New York: Boni & Liveright, 1926);
Him (New York: Boni & Liveright, 1927);
Christmas Tree (New York: American Book Bindery, 1928);
[No Title] (New York: Covici-Friede, 1930);
CIOPW (New York: Covici-Friede, 1931);
ViVa (New York: Liveright, 1931);
Eimi (New York: Covici-Friede, 1933);
No Thanks (Mount Vernon, N.Y.: Golden Eagle Press, 1935);
Tom (New York: Arrow Editions, 1935);
1/20 (London: Roger Roughton, 1936);
Collected Poems (New York: Harcourt, Brace, 1938);

E. E. Cummings (Sylvia Beach Collection, Princeton University)

50 Poems (New York: Duell, Sloan & Pearce, 1940);
1 x 1 (New York: Holt, 1944; London: Horizon Press, 1947);
Anthropos—The Future of Art (Mount Vernon, N.Y.: Golden Eagle Press, 1944);
Santa Claus—A Morality (New York: Holt, 1946);
Puella Mea (Mount Vernon, N.Y.: Golden Eagle Press, 1949);
XAIPE: Seventy-One Poems (New York: Oxford University Press, 1950);
i: six nonlectures (Cambridge: Harvard University Press, 1953);
Poems 1923-1954 (New York: Harcourt, Brace, 1954);
E. E. Cummings: A Miscellany, edited by George Firmage (New York: Argophile Press, 1958; enlarged edition, New York: October House, 1965; London: Owen, 1966);
95 Poems (New York: Harcourt, Brace, 1958);
100 Selected Poems (New York: Grove Press, 1959);
Selected Poems, 1923-1958 (London: Faber & Faber, 1960);
Adventures in Value (New York: Harcourt, Brace & World, 1962);

73 Poems (New York: Harcourt, Brace & World, 1963; London: Faber & Faber, 1964);

Fairy Tales (New York: Harcourt, Brace & World, 1965);

Complete Poems 1923-1962, edited by Firmage (2 volumes, London: MacGibbon & Kee, 1968; 1 volume, New York: Harcourt Brace Jovanovich, 1972);

Poems 1905-1962, edited by Firmage (London: Marchim Press, 1973);

Tulips & Chimneys: The Original 1922 Manuscript with the 35 Additional Poems from &, edited by Firmage (New York: Liveright, 1976).

PLAY PRODUCTION: *Him,* New York, Province-town Playhouse, 18 April 1928.

OTHER: Louis Aragon, *The Red Front,* translated by Cummings (New York: Contempo, 1933).

E. E. Cummings's experimentation with form and language places him among the most innovative of twentieth-century poets. His style eludes specific association with any one modern line. He was applauded by such various poets as Ezra Pound, William Carlos Williams, Marianne Moore, Robert Graves, Laura Riding, Allen Tate, Theodore Roethke, and Louise Bogan, but he remained peripheral to contemporary poetic movements. He was one of the earliest modern poets (Guillaume Apollinaire and Mina Loy preceded him) to introduce typographical eccentricities into writing. His dazzling linguistic risk taking was in fact painstakingly measured to control sound—pacing, syllable stress, juncture—and sight. The intricate spatial patterning led Marianne Moore to describe his poems as "a kind of verbal topiary-work." The strong visual character of Cummings's writing owes much to his parallel development as a painter. Indeed, his dismemberment of syntax derived from the advances in contemporary European visual art, particularly cubism.

However modern the stimulus for and the superficial appearance of his writing may have been, much of it arises from a nineteenth-century romantic reverence for natural order over man-made order, for intuition and imagination over routine-grounded perception. His exalted vision of life and love is served well by his linguistic agility. He was an unabashed lyricist, a modern cavalier love poet. But alongside his lyrical celebrations of nature, love, and the imagina-

tion are his satirical denouncements of tawdry, defiling, flat-footed, urban, and political life—open terrain for invective and verbal inventiveness. He trained his ear on the rhythms of American speech: he attacked the inauthentic and the manipulative; he twisted over-used words into punning submission; he mimicked familiar public slogans in despairing but vigorous poems, such as the justly celebrated "next to of course god america i/ love you land of the pilgrims' and so forth . . . ," and, from "POEM, OR BEAUTY HURTS MR. VINAL":

take it from me kiddo
believe me
my country, 'tis of

you,land of the Cluett
Shirt Boston Garter and Spearmint
Girl With The Wrigley Eyes(of you
land of the Arrow Ide
and Earl &
Wilson
Collars)of you i
sing: land of Abraham Lincoln and Lydia E. Pink-
ham,
land above all of Just Add Hot Water And Serve—
from every B.V.D.

let freedom ring[.]

Edward Estlin Cummings grew up in a Cambridge, Massachusetts, household which resounded with the verbally adroit and sententious speech of his self-made, civic-minded father, a Harvard professor and Unitarian clergyman, Edward Cummings. Family diaries provide copious documentation of young Estlin's early years and his resolve to become a poet. Rebecca, his mother, endorsed this ambition and orchestrated a delightful round of writing games and improvised theatrics to keep the young writer's imagination alert. In her long life, Cummings's devotion was constant—"if there are any heavens my mother will (all by herself) have/one." His Cambridge youth was happy, protected, homogenous. The family spent each summer on their property, Joy Farm, near Silver Lake in New Hampshire. Cummings would return to it nearly every summer of his life. Allusions to the idyll of childhood recur through his work, as in the early and much anthologized poem from *Tulips and Chimneys* (1923), "in Just/spring":

and eddieandbill come
running from marbles and

piracies and it's
spring

when the world is puddle-wonderful

the queer
old balloonman whistles
far   and   wee
and bettyandisbel come dancing

from hop-scotch and jump-rope and[.]

These years saw the beginnings of his abiding delight in mime, theater, and particularly the circus, which came to signify for him a devoted and pure artistry.

Between the ages of eight and twenty-two, Cummings wrote close to a poem a day. In his earnest application he imitated a wide variety of poetic forms—the ballad, the heroic couplet, the heroic quatrain, the rondeau, the rondel, the sonnet, the Spenserian stanza, and the triplet. The Cambridge tradition, as defined especially by Henry Wadsworth Longfellow, claimed his first allegiance. After he had entered Harvard in September 1911, John Keats and then Dante Gabriel Rossetti took precedence. Cummings was, of course, a superb mimic, but his grasp of the poetic potential of language was more than superficial. In the spring of his sophomore year he joined the editorial board of the literary magazine the *Harvard Monthly* and through this association began important friendships with S. Foster Damon, John Dos Passos, Schofield Thayer, J. Sibley Watson, and Stewart Mitchell: all conversant with new developments in the arts. Thayer and Watson, who had each inherited great wealth, would in the 1920s become joint owners of the *Dial,* with Mitchell as managing editor. Besides publishing his poems, they were to provide generous support for Cummings's painting and poetry.

The literary influence of these new friendships and the contact they provided with modern literature did not immediately alter Cummings's style. He continued to work doggedly within rigid, imposed forms. In his senior year, 1915, he wrote his first highly successful poem, a ballad which succeeds by its flaunting of discipline:

All in green went my love riding
on a great horse of gold
into the silver dawn.

four lean hounds crouched low and smiling
the merry deer ran before.

THE ENORMOUS ROOM

BY

E. E. CUMMINGS

 BONI AND LIVERIGHT
Publishers   :   New York

*Title page for Cummings's novel based on his experiences
as a prisoner during World War I*

Fleeter be they than dappled dreams
the swift sweet deer
the red rare deer.

Four red roebuck at a white water
the cruel bugle sang before.

The first clear indication of his affinity with a modern sensibility occurs in a term paper, "The New Art," which Cummings revised and presented as an address at the June 1915 Harvard commencement ceremony, where he received his A.B. "magna cum laude in literature especially Greek and English." This descriptive and impressionistic piece covered a range of avant-garde activities in the arts: developments from realism to cubism; overlaps between the visual arts and music and literature; achievements of artists such as Paul Cézanne, Marcel Duchamp, Igor Stravinsky, Arnold Schönberg, and Gertrude Stein. Cummings's introduction to the liberties of modern art prompted in his own conduct a new daring much opposed to the middle-class, high-minded ethos of his father-dominated home. Accompanied by his new friends, he became acquainted with the saloons and burlesque theaters of Boston, with popular arts and performers–clowns, acrobats, tap dancers, chorus girls–and with the drunks and prostitutes among their clientele. This was a magical netherworld for the sheltered Cambridge youth. The conservative Harvard style he had adopted in early work that Thayer referred to as "mortuary pieces" was gradually undermined. But through this early work Cummings had achieved a solid grounding in traditional verse forms against which he would bounce his teasing, acrobatic modernity. Many of his best poems allude with irony to traditional diction or form, often in amusing combinations of archaic with modern vocabulary and syntax:

(ponder,darling,these busted statues
of yon motheaten forum be aware
notice what hath remained[.]

Eight Harvard Poets (1917)–accepted for publication in fall 1916, after Cummings had earned his A.M. from Harvard the previous June–features the work of the Harvard Poetry Society–an informal group of poets associated with the *Harvard Monthly,* who met to read one another's work. Also including poems by Damon, Dos Passos, Robert Hillyer, Mitchell, William A. Norris, Dudley Poore, and Cuthbert Wright, *Eight Harvard Poets* contains eight poems by Cummings, all of which bear traces of his mature style and give evidence that he has heeded Pound's injunction against excessive verbiage. The poems are stark, and their staggered arrangement on the page draws attention to the densities of single words. In his earliest published experiments in subverting the conventions of punctuation, capitalization, and syntax, he aimed to uncover, beneath the mantle of custom and habit, a more interesting, more essential mechanism and dynamism of language. The poems are also quite clearly conceived as visual objects–they are typographic novelties. One poem from this period, which he excluded from the final selection for the book, required the reader to read back and forth across the page (for example: "I will wade out/ srewolf gninrub ni depeets era shgiht ym llit"). The poem "Crepuscule" marks the beginning of

his use of the lowercase first-person singular pronoun, which would become a Cummings trademark. (Though the *i*'s were capitalized when the poem appeared in *Eight Harvard Poets* because a copy editor decided they were typographical errors and "corrected" them.) The lowercase *i* suggests the somewhat contradictory impulse toward humility *and* uniqueness of his persona.

On 1 January 1917 Cummings moved to New York, where, he later recalled, "I also breathed: and as if for the first time." He worked at the mail-order book business for P. F. Collier, but the tedium of office work drove him to resign on 25 February from the only regular job he ever held. He preferred the vicissitudes of the life of full-time artist and poet.

Mounting war fever offended his pacifist leanings, but on 7 April 1917, the day after the United States entered the war, Cummings volunteered for the Norton-Harjes Ambulance Service, a frequent choice among young antimilitarist intellectuals. On board ship he met William Slater Brown, with whom he was to share much of his war experience and many subsequent years of friendship. The two men arrived in Paris to find that they had been separated from the rest of their unit, who had all gotten off the train at the wrong station. The bureaucratic muddle that ensued gave them a five-week holiday in Paris, enough to establish Cummings's lasting devotion to that city–"a divine section of eternity." Parisian lowlife provided him with endless entertainment and a brimming source of poetry.

But the ambulance service caught up with them, and on 13 June Cummings and Brown arrived at Section Sanitaire XXI, in the village of Germaine between St. Quentin and Ham. During three frustrating, idle months of service, boredom and disgust with their compatriots drove them to seek company among the ordinary French soldiers of nearby units. These actions raised suspicions that had already been alerted by Cummings's and particularly Brown's flagrant attempts to outwit and provoke the censors in letters home. (In one letter to his parents Cummings wrote that he was in "a place hardly *germain* to my malcontent.") On 23 September 1917 they were detained on suspicion of treason and sent, after questioning, to a Dépôt de Triage in the Normandy town of La Ferté-Macé, where aliens suspected of espionage and undesirable activities were detained. Three months of internment in a large chapel-like room in the Dépôt de Triage provided the material for Cummings's first lit-

E. E. Cummings, 1915

led in Paris and to share a studio with Brown, who arrived in April. Cummings gave most of his time to painting, which at that time presented greater challenges to him than poetry. Inspired by sights in Paris, particularly Pablo Picasso's sets for the ballet *Parade,* he worked at perfecting cubist technique. Schofield Thayer commissioned paintings and urged Cummings's poems on Martyn Johnson, editor of the *Dial.* In July 1918 his Greenwich Village artist's routine was interrupted; he was drafted for service in the U.S. Army and sent for training to Camp Devens, about forty miles west of Cambridge. He refused an opportunity to enter a training school for officers and NCO's, stubbornly holding to the nonheroic role of the *i*. Without the companionship of Brown's intelligent mind, he resented his curtailed freedoms and found no fascination in the heterogeneous assortment of men in his barracks. One of the abiding contradictions in his position of romantic individualism was his simultaneous admiration and scorn for ordinary people.

During his six months at Camp Devens he produced many of the poems that appeared in his next three published volumes, and a number of essays on theory of art and literature. He was especially interested in the finer discriminations of a reader's or viewer's senses, what he called "organic sensation"–kinesthetic experience of weight or resistance, subtle varieties of pressure or pain, a certain balance in the inner ear, and so on. How, he wondered, do the arts summon, mix, or muddle these sensations? Experimenting with his own poetry, he compiled extensive lists of rhyming or alliterating words and then composed from this palette of sounds. Many of these forays are indistinguishable from contemporary Dadaist or Surrealist jottings: "the Bar.tinkling luscious jigs dint of ripe silver with warmlyish wetflat splurging smells waltz the glush of squirting taps. . . ." Cummings dabbled in several of the -isms of early-twentieth-century art. He was attracted to futurism because of its dedication to movement. The adjective "alive" ranks in his vocabulary as the highest praise–it combines notions of being and becoming with movement, vigor, engagement, and delight.

In the spring of 1918 Schofield Thayer's wife, Elaine, had started to engage Cummings's own faculties of vigor, movement, and delight. Their growing attachment and subsequent affair were entirely sanctioned by Thayer. Elaine was a beauty, open to idealization by a romantic like Cummings. John Dos Passos remembered,

erary success, *The Enormous Room* (1922). At first he and Brown enjoyed the change of scene, the release from their inept compatriots, and the solidarity among the foreign prisoners. "I'm having *the time of my life!*" he told his parents. Indeed, it was not a typical prison experience; the confinement was intended more as a precaution than as a punishment. Cummings wrote poetry, kept notebooks, read Shakespeare with Brown–"days spent with an inimitable friend in soul stretching probings of aesthetics, 10 hour nights (9 pm–6.45 am) and fine folk to converse in five or six languages beside you–perfection attained at last." He wanted no intercession on his behalf. Even so, his father was outraged and interfered to secure his son's release. His father's correspondence with officialdom forms the preface to *The Enormous Room.* Cummings was freed on 19 December and returned undernourished to his parents' home. Over the next three years he wrote his prose account of the experience.

At the end of February 1918 he returned to New York to resume the bohemian life he had

"Those of us who weren't in love with Cummings were in love with Elaine." Scores of Cummings's best erotic poems, such as "i like my body when it is with your/body," were written for Elaine. In 1919, shortly after Cummings was discharged in January from the army, Elaine became pregnant and Cummings was, without doubt, the father. Nancy, born on 20 December 1919, was given Thayer's surname. After his discharge Cummings had returned to Greenwich Village to share a studio with Brown and to settle again into serious painting. He entered two works in the spring 1919 show of the New York Society of Independent Artists. By October 1920 he had finished *The Enormous Room* and, after finding little interest among New York publishers, left the manuscript in his father's resourceful hands.

The following year Cummings and Dos Passos toured Europe together, arriving in Paris, the final point of their journey, in mid-May 1921. There Cummings began his lifelong friendship with Ezra Pound, whom he described to his parents as "altogether, for me, a gymnastic personality." Elaine and Schofield Thayer were also in Paris for the July divorce that would unite Cummings with Elaine and his daughter, Nancy. He lived cheaply on money provided by Elaine's generous purse and by his father—family money would continue to supplement his meager earnings throughout his life. He drew and painted and, evidently, enjoyed Parisian cuisine: "I eat snails almost daily, oysters biweekly, mussels weekly, mermaids once a month."

Boni and Liveright accepted *The Enormous Room*, which appeared in May 1922 and was well received, even in the popular press. The *Boston Sunday Globe* gave their review the headline: "Harvard Man, Son of Prominent Preacher, Reveals His Terrible War Experience Involving High Officials." Like his poetry, this prose work (it is neither a novel nor a conventional memoir) subverts expectations: it is a high-spirited account of injustice and imprisonment in a freewheeling linguistic style that darts in and out of French and English in an unprecedented manner, as in the following excerpt: "lest the ordinarily tantalizing proximity of *les femmes* should not inspire *les hommes* to deeds which placed the doers automatically in the clutches of himself, his subordinates, and *la punition,* it was arranged that once a week the tantalizing proximity aforesaid should be supplanted by a positively maddening approach to coincidence. . . ." At the end, Cummings prevents his readers from seeing his release as a conven-

Elaine Orr (courtesy of Nancy T. Andrews)

tional resolution. The central focus of the book is, after all, romantic individualism. He attacks all attributes of government, believing that authority tramples on the development and expression of the individual being. His early fondness for Rossetti's allegorical mode resurfaces in a series of allusions to John Bunyan's *Pilgrim's Progress* (1678). These accumulated allusions elevate and focus the narrative.

Since his imprisonment Cummings had been writing poems. He had already tried unsuccessfully to place a manuscript he called *Tulips & Chimneys,* and, living in Paris in 1922, he revised the manuscript, removing several sexually explicit sonnets but leaving a remarkable collection of 152 poems which would not see publication, as a collection, during his lifetime. Between 1923 and 1925 the contents were scattered over three volumes of his poems. Only in 1976 was the complete manuscript finally published as Cummings had intended, under its original title, including the ampersand he preferred.

In April 1923 Cummings heard that Thomas Seltzer, father-in-law of Albert Boni of Boni and Liveright, would publish a condensed version of his manuscript, as *Tulips and Chimneys* (1923)–the tulips are free-verse lyrics and the chimneys are sonnets written in response to a sordid urban world. The collection opens with a number of his college poems, his formal declamatory "Epithalamion" written for the wedding of Elaine and Schofield Thayer in 1916 and his more sophisticated "Puella Mea" written for Elaine in 1919. His mature work is grouped under "Impressions," "Portraits," "Post Impressions," and the three sections of sonnets–"realities," "unrealities," and "actualities"–under the heading "Chimneys." The poems take liberties with poetic convention and public taste, as in his farewell to Cambridge morality: "the Cambridge ladies who live in furnished souls." But many are romantic invocations which exploit archaic language:

> spring omnipotent goddess thou dost
> inveigle into crossing sidewalks the
> unwary june-bug and the frivolous angleworm
> thou dost persuade to serenade his
> lady the musical tom-cat, thou stuffest
> the parks with overgrown pimply
> cavaliers and gumchewing giggly
> girls and not content
> Spring, with this
> thou hangest canary-birds in parlor windows[.]

The poem continues to mock its own grandiose manner though it never loses sight of its celebration of sensation and new life. In this early collection Cummings introduces an attitude that remains consistent throughout his work, an attitude that, in condemning mankind while idealizing the individual, is the basis for his portraits and his satires. The sarcastic verse

> Humanity i love you
> because you would rather black the boots of
> success than enquire whose soul dangles from his
> watch-chain which could be embarrassing for both–

ends with the statement, "Humanity/i hate you" (the poem was first collected in *XLI Poems*, 1925).

Portrait-poems held a strong appeal for Cummings the painter. *Tulips and Chimneys* in-

cludes his well-known "Buffalo Bill's" and others that take their subjects from the demimonde. Many of these poems employ the dialect of the lowbrow café dweller–a quasi-phonetic, comic approximation of their speech: "eet smeestaire steevensun/kum een, dare ease Bet, an LeeLee, an dee beeg wun" from "when you rang at Dick Mid's Place."

The proportion of sonnets in the volume, and indeed in all of Cummings's poetry, is high. He thrived on the disjunction of its formal constraints and his irreverent content. He liked to follow the rhyme scheme of the Petrarchan sonnet to which he added, in the final couplet, the characteristic Shakespearean modifying twist. The device could transform an initially romantic poem into a satire. In general, he reserved the sonnet or metrical forms for his more serious poems which embody a complex, transcendent vision. The looser, more experimental poems, on the other hand, aim to communicate concrete sensations and perceptions in all their existential immediacy. He shuns conventional syntax and punctuation as based on an arrangement of thoughts, feelings, and sensations already completed. His concern is with the instantaneous: "suddenly" is among his favorite words. Typography performs a dynamic function by approximating visually the actual object or experience that gave rise to the poem as in "breathing Spring twi (after rain) light."

Back in New York, Elaine and Cummings were married on 19 March 1924, and Cummings legally adopted Nancy on 24 April. Then four, she was a delight to him. He composed stories for her (some of which were published years later in *Fairy Tales*, 1965), and took her to the zoo and the circus as he had done in Paris. Life with Elaine was a pleasure too, with its round of restaurants, clubs, theaters, and friends' apartments. Dos Passos remembered, "After a couple of brandies on top of wine Cummings would deliver himself of geysers of talk. I've never heard anything that remotely approached it. It was comical ironical learned brilliantlycolored intricatelycadenced damnably poetic and sometimes just naughty."

Cummings continued to paint and to relish his role as experimental poet and iconoclast. *Tulips and Chimneys* was met by a number of hostile reviews, but this first major collection found more sympathy and interest than much of his subsequent work. In a review for *Poetry*, under the title "Flare and Blare," Harriet Monroe objected to his eccentricities of punctuation and typography;

yet, she added, "He is as agile and outrageous as a faun, and as full of delight over the beauties and monstrosities of this brilliant and grimy old planet. There is a grand gusto in him...." Edmund Wilson in the *New Republic* took accurate aim: "Cummings's style is an eternal adolescent, as fresh and often as winning but as half-baked as boyhood. A poet with a real gift for language, for a melting music a little like Shelley's, which rhapsodizes and sighs in soft vowels disembarrassed of their baggage of consonants, he strikes often on ethereal measures of a singular purity and charm—his best poems seem to dissolve on the mind like the flakes of a lyric dew; but he never seems to know when he is writing badly and when he is writing well. He has apparently no faculty for self-criticism."

The Dial Press sifted through the poems remaining from the original *Tulips & Chimneys* manuscript and selected forty-one for a volume entitled *XLI Poems*. Cummings then arranged for a private printing of the remainder of the manuscript plus some new poems. His title was *&* (1925) for the ampersand that he regretted was missing from Boni and Liveright's *Tulips and Chimneys*. The two additional volumes are distinguished from the first by a larger number of erotic poems.

In May 1924, two months after the Cummings's marriage, Elaine left for Europe to settle the estate of her deceased sister, Constance. In June she wrote that she had fallen in love with an Irish fellow passenger, Frank MacDermot, and wanted a divorce. The forlorn Cummings did all he could to dissuade her, and, after he failed, he entered into an extended custody battle over Nancy. But he was defeated and until 1948, when she heard the news directly from him, Nancy had no knowledge that he was her father.

Although 1925 was a year of great personal distress, it was also a year of literary achievement. *XLI Poems* and *&* both appeared and were well received. In a *Dial* review of *XLI Poems* Marianne Moore called him "fanciful, yet faithful to that verisimilitude of eye and of rhetoric which is so important in poetry," adding that he "shapes the progress of poems as if it were substance; he has 'a trick of syncopation Europe has,' determining the pauses slowly, with glides and tight-rope acrobatics, ensuring the ictus by a space instead of a period, or a semi-colon in the middle of a word, seeming to have placed adjectives systematically one word in advance of the words they mod-

ify, or one word behind, with most pleasing exactness." She went on to say, "The physique of the poems recalls the corkscrew twists, the infinitude of dots, the sumptuous perpendicular appearance of Kufic script; and the principle of the embedded rhyme has produced ... some sublimely Mohammedan effects."

Cummings was earning a steady if small income by writing comic sketches for *Vanity Fair*—mock interviews, parodies of theater reviews, letters to the editor—a job which he despised. At the end of 1925 he won the *Dial* award "for distinguished service to American letters." The prize of two thousand dollars equaled a full year's livelihood. He was a regular contributor to the *Dial*, which in ten years published thirty-seven of his poems, several critical articles, parts of his play *Him* (1927), and numerous drawings and paintings. The editors considered him their discovery among the moderns.

Encouraged by his success, Boni and Liveright contracted with Cummings early in 1926 for a volume of poems that would include a brief introductory reader's guide. He wrote to his mother about his choice of title: "IS FIVE (short for Twice Two Is Five, hasten to add.) But even so, how will M. et Mmme. Everyone compwehend? —such is the curse of awithmetic." The explanatory introduction became a characteristic statement about the superiority of process over product: "If a poet is anybody, he is somebody to whom things made matter very little—somebody who is obsessed by Making." The implication is that "making" is process and life giving, whereas "made" is stasis and death. The poems in *Is 5* (1926) mark no striking advance on the mature poems of *Tulips and Chimneys*. There is a larger proportion of satirical poems, particularly antiwar pieces such as the exasperated though gentle critique of American civilian concern—

my sweet old etcetera
aunt lucy during the recent

war could and what
is more did tell you just
what everybody was fighting

for,
my sister

isabel created hundreds
(and
hundreds)of socks ...

Anne Barton Cummings

—or such as the Siegfried Sassoon-type diatribe of "the season 'tis, my lovely lambs":

> braving the worst,of peril heedless,
> each braver than the other,each
> (a typewriter within his reach)
> upon his fearless derrière
> sturdily seated–Colonel Needless
> To Name and General You know who
> a string of pretty medals drew
>
> (while messrs jack james john and jim
> in token of their country's love
> received my dears the order of
> The Artificial Arm and Limb)[.]

As with all his books of poetry thus far, sales of *Is 5* were minimal.

Interest in drama and the theater was running high during the 1920s, and Cummings was drawn into Greenwich Village discussions of European and American dramatic expressionism. Out of this excitement he wrote the play *Him*, a somber, overcomplex Strindbergian drama, an ambitious effort to enact Freudian ideas. The play is a series of vignettes with circus sideshows, vaudeville skits, burlesque sketches, and Dada nonsense representing the unconscious. The main character, Him, is another manifestation of the nonhero, the lowercase *i*, the Everyman, the Anybody, but also the artist and playwright. Again,

Cummings's identity is barely concealed. However, the play represents one of his few extended attempts to make a considered composition out of the responses which constitute the poetic sensibility. Marianne Moore, managing editor for the *Dial*, recommended they print excerpts from *Him*, noting, "Some of it seems to me as imaginative and expert as anything of his I have read; and some of it to the contrary." The excerpts appeared in the August 1926 issue with a photograph of Cummings's painting *Noise Number 13*. Boni and Liveright's publication of the play prompted the Provincetown Playhouse to stage it. Under James Light's direction, it opened on 18 April 1928 to an amazed and fascinated audience. Cummings had written a "Warning" for the program: "Relax and give the play a chance to strut its stuff–relax, stop wondering what it's all 'about'–like many strange and familiar things, Life included, this Play isn't 'about,' it simply is. Don't try to enjoy it, let it try to enjoy you. DON'T TRY TO UNDERSTAND IT, LET IT TRY TO UNDERSTAND YOU." The play ran to full and delighted houses for twenty-seven performances.

On 1 May 1929 Cummings married Anne Barton, and together they departed for Europe. During the next two years they spent a great deal of time in Europe, probably because it was less expensive to live there than in the United States.

Cummings's book with no title, published by Covici-Friede in 1930, is an assemblage of nine nonsense stories, each preceded by an amusing line drawing. A narrative manner without narrative purpose or direction mingles, over sixty-three pages, clichés, epigrams, slogans, and puns: "Once upon a time, boys and girls, there were two congenital ministers to Belgium, one of whom was insane whereas the other was six-fingered. They met on the top of a churchsteeple and exchanged with ease electrically lighted visiting cards and the one who was not steering picked a rose and handed it to the waitress with the remark: 'Urinoir gratuit.' "

Another book followed in January 1931. The single published collection of his artwork, it was titled *CIOPW*, an acronym formed from the initial letters of the words *charcoal, ink, oil, pencil, watercolor*. Its subject is autobiographical, drawing on treasured features of Cummings's world: acrobats, burlesque dancers, Chaplin, a merry-go-round, portraits of his family, landscapes of Paris and of Joy Farm in New Hampshire.

at dusk
 just when
the Light is falled with birds
seriously
i begin

to climb the best hill,
driven by black wine.
a village does not move behind
my eyes

the windmills are
silent
their flattened arms
complain steadily against the west

one Clock dimly cries
nine, i stride among the vines
(my heart pursues
against the little moon

o here and then lank
    who; rises,

and; droops
as if upon a thread invisible)

A graveyard dreams through its
cluttered and brittle emblems, or
a field (and; pause among
the smell of minute mown lives) oh

my spirit you
Tumble
climb and mightily fatally

i remark how through deep sifted
fields Oxen distinctly move a
yellowandbluish cat (perched why
cunningly at this) windows yes

women standily meander in my
mind, woven by always upon
Sunset
crickets within me whisper

whose erect blood finally
trembles emerging to perceive
buried in cliff
    precisely

the Ending of this road,
a candle in a shrine:
its puniest flame persists
shaken by the sea

Final draft for a poem published in No Thanks *(© 1989 by the E. E. Cummings Trust; courtesy of the Clifton Waller Barrett Library, University of Virginia)*

With the demise of the *Dial* in 1929, few of Cummings's poems appeared in periodicals. However, in the early 1930s *This Quarter,* "a magazine of left-bank activities" edited by Edward Titus in Paris, published several of his poems, including those which reflect his troubled second marriage, which would end in 1932:

nothing is more exactly terrible than
to be alone in the house, with somebody and
with something)

    You are gone. there is laughter
and despair impersonates a street[.]

Such poems also appeared in *ViVa,* published in October 1931. The book contains seventy poems. Of the first sixty-three poems every seventh one is a sonnet, and the last seven poems are all sonnets. (Thus the book contains fourteen sonnets for the fourteen lines of the sonnet form.) Other-

wise the development is similar to that in all his books of poetry since *Is 5,* a tendency that Cummings described as "to begin dirty (world: sordid, satires) & end clean (earth: lyrical, love poems)." The collection indulges in the familiar linguistic manipulations. There are the by now predictable attacks on modern mass thinking; and a variety of portraits, many of them spoken in the subject's dialect. Play with language, such as the spoonerisms of poem 21, "helves surling out of eakspeasies per(reel)hapsingly," tends to turn serious, bitter, or occasionally strident. Among the satires is a poem which draws on his experience at Camp Devens, "i sing of Olaf glad and big/whose warmest heart recoiled at war: a conscientious object-or." As these lines suggest, it is one of Cummings's most trenchant antiwar pieces:

but—though all kinds of officers
(a yearning nation's blueeyed pride)
their passive prey did kick and curse

until for wear their clarion
voices and boots were much the worse,
and egged the firstclassprivates on
his rectum wickedly to tease
by means of skilfully applied
bayonets roasted hot with heat—
Olaf(upon what were once knees)
does almost ceaselessly repeat
"there is some shit I will not eat"

our president,being of which
assertions duly notified
threw the yellowsonofabitch
into a dungeon,where he died[.]

Olaf is an early type of the individual in a number of Cummings's poems. "Mostpeople" follow orders, do their duty; the individual is true to himself.

The mood of the volume is often affectionate: the poem for his mother, "if there are any heavens . . . ," the celebrations of his favorite phenomena–stars, birds, flowers, twilight–and the love poems such as "somewhere I have never traveled, gladly beyond/any experience."

In May 1931 Cummings had left Anne Cummings behind in Paris and traveled to the Soviet Union. American intellectuals, especially those–like Cummings and his friends–who expressed socialist ideals, had been quick to approve government sponsorship of art and literature in the Soviet Union and to note the optimistic reports on the current Soviet Five-Year Plan at a time when the West reeled under economic depression. Cummings's dissatisfaction with American culture predisposed him to enjoy his trip, yet his philosophy of individualism surely made him suspicious of collectivist ideology. During his stay he began to conceive of Russia as another Enormous Room, empty of laughter, fun, color, and spirit–an "uncircus of noncreatures." The travel diary he kept from 10 May to 14 June 1931 was much expanded for *Eimi*, published in 1933. The title, "I am" in Greek, asserts, once again, the individual against the collective. Within the mythic structure a journey to the Underworld–replete with allusions to Dante's *Inferno*–made by one Comrade Kem-min-kz (the Russian pronunciation of his name), the book traces various events that occurred on Cummings's journey, in their correct sequence. It is written in the same highly personal and mannered style of his poetry. In the following passage, for example, he is leaving Russia: "USSR a USSR a night-USSR a nightmare USSR home for the panacea Negation haven of all(in

life's name)Deathworshippers hopper of hate's Becausemachine(U for un- & S for self S for science and R for -reality)how it shrivels:how it dwindles withers;how it wilts diminishes wanes; how it crumbles evaporates collapses disappears–the verily consubstantial cauchemar of premeditated NYET." In the more than sixty reviews of *Eimi* in newspapers and magazines, reviewers expressed almost unanimous bafflement and impatience.

During the writing of *Eimi*, Cummings's antagonism to the Soviet Union became an obsession. He grew to despise both Communists *and* liberals. During the Roosevelt-Truman era his loathing for American culture grew, and his conservatism turned into reactionary bitterness. Before *Eimi* he had been regarded as a voice from the left because of the antiauthoritarian demeanor of the poems and *The Enormous Room*. He lost friends and the once unquestioning support of a literary world now increasingly sympathetic to literature fueled by a social conscience.

In 1932 while his divorce was being negotiated, Cummings met Marion Morehouse, a generous spirit who would remain his companion and common-law wife (it appears they never married) until his death. She was, like Elaine and Anne, a great beauty. Cummings's persistent financial worries lifted when, in the spring of 1933, he was awarded a Guggenheim Fellowship on the strength of the briefest proposal for "a book of poems."

At about the same time Lionel Kirstein, editor of the *Hound and Horn*, persuaded Cummings to compose a ballet scenario; at Marion's suggestion, he adapted *Uncle Tom's Cabin*. *Tom* was published in 1935, but not staged even though David Diamond completed the score in 1936. Both Diamond and Kirstein were among a number of young people who became close friends of Cummings's. He enjoyed preaching his doctrine of individualism and devotion to art. These new friendships filled the gap left by the deaths and disaffections of older friends.

Meanwhile Cummings could find no publisher for his new collections. Fourteen houses turned him down, partly because of the Depression economy and partly because his recent sales (for *Is 5*, *[No Title]*, *ViVa*, *Eimi*) had all been low. At last, *No Thanks* (1935), dedicated to the publishers who had rejected the book–their names arranged on the page in the shape of a funeral urn–was published by the Golden Eagle Press. Cummings's mother subsidized the printing. As

Marion Morehouse Cummings (photograph by Edward Mueller)

with all his books, the poems are carefully assembled in a symbolic schema. In *No Thanks,* the seventy poems are arranged in a pattern of three poems followed by a sonnet; with a cluster of three sonnets at the halfway point. Cummings visualized the book in the shape of a V: moving from two "moon" poems, descending to "earth" poems at the center of the book, and then rising to two "star" poems at the conclusion. His selection presents a fully developed view of life: his reverence for the instinctive self and the world of feeling against his contempt for the analytical mind and its imprisoning intellectual systems. Early in the collection "sonnet entitled how to run the world" offers the advice, "don't." Another attacks a man who "does not feel because he thinks" or, worse, one who "does not have to think because he knows." American culture takes its usual beating, as does "progress":

o pr
gress verily thou art m

mentous superc
lossal hyperpr
digious etc i kn
w & if you d[,]

and the slaves of the totalitarian state:

kumrads die because they're told)
kumrads die before they're old
(kumrads aren't afraid to die
kumrads don't
and kumrads won't
believe in life)and death knows whie[.]

These cantankerous poems are matched by open, more felicitous tributes to the natural world, to the promise of beginnings, of spring and of love.

Certain words in Cummings's vocabulary carry a rather full evaluative cargo–apart from his special veneration for the word "alive," he pays tribute to "is" ("Is will still occur" despite threats from "knowings" and "credos"), "guess," "dare," "open," "dream," and "yes." Words singled out for loathing are "same," "reason," "shut," "numb," and "mostpeople." "Who" is the acceptable relative pronoun since it always refers to an individual; "which" is despicable since, in his usage, it refers to a depersonalized human being, a nonperson. Nikita Khrushchev, for instance, is "a which that walks like a who." In *No Thanks,* Cummings takes his customary liberties with word forms. He is specially fond of the prefix "un-" which, placed before any noun, deprives it of its essence, its "thingness." Furthermore, in an effort to steer language away from abstraction, he constructs nouns out of verbs, adjectives, or adverbs, thereby suggesting motion where conventional language would suggest stasis and mere function. His polymorphous use of ordinary words extends their range of connotations and their capacity to become metaphors.

The two "star" poems which end the volume introduce a religious tone that is new in Cummings's work. Words such as "holy," "miraculous," "lifting hopes and hands," and an aspect of humble wonder before a higher force suggest that his father's Unitarian message had left its mark after all.

Because *No Thanks* was not published by a major house it had little promotion and very few notices. In 1938 Harcourt, Brace decided to gather Cummings's scattered work into a *Collected Poems.* It was more widely reviewed and better received than any of his other books, but sales were still slow. At the publisher's request, Cummings included a preface which reiterates his values:

> The poems to come are for you and for me and are not for mostpeople–it's no use trying to pretend that mostpeople and ourselves are alike. Mostpeople have less in common with ourselves than the squarerootofminusone. You and I are human beings; mostpeople are snobs. . . .
>
> Life,formostpeople,simply isn't. Take the socalled standardofliving. What do mostpeople mean by "living"? They don't mean living. Theymean the latest and closest plural approximation to singular prenatal passivity which science, in its finite but unbounded wisdom,has succeeded in selling their wives. If science could fail, a mountain's a mammal. Mostpeople's wives can spot a genuine delusion of embryonic omnipotence immediately and will accept no substitutes. . . .
>
> Miracles are to come. With you I leave a remembrance of miracles: they are by somebody who can love and who shall be continually reborn,a human being; . . .

Vitriol churns beneath the intimate, chatty surface and raises questions about the snobbery and elitism that Cummings wanted to repudiate. It is an abstract notion of humanity that Cummings hates.

There were 315 poems in the book, including twenty-two new ones. Among them, Yvor Winters found too much evidence of "infantile exhibitionism"; and Horace Gregory found too little evidence of development over the years. Yet Dudley Fitts wrote for the *Saturday Review of Literature:* "With all its failures and beauties, its clashing styles, its brainsmashing complexities and moving simplicities, this is the poetry of a man of complete artistic integrity."

During World War II, in 1940, *50 Poems* appeared. They are more compact and philosophical but otherwise not strikingly different from the usual collection of syntactically daring satires and love poems. The volume contains such frequently anthologized pieces as his small myth of a secret self, "anyone lived in a pretty how town," and the poem for his father, "my father moved through dooms of love." In retrospect, Cummings regarded this poem for his father as the start of a new development where he began to speak with a morally responsible voice and with greater concern for others.

Critics attacked the book for its now overfamiliar style and subject matter. A wartime publication, it made no mention of the contemporary global crisis. Babette Deutsch wrote a scathing review for the *Nation* (17 May 1941) in the form of a pastiche letter-poem addressed to Cummings, parodying his manner and pointing to, among other things, the formulaic ease of his method:

> ;but
> it is
> nineteenfortyone mrcummings
> ,and you must forgive us
> if we sometimes
> y
>   aaaw
>   n
> ....
> . . . we are not asking you for
> something new ,simply
> few
> and (er
>)or better
> ?poems

Sales were slow but steady; his reputation continued to grow, gradually, until by the 1960s the book was earning him four hundred dollars per year in royalties.

The entry of the United States into the war did not escape Cummings's notice. His revulsion against the growing hatred for the Japanese prompted him to write a skillfully patterned satire on incoherent, racist anger:

> ygUDuh
>
>   ydoan
>   yunnuhstan
>
>   ydoan o
>   yunnuhstan dem
>   yguduh ged
>
>   yunnuhstan dem doidee
>   yguduh ged riduh
>   ydoan o nudn[.]

In 1941 Cummings began to have pains in his left leg and back and was diagnosed as having osteoarthritis of the spine, which caused him pain for the rest of his life. He wore an uncomfortable metal corset, which he referred to as "the iron maiden," and unrelenting physical discomfort made him moody and irascible.

In 1944, with the publication of *1 x 1*, Henry Holt and Company became Cummings's publisher for what would be the peak years of his career. *1 x 1* is his most important volume of poems. The selection reflects universal concerns and a greater joy in life; it has less bitterness and fewer satires. Looking back on this period he said, "The 2nd 'world war' finds me trying to cheer up my native land; I feel responsible to certain anonymous-or-otherwise admirers."

1 x 1 is divided into three parts and progresses from dark to light, a schematic orderliness that is familiar from earlier collections. Section 1 opens with an imagistic piece about a dull November day, the sky a "nonsun blob," and moves on in "it's over a (see just," to a modern rendering of man's fall from grace:

> then over our thief goes
> (you and i)
> has pulled(for he's we)
> such fruit from what bough
> that someone called they
> made him pay with his now.

A few dark poems are clustered in this first section: "ygUDuh," "a salesman is an it that stinks Excuse," "a politician is an arse upon," "pity this monster manunkind/not." At the end of the section Cummings strikes the theme implicit in the title—oneness and love, the means (one times one) whereby oneness is reached. Variations on the theme occur throughout the book, as in the following lines reminiscent of Donne:

> one's not half two. It's two are halves of one:
> which halves reintegrating,shall occur
> no death and any quantity;but than
> all numerable mosts the actual more[.]

Section 2 ("X") contains some of his more compact and obscure poems, and also some of his more fragmented:

> old mr ly
> fresh from a fu
> ruddy as a sun
> with blue true two
>
> man
> neral
> rise
> eyes[.]

His memorable elegy for Sam Ward, the handyman at Silver Lake, is here too:

> rain or hail
> sam done
> the best he kin
> till they digged his hole
>
> :sam was a man[.]

In Section 3 ("1") Cummings's manner is lyrical and optimistic. Oneness in the natural world moves to oneness in human life with poems about the growth of a flower, the approach of dawn, the shock of spring, and on to love poems (some of which are very sentimental). He places his dedication to Marion Morehouse at the emotional high point of the book, the end.

1 x 1 was well received by a war-weary country. Theodore Spenser called it "a poetry of joy, that seeks for joy and, perhaps at the cost of wearing blinkers, finds and succeeds, to our great delight, in expressing it." William Reisen in the *Cincinnati Enquirer* wrote of the change in the poems: "Cummings, whose lower case poems were once regarded as the 'dernier cri' in modernism, has developed beyond mere sensationalism into a sincere and responsible artist although he still clings to his forms." For *1 x 1* Cummings received the Shelley Memorial Award from the Poetry Society of America. It was published in Great Britain in 1947, the second British edition of his poetry. *1/20* (1936) was the first.

In 1945 he made an exception to his rule of avoiding causes and, with William Carlos Williams, Karl Shapiro, Conrad Aiken, and others, he published a statement in the newspaper *PM*, 26 November 1945, in defense of Ezra Pound. His argument was: "Every artist's strictly illimitable country is himself." (Later he would use the same argument against charges of anti-Semitism in his own work.) He also gave money he could ill afford in order to help pay for Pound's medical treatment.

In 1946 the *Harvard Wake* published a special Cummings number, which contained his new play *Santa Claus* (subtitled *A Morality*), a fairy tale, and a poem as well as several tributes by other writers. William Carlos Williams praised Cummings's linguistic achievement and the moral quality with which he addresses the private consciences of his readers. Other leading writers who contributed to the issue were Marianne Moore, Theodore Spenser, Lionel Trilling, Jacques Barzun, Paul Rosenfeld, and Dos Passos.

Santa Claus, published separately by Henry Holt before Christmas in 1946, was a hybrid morality play and children's pantomime. Its archetypal characters and its action, which includes sudden reversals, derive from the tradition of the marionette theater.

In 1950 Oxford University Press published

E. E. Cummings, summer 1939 (photograph by Marion Morehouse Cummings)

a collection of poems called *XAIPE,* pronounced *Kyereh* and meaning in Greek "Rejoice." Its seventy-one poems begin with a sunset and end with a new moon, "luminous tendril of celestial wish." There are elegies for friends such as Paul Rosenfeld and Peter Munro Jack, satires, and these lines in a sonnet about the atom bomb:

> whose are these(wraith a clinging with a wraith)[.]
>
> ghosts drowning in supreme thunder?ours
> (over you reels and me a moon,beneath,
>
> bombed the by ocean earth bigly shudders)[.]

XAIPE and the fellowship given to Cummings by the American Academy of Poets after its publication became the center of accusations of anti-Semitism in the following lines:

> a kike is the most dangerous
> machine as yet invented
> by even yankee ingenu
> ity(out of a jew a few
> dead dollars and some twisted laws)
> it comes both prigged and canted[.]

His publishers had tried to persuade him to drop the poem but he resisted all interference, saying,

> it is more than most kind of thee, monsieur, to warn me of le public's reaction to 2 Wild Words (see how they run). And yet the (however painful) fact that America is not a free country doesn't, I feel, justify anyone's behaving like a slave or three or (in the lines of the Bad Bald Poet) steady
> there once was a cuntry of owe

such lofty ideals that know
man ever could mension
(imagine the tention)
     what might have offended jane dough
selah[.]

Seven out of thirty-two essays in the first collection of Cummings criticism, S. V. Baum's *EETI: eec: E. E. Cummings and the Critics* (1962), are devoted to the question of anti-Semitism in his poetry.

In February 1952 Cummings was invited to be the Charles Eliot Norton Professor at Harvard for the academic year 1952-1953. He accepted somewhat reluctantly since Harvard seemed to him a center of misguided intellectualism, and he found Harvard politics too lax. To his sister he wrote: "Have yet to encounter anybody in any manner connected with Harvard who isn't primevally pink." He chose, however, to keep his support for Joseph McCarthy and Eisenhower-Nixon Republicanism to himself, and he accepted the position, which required only that he deliver six lectures in return for a salary of fifteen thousand dollars.

His six lectures were published by Harvard University Press in 1953 in two forms: a printed text of the lectures and the readings he gave at the end of each as well as a full set of recordings made during the lectures. *i: six nonlectures* also includes selected key passages from his own work as well as an idiosyncratic selection of what he considered the best poems of Western literature. The lectures are autobiographical rambles. The first two describe his father and mother, his childhood home, his early friends and books. (Robert Graves found these lectures too "corny," preferring the poet's "Old Carnality.") Lecture 3 is a reminiscence about Harvard, New York, and Paris:

Thus thru an alma mater whose scholastic bounty appeared the smallest of her blessings–and by way of the even more magnificent institutions of learning, New York and Paris–our ignoramus reaches his supreme indebtedness. Last but most, I thank for my self-finding certain beautiful givers of illimitable gladness
   whose any mystery makes every man's
   flesh put space on; and his mind take
      off time[.]

The last three lectures–"i & you & is," "i & now & him," and "i & am & santa claus"–present his stance as a writer. A large proportion of each lecture contains quotations from his writing. He concluded the series as follows:

I am someone who proudly and humbly affirms that love is the mystery-of-mysteries, and that nothing measurable matters "a very good God damn:" that "an artist, a man, a failure" is no mere whenfully accreting mechanism, but a givingly eternal complexity–neither some soulless and heartless ultrapredatory infra-animal nor any un-understandingly knowing and believing and thinking automaton, but a naturally and miraculously whole human being–a feelingly illimitable individual; whose only happiness is to transcend himself, whose every agony is to grow.

Ecstasy and anguish, being and becoming; the immortality of the creative imagination and the indomitability of the human spirit–these are the subjects of my final poetry reading: which (I devoutly hope) may not wrong a most marvellous ode by Keats, and the magnificent closing stanzas of Shelley's Prometheus Unbound.

The nonlectures were a popular success among undergraduates and visitors, but graduate students and faculty were disappointed. David Perkins, a graduate student, reported, "I thought them elegantly phrased and delivered but empty of content. This was the general response of students and faculty." By all accounts Cummings's delivery was masterful.

In the 1950s Cummings began to draw an income through his poetry readings. He had become a superb reader of his own work and possibly one of the best readers of his time. Across America he attracted capacity audiences. He read slowly and precisely, registering every nuance that typography indicated. His agent, Betty Kray, arranged a schedule each fall and spring at colleges, museums, and art centers, and she supervised payment, travel, and other details, such as "There will be no provision for autographing books, attending dinners, receptions, and other social functions as part of the total reading engagement. . . . there will be no commentary with the reading." Despite his physical discomfort ("a casually dressed elderly man . . . stiff-legged, with one shoulder raised as though bearing a chip of contention") he continued performing–he enjoyed his own accomplishment and also the applause and adulation of his audiences.

The first full collection of Cummings's poems, *Poems 1923-1954* (1954), was met, on the whole, with enthusiasm and with the respect accorded to one of the country's foremost poets. In

1957 he accepted the role of Festival Poet at the Boston Arts Festival (three previous Festival Poets had been Robert Frost, Carl Sandburg, and Archibald MacLeish). Required to compose a festival poem, Cummings violated the expectations of his audience and the benign mood of the festival by reading his savagely satiric "THANKSGIVING (1956)." The ironical title reflects the anger and grief felt by Americans at the invasion of Hungary on their day of national celebration. Cummings had written to his daughter, Nancy, in a "shaggyblack chasm of shame & anger created by UNamerica's absolute D'abord encouragement & utter ensuite abandonment of that handful of humanbeings who did the bravest thing since Finland." The poem begins:

> a monstering horror swallows
> this unworld me by you
> as the god of our fathers' fathers bows
> to a which that walks like a who
>
> but the voice-with-a-smile of democracy
> announces night & day
> "all poor little peoples that want to be free
> just trust in the u s a"
>
> suddenly uprose hungary
> and she gave a terrible cry
> "no slave's unlife shall murder me
> for i will freely die[.]"

In 1958 he won the Bollingen Prize in Poetry, one thousand dollars, from Yale University and published a collection of prose pieces, *E. E. Cummings: A Miscellany*, which included his early Harvard commencement speech, "The New Art," and essays written for the *Dial* and *Vanity Fair*. In 1965 George Firmage revised and expanded the book to include other prose pieces. *95 Poems*, also published in 1958, was the last book of new poems to be published in Cummings's lifetime. It was as youthful in outlook as his earlier work. The sixty-four-year-old poet could still assert:

> Time's a strange fellow;
>   more he gives than takes
> (and he takes all)nor any marvel finds
> quite disappearance but some keener makes
> loser,gaining
>   –love!if a world ends
>
> more than all worlds begin to(see?)begin[.]

As Betty Kray remembered his last years in New York, "every night around ten o'clock he

would come by, tap on my window, and I would go with him on a long prowl through the Village streets. We walked and I listened and he talked about himself, about the world, about the things he loved. I disagreed with much of his political belief but held my tongue; he was quite vulnerable during this period. . . . He would disprove over and over again the critics' charge that neither his poems nor his paintings showed 'development'; that was the most intolerable of all the criticism."

He and Marion spent their summers and falls on Joy Farm taking close interest in raccoons, deer, a red fox who chased crickets, a gray fox, a porcupine, woodchucks, and chipmunks. Birds and flowers were his special delight: "Hummingbirds, a robin, phoebes, an indigo bunting, thrushes, a purple finch, swallows–buttercup, vetch, iris, sweet rocket & wild roses–backed by our seven mountains–what more could any human creature ask?"

Cummings collapsed at Joy Farm on 2 September 1962 and died the following day from a brain hemorrhage. He was sixty-seven. That summer he had been preparing another book of poems. George Firmage and Marion Morehouse assembled *73 Poems* for publication by Harcourt, Brace and World in 1963. It is a peaceful register of the birds, flowers, stars, springtimes and churchbells of the Joy Farm of his youth and old age.

From midcareer onward, Cummings's poetry had been criticized for its lack of development. There are certainly no identifiable, discrete periods in his work as there are with other modern poets such as Yeats, Pound, and Eliot. He said of people and poetry: "There are two types of human beings children & prisoners. Prisoners are inhabited by formulae. Children inhabit forms. A formula is something to get out of oneself, to rid oneself of–an arbitrary emphasis deliberately neglecting the invisible and significant entirety. A form is something to wander in, to loose oneself in–a new largeness, dimensionally differing from the socalled real world." Cummings's own wanderings within a form led, regrettably, to a formula. But he did perfect his style and, through beautifully calibrated readings, brought a love of poetry to many followers of the arts. In the 1950s he became one of the best-known poets in the country, particularly to college students. He was equally popular in the 1960s, since he spoke, in an antiauthoritarian language, for the expression of impulse and emotion. Reliably a maverick, he might well have shied away from the generation of imitators he unintentionally spawned (but, as Babette Deutsch proved in her "review," his style was easy to copy).

Relatively little critical attention has been given to his work, which does not lend itself to detailed academic study. But his poems themselves are still widely available and never fail to appear in anthologies of modern or American poetry.

Cummings's achievement deserves acclaim. He established the poem as a visual object (he can be seen, in fact, as a forerunner of concrete poetry); he revealed, by his X-ray probings, the faceted possibilities of the single word; and like such prose writers as Vladimir Nabokov and Tom Stoppard, he promoted sheer playfulness with language. Despite a growing abundance of second-rate imitations, his poems continue to amuse, delight, and provoke.

Letters:

Selected Letters of E. E. Cummings, edited by F. W. Dupee and George Stade (New York: Harcourt, Brace & World, 1969).
Letters written between 1899 and 1962 to family members (particularly his mother) and friends (particularly Ezra Pound), often in the riddling, playful style of the poems.

Bibliographies:

George J. Firmage, *E. E. Cummings: A Bibliography* (Middletown, Conn.: Wesleyan University Press, 1960).
A descriptive bibliography of primary works.

Guy L. Rotella, *E. E. Cummings: A Reference Guide* (Boston: G. K. Hall, 1979).
A comprehensive guide to reviews and criticism.

Biographies:

Charles Norman, *E. E. Cummings: The Magic Maker* (New York: Macmillan, 1958; revised edition, New York: Duell, Sloan & Pearce, 1964).
While the biography is a valuable repository of facts and anecdotes, it is an appreciation by a friend of Cummings rather than a work of critical scholarship.

Bethany K. Dumas, *E. E. Cummings: A Remembrance of Miracles* (London: Vision Press, 1974).

A short dash through Cummings's life and times followed by a brief survey of his poetry, prose, and drama.

Richard S. Kennedy, *Dreams in the Mirror: A Biography of E. E. Cummings* (New York: Liveright, 1980).
The definitive biography—a thorough and fascinating account of Cummings's life plus some excellent literary analysis.

References:

S. V. Baum, ed., *EETI: eec: E. E. Cummings and the Critics* (East Lansing: Michigan State University Press, 1962).
Twenty-six reviews of and essays on Cummings's work beginning with *The Enormous Room* (1922) and including a critical discussion of Cummings's anti-Semitism.

Irene Fairley, *E. E. Cummings & Ungrammar; a Study of Syntactic Deviance in His Poems* (Stamford, Conn.: Windmill Press, 1975).
A formal linguistic analysis of Cummings's syntactic rule breaking.

Norman Friedman, *E. E. Cummings: The Art of His Poetry* (Baltimore: Johns Hopkins Press, 1960).
A study of the major themes and techniques in Cummings's poetry up to *95 Poems*, tracing, in one chapter, the development of a poem through its manuscript variants.

Friedman, *E. E. Cummings: The Growth of a Writer* (Carbondale: Southern Illinois University Press, 1964).
An introductory survey of all of Cummings's writings published in his lifetime, with special consideration of his artistic vision.

Friedman, ed., *E. E. Cummings: A Collection of Critical Essays* (Englewood Cliffs, N.J.: Prentice-Hall, 1972).
A collection of fourteen essays covering Cummings's view of life, his language and style, and his longer prose works.

Rushworth Kidder, "E. E. Cummings, Painter," *Harvard Library Bulletin*, 23 (April 1975): 117-138.

Close analyses of poems–including information on sources and allusions–arranged chronologically by volume.

Gary Lane, *I AM: A Study of E. E. Cummings's Poems* (Lawrence: University Press of Kansas, 1976).
Close analysis of twenty-five poems to demonstrate Cummings's development of five ideas: seduction; the individual and heroism; the transcendent unity of life and death; death-in-life; and love as the means to and goal of transcendence.

Barry Marks, *E. E. Cummings* (New York: Twayne, 1964).
Analyzes individual poems; Cummings's vision of children and of sexuality; his place in the contemporary arts; his responses to American culture.

Guy L. Rotella, *Critical Essays on E. E. Cummings* (Boston: G. K. Hall, 1984).
A large and illuminating selection of reviews and essays covering a wide range of critical responses to all of Cummings's work.

Papers:
The Cummings collection in the Houghton Library at Harvard University contains nearly all the papers that were in Cummings's possession at the time of his death. Other important collections are in the Harry Ransom Humanities Research Center at the University of Texas, Austin; the Clifton Waller Barrett Library at the University of Virginia; and the National Archives, in Washington, D.C.

John Dos Passos

This entry was updated by Lisa Nanney (Emory University) from the entry by A. S. Knowles, Jr. (North Carolina State University) in DLB 9, American Novelists, 1910-1945.

Places	London Harvard University	Moscow Western Europe	New York City
Influences and Relationships	Ernest Hemingway E. E. Cummings Theodore Dreiser	Classical Greek and Roman Writers	James Joyce Walt Whitman
Literary Movements and Forms	Biography Realism Journalism	Stream of Con- sciousness	Cinematic Devices in Fiction
Major Themes	The Artist as Social Critic Monopoly Capitalism Materialism Poetry	Politics Failure of Com- munist Idealism History Harvard Aesthetes	Historical Development of American Democracy Proletarian Writing
Cultural and Artistic Influences	New Playwrights Thea- tre	Modern Art	
Social and Economic Influences	Disillusion with Liber- alism/Reactionary Conservatism	World War I Execution of Sacco and Vanzetti	The Spanish Civil War World War II Roosevelt's New Deal

See also the Dos Passos entries in DLB 4, American Writers in Paris, 1920-1939 *and* DLB: Documentary Series 1.

BIRTH: Chicago, Illinois, 14 January 1896, to John R. Dos Passos and Lucy Addison Sprigg Madison.

EDUCATION: B.A., Harvard University, 1916.

MARRIAGES: 21 August 1929 to Katherine F. Smith (deceased). 6 August 1949 to Elizabeth H. Holdridge; child: Lucy Hamlin.

AWARDS: Guggenheim Fellowships, 1939, 1940, 1942; elected to the American Academy of Arts and Letters, 1947; National Institute of Arts and Letters Gold Medal for Fiction, 1957; Academia Nazionale dei Lincei, Antonio Feltrinelli Prize, 1967.

DEATH: Baltimore, Maryland, 28 September 1970.

BOOKS: *One Man's Initiation–1917* (London: Allen & Unwin, 1920; New York: Doran, 1920); republished as *First Encounter* (New York: Philosophical Library, 1945); republished as *One Man's Initiation–1917,* unexpurgated edition (Ithaca: Cornell University Press, 1969);

Three Soldiers (New York: Doran, 1921; London: Hurst & Blackett, 1922);

Rosinante to the Road Again (New York: Doran, 1922);

A Pushcart at the Curb (New York: Doran, 1922);

Streets of Night (New York: Doran, 1923; London: Secker, 1923);

Manhattan Transfer (New York & London: Harper, 1925; London: Constable, 1927);

The Garbage Man: A Parade with Shouting (New York & London: Harper, 1926; London: Constable, 1929);

Orient Express (New York & London: Harper, 1927; London: Cape, 1928);

Facing the Chair: Story of the Americanization of Two Foreignborn Workmen (Boston: Sacco-Vanzetti Defense Committee, 1927);

Airways, Inc. (New York: Macaulay, 1928);

The 42nd Parallel (New York & London: Harper, 1930; London: Constable, 1930);

1919 (New York: Harcourt, Brace, 1932; London: Constable, 1932);

John Dos Passos (courtesy of Elizabeth H. Dos Passos)

Three Plays: The Garbage Man, Airways, Inc., Fortune Heights (New York: Harcourt, Brace, 1934);

In All Countries (New York: Harcourt, Brace, 1934; London: Constable, 1934);

The Big Money (New York: Harcourt, Brace, 1936; London: Constable, 1936);

The Villages are the Heart of Spain (Chicago: Esquire-Coronet, 1937);

Journeys Between Wars (New York: Harcourt, Brace, 1938; London: Constable, 1938);

U.S.A. (New York: Harcourt, Brace, 1938; London: Constable, 1938);

Adventures of a Young Man (New York: Harcourt, Brace, 1939; London: Constable, 1939);

The Ground We Stand On (New York: Harcourt, Brace, 1941; London: Routledge, 1942);

Number One (Boston: Houghton Mifflin, 1943; London: Constable, 1944);

State of the Nation (Boston: Houghton Mifflin, 1944; London: Routledge, 1945);

Tour of Duty (Boston: Houghton Mifflin, 1946);

The Grand Design (Boston: Houghton Mifflin, 1949; London: Lehmann, 1949);

The Prospect Before Us (Boston: Houghton Mifflin, 1950; London: Lehmann, 1951);

Life's Picture History of World War II, full-page texts by Dos Passos (New York: Simon & Schuster/Time, Inc., 1950);

Chosen Country (Boston: Houghton Mifflin, 1951; London: Lehmann, 1952);

District of Columbia (Boston: Houghton Mifflin, 1952);

The Head and Heart of Thomas Jefferson (Garden City, N.Y.: Doubleday, 1954; London: Hale, 1955);

Most Likely to Succeed (New York: Prentice-Hall, 1954; London: Hale, 1955);

The Theme Is Freedom (New York: Dodd, Mead, 1956);

The Men Who Made the Nation (Garden City, N.Y.: Doubleday, 1957);

The Great Days (New York: Sagamore Press, 1958; London: Hale, 1959);

Prospects of a Golden Age (Englewood Cliffs, N.J.: Prentice-Hall, 1959);

Midcentury (Boston: Houghton Mifflin, 1961; London: Deutsch, 1961);

Mr. Wilson's War (Garden City, N.Y.: Doubleday, 1962; London: Hamilton, 1963);

Brazil on the Move (Garden City, N.Y.: Doubleday, 1963; London: Sidgwick & Jackson, 1964);

Occasions and Protests (Chicago: Regnery, 1964);

Thomas Jefferson: The Making of a President (Boston: Houghton Mifflin, 1964);

The Shackles of Power: Three Jeffersonian Decades (Garden City, N.Y.: Doubleday, 1966);

An Informal Memoir: The Best Times (New York: New American Library, 1966; London: Deutsch, 1968);

The Portugal Story: Three Centuries of Exploration and Discovery (Garden City, N.Y.: Doubleday, 1969; London: Hale, 1970);

Easter Island, Island of Enigmas (Garden City, N.Y.: Doubleday, 1971);

Century's Ebb: The Thirteenth Chronicle (Boston: Gambit, 1975).

OTHER: *Eight Harvard Poets,* includes poems by Dos Passos (New York: Gomme, 1917).

For readers familiar with his work in the 1920s and 1930s, John Dos Passos's public image seemed clearly defined. His friends and colleagues were expatriate writers such as Ernest Hemingway, experimental dramatists such as John Howard Lawson, and modernist visual artists such as Fernand Léger. During these decades Dos Passos worked for radical political and artistic causes, serving on the executive board of the *New Masses* and publicly defending Sacco and Vanzetti in the mid 1920s. Photographs of the author suggested a certain intensity; it was the face of the tough-minded intellectual. *Three Soldiers* (1921), *Manhattan Transfer* (1925), and *U.S.A.*

(1938) were clearly indictments of the capitalist system. It appeared obvious that Dos Passos was one of that species even more numerous among European writers than American, the radical intellectual. When Jean-Paul Sartre hailed him as "the greatest writer of our time" in 1938, it seemed a perfectly appropriate mating of author and critic.

But then, so the story went, something seemed to go wrong with Dos Passos. In the later 1930s his work began to attack the Left; he made heroes of free-enterprise capitalists. The radical intellectual had lost his bearings, and reactions ranged from anger to pity. It was only in the 1950s, when new interest in Dos Passos stirred after a period of relative neglect, that some more accurate image of the man, and of the work, could be formulated. The process was helped immeasurably by Dos Passos himself, who began in a modest way to make himself available to his public and let himself be known. This was Dos Passos in his early sixties, to be sure–inevitably different from what he had been in earlier years–but it seemed clear to those who talked to him that his was a whole and healthy personality, with nothing in his manner to suggest that there had been some cataclysmic change. In appearance he was the perfect country squire: tall, portly, dressed in rumpled tweeds. He smoked cigars, enjoyed a glass of bourbon, and radiated amiability. He liked jazz and had a boyish sense of humor.

Dos Passos preferred not to make speeches, but he would read from his work in a gravelly voice whose accents still bore lingering traces of his long childhood stays in Europe and his elite education at Choate and Harvard. It was perhaps not an ideal voice for public performance, but audiences found themselves captivated both by his charm and by their realization that the voice, whatever its obscurities, was the real thing. In the classroom he was forthright both about his own work and that of others, but if he found it necessary to speak unfavorably of another writer, he was without malice. Wherever he went, he was asked why he had changed, why he had moved from radicalism to conservatism (he freely admitted supporting Barry Goldwater and, in Virginia politics, Harry Byrd). If the question was, as it must have been, a bore, Dos Passos answered it politely. He had not changed, he said; the world around him had: when he was young, industrial capitalism was the villain; in later years, communism, labor unions, and big government would all want to enslave us. To his own way of thinking, Dos Passos had been like a soldier continually defending the

Dos Passos with his parents at Niagara Falls, circa 1908 (courtesy of Elizabeth H. Dos Possos)

same ground but facing a different enemy in each war.

As Dos Passos the man emerged from his public persona, we were able to understand more clearly what the influences on him had been. He was born in Chicago (in a hotel room), but his roots were in the East. His father, John R. Dos Passos, was a successful corporation lawyer born in Philadelphia, the son of a Portuguese immigrant; his mother, Lucy Addison Sprigg Madison, came from Virginia and Maryland people. Dos Passos's parents were not free to marry until 1910, when he was fourteen and John R.'s legal wife was no longer living. As a consequence, young Dos Passos experienced what he later called "a hotel childhood." He and his mother lived to themselves, traveling frequently in Europe and sometimes living abroad. As Dos Passos tactfully explained his unusual childhood in *An Informal Memoir: The Best Times:* (1966), "Since [my father's] tenderly affectionate relations with my mother remained technically irregular as long as his first wife lived, it was only in Europe that they could travel openly together." Despite the unsettled circumstances of his youth, Dos Passos re-

membered John R., "The Commodore," with obvious pleasure and affection: "He was a lavish spender. He was known among the gayest of entertainers in a period when social life in New York still had a little of the cordiality of the small town. He was an accomplished public speaker. His fine singing voice was an asset in those days when singing was an after-dinner accomplishment. . . . He was known for his ability to recite whole scenes out of Shakespeare's plays. He had a great flow of conversation and rarely lost his sense of humor.

"He was a warmhearted man besides. He supported needy relatives and was always ready to bail out an unfortunate friend. . . . One of his partners once told me that, though Jack Dos Passos pulled in larger fees than anyone in the firm, every year's end found him in the red."

After a stay in an English school, young Dos Passos was brought back to America and in 1907 entered The Choate School in Connecticut under the name of Madison. He disliked boarding school, but he was a good student. In 1911, at the age of fifteen, he was accepted at Harvard, and following a six-month tour of Europe he began classes in the autumn of 1912. The Harvard years were happy and active. Dos Passos made life-long friends in Cambridge and gathered into his maturing consciousness a vast array of art and literature, especially painting and music. World War I had broken out in 1914, but as late as 1916 it had made little impression on Dos Passos and his circle: "The sound of marching feet came dimly through the walls of the sanctum upstairs in the Harvard Union where we edited the *Monthly.* Except for [E. E.] Cummings who was deep in Greek (he had graduated *summa cum laude* in Greek the year before) and in the invention of his special poetic typography, many of us chose to live in the eighteen-nineties. The *Yellow Book* and *The Hound of Heaven* and Machen's *Hill of Dreams* seemed more important, somehow, than the massacres round Verdun." By 1917, however, both Dos Passos's parents were dead, and he found himself increasingly anxious to see the great spectacle in Europe. In the spring of that year he joined the Norton-Harjes ambulance unit and became a "gentleman volunteer."

The Dos Passos who went to war had already seen life from a variety of perspectives: he had had a rather lonely childhood, but he had visited more of the world than the average American youngster; he had become fascinated with the new century's innovations in the arts, but Gib-

Dos Passos (seated) and Rumsey Marvin in France, 1920

bon and Thucydides had given him a familiarity with the culture of the ancient world; he had left his mark on the late-blooming decadence of the Harvard aesthetes, but their poses and self-conscious removal made him eager for closer experience of the "real world"; he had had the sort of education reserved for sons of the privileged classes, but by the time he sailed for France he had become convinced he was a socialist. If all this was enough to produce bewilderment in a more fragile sensibility, it had no such effect on Dos Passos, who then and for the rest of his life was a man of resilient temperament.

In France, Dos Passos served as a volunteer with an ambulance unit at Verdun, scene of some of the bloodiest fighting of the war, and, after the entry of America, as an enlisted man with an army medical unit. He had begun writing at Harvard; seven poems from that period would be published in *Eight Harvard Poets* (1917), and a novel begun in his Cambridge days and finished later would appear in 1923 under the title *Streets of Night*. But it was the war that really made Dos Passos a writer. The first two of his novels to be

published, *One Man's Initiation–1917* (1920) and *Three Soldiers*, are about the war, and he would return to it in the second volume of the *U.S.A.* trilogy, *1919* (1932).

One Man's Initiation–1917 was hastily written, and while Dos Passos would never disown it, he viewed it as a "greenhorn" book, redeemed only by a certain youthful sharpness of observation. Published first in England, it sold only sixty-some copies in the first six months. The novel was to have been part of a larger work jointly written by Dos Passos and his friend Robert Hillyer; *Streets of Night* was probably to have been incorporated too. As it was, *One Man's Initiation* turned out to be a novel of less than two hundred pages, a modest prelude to *Three Soldiers*. The hero of *One Man's Initiation*, Martin Howe, is clearly based on the author; his companion, Tom Randolph, on Hillyer. Their experiences on the Western Front are presented in a series of impressionistic sketches. An early interest in visual arts had led Dos Passos to take up painting, and he kept a sketching pad with him even at the Front. His narrative illustrates his painter's sensibility in its vivid compositions: "Someone had propped up the fallen crucifix so that it tilted dark despairing arms against the sunset sky where the sun gleamed like a huge copper kettle lost in its own steam. The rain made bright yellowish stripes across the sky and dripped from the cracked feet of the old wooden Christ, whose gaunt, scarred figure hung out from the tilted cross, swaying a little under the beating of the rain. Martin was wiping the mud from his hands after changing a wheel. He stared curiously at the fallen jowl and the cavernous eyes that had meant for some country sculptor ages ago the utterest agony of pain."

At the end of the novel Howe joins in a debate among three Frenchmen–a Catholic, a Communist, and an anarchist–that is full of youthful rhetoric: "They seated themselves round the table again. Martin took in at a glance the eager sunburned faces, the eyes burning with hope, with determination, and a sudden joy flared through him.

" 'Oh, there is hope,' he said, drinking down his glass. 'We are too young, too needed to fail. We must find a way, find the first step of a way to freedom, or life is a hollow mockery.' " But a short time later, the three Frenchmen are dead, leaving the uncertain future in the hands of the American. Dos Passos later wrote that whatever its failures as art, the debate "still expresses, in the language of the time, some of the enthusi-

Dos Passos's sketch of Italy (courtesy of Elizabeth H. Dos Passos)

asms and some of the hopes of young men." The same can be said of the novel as a whole; it is a slight but surprisingly authentic work.

Although Dos Passos's late father had had no trouble earning money, his generosity during his lifetime had left his heirs only a small inheritance, and for years Dos Passos would have trouble securing his share of that. He managed to support himself meagerly as a writer. Before *One Man's Initiation* came off the presses, he was at work on *Three Soldiers*, written in France and Spain. It was published in 1921, its orange dust jacket decorated with praise from such reviewers as H. L. Mencken, who called it "unquestionably the best war story yet produced in America," and Heywood Broun, who found the novel "deep rooted, passionate, sincere and moving." The *New York Herald*'s critic was impressed enough to suggest that "the rulers of the world, presidents, prime ministers, diplomats, will have to take [Henri Barbusse's] 'Under Fire' and 'Three Soldiers' and the facts they represent into account in any future international steps they take."

The novel would announce the arrival of John Dos Passos as an important American writer. It received an initial printing of two or three thousand copies and went on to be widely read. While *Three Soldiers* may not seem as impressive an accomplishment today as it did then, it marks a long stride forward in its author's development. Over four hundred pages in length, the novel is an attack upon war as the lethal agency of a system intent upon destroying the spirit and crushing the freedom of the individual. To give breadth to his message, Dos Passos selected a trio of national types: Fuselli is an Italian-American from San Francisco, Chrisfield a farm boy from Indiana, and John Andrews a well-bred Virginian who had been studying music at Harvard. We follow their fortunes through a narrative of six parts to which Dos Passos gave titles clearly indicative of both the thesis and the plot structure of the novel: "Making the Mould," "The Metal Cools," "Machines," "Rust," "The World Outside," and "Under the Wheels." War is a machine, the titles tell us, that will take the individual and either mold him to serve its purposes or destroy him. There is a "world outside"–an alternative life–but those who seek it will probably be caught and crushed "under the wheels" of the juggernaut. It is a powerful idea, yet the novel seems forced, as polemical novels often do. That Fuselli, who wants nothing so much as to succeed within the system and become a corporal, should end up in a labor battalion; that Chrisfield should become so brutalized that he kills not only Germans but one of his own officers and becomes a fugitive; and that John Andrews should be arrested for desertion as he sits composing his first major work are ironies too perfect to seem uncontrived.

Nevertheless, *Three Soldiers* was Dos Passos's first major work, and it created a model for numerous war novels to come. As George J. Becker points out, Dos Passos shifted "the focus from men at war to war itself," a perspective that would continue to be employed as late as Mailer's *The Naked and the Dead* (1948). Indeed Dos Passos himself, speaking once to college students, would express particular admiration for John Horne Burns's *The Gallery* (1947) because he felt that, of all the many novels of World War II, it did not imitate *Three Soldiers*. In terms of Dos Passos's own development, the novel enlarged the scope of his fiction to allow him to embrace contrasting scenes and moods: the grimness of the Western Front, the beauty of Paris. The use of three varied protagonists, although not an original idea, enabled Dos Passos to crosscut between story lines, a narrative technique similar to film montage. With this innovation, which he later refined in *Manhattan Transfer* and *U.S.A.*, he created a more total image of society than a single unified narrative could accomplish, and he showed how the machinery of capitalism could destroy those who were naive about the system or who resisted it, regardless of their background.

As one reads *Three Soldiers,* he is continually reminded that Dos Passos was immersed in music and painting: "He hurried along the road, splashing now and then in a shining puddle, until he came to a landing place. The road was very wide, silvery, streaked with pale green and violet, and straw-color from the evening sky. Opposite were bare poplars and behind them clusters of buff-colored houses climbing up a green hill to a church, all repeated upside down in the color-streaked river. The river was very full, and welled up above its banks, the way the water stands up above the rim of a glass filled too full. From the water came an indefinable rustling, flowing sound that rose and fell with quiet rhythm in Andrews's ears.

"Andrews forgot everything in the great wave of music that rose impetuously through him, poured with the hot blood through his veins, with the streaked colors of the river and the sky through his eyes, with the rhythm of the flowing river through his ears."

For all its youthful romanticism *Three Soldiers* is clearly the work of a comprehensive sensibility that could draw the imagery of Cézanne and Monet into this novel as easily as it was to draw cubism and expressionism into later works. In the Paris scenes the sound of Debussy can be sensed as clearly as the tauter rhythms of ragtime and Tin Pan Alley in the fiction ahead.

For Dos Passos, America's involvement in World War I seemed to betray the very foundations on which the nation was founded. In *Three Soldiers* he tried to dramatize that long moment when industrial capitalism gripped freedom by the throat and threatened to destroy it. It is an angry book, one in which the author seems at times to be admonishing himself to subordinate art to rhetoric: the autobiographical John Andrews changes his projected tone poem from a work based on a vision of the Queen of Sheba to one entitled "The Body and Soul of John Brown." Yet as Andrews contemplates the uses of revolt, he finds himself confronting another and

Dust jacket, with art by Dos Passos, for the 1926 publication of his play

more dispiriting vision: " 'It seems to me,' he said very softly, 'that human society has always been like that, and perhaps will be always that: organizations growing and stifling individuals, and individuals revolting hopelessly against them, and at last forming new societies to crush the old societies and becoming slaves again in their turn. . . .' "

In the 1920s the astonishing diversity and energy of Dos Passos's career seemed to embody the artistic and cultural revolutions of the era. He painted and sketched, showing his work in galleries in New York and reviewing the work of painters such as Georgia O'Keeffe. He committed himself to leftist causes and befriended a wide array of artists, writers, and political activists. Among his circle were Ernest Hemingway, the Fitzgeralds, Gerald and Sara Murphy, Malcolm Cowley, Edmund Wilson, and many other prominent figures of the 1920s. During these years many American writers shuttled between glamorous settings romanticized by "Jazz Age" stories. Dos Passos too traveled constantly, not to pursue the expatriate lifestyle but to enrich his writing in such varied places as Damascus, Paris, New Orleans, Savannah, Pamplona, Tangiers, Okracoke, Key West, Chicago, Mexico City, Provincetown, Billings, and Moscow. And he wrote constantly. Between 1920 and 1929, he published four novels, two travel books, two plays, a volume of poetry, and a political pamphlet.

Today, only *Three Soldiers* and *Manhattan Transfer* are still read. The poems in *A Pushcart at the Curb* (1922) are principally the observations of a traveler—many written in an objective, imagistic manner—reflecting some of the concerns of the new poetry of the period. Dos Passos would achieve no reputation as a poet, but, as the "Camera Eye" sections of *U.S.A.* reveal, he had a good ear to go with his painter's eye:

Rain slants on an empty square

Across the expanse of cobbles
rides an old shawl-muffled woman
black on a donkey with pert ears
that places sharp hoofs
as if the cobbles were eggs.
The paniers are full
of bright green lettuces
and purple cabbages
and shining red bellshaped peppers,
dripping, shining, a band in marchtime,
in the grey rain,
in the grey city.

A few of the poems are more personal, giving glimpses of an introspective author aware of the problems of heritage:

In me somewhere is a grey room
my fathers worked through many lives to build;
through the barred distorting windowpanes
I see the new moon in the sky.
....
Through all these tears the walls have writhed
with shadow overlaid upon shadow.
I have bruised my fingers on the windowbars
so many lives have cemented and made strong.
While the bars stand strong, outside
the great processions of men's lives go past.
Their shadows squirm distorted on my wall.

Tonight the new moon is in the sky.

Rosinante to the Road Again (1922) is a homage to Spain, which Dos Passos had visited both before and after his time at war. It approaches the subject from two perspectives, the fictional and the actual. In the first, we are in the company of Telemachus and Lyaeus:

Telemachus had wandered so far in search of his father he had quite forgotten what he was looking for. He sat on a yellow plush bench in the cafe El Oro del Rhin, Plaza Santa Ana, Madrid, swabbing up with a bit of bread the last smudges of brown sauce off a plate of which the edges were piled with the dismembered skeleton of a pigeon. Opposite his plate was a similar plate his companion had already polished. Telemachus put the last piece of bread into his mouth, drank down a glass of beer at one spasmodic gulp, sighed, leaned across the table and said:
   "I wonder why I'm here?"
   "Why anywhere else than here?" said Lyaeus, a young man with hollow cheeks and slow-moving hands, about whose mouth a faint pained smile was continually hovering, and he too drank down his beer.

Telemachus is Dos Passos's version of himself, Lyaeus a Bacchic foil to his more inhibited companion. The voyaging of Dos Passos, here as in the later *Orient Express*, is both a voyage into the world and a voyage into the self. Like Martin Howe and John Andrews, Telemachus-Dos Passos is trying to understand himself by observing his reactions within a certain context of persons, places, and events. In the second perspective Dos Passos analyzes the culture of Spain and its inevitable erosion "in the flood of industrialism that for the last twenty years has swelled to obliterate landmarks, to bring all the world to the same level of nickel-plated dullness." *Rosinante to the Road Again* closes in Toledo, where Telemachus is for a moment convinced that he has felt the eternal "gesture" of Spain and perhaps, gained some fleeting sense of himself, but Dos Passos, with characteristic self-mockery, has him doused with cold water thrown from a window above and intended for Lyaeus: " 'Speaking of gestures,' says Lyaeus, and bursts into laughter."

In 1923 Dos Passos released the revised early novel, *Streets of Night*. Linda W. Wagner and Michael Clark make sound cases for giving it something more than passing attention, but the great originality and broader scope of works published after it limits interest in *Streets of Night* to Dos Passos's most devoted readers. He is said to have described the novel as "an effort to recapture that strange stagnation of the intellectual class I'd felt so strangling during college." Certainly *Streets of Night* reminds us that the young Dos Passos has known the same milieu that produced the young T. S. Eliot and the poems of *Prufrock and Other Observations* (1917). It reminds

Dust jacket for Dos Passos's fourth novel

us also that a young novelist's first book is likely to be about the torments of youth; in that respect *Streets of Night* bore much the same relationship to Dos Passos's career as Fitzgerald's *This Side of Paradise* (1920) did to his. Its three principal characters find themselves unable to achieve fulfillment in a society that continues to be fundamentally puritanical and inimical to the life force. Wenny, full of joy, freedom, and physical life, kills himself when he finds he cannot escape the past. Fanshawe the intellectual resigns himself to "Massachusetts Avenue and the College Yard, and the museum and tea with professors' wives." Nan, the girl who could neither give herself to Wenny nor resign herself to Fanshawe, retreats to her room to summon up the spirit of Wenny with a ouija board. The style of the novel is occasionally jejune ("I'll . . . walk into Boston through terrible throbbing streets"), often reminiscent of Eliot ("the plateglass windows of cheap furniture stores and the twisted glint of tinware in the window of Woolworth's"), but *Streets of Night* is at least interesting for its autobiographical implications: in Fanshawe, as in Telemachus, Dos

Passos seems to be examining what he felt to be a certain disturbing priggishness in his own personality.

In the later 1920s another book of travel, *Orient Express* (1927), was published, as well as two of his three plays: *The Garbage Man* (1926) and *Airways, Inc.* (1928). In them Dos Passos demonstrated an unripened but lively theatrical sense. Drawn by John Howard Lawson into the New Playwrights Theatre in 1926, he was able to offer them an expressionistic play, *The Moon Is a Gong* (later called *The Garbage Man*), which they promptly put on the stage that year. It is, as a number of critics have noted, a somewhat incoherent piece, but the message embodied in the experiences of its protagonists, Tom and Jane, is clearly another reflection of the themes of *Streets of Night:* in the stifling wasteland of modern American society, this land of the walking dead, we must discover how to break out and live. *Airways, Inc.*, staged in 1929, focuses in a more naturalistic manner upon the economic, political, and spiritual ills of the capitalist system, reflected in the experiences of an American family, the Turners. Employing analogies to both the Lindbergh flight of 1927 and the execution of Sacco and Vanzetti in the same year, the play argues that inventiveness and heroism will be turned to dishonest profit and that those who seek change will be repressed. The final play, *Fortune Heights*, produced by the Chicago Workers' Theatre in 1934 and twice the same year in Russia, dramatizes the world of the uprooted and disinherited, seen so vividly in the opening and closing passages of *U.S.A.* The play takes place in one of those way-stations for the wanderer, a filling station with a row of overnight cottages on a cross-country highway. In that melancholy, middle-American setting Dos Passos studies the plight of the rootless proletariat desperate for something to believe in and so easily victimized by promoters and schemers.

We now regard the poems, the books of travel, and the two dramas of the period as relatively minor works, but it is clear that, apart from their inherent interest, they were important in providing Dos Passos with some portion of the broad range of experience–both real and literary–his greatest works would require. From that standpoint, *Manhattan Transfer* is easily the most important of the books published before *U.S.A.* In it he would create what he is now known for, a densely populated, many-layered study of the American character.

Dos Passos (standing right) and Katy (seated left) with acquaintances aboard ship at Key West, spring 1928

Manhattan Transfer is a cross-section novel, defined by George J. Becker as "a kind of mosaic, or, better, a revolving stage that presents a multitude of scenes and characters which, taken together, convey a sense of the life of a given milieu and by extension the tone of contemporary life generally." The milieu in this case is New York in the period between the first years of this century and the early 1920s. All of Dos Passos's characters are involved in the life of the city, all are affected by it, and it is their interaction with the pressures of Manhattan–and, by extension, with the pressures of modern, urban, industrial, and mercantile America–that he examines. The novel opens with two differently focused but complementary images:

Three gulls wheel above the broken boxes, orangerinds, spoiled cabbage heads that heave between the splintered plankwalls, the green waves spume under the round bow as the ferry, skidding on the tide, crashes, gulps the broken water, slides, settles slowly into the slip. Handwinches whirl with jingle of chains. Gates fold upwards, feet step out across the crack, men and women

press through the manuresmelling wooden tunnel of the ferry-house, crushed and jostling like apples fed down a chute into a press.

The nurse, holding the basket at arm's length as if it were a bedpan, opened the door to a big hot dry room with greenish distempered walls where in the air tinctured with smells of alcohol and iodoform hung writhing a faint sourish squalling from other baskets along the wall. As she set her basket down she glanced into it with pursed-up lips. The newborn baby squirmed in the cottonwool feebly like a knot of earthworms.

Both images speak of birth, beginnings, disorder, and helplessness. The passengers on the lurching ferry in the littered harbor are carried finally to a tunnel that will lead them, not into a world of open choices, but into a city that will "press" them into shape, or perhaps shapelessness. The newborn Ellen Thatcher, from the moment she is placed in the noisy and odiferous nursery, will respond to her reflexes. Any novel that opens with such images is clearly making a place for itself in the tradition of deterministic literature, but *Manhattan Transfer* is not a simple example of the species. Dos Passos's characters are molded by the city, but they also *are* the city. To some extent, the city is a reflection of what they are and, above all, of their incapacity to control the basic appetites. The determinants, in short, are both human and environmental. Take typical humans and put them in the chaos of the city, and the results will not be predictable but varied according to the random behavior both of the individual and the forces that work upon him. The forces may be external and mechanical (suggested by such chapter titles as "Tracks," "Steamroller," "Fire Engine," "Rollercoaster," and "Nickelodeon") or they may be the more internal forces of greed, lust for power, and sexuality. Ellen Thatcher grows up, becomes an actress, marries and divorces a homosexual actor, marries the observer-protagonist Jimmy Herf, becomes a successful editor, enters the world of the powerful, divorces Jimmy, and drifts toward another marriage. It is a seemingly ruthless life, yet we are not inclined to condemn her. There is a lack of real volition behind Ellen's career; like Dreiser's Carrie Meeber, she acts with little premeditation, moving reflexively in whatever direction, toward whatever person may help her achieve gratification. Near the end of the novel she is buying a dress at Madame Soubrine's when a seamstress, the hapless Anna Cohen, is accidentally burned. Ellen is momentarily shaken by this random exposure to tragedy, but the instincts regain control; we catch our last glimpse of her reaching out again, "advancing smiling toward two grey men in black and white shirt-fronts getting to their feet, smiling, holding out their hands."

In the reporter Jimmy Herf, Dos Passos created another partly autobiographical protagonist, less romantically conceived, however, than Martin Howe or John Andrews. The function of Herf is not simply to bring the author's experience into the novel; rather, as Becker points out, it is "to be odd man out, to be the uneasy seeker of a value system counter to that subscribed to by the rest, to refuse to make the compromises that worldly success demands." The last tentative but vaguely hopeful words of the novel are his, as he makes his way out of the wasteland: "Sunrise finds him walking along a cement road between dumping grounds full of smoking rubbishpiles. The sun shines redly through the mist on rusty donkey-engines, skeleton trucks, wishbones of Fords, shapeless masses of corroding metal. Jimmy walks fast to get out of the smell. He is hun-

gry; his shoes are beginning to raise blisters on his big toes. At a cross-road where the warning light still winks and winks, is a gasoline station, opposite it the Lightning Bug lunchwagon. Carefully he spends his last quarter for breakfast. That leaves him three cents for good luck, or bad luck for that matter." He secures a ride on a huge furniture truck, "shiny and yellow," which has drawn up outside.

While Herf's departure is subdued and his future uncertain, there is a degree of affirmation in the mere fact that he has survived without being corrupted; moreover, there is a slight qualification of Dos Passos's deterministic vision, for Herf has also expressed some independence of will and action, some ability to escape a destiny he cannot accept. But he is a rather passive character, and his survival does little to mitigate our sense that the novel is, in the end, as bleak as the landscape through which Herf last walks.

The lives of Jimmy and Ellen are given more attention in the novel than those of any other characters, but the impact of *Manhattan Transfer* depends upon our sense of being intimate witnesses to a series of interwoven human dramas: to the story of Stan Emory, the ebullient but drunken architect who commits suicide; of Joe Harland, failed financier turned alcoholic; of George Baldwin, an ambulance chaser who pursues, and catches, the brass ring; of Bud Korpenning, a country boy who is driven to his death by fear of the city; of Armand Duval, "Congo Jake," anarchist and bootlegger who learns how to flout the law and get away with it; of Anna Cohen, who dies while sewing dresses for the wealthy.

What emerges from this complex narrative is a vision of a morally undeveloped society where, as William Butler Yeats put it, "The best lack all conviction, while the worst/Are full of passionate intensity." Considering the nature of Dos Passos's fiction to this point, readers of the newly published novel might have expected it to be an attack upon the big city as an expression of the power of industrial capitalism–New York as another kind of battlefield, Manhattan as a symbol of society's compulsion to crush the freedom of the individual in a machinery of streets and subways. In fact, some such meaning is present in the novel. Yet *Manhattan Transfer* is far more a moral work than a political one. Often echoing *The Waste Land* (1922), it seems at times to be another version of "The Fire Sermon" section of Eliot's poem, full of references to fire engines, si-

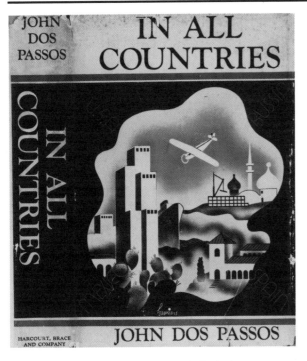

Dust jacket for Dos Passos's 1934 book of essays

rens, buildings in flames, death by fire. Its quarreling couples are as tense and desperate as Eliot's; Dos Passos had the same sense of how banal and degrading eroticism can be, and, like Eliot, he could write with a scalpel: " 'Get up on your toes and walk in time to the music. . . . Move in straight lines that's the whole trick.' Her voice cut the quick coldly like a tiny flexible sharp metalsaw. Elbows joggling, faces set, gollywog eyes, fat men and thin women, thin women and fat men rotated densely about them. He was crumbling plaster with something that rattled achingly in his chest, she was an intricate machine of sawtooth steel whitebright bluebright copperbright in his arms. When they stopped her breast and the side of her body and her thigh came against him. He was suddenly full of blood streaming with sweat like a runaway horse."

As Dos Passos moved toward *U.S.A.*, he was not only finding the vision he needed, but he was developing certain techniques that would lie at the very heart of his masterpiece. One of the most important of these is the indirect interior monologue, which allowed him to write in the third person while suggesting, through the use of selected words and phrases, the quality of a character's thoughts. When little Jimmy Herf returns from Europe with his mother, Dos Passos presents him objectively and subjectively without breaking stride: "He catches his toe on the brass threshold of the smoking room door and sprawls on deck, gets up rubbing his bare knee just in time to see the sun break through chocolate clouds and swash a red stream of brightness over the putty-colored water. Billy with the freckles on his ears whose people are for Roosevelt instead of for Parker like mother is waving a silk flag the size of a handkerchief at the men on a yellow and white tugboat." It is a Joycean technique, one that Dos Passos used with complete mastery.

In the late 1920s and early 1930s Dos Passos became a hero of the Left. *Manhattan Transfer* was taken, oversimply but not inaccurately, to be a portrayal of capitalist corruption. His activities on behalf of Sacco and Vanzetti, culminating in the tract titled *Facing the Chair* (1927), his visit to Russia in 1928, the trip with Dreiser in 1931 to investigate the condition of miners in Harlan County, Kentucky, all contributed to the image of a writer moving directly toward communism. In one of his indispensable biographical narratives in *The Fourteenth Chronicle* (1973), Townsend Ludington speaks of this, Dos Passos's "most left wing period": "Communists had every reason to believe he was one of them. Granville Hicks, himself a Party member until disillusioned by the Soviet-Nazi pact in 1939, when writing about 'The Politics of John Dos Passos' in 1950 for *Antioch Review,* asserted that 'no one had more influence on the leftward swing of the intellectuals in the early '30s.' Radicals saw what they wanted to in his work which, hypercritical of American society, suited their needs. They simply overlooked or reinterpreted his tendency toward liberalism and individualism although he stated his position explicitly. For in the *New Republic* in 1930 he had called himself 'a middle-class liberal, whether I like it or not,' and he located himself politically as neither a member of the Communist party nor procapitalist. In 1932 he referred to himself as a 'middle-class intellectual' and a 'camp follower of radical parties.' To the question, 'Do you believe that becoming a communist deepens an artist's work?' he answered, 'I don't see how a novelist or historian could be a party member under present conditions.' " As the three novels of *U.S.A.* (*The 42nd Parallel, 1919, The Big Money*) began to appear, they were assumed to represent the voice and conscience of the radical Left. That is not the way they are seen now.

It is true that Dos Passos was concerned with the victimization of the American proletariat; true that he deplored power-grabbing laissez-faire capitalists like Morgan; true that he re-

Dos Passos as a war correspondent in the Pacific, 1945

garded our participation in the First World War ("Mr. Wilson's War") as a betrayal of the old American ideals of peace and independence. Yet, taken as a whole, *U.S.A.* has no messages, as literature from the radical Left characteristically did; it is not a rallying cry. Toward the close of the final volume, in fact, the Communist party is portrayed as simply another ruthless collective. What fascinated Dos Passos was history. The problem was finding a way to understand it and present it. His answer was a new kind of narrative, a weaving together of the actual, the fictional, and the personal, and *The 42nd Parallel* (1930) was his first expression of it. With this new kind of book he could tell his real story, the collapse of the American Dream.

The structure of *The 42nd Parallel,* maintained in principle in *1919* and *The Big Money* (1936), is grounded in twenty narrative sections chronicling the lives of five fictional characters in the period between 1900 and 1917: Fenian McCreary, a laboring-class youngster who will be drawn into the revolutionary movement, lose momentum, and fade out of the story; Janey Wil-

liams, a stenographer who goes to work for J. Ward Moorehouse; Moorehouse, a self-made entrepreneur who moves into public relations; Eleanor Stoddard, a self-consciously arty young woman who opens an interior decorating shop with her friend Eveline Hutchins, becomes a theatrical designer, and later the confidante of Moorehouse; and Charley Anderson, a mechanic from North Dakota who goes overseas in an ambulance unit.

Woven through the fictional narratives are three other perspectives: the "Newsreels," made up of headlines, bits of newspaper stories, and snatches of popular songs, reflecting the events and ideas of America and the world in the first seventeen years of the century; the "Camera Eyes," impressionistic sketches drawn from the memories of the author; and the celebrated biographies of actual Americans. *The 42nd Parallel* opens with a "Newsreel," setting the time. America is triumphant in its war with Spain, the British have been defeated at Mafeking. The new century is being welcomed in. Ex-President Benjamin Harrison warns against "territorial expansion," while Senator Beveridge hails the American future and links it to the introduction of "civilization" in Asia. The choice of materials is significant, although Dos Passos disarms the reader by seasoning the "Newsreels" with amusing trivia– "GAIETY GIRLS MOBBED IN NEW JERSEY"– as if he did not want us to guess his themes too quickly. Here in the first moments of the novel, however, we have intimations of one of the major ideas of *U.S.A.*, that America lost its innocence when it sought to become a world power.

The first "Camera Eye" follows. We are in Dos Passos's memories, and again the theme is international conflict. He is with his mother in Belgium at the time of the Boer War, and they are being pursued by an angry crowd that believes the woman and child are English: "they're throwing stones grownup people throwing stones She's walking fast and we're running her pointed toes sticking out sharp among the poor trodden grassblades under the shaking folds of the brown cloth dress Englander." Then the first fictional narrative begins, the story of Fenian McCreary, "Mac." We follow Mac from some moments of his childhood in Middletown, Connecticut, through the death of his mother and the family's departure for Chicago, all written in a style that is part straight story telling, part indirect interior monologue, and part indirectly reported speech: "The funeral was from the undertaking parlors on Riverside Avenue on the next block. Fainy felt very proud and important because everybody kissed him and patted his head and said he was behaving like a little man. He had a new black suit on, too, like a grownup suit with pockets and everything, except that it had short pants. There were all sorts of people at the undertaking parlors he had never been close to before . . . and it smelt of whiskey and beer like at Finley's."

As Mac boards the coach for Chicago, having had breakfast at the station lunch counter, "Camera Eye (2)" interrupts with a contrasting scene from Dos Passos's childhood: expensive toy in hand, he boards a parlor car with his parents, who, traveling in luxury, are discussing the social acceptability of "colored people." Mac's story resumes, bringing him to the age of seventeen and the brink of his association with the old con-artist, Doc Bingham. "Newsreel II" interrupts with excerpts from Governor Pingree's speech to the Michigan legislature warning that inequality (Mac and the child Dos Passos; the coach and the parlor car) will lead to revolution; from Andrew Carnegie's speech extolling the virtues of manual labor (while Mac hopes that answering Doc Bingham's ad will make him a businessman); and from a story about the aviation pioneer Santos-Dumont (the reference to the Brazilian flier introduces another theme, Dos Passos's celebration of daring and inventiveness). "Camera Eye (3)" remembers the author's childish fright at seeing from a train window the smoke and flame of potteries at night, his mother's telling him that people "work there all night . . . Workingmen and people like that laborers travailleurs greasers," and her account of the shooting of a "greaser" in Mexico.

After the phrase "shooting a greaser" we are quickly confronted with the words *"Lover of Mankind,"* a perfect example of Dos Passos's ironic juxtapositions. The lover of mankind is the great Socialist Eugene Debs, the subject of the first of the biographies. Setting up his lines in the manner of a Whitman poem, Dos Passos tells the story of Debs's desire to create "a world brothers might own/where everybody would split even," and of his betrayal not only by the bosses but by his own proletarian followers:

> But where were Gene Debs's brothers in nineteen eighteen when Woodrow Wilson had him locked up in Atlanta for speaking against war

where were the locomotive firemen and engineers when they hustled him off to Atlanta Penitentiary?

> they were afraid to be with him,
> or to think much about him for fear they might believe him;
> for he said:
> *While there is a lower class I am of it, while there is a criminal class I am of it, while there is a soul in prison I am not free.*

An important point is made here. The collapse of the American Dream, in Dos Passos's view, was no simple matter of the suppression of a heroic proletariat by capitalist tyrants. It was far more a matter of some pervasive inability of Americans from all walks of life to find the moral resources the dream demanded. Mac's story is a case in point: when we last see him, the once-eager revolutionary is slipping into the pleasures of domesticity.

A close reading of as little as the first twenty-seven pages of *The 42nd Parallel* (to the end of the Debs biography) awakens us to the nature of the whole trilogy. Despite its "realism," the work is a carefully constructed artifice. Alfred Kazin has written that "we soon recognize that Dos Passos's contraption, his new kind of novel, is in fact (reminding us of Frank Lloyd Wright's self-dramatizing Guggenheim Museum) *the greatest character in the book itself.* Our greatest pleasure in reading *The 42nd Parallel* is in being surprised, delighted, and provoked by the 'scheme,' by Dos Passos's shifting 'strategy.' We recognize that the exciting presence in *The 42nd Parallel* is the book itself, which is always getting us to anticipate some happy new audacity. A mobile by Alexander Calder or a furious mural design by Jackson Pollock makes us dwell on the specific originality of the artist, the most dramatic thing about the work itself. So *The 42nd Parallel* becomes a book about writing *The 42nd Parallel.* That is the tradition of the romantic poet, and reading him we are on every side surrounded by Dos Passos himself: his 'idea.' "

There is no way that the fictional narratives of *U.S.A.* can be gracefully summarized without destroying their essential nature. They are deliberately verbose, tedious, banal, and unselective, meant to give a precise effect of real people thinking, talking, and acting their way through series of experiences to which they can bring only a limited understanding. The narratives are, in short, accounts of human beings stumbling through history, an effect heightened by the sporadic clatter of the "Newsreels." *The 42nd Parallel* takes its characters from the beginning of the century to World War I. The principal figure is Ward Moorehouse, born, like Yankee Doodle Dandy, on the Fourth of July. Mac and Charley Anderson stand virtually clear of him; the others—Janey, Eleanor, Eveline—are part of the making of what is essentially a new man for the new century, the artificial man in the synthetic career. Moorehouse is opportunistic, pompous, hypocritical, self-important. His careers rest principally upon his ability to do and say—without a hint of self-mockery—what is expected of him. He must be able to proclaim, when war breaks out, "I have offered my services to the government to serve in whatever capacity they see fit for the duration of the war . . . Of course I shall serve without pay," without once sensing that he is parodying himself. Moorehouse's rise through "public relations" to the inner sanctums of the big corporations is, like the rise of a scheming noble in an Elizabethan drama, in itself a comment on the age.

1919 is about the great betrayal, the war. New characters appear: Joe Williams, Janey's brother, a bewildered merchant seaman who dies on Armistice Day in a barroom brawl; Daughter, a Dallas ingenue who goes to Europe with Near East Relief at the end of the war and is killed larking in an airplane over Paris; Richard Ellsworth Savage, who leaves Harvard and joins the Norton-Harjes ambulance unit; Ben Compton, a radical who is sent to prison for refusing to be conscripted. But the dominant figure, once again, is Moorehouse, who turns his talents to the peace conference at Versailles and helps to see that the world is delivered into the hands of the money interests. As Kazin points out, *1919* is a book with "fury behind it . . . a picture of waste, hypocrisy, and debauchery."

The Big Money is a portrait of a disintegrating social order. Charley Anderson, having become a flying ace, returns from the war and goes into the aviation business. He is after the "big money." His rise and fall is a study of the corrupting power of that pursuit, a sinister version of the Horatio Alger myth in which the road from rags to riches becomes a journey into moral collapse. It is significant that Charley's fall crosses the rise of the actress Margo Dowling, who epitomizes the triumph of a fatuous and typically American kind of vulgarity. Ward Moorehouse appears again, slipping silently into the vacuum of his own character. Even as he falls, Richard Sav-

age, who pursues Moorehouse's place in the halls of power, is obviously beginning to come apart. The novel ends with the agony of Mary French, who pours herself into the unsuccessful defense of Sacco and Vanzetti. Thus, as *U.S.A.* concludes, events in the fictional narrative have merged with events in the recent life of the author; Dos Passos's novel has very nearly caught up with his own life.

The fictional narratives are the heart of *U.S.A.* Reading them, we feel that all this is happening to us, or to people like us, not just to people who will be in history books. This is the effect, of course, that realistic fiction always strives for, to put the reader on recognizable streets, in familiar rooms, with believable characters. Dos Passos, however, takes us further than that; with his technique of adopting the narrative manner to a particular voice, and sustaining the narrative over long stretches, we find the narrative voice taking over our imagination and becoming our voice: we seem to be telling our own story. It is a remarkable technique, especially when we consider that the average reader, standing on some relatively uneventful middle ground of American experience, really has little in common with Dos Passos's desperate "Gullivers," as Arthur Mizener calls them. Yet the stories of Mac, of Joe Williams, of Charley Anderson, of Margo Dowling seem finally to spring from our own memories.

As effective as the narratives are, however, it has long been the critical consensus that the biographies are the most brilliant tiles in the mosaic of *U.S.A.* The real heroes, the real villains who are not to be found in the fictional narratives, stand before us here: Debs, Burbank, and Frank Lloyd Wright; Carnegie, Morgan, and William Randolph Hearst. There are biographies of thinkers—Randolph Bourne, Jack Reed, Paxton Hibben—and entertainers—Rudolph Valentino and Isadora Duncan; inventors—Edison, Steinmetz, the Wright Brothers—and politicians—Teddy Roosevelt, Woodrow Wilson, and Robert La Follette. Their presence affirms the Plutarchian assumption, ratified by Gibbon and Emerson: a nation's destiny is molded in the personalities, the dreams, the actions of representative men. While the biographies are not lacking in inspirational figures, the story they tell, finally, is of an America that has become the captive of a greedy, powerful few. In carefully controlled cadences, and with the most finely tuned irony, Dos Passos shows us the ascendant personalities of the nation:

John Dos Passos with his wife Elizabeth, her son Chris, and their daughter Lucy (courtesy of Elizabeth H. Dos Passos)

Bessemer Duquesne Rankin Pittsburgh
Bethlehem Gary
Andrew Carnegie gave millions for
peace
and libraries and scientific institutes
and endowments and thrift
whenever he made a billion dollars he
endowed an institution to

promote universal peace
    always
    except in time of war.

J. P. Morgan is a silent man, not given to public utterances, but during the great steel strike he wrote Gary: *Heartfelt congratulations on your stand for the open shop, with which I am, as you know, absolutely in accord. I believe American principles of liberty are deeply involved, and must win if we stand firm.*

(Wars and panic on the stock exchange,
machinegunfire and arson,
bankruptcies, warloans,
starvation, lice, cholera and typhus:
good growing weather for the House of
Morgan.)

The most famous of the biographies, however, and arguably the finest piece of writing in *U.S.A.*, is about the Unknown Soldier. He is portrayed at the end of *1919* as a bewildered American Everyman, literally torn to bits by the machinery of "Mr. Wilson's War":

John Doe
heart pumped blood:
alive thudding silence of blood in your ears
down in the clearing in the Oregon forest
where the punkins were punkincolor pouring
into the blood through the eyes and the
fallcolored trees and the bronze hoopers were
hopping through the dry grass, where tiny
striped snails hung on the underside of the
blades and flies hummed, wasps droned, bumblebees
buzzed, and the woods smelt of wine and
mushrooms and apples, homey smell of fall pouring
into the blood,
    and I dropped the tin hat and the sweaty
pack and lay flat with the dogday sun licking my

throat and adamsapple and the tight skin over the breastbone.

The shell had his number on it.

The blood ran into the ground.
....
Where his chest ought to have been they
                                        pinned

the Congressional Medal, the D.S.C., the Médaille Militaire, the Belgian Croix de Guerre, the Italian gold medal, the Vitutea Militara sent by Queen Marie of Rumania, the Czechoslovak War Cross, the Virtuti Militari of the Poles, a wreath sent by Hamilton Fish, Jr., of New York, and a little wampum presented by a deputation of Arizona redskins in warpaint and feathers. All the Washingtonians brought flowers.

Woodrow Wilson brought a bouquet of poppies.

The indignation that fires Dos Passos's writing here is matched only by the heartbreak of "Camera Eye (50)," near the end of *The Big Money,* in which Dos Passos recalls the execution of Sacco and Vanzetti:

all right we are two nations
America our nation has been beaten by strangers who have bought the laws and fenced off the meadows and cut down the woods for pulp and turned our pleasant cities into slums and sweated the wealth out of our people and when they want to they hire the executioner to throw the switch

but do they know that the old words of the immigrants are being renewed in blood and agony tonight do they know that the old American speech of the haters of oppression is new tonight in the mouth of an old woman from Pittsburgh of a husky boilermaker from Frisco who hopped freights clear from the Coast to come here in the mouth of a Back Bay socialworker in the mouth of an Italian printer of a hobo from Arkansas the language of the beaten nation is not forgotten in our ears tonight

What can one hope to say about *U.S.A.?* One is tempted to say that it is both a more daring and a more significant work than any other American novel of this century—something akin to *Moby-Dick* (1851) in the century before. It is unquestionably Dos Passos's masterpiece. Like all masterpieces that come in mid career, it has haunted the reactions to everything that followed.

By the year *The Big Money* was in print, the Spanish civil war had broken out, and Dos Passos, like Hemingway, felt compelled to go to this beloved and familiar country. But while his sympathies were with the Left–the Republic–in its struggle against the Fascist rebels, the war marked his final and irrevocable turn against communism. An old friend, José Robles, was an apparent victim of the bloody purge Communists were carrying out in the ranks of the Left; Dos Passos's long friendship with Hemingway was ruptured in the wake of that tragic affair. When Dos Passos tried to find out when and why Robles had been executed, he was dismayed by the insensitivity of Hemingway who, speaking with the authority of one who had the ears of the commissars, brushed aside Robles's death as a necessity of war. Over this affair, as well as over their growing disagreement about the whole situation in Spain, the long friendship of the two writers was ended until it was briefly resumed following the death of Dos Passos's first wife in 1947.

As he left Spain in the spring of 1937, Dos Passos was also beginning to break his long-standing ties with Europe. For the remaining thirty-three years of his life, he would see himself as clearly American–an often restless American, to be sure, but one whose roots had taken firm hold in American soil. The disaster of Spain had blighted the old scenes; the clash of fascism and communism, with its mixture of violence and deceit, had suggested how treacherous the intellectual climate of Europe had become. In an essay in *Common Sense,* Dos Passos spoke of his relief at returning: "An American in 1937 comes back from Europe with a feeling of happiness, the relief of coming up out into the sunlight from a stifling cellar, that some of his grandfathers must have felt coming home from Metternich's Europe after the Napoleonic wars, the feeling all the immigrants have had when they first saw the long low coast and the broad bays of the new world. At least we still have alternatives."

In the 1940s Dos Passos would finally establish his claim to his father's farm in Virginia. He had had a house in Provincetown, at the tip of Cape Cod, since the early 1930s. Massachusetts and Virginia, Puritans and presidents: Dos Passos had finally planted his feet squarely upon the spiritual and temporal cornerstones of America. Although his fame was based on searching analyses of the failure of the American Dream, he was becoming increasingly convinced that America, whatever its failures, was the last hope

John, Elizabeth, and Lucy Dos Passos on the front steps of the house at Spence's Point, circa 1957 (courtesy of Elizabeth H. Dos Passos)

of human freedom. He was immersing himself in American history, particularly the age of Jefferson, and was well on his way to assuming the political posture that he would maintain for the rest of his life: that of the independent Jeffersonian democrat.

In 1939 Harcourt, Brace published the first novel of a trilogy that addressed itself to Dos Passos's new concerns. *Adventures of a Young Man* (1939) concludes with the death of Glenn Spotswood in Spain, shot either by Fascist snipers or by his Communist colleagues, but clearly because he was marked for extermination by the Communists. The story that precedes this starkly written conclusion ("Then suddenly something split and he went spinning into blackness. He was dead.") traces the path that brings young Glenn to die in a Spanish village, a victim of international politics. The journey begins, ironically, in innocent American idealism, which encourages Glenn to want to do good in a murderously pragmatic world. Influenced by the high-minded liberal ideologies that flooded the thinking of American intellectuals in the 1920s and 1930s, Glenn conceives his destiny in what will turn out to be fa-

tally simple terms: "Glenn got to talking about how he felt he'd wasted the last three years, taking all that trouble putting himself through college just because nobody of the whitecollar class could think of anything better to do. And all the time what he'd really wanted to be doing was beat his way around the country living like working people lived. The whitecollar class was all washed up. It was in the working class that real things were happening nowadays. The real thing was the new social order that was being born out of the working class. Of course, some things had been real, there had been a girl named Gladys. But gosh, it was hard to keep your life from getting all balled up. What he'd decided was to hell with your private life. He'd live for the working class. That was real."

The vision of *Adventures of a Young Man* was not the sort that would win the applause of a critical establishment largely committed to the Left. Although Dos Passos intended the spirit of the novel to be lightened by moments of satire, his critics found nothing amusing in the story and were offended by Dos Passos's rhetoric in the passages of poetic prose with which he bracketed sections of the novel:

> In America the Communist Party
> grew powerful and remarkably rich
> out of the ruin of freedom in Europe
> and the sacrifice of righteous men.
>
> Agents of the Kremlin plan
> were able to play on the benevolence of busybodies, the blindness of charitable dogooders, and the vanity of welltodo young men with windy brains.

It was in this period of his long career that Dos Passos's reputation went into a decline from which it would not entirely recover in his lifetime. Part of that decline had to do with his ideological estrangement from critics who deplored his break with left-liberalism, but part had to do with the altered nature of his fiction. As Dos Passos's writing sprang ever more quickly from current events, he put the "art" novel aside in favor of the one-dimensional, plainly written narrative. Something seemed to go out of his style, as if the shrunken boundaries of his vision had diminished the scope of his talent. The second novel of the trilogy, *Number One* (1943), was even simpler than the first in conception and execution. The focus is upon Glenn's brother, Tyler, who throws in his lot with a Huey Long-like politician, Chuck Crawford. Excited at first by Crawford's flamboyant energy, Tyler comes to realize that Crawford is a dangerous man, corrupt, power-hungry, and—as the title of the novel implies—utterly selfish. He breaks with Crawford in time to salvage a little self-respect, his decision influenced by a letter written by Glenn

> After all it's what you do that counts, not what you say.
> ....
> Tyler, what I'd started to write you about was not letting them sell out too much of the for the people and by the people part of the oldtime United States way. It has given us freedom to grow. Growing great people is what the country's for, isn't it?

Thus, as Linda W. Wagner points out, the phrase "number one" has yet other meanings: the need of the individual to be aware of the moral significance of his actions; the need of the nation to allow its people—its individuals—"freedom to grow," to achieve their full moral stature. Dos Passos says, in the last words of the novel,

> neighbors, wives, children, the postman who comes to the door, the woman who works in the kitchen, the man higher up;
> weak as the weakest, strong as the strongest,
> the people are the republic,
> the people are you.

The final novel, *The Grand Design* (1949), examines Roosevelt's New Deal. Its title is also double-edged, for it refers both to the "grand design" of the founding fathers, based on individual liberty, and to the complex and finally self-defeating vision of the Roosevelt administrations, a vision based on the assumption that government must shape the national destiny. Again, Dos Passos is observing the fallacies of collective thinking and the many ways in which idealism can come to grief in a welter of plans and programs that make no sense in practical application. The novel focuses upon another of Dos Passos's long-standing concerns, the temptations and abuses of power. His portrait of a declining Roosevelt speaks in melancholy tones of the price we have paid for the persuasive charms of Rooseveltian rhetoric:

> The President of the United States
> was a man of great personal courage
> and supreme confidence in his powers of persua-

sion. He never spared himself a moment, flew to Brazil and Casablanca, Cairo
> to negotiate at the level of the leaders;
> at Teheran the triumvirate
> without asking anybody's leave got to
> meddling with history; without consulting their constituents, revamped geography,
> divided up the bloody globe and left the freedoms out.
> ....
> We learned . . .
> ....
> but we have not learned . . .
> ....
> how to put power over the lives of men
> into the hands of one man
> and to make him use it wisely.

Of the three novels (published together in 1952 as *District of Columbia*), *The Grand Design* is the most richly developed and atmospheric. Dos Passos's evocation of Washington in the years of the New Deal and World War II is superb, a return to the sort of brilliant portrait of a city he had rendered earlier in *Manhattan Transfer*.

Through the war years Dos Passos had traveled about the country, observing the behavior of America in crisis (reported in *State of the Nation*, 1944) and immersing himself further in the historical and philosophical sources of the nation (*The Ground We Stand On*, 1941; *The Head and Heart of Thomas Jefferson*, begun in the early 1940s, published in 1954). In 1945 he had toured Germany and the still-active Pacific fronts, gathering his impressions in *Tour of Duty* (1946). While these and the other nonfiction works of the 1940s, 1950s, and 1960s are genuine reflections of their author's interests, they are also testimony to the fact that Dos Passos made his living by writing and could not have afforded—even if he had wished—to live off the rewards of art alone. Especially as his reputation as a novelist declined in the years after *U.S.A.*, he found the income from his fiction often precarious; simple necessity required that he be ready to apply his skills where the rewards were more certain.

In 1947, eighteen years after their marriage, Dos Passos's wife, the beloved Katy, was killed in an automobile accident. Dos Passos was also injured, losing an eye. Although he would remarry in 1949, Katy's death was a terrible blow, but it seems to have set Dos Passos's fiction on the path it would follow through the 1950s. *Chosen Country* (1951), *Most Likely to Succeed* (1954), and *The Great Days* (1958) are all more "personal"

Dos Passos in Rome with President Giuseppe Saragat of Italy, 1967, after receiving the Antonio Feltrinelli Prize for Fiction

than the work of the preceding twenty-five years, as if Dos Passos felt that the time had come to provide a fuller account of himself. *Chosen Country* is in many respects a tribute to Katy, portrayed in the figure of Lulie. It also marks the creation of an alter-ego Dos Passos would use again, Jay Pignatelli. Going back over the years sketched in the "Camera Eyes" of *U.S.A.*, he retells his early life in terms of two quests: for love, fulfilled in his marriage; and for a sense of country, fulfilled in his realization that America was not simply the land of his birth, it was the land in which he chose to live. It is a sentimental novel (notwithstanding a scathing portrait of Hemingway as "George Elbert Warner"), but it is so nostalgic, so idyllic, so sure of its values that it seems churlish to criticize it. It is harder to speak favorably of *Most Likely to Succeed* and *The Great Days*, however. By the 1950s Dos Passos was calling his novels "Chronicles," arranging them according to internal chronology with *Chosen Country*, since it covers the early years, heading the list. The chronicles, then, are of two kinds: those that focus closely on the author's life, and those that are part of the great social epic that comprises Dos

Passos's finest work. *Most Likely to Succeed* and *The Great Days*, like *Chosen Country*, are clearly of the former kind and seem to spring principally from Dos Passos's compulsion to analyze himself as he had analyzed the nation. But Dos Passos was not naturally that kind of writer; his soul-searching tends to be embarrassing. In the career of Jed Morris, the protagonist of *Most Likely to Succeed*, he seems to be entertaining, in part, a vision of his worst self, a self that was not, but might have been. His analysis of the machinations of the theater and the film industry has, as always, the authority of a writer who was careful to find out how things work, but the novel is a bitter and seemingly gratuitous addition to the chronicles. *The Great Days* fills in the period of World War II by dwelling upon the midlife crisis of Ro Lancaster, a journalist who finds himself trying to recover his momentum by winning the love of a much younger woman. For Ro, the "great days" are all in the past; the only hope lies in Elsa, a self-centered girl who is hardly in a position to understand him or his life (James T. Farrell, who liked the book, sagely remarked that she "is like a daughter of a character in *U.S.A.*"). This is an autumnal novel, full of the sense of how little a man's life adds up to no matter where he has been or what he has done. Nevertheless, *The Great Days* gave Dos Passos an opportunity to describe wartime Washington again, to reflect again upon his first marriage, and to write about the Nuremburg trials and postwar Paris. It has a place, if not a strong one, in his long chronicle of our age.

If the novels of the 1950s seemed to suggest that Dos Passos had lost the desire to write the broader, more objectively conceived fiction that he was known for, *Midcentury* (1961) was, in part, reassuring. Returning to some of the techniques of *U.S.A.*, Dos Passos moved outside himself to record the decline and fall of the labor movement as an expression of the just aspirations of the American worker. It is a big novel (496 pages), and more than once it strikes some of the old sparks. A brilliant biography of the ill-fated young actor James Dean demonstrated that Dos Passos had lost none of his ability to sculpt a significant personality in granitic prose: "They took him on to study at the Actor's Studio. The Actor's Studio was celebrity's lobby in those days. That year Marlon Brando was the artistic idol of the screen. Directors saw a young Brando in Dean (the hepcat school, sideburns and a rat's nest for hair, leather jackets, jackboots and a motorcycle at the curb. These are tough guys, delinquents; but sensitive: Great God how they're sensitive). Elia Kazan hired him to play a sinister adolescent: 'Live the part,' Stanislavski told his actors." The fictional narratives of the beat-up, dying old Wobbly, Blackie Bowman, are marvelous: the essential Dos Passos, finding the right voice to express the rambling memories of an American "prole" who has been through the wars and seen the cause betrayed: "The fall I decided to take a spell on the beach in San Pedro while I looked for better paying work was the fall they blew up the *Los Angeles Times*. To tell the truth I got my first job because the cops rounded up so many bridgemen that work was at a standstill on a new downtown hotel. At least in the merchant marine I'd learned how to balance on a scaffolding and paint. The day they arrested the McNamaras, just to prove I wasn't a scab, I went around and joined the International Association of Bridgemen and Structural Iron Workers, not that I approved of killing innocent people–that was no way to fight the class war–but I honestly believed the McNamara brothers were being framed."

Like *U.S.A.*, *Midcentury* uses a variety of materials–fiction, biographies, headlines and news stories, authorial meditations–to assemble a picture of American civilization as Dos Passos perceived it in the later 1950s. The central fictional figure is Terry Bryant, a World War II veteran who believes that he has found true brotherhood in the unions, only to discover that the labor movement has become repressive, self-serving, and infiltrated by gangsters. In addition there are such figures as Blackie, who embodies both the turbulent history of labor radicalism and the defeat of the old ideals, and Jasper Milliron, who resurrects the dying spirit of free enterprise by deciding to leave the family corporation and strike out on his own. Their stories are augmented by five segments called "Investigator's Notes," in which a union member tells his story–in each case a story of corruption, violence, and betrayal–to a Senate committee.

The biographies speak, from differing perspectives, of an America that has been undermined by various kinds of fatuity and self-indulgence, expressed in the glorified punkdom of a James Dean or perhaps in the pernicious influence of Freud:

> By crying up inhibition as the ulti-
> mate ill Freud disposed of thou shalt not. God

is a father image to be talked out of the
system. The Marxists at least
made transcendent their anti-God principle;
for Paraclete read Dialectic; Man worships History,
Thesis, Antithesis, Synthesis
form another new Trinity: by scrupulous
adherence to the Party Line a man may be
assured of salvation

by dialectical materialism;

these are the brainwashers, the twin myths of Marx and Freud, opposed yet interlocking, as victory interlocks with defeat, which soared out of the scientific ruminations of the late nineteenth century

to hover like scavenger birds
over the disintegration of the Western
will:

Weighing heavily in the impact of the biographies are studies of such labor leaders as Bridges, Tobin, Beck, and Hoffa, telling a composite story of the subversion of the movement. There is a degree of mitigation in such a life as that of General William Dean, the self-disciplined hero of Korea, but it is clear from the biographies as a whole that Dos Passos's view of our "representative men" was not a hopeful one.

Midcentury is an impressive book but not an altogether satisfactory one. Its main defect is a troubling incongruity of perspectives. The title implies a novel of breadth, and the biographies, documentaries, and meditations support that promise in varying degrees: the opening meditation, for instance, places the author against a vast backdrop of space and time:

> *Walking the earth under the stars,*
> *musing midnight in midcentury,*
> *a man treads the road with his dog;*
> *the dog, less timebound in her universe of*
>   *stench and*
> *shrill, trots eager ahead.*
> ....
> *A million men on a million nights, heirs of a*
> *million generations, ponder the proliferation of*
> *their millions to the millionth power till*
>   *multitude bursts into nothingness,*
>   *and numbers fail.*

The fictional narratives, however, leave us with the impression that we have read an expose of the labor movement. While this is not literally true, it is nevertheless a strong enough impression to leave the reader a little uncertain of the real import of *Midcentury*.

The same uncertainty may trouble the reader of *Century's Ebb* (1975). Published five years after Dos Passos's death, this final chronicle often seems to be focused upon too narrow a range of materials to speak for the century. While its reach of time is wide–from the Spanish civil war to the moon-landing–its fictional perspective is embodied in characters who take us over historical ground that Dos Passos had to a large extent covered before and whose lives are expressive of certain themes that had become nearly obsessive. There is Jay Pignatelli, who takes us back to Dos Passos's experiences in the Spanish war–the Robles affair and the break with Hemingway–and on through the death of Katy Dos Passos (told with heartbreaking restraint) and the second marriage. In the Bobby Baker-like Danny DeLong we follow the career of a not unlikable "Boy Wizard of Wall Street" whose shady operations put him in Sing-Sing. In Paul Edwards we have the story of a decent, happily married young midwesterner who develops a successful career in the Farm Administration but finds his future darkened by the discovery that his children are using drugs. The DeLong and Edwards narratives are Dos Passos's way of dramatizing once again the moral confusions prevalent in government, law court, business, and home, but there is little in them that could be called fresh light. This is equally true of the whole emphasis upon the evils of communism, which at one point leads Dos Passos to offer a sympathetic biography of Joe McCarthy. Even a devoted reader may wince when Dos Passos writes: "Perhaps the oddest thing about McCarthy's career was that the Senate which had repudiated him gave him the rare honor of a funeral service in the Senate chamber. It was as if the Senators were trying to make up to the poor corpse all the agony they had visited on the living man."

Nevertheless, *Century's Ebb* has splendid moments (the biography of George Orwell could hardly be better) and makes some important contributions to our understanding of Dos Passos and his work. The spirit of Walt Whitman pervades the novel, establishing its presence in the very opening words:

> You, Walt Whitman,
> who rose out of fish-shape Paumanok
> to go crying, like the spotted hawk,

> your barbaric yawp over the roofs,
> to utter "the password primeval,"
> and strike up for a new world;
> what would you say, Walt, here, now, today,
> of these States that you loved,
> Walt Whitman, what would you say?

Inevitably, one thinks of that passage in Whitman's *Democratic Vistas* (1871) beginning, "I say we had best look our times and lands searchingly in the face, like a physician diagnosing some deep disease," for that is what Dos Passos had been doing for fifty years. With the invocation of Whitman, Dos Passos affirmed his own long career as observer, patriot, individualist, critic, and–ultimately–yea-sayer; despite its vistas of corruption and confusion, *Century's Ebb* concludes with a vision of American daring and ingenuity that would have inspired Whitman as it did Dos Passos: " 'Two minutes, thirtysix seconds and counting . . . all systems go.' Ears throbbed in anticipation, hearts beat a tattoo. Suppose something went wrong. 'Thirty seconds and counting.' Now the fire. Red and yellow flames. The great white pencil lifted itself slowly out of its billow of brown smoke. An enormous rumbling roar filled the sky. Faster, higher. The flaming rocket curves into the clouds. Frantic throats answer the jet engines' roar only to be hushed when the quiet workaday voices of the spacecraft's crew take over the radio. Worldwide, uncounted millions of television viewers joined in a prayer for the men in that golden bullet. In every one of them the need to know, the smouldering spirit of adventure, buried deep down under the routine of every day, flared for a moment like the rocket engine into soaring flame."

Dos Passos was, above all, a writer. He lived his life without the high drama, the scandal, or the gossip that biographers so often associate with the generation of writers who came of age in the early twentieth century. Even the once mildly shocking story of his parentage now rests quietly among the vital statistics. Yet to know the man through his work is as rewarding an experience as American literature can offer. The author of *Manhattan Transfer* and the vast *U.S.A.* trilogy left a chronicle of his country and his times that continues to vibrate with remarkable creative energy and truth. The person, John Dos Passos, left the solid, invaluable image of a good man.

Letters:

The Fourteenth Chronicle: Letters and Diaries of John Dos Passos, edited by Townsend Ludington (Boston: Gambit, 1973).

Organized chronologically and accompanied by a focused, illuminating biographical narrative; primary sources and editor's overview together constitute an invaluable guide to Dos Passos's life and work.

Bibliographies:

Jack Potter, *A Bibliography of John Dos Passos* (Chicago: Normandie House, 1950).

Selected primary works and secondary sources through 1949.

John C. Rohrkemper, *John Dos Passos: A Reference Guide* (Boston: G. K. Hall, 1980).

Annotated secondary bibliography.

David Sanders, *John Dos Passos: A Comprehensive Bibliography* (New York: Garland, 1987).

The most complete of the bibliographies; extensive publication information on primary listings and helpful annotations on secondary sources through 1983.

Biographies:

Melvin Landsberg, *Dos Passos's Path to U.S.A.: A Political Biography 1912-1936* (Boulder: Colorado Associated University Press, 1972).

Emphasizes the political aspects of Dos Passos's intellectual and literary development through the first half of his career.

Townsend Ludington, *John Dos Passos: A Twentieth Century Odyssey* (New York: Dutton, 1980).

A balanced, readable biography with helpful notes; explains the relationships among the biographical, cultural, artistic, and political bases of Dos Passos's literary development.

Virginia Spencer Carr, *Dos Passos: A Life* (Garden City, N.Y.: Doubleday, 1984).

Offers exhaustive details about Dos Passos's youth, his family, and life after his experiences in the Spanish civil war.

References:

Daniel Aaron, *Writers on the Left: Episodes in American Literary Communism* (New York: Harcourt, Brace, 1961).

Discusses the reasons for Dos Passos's political shift to conservatism in mid career and the results of that shift on his writing and finds the changes in Dos Passos's political attitudes consistent with his lifelong beliefs.

George J. Becker, *John Dos Passos* (New York: Ungar, 1974).

Critical overview of Dos Passos's works; biographical outline; brief summaries of novels; and separate chapters on *Manhattan Transfer* and *U.S.A.*.

Allen Belkind, ed., *Dos Passos, the Critics, and the Writer's Intention* (Carbondale: Southern Illinois University Press, 1971).

A collection of previously published essays including seminal articles by critics such as Malcolm Cowley, Blanche Gelfant, Alfred Kazin, and Jean-Paul Sartre.

C. W. Bigsby, *A Critical Introduction to Twentieth-Century American Drama, I, 1900-1940* (New York: Cambridge University Press, 1982).

Discusses Dos Passos's plays, emphasizing their modernist form and political direction.

John D. Brantley, *The Fiction of John Dos Passos* (The Hague: Mouton, 1968).

A study of Dos Passos's novels through *Midcentury* (1961); highlights the "machine" as symbol of impersonal forces that threaten individuality in U.S. culture.

Michael Clark, *Dos Passos's Early Fiction, 1912-1938* (London: Associated University Presses, 1987).

Explores the influence of American intellectual history on Dos Passos's work through *U.S.A.*; especially helpful discussions of the apprentice works, published and unpublished.

Andrew Hook, ed., *Dos Passos: A Collection of Critical Essays* (Englewood Cliffs, N.J.: Prentice-Hall, 1974).

Features Dos Passos's own comments on the "situation in American writing" along with important essays by E. D. Lowry, Claude-Edmonde Magny, and John William Ward.

Alfred Kazin, Introduction to Dos Passos's *The 42nd Parallel* (New York: New American Library, 1969).

A clear preface that places Dos Passos's life and trilogy in the context of the history, culture, and artistic achievements of the "Lost Generation."

Donald Pizer, *Dos Passos' U.S.A.: A Critical Study* (Charlottesville: University Press of Virginia, 1988).
A helpful guide to the composition, organization, and style of the trilogy, with a separate chapter explaining the four "modes" of the novels.

Cecelia Tichi, *Technology, Literature, Culture in Modernist America* (Chapel Hill: The University of North Carolina Press, 1987).
Illustrates vividly how Dos Passos's literary style and structures reflect the technological

revolution in early twentieth-century America.

Linda W. Wagner, *Dos Passos, Artist as American* (Austin: University of Texas Press, 1979).
Comprehensive critical overview of Dos Passos's development as a chronicler of America; includes discussions of some often-neglected early essays, stories, and poems as well as an extensive selected bibliography.

Papers:
The Alderman Library, University of Virginia, has the most extensive collection of manuscripts and other working materials.

T. S. Eliot

This entry was updated by Jewel Spears Brooker (Eckerd College) from her entry in
DLB 45, American Poets, 1880-1945, First Series.

Places	St. Louis Massachusetts	Paris Harvard	London

Influences and Relationships	Elizabethan and
	    Jacobean Dramatists
	Sir James G.
	    Frazer (*The Golden
	    Bough*)
		Jules Laforgue
		Stéphane Mallarmé
		Ezra Pound
		Dante
		Charles Baudelaire
			James Joyce
			Virginia Woolf
			Jessie Weston (*From
			    Ritual to Romance*)

Literary Movements and Forms	Imagism
	French Symbolism
	New Criticism
		Modernism
		The "Mythical
		    Method"
			The Bloomsbury
			    Group

Major Themes	The Nature and
	    Limitations of
	    Language
	Tension between
	    Faith and Doubt
		Justification of
		    God's Ways
		    to Man
		Greek and Roman
		    Myth
			Twentieth Century
			    Urban Life
			Breakdown of
			    Tradition
			Alienation

Cultural and Artistic Influences	Philosophical
	    Neorealism
		Christianity
		Vorticism
			Philosophical
			    Neoidealism

Social and Economic Influences	World War I	World War II	The Great Depression

See also the Eliot entries in DLB 7, Twentieth-Century American Dramatists; DLB 10, Modern British Dramatists, 1900-1945; *and* DLB 63, Modern American Critics, 1920-1955.

BIRTH: St. Louis, Missouri, 26 September 1888, to Henry Ware and Charlotte Chauncy Stearns Eliot.

EDUCATION: A.B., 1909; A.M., 1910; Harvard University; University of Paris (Sorbonne), 1910-1911; Harvard University, 1911-1914; Oxford University, 1914-1915; Ph.D. dissertation accepted by Harvard University, 1916.

MARRIAGES: 26 June 1915 to Vivien (Vivienne) Haigh-Wood; 10 January 1957 to Esme Valerie Fletcher.

AWARDS AND HONORS: Sheldon Traveling Fellowship (Harvard), 1914; *Dial* Award for *The Waste Land,* 1922; Litt.D., Columbia University, 1933; LL.D., University of Edinburgh, 1937; Litt.D., Cambridge University, 1938; Litt.D., University of Bristol, 1938; Litt.D., University of Leeds, 1939; Litt.D., Harvard University, 1947; Litt.D., Yale University, 1947; Litt.D., Princeton University, 1947; D.Litt., Oxford University, 1948; Nobel Prize for Literature, 1948; Order of Merit of the British Empire, 1948; Honorary Fellow, Magdalene College, Cambridge University, 1948; Honorary Fellow, Merton College, Oxford University, 1949; Commander, Ordre des Arts et des Lettres, 1950; Officier de la Légion d'Honneur, 1950; D.Litt., University of London, 1950; New York Drama Critics Circle Award for *The Cocktail Party,* 1950; Litt.D., Washington University (St. Louis), 1953; LL.D., St. Andrews University, 1953; Hanseatic Goethe Prize (Hamburg), 1954; Litt.D., University of Rome, 1958; Dante Gold Medal (Florence), 1959; Litt.D., University of Sheffield, 1959; D. ès L., University of Paris (Sorbonne), 1959; D. ès L., University of Aix-Marseille, 1959; D. ès L., University of Rennes, 1959; Orden Pour le Merite (West Germany), 1959; D.Philos., University of Munich, 1959; Emerson-Thoreau Medal of the American Academy of Arts and Letters, 1959; Honorary Citizen, Dallas, Texas, 1959; Honorary Deputy Sheriff, Dallas County, Texas, 1959; Campion Medal of the Catholic Book Club, 1963; U.S. Medal of Freedom, 1964; Litt.D., University of Bologna, 1967.

DEATH: London, England, 4 January 1965.

BOOKS: *Prufrock and Other Observations* (London: The Egoist, 1917);
Ezra Pound: His Metric and Poetry (New York: Knopf, 1918);
Poems (Richmond: Leonard & Virginia Woolf at The Hogarth Press, 1919);
Ara Vos Prec (London: Ovid Press, 1920); republished, with one substitution and one title change, as *Poems* (New York: Knopf, 1920);
The Sacred Wood: Essays on Poetry and Criticism (London: Methuen, 1920; New York: Knopf, 1921);
The Waste Land (New York: Boni & Liveright, 1922; Richmond: Leonard & Virginia Woolf at The Hogarth Press, 1923);
Homage to John Dryden: Three Essays on Poetry of the Seventeenth Century (London: Leonard & Virginia Woolf at The Hogarth Press, 1924);
Poems 1909-1925 (London: Faber & Gwyer, 1925; New York & Chicago: Harcourt, Brace, 1932);
Journey of the Magi (London: Faber & Gwyer, 1927; New York: Rudge, 1927);
Shakespeare and the Stoicism of Seneca (London: Oxford University Press, 1927);
A Song for Simeon (London: Faber & Gwyer, 1928);
For Lancelot Andrewes: Essays on Style and Order (London: Faber & Gwyer, 1928; Garden City, N.Y.: Doubleday, Doran, 1929);
Dante (London: Faber & Faber, 1929);
Animula (London: Faber & Faber, 1929);
Ash-Wednesday (London: Faber & Faber, 1930; New York & London: Putnam's, 1930);
Marina (London: Faber & Faber, 1930);
Thoughts After Lambeth (London: Faber & Faber, 1931);
Triumphal March (London: Faber & Faber, 1931);
Charles Whibley: A Memoir (London: Oxford University Press, 1931);
Selected Essays 1917-1932 (London: Faber & Faber, 1932; New York: Harcourt, Brace, 1932);
John Dryden: The Poet The Dramatist The Critic (New York: Terence & Elsa Holliday, 1932);
Sweeney Agonistes: Fragments of an Aristophanic Melodrama (London: Faber & Faber, 1932);
The Use of Poetry and The Use of Criticism: Studies in the Relation of Criticism to Poetry in England (London: Faber & Faber, 1933; Cambridge: Harvard University Press, 1933);

T. S. Eliot

After Strange Gods: A Primer of Modern Heresy (London: Faber & Faber, 1934; New York: Harcourt, Brace, 1934);

The Rock: A Pageant Play (London: Faber & Faber, 1934; New York: Harcourt, Brace, 1934);

Elizabethan Essays (London: Faber & Faber, 1934); republished, with omission of three essays and addition of one, as *Essays on Elizabethan Drama* (New York: Harcourt, Brace, 1956); republished as *Elizabethan Dramatists* (London: Faber & Faber, 1963);

Words for Music (Bryn Mawr, Pa., 1934);

Murder in the Cathedral, acting edition (Canterbury: H. J. Goulden, 1935); complete edition (London: Faber & Faber, 1935; New York: Harcourt, Brace, 1935);

Two Poems (Cambridge: Cambridge University Press, 1935);

Essays Ancient & Modern (London: Faber & Faber, 1936; New York: Harcourt, Brace, 1936);

Collected Poems 1909-1935 (London: Faber & Faber, 1936; New York: Harcourt, Brace, 1936);

The Family Reunion (London: Faber & Faber, 1939; New York: Harcourt, Brace, 1939);

Old Possum's Book of Practical Cats (London: Faber & Faber, 1939; New York: Harcourt, Brace, 1939);

The Idea of a Christian Society (London: Faber & Faber, 1939; New York: Harcourt, Brace, 1940);

The Waste Land and Other Poems (London: Faber & Faber, 1940; New York: Harcourt, Brace, 1955);

East Coker (London: Faber & Faber, 1940);

Burnt Norton (London: Faber & Faber, 1941);

Points of View (London: Faber & Faber, 1941);

The Dry Salvages (London: Faber & Faber, 1941);

The Classics and the Man of Letters (London, New York & Toronto: Oxford University Press, 1942);

The Music of Poetry (Glasgow: Jackson, Son & Company, Publishers to the University, 1942);

Little Gidding (London: Faber & Faber, 1942);

Four Quartets (New York: Harcourt, Brace, 1943; London: Faber & Faber, 1944);

What Is a Classic? (London: Faber & Faber, 1945);

Die Einheit der Europäischen Kultur ["The Unity of European Culture"–bilingual] (Berlin: Carl Habel, 1946);

A Practical Possum (Cambridge: Harvard Printing Office & Department of Graphic Arts, 1947);

On Poetry (Concord, Mass.: Concord Academy, 1947);

Milton (London: Geoffrey Cumberlege, 1947);

A Sermon (Cambridge: Cambridge University Press, 1948);

Selected Poems (Harmondsworth: Penguin/Faber & Faber, 1948; New York: Harcourt, Brace & World, 1967);

Notes Towards the Definition of Culture (London: Faber & Faber, 1948; New York: Harcourt, Brace, 1949);

From Poe to Valéry (New York: Harcourt, Brace, 1948);

The Undergraduate Poems of T. S. Eliot published while he was in college in The Harvard Advocate, unauthorized publication (Cambridge, 1949);

The Aims of Poetic Drama (London: Poets' Theatre Guild, 1949);

The Cocktail Party (London: Faber & Faber, 1950; New York: Harcourt, Brace, 1950; revised edition, London: Faber & Faber, 1950);

Poems Written in Early Youth (Stockholm: Privately printed, 1950; London: Faber & Faber,

1967; New York: Farrar, Straus & Giroux, 1967);

Poetry and Drama (Cambridge: Harvard University Press, 1951; London: Faber & Faber, 1951);

The Film of Murder in the Cathedral, by Eliot and George Hoellering (London: Faber & Faber, 1952; New York: Harcourt, Brace, 1952);

The Value and Use of Cathedrals in England Today (Chichester: Friends of Chichester Cathedral, 1952);

An Address to Members of the London Library (London: London Library, 1952; Providence, R.I.: Providence Athenaeum, 1953);

The Complete Poems and Plays (New York: Harcourt, Brace, 1952);

Selected Prose, edited by John Hayward (Melbourne, London & Baltimore: Penguin, 1953);

American Literature and the American Language (St. Louis: Department of English, Washington University, 1953);

The Three Voices of Poetry (London: Cambridge University Press, 1953; New York: Cambridge University Press, 1954);

The Confidential Clerk (London: Faber & Faber, 1954; New York: Harcourt, Brace, 1954);

Religious Drama: Mediaeval and Modern (New York: House of Books, 1954);

The Cultivation of Christmas Trees (London: Faber & Faber, 1954; New York: Farrar, Straus & Cudahy, 1956);

The Literature of Politics (London: Conservative Political Centre, 1955);

The Frontiers of Criticism (Minneapolis: University of Minnesota Press, 1956);

On Poetry and Poets (London: Faber & Faber, 1957; New York: Farrar, Straus & Cudahy, 1957);

The Elder Statesman (London: Faber & Faber, 1959; New York: Farrar, Straus & Cudahy, 1959);

Geoffrey Faber 1889-1961 (London: Faber & Faber, 1961);

Collected Plays (London: Faber & Faber, 1962);

George Herbert (London: Longmans, Green, 1962);

Collected Poems 1909-1962 (London: Faber & Faber, 1963; New York: Harcourt, Brace & World, 1963);

Knowledge and Experience in the Philosophy of F. H. Bradley (London: Faber & Faber, 1964; New York: Farrar, Straus, 1964);

To Criticize the Critic and Other Writings (London: Faber & Faber, 1965; New York: Farrar, Straus & Giroux, 1965);

The Waste Land: A Facsimile and Transcript of the Original Drafts Including the Annotations of Ezra Pound, edited by Valerie Eliot (London: Faber & Faber, 1971; New York: Harcourt Brace Jovanovich, 1971);

Selected Prose of T. S. Eliot, edited by Frank Kermode (New York: Harcourt Brace Jovanovich/Farrar, Straus & Giroux, 1975).

OTHER: Charlotte Eliot, *Savonarola: A Dramatic Poem,* introduction by Eliot (London: Cobden-Sanderson, 1926);

Edgar Ansel Mowrer, *This American World,* preface by Eliot (London: Faber & Gwyer, 1928);

Ezra Pound, *Selected Poems,* edited, with an introduction, by Eliot (London: Faber & Gwyer, 1928);

Charles Baudelaire, *Intimate Journals,* translated by Christopher Isherwood, introduction by Eliot (London: Blackamore Press/New York: Random House, 1930);

St.-J. Perse, *Anabasis a Poem,* translated, with an introduction, by Eliot (London: Faber & Faber, 1930; New York: Harcourt, Brace, 1938; revised edition, New York: Harcourt, Brace, 1949; London: Faber & Faber, 1959);

Pascal's Pensées, translated by W. F. Trotter, introduction by Eliot (London & Toronto: Dent/New York: Dutton, 1931);

"Donne in Our Time," in *A Garland for John Donne, 1631-1931,* edited by Theodore Spencer (Cambridge: Harvard University Press, 1931), pp. 1-19;

"Address by T. S. Eliot, '06, to the Class of '33, June 17, 1933," *Milton Graduates Bulletin,* 3 (November 1933): 5-9;

Harvard College Class of 1910. Seventh Report, includes an autobiographical note by Eliot (June 1935), pp. 219-221;

Marianne Moore, *Selected Poems,* edited, with an introduction, by Eliot (New York: Macmillan, 1935; London: Faber & Faber, 1935);

Alfred Tennyson, *Poems of Tennyson,* introduction by Eliot (London, Edinburgh, Paris, Melbourne, Toronto & New York: Nelson, 1936);

Djuna Barnes, *Nightwood,* introduction by Eliot (New York: Harcourt, Brace, 1937); introduction and preface by Eliot (London: Faber & Faber, 1950);

Rudyard Kipling, *A Choice of Kipling's Verse,* edited, with an introduction, by Eliot (London: Faber & Faber, 1941; New York: Scribners, 1943);

Samuel L. Clemens (Mark Twain), *The Adventures of Huckleberry Finn,* introduction by Eliot (London: Cresset Press, 1950);

"Ezra Pound," in *Ezra Pound: A Collection of Essays,* edited by Peter Russell (London & New York: Peter Nevill, 1950), pp. 25-36;

Joseph Chiari, *Contemporary French Poetry,* foreword by Eliot (Manchester: Manchester University Press, 1952);

Pound, *Literary Essays,* edited, with an introduction, by Eliot (London: Faber & Faber, 1954; Norfolk, Conn.: New Directions, 1954);

Chiari, *Symbolisme from Poe to Mallarmé,* foreword by Eliot (London: Rockliff, 1956);

Paul Valéry, *The Art of Poetry,* translated by Denise Folliot, introduction by Eliot (New York: Pantheon, 1958);

From Mary to You, includes an address by Eliot (St. Louis: Mary Institute, 1959), pp. 133-136;

"The Influence of Landscape upon the Poet," *Daedalus,* 89 (Spring 1960): 420-422;

The Criterion 1922-1939, 18 volumes, edited by Eliot (London: Faber & Faber, 1967).

T. S. Eliot is one of the giants of modern literature, highly distinguished as poet, literary critic, dramatist, and editor/publisher. In 1910-1911, while still a student, he wrote "The Love Song of J. Alfred Prufrock" and other poems which are landmarks in the history of literature. In these college poems, written with virtually no influence from his contemporaries (William Butler Yeats was well known, but not yet modern; Ezra Pound at this time was neither well known nor modern), Eliot articulated distinctly modern themes in forms which were both a striking development of and a striking departure from those of nineteenth-century poetry. Within a few years, he had composed another landmark poem, "Gerontion" (1920), and within a decade, the century's most famous and influential poem, *The Waste Land* (1922). While the origins of *The Waste Land* are in a sense personal, the voices projected are universal. Perhaps without having intended to do so, Eliot diagnosed the malaise of his generation and indeed of Western civilization in the twentieth century. In 1930 he published his next major poem, *Ash-Wednesday,* written after his conversion to Anglo-Catholicism. Conspicuously different in

style and tone from his earlier work, these confessional lyrics chart his continued search for order in an age of chaos. The culmination of this search as well as of Eliot's poetic writing is his great meditation on the nature of time and of human history, *Four Quartets* (1936-1942). With *Four Quartets,* Eliot virtually concluded his career as a poet.

Eliot was almost as distinguished a literary critic as he was a poet. From 1916 through 1921, he contributed approximately one hundred reviews and articles to perhaps a dozen periodicals. This early criticism was produced at night under the pressure of supplementing his meager salary, first as a teacher, then as a bank clerk; and not, as is sometimes suggested, under the compulsion to rewrite literary history. He did much, it is true, to generate a revolution in literary taste, but this was not part of his intention. Possessing a special critical intelligence and superb training in philosophy and literature, he wrote with such elegance and incision that his essays, however hastily written and for whatever motive, had an immediate impact. His ideas quickly solidified into doctrine and became, with the early essays of I. A. Richards, the basis of the most influential school of literary criticism in this century, the so-called New Criticism. Three of these essays—"Tradition and the Individual Talent," "Hamlet and His Problems," and "The Metaphysical Poets"—outline in canonical form such modern critical doctrines as "tradition," "impersonality," "irrelevancy of belief," "objective correlative," and "unified sensibility."

Through half a century of critical writing, Eliot's concerns remained more or less constant; his position regarding those concerns, however, was frequently refined, revised, or, occasionally, reversed. He discovered, though, that those early and tentative formulations had taken on a life of their own. Even today, most commentators seem to be unaware of the complexity of Eliot's developing critical mind and of the distortion which results from the assumption that those well-known phrases do justice to that mind. Beginning in the late 1920s, Eliot's literary criticism was supplemented by, at times supplanted by, religious and social criticism. In these writings, such as *The Idea of a Christian Society* (1939), he can be seen as a deeply involved and thoughtful Christian poet in the process of making sense of the world *l'entre deux guerres.* "Orthodoxy," "heresy," and other terms from seventeenth-century Christian rhetoric replace such earlier terms as "tradition" and

T. S. Eliot, 1896, in the schoolyard at Mary Institute, the St. Louis girls' school founded by his grandfather, William Greenleaf Eliot (courtesy of the Hayward Collection, King's College Library, Cambridge)

"impersonality." These writings, sympathetically read, suggest the dilemma of the serious student of Western culture in the 1930s, and rightly understood, they complement his poetry, his plays, and his earlier literary journalism.

As a dramatist also, Eliot is an important figure in the twentieth century. He was inclined from the first toward the theater–his early poems are essentially dramatic; many of his early essays and reviews are on drama or dramatists. By the mid 1920s he was writing a drama, *Sweeney Agonistes;* in the 1930s he wrote *The Rock* (1934), *Murder in the Cathedral* (1935), and *The Family Reunion* (1939); in the 1940s and 1950s he devoted himself almost exclusively to plays, of which *The Cocktail Party* (1950) has been the most popular. His goal, realized only in part, was the revitalization of poetic drama in terms which would be consistent with the modern age. He experimented endlessly with language which, though close to contemporary speech, is essentially poetic and thus capable of extraordinary spiritual, emotional, and intellectual resonance. He did more,

perhaps, than any other person to reestablish poetic drama and to create an audience for it. His work has influenced many important twentieth-century dramatists, including W. H. Auden and Harold Pinter.

Eliot also made significant contributions as an editor and publisher. From 1922 to 1939 he was the editor of a major intellectual journal, the *Criterion,* and from 1925 to 1965, an editor/ director in the publishing house of Faber and Faber. In both capacities, he worked tirelessly behind the scenes to nurture the intellectual and spiritual life of his time.

Because Eliot's personal papers are restricted and most of his letters are still unpublished, any discussion of his life must be tentative. A number of basic facts, of course, are part of the public record, and others have been revealed in occasional remarks by the poet himself. Thomas Stearns Eliot was born 26 September 1888; he was the second son and seventh child of Charlotte Stearns and Henry Ware Eliot, members of a distinguished Massachusetts family recently transplanted to Missouri. Eliot's family tree includes settlers of the Massachusetts Bay Colony, prominent clergymen and educators, a president of Harvard University (Charles William Eliot), and three presidents of the United States (John Adams, John Quincy Adams, and Rutherford B. Hayes). The move from Boston to St. Louis had been made by the poet's grandfather, William Greenleaf Eliot, a Unitarian minister, educator, and civic leader. In St. Louis he established the first Unitarian church and founded both Smith Academy and Washington University. Although William Greenleaf Eliot died a year before T. S. Eliot was born, he remained at the center of his family's moral and ethical life. On the occasion of the one hundredth anniversary of the founding of Washington University, T. S. Eliot remarked that he had been brought up to be ever mindful of his grandfather's moral judgments: "our decisions between duty and self-indulgence, were taken as if, like Moses, [my grandfather] had brought down the tables of the Law, any deviation from which would be sinful." The Eliot family lived in downtown St. Louis, not far from the Mississippi River, and the poet was born and spent his formative years at 2635 Locust Street. Although tireless in their service to St. Louis, the Eliot family never felt entirely at home in the west and carefully maintained the Massachusetts connection. They summered in New England, and in 1897, Henry Ware Eliot built a house near the sea at Gloucester. The summers on Cape Ann provided the poet with some of his happiest memories, memories tapped some forty years later when he was writing *The Dry Salvages*. When the time came to send their sons to university, Charlotte and Henry Ware Eliot sent them back to Massachusetts. Henry spent two years at Washington University before going on to Harvard, but Tom went directly from Smith Academy to the northeast, first to Milton Academy and then to Harvard.

From these few facts, several points emerge as relevant to Eliot's future mind and art. First, he was to become extremely conscious of history—his own, that of his family, his civilization, his race—and of the ways in which the past constantly impinges on the present and the present on the future. Second, he was early possessed by a sense of homelessness. As he explained in a 1928 preface, "The family guarded jealously its connections with New England; but it was not until years of maturity that I perceived that I myself had always been a New Englander in the South West, and a South Westerner in New England." In 1919, having settled in London, he wrote his brother that "one remains always a foreigner," that "one is always coming up against differences of feeling that make one feel humiliated and lonely." As late as 1945, he would call himself "Metoikos" (meaning exile), and this feeling of being everywhere homeless, everywhere in exile, haunts most of his poetry.

Third, Eliot's thoroughly urban imagination took its shape from his childhood experience in the streets of St. Louis. As he revealed in a 1930 letter quoted in an appendix to *American Literature and the American Language* (1953), "St. Louis affected me more deeply than any other environment has done." His most powerful and typical images—city streets and city slums, city rivers and city skies—(though eventually mediated through such literary sources as Charles Baudelaire's images of Paris) were etched on his mind in the streets of St. Louis. In Eliot's childhood, his widowed grandmother lived around the corner, and out of respect for her wish to continue living in the house her husband had built, the family resisted the flight to the suburbs. In "The Influence of Landscape upon the Poet" (1960), he explained that they chose to stay in "a neighborhood which had become shabby to a degree approaching slumminess. . . . for nine months of the year my scenery was almost exclusively urban, and a good deal of it seedily, drably

urban at that. My urban imagery was that of St. Louis, upon which that of Paris and London had been superimposed." City scenes, even sordid ones, as he suggested in a 1914 letter to Conrad Aiken, helped him to feel alive, alert, and self-conscious. St. Louis was his urban nursery, the site of his first encounter with powerful scenes and smells retrieved for us in his early poems with their littered labyrinthine streets, the faint stale smells of beer, and the yellow fog that rubs its muzzle on the window panes, that lingers, leaps, slips, falls, and curls up for a nap. The river imagery which pervades his poetry from beginning to end also comes from St. Louis, from the great Mississippi. In the 1930 letter just quoted, Eliot says "Missouri and the Mississippi have made a deeper impression on me than any other part of the world." The early poems are strewn with images of city rivers—the Mississippi, the Charles, the Seine, and the Thames—rivers littered with "empty bottles, sandwich papers—Silk handkerchiefs, cardboard boxes, cigarette ends/ Or other testimony of summer nights." And one of his last major poems, *The Dry Salvages*, evokes this rhythm known from the nursery bedroom, the implacable unpropitiated brown god with its cargo of dead Negroes and chicken coops.

Eliot was educated at Smith Academy in St. Louis (1898-1905), at Milton Academy in Massachusetts (1905-1906), at Harvard University (A.B., 1909; A.M., 1910; Ph.D. courses, 1911-1914), at the University of Paris (Sorbonne, 1910-1911), and at Merton College, Oxford University (1914-1915). He devoted a further year (1915-1916) to a doctoral dissertation on the philosophy of F. H. Bradley. In 1916 he booked passage to return to Harvard to defend his dissertation but was hindered by the complications of wartime travel and sent the dissertation by mail. It was accepted by the philosophy department, with Josiah Royce calling it the work of an expert.

The first two decades of the twentieth century were golden years for the Harvard University philosophy department. During his time there, Eliot had some of the century's most distinguished philosophers as teachers, including George Santayana, Josiah Royce, and Bertrand Russell. As an undergraduate, Eliot emphasized language—Latin, Greek, German, and French; as a graduate student, he emphasized Indic Religion and Idealist philosophy. One of the distinctive traits of his poetry can be directly associated with his splendid education. His early masterpieces are distinguished by a curious combination of sensuous imagery and intellectuality; in his mind, the smell of cooking and the philosophy of Spinoza meet and form new wholes. This combination, which he was later to remark in the metaphysical poets, derives in part from his decade-long immersion in philosophy and language. Eliot's most fruitful extracurricular activity at Harvard was his association with the college literary magazine, the *Harvard Advocate*. Many of his earliest poems were first published by the *Advocate*, and at least one of his lifelong friendships, that with fellow poet Conrad Aiken, was formed in this well-known nursery of writers and poets.

The most far-reaching consequence of Eliot's undergraduate career at Harvard was his accidental discovery of Arthur Symon's *Symbolist Movement in Literature* (1899), a book which Eliot later said had changed the course of his life. Symons introduced him to the poetry of Jules Laforgue, and Laforgue, Eliot claimed, helped him to discover himself as a poet, to find his own voice. Reading Laforgue taught him how to handle emotion in poetry, through irony and through a quality of detachment which enabled him to see himself and his own emotions essentially as objects for analysis. By feeding his increasing Francophilia, Symons also led Eliot in 1910 to take a course in French literary criticism from Irving Babbitt. Babbitt became perhaps the single most important influence on Eliot's mind. Babbitt's antipathy toward romanticism and his advocacy of tradition, for example, are cornerstones of Eliot's later criticism. And finally, at least indirectly, Symons led Eliot to spend the academic year 1910-1911 reading literature and philosophy at the Sorbonne in Paris, immeasurably augmenting his indebtedness to France. It was during this academic year that Eliot met and became close to Jean Verdenal, a medical student who shared his interests in art and literature. Verdenal served as a medical officer on the Western Front and in May 1915 was killed while tending a wounded soldier. His death occasioned special grief in Eliot, who dedicated his first volumes of poetry to the memory of his fallen friend. Paris was also important in Eliot's development for directing his attention to Charles Baudelaire, who showed him how to transform the sordid images of quotidian urban life into art, and for pointing him toward Stéphane Mallarmé, who showed him how to gain the collaboration of readers by impregnating the blank spaces between words and by underpinning poetic structures with ritualistic ones. Dur-

ing this year in Paris, Eliot attended the lectures of Henri Bergson and began to ponder the questions on time and consciousness which are at the center of *Four Quartets* and which hover just above and just below everything he wrote.

One of the special pleasures of Eliot's Harvard years was the close relationship which developed with his cousin Eleanor Hinkley, three years his junior. As a student at Radcliffe College, she had taken George Pierce Baker's famous "47 Workshop" in theatre. In 1912, through amateur theatricals at her house, Eliot met and fell in love with Emily Hale. In early 1914, Eleanor cast Tom and Emily together in a skit based on Jane Austen's *Emma*. Eliot's letters to Eleanor are among his most high-spirited and preserve intact his youthful wit and urbanity.

Eliot's career as a poet can be divided into three periods–the first coinciding with his studies in Boston and Paris and culminating in "The Love Song of J. Alfred Prufrock" in 1911; the second coinciding with World War I and with the financial and marital stress of his early years in London and culminating in *The Waste Land* in 1922; and the third coinciding with his melancholy and alarm at the economic depression and the rise of Nazism and culminating in the wartime *Quartets* in 1942. The poems of the first period were preceded only by a handful of schoolboy exercises, clever after a fashion, but in no way suggestive of the creative intelligence which was to manifest itself in 1910-1911, when with four poems– "Portrait of a Lady," "Preludes," "Rhapsody on a Windy Night," and "The Love Song of J. Alfred Prufrock"–Eliot virtually invented modern English poetry. In the earlier poems, he had been concentrating on form. As he told Donald Hall in a 1959 interview, "My early *vers libre* . . . was started under the endeavor to practice the same form as Laforgue . . . merely rhyming lines of irregular length, with the rhymes coming in irregular places." In the four greater poems, he told Hall, he was burdened with material which had been incubating in his mind for years, and was not concerned with form *per se*: "There were things in the next phase which were freer, like 'Rhapsody on a Windy Night.' I don't know whether I had any . . . model . . . in mind . . . It just came that way." And until the form "just came," he said in *The Use of Poetry and The Use of Criticism* (1933), he himself was unable to understand the material to which it gave birth. These poems perfectly illustrate his idea, not articulated until years later, of tradition and the individual tal-

T. S. Eliot at Harvard (courtesy of the Hayward Collection, King's College Library, Cambridge)

ent, in that they issue from a marriage of the classics of the Western past—that which educated Westerners have in common—and the experience of a unique mind of the present. In these early poems, Homer, the Greek dramatists, the biblical writers, Dante, Shakespeare, even Alfred Tennyson and Rudyard Kipling, meet the fastidious and sensitive youth from St. Louis, producing totally new works of art which modify and reshape the tradition from which they sprang.

The early poems introduce themes to which, with variation and development, Eliot was to return time and again. These themes are all related in one way or another to the problem of isolation and to the causes and the consequences in the contemporary world of isolation. In a minor poem of 1909, "Conversation Galante," a man and a woman speak to each other, but neither comprehends what the other is saying. In "Portrait of

a Lady," a man and woman meet, but the man is inarticulate, imprisoned in thought. In this ironic dramatization of a "conversation galante," the woman speaks without thinking and the man thinks without speaking. Her words are juxtaposed against his thoughts—an "insistent out-of-tune/Of a broken violin" juxtaposed against "a dull tom-tom . . ./Absurdly hammering a prelude of its own" inside his brain.

The profound isolation of the lady in "Portrait of a Lady," who decorously extends her hand across the abyss, becomes in "The Love Song of J. Alfred Prufrock" an isolation which is absolute. The specific lady is succeeded by generalized women; the supercilious youth by the middle-aged intellectual he will become, for whom women and indeed the entire universe exist as abstractions. The poignance of this superb poem derives in part from a tension between Prufrock's self-generated isolation and his obsession with language. Although he is afraid to speak, he can think only in the language of dialogue. This dialogue with himself, moreover, consistently turns on the infinite possibilities (or impossibilities) of dialogue with others. The tension created by this obsession with language is reinforced by another quality which implies the real existence of other people—fear. Interestingly, though, he is not so much afraid of other people as of other people's language. These women who (simply by talking) can transform the greatest of artists, Michelangelo, into a meaningless, tea-party abstraction will have no trouble with Prufrock. His anguished refusal to be formulated and pinned (wriggling) to the wall is one of the greatest expressions of isolation in modern European literature. In "Preludes" and "Rhapsody on a Windy Night," the lady and Prufrock's women are succeeded by a woman who exists only as one of "the thousand sordid images/Of which [his] soul [is] constituted." And his sordid image of her includes the sordid image of himself that she sees flickering on the ceiling.

In these early poems, the progression from a feeble attempt to build a bridge in "Conversation Galante" to a failure in "Portrait of a Lady" to an impossibility in "The Love Song of J. Alfred Prufrock" is paralleled on other levels, and understanding these levels is crucial in getting to the heart of Eliot. The isolation of man from woman is paralleled by the isolation of man from man, of man from God, and of poet from reader; isolation is sexual, human, religious, and since Eliot is a poet, vocational. In "Conversation

Galante" and "Portrait of a Lady," other people and perhaps God exist, but they are unreachable; in "The Love Song of J. Alfred Prufrock," they exist, but only as aspects of Prufrock's mind; in "Preludes" and "Rhapsody on a Windy Night," the other, whether human or divine, has been so thoroughly assimilated that it can no longer be defined. This situation is explicitly aesthetic. The poet-persona of "Conversation Galante" bores his companion with baffling metaphors. The protagonist of "Portrait of a Lady" is paralleled by an artist in the concert room, and both the suitor and the pianist fail to reach their listeners. In both cases, this failure is described in ceremonial terms which act to superimpose the religious on the sexual and aesthetic. J. Alfred Prufrock—as lover, as prophet, as poet—also fails to reach his audience. These failures are skillfully layered by the use of imagery which defines Prufrock's problem as sexual, as religious (how to raise himself from the dead, how to cope with his own flesh on a platter), and as rhetorical (how to sing, how to say, how to revise). And as "The Love Song of J. Alfred Prufrock" shows most clearly, the horizontal and vertical gaps mirror a gap within, a gap between thought and feeling, a partition of the self.

The techniques of Eliot's early poems owe something to the Jacobean dramatists and to Robert Browning, but these essentially dramatic ancestors were transformed in his mind by an encounter with the French symbolist poets and by his own impulse toward idealism. Browning's dramatic monologue, a recognizable ancestor, becomes in "The Love Song of J. Alfred Prufrock" interior monologue. Formally, Browning's logical and psychological continuity gives way to Eliot's systematic juxtapositions, both linear and vertical. In part, the form in these early poems is a protest against the immediate past; in part (and more important), an attempt to solve a very practical problem. Because art is at bottom a collaborative achievement which the artist initiates and the audience completes, it becomes virtually impossible unless the artist and his audience have enough in common to permit communication on some level. The early-twentieth-century shattering of shared meanings puts the artist in a situation analogous to that of Prufrock. Prufrock can never get beyond the corridors of his own mind, can never speak to the chattering abstractions who convert him into an abstraction. But Eliot did reach beyond his own mind. By using formal techniques which force the reader to do his part

of art's labor, he has spoken to and has moved countless readers. The once shocking techniques of these early poems—deliberate open-endedness, concentrated allusiveness, juxtaposition, irony—all work to gain the creative collaboration of readers with whom Eliot had almost nothing in common. Of reader collaboration, he had learned much from the symbolists, whose methods were especially contrived to generate poems in the minds of readers.

Between the great poems of 1910-1911 and *The Waste Land,* Eliot lived through a number of experiences which are crucial in understanding his development as a poet. First, from 1911 to 1916, he studied for a Ph.D. in philosophy—from 1911 to 1914 at Harvard; in the 1914-1915 academic year at Oxford; and in 1915-1916 in London working on his dissertation. Eliot's 1911-1914 work at Harvard included serious study of both Eastern and Western philosophy. His Indic studies (two years of Sanskrit and of Indian philosophy) abetted his innate asceticism and provided a more comprehensive context for his understanding of culture. Inevitably, these studies entered his poetry. The Indian myth of the thundergod, for example, provides the context for section 5 ("What the Thunder Said") of *The Waste Land,* and Buddha's fire sermon the context for section 3 ("The Fire Sermon"). In his study of European philosophy, Eliot concentrated on problems in contemporary epistemology. His immersion in the neo-idealism of F. H. Bradley and the neorealism of Bertrand Russell had many effects, of which two proved especially important. Positively, these studies suggested methods of structure which he was able to put to immediate use in "Gerontion" and *The Waste Land.* Negatively, these studies convinced him that the best and most sophisticated answers to the cultural and spiritual crises of his time were finally inadequate. This conclusion contributed to his decision to abandon the career for which his education had prepared him. To the great disappointment of his family, he chose not to return to America and settle down as a professor of philosophy, but rather to remain in England and follow a literary career.

Eliot's decision to put down roots, or to discover roots, in Europe stands, together with his first marriage and his conversion, as the most important of his entire life. With the original intention of staying for one year, Eliot left Boston in June 1914 for the University of Marburg in Germany. He was forced by the outbreak of war to abandon his fellowship and in August arrived in

London, an intellectual hothouse with "isms" proliferating in every field, especially the arts.

He had been preceded by his Harvard friend Conrad Aiken, who had come to London with the idea, as he put it in a letter of June 1914, of doing a little "self-advertising" and with the secondary intention of helping his friend Tom Eliot. Aiken had seen a longer early version of "The Love Song of J. Alfred Prufrock," had made suggestions, which Eliot accepted, about dropping part of it, and in the summer of 1914, carried it and another Eliot poem, "La Figlia che Piange," with him to London. Either on this occasion or an earlier one he tried unsuccessfully to interest Harold Munro in Eliot's work. He also showed "The Love Song of J. Alfred Prufrock" to the American Ezra Pound and left Eliot an introduction to Pound. In September, Eliot called on Pound, a meeting with enormous consequences for modern poetry. Pound discovered that Eliot had modernized himself by himself and immediately adopted him as a cause, peddling his poetry, introducing him to Yeats and other artists, convincing him to settle in London, reassuring his nonplussed and disappointed father. In a letter written one week after his first meeting with Pound, Eliot told Aiken that "Pound has been *on' n'est pas plus aimable*," adding he expected to dine with Pound and Yeats at a Chinese restaurant the following Monday. In 1915, at a time when Eliot was close to giving up, Pound arranged for the publication of "The Love Song of J. Alfred Prufrock" in *Poetry*, and in 1917 he facilitated the publication of *Prufrock and Other Observations*.

The impact of Ezra Pound, however, pales beside that of Vivien Haigh-Wood, the pretty but nervous English girl Eliot married in June 1915. In a late April letter to Eleanor Hinkley describing his social life at Oxford, Eliot mentioned that he had met an English girl named Vivien, and on 26 June, encouraged by Pound, he married her (without notifying his family) at the Hampstead Registry Office with her aunt and one of her friends as witnesses. However lovingly begun, the marriage was in most respects a disaster. In the 1960s, in a private paper, Eliot admitted that it was doomed from the start: "I think that all I wanted of Vivienne was a flirtation or a mild affair: I was too shy and unpractised to achieve either . . . I came to persuade myself that I was in love with her simply because I wanted to burn my boats and commit myself to staying in England. And she persuaded herself (also under the influence of Pound) that she would save the

poet by keeping him in England." The tragic nature of Eliot's misalliance was at once evident to outsiders. A few weeks after the marriage, Bertrand Russell dined with the Eliots and described Vivien as "light, a little vulgar, adventurous, full of life" and Eliot as "exquisite and listless." A few months later, in October, Russell observed that Eliot "has a profound and quite unselfish devotion to his wife," but she had impulses of a "Dostojevsky type of cruelty" toward him. "She is a person who lives on a knife-edge, and will end as a criminal or a saint." In fact, she ended in madness, a development which in retrospect seems inevitable but for which Eliot felt partially responsible and for which he forgave himself only in old age, if ever. This burden is the biographical shadow behind a motif recurrent in the poems and plays—the motif of "doing a girl in," of wife murder. The struggle to cope emotionally and financially with Vivien Eliot's illness almost, in truth, did Eliot in, leading him first to exhaustion, and then, in 1921, to collapse. His conscientious effort between 1915 and 1922 to build a bridge across the gulf which separated them, reflected most conspicuously in part 2 of *The Waste Land*, is a lived experience behind all of his subsequent work.

Eliot's marriage and his determination to make it as a literary man in London had two other immediate and far-reaching consequences. The first was estrangement from his family, particularly his father. Eliot was mindful of the love and financial support that his father had given him and hoped to vindicate his geographical, vocational, and marital choices by becoming an acclaimed poet. But his father died before Eliot could prove himself, and the poet wrote in grief to his mother: "If I can think at the end of my life that I have been worthy to be his son I shall be happy." Eliot continued to brood over the fact that his dying father believed that his son had made a mess of his life. This lingering sadness can be seen, perhaps, in the persistent but ambiguous interest in father death which appears in *The Waste Land* and in the plays.

The second consequence of his decision was severe financial distress. To support himself and his chronically ill wife, he took a job as a teacher—in the fall of 1915 at High Wycombe Grammar School, and throughout 1916 at Highgate Junior School. Finding the teaching of young boys extremely draining work, he gave it up at the end of 1916 and in March of 1917 began work in the Colonial and Foreign Department of Lloyds

Bank. Although he was to stay with Lloyds for the next nine years, he discovered that banking, like teaching, did not produce nearly enough income to cover his expenses and Vivien's medical bills. He was thus forced to supplement his duties as a teacher, as banker, and as nurse to his wife with a great deal of night work as lecturer, reviewer, and essayist. Working from 1916 to 1920 under incredible pressure (a fifteen-hour work day was common for him), he wrote the essays, published in 1920 as *The Sacred Wood*, which reshaped literary history.

The focus in Eliot's early essays is essentially the same as in the poetry–the problem of isolation, its causes and its consequences. In the poems, the emphasis is on man's isolation from man (from woman, too, of course) and his related isolation from God. In the literary criticism, the emphasis is on the artist in isolation, cut off from his audience and from great artists and thinkers of both the present and the past. In "Tradition and the Individual Talent" (1919), one of this century's most celebrated essays, Eliot attempts to cope with the isolation of the artist resulting from the early-twentieth century's massive repudiation of the past, a repudiation which severed man's intellectual and spiritual roots. Eliot deals with the implications of this disaster by defining "tradition" as an ideal (that is, mental) structure in which the "whole of the literature of Europe from Homer and within it the whole of the literature of [the artist's] own country has a simultaneous existence and composes a simultaneous order." To put it more simply, he defines tradition not as a canon, but as an ongoing relationship of Western masters, living and dead, within the mind and bones of the contemporary poet. Eliot's reaction against romanticism, similarly, is related to the fact that romanticism celebrates the artist in isolation; his dedication to order, to the fact that order by definition is an organized assembly of what otherwise would be isolated fragments. Eliot's notion that modern poetry should be complex derives in part from his attempt to overcome his isolation from his readers by forcing them to become involved as collaborators in his poetry. When he began to turn, a decade later, to religious and social criticism, he explored in new areas the same problem and suggested tentative solutions.

Eliot's early literary criticism developed from his formal and systematic study in philosophy and the history of religion. Like his mentor Bradley, he was a thoroughgoing skeptic and in special ways a relativist. But Eliot's skepticism included an insistence upon faith (in a non-religious sense) as the foundation of thought and the dynamic of history. Eliot rejected orthodox Hegelianism, but perhaps unconsciously, he used a methodology which was essentially dialectical. His critical imagination, in fact, was strongly dialectical, and each of his famous critical dictims should be understood in terms of a fragile tension between opposites which is tentatively synthesized in a more comprehensive term which *retains* rather than dissolves the tension. For example, "tradition" and "individual talent" are in normal usage opposites, but in his revision of these terms, they are complements, held in tension through a definition of "tradition" which includes the individual, the dynamic, the subjective, and the contemporary. In campaigning against "subjectivity," he was campaigning against *mere* subjectivity. His "objectivity" includes the subjective; similarly, his "impersonality" includes the "personal." As he puts it "Tradition and the Individual Talent," "only those who have personality and emotions know what it means to want to escape from those things." He posits an "ideal order of monuments," but insists that this ideal order is not fixed but constantly being modified and shaped by individual artists. He suggests that a text is a self-sufficient object and at the same time a construct collaboratively achieved by a reader. His account of the way a poet's mind works by unifying disparate phenomena is consistent with his dialectical imagination, as is his account of literary history.

Eliot's prose, then, abounds with opposites. This sort of rhetoric tends to produce parallel constructions of some elegance and in this tendency often seduces its readers to undue focus on the parallelism. Although he typically undercut or moved beyond most of his famous "formulas" in the same speech or essay (often in the same sentence) in which he introduced them, it has long been fashionable to (1) focus on one of his polarities and make it into a fixed principle, or to (2) focus on both and remark that he contradicts himself. Both positions result from a superficial reading of his work and a failure to grasp the complexity of his dialectical imagination. He was himself aware of this dilemma and often remarked his embarrassment at the notoriety of some of his phrases. Part of the problem in commenting on Eliot's critical mind and influence, of course, is that his mind, like the mind of Europe, was always developing and never quite abandoned any-

T. S. Eliot in 1938; portrait by Wyndham Lewis (courtesy of the Durban Municipal Art Gallery)

thing *en route*. His mind cannot be understood by trying to abstract it from the work of his disciples, such as the New Critics, but it can be experienced in his own essays and journalism.

In regard to poetry, the decade between the Harvard poems and *The Waste Land* is for the most part a long dry stretch. Although Eliot had written a few short pieces at Oxford in 1915, he was afraid by 1916 that "The Love Song of J. Alfred Prufrock" was his swan song. And by 1917, he had become, by his own testimony, quite desperate. To get going again, Eliot wrote a handful of poems in French, one of which, "Dans le Restaurant," in a truncated English version, ended up in *The Waste Land*. Eliot and Pound were at their closest during these years, and some of the impetus for Eliot's revival as a poet came from his flamboyant friend. Both felt that the freedom

achieved in the previous decade of revolution in the arts had degenerated to license, and they decided to move back toward more precise forms, a move analogous to Picasso's move a few years later from Cubism to neoclassicism. In Eliot, the result was the quatrain poems, so-called because they were modeled, at Pound's suggestion, on the quatrains of Théophile Gautier's *Emaux et Camées* (1852). These Gautier-inspired poems, all highly polished satires, include "The Hippopotamus," "Sweeney Erect," "Sweeney among the Nightingales," "Burbank with a Baedeker," "Mr. Eliot's Sunday Morning Service," "Whispers of Immortality," and "A Cooking Egg." The themes of the French poems and of the quatrain poems are those of Eliot's great poems of 1910-1911 and of the criticism–the absence of a common ground, isolation, consequent sterility, death which is final, death which leads to regeneration. Largely as a result of World War I, Eliot's focus– international, cultural, institutional–is broader than in the earlier poems. Prufrock is primarily an individual; Burbank and Sweeney are primarily types.

The difference between the "The Love Song of J. Alfred Prufrock" and the Sweeney poems, however, is only partially due to expanded focus; much more important is enlarged technique. For Eliot, the quatrain poems were experiments; for the critic, they are a laboratory for studying his developing poetic. Form rather than content is uppermost. He settled on the quatrain form, in fact, before he had any idea of what he was going to say. The form of the stanza is Gautier's; in every other way, though, the form is Eliot's–a natural development of his inclusive and systematic mentality. In the 1910-1911 poems, Eliot had used allusions as a means of layering texts and of forcing the reader to reevaluate (and thus reinvigorate) the entire Western tradition. For example, beneath Eliot's ironic love song, the perceptive reader cannot but hear the sentimental love songs of the nineteenth century; beneath Prufrock's debate with himself, the reader may discover the medieval debate of body and soul; beneath Prufrock's paralysis, that of Hamlet; beneath Prufrock's burial, that of Lazarus; beneath Prufrock's hell, Dante's inferno. The careful reader not only sees this complex layering of texts but is literally forced to see with new eyes the entire tradition in which these texts exist.

In the quatrain poems, allusions are used in much the same way, but in much greater density, becoming a means for remarkably intricate, highly systematic intellectual gymnastics. Critic William Arrowsmith aptly dubs this highly deliberate and systematic layering of texts "the poem-as-palimpsest." The poem-as-palimpsest, although never again used as conspicuously as in these poems, is basic to *The Waste Land*. Eliot continued to use allusions to layer texts in a complex way, but beginning with "The Hollow Men," he used them more sparingly. In that it requires special knowledge and much work from the reader–at least as much work, Eliot wryly notes, as would be required of a barrister preparing a difficult court case–the poem-as-palimpsest enables the poet to gain from his audience the sort of creative co-labor without which the greatest art cannot exist.

Eliot's most important single poem between 1911 and 1922 is "Gerontion." Important in itself, it also serves as a transition to *The Waste Land,* to which, for thematic reasons, Eliot considered it an appropriate prelude, and to which, until dissuaded by Pound, he considered attaching it. The emphasis in the early poems had been on the isolation of the individual (Mr. Prufrock and company), on its causes and consequences. In "Gerontion" and *The Waste Land,* the individual crisis is seen as part of a cultural crisis; the causes and consequences are seen to be embedded in contemporary history. On all levels, the causes are more or less the same. Isolation is produced, first, by the collapse of common ground in culture, the loss of that mythic substructure which enables man to understand his relatedness to anyone or anything, to place himself in his world. In the early part of the twentieth century, the collapse of shared assumptions in many fields–religion, physics, philosophy, art– produced a crisis in epistemology, in knowing, and this crisis is basic to all of Eliot's work. The second cause is related to the first. To Eliot and to many intellectuals, the villain is knowledge; or from a slightly different angle, the villain is human intelligence. Knowledge, in leading modern man to know that he cannot know anything, in robbing him of shareable assumptions about reality, has banished his brothers and maimed his gods. The situation ends, as W. H. Auden once said, with each confined in the cell of himself.

Among the special ironies of literary history is the fact that Eliot, his fine intelligence burnished to a rare brilliance, was always painfully aware of intelligence as destroyer. The villain in all of his poems through *The Waste Land* is think-

ing, intellection. From "Conversation Galante" through "Portrait of a Lady" to "The Love Song of J. Alfred Prufrock" and "Preludes," the persona moves into increasingly purer realms of abstraction, and consequently into deeper and deeper isolation. It is "thinking" that dissolves the unity of felt thought or thought feeling, producing the divided self; thinking that first generates and then perpetuates self and other. The young man in "Portrait of a Lady" is encased in silence by "thinking"; Prufrock is etherized upon the table of his mind by continuous thinking and rethinking. Gerontion and the inhabitants of the waste land are also thought-trapped creatures, sealed in the prison of solipsism, in which thinking, particularly thinking of the key with which to break out, only confirms the prison. That no lover, human or divine, that no friend can reach through the wall of thought is one of Eliot's special themes. The consequences of isolation– fragmentation, sterility, and death–are parallel on all levels: sexual, cultural, religious, and aesthetic. The cure for isolation similarly is parallel. Generation and renewal are contingent on transcendence of the self, on collaboration between human beings.

In the early poems, then, Eliot's great themes had been established. Preeminent is the profound isolation of modern urbanites, isolation from friends, enemies, lovers, gods, readers. The cause is the collapse of the common ground–in language, in culture, in religion, in art–which serves as a bridge, as a means of self-transcendence. And the consequences of isolation are sterility and death. This accounts for Eliot's perennial preoccupation in life and in art with the necessity for and, in the early poems, the impossibility of resurrection or regeneration. In "Gerontion" and *The Waste Land,* Eliot begins to explore possibilities for overcoming the consequences of isolation. In "Gerontion," he experiments with a solution suggested by his readings in philosophy; in *The Waste Land,* with solutions suggested by his readings in anthropology.

"Gerontion" is the most negative of all Eliot's major poems, reflecting among other things his melancholy over the war; his conclusion that philosophy and religion, like sexual love, promise more than they deliver; his fear that great art is impossible in the twentieth century; his conviction that Western civilization is, in Pound's well-known line, "an old bitch gone in the teeth" ("Ode pour l'Election de Son Sepulchre"). Civilization in Eliot's poem is a shrivelled old man, not only gone in the teeth, but also gone in the eyes, gone in the head, gone in the groin. His name, a transliteration of the Greek word for "little old man," is also a description. The poem is a representation of the state of this old man's mind; and his mind, consisting of bits and pieces of floating cultural, intellectual, spiritual, and sexual debris, is an image of contemporary civilization. Here displayed in all their horror are the consequences of that isolation Eliot had been brooding on and living in for years.

In the opinion of many critics, "Gerontion" is Eliot's most difficult poem. The difficulty derives not so much from content as from form, or as some would have it, from absence of form. What appears at first to be a Prufrockian interior monologue proves to be totally lacking in psychological coherence. In truth, the structure of "Gerontion" is far more complex than that of "The Love Song of J. Alfred Prufrock," due in part to Eliot's assimilation of the idealism of F. H. Bradley, on whose epistemology he had recently completed a dissertation. An understanding of one of Bradley's basic ideas, the systematic nature of truth and judgment, makes "Gerontion" far more accessible. (See Jewel Spears Brooker, "The Structure of Eliot's Gerontion," *ELH*, Summer 1979.)

Common to all absolute idealists and endorsed in Eliot's thesis, the doctrine, simply stated, is that reality consists of parts which are all interconnected in a single system. On the intellectual level, Bradley's doctrine explains away the fragmentation and chaos which seem to characterize contemporary culture. Everything that exists, simply by virtue of existing, is included in the Absolute, which is an overarching, all-inclusive whole. From the fact that the Absolute is all-inclusive, it follows that every perception, every object, every thing in the universe, is a part rather than a whole. Any fragment, no matter how isolated it may appear, is connected to other fragments; every fragment is self-transcendent, that is, it reaches beyond itself and participates in successively greater fragments until it reaches the all-inclusive whole. More simply, every fragment has a context which in turn has a context which in turn again has a context which finally is the Absolute. Because these fragments are all part of one single thing, they are necessarily and systematically related. No fragment has its meaning alone; it exists as part of a unitary and timeless system. Most of Eliot's criticism, including his notion of "tradition," is rooted in this Bradleyean doc-

trine, and most of his poetry, "Gerontion" noticeably, takes it as a structural principle.

In "Gerontion" the dynamic controlling movement from one part to another is not the flow of an old man's consciousness, but the expansion and contraction of the contexts of fragments. The poem is arranged into an almost endless number of superimposed contexts by using the image of houses within houses. By placing houses within houses within houses, Eliot is able to show that every fragment is part of a context which is itself part of a larger context. The objects contained within the houses become less inclusive houses which in turn contain other houses; at the same time, all of the houses are included in more inclusive houses. The house which serves as the model for all of the others is Gerontion's literal house. In the first stanza this house, its tenants, and its surroundings are described. In subsequent stanzas other major houses are superimposed. Although the house image appears at the beginning of the poem, its function as a structural element is not clear until one has read the entire poem and then returned to the beginning. The coda of the poem— "Tenants of the house,/Thoughts of a dry brain in a dry season"–becomes a structural key when it is in the mind of a reader who is re-reading the poem.

As Gerontion describes his literal house and its desiccated tenants, the reader who has the final image in his mind will immediately perceive that Gerontion is more than a tenant in this old house. Gerontion himself, his body, is also an old house with dying tenants, one of which, his brain, is another ruined house with diseased tenants, his thoughts. The idea that all fragments exist necessarily within more inclusive contexts is perfectly illustrated by these images, because a brain can only exist as part of a more inclusive whole. In that the crucial clue is placed at the end of the poem, "Gerontion" illustrates the point made long ago by Joseph Frank: modern literature cannot be read; it can only be re-read, because the whole, of which the last lines are a part, must be in the reader's mind throughout.

The house in which Gerontion lives, clearly on the edge of doom, is old, decayed, brittle, windowless, drafty; it is located in a neglected yard filled with rocks, moss, excreta. The tenants– Gerontion and a woman–are old and sick, and they are transients in a rented house. The owner, a depraved contemporary Jew, squats on the windowsill. The "dry season" is upon them all, and wind batters the house. From this house, there is a proliferation of houses in many directions, and all of them are replicas of the first one. All of the houses are, from a larger point of view, tenants; all of the tenants, from a smaller point of view, are houses. In the first stanza alone, there is a series of houses (tenants): Gerontion's thoughts, his brain, his body, his house, the yard, the field, and Europe. All of these tenants are dying transients in houses rented from a predator who represents both ancient religion and modern capitalism.

To these doomed houses are added in subsequent stanzas the houses of history and of hell; the houses of David (Israel) and of Lancelot Andrewes (the Christian church); of the whore's womb and the messiah's tomb; and many more, all precisely modeled on the first one. The cause of ruin in all is related to a loss of feeling, a decay of religion, and an expansion of knowledge. United in decay, the houses are also to be united in judgment. The coda of the poem returns the reader to the house which, though small, includes all of the others: the arid brain of the withered intellectual whose memories and thoughts, visions and revisions, furnished Eliot with a perfect metaphor for his vision of postwar civilization.

Eliot's first years as a literary man bore tangible fruit in 1920 with the publication of *Ara Vos Prec* (American title, *Poems*), collecting most of his poetry through the quatrains and "Gerontion," and the publication of the best of his literary essays, including "Tradition and the Individual Talent," in *The Sacred Wood*. As Eliot wrapped up the details surrounding these projects, he moved on to what was to prove a watershed experience not only in his life as a poet but also in the history of European poetry. In December 1919 he wrote his mother in America that his New Year's resolution was "to write a long poem I have had on my mind for a long time." That long poem, *The Waste Land*, continues Eliot's exploration of what he saw as the decay of European civilization. In "Gerontion" Eliot had managed to impose order on the chaos by seeing all fragments as part of a system. In the last analysis, however, this purely philosophic solution, even if true, is woefully inadequate. Gerontion's ruined houses, even if seen as parts of a whole, are still ruined. That all the fragments are ordered may be great comfort for the philosopher, or even to the artist, but it is little comfort to the individual who must live and work among the ruins. Bradley's notion was push-

ed into the background because Eliot's long poem is much more than an account of the breakdown of civilization; *The Waste Land*, unlike "Gerontion," is an account of a breakdown in the poet's personal life.

In the five years between his marriage and composition of *The Waste Land*, Eliot had suffered continuously from overwork, financial strain, and marital anxiety. The death of his father took a heavy toll, as did the loss of friends in the war. Eliot's most severe distress, however, was that associated with the breakdown of his marriage. It had become increasingly clear that Thomas and Vivien Eliot were not good for each other. His comments about her in the letters that have surfaced are in no way disrespectful (they reflect, mainly, concern for her health and respect for her resourcefulness), but if the poems "Hysteria" (written in 1914-1915) and "Ode" (written in 1918) are any indication, his feelings were more negative than he could admit to his family or friends, or even to himself. In the 1960s he finally acknowledged what had long been evident: "To her the marriage brought no happiness . . . to me, it brought the state of mind of which came *The Waste Land*."

These years of unmitigated anxiety culminated, finally, in serious illness. In 1921, on the verge of a nervous breakdown, he was forced to take a leave from the bank. For rest, he went in October for a month to Margate; and then, leaving Vivien Eliot in Paris, he went to a sanatorium in Switzerland. From Lausanne, he wrote his brother that he was trying to learn "to use all my energy without waste, to be *calm* when there is nothing to be gained by worry, and to concentrate without effort." In this protected environment, he devoted himself to writing the "long poem" that had been on his mind, a work in which his illness is included as part of the material. "On Margate Sands/I can connect nothing with nothing." "By the waters of Leman [Lake Geneva] I sat down and wept." In the original typescript, there is a reference to leaving Vivien: "I left without you/There I left you/Clasping empty hands."

In January 1922 Eliot returned to London, stopping briefly in Paris, where he left the manuscript of *The Waste Land* with Ezra Pound. Pound immediately recognized it as a work of genius ("About enough, Eliot's poem, to make the rest of us shut up shop"), but he thought it needed cutting and suggested revisions to bring it down to size. Eliot accepted most of Pound's suggestions

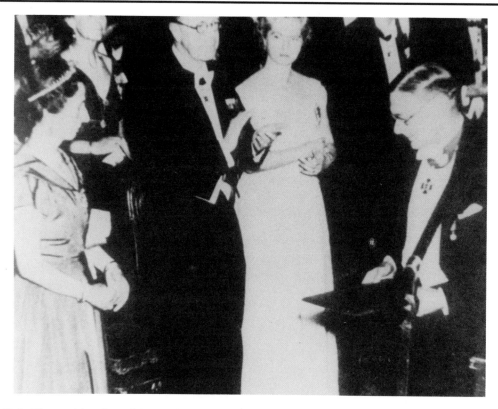

T. S. Eliot receiving the Nobel Prize for Literature, 10 December 1948 (courtesy of Keystone Press Agency)

and later testified that Pound was "a marvelous critic because he . . . tried to see what you were trying to do." In October 1922 *The Waste Land* appeared in England in the first issue of the *Criterion,* the journal Eliot was to edit for most of the next two decades; three weeks later, on 5 November, it appeared in America in the *Dial,* with Eliot receiving the *Dial* award of two thousand dollars.

The Waste Land* was taken by some critics as a tasteless joke, by others as a masterpiece expressing the disillusionment of a generation. As far as Eliot was concerned, it was neither. He needed, he explained in the *Paris Review* interview, to get something off his chest, adding, "one doesn't know quite what it is that one needs to get off the chest until one's got it off"; or as he put it in the conclusion to *The Use of Poetry and The Use of Criticism,* he did not know until the shell broke what sort of egg he had been sitting on. In a lecture at Harvard, quoted in *The Waste Land* facsimile, he gave another explanation, astonishing in its simple honesty, its humility. Responding to those who considered *The Waste Land* "an important bit of social criticism," he remarked, "To me it was only the relief of a personal and wholly insignificant grouse against life; it is just a piece of

rhythmical grumbling." The grumbling is personal, of course, which is why he calls it insignificant, but in that its causes are inseparable from those that set a generation or more of intelligent and talented Westerners to grumbling, it is more than personal. Eliot's "grouse against life," certainly, is part of a larger and shared discontent about the decay of the West and the conditions of modern urban life.

Another aspect of Eliot's "grumbling" which is more than personal is his anxiety about possibility in art. A major theme in his poetry and prose from 1910 had been the situation of the artist who is isolated from his audience by a collapse of common ground in culture. Deprived of a shared mythic or religious frame, the modern artist was forced to come up with other means of unity, other grounds for collaboration with an audience. He had to find, as Eliot put it in *"Ulysses,* Order, and Myth" (*Dial,* November 1923), his review of James Joyce's *Ulysses* (1922), "a way of controlling, of ordering, of giving a shape and a significance to the immense panorama of futility and anarchy which is contemporary history." The "narrative method," rooted in sequence, in continuity, in an orderly flow of life (and stories) from beginning to end, had been rendered obsolete by modern science and by conditions of history. The philosophic method, Eliot had concluded, was an elusion. Consequently, in *The Waste Land,* he experimented with a new method which he hoped was "a step toward making the modern world possible for art." This method, "already adumbrated by Mr. Yeats," Eliot called the "mythical method." He defined it as the manipulation of a continuous parallel between an ordered world of myth (an abstraction) and a chaotic world of history, contemporary or otherwise. In keeping the chaos of his own time on the surface, the artist is being true to history; in referring this chaos to a timeless order, he is being true to art. And in forcing the reader to know (or to learn) the myth, to hold it in his mind as a reference point, and to manipulate the parallel between the world of myth and the world of time, the modern artist is forcing the reader into a collaborative role. This reader must be competent and active, for he is the cowriter in whose mind works such as *Ulysses* and *The Waste Land* take their shape and find their meaning.

Eliot claimed that the mythical method would have been impossible a few years earlier and had become possible only because of recent work in psychology and ethnology, and because of Sir James Frazer's *The Golden Bough* (1890-1915). (See Jewel Spears Brooker, "The Case of the Missing Abstraction: Eliot, Frazer, and Modernism," *Massachusetts Review,* Winter 1984.) Frazer's monumental twelve-volume work is an attempt to interpret the history of religion in terms consistent with Darwinian science. As Darwin had attempted to discover the origin of species and chart the descent of man, anthropologists attempted to discover the origin of religion and chart the descent of the gods. The controlling idea, consistent with the Newtonian/Darwinian assumption of continuity, was that all religions, all myths, originated from a single parent myth. And by examining literally thousands of myths, anthropologists were able to reconstruct this parent myth. To artists trying to find a genuine common ground upon which to unify their art, these ideas proved invaluable. Theoretically, the monomyth is a perfect common ground in that it is shared by all. Religion in the modern world exists only in fragments, but if all of the fragments have a common parent, they can be unified by reference to this Urmyth. All beliefs, no matter how bizarre, are part of one belief; all believers, part of one family.

Eliot saw in this thesis a solution to his problem as an artist–how both to respect and to transcend not only his own isolation, but also the chaos of contemporary history. In the notes to *The Waste Land,* he acknowledged his general debt to Frazer; and his specific debt to Jessie Weston, who in 1920 had published a book called *From Ritual to Romance,* in which she tried to find the origin of all stories having to do with the Holy Grail. Some scholars had postulated a Christian origin, others a folk origin; Weston traces both Christian and folk elements to a common parent, in her words, to "an ancient Ritual, having for its ultimate object the initiation into the secret of the sources of Life, physical and spiritual." In other words, she tried to find the monomyth for the Grail legends. Most important, the monomyth itself exists only as an abstraction, a mental reconstruction made up from many surviving fragments. As a reconstruction in the mind of Frazer or Weston, it serves to structure and unify all fragments of religion and myth; in the mind of the poet, it serves to unify all fragments of religion and culture in twentieth-century Europe; in the mind of the reader of *The Waste Land,* it serves to structure the religious and cultural fragments which make up the poem.

The fragments of myth and religion in *The Waste Land* come from all over the globe and from all periods of history. Christianity in this poem is just one more religion, and fragments of it exist side by side with fragments of Buddhism, ancient fertility cults, contemporary fortune-tellers. All derive ultimately from and find their unity in the Urmyth. One myth, however, has special importance for the poem because it supplied Eliot with the title and much of the symbolism of his poem. That myth, found in *From Ritual to Romance,* tells of a kingdom in which the vitality of the king and that of his kingdom are mysteriously intertwined. The king has suffered a wound (from war, sickness, old age, or whatever) in his genitals, and this sexual wound affects his entire kingdom, depriving it of regenerative power, turning it into a waste land. The land may be restored by a hero who undergoes certain trials and asks certain questions. In Eliot's poem, this myth exists in the same form as it exists in the modern world, that is, in fragments which in the mind of a Jessie Weston or a T. S. Eliot or an intelligent reader may be reconstructed into a whole. As structural principle, then, the monomyths of Weston and Frazer enable the informed reader to unify all fragments in Eliot's poem. As symbol, Weston's myth enables Eliot to construct parallels between contemporary civilization and the mythic waste land and between diseased religion in history and the sexually wounded god-king; and it enables the poet to suggest that, in history as in myth, the wounding of god and the decay of culture are interrelated.

In *The Waste Land,* then, as in "Gerontion," the overall theme is the breakdown of contemporary civilization. In *The Waste Land,* this theme is illustrated and reinforced by juxtaposition to breakdown in Eliot's personal life on the one hand, and on the other to the repeated breakdowns of many, perhaps all, temporal civilizations. Also as in "Gerontion," the structural method is spatial rather than narrative: meaning does not emerge from the sequential arrangement of parts on a page, but from the spatial arrangement of parts in the mind of the reader. In neither poem, however, does the insistence on spatiality amount to a denial of temporality. The poem in the mind is *in time*–it is not given all at once and not given once for all; and it is dynamic rather than static.

The major differences in "Gerontion" and *The Waste Land* are related to point of view. In "Gerontion," unity is inextricable from the consciousness of a single narrator. His mind is an image of civilization. In *The Waste Land,* there is no single narrator, but a multiplicity of superimposed minds, one of which, that of the blind and impotent prophet Tiresias, has a special status. Far more important than the mind of Tiresias, however, is the mind of the reader. The basic structural principle, learned from Bradley, of the systematic nature of reality is modified as Eliot moves from "Gerontion" to *The Waste Land.* In "Gerontion," unity is achieved by referring fragments to ever more inclusive houses or contexts until the Absolute, in which all contexts are systematically contained, is reached. In *The Waste Land,* unity is achieved by referring all fragments to increasingly inclusive parents until the original is reached. There are several important groups of fragments, each leading to its own parent, for example, linguistic fragments leading to Indo-European or some parent language. But the most important group of fragments is the religious or mythic, and the most important parent, the monomyth. The origin of all fragments, even of those seemingly most unconnected to religion, is ultimately religious. The fragments of art, for example, descend from ritual; this, of course, is

the meaning of Weston's title, *From Ritual to Romance.*

The Waste Land consists of five parts which, by traditional standards, seem unrelated. In each part, Eliot's own verse is mixed with fragments of the verse of others, all joined without transitions. This montage includes fragments from several languages and allusions to hundreds of other texts. On one level, these fragments refer primarily to contemporary civilization; on another level, to other temporal civilizations; on the deepest level, to a world of myth. The meaning of the poem exists in all of the fragments taken together, as a whole. The emergence of order and simplicity from this bewildering complexity can perhaps be suggested by a brief survey of the poem.

The primary subject of the first section of the poem–"Burial of the Dead"–is death; death which is just a problem in waste disposal, death which is part of a natural cycle, death as a prelude to life, death as a part of life, life which is a death-in-life, death as an end, death as a beginning. Eliot's montage includes the death of the year, death of individuals, of cities, of civilizations. The title of the first section is a fragment of the title of the majestic burial service in the *Book of Common Prayer,* "The Order for the Burial of the Dead." This service affirms the belief that the burial of the dead is a prelude to the resurrection of the body and to everlasting life. The Anglican church is a descendant of medieval Catholicism, nurturer of the Grail legends, and medieval Catholicism, in turn, descends from first-century Christianity, which has for its major doctrine the death and resurrection of Christ. All of these go back in Frazer's genealogy to primitive rituals in which burial is a ritualistic "planting" intended to insure a rich harvest. Eliot refers specifically to such rituals in the lines "That corpse you planted last year in your garden/Has it begun to sprout?" The ritualistic planting, in April, of a male corpse (or part of one, usually the genitals) in mother earth is at the center of many ancient fertility ceremonies. But Eliot's lines refer also to the contemporary world, where planting the corpse insures harvest by acting as organic fertilizer, and where April is cruel because, in "breeding/Lilacs out of the dead land," it promises what it does not deliver, new life.

The last line of "Burial of the Dead" is a quotation from the prefatory poem of Baudelaire's *Les Fleurs du Mal* and may be translated "You! Hypocrite reader!–my double–my brother!" In this poem, entitled "Au Lecteur" ("To the Reader"),

Baudelaire addresses his reader directly and indicts him as a fellow sinner. In appropriating Baudelaire's line, Eliot indicts his reader not only as a fellow sinner, but also as a partner in the wasting of the land and of civilization. This is so because in his "menagerie of vices," Baudelaire ranks sins, placing at the top, as the most hideous and most evil, the very sin which in Eliot's view swallows up all meaning and turns the world into a waste land. The deadliest sin to Baudelaire and to Eliot is not pride, not greed or rape or murder. The vice of all vices which Baudelaire and Eliot discern both in their readers and in themselves is *ennui*, an inability to invest everyday life with meaning and structure. This monster, the hound devouring the inhabitants of the contemporary waste land, makes a grand entrance in section 2 of Eliot's poem.

The underlying subject of the second section–"A Game of Chess"–is sex, in myth part of a larger interest in life and life-giving forces. In history, though, as Eliot shows, sex is often not associated with life at all. He juxtaposes two "love" scenes–minidramas from opposite ends of the social scale, both displaying sterile and meaningless relationships. The relationship of the upper-class couple is structured by a game of chess, and that of the Cockney couple by visits to the pub. The title of the section alludes to the origin of the game of chess in Hindu agrarian ritual, a context emphasizing enrichment of life for the individual and the community. The original meaning of the game of chess is lost, but the game itself survives, a remnant of a lost and barely glimpsed whole. In this part of *The Waste Land*, Eliot focuses on two relatively modern uses of the game of chess, both related to sexual rituals, but neither to life enhancement. The first modern use of the game is introduced by an allusion to two seventeenth-century plays by Thomas Middleton–*A Game of Chess* and *Women Beware Women*. In *Women Beware Women*, a chess game is used to structure a seduction which is also a betrayal and a rape. The second modern use of a game of chess is introduced in the non-conversation between the upper-middle-class couple. Finding themselves totally bored, they play a game of chess to structure (and to kill) time. Through allusion, other sterile sexual situations– Ophelia's, Cleopatra's, Philomela's–are superimposed. In Philomela, sex is associated with brutality; in Cleopatra, with passion; in Ophelia, with betrayal; in Eliot's characters, with boredom. All of these situations involve sex and sexual games.

Sex is not associated with regeneration in any of the situations, but only in the contemporary situation is it associated with the ultimate evil of *ennui*.

The underlying subject of section 3–"The Fire Sermon"–is again the sexual wound behind civilization's decay. As in "A Game of Chess," there are two contemporary sexual situations– one, a homosexual proposition; the other, a mechanical sexual transaction between a typist and a clerk. Both situations issue from boredom; both, obviously, are loveless and fruitless. The theme is enlarged by including references to loveless couples through the centuries and to fallen gods in Wagner's *Gotterdammerung*. The title–"The Fire Sermon"–refers to the sermon in which Buddha advocates extinguishing the fires of lust. In the contemporary world Buddha's admonition has been fulfilled in a most ironic way. There is no lust because there is no feeling.

The underlying subject in the short fourth section–"Death by Water"–is again death. The drowning of a sailor, followed by dissolution of his body, is juxtaposed, through allusion, to the death by water of Christian baptism and of Frazer's vegetation myths, both of which are ritualistic preludes to rebirth. The ritualistic death by water involves purification; the contemporary death by water is also, ironically, a purification, a cleansing of bones.

The underlying subject of the fifth section of *The Waste Land*–"What the Thunder Said"–is restoration, not as a fact, but as a distant possibility. The previous images of desolation and drought and sterility reappear, but now accompanied by images suggesting the possibility of revitalization. Thunder sounds in the distance; Christ, the slain and resurrected hero whose death effects restoration, walks in the land; the mythic questor whose personal trials can secure communal blessing approaches the Chapel Perilous. The title of this section refers to an Indian legend in which men, gods, and devils listen to the thunder and then construct from that sound the positive message which can restore the waste land and make its inhabitants fruitful again. The poem ends, however, not with restoration, but with an avalanche of fragments, the most concentrated in the entire poem. Two are questions indicating a desire for purification and rebirth; they are answered, unfortunately, with a fragment indicating the persistence of violence, madness, and death. The last fragment, by chance a benediction, is the cruelest in that, like April, and perhaps like thunder, it awakens expectations that it does not satisfy. In conclusion, restoration remains only as a possibility; it all hinges, finally, on a willingness to take the given–thunder, for example–and to construct something which will enable reclamation of structure and meaning. The waste land is not a result of the lack of water, but of the lack of belief. The waste land is filled with water, but it is demythologized water, water that drowns. All of the mythic acts–such as burial in the earth, immersion in water, sexual intercourse–are practiced in the waste land. But they have all been demythologized by the absence of belief. What is needed to restore the waste land is a re-mythologizing of the events of everyday life, a resacramentalization which will reinvest life with structure and meaning. The last lines seem to make a distinction which will become crucial in Eliot's own life: it is probably impossible to restore the waste land which is Western civilization, but it may be possible to create order in the waste land of one's personal life.

The Waste Land was both an end and a beginning; it was also a continuation. The distance traveled in the following decade can be gauged by the fact that in 1932, Eliot, now a world-famous poet, returned to Harvard as Charles Eliot Norton Professor of Poetry. Three events of the intervening decade are important in following the shape of his life and art. First, his financial and in a sense his vocational situation was resolved when, in 1925, he left Lloyds Bank for the publishing house of Faber and Gwyer (later Faber and Faber). Second, his marital situation continued to deteriorate, ending with his permanent separation from Vivien Eliot in 1932; and third, his spiritual odyssey culminated in 1927 in baptism into the Anglican church and in naturalization as a British subject. The financial nightmare had begun to fade in 1922 when he launched the *Criterion*. When, on the eve of World War II, a weary Eliot announced that he was bringing the *Criterion* to a close, he was able to look back with considerable pride on the quality and range of its accomplishments. By publishing such distinguished writers as Paul Valéry, Marcel Proust, James Joyce, Virginia Woolf, D. H. Lawrence, W. H. Auden, Jacques Maritain, Charles Maurras, and Wilhelm Worringer, he had greatly enhanced intellectual fellowship in Europe *l'entre deux guerres*. At Faber, Eliot found a congenial and enduring group of associates, a community. And through Faber, he was able to be a mentor and friend to younger writers. Stephen Spender reports that Eliot, in his dealings with younger poets, was "gentle, helpful, and tolerant, and never expressed disapproval of their politics." W. H. Auden, according to Spender, claimed "that of all the older writers with whom we had dealings, Eliot was the most consistently friendly, the least malicious, envious, and vain." The reciprocally rewarding relationship with Faber continued for the rest of Eliot's life.

The community of intellectuals and artists of which, through the *Criterion* and Faber, Eliot became a part assuaged somewhat the sense of fragmentation which had always haunted him. The sexual and the religious aspects of his isolation, however, proved resistant to transcendence. He and Vivien Eliot were unable to forge any sort of unity, and, as their relationship and her health continued to deteriorate, he suffered in ways which could not help but surface in his poetry. Inseparable from his realization that human love, and in particular, sexual love, had failed is his turn toward God and the church. The emptiness and desolation of this period are perfectly caught in a poem thought by I. A. Richards to be Eliot's most beautiful, "The Hollow Men."

"The Hollow Men," composed in fragments over a two- or three-year period, appeared as a single poem in *Poems 1909-1925* (1925). Written in the style of what Eliot once said was the best part of *The Waste Land,* the water-dripping song in "What the Thunder Said," "The Hollow Men" is based on four main allusions–to Dante's *The Divine Comedy,* to Shakespeare's *Julius Caesar,* to Joseph Conrad's *Heart of Darkness,* and to an event in English history, the Gunpowder Plot of 1605. Dante, Shakespeare, and Conrad are arguably the most important writers in the background of Eliot's art, and *Heart of Darkness* is probably second only to *The Divine Comedy* as an intellectual/ spiritual resource. Conrad's hero, Mr. Kurtz, a cultivated European idealist and carrier of civilization to dark places, glimpses as he dies a vision which he expresses as "The horror! The horror!" These words, included in Eliot's original epigraph for *The Waste Land,* describe the vision both Conrad and Eliot saw beneath the veneer of European civilization. And they describe what Conrad probably and Eliot certainly saw beneath the veneer of modern idealism.

In "The Hollow Men" Eliot focuses on the idealism shared by such figures as Brutus, Guy Fawkes, and (as in *The Waste Land*) Mr. Kurtz, and in an epigraph which is also a conclusion, he quotes from *Heart of Darkness* the simple announce-

T. S. Eliot with his wife, Valerie, 1957 (photograph by Angus McBean)

ment by a jungle boy–"Mistah Kurtz–he dead." The death of Mistah Kurtz and all that he stands for is, of course, at the center of the meaning of this poem. From one point of view, however, the most interesting of the disillusioned and defeated idealists is not Mistah Kurtz, but Mistah Eliot, who in 1925 wrote to Bertrand Russell "I am quite desperate." Physically and spiritually worn out, Eliot presents an unforgettable picture of exhaustion and emptiness. The "Old Guy" of the epigraph is not only Guy Fawkes, but also "the old man" whose death, according to St. Paul, is the condition of new life. Many figures in Eliot's early poems, including all the gods and semigods from Frazer, have to die or be put to death as the condition for the continuation of life. Those who cannot die cannot really live. The most striking of these death-in-life figures, of course, is the Sibyl of Cumae who presides over *The Waste Land.* In "The Hollow Men," Eliot does not go beyond a presentation of emptiness, but in presenting it, he seems to accept the death that is the essential step toward his own *vita nuova.* In "Gerontion" and *The Waste Land,* Eliot

had seen the death-in-life figures as primarily other than himself. But in "The Hollow Men," in trying to articulate his own inarticulate emptiness, he numbers himself among the living dead. His idealism, like that of Brutus, Fawkes, and Kurtz, has led him to the cactus land.

The way out of the cactus land led Eliot to his own "death by water" in a small church at Finstock near Oxford, where on 29 June 1927 he was baptized into the Anglican Communion. In November, in what seemed to him part of the same ritual, he was naturalized as a British citizen. Many of Eliot's contemporaries, having adopted him as a sort of spokesman, felt that in embracing traditional Christianity he had abandoned them in the desert. He gently explained that he had never intended to be the spokesman for a generation; that he had been trying all along to work out his own salvation; and that, for "powerful and concurrent reasons," he had been drawn inexorably toward Christianity. As he said in "Christianity and Communism" (*Listener,* March 1932), "In my own case, I believe that one of the reasons was that the Christian scheme seemed to me the only one which would work . . . the only possible scheme which found a place for values which I must maintain or perish." Like Pascal, Eliot had proceeded to the Christian position by a careful process of rejection and elimination. He had tried schemes from philosophy and from anthropology, and he discovered that in the end these schemes failed to account for the world as he saw it and were a less-than-satisfactory basis for order in life and in art.

The Christian scheme, at once personal and communal, which Eliot chose for a basis of order carries as its first condition death and rebirth. The truth that rebirth involves its own pain can be seen in retrospect as a major theme of *The Waste Land,* caught in the opening line, "April is the cruellest month." The painful journey through death into new life is dealt with explicitly in *Journey of the Magi,* a dramatic monologue published as a pamphlet a month after Eliot's baptism. "A cold coming we had of it," say the wise men. In coming to this birth, the incarnation of Christ, they come also to the crucifixion, and to something bitter, "like Death, our death." Eliot's coming, his turning, forms the material for *Ash-Wednesday,* his main poem between *The Waste Land* and *Four Quartets.*

The second poem in the *Ash-Wednesday* sequence appeared in the *Saturday Review of Literature* (10 December 1927) a few months after

Eliot's baptism. Titled "Salutation," it demonstrates that the old guy, in the pun of "The Hollow Men," is dying, the new guy coming to life; and it introduces not only the new man, but also the new style. The scene of "Salutation" is the waste land, the cactus land of his earlier work; the subject is certain death and possible new life. The fact that the setting and subject are the same only serves to underscore the great difference in tone and general import. "Lady, three white leopards sat under a juniper-tree/In the cool of the day, having fed to satiety/On my legs my heart my liver and that which had been contained/In the hollow of my skull. And God said—shall these bones live?" Allusions to the Garden of Eden, to Ezekiel's Valley of Dry Bones, to Saint Paul, and to Dante show that the old man has been dismembered, that his now clean, dry bones patiently await oblivion or resurrection. The bones sing a litany celebrating the "End of the endless/Journey to no end" and the arrival at "the Garden/Where all love ends." The resonance of these lines derives in part from the religious and philosophic richness of Eliot's use of the word "end." An "end" is a cause or source, a purpose or raison d'être, a cessation, a logical conclusion, and a fulfillment. An "end" is also the place where the "end" happens. Thus the endless (unceasing, unfulfilling, pointless, placeless) journey through the dark wood of his life with and to no end (purpose, conclusion, haven) finds an end (conclusion, purpose, and thus a beginning and a cause) in the Incarnation, and in the Garden where all love ends (meets its source and cause, finds its fulfillment, ceases in itself to become part of larger love).

Eliot uses the word "end" with similar richness in *Four Quartets,* his most magnificent meditation on beginnings and ends. A major theme of *East Coker,* for example, is carried in the lines: "In my beginning is my end . . . In my end is my beginning." And the aesthetic and the theodicy of *Little Gidding* culminate in "What we call the beginning is often the end/And to make an end is to make a beginning./The end is where we start from." and "We shall not cease from exploration/And the end of all our exploring/Will be to arrive where we started/And know the place for the first time." The exploration of ends and beginnings which came to dominate his later poetry and his plays had its beginning in this poem of *Ash-Wednesday,* "Salutation," a poem that "ends" with "This is the land. We have our inheritance." In that this "ending" echoes the "end" of *The Waste Land*—"Shall I at least set my lands in order?" and the fragment from Nerval's "El Desdichado" ("The Disinherited")—"Salutation" constitutes an important bridge between the two major parts of Eliot's career as a poet.

Ash-Wednesday is composed of six parts, three of which had been published separately before the 1930 publication of all six under one title. The title refers to the first day of Lent, a day of repentance and fasting in which Christians acknowledge their mortality and begin the forty-day period of self-examination leading to the new life of Easter. The structure of this sequence comes from Eliot's new principle of order, the Christian scheme which for him had subsumed both Bradley and Frazer. In place of the monomyth as a reference point, Eliot now uses the Incarnation of Christ—not only in *Ash-Wednesday,* but also in *Four Quartets* and the plays. The Incarnation represents a unique intersection of the human and the divine, of time and the timeless, of movement and stillness. Eliot's earlier schemes had been a means of making art possible in the chaos of contemporary history; his new scheme, however, is a means of making life, of which art is only a part, possible. The integration of life and art can be seen in the fact that *Ash-Wednesday* is at once more personal, confessional even, and at the same time more formal and stylized than the earlier work.

The *Ash-Wednesday* sequence as a whole celebrates the turning point in Eliot's life—turning from one blessed face to a higher one, from fragmentation to unity, from a world of ambition to a God of peace. The personal and the universal turning which is the poem's major subject—the "unstilled world still whirled/About the centre of the silent Word"—is also the basis of structure. The first lines circle and hover as they introduce the theme of turning—"Because I do not hope to turn again/Because I do not hope/Because I do not hope to turn." The circling continues in line after line as the penitent turns in his attempt to stay still and to build something upon which to rejoice. The turning of the first poem is followed in the second by stillness—the bright vision of the leopards who have fed on the dry bones of the penitent's former self. Then in the third poem, the turning resumes as the penitent ascends a spiral staircase, leaving his previous self to struggle with the devil of the stairs. The fourth poem, like the second, is a vision, but the desert has been succeeded by a garden, the stillness by movement, and death by life. The fifth is a meditation on the still point, the Word, which is the source and end of all turning. The last poem circles back on the first, but with a slight advance–"Because I do not hope to turn again" has become "Although I do not hope to turn again." The poem returns at last to its opening prayer, "Teach us to care and not to care./Teach us to sit still."

For all its brightness, *Ash-Wednesday* remains a poem about twilight, about "the time of tension between dying and birth." The tension is resolved in *Marina* (published as a pamphlet in 1930), frequently regarded as Eliot's most beautiful short poem. It consists of an interior monologue spoken by Pericles, the Prince of Tyre, who in Shakespeare's play sails the seas in search of his beloved wife, lost after giving birth at sea to an infant daughter, also lost and presumably dead. Eliot's monologue, inspired by Shakespeare's recognition scene, conveys the wonder and awe the old prince experiences in realizing that the beautiful girl standing before him is Marina, his daughter. What "Gerontion" is to *The Waste Land*, this joyous celebration of new life is to *Four Quartets*.

The decade inaugurated with *Ash-Wednesday* was an eventful one for Eliot. In 1932 he published *Selected Essays*, a collection of his literary journalism through the 1920s; in 1933, *The Use of Poetry and The Use of Criticism*, his lectures as Charles Eliot Norton Professor of Poetry at Harvard in 1932-1933. In the spring of 1933, he gave lectures at the University of Virginia, which were published in 1934 as *After Strange Gods*. He also lectured at Edinburgh and at Cambridge; the Cambridge lectures were later collected as *The Idea of a Christian Society* (1939). Also in the 1930s, he realized his longstanding ambition of becoming a dramatist, finishing both *Murder in the Cathedral* (1935) and *The Family Reunion* (1939). Eliot also published *Old Possum's Book of Practical Cats* (1939), light poems composed for his godchildren. This book became, some fifteen years after Eliot's death, the text for a spectacular musical with score by Andrew Lloyd Webber. Having loved the English music hall, Eliot would have been delighted with *Cats*.

Eliot's major poetic achievement during the 1930s was *Burnt Norton*, composed in 1935, initially considered as an independent work–and included as such in *Collected Poems 1909-1935* (1936)–but becoming during the war the first of four comparable works which together are known as *Four Quartets*. This magnificent sequence–*Burnt Norton* (1936; published separately in 1941), *East Coker* (1940), *The Dry Salvages* (1941), and *Little Gidding* (1942)–is widely regarded as Eliot's masterpiece. He himself thought *Four Quartets* his greatest achievement, and *Little Gidding* his best poem.

Burnt Norton originated from some lines Eliot cut from *Murder in the Cathedral*. In the play, Becket is confronted by a tempter who suggests a return to the past as a way to escape the dangerous present: "The Chancellorship that you resigned/When you were made Archbishop–that was a mistake/On your part–still may be regained." In this scene, requiring a reexamination of the whole of life in the light of the present moment, a priest originally responded with the following words: "Time present and time past/Are both perhaps present in the future./Time future is contained in time past. . . . What might have been is a conjecture/Remaining a permanent possibility/Only in a world of speculation. . . . Footfalls echo in the memory/Down the passage which we did not take/Into the rose-garden." These beautiful lines, only slightly modified, now form the opening section of *Burnt Norton*. The temptation to try to go back and take a different road, to cancel history and create an alternative present, constitutes an intersection where the lives of Becket, of Christ, and of Eliot come together. This intersection generated Eliot's meditation on time and timelessness, on history and consciousness, on life and art, and on God.

Eliot's exploration of these great subjects is resumed and completed in the other three *quartets*, written some five years after *Burnt Norton*. Whereas his earlier poems had been centered on the isolated individual, *Four Quartets* is centered on the isolated moment, the fragment of time which takes its meaning from and gives its meaning to a pattern, a pattern at once in time, continuously changing until the supreme moment of death completes it, and also out of time. Since the individual lives and has his being only in fragments, he can never quite know the whole pattern, but in certain moments, he can experience the pattern in miniature. These timeless moments in time–"the moment in the rose-garden,/ The moment in the arbour where the rain beat,/ The moment in the draughty church at smokefall" (*Burnt Norton*)–provide for Eliot the means of conquering time. This moment of sudden illumination, in and out of time, Eliot associates with the Word-made-flesh, the Incarnation; and also with the word-made-art, poetry. The part-pattern configuration, especially in these three dimensions, is both the main subject and the main principle of form in *Four Quartets*. Both idea and form issue ultimately from Eliot's new "scheme," the Christian religion; and his masterpiece, like Milton's, is a theodicy, a vindication of the ways of God to man. "Love is the unfamiliar Name/Behind the hands that wove/The intolerable shirt of flame/Which human power cannot remove./We only live, only suspire/Consumed by either fire or fire"; "All manner of thing shall be well/When the tongues of flame are in-folded/Into the crowned knot of fire/And the fire and the rose are one" (*Little Gidding*).

The fact that *Four Quartets* is a meditation on time and a celebration of pattern points to a secondary principle of form, albeit the one usually mentioned first by literary critics. From the title and from a lecture called *The Music of Poetry* (1942), delivered early in the year he finished *Little Gidding*, it is clear that Eliot was working with a musical analogy throughout *Four Quartets*, especially in regard to structure: "There are possibilities for verse which bear some analogy to the development of a theme by different groups of instruments; . . . possibilities of transitions . . . comparable to the different movements of . . . a quartet, . . . possibilities of contrapuntal arrangement of subject-matter." There can be no doubt that Eliot is here describing his own composition of *Four Quartets*. The most conspicuous analogies to music include statement and counterstatement, theme and variation, tempo variation, and mood variation. By using the musical analogy, Eliot was able to avoid monotony, the plague of long and complex philosophical poems. He is returning, furthermore, to his beginnings as a poet and thus demonstrating one of the themes of *Four Quartets:* "We shall not cease from exploration/And the end of all our exploring/Will be to arrive where we started/And know the place for the first time" (*Little Gidding*). In three of his four early masterpieces, "The Love Song of J. Alfred Prufrock," "Preludes," and "Rhapsody on a Windy Night," an analogy with music is established in the title (in the fourth, "Portrait of a Lady," an analogy is established through imagery). The analogy with music is useful in clarifying the nondiscursive nature of *Four Quartets*, but as Eliot warns in *The Music of Poetry* and in essays on the symbolists, it should not be pushed too far.

One other major aspect of form in *Four Quartets* is noteworthy in view of the status of this se-

quence as both the pinnacle of Eliot's achievement and also a pinnacle of modern art. In *Four Quartets*, Eliot brilliantly solved a problem at the core of most modern art, a problem which could be called the case of the missing abstraction. (See Jewel Spears Brooker, "The Case of the Missing Abstraction," *Massachusetts Review*, Winter 1984.) In a 1924 essay, "Four Elizabethan Dramatists," written a year or so after he completed *The Waste Land*, Eliot explained that great art always consists of a relationship between actual life, which is its material, and an abstraction, which is its basis of form. And because great art is always a collaboration between an artist and his audience, this abstraction must be common; that is, it must exist (or be capable of existing) not only in his mind, but in his reader's. Yeats solved the case of the missing abstraction by making up an elaborate system and publishing it as a sort of mythic handbook for his readers. Eliot solved it in *The Waste Land* by giving his readers the fragments from which they could construct (or reconstruct) the missing abstraction, the Urmyth; and then by referring them to Frazer and Weston, whose work provides a precise model for do-it-yourself mythmakers.

In *Four Quartets* Eliot solved the case of the missing abstraction by allowing the poem itself to generate the pattern which undergirds it and gives it meaning. On the simplest level, the abstraction is born of the fact that there are *four* meditations, all different, and yet obviously all of a kind. Just as from many myths, Frazer abstracted one myth; just as from forty-one symphonies, the listener abstracts a Mozartian symphony, heard only in the mind's ear; just as from six tragedies, the theatergoer or reader abstracts a Shakespearean tragedy, performed only in the theater of the mind; so the reader of *Four Quartets* inevitably if unconsciously abstracts an Eliotian quartet. This poem in the mind is private to each reader, but because it is generated by the text all readers share, it agrees to a remarkable extent with the abstractions constructed by other readers. The poem in the mind is at once spatial (it exists all at once in mental space) and temporal (it is always changing): "The knowledge imposes a pattern, and falsifies,/For the pattern is new in every moment/And every moment is a new and shocking/Valuation of all we have been" (*East Coker*). In order to perceive the pattern, one must temporarily spatialize it. Such spatialization inevitably falsifies, but it is necessary because it is the only way of glimpsing the still point at the center of all movement: "Only by the form, the pattern,/Can words or music reach/The stillness, as a Chinese jar still/Moves perpetually in its stillness" (*Burnt Norton*).

The Quartet in the mind, the pattern, emerges automatically from the fact that each of the *Four Quartets* explores the same general subject; each is named for a place; and each has approximately the same form. The subject–the intertwined mysteries of part-pattern and of movement-stillness–has many faces and can be viewed from many angles. The meaningfulness of Eliot's treatment is immeasurably enriched by the fact that the form of the sequence is itself a perfect illustration of the twin mysteries.

The title of each meditation refers to a specific place important to the poet. Burnt Norton is the name of a country house in Gloucestershire, which Eliot visited in the summer of 1934 in the company of his American friend Emily Hale, an amateur actress and a professor of drama whom Eliot had known well during the Harvard years (after he had settled in England, he asked Conrad Aiken to dispatch flowers to her on opening night). Pending the availability of Eliot's many letters to this friend of more than half a century (letters sealed at Princeton University until the year 2020), the details of their relationship cannot be known. But it seems likely that on this summer day in the rose garden, Eliot, guilt-torn and exhausted from his disastrous marriage and recent separation, experienced a temptation to deny the present by returning to the road not taken in 1914, a temptation exactly analogous to that of Thomas Becket which generated the lines which now open *Burnt Norton*.

The title of the second quartet, *East Coker*, refers to the village in Somersetshire from which in the seventeenth century Eliot's family had immigrated to America, and to which, after his death, Eliot's own ashes were to be returned. The mystery of man's beginnings and his ends–"In my beginning is my end"; "In my end is my beginning"–in and out of history is explored in this quartet. The third quartet takes its title from a small but enormously treacherous group of rocks, the Dry Salvages, located off the coast of Cape Ann, Massachusetts, where Eliot had passed his childhood summers. These rocks, the cold and seemingly limitless ocean in which they are anchored, and the great Mississippi River of his childhood are the major symbols in this meditation.

The last quartet takes its title from a tiny village in Huntingdonshire, Little Gidding, which in the seventeenth century had been a community of dedicated Christians under the leadership of Nicholas Ferrar. Eliot, who visited Little Gidding in 1936, admired the example of this small group who had renounced position and wealth for a life of work and prayer. Each of these four places is associated with Eliot's part-pattern, stillness-movement theme. He insists on the importance of specific places as he does of specific moments. The timeless moment, in fact, can only occur in a specific place–a rose garden, a drafty church, a rain-washed arbor. The places are only fragments of the pattern; they constitute, nevertheless, the only way to transcendence. "Only through time time is conquered" (*Burnt Norton*); only through place place is conquered.

As all the quartets explore the same theme, as all point to a specific place, so all have the same general form. The first part of each consists of a meditation on time and consciousness, arranged as statement-counterstatement-recapitulation. The second consists of a highly structured poetical passage followed by a relatively prosaic passage, both on the general subject of being trapped in time. The third explores implications of the first two in terms of a journey metaphor, of some concept of movement of the self in and out of time. The fourth is a brief lyric treating of death and rebirth. The fifth begins with a colloquial passage and then ends with a lyric which secures closure by returning to the beginning and by gathering the major images. This fifth section in each quartet also incorporates a meditation on the problem of the artist, who must still move in stillness, keep time in time (both continuously move in step and continuously be still).

In "Four Elizabethan Dramatists" Eliot had argued that the greatest artists have achieved consistency not by copying life, but by anchoring their work in an abstraction from life. Eliot's remarkable achievement in *Four Quartets* is that he simultaneously anchored his work and generated the abstraction in which to anchor it. As an individual, he accepted the Christian religion, but as an artist, he accepted the limitation posed by a post-Christian civilization. He therefore eschewed anchoring his art in the Christian myth, or as Yeats had done, in a private myth, choosing the more difficult way of anchoring it in an abstraction rising from its own creation. That he created *Four Quartets* within these limitations places him among the greatest artists to have ever written in English.

Eliot's career as a poet virtually ends with *Four Quartets*. The remainder of his creative energy was put into his comedies and his many public addresses. His long-standing despair over Western civilization, at the heart of "Gerontion" and *The Waste Land*, still conspicuous in 1939 in his farewell editorial for the *Criterion*, was modified by the onset of World War II. He suddenly realized that there were traditions and principles worth dying for, and he did what he could to help preserve them. In January 1947 the most painful chapter in his personal history came to an end when Vivien Eliot, after years of madness, died in an institution. Ezra Pound, the old friend who had urged him to marry the vivacious English girl, was himself confined in a mental hospital, St. Elizabeths in Washington, D.C., charged with treason for the radio speeches he had made during the war. With other concerned friends of letters, Eliot did what he could to improve the situation of his old benefactor. Against these shadows, Eliot must have experienced some pleasure in his growing reputation as the world's greatest living poet and the century's most-distinguished man of letters.

Beginning in the mid 1940s, he received almost every accolade the West had to offer a poet. The world's oldest and most prestigious universities, including his alma mater, bestowed honorary doctorates. In 1948, he received England's most exclusive and prestigious civilian prize, the Order of Merit, and, in the same year, the Nobel Prize for Literature. In subsequent years, he was awarded the most coveted international prizes in the humanities. The superstar status of this most private and difficult poet is indicated by other awards (for example, he was made an "Honorary Deputy Sheriff" of Dallas County, Texas); by coverage in popular magazines (for example, in March 1950 *Time* did a cover story on him); and by the size of his audiences (for example, nearly fifteen thousand came to his 1956 lecture in Minneapolis). Eliot accepted all of this attention with characteristic grace and good humor. "He was, above all, a humble man; firm, even stubborn at times, but with no self-importance; quite unspoilt by fame; free from spiritual or intellectual pride"– this quotation from his obituary in the *Times* (London) is substantiated by the testimony of those who knew him as a person rather than as a monument.

The most important event in Eliot's later life was his second marriage. In his sixty-ninth year (1957), he married Esme Valerie Fletcher,

his devoted secretary at Faber since 1949, and almost forty years his junior. By all accounts, this happy marriage rejuvenated the poet. His obvious contentment may seem to contradict all or most of his earlier references to sexual love. In fact, the marital bliss reveals with special clarity a larger pattern in his life and art. That pattern involves a continuous dissatisfaction with brokenness, a continuous quest for wholeness. His early obsession with brokenness and isolation can easily be seen in retrospect as the negative expression of a quest for wholeness and communion. Such a quest is religious in the most radical sense, for "religion" (*re* "again"; *ligare* "to tie or bind") is literally a reconnecting of pieces into a whole, a rebinding of fragments. Religion begins with an awareness of brokenness, of isolation from something or someone; religious activity by definition is motivated by dissatisfaction with isolation, with partness. Eliot's universality (the quality he admired most in Virgil and Dante) is inseparable from the fact that, both in poetry and in life, he represents a man of great feeling and intelligence in quest of wholeness. The quest for unity in art was realized in different ways in different periods, with "The Love Song of J. Alfred Prufrock," "Gerontion," *The Waste Land*, *Ash-Wednesday*, and *Four Quartets* representing various solutions. Inseparable from the quest for unity in art is the quest for a system or an abstraction which would allow for philosophical wholeness, a quest which includes encounters with Bradley, Frazer, Saint Paul, and others. Inseparable too is the quest for self-transcendence through human love. For most of his life, he believed that this sort of transcendence was a chimera ("April is the cruellest month"). His second marriage is important because it is the complement in his personal life of the religious unity he found through commitment to the Incarnation and of the aesthetic unity he achieved in *Four Quartets*. The personal unity, the "new person/Who is you and me together," is celebrated in his last play, *The Elder Statesman* (1959), and in the last poem in his *Collected Poems 1909-1962* (1963), "A Dedication to My Wife." Eliot's last years, though happy, were darkened by illness. He died in London of emphysema and related complications on 4 January 1965. The *Times* (London) obituary was entitled "The Most Influential English Poet of His Time." And the long obituary in *Life* magazine concluded with "Our age beyond any doubt has been, and will continue to be, the Age of Eliot." Such claims inevitably provoke reaction and reeval-

Robert Crawford, *The Savage and the City in the Work of T. S. Eliot* (Oxford: Clarendon Press, 1987).
Explores the twin concerns of primitive and urban life in Eliot's early work.

Lois Cuddy and David H. Hirsch, eds., *Critical Essays on T. S. Eliot's The Waste Land* (Boston: G. K. Hall, 1989).
Excellent selection of interpretative essays on *The Waste Land*.

Harriet Davidson, *T. S. Eliot and Hermeneutics: Absence and Interpretation in The Waste Land* (Baton Rouge: Louisiana State University Press, 1985).
Brings theories of Paul Ricoeur and Jacques Derrida to bear on *The Waste Land*.

Elizabeth Drew, *T. S. Eliot: The Design of His Poetry* (London: Eyre & Spottiswoode, 1950).
Survey of Eliot's poetry with focus on Jungian myth criticism.

Joseph Frank, "Spatial Form in Modern Literature," in his *The Widening Gyre: Crisis and Mastery in Modern Literature* (Bloomington: Indiana University Press, 1968), pp. 2-63.
Extremely helpful and influential essay about the crisis in modern literature and the attempt of writers to shift basis of structure in literature from narrative (temporal) to juxtapositional (spatial) form.

Helen Gardner, *The Art of T. S. Eliot* (London: Cresset Press, 1949).
An early but still valuable overview of Eliot's poetry.

Gardner, *The Composition of Four Quartets* (London: Faber & Faber, 1978; New York: Oxford University Press, 1978).
A detailed account of the origin and growth of *Four Quartets*. Includes texts of poems and comments by Eliot and his friends.

Lyndall Gordon, *Eliot's Early Years* (Oxford & New York: Oxford University Press, 1977).
A psycho-biography of the poet's early life in terms of a spiritual quest. Contains much biographical and interpretative commentary.

Gordon, *Eliot's New Life* (New York: Farrar Straus Giroux, 1988).
A sequel to *Eliot's Early Years*, taking the poet from his 1927 conversion to the end of his life, with focus on his relations to women.

Michael Grant, ed., *T. S. Eliot: The Critical Heritage*, 2 volumes (London: Routledge & Kegan Paul, 1982).
Representative commentary on Eliot's work from 1916-1963. A valuable sourcebook.

Piers Gray, *T. S. Eliot's Intellectual and Poetic Development, 1909-1922* (Atlantic Highlands, N.J.: Humanities Press, 1982).
A valuable discussion of the relation of Eliot's ideas and education to his poetry through *The Waste Land*.

Donald Hall, "Notes on T. S. Eliot," in *Remembering Poets* (New York: Harper & Row, 1977), pp. 77-110.
A valuable reminiscence of Eliot in later life by a junior poet who knew him.

Nancy Duvall Hargrove, *Landscape as Symbol in the Poetry of T. S. Eliot* (Jackson: University Press of Mississippi, 1978).
Discusses Eliot's use of landscape as symbol in his poetry. Contains photographs of places associated with Eliot's poetry.

Herbert Howarth, *Notes on Some Figures Behind T. S. Eliot* (Boston: Houghton Mifflin, 1964; London: Chatto & Windus, 1975).
Provides valuable backgrounds of Eliot's life and work.

Cleo McNelly Kearns, *T. S. Eliot and Indic Traditions: A Study in Poetry and Belief* (Cambridge & New York: Cambridge University Press, 1987).
Helpful exploration of Eliot's Indic studies and the use he made of them in his poetry.

Hugh Kenner, *T. S. Eliot: The Invisible Poet* (New York: McDowell, Obolensky, 1959).
An overview of Eliot's life and work with emphasis on Eliot's ideas of impersonality in art.

Kenner, ed., *T. S. Eliot: A Collection of Critical Essays* (Englewood Cliffs, N.J.: Prentice-Hall, 1962).
Collection of essays on Eliot's writings.

A. Walton Litz, ed., *Eliot in His Time: Essays on the Occasion of the Fiftieth Anniversary of The Waste Land* (Princeton: Princeton University Press, 1973).
Essays by various scholars on *The Waste Land.*

Edward Lobb, *T. S. Eliot and the Romantic Critical Tradition* (London: Routledge & Kegan Paul, 1981).
Explores Eliot's relation to Romanticism.

John D. Margolis, *T. S. Eliot's Intellectual Development 1922-1939* (Chicago & London: University of Chicago Press, 1972).
Valuable survey of intellectual backgrounds with emphasis on Eliot's editorship of the *Criterion.*

Jay Martin, ed., *A Collection of Critical Essays on The Waste Land* (Englewood Cliffs, N.J.: Prentice-Hall, 1968).
Essays on *The Waste Land.*

Timothy Materer, *Vortex: Pound, Eliot, and Lewis* (Ithaca & London: Cornell University Press, 1979).
Explores Eliot's relationships with Ezra Pound and Wyndham Lewis and the significance of vorticism in modern literature.

F. O. Matthiessen, *The Achievement of T. S. Eliot: An Essay on the Nature of Poetry* (London & New York: Oxford University Press, 1935; revised and enlarged, 1947).
Early overview of Eliot's poetry.

A. D. Moody, *Thomas Stearns Eliot: Poet* (Cambridge & New York: Cambridge University Press, 1979).
Valuable survey of Eliot's poetry.

Moody, ed., *The Waste Land in Different Voices* (New York: St. Martin's Press, 1974).
Collection of essays on *The Waste Land.*

James Olney, ed., *T. S. Eliot* (Oxford: Clarendon Press, 1988).

Important collection of essays on all aspects of Eliot's work. Includes essays by Brand Blanchard, Valerie Eliot, and many others.

Gertrude Patterson, *T. S. Eliot: Poems in the Making* (Manchester: University of Manchester Press, 1971; New York: Barnes & Noble, 1971).
Fine discussion of the poetry, with emphasis on its structure and with comparison to form in other modern arts.

Jeffrey M. Perl, *Eliot's Unwanted Scepticism* (Baltimore: Johns Hopkins University Press, forthcoming 1989).
Valuable exploration of Eliot's early philosophical studies and of his politics.

Perl and Andrew P. Tuck, "Foreign Metaphysics: The Significance of T. S. Eliot's Philosophical Notebooks," *Southern Review,* 21 (January 1985): 79-88.
Relates Eliot's early philosophical studies to his concept of tradition.

Balachandra Rajan, ed., *T. S. Eliot: A Study of His Writing By Several Hands* (London: Dobson, 1947).
Collection of essays on Eliot's writing.

Elisabeth W. Schneider, *T. S. Eliot: The Pattern in the Carpet* (Berkeley: University of California Press, 1975).
Overview of Eliot's poetry.

Ronald Schuchard, "Eliot and Hulme in 1916: Toward a Revaluation of Eliot's Critical and Spiritual Development," *PMLA,* 88 (October 1973): 1083-1094.
Explores the important relationship of Eliot and T. E. Hulme.

Schuchard, " 'First-Rate Blasphemy': Baudelaire and the Revised Critical Idiom of T. S. Eliot's Moral Criticism," *ELH,* 42 (Summer 1975): 276-295.
Explores Eliot's moral philosophy in terms of his admiration of Charles Baudelaire.

Sanford Schwartz, *The Matrix of Modernism: Pound, Eliot, & Early 20th-Century Thought* (Princeton: Princeton University Press, 1985).

Valuable discussion of modernism and intellectual backgrounds of Eliot and his contemporaries.

Martin Scofield, *T. S. Eliot: The Poems* (Cambridge & New York: Cambridge University Press, 1988).
Valuable overview of Eliot's poetry.

Richard Shusterman, *T. S. Eliot and the Philosophy of Criticism* (New York: Columbia University Press, 1988).
A significant reevaluation of Eliot's philosophical bearings.

William Skaff, *The Philosophy of T. S. Eliot: From Skepticism to a Surrealist Poetic 1909-1927* (Philadelphia: University of Pennsylvania Press, 1986).
Valuable survey of Eliot's reading through 1927.

Kristian Smidt, *Poetry and Belief in the Work of T. S. Eliot* (Oslo: J. Dybwad, 1949; revised edition, London & New York: Humanities Press, 1961).
Discussion of tradition and belief in Eliot's poetry.

Grover Smith, *T. S. Eliot's Poetry and Plays: A Study in Sources and Meanings,* enlarged edition (Chicago: University of Chicago Press, 1974).
Standard discussion of allusions in Eliot's writing.

Stephen Spender, *T. S. Eliot* (New York: Viking, 1975).
Overview by younger poet befriended by Eliot.

Sheila Sullivan, ed., *Critics on T. S. Eliot* (London: Allen & Unwin, 1973).
Collection of critical essays on Eliot's work.

Allen Tate, ed., *T. S. Eliot: The Man and His Work* (New York: Delacorte, 1966; London: Chatto & Windus, 1967).
An essential collection of memoirs and impressions by Eliot's friends and admirers.

Leonard Ungar, *T. S. Eliot: Movements and Patterns* (Minneapolis: University of Minnesota Press, 1966).
Helpful discussion of theme and structure in Eliot's poetry.

Linda Wagner, ed., *T. S. Eliot: A Collection of Criticism* (New York: McGraw-Hill, 1974).
Collection of essays on Eliot's work.

Papers:
The most valuable collections of Eliot's papers are located in the Eliot Collection of Houghton Library at Harvard University; the Berg Collection of the New York Public Library; the Hayward Collection of King's College Library at Cambridge University; and the Princeton University Library. Many of these papers are restricted, and one major collection (the Emily Hale papers at Princeton) is sealed until the year 2020. Smaller collections are located in numerous universities around the world.

William Faulkner

This entry was updated by Linda Wagner-Martin (University of North Carolina, Chapel Hill) from her entry in DLB 9, American Novelists, 1910-1945.

Places	Mississippi	New Orleans	Hollywood
Influences and Relationships	James Joyce Malcolm Cowley	Sherwood Anderson	Howard Hawks
Literary Movements and Forms	Stream-of-Consciousness Narrative	Realism Southern Renaissance	Family Saga
Major Themes	Family Relationships Ambiguity of Comedy and Tragedy The Nature of Evil	The Search for Identity Incest Miscegenation	The Demands of Honor Madness
Cultural and Artistic Influences	Freudian Psychology	The Bible	
Social and Economic Influences	World War I	Racism	Civil War

See also the Faulkner entries in DLB 11, American Humorists, 1800-1950; DLB 44, American Screenwriters, Second Series; DLB: Documentary Series 2; *and* DLB Yearbook 1986.

BIRTH: New Albany, Mississippi, 25 September 1897, to Murry Cuthbert and Maud Butler Falkner.

EDUCATION: University of Mississippi, 1919-1920.

MARRIAGE: 20 June 1929 to Lida Estelle Oldham Franklin; children: Alabama, Jill.

AWARDS AND HONORS: Elected to National Institute of Arts and Letters, 1939; O. Henry Award for "Barn Burning," 1939; elected to American Academy of Arts and Letters, 1948; Nobel Prize, 1949; William Dean Howells Medal of the American Academy of Arts and Letters, 1950; National Book awards for *Collected Stories*, 1951, and *A Fable*, 1955; Pulitzer Prize for *A Fable*, 1955; Gold Medal for Fiction from the National Institute of Arts and Letters, 1962; Pulitzer Prize for *The Reivers*, 1963.

DEATH: Byhalia, Mississippi, 6 July 1962.

SELECTED BOOKS: *The Marble Faun* (Boston: Four Seas, 1924);
Soldiers' Pay (New York: Boni & Liveright, 1926; London: Chatto & Windus, 1930);
Mosquitoes (New York: Boni & Liveright, 1927; London: Chatto & Windus, 1964);
Sartoris (New York: Harcourt, Brace, 1929; London: Chatto & Windus, 1932); original uncut version *Flags in the Dust*, edited by Douglas Day (New York: Random House, 1973);
The Sound and the Fury (New York: Cape & Smith, 1929; London: Chatto & Windus, 1931);
As I Lay Dying (New York: Cape & Smith, 1930; London: Chatto & Windus, 1935);
Sanctuary (New York: Cape & Smith, 1931; London: Chatto & Windus, 1931); unrevised version, *Sanctuary: The Original Text*, edited by Noel Polk (New York: Random House, 1981);
These 13 (New York: Cape & Smith, 1931; London: Chatto & Windus, 1933);
Light in August (New York: Smith & Haas, 1932; London: Chatto & Windus, 1933);

William Faulkner (courtesy of Louis Daniel Brodsky)

A Green Bough (New York: Smith & Haas, 1933);
Pylon (New York: Smith & Haas, 1935; London: Chatto & Windus, 1935);
Absalom, Absalom! (New York: Random House, 1936; London: Chatto & Windus, 1937);
The Unvanquished (New York: Random House, 1938; London: Chatto & Windus, 1938);
The Wild Palms (New York: Random House, 1939; London: Chatto & Windus, 1939);
The Hamlet (New York: Random House, 1940; London: Chatto & Windus, 1940);
Go Down, Moses and Other Stories (New York: Random House, 1942; London: Chatto & Windus, 1942);
The Portable Faulkner, edited by Malcolm Cowley (New York: Viking, 1946);
Intruder in the Dust (New York: Random House, 1948; London: Chatto & Windus, 1949);
Knight's Gambit (New York: Random House, 1949; London: Chatto & Windus, 1951);
Collected Stories of William Faulkner (New York: Random House, 1950; London: Chatto & Windus, 1951);

Requiem for a Nun (New York: Random House, 1951; London: Chatto & Windus, 1953);

A Fable (New York: Random House, 1954; London: Chatto & Windus, 1955);

The Town (New York: Random House, 1957; London: Chatto & Windus, 1958);

New Orleans: Sketches, edited by Carvel Collins (New Brunswick: Rutgers University Press, 1958; London: Sidgwick & Jackson, 1959);

The Mansion (New York: Random House, 1959; London: Chatto & Windus, 1961);

The Reivers (New York: Random House, 1962; London: Chatto & Windus, 1962);

Early Prose and Poetry, edited by Collins (Boston: Little, Brown, 1962; London: Cape, 1963);

The Marble Faun and A Green Bough (New York: Random House, 1965);

Essays, Speeches & Public Letters, edited by James B. Meriwether (New York: Random House, 1966; London: Chatto & Windus, 1967);

The Wishing Tree (New York: Random House, 1967; London: Chatto & Windus, 1967);

A Faulkner Miscellany, edited by Meriwether (Jackson: University Press of Mississippi, 1974);

Uncollected Stories of William Faulkner, edited by Joseph Blotner (New York: Random House, 1979).

PLAY PRODUCTION: *Requiem for a Nun,* London, Royal Court Theatre, 26 November 1957; New York, John Golden Theatre, 30 January 1959.

MOTION PICTURES: *Today We Live* (M-G-M, 1933), story and dialogue;

The Road to Glory (20th Century-Fox, 1936), screenplay by Faulkner and Joel Sayre;

Slave Ship (20th Century-Fox, 1937), story and additional dialogue;

To Have and Have Not (Warner Bros., 1944), screenplay by Faulkner and Jules Furthman;

The Big Sleep (Warner Bros., 1946), screenplay by Faulkner, Furthman, and Leigh Brackett;

Land of the Pharaohs (Warners Bros., 1955), story and screenplay by Faulkner, Harry Kurnitz, and Harold Jack Bloom.

TELEVISION: *The Graduation Dress* (CBS, 1960), teleplay by Faulkner and Joan Williams.

William Faulkner is considered by many readers to have been America's greatest modern writer. His fiction satisfies the critical demands that writing be inventive and invigorating, as

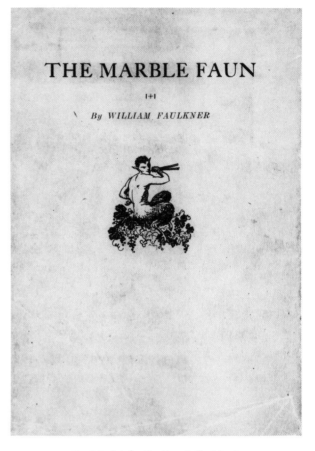

Dust jacket for Faulkner's first book

ready to release the imagination as it is to channel it. Each of Faulkner's novels is a distinct structure of language, carefully shaped to achieve its own distinct meaning. Faulkner faces the problematic existence of the modern world, and he insists that human beings can surmount those problems. As he said in his Nobel Prize address, "I believe that man will not merely endure: he will prevail. He is immortal, not because he alone among creatures has an inexhaustible voice, but because he has a soul, a spirit capable of compassion and sacrifice and endurance." Faulkner portrays in his fiction all the qualities he finds necessary for truly human and humane existence—honor, respect, love, bravery, loyalty, humor, responsibility, reverence, fear. The vividness of his characterizations places him with such writers as Shakespeare, Dostoyevski, and Dickens; his moral point of view places him with these and other less likely compatriots—Milton, for one, and perhaps Dante.

Faulkner's stable and ultimately moral perspective was less apparent early in his career because he often worked through negative characterization. Mrs. Compson of *The Sound and the Fury* (1929) illustrates the character of the ideal mother because she is not; she is brilliantly portrayed as nonmaternal. The Reverend Gail Hightower of *Light in August* (1932) is similarly warped–a nonministering minister. Because Faulkner's fiction is not obviously judgmental, readers had to learn to find patterns in his work before they could relate method to authorial perspective. Once it was understood that Faulkner was exploring a range of personalities (through a series of credible characters) in order to lead readers to an understanding of the personal dilemma ("the human heart in conflict with itself"), his work became more fully appreciated.

Because he could so vividly portray all types of characters–aggressive and passive, male and female, crippled and healthy, old and young–Faulkner successfully employed a large variety of narrative voices. Not until his later books and the arrival of the wise and loving V. K. Ratliff in *The Hamlet* (1940) was there a character who came close to representing Faulkner's point of view. Faulkner's fiction comes very near to being a pure example of the storytelling art that focuses on characters–"flesh-and-blood, living, suffering, anguishing human beings"–rather than the subjective author-as-narrator mode of other important modernists such as Ernest Hemingway.

We recognize Faulkner's art less for its geographical accuracy than for its human accuracy. That he lived and wrote in the South has relatively little to do with his technical prowess or many of his thematic concerns. Widely read, reasonably well-traveled, Faulkner lived and wrote in Mississippi because living there was relatively inexpensive, because his and his wife's families were there, and because he liked both the rural simplicity and the comparative freedom to live as he wanted. To label him a "Southern writer" with any sense of denigration or limitation is surely inaccurate. Critical opinion once took that tack, but since Malcolm Cowley edited *The Portable Faulkner* in 1946 and prefaced it with his perspicacious critical assessment, the level of published criticism has improved greatly. There now is more work published on Faulkner than on any other American author, proving that Faulkner's fiction continues to speak to contemporary readers. The present Faulkner scholar is further aided by the recent publication of many personal papers–Faulkner's letters, manuscripts, and unpublished writings–and many scholarly books such as Joseph Blotner's biographies, concordances, anno-

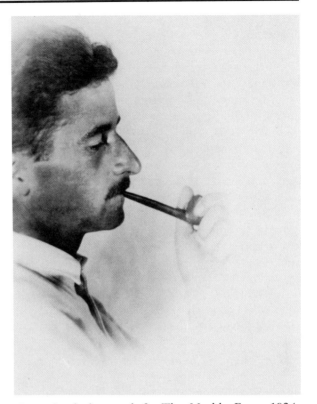

Promotional photograph for The Marble Faun, *1924 (photo by Willa Johnson; William Faulkner Collection [# 6074], Special Collections Department, Manuscripts Division, University of Virginia Library)*

tated bibliographies of existing criticism, and correlations of manuscripts.

Before the Blotner biography was published in 1974, Faulkner's enigmatic life had given rise to some erroneous directions in criticism. Because many modern writers contemporary with Faulkner were using autobiography in their fiction, readers sought correspondences between Faulkner as a person and his characters. There are few direct correlations; instead Faulkner uses his knowledge and experience as a sentient human being to give credibility to all his characters. His sense of "experience" is that of Henry James in his "The Art of Fiction" (1884): "Experience is never limited, and it is never complete; it is an immense sensibility, a kind of huge spiderweb of the finest silken threads suspended in the chamber of consciousness, and catching every airborne particle in its tissue. It is the very atmosphere of the mind; and when the mind is imaginative–much more when it happens to be that of a man of genius–it takes to itself the faintest hints of life. . . . The young lady living in a village has only to be a damsel upon whom nothing is lost to make it quite unfair . . . to declare to her that she shall have nothing to say about the military."

Faulkner's characters surely gain from the fact that he was descended from a colorful Southern family, the Falkners. (Faulkner added the *u* when he joined the Canadian RAF in 1918.) His great-grandfather, William Clark Falkner, a prominent citizen of Ripley, Mississippi, was a lawyer, a planter, a colonel in the Confederate army, a railroad builder, and a writer of poetry, novels, a play, and travel sketches. His novel *The White Rose of Memphis,* published serially in 1880 and in book form in 1881, was well received. Faulkner's grandfather, John Wesley Thompson Falkner, was a lawyer, railroad owner, and banker, who moved his family from Ripley to Oxford, Mississippi, in 1885. Both men figure in Faulkner's fiction–William C. Falkner in *The Unvanquished* and *Sartoris,* where he is the prototype for the character of Colonel John Sartoris; and John Wesley Falkner in *The Town, Sartoris,* and *The Unvanquished,* where he is the model for the Colonel's son Bayard. The death of William C. Falkner, who was killed on the street in Ripley, Mississippi, by his former business partner, is recreated several times in Faulkner's fiction. With Faulkner such recreation is never simple biographical recollection; it is rather an attempt to understand the meaning of the act within the context of Southern history.

Faulkner's own father, Murry Falkner, led a life that was less glamorous. He married Maud Butler in 1896, and they spent the early years of their marriage in New Albany and then Ripley, Mississippi, while he worked for the family railroad. After the railroad was sold in 1902, he took his family back to Oxford, where he engaged in several business ventures largely financed by his father–including a livery stable and a hardware store–before becoming secretary of the University of Mississippi in Oxford, in 1918. He later became the university's business manager.

Faulkner's childhood was filled with projects and games involving his three younger brothers (Murry, born in 1899; John, born in 1901; and Dean, born in 1907) and his cousin Sallie Murry Wilkins, who was the same age as Murry Falkner. Estelle Oldham, his wife-to-be, was another close playmate. Faulkner was a good student in his younger elementary days, but by sixth grade he was playing hooky whenever he had the opportunity. In high school, he was more interested in playing football than in studying. He liked to write

and draw, and he illustrated the stories and poems he had written. He seemed often to live in a world of imaginary characters and events, and was eager to miss social events if his parents would permit him to.

Faulkner stopped attending school midway through the eleventh and final grade at Oxford High School. He went back briefly in the fall of 1915 because he wanted to play football once again and, despite his slight stature (he was 5'5" at the time and grew only another half inch), he made the first string (for the first time), as quarterback. Leaving high school for good once the season was over, he was put to work in early 1916 as a bookkeeper in his grandfather's bank. He had no interest in the job and did little work. His real interest was in reading the avant-garde literature to which he had been introduced by Phil Stone. A native of Oxford and four years older than Faulkner, Stone had cum laude bachelor's degrees from both the University of Mississippi and Yale. Returning to Oxford in the summer of 1914 to study law at the university, he and Faulkner soon became friends, and he was to contribute much to Faulkner's literary education, commenting on Faulkner's writing and introducing him to new books. He also introduced Faulkner to another Oxford native, the writer Stark Young, who, although he had left his job at the University of Mississippi to teach literature at the University of Texas, returned to Oxford each summer. Young proved to be another of Faulkner's early mentors. In the fall of 1916, after Stone had completed his law degree at the University of Mississippi and gone to Yale to pursue a second LL.B., Faulkner began to spend more time around the university campus, forming another important friendship with a freshman named Ben Wasson, who was later to serve as his literary agent. Although he was not a student at the university, drawings by Faulkner were included in the school's yearbooks for 1916-1917 and 1917-1918.

Still discontent with his job at the bank, where he was actually spending very little time, Faulkner had further cause for unhappiness in early 1918 when Estelle Oldham announced her engagement to Cornell Franklin. She and Faulkner had planned to marry, but both sets of parents forbade their union. Faulkner had no profession; Franklin was an established lawyer. Estelle Oldham offered to elope with Faulkner, but he wanted her father's consent so she drifted into a marriage that proved to be unhappy, and Faulkner vowed to enter the military as soon as possi-

Faulkner in Paris, 1925

ble. After being turned down for aviation training in the U.S. Army Signal Corps, he went to New Haven to spend some time with Phil Stone. In July he enlisted in the Canadian division of the RAF, but World War I ended before he could complete his flight training. He remained fascinated with flying throughout his life, and he returned home from Canada wearing his RAF uniform and telling stories that suggested that he had had a glowing military career.

Back in Oxford, Faulkner began writing poetry in earnest, and at Stone's suggestion, he sent "L'Apres-Midi d'un Faune" to the *New Republic,* where it was accepted. He enrolled at the University of Mississippi as a special student for the 1919-1920 academic year. His first semester courses were French, Spanish, and English (Shakespeare). After receiving an *A* and a *B* respectively in French and Spanish, but only a *D* in his Shakespeare course, he dropped English for the second semester. Blotner suggests that Faulkner preferred the French course to Shakespeare anyway and points to Faulkner's growing interest during that period in the poetry of Paul Verlaine. During that year, thirteen of his poems and a short story ("Landing in Luck," about an aviation cadet's first solo flight) appeared in the student newspaper, the *Mississippian,* and he contributed many drawings and a sonnet, "To a Co-ed," to *Ole Miss,*

the yearbook. He also won the university's annual prize for the best poem. Although he pledged the S.A.E. fraternity, he took little part in its activities. His almost foppish dress and seemingly arrogant attitudes won for him the nickname "Count No 'Count," but Blotner suggests that Faulkner was very shy during this college experience and may have had difficulty making friends with any but the literary crowd he was most interested in. Faulkner reentered the university for the 1920-1921 academic year, but after a few weeks he stopped attending classes, and he officially withdrew on 5 November. He continued to contribute to campus publications.

While still a student, he and some friends had formed a dramatic club, and for them he produced by hand six copies of a one-act play with accompanying illustrations, *Marionettes.* He also put together a collection of his poems, *Vision in Spring,* of which he made a single copy and presented it to Estelle Franklin, who was visiting in Oxford that spring. In September 1921 Stark Young visited Oxford, after having spent a year in Italy, and suggested that Faulkner join him in New York and look for a job there. Faulkner took Young's advice, and Young introduced him to Elizabeth Prall (later Mrs. Sherwood Anderson), who gave him a job in the Fifth Avenue Doubleday Bookstore, which she managed. During the few months he was in New York, Faulkner continued to write poetry and fiction, but he was unhappy there and in late December, at Phil Stone's urging, he accepted the job of postmaster of the University of Mississippi post office. He did little work at this job and seems to have spent much of his time there reading and writing. On weekends he often went to New Orleans, where he met a number of the literati who edited the *Double Dealer.* His poem "Portrait" was published in the June 1922 issue of the *Double Dealer.* Faulkner also continued to write poetry and prose for the *Mississippian.* His reviews of contemporary writers such as Conrad Aiken, Edna St. Vincent Millay, and Eugene O'Neill show his acute interest in innovative writing. In May 1924, the Four Seas Company agreed to publish, at Phil Stone's expense, a collection of Faulkner's poems, *The Marble Faun.* The official publication date was 15 December 1924.

In October 1924, Faulkner lost his job in the post office because of undelivered mail, and he took the opportunity afforded by his new freedom to visit New Orleans to meet Sherwood Anderson, who was now married to Elizabeth Prall.

Dust jacket for Faulkner's second novel, which describes the relations among self-conscious artists in New Orleans

After a few months in Oxford writing and reading proofs for his forthcoming book, Faulkner returned to New Orleans on 4 January 1925, planning to embark from there to Europe. But, at the encouragement of Elizabeth Anderson, he stayed on, contributing essays, poems, and sketches to the *Double Dealer* and other sketches and short stories to the *New Orleans Times-Picayune* (some of these sketches and stories prefigure later short stories). He was also at work on a novel, which he called "Mayday," and he showed early portions of his work to Sherwood Anderson. Anderson was already a well-established writer. His most famous book, *Winesburg, Ohio*, had appeared in 1919, and his unconventional subject matter and treatment had been highly praised. Faulkner had been spending many hours with him, swapping stories, walking, drinking, and discussing literature. It was through the older writer's recommendation that Boni and Liveright accepted the manuscript, and it ap-

peared on 25 February 1926, after someone in the publisher's office had suggested that the title be changed to *Soldiers' Pay* and Faulkner had accepted the change. Faulkner left on his long-anticipated trip to Europe on 7 July 1925. Debarking at Genoa on 2 August, he traveled in Italy and Switzerland, before settling in Paris in mid-August. Except for brief tours through the French countryside and England, he remained in Paris until sailing for home on 8 December. During this time he was writing fiction, spending most of his time on "Elmer," a novel which he eventually decided to abandon before completion.

Soldiers' Pay is an unremarkable first novel. Caught up in the contemporary interest in World War I and its aftermath, Faulkner treated the fortunes of returning hero Donald Mahon with bitter sympathy. Wounded and terribly disfigured, Mahon has no chance of fitting into the society that would greet him with platitudes and praise. He loses his superficial fiancée, troubles his family (his father is a minister, who seems unable to understand the psychological damage his son has borne), and heads toward death with little regret. Some readers objected to Faulkner's evident pessimism and to his ironic deflation of patriotism, but many responded favorably.

The novel suffers from the unnecessary inclusion of minor characters and a sweepingly literary style, but its force remains clear even today. When the badly wounded Mahon needs assistance while returning home by train, Margaret Powers is drawn to him. Briefly married but widowed during the war, Powers is the first of Faulkner's unconventional fictional women—perceptive, loving, disdainful of restrictive traditional morality. She forms a partnership to care for Mahon with gruff but kindly veteran Joe Gilligan, Mahon's friend from the war, and together they help Mahon once he has returned home. Margaret Powers is an enigma—a woman who gives her time, and eventually her reputation, for a stranger.

The pathos of the novel is the predictability of Mahon's ending. He cannot return to normal living in any real sense. He is going blind. He is marked for death not only by his badly scarred face but by his attempts to fit back into the constraining morality of the small town. The hypocrisy of the townspeople is one of Faulkner's targets; they pretend to welcome Mahon back while they shudder at his disfigurement. After Mahon's fiancée, Cecily Saunders, breaks the engagement,

Drawing of Faulkner by Stephen Longstreet (collection of Matthew J. Bruccoli)

Margaret Powers agrees to marry the dying soldier. This second marriage for her will effectively cancel her hope of marriage in the future (a twice-widowed young woman would bear a sexual stigma). Marrying Mahon is then a sacrificial act because it allows him to die without having felt rejection. Faulkner's treatment of the townspeople, his focus on different kinds of love, and his emphasis on Donald Mahon and Margaret Powers as martyrs make *Soldiers' Pay* more than a war story.

Faulkner spent most of 1926 in New Orleans, where, having given up on "Elmer," he completed his second novel, *Mosquitoes* (1927). This novel drew on people he knew in New Orleans and Pascagoula, Mississippi, where he had visited during two summers. In September he sent the completed typescript to Boni and Liveright, where it received an enthusiastic report from a young reader named Lillian Hellman. The firm accepted the novel, and it was published on 30 April 1927. Hellman later reviewed the novel enthusiastically for the *New York Herald Tribune,* and

Conrad Aiken, whom Faulkner had long admired, wrote an encouraging review for the *New York Evening Post,* but other reviews were more critical.

Mosquitoes is a portrait of the artist becoming an artist. While Faulkner's early interest in literary and artistic characters was understandable, this book is filled with long and somewhat pretentious discussions of art and aesthetics. Some of the main characters are artists—Gordon the sculptor, Dawson the writer. More characters, however, are only hangers-on, eager to be seen with artists. A few of the characters manage to live apart from what Faulkner sees as a debilitating concern with art: Patricia Robyn is the essence of pagan youth and beauty, and her ill-fated attempt to elope leads to the book's title: when she and her lover leave the yacht and the rest of the literary party, they end up lost in a mosquito-infested swamp. While Faulkner's symbolism does not work consistently, the book suggests that no direction is as simple or as effective as it might appear. Sheer animal stamina does not succeed any better than effete cultural snobbery.

Faulkner's tendency toward overdone allusion and platitude is cut short, however, as he closes the story with a brief but serious conversation among three of the artists. Gordon has sculpted a head of Mrs. Maurier, the yachting party hostess, which catches the tragedy of her unfulfilled life. His art has clarified her character. Her friends recognize its accuracy even though that accuracy surprises them. The scene of their viewing the sculpture closes with Gordon's statement (with which Faulkner agreed) of the harmony among people—harmony based, often, on unhappiness: "Forget grief. . . . Only an idiot has no grief; only a fool would forget it. What else is there in this world sharp enough to stick to your guts?"

Faulkner's interest in grief, in the character who could survive the full range of life's often inexplicable treatment, permeates much of his fiction. Enduring becomes one criterion for nobility; it is overshadowed only by the capacity to be responsible, to care about others. In Faulkner's third novel, *Sartoris* (1929), the hero, young Bayard Sartoris, has neither of these traits. Instead, Bayard shows his grief over the death of his twin brother, John, in World War I, where they were both pilots, by living furiously, erratically, seeking release in fast cars, planes, and sexual passion.

Faulkner working in the library at Rowan Oak (courtesy of Jill Faulkner Summers)

After completing *Mosquitoes,* Faulkner had begun two novels, "Father Abraham," in which Flem Snopes appeared for the first time and which he soon abandoned, and *Flags in the Dust* (published in its entirety in 1973). Faulkner completed this novel in October 1927 and sent it to Horace Liveright, who had published his first two books, but on 30 November Liveright rejected the book, saying, "The story really doesn't get anywhere and has a thousand loose ends." Ben Wasson, newly hired as Faulkner's agent, placed the novel with Harcourt, Brace after agreeing to Alfred Harcourt's request that he cut the manuscript for Faulkner. This cut version was published as *Sartoris* on 31 January 1929 to mixed reviews.

Faulkner was to say later that while writing *Flags in the Dust,* "I realised that to make it truly evocative it must be personal, in order not only to preserve my own interest in writing, but to preserve my belief in the savor of bread-and-salt. . . . So I got some people, some I invented, others I created out of tales I learned of nigger cooks and stable boys of all ages. . . . Created, I say, because they are composed partly from what they were in actual life and partly from what they should have been and were not: thus I improved on God who, dramatic though He be, has no sense, no feel-

ing for, theatre." *Sartoris* is usually called the first typical Faulkner novel, not only because it is set in his part of the South, in what he later called "that little postage stamp of native soil" that Sherwood Anderson had advised him to write about, but also because it is a story-telling novel. Many legends, tall tales, and Mississippi gossip are either recounted or referred to; the reader is included in everything the narrator knows. After finishing *Sartoris,* the reader feels that he knows Yoknapatawpha County as though this fictional place were real. Most of Faulkner's subsequent books tell and retell the stories touched on peripherally in *Sartoris.*

The primary narrative line is the story of the Sartoris family. The Sartoris men are improvident, foolhardy, daring: Faulkner admires their defiance of convention, their rebellion, even while he sorrows over it. Jenny Du Pre, their venerable yet feisty old aunt, whose "indomitable spirit" gives her the force to cope with the Sartoris men in her care, loves them genuinely, for their wildness, their stubbornness, their dreams. And the tragedy of the young Sartoris men, the twins Bayard and John, is that so much has already been achieved, and so little is left to dream.

Once back from World War I, Bayard spends the rest of his short life in the search for something he can accomplish, but all he finds for himself, and creates for others, is waste and heartbreak. He hurts his wife, Narcissa Benbow, as well as his family; and he dies before their child is born. Bayard's life illustrates Aunt Jenny's pronouncement to Narcissa: she claims of women that "we can stand anything" and says of men, "Men can't stand anything. . . . Can't even stand helling around with no worry and no responsibility and no limit to all the meanness they can think about wanting to do." In contrast to the life of the naive young lawyer, Narcissa's brother Horace Benbow, Bayard's life seems preferable, Bayard meets fate head on, and if his death comes to illustrate the "blind tragedy of human events" set against the human will, it at least illustrates something. Benbow dwindles on into circumstances he has never chosen. He is always a victim.

In *Flags in the Dust*, the uncut version of *Sartoris*, more emphasis is given to Narcissa and Horace Benbow, foreshadowing Faulkner's later fascination with the brother-sister relationships which dominate such novels as *The Sound and the Fury, As I Lay Dying*, and *Absalom, Absalom!* Faulkner's fiction seldom conveys a single theme: his writing is a mirror that catches life's drama and humor in angles both direct and oblique.

After completing *Flags in the Dust*, Faulkner worked on several short stories; from one of these stories, "Twilight," grew his next novel, *The Sound and the Fury*, which he completed in October 1928. He was to remember later being moved by an image he had created in the story: "Caddy climbing the pear tree to look in the window at her grandmother's funeral while Quentin and Jason and Benjy and the negroes looked up at the muddy seat of her drawers," and he concluded, "I loved her so much I couldn't decide to give her life just for the duration of a short story. She deserved more than that. So my novel was created, almost in spite of myself."

Reacting to Liveright's rejection of *Flags in the Dust*, he became concerned with writing only to please himself. Five years later he said, "I wasn't even writing a book. I was thinking of books, publication, only in the reverse, in saying to myself, I won't have to worry about publishers liking or not liking this at all." Then, he remembered, "One day I seemed to shut a door between me and all publishers' address and book lists. I said to myself, Now I can write. Now I can

Faulkner receiving the Nobel Prize, 10 December 1950

make myself a vase like that which the old Roman kept at his bedside and wore the rim slowly away with kissing it."

The Sound and the Fury stands as a monument to the power of the written word. Albert J. Guerard says in *The Triumph of the Novel*, that with this novel, and with *As I Lay Dying*, Faulkner now seemed "to write only for himself and a happy few," as he experimented "in structure and in post-Joycean renderings of consciousness and of less-than-conscious mental life." Through this experimentation, says Guerard, Faulkner tried to present "the essence and *quidditas* of a character: his deepest drives and unrecognized anxieties." Quentin Compson, sensitive yet timorous; Jason, unscrupulous yet competitive, concerned only with business; and Benjy, retarded yet prescient, illustrate those deep drives and unrecognized anxieties Guerard mentions. Faulkner's accomplishment in *The Sound and the Fury* was to make understandable–even sympathetic–characters who fit no moral law accepted by readers. The oldest brother, Quentin, dreams of incest with his sister, Caddy; Jason dreams of punishing the niece he has consistently robbed of the money her mother sends for her; Benjy, castrated after showing signs of sexuality, dreams without benefit of vocabulary, of warm shapes and comfort. Human angst is the subject of Faulkner's novel, and yet touches of humor and joy make his account bearable.

Although none of the novel's four parts presents her point of view, the book centers on the only sister, Caddy. It is Caddy's journey through life–her discovery of sexuality, her pregnancy, her wedding, her eviction from her husband's home, the birth of her child, her visits back to the Compson home–that the novel documents. The brothers react to her, as she is the initiator, the actor, the strong character. Yet Caddy is never presented as fully as the brothers; her story is told only through the unreliable narration of her brothers, whom Faulkner makes appear to be the center of the book. Critics have often misunderstood this structural technique; because Benjy has one quarter of the novel given to him, to his point of view, he must be a major character. He is, of course, but rather than being a major *character* in a complete sense of the word, he is a major *observer,* a part of the story-telling process. Benjy is acted upon–his name is changed, he is castrated, punished, and secluded–rather than being permitted to act.

Much the same kind of narrative strategy pervades the other brothers' sections, although Quentin and Jason may seem to be somewhat more in control of their lives than is Benjy. Moved by events that they have not set in action, Quentin and Jason illustrate patterns of response recognizable in modern psychology: Quentin–denial, self-doubt, suicide; Jason–anger, vindication, revenge.

At the root of the Compson disaster–because the family unit finally disintegrates, becomes bereft of either position or sanity–is the loveless atmosphere in the original family group. The mother who is far from being maternal; the father who fears all action and, instead of motivation, gives his children a full dose of cynicism; the uncle who represents self-interest to the exclusion of all else–the all-important adults in the Compson family are poor examples to the developing children who look to them for role models. "Lost somewhere below even them without even a ray of light," in Quentin's words, are the children Caddy, Quentin, Jason, and Benjy. The only responsive adult in their lives is Dilsey, who endures and has done the best she can in loving them but cannot replace their natural parents. The Compson family tragedy is that of a self-centered family. More than a picture of the decline of traditional civilization and the rise of commercialism in the new South, *The Sound and the Fury* carries a timeless message–that people, especially families, must care for each other; that

only love keeps life bearable; and that without it, people choose ways to escape their human responsibilities.

The editor who had recommended *Flags in the Dust* to Alfred Harcourt was Harrison Smith. In late 1928 Smith left Harcourt, Brace to form a new firm with the British publisher Jonathan Cape. *The Sound and the Fury* was published by Cape and Smith on 7 October 1929. In Smith, Faulkner felt that he had a publisher who had confidence in his work. The reviews for *The Sound and the Fury* were generally enthusiastic, but in the unstable economic climate that surrounded the 29 October 1929 stock-market crash, these reviews did not lead to good sales. Faulkner's work was beginning to be widely noticed, but he was not faring well financially.

In January or February 1929, around the time Harrison Smith agreed to publish *The Sound and the Fury*, Faulkner set out to "invent the most horrific tale I could imagine" with the conscious intention of making money. The tale was *Sanctuary,* the most violent and sensational of Faulkner's novels. One of the reasons for Faulkner's increased concern about money was that he was about to marry a divorced woman with two children. Estelle Oldham Franklin had separated from Cornell Franklin in 1927, and in April 1929 her divorce became final. The immediate prospects for Faulkner's money-making project were not good, however. The consensus about the manuscript at the offices of Cape and Smith, where Faulkner had sent it in the late spring of 1929, was that it was too shocking, unpublishable. In the introduction for the 1932 Modern Library edition of *Sanctuary,* Faulkner remembered Smith's writing, "Good God, I can't publish this. We'd both be in jail." Despite this setback Faulkner and Estelle Franklin were married on 20 June 1929. After spending the summer in Pascagoula, Mississippi, they returned to Oxford, where Faulkner took a job working nights at the university power plant. To the hum of the dynamo at the power plant, he wrote *As I Lay Dying* (1930), which would prove to be his next published novel.

Faulkner later said of the composition of this novel, "I set out deliberately to write a tour-de-force. Before I ever put pen to paper and set down the first word I knew what the last word would be and almost where the last period would fall. . . . That other quality which *The Sound and the Fury* had given me was absent: that emotion definite and physical and yet nebulous to describe: that ecstasy, that eager and joyous faith

The Faulkners at Rowan Oak, May 1955 (courtesy of the William Faulkner Collection, University of Virginia Library, and U.P.I.)

and anticipation of surprise which the yet unmarred sheet beneath my hand held inviolate and unfailing, waiting for release.... I said, More than likely I shall never again have to know this much about a book before I begin to write it...." Despite the difference in the methods of composition, *The Sound and the Fury* and *As I Lay Dying* have often been paired by critics who point to them as Faulkner's most brilliant stylistic experiments. The sheer audacity of Faulkner's employing structures and narrative methods that conflicted with all the conventions of fiction has to be considered; yet if these novels did not deal with themes that speak to every reader, few people would have bothered to learn to appreciate the craft. For readers in the late 1920s, accustomed to the accumulation of details and straightforward plots of a realistic writer such as Theodore Dreiser, Faulkner's stylistic innovations posed many problems. That Faulkner's experimentation was accepted by a contemporary audience is a tribute to the centrality of his theme: the need for balance between the demands of

self and responsibility to one's society.

As I Lay Dying presents this responsibility as the family's obligation to fulfill their promise to Addie Bundren, their dying mother, who has asked to be buried with her kin. Although she is central to the novel, she speaks only one of the fifty-nine interior monologues into which the novel is divided. Mistrustful of language, of rhetoric, Addie has lived, and dies, through action. That she has Faulkner's sympathy is clear from the opposition he creates for her in her husband, Anse. One of the laziest characters in American fiction, Anse has a kind of bewildering charm (he believes that he will die if he even sweats, a wonderful ruse for one who lives in Mississippi before the days of air conditioning); he believes that his children and friends are put on earth purposely to care for him (and he is ever a God-fearing man); but the real evil in his character becomes clear as the novel progresses, and we see what living with such a man—emotionally dead from the beginning—has done to Addie. As Dr. Peabody and the neighbors Tull and Samson give reliable perspectives, it soon becomes poignantly clear how little Addie has had in her life.

Another family novel, the book's principal characters are the parents and the five children. Again one sister (Dewey Dell, pregnant with an illegitimate child) is set against her brothers. This time there are four: Cash, the builder who sacrifices self for his family; Darl, the clairvoyant and eventually insane child who wants his mother's love desperately; Jewel, the illegitimate son of the minister and his mother's favorite; and Vardaman, the youngest and the one most affected by his mother's death. Yet, unlike Caddy, Dewey Dell is not at the center of her brothers' existence; the novel's focus is more often on the mother's relationship with the children and on the brothers' interaction with each other. A range of emotion colors the chronological presentation of Addie's death, funeral, and what should have been a simple journey to Jefferson (some forty miles away). Anger, hatred, jealousy, loyalty, reverence, fear–Faulkner creates the panorama as he presents the characters dramatically. In *As I Lay Dying* he took his structure from the play script; the name of the speaker appears above each segment of the story. In the interweaving of parts lies the fantastic artistry of the novel, not only accomplishing the narrative proper but also creating a subtle blend of tone so that *As I Lay Dying* has been called comic as often as it has been called tragic. That it is both, and that part of its impact comes from the shifting points of view of fifteen different speakers that blend, contrast, and finally illuminate, is to Faulkner's highest credit.

Faulkner sets up polarities between male and female as often as he does between the cultured and the peasant (*As I Lay Dying* is usually considered different from *The Sound and the Fury* because its characters are common folk, a distinction that seems to have existed in critics' minds more regularly than in Faulkner's), between the old South and the new, and between the urban and the rural. Here, and in other Faulkner novels as well, the female is an active force–passionate, protective, and strong–as when Addie says with a deep irony, "I would be I; I would let him be the shape and echo of his word." For Anse and the Reverend Whitfield, rhetoric might suffice; for Addie, "words are no good.... I knew that motherhood was invented by someone who had to have a word for it because the ones that had the children didn't care whether there was a word for it or not. I knew that fear was in-

vented by someone that had never had the fear; pride, who never had the pride.... I would think how words go straight up in a thin line quick and harmless, and how terribly doing goes along the earth, clinging to it, so that after a while the two lines are too far apart for the same person to straddle from one to the other...." In his later fiction, Faulkner created male characters who are also chary of language and mistrustful of people (such as Gavin Stevens) who dissipate their feeling into fluency. In his early and middle fiction, these strong, silent characters were usually women.

As I Lay Dying was published on 6 October 1930. Most of the reviews expressed qualified praise, but again, while they added to Faulkner's stature as a novelist, their praise was not translated into good sales. As soon as he had sent off *As I Lay Dying,* Faulkner had turned, as he would often during the 1930s, to writing short fiction that he hoped would interest the editors of popular magazines. As the 1930s wore on, he became increasingly successful at placing short fiction in such high-paying magazines as the *Saturday Evening Post.* During that same time Faulkner's financial obligations increased as well. In April 1930 the Faulkners bought the old Shegog place, one of the oldest houses in the county, and renamed it Rowan Oak. It was a fine old house, but it was in total disrepair and lacked both electricity and plumbing. The cost of restoring and refurbishing the house was a considerable drain on Faulkner's income, as were the medical bills associated with the premature birth, on 11 January 1931, of Alabama Faulkner, who died several days later. With the birth of Jill Faulkner on 24 June 1933, the Faulkner household now included three children. In addition, after the death of his father in August 1932 and the death of his youngest brother, Dean, in November 1935, Faulkner contributed to the support of his mother and his brother's wife and child.

Around mid November 1930 Faulkner unexpectedly received galley proofs for *Sanctuary.* Harrison Smith, who, despite his qualms about the novel, continued to appreciate Faulkner's talent, had decided to take a chance on the book. When Faulkner read the galleys, however, he asked Smith not to publish the book, and after Smith told him that he had invested too much to abandon it, Faulkner made extensive revisions on the galleys, nearly rewriting the book. In his rewriting, he focused the novel on Temple Drake.

Temple Drake, a well-born Southern coed, is raped by the gangster Popeye and is so damaged by the experience that she lies to save his life. One conflict in the novel is between Popeye and Horace Benbow. Popeye has coldly murdered a man to gain access to Temple, whom he rapes with a corncob because he is impotent. He then sets her up in a brothel and becomes her procurer and a voyeur; his fascination with sex makes him in some ways much like Benbow in his relationship with his stepdaughter. Benbow, the naive, ineffectual lawyer, defends the man who has been implicated in the murder, but he fails to win his case because he understands so little about the extent of Temple's rape trauma. Temple, who has earlier agreed to testify for the defense, testifies instead (through what she does not say) for the prosecution; and fearfully seeks protection in the male family figures of the patriarchy–her father and brothers. Just as Faulkner understands Temple's psychology, so he also clarifies the enigma of the emotionally stunted Popeye. Even when Popeye awaits execution for another murder, one he did not commit, he remains inhuman and mechanistic–evil depersonalized. Influenced by Henry Bergson's theory of comedy–that mechanization is a way to create comic character–Faulkner added the deep irony that Popeye was a caricature in what should have been the most human of life's acts. Readers in the 1930s tried to avoid recognizing the horror of Popeye's inhumanity and the victimization of Temple by reading the ironically titled *Sanctuary* as an allegory of the post-Civil War South. More recent readers have come to appreciate Faulkner's skill at representing aberrant psychological states.

What this novel did for Faulkner's career is disproportionate to its merits as fiction. Published on 9 February 1931, it attracted international notice, largely because of its sensational plot, and by early April more than 7,000 copies had been sold. (The first printing of *The Sound and the Fury* was 1,789 copies, and there was no need for a second printing until almost a year and a half later.) Southern reviewers had been slightly more sympathetic than northern reviewers to the subject matter of *As I Lay Dying,* but with *Sanctuary* the tables were reversed. Reviewers throughout the South were outraged, and in Oxford, Blotner reports, the book "had become a scandal. Mac Reed loyally stocked copies, but a buyer usually wanted it wrapped in brown paper before he took it out of the drugstore. Professor

Faulkner at the University of Virginia, 1960 (photo by Ralph Thompson; William Faulkner Collection [# 6074], Special Collections Department, Manuscripts Division, University of Virginia Library)

Calvin Brown, bestower of Billy Faulkner's first literary prize, asked in shock, 'Now, why would *anybody* write a book like *that?*' " Faulkner's father saw a girl carrying a copy on campus and told her, "It isn't fit for a nice girl to read." Faulkner was somewhat taken aback by the reaction and later tended to disparage the novel, but on the grounds of its faulty technique rather than its sensationalism. Scholars have since suggested that Faulkner undervalued his artistry in this novel. In a July 1931 interview Faulkner called *As I Lay Dying* his best novel, but said, "I haven't written a real novel yet," adding, "I'm too young in experience. It hasn't crystallized enough for me to build a book upon one of the few fundamental truths which mankind has learned."

He was learning from his earlier writing, however. In *Light in August,* begun in August 1931, he drew from Addie Bundren of *As I Lay Dying* for Lena Grove's realistic assessment of her life, which contrasts sharply to the tortured questioning of both Gail Hightower, a former minister, and Joe Christmas, an orphaned outsider. Faulkner took from *Sanctuary* the delayed flashback technique, in which he had finally told his readers why Popeye was such a misfit, and applied the method to a comprehensive treatment of Joe Christmas's early history, depicting the reasons for Joe's alienation. Faulkner's recreation of the orphan's childhood became the heart of his 1932 study in community.

Joe Christmas is not unlike other displaced Faulkner characters–Bayard Sartoris, Donald Mahon, Quentin Compson–but in this instance, Joe's lack of surety about his identity is complicated because he may have black blood. The pretentious Rev. Gail Hightower has fallen away from his calling because he is self-interested, caught in a romance of ancestry, unable to love. Hidden from the very society he has been trained to help, Hightower lives an iconoclastic life–satisfied with what he pretends is his martyrdom–only to be brought back into full involvement with others through his part in the Joe Christmas story. Hightower's one connection with other human beings is Byron Bunch, a modest laborer who comes to act much as V. K. Ratliff does in Faulkner's later fiction, as the person who fuses story lines and, more important, characters. That he finally is paired with Lena Grove, an embodiment of the female principle, is proof of his real identity, and his as yet unproved virility.

Cleanth Brooks has called *Light in August* Faulkner's novel of humanity: people are called into relationships out of need rather than philosophy. Joanna Burden's fate is to be limited to seeing people as representatives of groups–she sees Joe Christmas as a nigger, only–and others in the community are similarly narrow. The process of Joanna Burden's death and Joe Christmas's execution at the hands of Percy Grimm is to bring to the community a recognition of its errors, in one sense to redeem all its citizens: "upon that black blast the man seemed to rise soaring into their memories forever and ever. They are not to lose it, in whatever peaceful valleys, beside whatever placid and reassuring streams of old age, in the mirroring faces of whatever children they will contemplate old disasters and newer hopes. . . ." The novel also deals with family, but here *family* becomes defined in a larger sense than in *The Sound and the Fury* and *As I Lay Dying*. Joe's treatment at the hands of his grandfather is unpardonable; so too is the behavior of his foster father, of Lena's family, and of other families. The obvious Christian symbols and images that punctuate Faulkner's fiction become especially meaningful here when all the biblical teachings about the role of family are considered.

The novel was published on 6 October 1932 by Harrison Smith and his new partner, Robert Haas. The reviews were laudatory, but, although Faulkner's genius was beginning to be widely recognized, his financial difficulties were not over. While in New York in late 1931 he had been approached about writing screenplays in Hollywood, and he spent much of 1932 there on contract with M-G-M. His first success with screen writing was his work on *Today We Live* (1933), for director Howard Hawks. In the course of their work together, Hawks discovered Faulkner's talent as "script doctor" and often used him to revise scenes in screenplays by other writers. Faulkner spent a few weeks doing script writing on location in New Orleans in April 1933, and in 1935 he went back to Hollywood where he spent five weeks working for 20th Century-Fox. The product of this visit was *The Road to Glory* (1936), for which he wrote the screenplay with Joel Sayre. Faulkner was in Hollywood for much of 1942-1945 and wrote the screenplay with Jules Furthman for the 1944 film version of Ernest Hemingway's *To Have and Have Not* and, with Furthman and Leigh Brackett, the screenplay for the 1946 production of Raymond Chandler's *The Big Sleep*. In 1953 and 1954 he worked on *Land of the Pharaohs* (1955) with Harry Kurnitz and Harold Jack Bloom, joining director Howard Hawks on location in Egypt in February 1954. The income from screen writing was welcome, but Faulkner disliked Hollywood.

By the time he wrote *Light in August*, Faulkner was already well into creating his Yoknapatawpha County. Locations were interrelated and specified in his mind, as were characters. Not that a character from one novel would duplicate exactly the character of the same name in another book, but Faulkner tended to keep the same sense of person connected with the name. With *Absalom, Absalom!* he began the practice of providing such aids to the reader as maps and chronologies. But during the mid 1930s Faulkner was not limited to working with only this Southern rural locale. *Pylon* (1935) is a good illustration of Faulkner's ability to move outside his mythical county and still create dynamic and moving fiction. Faulkner had always been fascinated with flying, and in February 1933 he had begun taking flying lessons. In February 1934 he attended the dedication of Shushan Airport in New Orleans and witnessed part of the festivities. The meet was plagued by bad weather, and there were several fatal and near-fatal accidents. Faulkner carried away with him an image of those pilots: "there was really no place for them in the culture, in the economy, yet they were there, at that time, and everyone knew they wouldn't last very long, which they didn't. . . . Something frenetic and almost immoral about it. That they were outside the range of God, not only of respectability, of love, but of God too. That they had escaped the compulsion of accepting a past and a future, that they were–they had no past. That they were as ephemeral as the butterfly that's born this morning with no stomach and will be gone tomorrow." From this experience and his own experiments with stunt flying, grew *Pylon,* which he began in late October of 1934 and completed by the end of November.

Joseph McElrath calls *Pylon* Faulkner's "Portrait of a Lady." It is that, centering on the character of Laverne Shumann, one of the toughest heroines in American fiction. As he did in *As I Lay Dying,* Faulkner echoed Hawthorne's *The Scarlet Letter.* He also borrowed from T. S. Eliot's *The Waste Land* and *The Love Song of J. Alfred Prufrock,* especially for the character of the unnamed and seemingly reliable narrator, the newspaper reporter. Set in a city like New Orleans, *Pylon* tells the story of three fliers, two men and the woman they share. Silhouetted against the common conventions of society, these three characters live defiant lives. They know the rules, but they are forced through economic need and some rare spirit of daring to defy them. The process of the novel undermines the conventional perspective, represented by the reporter. By the end of the book, he is seen as the most pathetic of all the characters. While Laverne Shumann may be desperate for love and a sense of belonging, she at least recognizes her need; the reporter only disguises it.

After Roger Shumann is killed flying, his suicide motivated by the need to provide money for Laverne, who is pregnant with a second child, she takes his son to Roger's father. She will have the second child and make a life with the other pilot, who has been her lover. Dr. Shumann warns her that if she leaves the child, she cannot reclaim him: "We are old; you cannot understand that, that you will or can ever reach a time when you can bear so much and no more; that nothing else is worth the bearing; that you not only cannot, you will not; that nothing is worth anything but peace, peace, peace, even with bereavement and grief–nothing! nothing!" Reminiscent of Joe Christmas's plea for peace, this answer confirms

the reader's perception that despite her abandonment of her child, Laverne is to be viewed sympathetically. Faulkner's characters are seldom faced with clearly marked choices, and his strategy of rarely making clear judgments about characters tends to increase the realism of their choices. Faulkner's interest in his characters was impartial: "The first thing that a writer has is compassion for all his characters. . . . He himself does not feel that he has the power to judge."

Published by Smith and Haas on 25 March 1935, *Pylon* was a shocking book and reviewers responded accordingly. Many, including Malcolm Cowley, praised Faulkner's artistry but criticized what Cowley called the novel's "lack of proportion between stimulus and response" and its "air of unnecessary horror and violence." Other reviews were more negative. John Crowe Ransom said, "William Faulkner is spent."

Faulkner was to say later that by the time the reviews of *Pylon* appeared, he was too busy working on his next novel to pay much attention to them. In *Absalom, Absalom!* (1936), as in his other novels of the late 1930s, *The Unvanquished* and *The Wild Palms,* he would again refuse to make overt authorial judgments. Going beyond his earlier theories of fictional technique and again employing socially unacceptable themes, Faulkner wrote about the demands of honor in widely different novels. Their characters are people who have known defeat yet continue their struggles. Society is inimical to their dreams or purposes, but the resolutions of these novels suggest that they have gained a wider kind of knowledge in the process. All these novels deal with intimacy between men and women, sometimes sexual, sometimes political. All deal with sexual situations that are at the least inappropriate; all are passionate novels.

Absalom, Absalom! has been called Faulkner's greatest novel. The novel's incest theme guaranteed that public response would be explosive, but a more important subject is Thomas Sutpen's dream of creating his own world, a territory with himself as proprietor. Great personal dedication and amazing energy go into the conquest; if his relations with other human beings are inhuman, his absorption in his mission is frighteningly magnificent. Sutpen's Hundred, the bizarre plantation he creates through the exploitation of a group of wild Negroes and an architect he has taken captive, affronts his southern neighbors; his life-style is offensive; rumors about him spread rapidly. What Faulkner created, finally, is the text–four of the texts–of this rumor mill. The fabrication of the Sutpen story folds back upon itself as Faulkner shows us the real characters of the four unreliable narrators: the venerable cynic, Mr. Compson; and his son Quentin, the romantic young Southerner (both from *The Sound and the Fury*); the jilted and wronged spinster Rosa Coldfield; and the ultrarational Canadian Shreve McCannon, Quentin's Harvard roommate.

Absalom, Absalom!, as its title suggests, is in part a lament for the relations of father and son. Thomas Sutpen has abandoned his first wife and son, Charles Bon, after he discovered that his wife has black blood. That Charles falls in love with his half sister, Judith Sutpen, without her knowing his relationship to her, and is killed by his half brother to prevent their incestuous union is the great irony of the novel, intensified because none of the novel's narrators knows if Charles was aware of his relationship to the others.

Faulkner's earlier experiments with style seem almost mechanical compared to the structural and tonal variety of *Absalom, Absalom!* More important, it is not experimentation for its own sake, but rather an attempt to call into question the human ability to know. If a person cannot recount "facts" so that listeners understand; if letters cannot really provide the information needed; if even the bravest imagination cannot reconsider situations and come to accurate suppositions–what is the basis, then, for human knowledge? What is the difference between history and fiction, fact and imagination?

Part way through the writing of the novel Faulkner was deeply bereaved by the death of his brother Dean in a flying accident, and Faulkner's sorrow is echoed in the tone of *Absalom, Absalom!* The novel was published on 26 October 1936 by Random House, which Smith and Haas had recently joined as partners. Reviewers recognized the power of the novel's tragic tone, while at the same time they were confused by the novel's technique. The anonymous reviewer for *Time* called it "the strangest, least readable, most infuriating and yet in some respects the most impressive novel that William Faulkner has written."

Despite the fairly disappointing sales of *Absalom, Absalom!*, Bennett Cerf of Random House was eager to add another Faulkner title to his firm's list, and in the early summer of 1937, Faulkner began shaping a group of his short stories into a novel. *The Unvanquished* (published on 15 February 1938) is written in the straightforward, unexperimental style that Faulkner had adopted for his stories for popular magazines, and it met with far more approval from the reviewers.

In *The Unvanquished* characters again face ridiculous odds. "How can you fight in the mountains, Father?," asks Bayard Sartoris, only to receive the most Faulknerian of answers, "You can't. You just have to." In this novel Faulkner allows a character to find the lost father. Here the Sartoris family reappears, and young Bayard learns full measure from his enduring and caring father. But once again the simple solutions shift and change before our eyes. Once a boy finds answers from his father, circumstances change and life demands new answers: Bayard Sartoris is the "unvanquished" of the title because he goes past his father in learning. He relinquishes the right to avenge his father's death with another killing and so rises past his culture's accepted standards of human behavior. Bayard has learned from Drusilla Hawk's vengeance and from Rosa Millard, too, and in her story Faulkner finds both humor and pathos.

The Unvanquished is the first of what might be called Faulkner's "blend tales," novels which are comprised at least partly from chapters published earlier as stories; and close study of the changes Faulkner made between stories and chapters in longer fiction will show that his intention and purpose changed with the move into longer form. The title of this novel appeared first on a short story which recounts the mule-trading exploits of Rosa Millard. Yet once into the novel Faulkner shifted the action so that the title refers only to Bayard: Rosa is, in fact, killed because of an error in judgment, and the novel is shaped to stress Bayard's initiation into the adult world. Rosa is finally no better tutor than the other adults, and Bayard leaves his family behind in his own quest for experience.

The Wild Palms, which Faulkner began writing in November 1937, might appear to be a blend tale too, because in it Faulkner counterpoints two stories, one of Charlotte Rittenmeyer and Harry Wilbourne's romance, the other of the tall convict's rescuing a pregnant damsel in distress during a raging flood. The stories have in fact been separated and published separately, but Faulkner intended them to appear in the arrangement he gave them. Faulkner later said that as he reached the end of the first section, "I realized suddenly that something was missing, it needed emphasis, something to lift it like counterpoint in music. So I wrote on the 'Old Man' story until 'The Wild Palms' story rose back to pitch. Then I stopped the 'Old Man' story at . . . its first section and took up 'The Wild Palms' again until it began to sag. Then I raised it to a pitch again with another section of its antithesis. . . ."

The relation between the two stories is mythic rather than thematic, with each male character being forced into a relationship with a woman who is both lover and destroyer. In "The Wild Palms" Wilbourne leaves medical school to run away with Charlotte, trying to find the idyllic love she imagines. During the course of the affair, Wilbourne becomes more of a romantic than she; his decisions lead them into progressively less stable situations. After Charlotte becomes pregnant, he bungles the abortion she has demanded, and the complications from that illegal operation lead to her death. She dies—withdrawn, angered at what she feels has been betrayal, but loyal to his right to freedom—having made her husband promise not to prosecute Wilbourne. When Charlotte's husband offers Wilbourne cyanide rather than life imprisonment, he refuses, having learned through Charlotte's dream of great passion, *"between grief and nothing I will take grief."*

Wilbourne spends the rest of his life in prison, hanging onto the memories for which he had traded his medical career and his future. Faulkner clearly sympathizes with his dilemma but uses "Old Man" to point to the comic elements inherent in Wilbourne's romanticism. The tall convict had committed his initial robbery so that he could buy gifts for a girl, who married another after he was sent to prison. On a work gang during the flood he is assigned to rescue a pregnant woman from a tree. After he saves her, the boat takes its own course, and the convict and the rescued lady find themselves stranded on an island and do not return to civilization for seven weeks. During this time the lady gives birth to a son, and in a series of amusing if horrific situations the convict heroically protects them and gets them back home. When the convict has ten years for attempted escape added to his sentence—an ironic reward for his superhuman recovery of both woman and boat—he accepts further punishment gladly; he so fears women that he sees prison as a sanctuary. The two men who end up in the same prison are ironic opposites. The doctor has botched Charlotte's abortion using dirty surgical instruments. The convict has successfully delivered a baby by using a tin-can lid to cut the

umbilical cord. The romantic has been unable to act heroically for his lady; the man who fears women has.

Published on 19 January 1939, *The Wild Palms* received reviews that were generally complimentary, but not enthusiastic. *Time* found the novel's publication significant enough to put Faulkner's picture on the cover, but some reviewers, including Malcolm Cowley, disliked the counterpointing of the two stories. When Cowley compiled *The Portable Faulkner* he included "Old Man" by itself. Despite such criticism of its structure *The Wild Palms* sold well, topping the sales records for *Sanctuary*, but Faulkner's money worries were not over.

Faulkner's fiction of the late 1930s may reflect some of the conflicts he was experiencing in his marriage. In addition to his continuing financial responsibilities, he had found his marriage less satisfying than either he or Estelle Faulkner had expected. At times both Faulkner and his wife drank heavily and argued violently. Living in Hollywood in 1932, Faulkner had become involved with a script girl, Meta Doherty. (David Minter suggests that this affair is reflected in *The Wild Palms*.) Faulkner considered divorce, but he was afraid that he would be kept from further contact with his daughter, Jill. Faulkner's preoccupation with the quest for honor in his fiction during these years may well mirror his own search for the honorable choices in his personal life.

A change in tone is apparent in Faulkner's next project. In December 1938 he mapped out a trilogy of novels, which would be published as *The Hamlet* (1940), *The Town* (1957), and *The Mansion* (1959). Although the second and third volumes were published long after the first, the basic concept of all three was formed in 1938, and they are all dedicated to the same person, Phil Stone, who, Faulkner says in the dedication to *The Town*, "did half the laughing for thirty years." Faulkner often saw comedy in tragedy, and the reverse; comedy often makes events bearable even to the most sensitive human spirits. In the trilogy most of the comedy is located in various members of the Snopes tribe, yet in an October 1938 interview, Faulkner describes the family as creeping over the town of Jefferson, Mississippi, like "mold over cheese," destroying all that is traditional and beautiful. The master stroke of Faulkner's trilogy is that Flem, the most successful of the tribe, is finally vanquished by another Snopes.

The three books of the trilogy have two primary strengths: a wide canvas for characters to populate, as the action moves from the tiny hamlet of Frenchman's Bend to Jefferson and finally to Flem's elegant Jefferson mansion. Faulkner brings many characters into play—hill people, villagers, the more sophisticated town dwellers, and V. K. Ratliff, the sewing-machine agent. Faulkner employs a variable point of view which gives the Snopes stories a more intellectual meaning: all action is reported by one of three characters, Ratliff; Chick Mallison, the young boy learning from his elders; and Gavin Stevens, an educated lawyer who is often wrong about his observations. Both Ratliff and Mallison are reliable narrators, even though they may not seem to be.

Flem Snopes's single-minded mission is to acquire property. His rise begins in *The Hamlet* when he marries Eula Varner, pregnant by Hoake McCarron, who has run off to avoid marrying her. Her father, concerned for the family name, convinces Flem to marry Eula in exchange for the Old Frenchman place. The impotent Flem is ironically mated with Eula, a woman so closely linked with the natural world that she is described in mythic terms as a goddess of nature and sexuality. One of her suitors has predicted such a marriage for her: "He could almost see the husband which she would someday have. He would be a dwarf, a gnome without glands or desire, who would be no more a physical factor in her life than the owner's name on the fly-leaf of a book. There it was again, out of the books again, . . . the crippled Vulcan to that Venus, who would not possess her but merely own her by the single strength which power gave, the dead power of money, wealth, gewgaws, baubles, as he might own, not a picture, statue: a field, say. He saw it: the fine land rich and fecund and foul and eternal and impervious to him who claimed title to it, oblivious, drawing to itself tenfold the quality of living seed its owner's whole life could have secreted and compounded, producing a thousandfold the harvest he could ever hope to gather and save."

In ironic contrast to this perversion of what is on the surface a normal love relationship is the idiot Ike Snopes's love affair with the cow. Ike's bestiality is in actuality pure love. Like Eula the cow is given mythic stature, compared to Juno and Helen of Troy, but unlike Flem, Ike is a lover, not an exploiter, of the natural world. By the end of *The Hamlet,* Flem has pulled off several financial coups and is getting ready to try his

skills in Jefferson, but he has made one mistake: he has refused to help his cousin Mink Snopes, who has been convicted of murder and sentenced to prison. V. K. Ratliff has called Mink "a different kind of Snopes like a cotton-mouth is a different kind of snake," and Mink will prove to be Flem's nemesis.

In *The Town* Flem firmly establishes his position in Jefferson and brings a whole brood of Snopeses with him. While the naive and idealistic lawyer Gavin Stevens sets himself in opposition to the Snopes's wheelings and dealings, he is also vying with Manfred de Spain for the attentions of Eula Snopes, with whom De Spain carries on an eighteen-year affair. When, in his quest for respectability, Flem is about to expose his wife's affair, Eula commits suicide to protect her daughter, Linda, and to keep Flem from bribing De Spain. The romantic Gavin Stevens sees Eula's suicide as heroic, a matter of honor, ignoring Eula's own words: "women aren't interested in poets' dreams. They are interested in facts."

In *The Mansion* Linda returns home from New York after her artist husband has been killed in the Spanish civil war. She resents Flem for his manipulation of her and her mother and waits patiently for an opportunity for revenge, which comes when Mink Snopes gets out of prison after thirty-eight years. Linda stands by passively while Mink shoots Flem; she helps Mink escape. Ironically, Flem, whose whole life has been geared toward acquisition, has been brought down by one who, as Brooks points out, "possesses only two things of value: his identity and the savage pride with which he defends that identity. He is mean, cruel, and callous to human claims of any sort; he is selfish and self-centered. . . . But because he owns nothing but himself, he must protect the honor of self with passionate ardor."

The reviews for *The Hamlet* were generally good, but *The Town* and *The Mansion* were met with less enthusiasm. At present Faulkner's major period is said to begin with *The Sound and the Fury* and to conclude with *Go Down, Moses*. This assessment may be unjust. In his later fiction Faulkner still exhibits a range of human emotion, albeit with more humor; complicated narratives which involve the reader in the process of narrative; and a deft wit which is evident in both plot and description. These traits continue into Faulkner's last novel, *The Reivers,* published in 1962 just before his death. His later fiction deserves more attention than it has thus far received.

In 1942, two years after the publication of *The Hamlet*, appeared *Go Down, Moses*, a blend tale which includes "The Bear" and other chapters in which characters both black and white engage in most of life's rituals. Because characters did not appear to continue from chapter to chapter, Random House titled the book *Go Down, Moses, and Other Stories*. Faulkner said later that he was surprised to see the subtitle and that "Moses is indeed a novel." The misleading title leads to misleading interpretations. "The Bear" in the context of the whole novel casts an unsympathetic light on the withdrawal of Ike McCaslin. Read separately, however, the section can be viewed as a positive statement about Ike's noninvolvement.

Go Down, Moses, along with *Intruder in the Dust* (1948), is Faulkner's fullest treatment of the life of the black in the South. Continuing his praise of black endurance, he develops the history of the McCaslin family, whose genealogy includes both whites and blacks. In almost every comparison of white McCaslin with black McCaslin, the black is depicted as more stable and more just. A key chapter in *Go Down, Moses*, "The Fire and the Hearth," establishes Molly and Lucas Beauchamp as moral barometers for the clan; these characters then continue into the other chapters, as well as into *Intruder in the Dust.* This latter novel is also important for Faulkner because in it he created Chick Mallison, the young boy who is to avenge all the mature whites' errors and who becomes one of the principal narrators of *The Town* and *The Mansion.* Just as Faulkner came to find great satisfaction in the character of V. K. Ratliff, so too did Chick Mallison give him pride. Like Mark Twain, Faulkner had found that emerging consciousness of a young boy which helped him recapture his own process of maturation.

Now in his mid-forties, Faulkner began spending much time in Hollywood writing screenplays to help alleviate his financial troubles. Although he was doing some fiction writing, six years elapsed between the publication of *Go Down, Moses* and *Intruder in the Dust.* By 1944 his reputation was at a low ebb. In 1946, however, the publication of *The Portable Faulkner,* edited by Malcolm Cowley, did much to bring Faulkner's work before the public eye once more, and the sale of the film rights to *Intruder in the Dust* for fifty thousand dollars in July 1948 helped to alleviate his financial worries. His 1948 election to the American Academy of Arts and Letters was followed by the 1949 Nobel Prize (which was announced in November 1950). Faulkner was now the most respected living American writer.

In November 1949 *Knight's Gambit*, a collection of short stories and a novella dealing with Gavin Stevens, was published. His *Collected Stories* (1950) received the 1951 National Book Award for fiction. In early 1950 Faulkner returned to the Temple Drake story with *Requiem for a Nun* (1951), where he treats Temple far more sympathetically than he did in *Sanctuary.* Here Temple and the black Nancy understand what has to be done to circumvent the evils of conventional society. When Temple's husband, Gowan Stevens, and his uncle Gavin Stevens allow their rhetoric to cloud human issues, the women characters are forced into action that seems antisocial, but may be purgative. Among the sections of dramatic dialogue, Faulkner interspersed monologues about the character of the Southern town, the courthouse, and justice. Much of his feeling of reverence for the earth and wise social conventions surfaces here, just as in *Go Down, Moses* Faulkner expressed his reverence for the earth and the hunt.

In 1951 and 1952 Faulkner worked with Ruth Ford, Lemuel Ayers, and Albert Marre on adapting *Requiem for a Nun* for the stage, but it was not produced until November 1957 in London and January 1959 in New York. Ruth Ford played Temple Drake; her husband, Zachary Scott, played Gavin Stevens; and Gowan Stevens was portrayed by Robert Keith. Albert Camus adapted *Requiem for a Nun* for the Paris stage, where is was successfully produced in 1956.

Although *A Fable* (1954) was to win both a National Book Award and a Pulitzer Prize in 1955, it was greeted with mixed reviews. Much less concrete, with fewer sharply defined characters, this World War I novel, begun in 1943 during World War II, was undermined by Faulkner's florid, square-block prose; stentorian as a military dirge. Readers found little to relate to in this story of World War I France. Faulkner intended *A Fable* to be one of his most affirmative books. As much of the novel's dialogue states, people must hope, they must "believe in belief" and must recognize foundations, ritual, and roots. The three women in the novel act to uphold their beliefs rather than speak about them: they find their half-brother, fight off a hostile crowd, ask for and receive his body, and take it home. The chapters devoted to the women are clear and well paced. The book becomes more cluttered when Faulkner focuses on the General (whose authority is questionable as he demands that a whole regiment be shot) or the Runner's activities on the battlefield.

In *A Fable* Faulkner uses the innocent spiritualism of the peasants to stress his belief in emotion over intellect: the military men are rational; the "idiot" Marya, however, understands much more than they and is tranquil as a result. Like Faulkner, Marya understands these wretched men. As for the Runner, purpose will endure even in the midst of physical torture. Faulkner's themes continuing from his Yoknapatawpha fiction are clear: people sin against others only by using them for personal ends; the ability to endure is of great value in this mad but sometimes humorous race with and for life; there is virtue in simple hope as well as in a readiness to accept change. Peace is not the normal human condition.

During the 1950s Faulkner became increasingly in demand as a lecturer. He made visits for the State Department to various places such as Latin America, Japan, and Greece, and he spoke on college campuses. In 1957, after completing *The Town,* he became writer-in-residence at the University of Virginia and began dividing his time between Charlottesville and Oxford. During these last years of his life he completed *The Mansion* (1959) and *The Reivers* (1962). His interest in flying had faded, but he continued to love riding, especially fox hunting. Beginning in 1959 he suffered a number of serious injuries as a result of falls from horses. A final fall on 17 June 1962 contributed to his already failing health. He entered the hospital on 5 July and died of a heart attack at 1:30 A.M. on 7 July.

The Reivers, published on 4 June 1962, a month before Faulkner's death, is his last nostalgic glance at Yoknapatawpha County. Set in 1905, it is a warm reminiscence of the days when cars were so rare in the Mississippi countryside that in order to "borrow" his boss's car to meet his girl in a brothel, Boon Hoggenbeck, too unlikely looking to pass as its owner, has to take along the owner's son, Lucius Priest, as cover, so that he can claim to be chauffeuring the young man. The wild drive, the complicating horse race, the scenes in the whorehouse are all memorable in themselves as the epitome of the Southern tall tale; but Faulkner simultaneously weaves the simple fiction into a strong statement of honor. Lu-

cius learns principled living from both Miss Corrie, the prostitute, and Uncle Parsham, a black man who serves as a grandfather surrogate. Lucius's return home to his own grandfather, and his punishment, reinforces those lessons. All Faulkner's emphasis on life as process, on learning as experience and the reverse, on the need for human beings to make their own judgments independent of convention or organized religion comes to fruition in the last exchange between Lucius and his grandfather, when Lucius asks how he can forget what has happened and his grandfather replies, "Nothing is ever forgotten. Nothing is ever lost. It's too valuable." Instead of forgetting experience, one must "Live with it," because, the grandfather says, "A gentleman can live through anything. He faces anything. A gentleman accepts the responsibility of his actions and bears the burden of their consequences, even when he did not himself instigate them. . . . "

Not so far from Dilsey's belief in "endurance" or the Sartoris's "You can't. You just have to" is Grandfather Priest's reaffirmation. The palm at the end of the road goes to that person who is willing to know love and duty, and to take responsibility, to be responsible. In Faulkner's fiction, those persons are both male and female, black and white. Whatever Faulkner wrote, whatever Faulkner would have written, bore that legend, no matter what its structure or image pattern. That he could approach the same themes repeatedly and yet each time capture readers with his innovative craft and fascinating characters is a tribute to his greatness.

Letters:

The Faulkner-Cowley File: Letters and Memories, 1944-1962, edited by Malcolm Cowley (New York: Viking, 1966).
  Presents the correspondence as well as an account of Cowley's impressions of Faulkner during their friendship of nearly twenty years.

Selected Letters of William Faulkner, edited by Joseph L. Blotner (New York: Random House, 1977).
  Selection of letters written by Faulkner to his family, friends, and publishers between 1918 and 1962.

Interviews:

Faulkner at Nagano, edited by Robert A. Jelliffe (Tokyo: Kenkyusha, 1956).

Collection of speeches, interviews, and colloquies given in Japan as part of the Nagano Seminar in August 1985.

Faulkner in the University: Class Conferences at the University of Virginia, edited by Frederick L. Gwynn and Joseph L. Blotner (Charlottesville: University of Virginia Press, 1959).
Records excerpts from the thirty-seven conferences held during Faulkner's year as writer in residence at the University of Virginia.

Faulkner at West Point, edited by Joseph L. Fant and Robert Ashley (New York: Random House, 1964).
An account of the question and answer sessions during Faulkner's 1962 visit to West Point; includes a transcript from his reading of *The Reivers,* which incorporated revisions made after the novel's publication.

Lion in the Garden: Interviews with William Faulkner, 1926-1962, edited by James B. Meriwether and Michael Millgate (New York: Random House, 1968).
Collects significant interviews with Faulkner including those given in Europe and Asia as well as in the United States.

Bibliography:
Thomas L. McHaney, *Faulkner: A Reference Guide* (Boston: G. K. Hall, 1976).
The most useful bibliography of Faulkner's works available.

Biographies:
Joseph Blotner, *Faulkner: A Biography,* 2 volumes (New York: Random House, 1974); revised edition, 1 volume (New York: Random House, 1984).
Treats Faulkner's life in the context of his Mississippi background and attempts to trace the intent and development of his fiction; includes a section on Faulkner's ancestors.

David Minter, *William Faulkner, His Life and Work* (Baltimore & London: Johns Hopkins University Press, 1980).
Surveys Faulkner's life and career.

References:
Richard P. Adams, *Faulkner: Myth and Motion*

(Princeton: Princeton University Press, 1968).
Focuses on the major novels, discusses Faulkner's use of T. S. Eliot's "mythical method," his moral sense, and his structures and techniques.

Cleanth Brooks, *William Faulkner: The Yoknapatawpha Country* (New Haven: Yale University Press, 1963).
A good introduction to Faulkner; perhaps the most important Faulkner study ever.

Brooks, *William Faulkner: Toward Yoknapatawpha and Beyond* (New Haven: Yale University Press, 1978).
A continuation of Brook's 1963 discussion of Faulkner.

Panthea Broughton, *William Faulkner: The Abstract and the Actual* (Baton Rouge: Louisiana State University Press, 1974).
Attempts to show that Faulkner's use of abstraction enhances rather than diminishes the philosophical and aesthetic import of his fiction.

Maurice Coindreau, *The Time of William Faulkner* (Columbia: University of South Carolina Press, 1971).
A collection of essays by Faulkner's French translator of thirty years discussing the novels, Faulkner's achievement and his critical reception in France, the American novel, and Faulkner the man; also reprints Coindreau's prefaces to his translations of works by Faulkner and several other Southern writers.

Malcolm Cowley, *—And I Worked at the Writer's Trade* (New York: Viking, 1978).
In this rebuttal to Irwin's *Doubling and Incest/ Repetition and Revenge,* Cowley criticizes Irwin's Freudian analysis of Faulkner's works as oversimplified and charges him with inconsistency and sexism, among other shortcomings.

Cowley, *A Second Flowering* (New York: Viking, 1973), pp. 130-155.
Includes Cowley's essay, *Faulkner's Yoknapatawpha Story,* which sees Faulkner's fictional county as a microcosm of the world

and its history as an unconventional, anti-romantic plantation legend.

Leland H. Cox, *William Faulkner: Biographical and Reference Guide, Gale Author Handbook 1* (Detroit, Mich.: Gale Research, 1982).
Contains a short biographical piece on Faulkner, a listing of the works, and reprints of the introductions to the novels.

Cox, *William Faulkner: Critical Collection, Gale Author Handbook 2* (Detroit, Mich.: Gale Research, 1982).
Collects six statements by Faulkner and twenty essays on the author and his works; includes a list of further readings.

Frederick J. Hoffman, *William Faulkner* (New York: Twayne, 1961; revised, 1966).
An introduction to Faulkner and his major works; focuses upon the effectiveness of his characterization, his concern with the problem of evil, his moral vision, and the folk elements in his fiction.

John T. Irwin, *Doubling and Incest/Repetition and Revenge: A Speculative Reading of Faulkner* (Baltimore: Johns Hopkins University Press, 1975).
Connects Faulkner's fiction to the philosophy of Nietzsche and the psychoanalytic theory of Freud, and treats the themes of incest, narcissism, "the phantasy of the reversal of generations," and repetition of the past in *Absalom, Absalom!* and *The Sound and the Fury*.

Martin Kreiswirth, *William Faulkner, The Making of a Novelist* (Athens: University of Georgia Press, 1983).
Examines notes, discarded versions, early drafts, and published works to document Faulkner's creative processes and evolution as a writer.

Michael Millgate, *The Achievement of William Faulkner* (New York: Random House, 1966).
Presents an overall critical response to the body of Faulkner's work; includes essays on his career, each of the novels, and his achievement.

Eric J. Sundquist, *Faulkner: The House Divided* (Baltimore, MD.: Johns Hopkins University Press, 1983).
Explores the theme of Southern race relations in Faulkner's novels and sees his treatment of miscegenation in *As I Lay Dying* as a turning point in his career.

Cathy Waegner, *Recollection and Discovery: The Rhetoric of Character in William Faulkner's Novels* (New York: Lanz, 1983).
Analyses Faulkner's use of rhetoric and narrative devices, such as interior monologue, repetition, and revision, to place the reader in the role of either "recollector" or "discoverer."

Linda W. Wagner, *Hemingway and Faulkner: inventors/masters* (Metuchen, N.J.: Scarecrow Press, 1975).

Wagner, *William Faulkner: Four Decades of Criticism* (East Lansing: Michigan State University Press, 1973).

Meta Carpenter Wilde and Orin Borsten, *A Loving Gentleman* (New York: Simon & Schuster, 1976).
A memoir by the Hollywood script girl (Wilde) with whom Faulkner became involved in 1935, ostensibly written to discourage a later sensational account of their time together.

Dashiell Hammett

Richard Layman

Places	Baltimore San Francisco	Hollywood	New York City
Influences and Relationships	Lillian Hellman		
Literary Movements and Forms	Hardboiled Literature *Black Mask* School	Crime Fiction	Screenwriting
Major Themes	Corruption Code Behavior	Social Responsibility	Emotional Callousness
Cultural and Artistic Influences	Drama		
Social and Economic Influences	World War I World War II	Communism	

See also the Hammett entry in DLB: Documentary Series 6, Hardboiled Writers.

BIRTH: Saint Mary's County, Maryland, 27 May 1894, to Richard and Annie Bond Hammett.

MARRIAGE: 7 July 1921 to Josephine A. Dolan (permanently separated 1929); children: Mary Jane, Josephine.

DEATH: New York City, 10 January 1961.

BOOKS: *Red Harvest* (New York & London: Knopf, 1929);
The Dain Curse (New York: Knopf, 1929; London: Knopf, 1930);
The Maltese Falcon (New York & London: Knopf, 1930);
The Glass Key (London & New York: Knopf, 1931);
The Thin Man (New York: Knopf, 1934; London: Barker, 1934);
Secret Agent X-9, books 1 and 2 (Philadelphia: McKay, 1934);
$106,000 Blood Money (New York: Spivak, 1943);
The Battle of the Aleutians, with Robert Colodny (Adak, Alaska: U. S. Army Intelligence Section, Field Force Headquarters, Adak, 1944);
The Adventures of Sam Spade (New York: Spivak, 1944); republished as *They Can Only Hang You Once* (New York: The American Mercury/Spivak, 1949);
The Continental Op (New York: Spivak, 1945);
The Return of the Continental Op (New York: Spivak, 1945);
Hammett Homicides, edited by Ellery Queen (New York: Spivak, 1946);
Dead Yellow Women, edited by Queen (New York: Spivak, 1947);
Nightmare Town, edited by Queen (New York: The American Mercury/Spivak, 1948);
The Creeping Siamese, edited by Queen (New York: Spivak, 1950);
Woman in the Dark, edited by Queen (New York: Spivak, 1951);
A Man Named Thin, edited by Queen (New York: Ferman, 1962);
The Big Knockover, edited by Lillian Hellman (New York: Random House, 1966); reprinted as *The Dashiell Hammett Story Omnibus* (London: Cassell, 1966);
The Continental Op, edited by Steven Marcus (New York: Random House, 1974);

Dashiell Hammett

Woman in the Dark (New York: Knopf, 1988).

OTHER: *Creeps by Night,* edited by Hammett (New York: Day, 1931; London: Gollancz, 1932);
After the Thin Man, in *New Black Mask 5* and *6,* edited by Matthew J. Bruccoli and Richard Layman (San Diego, New York & London: Harvest, 1986).

MOTION PICTURES: *City Streets,* original story by Hammett, Paramount, 1931;
Mister Dynamite, original story by Hammett, Universal, 1935;
After the Thin Man, original story by Hammett, Metro-Goldwyn-Mayer, 1936;
Another Thin Man, original story by Hammett, Metro-Goldwyn-Mayer, 1939;
Watch on the Rhine, screenplay by Hammett, Warner Brothers, 1943.

In March 1928, just after Dashiell Hammett had submitted his first novel for publication, he wrote to his editor, Blanche Knopf, that unlike most moderately literate people, he took detective fiction seriously: "Some day somebody's going to make 'literature' out of it . . . and I'm selfish enough to have my hopes." Hammett wrote only five novels and fifty-five short stories in his twelve-year writing career, but it is generally acknowledged that his impact on detective fiction is unequaled in this century.

When Hammett began writing in 1922 there was an abundance of mystery writers who satisfied a growing hunger among American readers for stories of murder and intrigue. Even so, the mystery was written largely by untrained and unskilled writers or by professionals as a diversion from their serious work. It was commonly agreed that the sole purpose of the mystery was to present a problem, usually a murder, to provide the clues to its solution, and then, after a proper interval, to reveal the criminal and his method. There was little place for character development, because it was only a distraction from the description of the crime and the clues. The crime, it was felt, had to be unusual to be interesting, and therefore fictional murderers bore little resemblance to actual criminals, and the methods of crime in fiction often tested the reader's credulity. The setting was typically in a middle- or upper-class society, because there the crime was more shocking and more worthy of the attention of a detective, most often a brilliant amateur who solved crimes as a hobby.

Hammett's mysteries were different. He was the most accomplished of a school of writers that emerged in the early 1920s who were called hardboiled. "Hammett took murder out of the Venetian vase and dropped it into the alley," Raymond Chandler explained. "Hammett wrote at first (and almost to the end) for people with a sharp, aggressive attitude to life. They were not afraid of the seamy side of things; they lived there. Violence did not dismay them; it was right down their street. Hammett gave murder back to the kind of people that commit it for reasons, not just to provide a corpse; and with the means at hand, not hand wrought dueling pistols, curare, and tropical fish. He put these people down on paper as they were, and he made them talk and think in the language they customarily used for these purposes." Hammett brought realism to mystery fiction and, by the time he wrote his last novel in 1933, he could boast, with the support of the literary establishment, that he had accomplished the goal he had expressed to Blanche Knopf five years earlier. He had written mysteries of lasting literary worth.

Dashiell Hammett was born in St. Mary's County, Maryland, about sixty miles southeast of

Hammett at the typewriter, 1934

Washington, D. C. Richard Hammett, his father, was a justice of the peace and tended the family farm called Hopewell and Aim owned by Samuel Hammett, Richard's father. Until about 1900, two families lived in the three-story house on Hopewell and Aim: Samuel Hammett, his second wife, and their three young children; Richard, his wife Anna, and their three children: Aronica Rebecca (called Reba) born 1893, Samuel Dashiell (called Dash-*eel*) born 1894, and Richard Thomas, Jr. (called Dick) born 1896. Anna Hammett worked as a nurse when she was able, but poor health and the duties of motherhood kept her home much of the time. Richard Hammett was an ambitious man who suffered from bad luck and impatience. He sought a political career in St. Mary's County by opportunistically switching parties, but such disloyalty was looked upon with disfavor and, according to one family account, he was run "out of the county, more or less, on a rail." In 1900 the Hammetts moved to Philadelphia, where they stayed for about a year before they went to Baltimore and entered Dashiell in public school. In 1908, after his first semester of high school at Baltimore Polytechnic Institute, Dashiell Hammett quit school to help his father salvage a business enterprise, probably selling fresh seafood and produce door-to-door. When the business failed, Hammett took a succession of temporary jobs to help support the family. "I became the unsatisfactory employee of various railroads, stock brokers, machine manufacturers, canners, and the like. Usually I was fired," he wrote later.

His instability ended in 1915, when, at the age of twenty-one, Hammett became an operative for Pinkerton's National Detective Agency. He worked at Pinkerton's until 1918 when he went into the army and, off and on, for two years after his discharge in 1919. It was the longest-lasting job Hammett would ever hold and the most important in terms of his development as a writer. In 1915 Pinkerton's was the largest detective agency in the country, and their work was varied. During labor disputes of the time Pinkerton's operatives acquired a reputation as strike-busters because they were often called upon to maintain order on picket lines. They also hunted lawbreakers, methodically and, according to their advertisements, tirelessly. As an operative, Hammett worked on a wide variety of cases. He broke strikes; he chased crooks; and he conducted surveillance. Hammett worked out of Pinkerton's Baltimore office, though his duties took him all over the Southeast. He boasted later in his life that as a Pinkerton he had once been hired to find a man who stole a Ferris wheel. On another occasion, he said, he had helped arrest a gang of blacks accused of stealing dynamite: "In the excitement I had a feeling something was wrong but I could not figure out what it was till I happened to look down and saw this negro whittling away at my leg."

His career was interrupted in June 1918 when he was inducted into the army. Though Hammett never got more than twenty miles from his home as a soldier, he left the service as a war casualty. He was stationed at Camp Meade, Maryland, in the ambulance corps and contracted Spanish influenza during the worldwide epidemic that claimed more American lives than military action during World War I. His influenza developed into tuberculosis, and Hammett was given a medical discharge with a twenty-five percent disability rating in May 1919. His illness afflicted him permanently, and he was never again fit for an occupation that required physical labor–including work as a private detective.

Nonetheless, Hammett tried to resume his career at Pinkerton's, working as his health permitted. After a year of sporadic work in Baltimore,

Hammett left in 1920 for Washington state, where he worked out of Pinkerton's Spokane office. He seems to have worked briefly in Montana at the Anaconda Copper Mines, where there had been labor troubles since before the war and Pinkerton's had been hired to maintain order. The experience in Montana provided the material for Hammett's first novel, written seven years later.

Just over six months after his move west, Hammett's health deteriorated seriously, and he was hospitalized in the U. S. Public Health Service Hospital in Tacoma, Washington, fully disabled. He stayed there from 6 November 1920 to 21 February 1921, when he was transferred to another USPHS hospital near San Diego, where he stayed until 15 May. In Tacoma, Hammett fell in love with his nurse, a twenty-four-year old named Josephine Dolan, who soon conceived a child. Their marriage came on 7 July 1921, a month after Hammett was released from the hospital in San Diego, and they established a residence in San Francisco. Mary Jane Hammett was born ten weeks later.

The early days of Hammett's marriage were difficult ones. He had a family to support and little prospect of steady employment. He worked briefly for Pinkerton's in San Francisco and later bragged about his role in several big cases, including the Fatty Arbuckle rape-murder case and the Sonoma gold specie theft in which $250,000 in gold coin was stolen from a freighter; but by the end of 1921, Hammett's Pinkerton days were over for good as worsening health caused him to be bedridden. Hammett had to find another occupation by which to support his family, and he chose writing.

In February 1922, he took advantage of a disabled veteran's rehabilitation program and signed up for an eighteen-month vocational training course in newspaper reporting at Munson's Business College. Though he never worked as a reporter, Hammett, now twenty-eight, began his writing career in October 1922 with a short publication in H. L. Mencken and George Jean Nathan's magazine *Smart Set*. Before the end of the year he managed four more publications of short stories and brief articles, and in 1923, he had fourteen stories and two articles published. With the exception of five early publications in *Smart Set*, all of Hammett's stories were published in detective fiction pulps, primarily in *Black Mask*, the most notable of that group.

Dust jacket for the British edition of The Thin Man

There was a movement underway in 1922 among certain *Black Mask* writers that would transform the detective story from fanciful, elaborate puzzles in fictional form to brutal, realistic accounts of life in the criminal underworld. The movement was particularly well suited to Hammett, whose fiction was based primarily on his experience as a detective and his knowledge of criminal behavior. In October 1923, Hammett's story "Arson Plus" was published in *Black Mask*. It introduced the dominant character of his short fiction and marked the beginning of his development as the most accomplished of the hard-boiled writers in the so-called *Black Mask* school. The character is the Fat Man, an unnamed operative—short, fat, and middle-aged—for the Continental Detective Agency. Hammett later said the Continental Op was based on his Pinkerton's supervisor in Baltimore, Jimmy Wright, and it is clear that the Continental Detective Agency is modeled after Pinkerton's, which had its Baltimore offices in the Continental Building.

The distinguishing characteristic of the Continental Op is his utter believability. Unlike the amateur super sleuths of the classic detective story or the invincible street fighters of the new hard-boiled fiction, Hammett's Fat Man was neither a genius nor a ruffian. "I see in him a little man going forward day after day through mud and

blood and death and deceit—as callous and brutal and cynical as necessary—towards a dim goal, with nothing to push or pull him towards it except that he's been hired to reach it," Hammett wrote.

Twenty-six of Hammett's Op stories were published between October 1923 and November, in addition to two related novelettes and two novels featuring the Op. By the time he had finished with that character Hammett had established a standard against which all hard-boiled detective fiction is measured.

Like most hard-boiled fiction, Hammett's stories were dominated by the character of his detective, who is the first-person narrator. He is tough, cynical, and realistic—he is not possessed of any notion that he can eliminate evil from the world; he simply does the best he can to make his small part of it livable. The Op, like Hammett's other detectives, is a code hero. He lives according to a personal sense of right and wrong that for him transcends both civil and religious law. The plots of Hammett's stories are of secondary importance. Normally he used conventional plot devices of the classic mystery writers, revived by realistic characters and a spare vernacular writing style.

By the mid 1920s Hammett was a successful pulp story writer. That means he had a story a month published, usually in *Black Mask,* had earned himself a reputation among the magazine's regular readers, and made perhaps $1000 a year from his writing.

In May 1926 Hammett's second daughter Josephine was born, and again he faced the problem of stretching his income to support his family. He decided to give up writing for advertising, an interest of his since he had left Pinkerton's. In March 1926 Hammett took a job at Samuels Jewelry Company in San Francisco as advertising manager. The money was good and the prospects were bright—but short-lived. On 20 July 1926 Hammett collapsed at work from a lung hemorrhage and was not able to continue his job. Moreover, his condition was considered infectious by the Public Health Service nurses who visited him at home, and Hammett was required to take up residence away from his wife and daughters. Bedridden and lonesome, he returned to writing.

In November 1926 there was a change of editors at *Black Mask*. Capt. Joseph Shaw, a World War I bayonet instructor with a paucity of magazine experience, took over the editorial reins and determined to make *Black Mask* the best magazine of its kind. Largely through self-promotion, Shaw was later celebrated as the innovator at *Black Mask* of the hard-boiled form, though Hammett had already refined it by 1926. Shaw's real importance was not as an innovator, but as a promoter and an organizer. His first move after he took over *Black Mask* was to lure the best writers who had previously been published in the magazine back as regulars. Hammett was chief among his priorities.

In February 1927 Hammett's first story in eleven months appeared in *Black Mask*. It was his most ambitious to date, the first installment of a two-part, 35,000-word novelette consisting of "The Big Knockover" and "$106,000 Blood Money" (published in May 1927). Hammett had now firmly dedicated himself to a literary career. Probably with Shaw's help, he had become a reviewer of mystery novels for the *Saturday Review of Literature*, a position he held from January 1927 to October 1929.

More important, he began writing longer works, again almost certainly at Shaw's urging, and in November 1927 the first installment of Hammett's first novel was published in *Black Mask*. The novel, then known as "The Cleansing of Poisonville," was episodic in structure because it was written for serial publication. It appeared in four monthly segments, concluding in February 1928. That same month, Hammett sent the manuscript of his novel, unsolicited, to Alfred A. Knopf Publisher. It caught the attention of Blanche Knopf, who was chief editor of the firm's mystery line, and by March Hammett's novel was accepted for book publication on the condition that he revise it extensively and change the title. *Red Harvest* was published by Knopf in February 1929.

In *Red Harvest*, the Op narrates the story of his involvement with the mining town of Personville. He was hired by Donald Willsson, the son of Elihu Willsson, the town's wealthiest and most powerful man, to help in an investigation of corruption. When Donald is murdered before the Op meets him, Elihu Willsson hires the Op to find his son's murderer. During the course of his investigation, the Op "blows the lid off the town," as he put it. He discovers that there are four gang leaders who, working under Elihu Willsson's protection, control illegal activities, and the Op destroys them by setting them against one another. There are twenty-four murders in the novel (revised down from twenty-six in the serial version), most arranged by the Op.

In the lawless environment of the town, "it's easier to have them killed off, easier and surer," he explains. At the end of the novel, the Op has cleaned up Personville. All of the gang leaders are dead, and Elihu Willsson, whose irresponsible use of power had caused the town's corruption, lives on, though he is old and withered. The Op does not provide a system of order for the town. He leaves the rubble behind him.

When the novel was published, some reviewers found the violence excessive and repulsive, despite the fact that Hammett had accurately described an area of the Northwest at a time when, according to a *New York Times* report, murders were common occurrences. Others saw real talent exhibited in Hammett's first novel. "It is doubtful if even Ernest Hemingway has ever written more effective dialogue," Herbert Ashbury stated in *The Bookman*. "We recommend this one without reservation. We gave it A plus before we'd finished the first chapter," was Walter R. Brook's verdict in *Outlook and Independent*.

Hammett did not need the encouragement of reviewers to go on. In February 1929, the same month that Knopf published *Red Harvest*, the last of four installments of his second novel, *The Dain Curse*, appeared in *Black Mask*, and he had substantially finished his third novel. *The Dain Curse* is generally considered to be Hammett's weakest novel–even he called it "a silly story"–and much of the blame lies with his attempt to write for two markets at once. *Black Mask* wanted long works broken into episodes for serial publication; Knopf wanted integrated novels. In an attempt to please them both, Hammett wrote a rambling novel in which the intensity of the action rises and falls too often to sustain the reader's interest. When he was asked for revisions by Harry Block, who edited his work at Knopf under Mrs. Knopf's supervision, Hammett resisted, making only the easiest changes. It was the summer of 1928, and he was working on *The Maltese Falcon*, a better book more worthy of his attention, Hammett thought.

The Dain Curse is about Gabrielle Leggett, a lady helpless before the forces of corruption and possessiveness. Gabrielle's family was broken up when she was five by her aunt, Alice Dain (who later became her step-mother). Both Dain sisters had been in love with the same man, and Alice's sister had married him. Determined to have her man, Alice tricked Gabrielle into shooting her mother. The plot failed when Gabrielle's father came home at the instant of the murder and deter-

Hammett speaking at an anti-Nazi rally, late 1930s

mined to take the blame for the murder himself to protect his daughter. The present action begins in San Francisco some thirteen years later after Gabrielle's father has escaped from Devil's Island, assumed the name Leggett, and fled to the United States, where Alice Dain, who has raised Gabrielle, has found him and blackmailed him into marriage.

A force as pernicious as Alice Dain was to Leggett is now intruding into Gabrielle's life. The evil writer Owen Fitzstephen, himself distantly related to the Dains, is in love with Gabrielle, who spurns him. So he sets out to torment her and possess her. The Op intercedes and rescues Gabrielle from a series of dangers before he exposes Fitzstephen and accomplishes Gabrielle's spiritual awakening.

The reviewers were complimentary about Hammett's second novel and often enthusiastic about his talent as a writer. By August 1929, the month after publication, *The Dain Curse* had gone into its third printing (indicating a respectable sale of, perhaps, ten thousand copies), and in January 1930 it became Hammett's first novel to be published in England.

The year 1929 was a turning point in Hammett's life. Hollywood moviemakers were beginning to take note of his work and, though it was two more years before he signed a movie contract, Hammett was beginning to realize that he could make big money from his writing. More important, in 1929 he completed work on *The Maltese Falcon*, the novel that many critics feel is his best and the book that earned Hammett permanent respect in literary circles.

The Maltese Falcon was the first of Hammett's novels not written specifically for serial publication in *Black Mask*. Shaw did publish Hammett's third novel in five parts, but Hammett made no concession to his magazine audience this time. *The Maltese Falcon* is a tightly organized novel, not a long work patched out of related stories as *Red Harvest* and *The Dain Curse* had been.

The Maltese Falcon introduces a new detective, Sam Spade. Like the Continental Op, Spade lives by the detective's code, but his motives are more ambiguous than those of the Op. Spade does not work for a detective agency; he is a loner who keeps his own confidence and answers

142

Hammett as a newly enlisted private in the Army, 1942

to no one but himself. Much of the success of the novel is due to the enigma of Spade's character and Hammett's skill at manipulating point of view in drawing Spade's characterization. Unlike most hard-boiled detective fiction, Hammett's included, *The Maltese Falcon* is narrated in the third person so that Spade can be as mysterious a man to the reader as to the other characters in the novel, so that Hammett can reveal information to the reader as the detective obtains it, and so that Spade's reaction to the evidence can be related objectively.

The Maltese Falcon, published by Shaw in monthly installments from September 1929 to January 1930 and by Knopf, virtually without editorial changes in March 1930, is set in San Francisco during a five-day period in December 1928. Spade is visited by a duplicitous and lovely client who, under the guise of seeking her lost sister, tries to enlist his help in securing a priceless artifact–a jewel-encrusted, solid-gold falcon given as a tribute to Charles V by the Hospitallers of

St. John in the early sixteenth century. Brigid is one of five fortune seekers trying to get the bird. Spade becomes personally interested in Brigid when his partner, Miles Archer, is murdered while working on her case. As he becomes more and more involved, Spade uncovers her lies and seems to fall in love with her. The climax of the novel comes when Spade proves that Brigid is a murderess–that she killed Archer among others–and he must resist her bribes of money and love and hand her over to the police.

Spade's hard pragmatism and his motivation throughout the book are expressed in terms of the tribute he must pay to live in relative freedom. Like the Hospitallers of St. John, who paid an annual tribute to Charles V in the form of a falcon to ensure they would be allowed to inhabit lands under his domain, Spade feels that he must provide regular tributes to the civil authorities in San Francisco by solving crimes.

As the porcine Casper Gutman, who discovered the Maltese Falcon's existence and enlisted the aid of "agents" to steal it for him, explained, the rental agreement between the Hospitallers and Charles V stipulated that if they ever left the island it was to revert to Spain. "Understand? He was giving it to them, but not unless they used it . . . ." San Francisco is Spade's city–"This is my city and my game," he tells Gutman–and Spade accepts a similar implicit agreement with those who control his city. "I never forget that when the day of recovery comes I want to be all set to march into headquarters pushing a victim in front of me. As long as I can do that I can put my thumb to my nose and wriggle my fingers at all the laws in the book. . . ." That blend of responsibility, pragmatism, and hard-boiled code morality defines Spade's character and sets up the climactic scene in the novel, the best known in all of Hammett's fiction, in which he explains to Brigid why he must hand her over to the police despite her pleas for freedom and her promises of love:

> You'll never understand me, but I'll try once more and then I'll give it up. Listen, when a man's partner is killed he's supposed to do something about it. It doesn't make any difference what you thought of him. He was your partner and you're supposed to do something about it. Then it happens we were in the detective business. Well, when one of your organization gets killed it's bad business to let the killer get away with it. It's bad all around–bad for that one organization, bad for every detective everywhere. Third, I'm a detective and expecting me to run

criminals down and then let them go free is like asking a dog to catch a rabbit and then let it go. It can be done all right, and sometimes it is done, but that's not the natural thing.

Fourth, no matter what I wanted to do now it would be absolutely impossible for me to let you go without having myself dragged to the gallows with the others. Next, I've no reason in God's world to think I can trust you and if I did this and got away with it you'd have something on me that you could use whenever you happened to want to. That's five of them. The sixth would be that, since I've also got something on you, I couldn't be sure you wouldn't decide to shoot a hole in me some day. Seventh, I don't even like the idea of thinking that there might be one chance in a hundred that you'd played me for a sucker. And eighth–but that's enough. All those one side. Maybe some of them are unimportant. I won't argue about that. But look at the number of them. Now on the other side we've got what? All we've got is the fact that maybe you love me and maybe I love you."

The reception of *The Maltese Falcon* was flattering for Hammett. Aside from rave notices about the novel as an exciting mystery, including Alexander Woollcott's claim that it was "the best detective story America has yet produced," Hammett was beginning to command respect as a mainstream writer. L. F. Nebel of the St. Louis *Post-Dispatch* wrote, "It seems a pity that this should be called a detective story. . . . Truly, it is a story about a detective, but it is so much about a detective that he becomes a character, and the sheer force of Hammett's hard, brittle writing lifts the book out of the general run of crime spasms and places it aloof and above as a brave chronicle of a hard-boiled man, unscrupulous, conscienceless, unique." William Curtis in *Town & Country* went further: "I think Mr. Hammett has something quite as definitive to say, quite as decided an impetus to give the course of newness in the development of an American tongue, as any man now writing."

Sales were brisk–seven printings during the first year after publication–and there were serious inquiries from Hollywood about rights to Hammett's works. The money was beginning to come for Hammett; his health was better; and he had a girlfriend–a writer named Nell Martin. In October 1929 Hammett left his family in San Francisco and went with Nell Martin to New York, where he was received as a literary celebrity. By that time his fourth novel, *The Glass Key*, was well underway.

Hammett's sister, Reba

The Glass Key was completed in February 1930 and published in four parts by *Black Mask* between March and June. Book publication by Knopf was in April 1931. In *The Glass Key* Hammett's experiment with the objective third-person point of view is carried a step further than in *The Maltese Falcon*. In his fourth novel, Hammett depersonalizes the narration to the point that the book's primary character, Ned Beaumont, is always referred to by his full name, removing any hint of narrative familiarity with him.

The Glass Key is not a detective novel, though it is Hammett's most hard-boiled novel, and it utilizes the narrative elements of the detective novel. Ned Beaumont is a gambler and the chief assistant to his friend, political boss Paul Madvig. While arranging support for the inept Senator Henry, Madvig foolishly falls in love with the Senator's daughter, Janet. During a meeting at Henry's house between Madvig and the Senator, Henry's son is murdered, and suspicion falls on Madvig. Though he is at first able to resist the charges because of his political power, Janet Henry, who is repulsed by Madvig, is certain of his guilt and sets out to destroy him. During the course of her amateurish investigation, she encounters Beaumont, who is also trying to solve the murder because he realizes that Madvig is being damaged politically by the growing pressure for his indictment.

Janet Henry falls in love with Ned Beaumont and Beaumont with her, though he still feels loyalty to his friend Madvig. The novel ends as Beaumont exposes the senator as his son's murderer—saving Madvig from what is by that time sure prosecution—and leaves town with Janet, whom Madvig still loves.

The Glass Key is a complex novel about friendship and its responsibilities, about the corrupting nature of political power, and about the terrible aspect of knowledge—certain facts are painful to know (as when Janet Henry learns her father murdered her brother), but once they are revealed, they must be acted upon. Thus Janet Henry must react against the corruption her father represents. Similarly, Ned Beaumont has to face up to the knowledge of Paul Madvig's foolishness and his own affection for Janet Henry. The only responsible course of action for him is to leave the city where Madvig operates.

When book publication for *The Glass Key* came, the novel received even higher praise than *The Maltese Falcon* and sold about as well. Twenty thousand copies were sold by the end of the year, and Hammett was hailed again as one of the hottest authors in the country.

Since 1930, Hammett, who had left Nell Martin behind, had been in Hollywood writing original movie scripts and arranging to have his novels adapted into film. In February 1930 *Roadhouse Nights,* based on *Red Harvest,* was released by Paramount, and by summer 1930 Hammett had signed a short-term contract to write original screenplays for that studio, which proved unfruitful for Paramount. Throughout the 1930s Ham-

Hammett testifying before the McCarthy Committee

mett maintained what amounted to a dual residence in Hollywood and New York, spending roughly equal amounts of time on each coast. He was finished as a serious writer by 1931 when he became assured of a steady income from Hollywood. It was the era of hard-boiled detective films, and Hammett was acknowledged as the best of the tough mystery writers. Between 1930 and 1935 five movies were made from his works, and in 1934 he signed a generous contract with M-G-M that assured him, along with other earnings from previously published work, in excess of $100,000 a year. That spelled the ruin of a writer who had always written for money: now he did not need new sources of income, so he devoted himself to flamboyant living. He spent money lavishly; he displayed freely what Raymond Chandler called his "shocking capacity for liquor"; he took shameless advantage of the availability of starlets and harlots; and he exploited his position as a full-blown literary celebrity.

In 1931 Hammett began a novel called "The Thin Man," but when his agent illegally sold serial rights to a magazine, Knopf, who had a contract for the novel, objected, and Hammett abandoned the project. In 1933 he wrote a new novel, again called *The Thin Man* (1934). Perhaps because Hammett felt he could not afford to spend much time on the novel because of its poor earning potential relative to screenwriting, *The Thin Man* is a facile work and, with the possible exception of *The Dain Curse,* it is his weakest. It was also his best-selling.

Since the winter of 1930, Hammett had been keeping company with the woman who would be his steadiest companion for the rest of his life, Lillian Hellman, then a script reader at M-G-M attempting to become a playwright. Her spirit of self-indulgent independence matched his own, and together Hammett and Hellman spent everything he earned, living high. Hammett modeled his dissolute Nick and Nora Charles in *The Thin Man* on himself and Hellman, a fact made obvious by the novel's dust jacket, for which Hammett himself posed as the suave Nick Charles, and the dedication, "To Lillian."

The Thin Man is set during the week of Christmas, 1932. Nick Charles has married rich and given up detective work to manage his wife's money. During a visit to New York, he becomes interested in the murder of an old friend (the thin man of the title). In an alcoholic haze, between shopping trips and seemingly endless parties, Nick Charles conducts an unconventional investigation and solves the murder–a little too easily and a little too smugly.

The novel is poorly structured, implausible, and impossibly flippant, but it is redeemed by the creation of the Charleses, a couple who transcended their literary origins. "Maybe there are better writers in the world," Hammett wrote Hellman in 1937, "but nobody ever invented a more insufferably smug pair of characters." *The Thin Man* was filmed in 1934, with William Powell and Myrna Loy as the Charleses, and the movie was successful enough to warrant five sequels, the last of which appeared in 1947. Moreover, the characters were the subject of a radio serial, *The Adventures of the Thin Man,* from 1941 to 1950, and an NBC television series starring Peter Lawford and called *The Thin Man* from 1957 to 1958.

The Thin Man was published in an expurgated version in *Redbook* magazine in December 1933 and by Knopf in January 1934. It was Hammett's last novel. Reviewers were respectful, though most agreed that *The Thin Man* was not up to the standard set by *The Maltese Falcon* and *The Glass Key.* Hammett said twenty-three years later that *The Thin Man* had always bored him.

When Hammett's career as a professional writer ended in 1934 he was forty years old, and he had twenty-seven years to live. He was supported well by his income from his literary works throughout the 1930s and 1940s. He continued to be a literary man–he was respected for his literary judgment, and he took an active interest in the career of his friend Lillian Hellman, whose first play, *Children's Hour* (1934), was developed from an idea suggested by Hammett. He always planned to write another novel, and on at least six occasions began work, but he rarely got beyond an outline and only in the case of "Tulip" in the early 1950s got as far as a partially finished draft.

From 1934 to 1937, Hammett was under contract to M-G-M as a screenwriter, but although he produced original stories for two of the Thin Man sequels, the work was careless, and he was chronically undependable. In 1937 he became interested in politics and probably joined the Communist party. Regardless of his official political affiliation, Hammett worked actively for a variety of leftist organizations and was one of the founders of Equality Publishers, a short-lived enterprise dedicated to "an uncompromising fight against the enemies of humanity."

In 1942, although he was forty-eight, in uncertain health, and considered subversive, Hammett managed to join the U. S. Army. He was stationed in Alaska from 1943 until his discharge in 1945, and during much of that time he edited a camp newspaper called *The Adakian,* which he founded, on the island of Adak. In 1943 Hammett took a screen credit from M-G-M for adapting Lillian Hellman's anti-Nazi play *Watch on the Rhine* into a screenplay, though his true contribution would be better described as transcription rather than adaptation. The movie is faithful to the play, and the additional dialogue included in the film version was supplied by Hellman.

When Hammett left the army, he returned to New York, where he lived quietly and well, supported primarily by radio serials based on characters from his works. Though Hammett had no hand in the scripts, he earned an average of $400 a week from each of the three long-running serials: *The Adventures of the Thin Man* (1941-1950), *The Fat Man* (1946-1950), and *The Adventures of Sam Spade* (1946-1951). Less rewarding financially, but important to his reading audience, was the publication between 1944 and 1951 of nine paperback collections of his stories edited by Ellery Queen. Nothing he had written since

The radio serial Adventures of Sam Spade *(1946-1951) was sponsored by the Wildroot Company, which advertised the show in a long-running series of ads, such as the one above, in the Sunday comic sections of newspapers all over the country*

1934 was included in these collections and most of the stories date from the 1920s, yet they sold well, giving evidence to the fact that Hammett's reputation had lost none of its luster because of his inactivity.

In the summer of 1950 Hammett's political concerns caused a turning point in his life. Since 1946 he had been National Vice Chairman and New York State Chairman of the Civil Rights Congress, a humanitarian organization considered subversive by the federal government. He also served as chairman of a CRC bail fund committee which provided bail for jailed left-wing political activists. In July 1951 Hammett was called to testify before a U. S. District Court trying to determine the whereabouts of four Communists convicted under the Smith Act who had skipped bail put up by Hammett's CRC committee. He refused to testify and was sentenced to six months in prison for contempt of court.

When Hammett got out of jail in December 1951, having served five months of his sentence, he was without income. His radio serials had all been canceled because of his political problems. Moreover, the Internal Revenue Service had placed a lien against Hammett's estate for unpaid taxes amounting, finally, to over $180,000. Hammett had never saved; he was destitute in 1951.

He spent the last nine years of his life as a recluse, living most of the time rent-free in the gatehouse cottage of a friendly doctor in Katonah,

New York. He tried a last time in 1953 to write another novel; the result is the autobiographical fragment "Tulip" which ends with the words: "When you are tired you ought to rest, I think, and not try to fool your customers with colored bubbles." Hammett had rested for a long time before his death of various ailments, including lung cancer, on 10 July 1961. He was buried in Arlington National Cemetery.

Although Hammett's career as a writer lasted only twelve years, his influence was profound. He not only infused mystery fiction with tough realism, he made the crime novel respectable by writing works that were not bound by the artificial structures of a form. It is inaccurate to say that his best works are fine mystery novels; they are fine novels–by any standard.

Bibliography:

Richard Layman, *Dashiell Hammett: A Descriptive Bibliography* (Pittsburgh: University of Pittsburgh Press, 1979).
Lists primary and selected secondary works.

Biographies:

Richard Layman, *Shadow Man: The Life of Dashiell Hammett* (New York: Harcourt Brace Jovanovich, 1981).
The first full biography of Hammett; stubbornly adheres to the facts of Hammett's life; all his published fiction is described.

Hammett, near the end of his life, with Mrs. Richard Wilbur

Diane Johnson, *Dashiell Hammett: A Life* (New York: Random House, 1983).
   The authorized biography drawing on family materials unavailable to other biographers; a novelistic approach to Hammett's life.

William F. Nolan, *Hammett: A Life at the Edge* (New York: Morrow, 1983).
   Biographical interpretation by the mystery writer and popular biographer who wrote the first book-length study of Hammett's life and career.

Julian Symons, *Dashiell Hammett* (San Diego and New York: Harcourt Brace Jovanovich, 1985).
   An overview of Hammett's life and career by the noted literary critic and historian.

References:
David T. Bazelon, "Dashiell Hammett's Private Eye," in *The Scene before You: A New Approach to American Culture,* edited by Chandler Brossard (New York: Rinehart, 1955), pp. 180-190.

Early critical essay arguing that Hammett is best at writing formula fiction in which motivation is not carefully analyzed.

Christopher Bentley, "Radical Anger: Dashiell Hammett's *Red Harvest*," in *American Crime Fiction: Studies in the Genre*, edited by Brian Docherty (New York: St. Martin's, 1988), pp. 54-70.
   A Marxist reading of Hammett's first novel.

Raymond Chandler, "The Simple Art of Murder," *Atlantic Monthly* (December 1944): 53-59.
   Pioneering essay in which Hammett's writing is discussed in terms of tradition of American crime fiction.

City of San Francisco, special Hammett issue (4 November 1975).
   Includes documents and interviews obtained by private detective David Techheimer in his investigation of Hammett's life; includes an interview with Hammett's wife and the text of an early version of "The Thin Man."

Gary Day, "Investigating the Investigator: Hammett's Continental Op," in *American Crime Fiction: Studies in the Genre*, edited by Brian Docherty (New York: St. Martin's, 1988), pp. 39-53.
A discussion of the narrative strategies Hammett employed in the characterization of the unnamed detective hero of his first two novels and most of his short stories.

Robert I. Edenbaum, "The Poetics of the Private-Eye: The Novels of Dashiell Hammett," in *Tough Guy Writers of the Thirties*, edited by David Madden (Carbondale: Southern Illinois University Press, 1968), pp. 80-103.
Describes the code of toughness in Hammett's novels and points out that the mask of stoicism worn by Hammett's heroes is never lifted to show the reader their volnerability.

Sinda Gregory, *Private Investigations: The Novels of Dashiell Hammett* (Carbondale & Edwardsville: Southern Illinois University Press, 1985).
Critical and interpretive study of Hammett's fiction.

Richard Layman, "Dashiell Hammett" in *Dictionary of Literary Biography: Documentary Series 6—Hardboiled Writers*, edited by Matthew J. Bruccoli and Layman (Detroit: Gale Research, 1989).
A documentary record of Hammett's life and career, including much previously uncollected material.

Ross Macdonald, "Homage to Dashiell Hammett," in *Self-Portrait: Ceaselessly in the Past* (Santa Barbara, Cal.: Capra, 1981), pp. 109-112.
Essay by the crime writer describing Hammett's literary influence.

Irving Malin, "Focus on 'The Maltese Falcon': The Metaphysical Falcon," in *Tough Guy Writers of the Thirties*, edited by David Madden (Carbondale: Southern Illinois University Press, 1968), pp. 104-109.
Argues that *The Maltese Falcon* describes a mysterious world in which the falcon itself is the deity.

William Marling, *Dashiell Hammett* (New York: Twayne, 1983).
Biographical and critical study in the standard format of the Twayne United States Authors series.

Walter Raubicheck, "Stirring It Up: Dashiell Hammett and the Tradition of the Detective Story," *Armchair Detective*, 20 (Winter 1987): 20-25.
Examination of the innovations Hammett introduced to the detective story through irony and characterization.

Robert Shulman, "Dashiell Hammett's Social Vision," *The Centennial Review*, 29 (Fall 1985): 400-419.
An attempt to reconcile the social views of *Red Harvest*, *The Maltese Falcon*, and *The Glass Key* with Hammett's later political view.

George J. Thompson, "The Problem of Moral Vision in Dashiell Hammett's Detective Novels," *Armchair Detective*, 6 (May 1973): 153-156; 6 (August 1973): 213-225; 7 (November 1973): 32-40; 7 (May 1974): 178-192; 7 (August 1974): 270-280; 8 (November 1974): 27-35; 8 (February 1975): 124-130.
Long essay discussing Hammett's fiction in terms of the value system it advocates.

Peter Wolfe, *Beams Falling: The Art of Dashiell Hammett* (Bowling Green, Ohio: Bowling Green University Popular Press, 1980).
Critical discussion of Hammett's fiction.

Papers:
Hammett's papers are at the Humanities Research Center, University of Texas.

Langston Hughes

This entry was updated by R. Baxter Miller and Evelyn Nettles (University of Tennessee) from Miller's entry in DLB 51, Afro-American Writers from the Harlem Renaissance to 1940.

Places	Joplin, Missouri Cleveland, Ohio	Russia Mexico City	New York City The Orient
Influences and Relationships	Alain Locke Countee Cullen Arna Bontemps	Carl Van Vechten Arthur Spingarn Charlotte Mason	Zora Neale Hurston Margaret Walker Arthur Koestler
Literary Movements and Forms	Lyric Poetry The Novel	Political Essay Realism	Folk Humor Satire

Major Themes	The Role of
	    Blacks in the
	    Modern World
	Misplaced Values
		Poor Rural Blacks
		    vs. the Black
		    Middle-Class
		Folk Philosophy
			The Endurance of
			    Human Spirituality
			Miscegenation

Cultural and Artistic Influences	Jazz and the Blues	The Theater	Afro-American History
Social and Economic Influences	Socialism	Racism	Spanish Civil War

See also the Hughes entries in *DLB 7: Twentieth-Century American Dramatists* and *DLB 48: American Poets, 1880-1945, Second Series.*

BIRTH: Joplin, Missouri, 1 February 1902, to James Nathaniel and Carrie Mercer Langston Hughes.

EDUCATION: Columbia University, 1921-1922; B.A., Lincoln University (Pennsylvania), 1929.

AWARDS AND HONORS: *Opportunity* magazine poetry prize, 1925; Amy Spingarn Contest (*Crisis* magazine) poetry and essay prizes, 1925; Harmon Gold Medal for *Not Without Laughter*, 1931; Rosenwald Fellowships, 1931, 1941; Guggenheim Fellowship, 1935; Litt.D., Lincoln University (Pennsylvania), 1943; National Institute and American Academy of Arts and Letters Award in Literature, 1946; Anisfield-Wolf Award, 1953; Spingarn Medal, 1960; Litt.D., Howard University, 1963; Litt.D., Western Reserve University, 1964.

DEATH: New York, New York, 22 May 1967.

Langston Hughes

BOOKS: *The Weary Blues* (New York: Knopf, 1926; London: Knopf, 1926);

Fine Clothes to the Jew (New York: Knopf, 1927; London: Knopf, 1927);

Not Without Laughter (New York & London: Knopf, 1930; London: Allen & Unwin, 1930);

Dear Lovely Death (Amenia, N.Y.: Privately printed at Troutbeck Press, 1931);

The Negro Mother and Other Dramatic Recitations (New York: Golden Stair Press, 1931);

The Dream Keeper and Other Poems (New York: Knopf, 1932);

Scottsboro Limited: Four Poems and a Play in Verse (New York: Golden Stair Press, 1932);

Popo and Fifina: Children of Haiti, by Hughes and Arna Bontemps (New York: Macmillan, 1932);

A Negro Looks at Soviet Central Asia (Moscow & Leningrad: Co-operative Publishing Society of Foreign Workers in the U.S.S.R., 1934);

The Ways of White Folks (New York: Knopf, 1934; London: Allen & Unwin, 1934);

A New Song (New York: International Workers Order, 1938);

The Big Sea: An Autobiography (New York & London: Knopf, 1940; London: Hutchinson, 1940);

Shakespeare in Harlem (New York: Knopf, 1942);

Freedom's Plow (New York: Musette Publishers, 1943);

Jim Crow's Last Stand (Atlanta: Negro Publication Society of America, 1943);

Lament for Dark Peoples and Other Poems (N.p., 1944);

Fields of Wonder (New York: Knopf, 1947);

One-Way Ticket (New York: Knopf, 1949);

Troubled Island [opera], libretto by Hughes, music by William Grant Still (New York: Leeds Music, 1949);

Simple Speaks His Mind (New York: Simon & Schuster, 1950; London: Gollancz, 1951);

Montage of a Dream Deferred (New York: Holt, 1951);

Laughing to Keep from Crying (New York: Holt, 1952);

The First Book of Negroes (New York: Franklin Watts, 1952; London: Bailey & Swinfen, 1956);

Simple Takes a Wife (New York: Simon & Schuster, 1953; London: Gollancz, 1954);

The Glory Round His Head, libretto by Hughes, music by Jan Meyerowitz (New York: Broude Brothers, 1953);

Famous American Negroes (New York: Dodd, Mead, 1954);

The First Book of Rhythms (New York: Franklin Watts, 1954; London: Bailey & Swinfen, 1956);

The First Book of Jazz (New York: Franklin Watts, 1955; London: Bailey & Swinfen, 1957);

Famous Negro Music Makers (New York: Dodd, Mead, 1955);

The Sweet Flypaper of Life, text by Hughes and photographs by Roy DeCarava (New York: Simon & Schuster, 1955);

The First Book of the West Indies (New York: Franklin Watts, 1956; London: Bailey & Swinfen, 1956); republished as *The First Book of the Caribbean* (London: Edmund Ward, 1965);

I Wonder As I Wander: An Autobiographical Journey (New York & Toronto: Rinehart, 1956);

A Pictorial History of the Negro in America, by Hughes and Milton Meltzer (New York: Crown, 1956; revised, 1963; revised again, 1968); revised again as *A Pictorial History of Black Americans,* by Hughes, Meltzer, and C. Eric Lincoln (New York: Crown, 1973);

Simple Stakes a Claim (New York & Toronto: Rinehart, 1957; London: Gollancz, 1958);

The Langston Hughes Reader (New York: Braziller, 1958);

Famous Negro Heroes of America (New York: Dodd, Mead, 1958);

Tambourines to Glory (New York: John Day, 1958; London: Gollancz, 1959);

Selected Poems of Langston Hughes (New York: Knopf, 1959);

Simply Heavenly, book and lyrics by Hughes, music by David Martin (New York: Dramatists Play Service, 1959);

The First Book of Africa (New York: Franklin Watts, 1960; London: Mayflower, 1961; revised edition, New York: Franklin Watts, 1964);

The Best of Simple (New York: Hill & Wang, 1961);

Ask Your Mama: 12 Moods for Jazz (New York: Knopf, 1961);

The Ballad of the Brown King, libretto by Hughes, music by Margaret Bonds (New York: Sam Fox, 1961);

Fight for Freedom: The Story of the NAACP (New York: Norton, 1962);

Something in Common and Other Stories (New York: Hill & Wang, 1963);

Five Plays by Langston Hughes, edited by Webster Smalley (Bloomington: Indiana University Press, 1963);

Simple's Uncle Sam (New York: Hill & Wang, 1965);

The Panther & The Lash (New York: Knopf, 1967);

Black Magic: A Pictorial History of the Negro in American Entertainment, by Hughes and Meltzer (Englewood Cliffs, N.J.: Prentice-Hall, 1967);

Black Misery (New York: Knopf, 1969);

Good Morning Revolution: Uncollected Social Protest Writings by Langston Hughes, edited by Faith Berry (New York & Westport, Conn.: Lawrence Hill, 1973).

PLAY PRODUCTIONS: *Mulatto,* New York, Vanderbilt Theatre, 24 October 1935;

Little Ham, Cleveland, Karamu House, March 1936;

When the Jack Hollers, by Hughes and Arna Bontemps, Cleveland, Karamu House, April 1936;

Troubled Island, Cleveland, Karamu House, December 1936; opera version, libretto by Hughes, music by William Grant Still, New York, New York City Center, 31 March 1949;

Joy to My Soul, Cleveland, Karamu House, March 1937;

Soul Gone Home, Cleveland, Cleveland Federal Theatre, 1937;

Don't You Want to Be Free?, New York, Harlem Suitcase Theatre, 21 April 1938;

Front Porch, Cleveland, Karamu House, November 1938;

The Organizer, libretto by Hughes, music by James P. Johnson, New York, Harlem Suitcase Theatre, March 1939;

The Sun Do Move, Chicago, Good Shepherd Community House, Spring 1942;

Street Scene, by Elmer Rice, music by Kurt Weill, lyrics by Hughes, New York, Adelphi Theatre, 9 January 1947;

The Barrier, libretto by Hughes, music by Jan Meyerowitz, New York, Columbia University, January 1950; New York, Broadhurst Theatre, 2 November 1950;

Just Around the Corner, by Amy Mann and Bernard Drew, lyrics by Hughes, Ogunquit,
Maine, Ogunquit Playhouse, Summer 1951;

Esther, libretto by Hughes, music by Jan Meyerowitz, Urbana, University of Illinois, March
1957;

Simply Heavenly, New York, Eighty-fifth Street Playhouse, 20 October 1957;

The Ballad of the Brown King, libretto by Hughes,
music by Margaret Bonds, New York, Clark
Auditorium, New York City YMCA, 11 December 1960;

Black Nativity, New York, Forty-first Street Theatre, 11 December 1961;

Gospel Glow, Brooklyn, New York, Washington
Temple, October 1962;

Tambourines to Glory, New York, Little Theatre, 2
November 1963;

Let Us Remember Him, libretto by Hughes, music
by David Amram, San Francisco, War Memorial Opera House, 15 November 1963;

Jerico-Jim Crow, New York, Village Presbyterian
Church and Brotherhood Synagogue, 28 December 1964;

The Prodigal Son, New York, Greenwich Mews Theatre, 20 May 1965.

OTHER: Alain Locke, ed., *The New Negro,* includes nine poems by Hughes (New York:
A. & C. Boni, 1925);

Four Negro Poets, includes twenty-one poems by
Hughes (New York: Simon & Schuster,
1927);

Four Lincoln University Poets, includes six poems by
Hughes (Lincoln University, Penn.: Lincoln
University Herald, 1930);

Elmer Rice and Kurt Weill, *Street Scene,* lyrics by
Hughes (New York: Chappell, 1948);

The Poetry of the Negro, 1746-1949, edited by
Hughes and Arna Bontemps (Garden City,
N.Y.: Doubleday, 1949);

Lincoln University Poets, edited by Hughes, Waring
Cuney, and Bruce McM. Wright (New York:
Fine Editions Press, 1954);

The Book of Negro Folklore, edited by Hughes and
Bontemps (New York: Dodd, Mead, 1958);

*An African Treasury: Articles/Essays/Stories/Poems by
Black Americans,* selected, with an introduc-
tion, by Hughes (New York: Crown, 1960;
London: Gollancz, 1961);

Poems from Black Africa, edited by Hughes (Bloomington: Indiana University Press, 1963);

New Negro Poets: U.S.A., edited by Hughes (Bloomington: Indiana University Press, 1964);

Hughes as an infant with his mother, Carrie Hughes, 1902

The Book of Negro Humor, edited by Hughes (New
York: Dodd, Mead, 1966);

The Best Short Stories by Negro Writers, edited, with
an introduction, by Hughes (Boston & Toronto: Little, Brown, 1967).

TRANSLATIONS: Federico García Lorca, *San Gabriel* (N.p., 1938);

Jacques Roumain, "When the Tom-Tom Beats"
and "Guinea"; Refino Pedroso, "Opinions
of the New Chinese Student," in *Anthology
of Contemporary Latin-American Poetry,* edited
by Dudley Fitts (Norfolk, Conn.: New Directions, 1942), pp. 191-193, 247-249;

Roumain, *Masters of the Dew,* translated by
Hughes and Mercer Cook (New York:
Reynal & Hitchcock, 1947);

Nicolas Guillén, *Cuba Libre,* translated by Hughes
and Ben Frederic Carruthers (Los Angeles:
Ward Richie Press, 1948);

Leon Damas, "Really I Know," "Trite Without
Doubt," and "She Left Herself One Evening," in *The Poetry of the Negro, 1746-1949,*

edited by Hughes and Arna Bontemps (Garden City, N.Y.: Doubleday, 1949), pp. 371-372;

García Lorca, *Gypsy Ballads*, Beloit Poetry Chapbook, no. 1 (Beloit, Wis.: Beloit Poetry Journal, 1951);

Gabriela Mistral (Lucila Godoy Alcayaga), *Selected Poems* (Bloomington: Indiana University Press, 1957);

Jean-Joseph Rabearivelo, "Flute Players"; David Diop, "Those Who Lost Everything" and "Suffer, Poor Negro," in *Poems from Black Africa*, edited by Hughes (Bloomington: Indiana University Press, 1963), pp. 131-132, 143-145.

As a household name for so many readers of varying persuasions, Langston Hughes was perhaps the most significant black American writer in the twentieth century. From the Harlem Renaissance of the early twenties, to the Black Arts reorientations of the sixties, his short stories, novels, dramas, translations, and seminal anthologies of the works of others at home and abroad, helped unify peoples in the African diaspora. He helped nurture, in other words, so profoundly the generations after him. His early work was an innovative complement to the talent of his contemporaries, including the Keatsian verse of Countee Cullen, the avant-garde and even prophetic painting of Aaron Douglass, and the musical flamboyance of Josephine Baker. In his late twenties and early thirties, he helped inspire writers Margaret Walker and Gwendolyn Brooks. Later he encouraged writers of a third generation, including Ted Joans, Mari Evans, and Alice Walker. And, all the while, he indirectly helped open the doors of publishing to them and others of various races; he helped charm the American audience to the future of ethnic equality and pluralism. In many ways, he crafted, better perhaps than any poet since Walt Whitman, whom he celebrated and came to be suspicious about, the noblest visions of what America could be.

Between 1921 and 1967 Hughes became both famous and beloved. Even before he had helped young blacks gain entry to the major periodicals and presses of the day, his innovations in literary blues and jazz were acclaimed. As he worked to free American literature from the plantation tradition, he introduced new forms that reflected confidence and racial pride. He displayed social awareness in his fictional characters and technical mastery in his works.

James Langston Hughes was born to Carrie Langston Hughes and James Nathaniel Hughes on 1 February 1902 in Joplin, Missouri. Carrie's father, Charles Howard Langston, moved to Kansas in search of greater racial and financial freedom. His penchant for the literary and his desire to transcend the farm and the grocery store in Lawrence, Kansas, were passed on to Hughes. Charles's brother, John Mercer Langston, the poet's great-uncle, contributed to the family's literary efforts by penning an autobiography, *From the Virginia Plantation to the National Capital* (1894). The financially secure John Mercer Langston willed to his descendants a big house as well as stocks and bonds.

Hughes's mother, Carrie Langston, briefly attended college, and she demonstrated a dramatic imagination through writing poetry and delivering monologues in costume. James Nathaniel Hughes, the poet's father, studied law by correspondence course, but when he was denied permission by the all-white examining board to take the Oklahoma Territory bar examination, he moved to Joplin with his wife in 1899. There, after four years of marriage and the death of his first child (in 1900), angered by unremitting poverty and faced with supporting an eighteen-month-old child, James Hughes left the United States in October 1903 for Mexico, where he eventually prospered and thus was able to contribute to the support of his son. Carrie Hughes refused to accompany him, and, unable to get even menial jobs in Joplin, she moved constantly from city to city looking for work, occasionally taking the young Langston with her. For most of the next nine years, however, the poet lived in Lawrence with his maternal grandmother, Mary Leary Langston, although he visited his mother briefly in Topeka, stayed with her in Colorado, and traveled with her to Mexico in 1908 to see his father.

As a youngster, Hughes was acutely aware of the luxury in which his cousins lived in Washington in contrast to the poverty in which he and his grandmother lived, but she never wrote to them for help. He learned early that bills do not always get paid but that resourcefulness was essential to survival. Unlike most other black women in Lawrence, Kansas, his grandmother did not earn money by domestic service. She rented rooms to college students from the University of Kansas, and sometimes she would even live with a friend and rent out her entire house for ten or twelve dollars a month.

In 1907 Langston's mother took him with her to a library in Topeka, where he fell in love with books, in part because he was impressed that the library did not have to pay rent. Through the double perspective of boy and man, he recalled: "even before I was six books began to happen to me, so that after a while there came a time when I believed in books more than in people—which, of course, was wrong."

Hughes's grandmother influenced his life and imagination deeply. She was a gentle and proud woman of Indian and black blood. He remembered that she once took him to Osawatomie. There, she shared the platform as an honored guest of Teddy Roosevelt because she was the last surviving widow of the 1859 John Brown raid. Following her death in April 1915, Hughes lived briefly with his mother, who had by then (possibly in the previous year) married Homer Clark. When Clark left town to seek a job elsewhere, Carrie Hughes left Langston with his grandmother's friend Auntie Reed and her husband, who owned a house a block from the river near the railroad station. Devout Christians, they constantly urged Hughes to join the church. In a revival meeting, Hughes saw his friend bow to adult pressure and confess to having seen Jesus. The boy was immediately saved, or at least his elders thought so. Feeling guilty for keeping the elders up late, Hughes feigned a religious conversion, but that night he could not stop crying alone in bed. The Reeds thought he was pleased with the change in his life, but Hughes marked the incident as the beginning of his disbelief because Jesus had not intervened to save him.

In the seventh grade, Hughes secured his first regular job—cleaning the lobby and toilets in an old hotel near school—which would later inspire "Brass Spittoons," a poem he published in *Fine Clothes to the Jew* (1927). Late in the summer of 1915, Hughes rejoined his mother, stepfather, and Clark's son Gwyn. They lived in Lincoln, Illinois, for a year, and in 1916 Homer Clark moved the family to Cleveland. Hughes entered Central High School that autumn and had a successful four years there. He wrote poems for the *Belfry Owl*, the student magazine, helped win the city championships in track, was on the monthly honor roll, and edited the school yearbook. Among the teachers, many of whom he found inspirational, was Latin teacher Helen Chesnutt, daughter of well-known novelist Charles W. Chesnutt.

From 1916 to 1920 Hughes had many Jewish friends, because he found the children of foreign-born parents to be more democratic than those of other white Americans. He escorted a Jewish girl when he first attended a symphony-orchestra concert. Fellow students introduced Hughes to socialist ideas; they lent him Ethel Boole Voynich's *The Gadfly* (1891), copies of the *Liberator* and the *Socialist Call,* and took him to hear Eugene Debs, a socialist leader. Though Hughes never became an extreme leftist, his early years shaped his commitment to the poor and led him to read Arthur Schopenhauer, Friedrich Nietzsche, Edna Ferber, and Guy de Maupassant, whom he found fascinating.

Hughes spent the summer of 1919 with his father in Mexico. Unfortunately Hughes found he disliked his father's materialistic outlook. Depressed most of the time, Hughes contemplated but rejected the idea of committing suicide.

Back in the United States, Hughes dated a seventeen-year-old black woman, who was newly arrived from the South. They had met at a dance in a school gym and she inspired the lyric "When Sue Wears Red," the first of many poems in which Hughes would celebrate the beauty of black women.

> When Susanna Jones wears red
> Her face is like an ancient cameo
> Turned brown by the ages.
>
> Come with a blast of trumpets,
> Jesus!

In July 1920 on the train to visit his father in Mexico, crossing the Mississippi River to St. Louis, Hughes wrote the short lyric "The Negro Speaks of Rivers." Through the images of water and pyramid, the verse suggests the endurance of human spirituality from the time of ancient Egypt to the nineteenth and twentieth centuries. The muddy Mississippi made Hughes think of the roles in human history played by the Congo, the Niger, and the Nile, down whose water the early slaves once were sold. And he thought of Abraham Lincoln, who was moved to end slavery after he took a raft trip down the Mississippi. The draft he first wrote on the back of an envelope in fifteen minutes has become Hughes's most anthologized poem:

> I've known rivers;
>   I've known rivers ancient as the world and
>   older than the flow of human blood in human
>   veins.

notice

Monday 1927

Not "Lincoln, Pa.," but, —
Lincoln University, Pa.

Dear Alain,

It was good to hear from you and to hear how lucky you are. I hate to be "snowed-under" all by myself! I've got so much to do and so many letters to answer that I've stopped doing anything, and have been playing somebody's banjo all evening till I thought about writing to you..... "Fine Clothes" is still getting grand reviews, — all the way from "He's a great poet" to "He's a low-down hound." How they do vary! Did you see Alice Dunbar's in the Washington Eagle this week?.... Has yours come out?.... If you do see any you can clipp for me, do so, as my clipping bureau is missing everything but the pictures. I think they see only the tabloids, or else they don't know how to read. .... There have been some grand letters, too, from all points of the compass. Even from folks who haven't seen me for 20 years

A 1927 letter to Alain Locke, written after the publication of Hughes's second book (courtesy of the Alain Locke Papers, Mooreland-Spingarn Research Center, Howard University)

yet knew me at once from the Opportunity picture,— which proves the genius of Reiss.... The American Legion is trying to put poor Kerlin's Liberal Club out of West Chester. .... Woodson was to come out to speak for us Sunday but fell ill of a cold.... I've got one, too,... When will our phamplet come out? I'm sure it'll be fine and am anxious to see it.... The Messenger took my stories and are using one in the April number with illustrations.... Camden was great. You must meet Mr. Livery and Vernon Rich when you go there. They're both at Walt's house. You might make a Tues. evening talk or something there. Camden papers give great publicity.—I went to a Med. clinic at Penn and saw Dr. D ever remove kidneys, appendices, hernias, and uteruses. I didn't know Philly could furnish anything quite so intense. Even students fainted,— but not I. It was much less gruesome than a bull fight...... I want to see you, (because I've decided to go South) but New York is impossible at the moment. You see I'm even reduced to tablet paper for my letters. As Clara says "City fo' me!" It's a hard world.... I'll have to order a "Weary Blues" for Newman. Haven't even one of those. (I've got to find a 1st edition copy for myself somewhere.)

Bien a toi,   Langston   :?? P?9...?9 ?

My soul has grown deep like the rivers.

I bathed in the Euphrates when dawns were young.
I built my hut near the Congo and it lulled me to
  sleep.
I looked upon the Nile and raised the pyramids
  above it.
I heard the singing of the Mississippi when Abe
    Lincoln went down to New Orleans, and I've
    seen its muddy bosom turn all golden in the
    sunset.

I've known rivers:
  Ancient, dusky rivers.

My soul has grown deep like the rivers.

Hughes lived with his father in Mexico until September 1921 between agonizing his father's desire for him to attend a European university and his own preference for attending Columbia University in New York. As an escape he went to bullfights in Mexico City almost every weekend. He was unsuccessful in writing about them, but he did write articles about Toluca and the Virgin of Guadalupe. The *Brownies' Book,* a magazine just begun by W. E. B. Du Bois's staff at the *Crisis,* published two poems by Hughes in the January 1921 issue and *The Gold Piece,* his one-act play for children, in the July 1921 issue. Jessie Fauset, the literary editor, also accepted one of his articles and the poem "The Negro Speaks of Rivers" for the June 1921 issue of *Crisis.*

In the fall of 1921, with his father's permission, Hughes enrolled at Columbia University. His dream quickly turned into grim reality: the cold weather was depressing, the buildings were like factories, and the program and students were not to his liking. He abandoned school in favor of attending Broadway shows and lectures at the Rand School; he read what he wanted. In the spring he missed an important exam to attend the funeral for the black performer Bert Williams, and each night he went to see *Shuffle Along,* where he sat in the gallery and adored Florence Mills. After finals, Hughes dropped out of Columbia and worked at various odd jobs while he gave his undivided attention to the milieu and the people who would shape the Harlem Renaissance.

During the winter of 1923 Hughes wrote the poem that would give the title to his first volume of poetry. "The Weary Blues," about a piano player in Harlem, captures the flavor of the night life, people, and folk forms that would become characteristic of the experimental writing of the renaissance. The piano player uses his instrument to create the "call and response" pattern essential to the blues. He is alone and lonely: "Ain't got nobody in all this world,/Ain't got nobody but ma self./I's gwine to quit ma frownin'/And put ma troubles on the shelf," but his piano "talks" back to him. Through the process of playing the piano and singing about his troubles, the man is able to exorcise his feelings and arrive at a state of peace:

And far into the night he crooned that tune.
The stars went out and so did the moon.
The singer stopped playing and went to bed
While the Weary Blues echoed through his head.
He slept like a rock or a man that's dead.

In structure and subject matter the poem varies from traditional forms. Although there are rhymes and onomatopoeic effects ("Thump, thump, thump, went his foot on the floor"), there are also unusual lines, such as

Sweet Blues!
Coming from a black man's soul.
O Blues!

Such lines serve to move the poem beyond its traditional components and to locate the ethos in Afro-American culture. A frequently anthologized poem, "The Weary Blues" treats blues as theme and structure and was a fitting choice as the title of a volume designed to focus on the masses of black people rather than the elite.

Alain Locke, a philosophy professor at Howard University, wrote to commend Hughes on the poems which had appeared in *Crisis.* But when Locke, a former Rhodes scholar, asked to visit Hughes, the young poet declined fearfully because he did not think he was prepared for such distinguished company.

In the spring of 1923 Hughes left Harlem for sea travel; he secured work as a cabin boy on a freighter to Africa. Off the point of Sandy Hook, New Jersey, he threw into the sea a box of books that reminded him of hardships of his past: attics and basements in Cleveland, lonely nights in Toluca, dormitories at Columbia, and furnished rooms in Harlem. He wrote, in *The Big Sea* (1940), of his first reaction to seeing Africa: "My Africa," he says, "Motherland of the Negro

Peoples! And me a Negro! Africa! The real thing."

Hughes returned to the United States late in 1923 but was in Paris by the spring of 1924. Locke visited him there to solicit poems for a special issue of the *Survey Graphic,* an issue which was the basis for the book *The New Negro* (1925).

Locke, who invited Hughes to Venice and gave him a personally guided tour, knew who the architects of the stately old buildings were and where Wilhelm Wagner, the nineteenth-century German composer, had died. Hughes was not impressed; in less than a week, he was bored with palaces, churches, and paintings, as well as English tourists. He confirmed that Venice, too, had back alleys and poor people. He left for New York, where he took a few poems to Countee Cullen, whom he had already met and whose work he admired. With Cullen he attended an NAACP benefit party, where he met Carl Van Vechten.

In 1924 Hughes met Arna Bontemps, a crossing of paths that would have happy consequences for the two writers throughout their lives. They formed a mutual fan club, with Hughes greatly admiring Bontemps's ability to create in the midst of a demanding domestic life and Bontemps perhaps admiring Hughes's freedom and ability to write in spite of constant movement. The two writers complemented each other and worked well on a number of projects that extended for decades, including collaboration on children's books and a plethora of anthologies. Hughes, the faster writer of the two, sometimes had to wait for the slower Bontemps to complete his share of a promised work, but the delays did not harm their friendship or the quality of the work. When Bontemps became librarian at Fisk, he kept in touch with Hughes as he traveled to various parts of the world; indeed, perhaps Bontemps formed one of the centers around which Hughes would revolve for the remainder of his life.

The winter of 1925 found Hughes working in Washington, D.C., with Carter G. Woodson at the Association of Negro Life and History. This employment turned out to be brief because the paperwork hurt his eyes. He quit the "position" to take a "job" as a busboy at the Wardman Park Hotel, where he met the poet Vachel Lindsay. One afternoon Hughes put copies of his poems "Jazzonia," "Negro Dancer," and "The Weary Blues" beside Lindsay's dinner plate and went away. On his way to work the next day, Hughes read in the headlines that Lindsay had discovered a Negro busboy poet. Lindsay advised Hughes to continue writing and to seek publication for his poems.

In 1925 Hughes won his first poetry prize in a contest sponsored by *Opportunity,* the official magazine of the Urban League, and Casper Holstein, a wealthy West Indian numbers banker. At the gathering at which prizes were awarded, Hughes met Mary White Ovington and James Weldon Johnson and renewed his acquaintance with Carl Van Vechten, who asked Hughes if he had sufficient poems for a book. Hughes sent a manuscript to him, and Van Vechten liked the verses well enough to forward the volume to Alfred A. Knopf, his publisher. Blanche Knopf informed Hughes of her intention to publish the book.

Through Van Vechten Hughes met Arthur Spingarn, a prominent lawyer. Earlier that day he had accepted a long-standing invitation to tea from Spingarn's sister-in-law, Amy Spingarn. In Faith Berry's words: "emotional ties were formed between Hughes and the Spingarn family that lasted for the rest of their lives. As Hughes's attorney and personal friend for more than forty years, Arthur Spingarn made the poet's personal concerns his own and was unstinting in his public praise and admiration for Hughes." Amy Spingarn became a secret benefactor of the poet and provided him continual encouragement. She even offered to finance his education.

Hughes's poetry during this period is youthfully romantic. In the elevated lyric "Fantasy in Purple," the African drum of tragedy and death becomes a metaphor for humanism and survival. "As I Grew Older" blends reflection and nostalgia as the speaker, framed by light and shadow, seeks to rediscover his dream. In "Mexican Market Woman," Hughes's narrator uses simile to create a dark mood of weariness and pain. And through the persona in "Troubled Woman," the narrator portrays humanity similarly bowed but unbroken. With blues irony the voice modifies implicitly the pessimistic side of the spirituals ("nobody knows de trouble I seen") into the more optimistic side ("I know trouble don't last always"). "Mother to Son," a dramatic monologue, shows how dialect can be used with dignity. The image of the stair as a beacon of success inspires hope in both the son and the reader. All of the poems appeared in *The Weary Blues,* which was published in January 1926.

Critical response to *The Weary Blues* was mixed. Reviews in the *New York Times, Washington*

Langston Hughes, 1933 (courtesy of the Schomburg Center for Research in Black Culture, the New York Public Library, Astor, Lenox and Tilden Foundations)

Post, Boston Transcript, New Orleans Times-Picayune, New Republic, and elsewhere were laudatory; the only derogatory review in a white publication was in the *Times Literary Supplement,* which called Hughes a "cabaret poet." Reviewing the book in the February 1926 issue of *Opportunity,* however, Cullen found some of the poems "scornful in subject matter . . . and rhythmical treatment of whatever obstructions time and tradition . . . placed before him" and called Hughes one of those "racial artists instead of artists pure and simple." In the *Crisis* Fauset praised Hughes's liberation from established literary forms. No other poet, she said, would ever write "as tenderly, understandingly, and humorously about life in Harlem." Admiring the book for its cleanness and simplicity, Locke viewed Hughes, in *Palms,* as the spokesman for the black masses.

After a brief visit to Lincoln, Illinois, in February 1926, Hughes enrolled at Lincoln University in Pennsylvania. When classes were over for the summer, he moved to New York and into a rooming house on 137th Street, where novelist Wallace Thurman also lived. Thurman, managing editor of the *Messenger,* joined with Hughes, John P. Davis, Bruce Nugent, Zora Neale Hurston, Aaron Douglas, and Gwendolyn Bennett to sponsor *Fire!!,* a progressive and innova-

tive periodical. Its first and only issue earned indignation from Du Bois and dismissal from Rean Graves, a critic for the *Baltimore Afro-American:* "I have just tossed the first issue of *Fire* into the fire. . . . Langston Hughes displays his usual ability to say nothing in many words."

Hughes attended lively parties sponsored by heiress A'Lelia Walker and Van Vechten. Many of the same people usually attended the gatherings of the two sponsors, though more writers typically visited Van Vechten's. There Hughes met Somerset Maugham, Hugh Walpole, and Zora Neale Hurston's one-time employer Fannie Hurst, as well as William Seabrook and Louis Untermeyer.

In New York that summer Hughes wrote and rewrote the poem "Mulatto," which would appear in *Saturday Review of Literature* and in the collection *Fine Clothes to the Jew* (1927). When he read the poem one evening at James Weldon Johnson's, Clarence Darrow called it the most moving poem he had heard. While Hughes himself said the verse was about "white fathers and Negro mothers in the South," the craft transcends the autobiographical paraphrase. Through the view of one son, a victim of miscegenation, the speaker judges the father's contemptuous indifference and illustrates the callousness of white America in particular and humanity in general. Finally, he shows the hatred of the legitimate son for the bastard speaker, for the former signifies the inner collapse of the human family through racism.

"Mulatto" reinforces the techniques used in the ballad "Cross," published earlier but also collected in *Fine Clothes to the Jew.* In the poems Hughes enlarged the basic inequality among blacks into social and symbolic meaning, the "problem of mixed blood . . . one parent in the pale of the black ghetto and the other able to take advantage of all the opportunities of American democracy." He also emphasized the peculiar plight of the mulatto. "Cross" proclaims:

My old man died in a fine big house.
My ma died in a shack.
I wonder where I'm gonna die,
Being neither white nor black?

Critics in the black middle class objected to *Fine Clothes to the Jew* on ideological grounds. Their philosophical differences with Hughes went back to 1922, for he had decided then to serve the black masses and to avoid middle-class affectation. Black academicians had insisted, on the contrary, on a social image which would still promote racial integration. When it became apparent that Hughes had not complied, a headline in the *Pittsburgh Courier* read "Langston Hughes's Book of Trash," and another appeared in the *New York Amsterdam News:* "Langston Hughes, the Sewer Dweller."

During his ensuing years of study at Lincoln, Hughes met Charlotte Mason (who liked to be known as "Godmother") on a weekend trip to New York in 1927. A friend had introduced him to the elderly white lady, who delighted Hughes immediately and who, despite her age, was modern in her ideas about books, Harlem theater, and current events. She became his literary patron, a title both disliked. With her support Hughes began work on his first novel, *Not Without Laughter* (1930), which he envisioned as a portrait of a typical black family in Kansas. His personal background could not serve as a resource since his grandmother never worked in domestic service and rarely attended church: his mother had been a newspaperwoman and stenographer. Hughes began writing furiously, tacking short biographical sketches of characters to the walls in his room. At first he wrote a chapter or two a day and revised them, but the revisions were so unsatisfactory that he decided to write the book straight through. After the completion of the first draft in about six weeks, he went to Provincetown for a vacation before classes started. In the summer and fall of 1929, his senior year at Lincoln, Hughes revised the novel, continuing the process after graduation and through the summer. What had seemed acceptable to him before he went to Canada seemed to have diminished in quality upon his return. Yet the novel was accepted for publication and appeared in 1930.

In *Not Without Laughter* Hughes chose fidelity to the folk spirit instead of abandoning it for the middle-class trappings of his Lincoln education. The novel relates the growth of Sandy Williams, who lives with and is greatly influenced by Hagar, his religious grandmother. Sandy's mother Anjee spends most of her time working as a domestic and waiting restlessly for Jimboy, her guitar-playing, rambling husband, to make one of his trips home. Hagar's oldest daughter, Tempy, has separated herself from the family by assimilating middle-class culture and adopting values alien to her upbringing; Harriett, the youngest daughter, is the vibrant lover of life who defies her mother by attending parties and aspiring

Cover for the first paperback edition of the book that combines De Carava's photographs and Hughes's text to present a positive view of Harlem life

to be a blues singer. After Hagar's death, it is the unlikely Harriett who carries on her values and encourages Sandy to continue his education.

Family and home unify the novel, with Hughes combining fiction and history in his depiction of social setting and character. In his portrayal of the Williams family's disintegration and reunification, he draws upon his familiarity with the barbershop in Kansas City and his experience with a wandering stepfather. He includes songs from childhood and has Sandy go to Chicago as he once did. The book is successful in capturing the folk flavor so vital to Hughes.

In the early winter of 1930 Hughes broke irreparably with Mason. He had loved her kindness and generosity, including her sincere support for black advancement and liberal causes. He had admired her awareness of then-budding stars Duke Ellington and Marian Anderson, and he had appreciated the humility which had made her remain his anonymous patron. In providing excellent supplies for his creative work, she had broadened his cultural life through visits to the Metropolitan Museum of Art, to concerts at Carnegie Hall, and to the musicals of the day. Yet they had disagreed on political philosophy and race. Mason believed that blacks linked American whites to the primitive life and should only concern themselves with building on their cultural foundations. Hughes rejected such a simplistic view of the role of blacks in the modern world. Although he did not openly criticize Mason, he became psychosomatically ill following his final meeting with her.

Hughes also severed his ties with Hurston that winter. After one of her many trips to the Deep South, Hurston and Hughes began to work on the folk comedy "Mule Bone," a play based on an amusing tale she had collected, one which portrayed a quarrel between two church factions. Apparently Hughes outlined the plot while Hurston embellished the dialogue and strengthened the humor. Before Hurston returned south, the two were supposed to complete a first draft from which Hughes was to write the final revision. Back in Cleveland to live with his mother, Hughes attended a performance by the Gilpin Players, after which he learned that Rowena Jelliffe, the director, had just received an excellent Negro folk comedy from Hurston. Though a group in New York had turned down the play, an agent had given Jelliffe permission to try it out in Cleveland. Unable to reach Hurston by phone, Hughes wired her unsuccessfully, and, after three unanswered letters, Hurston replied finally from New York. She admitted sending the play to her agent and speculated angrily that Hughes would only have spent his half of the royalties on some girl she disliked. She went to Cleveland later to close the deal but then recanted. The incident led to a rift that was never mended and has become one of the classic break-ups in Afro-American literary history.

Now almost thirty, Hughes was determined to make a living from writing. He set out with Zell Ingram, a student at the Cleveland School of Art, to tour the South by car. In Daytona Beach he met Mary McLeod Bethune, who suggested that Hughes do readings throughout the region since his achievements could be inspiring in the prevailing climate of racial restriction. Hughes considered the advice but did not act upon it until his trip was over. He and Ingram spent the summer in Haiti. Although he did not use the letters of introduction from Walter White, William

Seabrook, Arthur Spingarn, and James Weldon Johnson to meet upper-class Haitians, he did meet Jacques Roumain, a cultured Haitian who appreciated indigenous folklore. Later, with approximately four dollars between them, Hughes and Ingram arrived back in Miami. When they returned to Daytona Beach, Bethune cashed a thirty-dollar check for them and asked to share the ride back to New York.

Hughes received a grant for $1,000 from the Rosenwald Fund to tour black colleges in the South. He purchased a Ford and then, having no license, he struck a deal with Lucas Radcliffe, a fellow alumnus of Lincoln. Radcliffe would drive and manage accounts while Hughes would read poetry. Both men would share the profits.

The trip, starting in the fall of 1931, deepened Hughes's commitments to racial justice and literary expression. When the nine Scottsboro boys were accused unjustly of raping two white prostitutes, he observed unhappily that black colleges were silent. "Christ in Alabama," a poem comparing the silence of the black colleges to that of the bystanders at the Crucifixion, caused a sensation in Chapel Hill, North Carolina, where playwright Paul Green and sociologist Guy B. Johnson had invited Hughes to read in November. About a week before the scheduled arrival, Hughes received a note from a white student, Anthony Buttitta, who invited him to share a room. Buttitta and his roommate, Milton Abernethy, had printed two of Hughes's publications, "Christ in Alabama" and an article, in *Contempo*, an unofficial student magazine. The poem had included lines such as:

Christ is a Nigger
Beaten and black—
O, bare your back.

....

Most holy bastard
Of the bleeding mouth:
*Nigger Christ
On the cross of the South.*

The subsequent appearance by Hughes nearly caused a riot, but his rescue from the angry crowd that attended the reading did not deter his challenge to racial segregation. He ate with the editors in a southern restaurant and thereby helped to set a new tone for race relations in Chapel Hill.

At various stops in other towns, the poet's audiences overflowed. Blacks admired the young poet who had "walked into a lion's den, and

Amy Spingarn's portrait of Hughes (courtesy of the Schomburg Center for Research in Black Culture, the New York Public Library, Astor, Lenox and Tilden Foundations)

come out, like Daniel, unscathed." Bethune praised the same heroism in Hughes's poetry. For her and others he read "The Negro Mother," which projects spiritual inspiration and endurance through images of fertility. In the remembrance of suffering, the speaker urges her children to transform the dark past into a lighted future. When Hughes completed the reading, Bethune embraced and consoled him: "My son, my son."

Communal love and history informed the poet's life and work. Following a program in New Orleans, he took an hour to encourage the then-adolescent poet Margaret Walker. In preparing for a reading at Tuskegee Institute in February, he thought about educator Booker T. Washington, who had founded the institution in 1881. Often at odds with the more militant Du Bois, a Hughes mentor during the renaissance, Washington had at least won partial approval from Sandy in *Not Without Laughter.*

As a youngster in Lawrence, Hughes had been taken to hear Washington speak at Topeka. Later Hughes had read *Up From Slavery* (1901), Washington's well-known autobiography. At Tuskegee, Hughes met the current president, Robert

Moten, as well as the famous scientist George Washington Carver. His talks with many English classes continued to be a source for his literary imagination, as did his whole trip.

The 1932 trip, which ended in San Francisco (at the home of Noel Sullivan, who would later be helpful to Hughes) after stops in Arkansas and other places, encouraged the literary relationships which shaped Hughes's imaginative life and made him speculate on both the nature and the obligation of art. This heightened awareness framed his journey to Russia that year as part of a film company. When Hughes met the Hungarian-born British writer Arthur Koestler in Ashkhabad, the two explored Soviet Asia together. Koestler provided the opportunity for Hughes to reflect on emotion and creativity: "There are many emotional hypochondriacs on earth, unhappy when not happy, sad when not expounding on their sadness. Yet I have always been drawn to such personalities because I often feel sad inside myself, too, though not inclined to show it. Koestler wore his sadness on his sleeve." Schooled in Western individualism, Hughes defended the artist's autonomy against the political directives of bureaucrats. Koestler retorted that the simultaneous expression of politics and individuality were difficult, especially when politicians lacked appreciation for creativity. At certain moments, Koestler argued, social aims transcended personal desires, though the Russian writer had begun to see Stalinist repression and to turn against communism. Grateful for the discussions with Koestler, Hughes probably thought his own ideas unchanged, but the encounter had renewed his leftist inclinations.

Hughes's meeting with Marie Seton furthered his leftist leanings. When he moved into a Moscow hotel, she lent him a copy of D. H. Lawrence's short story collection *The Lovely Lady* (1933). He liked "The Rocking Horse Winner" particularly because the possessive, terrifying, and elderly woman reminded him of Charlotte Mason. In attempting futilely to write an article about Tashkent, he began to remember a story told once by Loren Miller, a young lawyer in California. In a small Kansas town, a very pretty black woman attracted the attention of the only black doctor, undertaker, and minister. While all three enjoyed her favors, she became pregnant, but wasn't sure who was the father. When the doctor performed an abortion, the girl died. The undertaker took charge of her body, and the minister preached at her funeral. Hughes reworked the tale into an interracial story which would appear in *The Ways of White Folks* (1934). The black "girl" became a white middle-class youngster, Jessie Studevant, whose parents did not want her to have a relationship with a Greek boy, Willie Matsoulos, an immigrant whose father ran an ice-cream stand. When the girl's mother forced her to have an abortion, Jessie died. Hughes revised his source satirically to picture the deep pathos and hypocrisy in American society.

Yet the craft of the story transcended any social message. Through the setting of Melton, a small town in Iowa, the shrewd narrator clarifies misplaced values. He sets Cora's daughter, the black Josephine, against Mrs. Art's white Jessie. Whereas the first dies from unavoidable neglect, the second dies through willful decisions. Indeed even the name "Art" allegorizes coldness in Western creativity. Through the omniscient, ironic narrator, Hughes reflects on aborted life while he implies the need for human sympathy.

In 1933 the stories "Home" (*Esquire*, 1934) and "Blues I'm Playing" (*Scribner's*, May 1934) were accepted for publication. "Home" juxtaposes the artist's quest for beauty and truth with the lyncher's self-indulgent animalism. Roy Williams, a violinist by day and jazz player by night, returns from Europe to Hopkinsville, Missouri, where he provokes envy in the local whites. When he bows to Mrs. Reese, a benevolent white music teacher, he is killed by the whites who are jealous of his talent, clothing, and education. The story shows that music can neither transform such mobs nor protect the artist from vicious attack. Despite the apparent defeat, the humane greeting of the two musicians survives spiritually.

In "The Blues I'm Playing," Hughes reworks the disturbing break with Mason into a plot involving a black pianist, Oceola Jones, who abandons the Western classics. Though her patron, Dora Ellsworth, a childless widow, believes in art alone, Jones believes in both art and life (Mason actually preferred "primitive folk art" to the classics), but a more complex psychology informs the story. To accept the innovative ideas of Oceola would mean to admit the misdirection of Ellsworth's own life and to transcend Western dualism. When Ellsworth refuses to do so, the two women represent a theoretical and ideological struggle over aesthetics. In the story, Oceola's wildly syncopated jazz is contrasted with both the classical music and the slow-singing blues. In the onomatopoeic climax of Oceola's final song, music becomes both a personal and cultural libera-

tion. Oceola has the last word, as through her the writer transmutes the personal life into the symbolic quest for self.

In Russia Hughes had learned well the relationship between writing and mythmaking. The representative of a leading American newspaper had intentionally printed a story in New York that the film company with which Hughes was traveling was stranded and starving in Moscow. When the filmmakers showed the reporter the clippings, he merely grinned. But Hughes, to provide a clearer picture, praised the many positive changes which Americans ignored in revolutionized Russia, particularly the open housing and reduced persecution of Jews. Yet Hughes turned away from Russia eventually because he refused to live without jazz, which the communists banned, for they limited artistic freedom generally.

Determined to confront worldwide fascism and racism, Hughes returned to San Francisco by way of the Orient in 1933. His trip home demonstrates his headstrong personality. Though Westerners in Shanghai had warned him that the watermelons were tainted and potentially fatal there, he ate well, enjoyed the fruit, and lived to write the story. Warned to avoid the Chinese districts, he visited those areas and found the danger illusory. In Tokyo the police interrogated, detained, and finally expelled him. In the Japanese press's inflated stories of Korean crimes, he read the pattern of racism so familiar in the States. Aware that victims become victimizers in turn, he understood the Japanese debasement of the Chinese, and, on the way back to the United States, he warned that Japan was a fascist country.

Between 1933 and 1934 Hughes retired temporarily from world politics. In Carmel, at Sullivan's home "Ennesfree," he completed a series of short stories which were later included in *The Ways of White Folks*. He also wrote articles, including one on the liberation of women from the harems of Soviet Asia. Grateful to Noel Sullivan for the time to write, Hughes worked from ten to twelve hours a day, producing at least one story or article every week and earning more money than he ever had. He sent most of his earnings to his mother, who was ill at the time. Having broken with his father in 1922, Hughes learned, too late to attend the funeral, that his father had died in Mexico on 22 October 1934. Hughes traveled to Mexico and remained there from January to April of 1935, during which time he read Cervantes's *Don Quixote*. From Cervantes he de-

LANGSTON HUGHES

THE PANTHER
AND THE LASH

POEMS OF OUR TIMES

$1.95

Front cover for the last volume of Hughes's poetry to be published in his lifetime

rived a masterful blend of tragedy and comedy to complement the appreciation of natural beauty he had learned from Maupassant and the complexity of literary psychology he had learned from Lawrence.

He needed the humor for the Broadway production of *Mulatto*, the dramatic rewrite of the short story "Father and Son." Hughes was amazed at the changes proposed. The character played by Sally Williams, sister of the protagonist Bert, should have gone away to school; instead, she remained at home to provoke sexual sensationalism by getting raped. The play was banned in Philadelphia and nearly prohibited from playing in Chicago. But on Broadway it had a long run. *Mulatto* played there for a year, from 1935 to 1936, and it was on the road for two more seasons.

As a correspondent in 1937 for the *Baltimore Afro-American* during the Spanish Civil War, Hughes was deeply impressed by Pastora Pavón, the famous flamenco singer known as La Niña de los Peines, whose bluesy art resisted both war and death. When Hughes heard that she had refused to leave besieged Madrid, he traveled there to see her. Her midmorning appearance among hand-clapping, heel-tapping guitarists was striking. She sat in a chair and dominated the performance as she half-spoke and half-sang a *solea*. To Hughes her voice was wild, hard, harsh, lonely, and bittersweet, reminding him of black Southern blues because, despite the heartbreak implied, it signified the triumph of a people.

Hughes stayed on the top floor of the Alianza de Intelectuales in 1937; his room faced the fascist guns directly. Yet he stayed and met with the white American writers visiting Spain, including Ernest Hemingway, Martha Gelhorn, Lillian Hellman, and critic Malcolm Cowley. Nancy Cunard and Stephen Spender turned up as well, as did non-English-speaking writers such as the French novelist André Malraux and Pablo Neruda, the leftist poet from Chile. Of these writers, Hemingway influenced Hughes most deeply. Hemingway had won a fight with an Englishman over some misunderstanding concerning the man's wife. When the squabble resurfaced as a short story, Hemingway described the incident so pointedly that few people in Madrid at the time could mistake the source, though he had exaggerated the other man's slightness and the woman's stockiness. He portrayed the man as hiding under a table as shots rang out, thereby leaving his wife unprotected. Actual witnesses, however, claimed that the Englishman took cover only after assurances that his wife was safe.

Hughes appreciated the writer's imaginative revision of the event but hoped to disguise better the autobiographical sources for his own fiction. Still, Hemingway had melded history and autobiography successfully into imaginative writing.

In December 1937 Hughes went to Paris for the holidays, where he saw Nancy Cunard, Bricktop, and the Roumains. Louis Aragon introduced him to George Adam, who translated short stories into French, and Pierre Seghers, who would become Hughes's publisher. Hughes had heard from Russian intellectuals that Spain was to be considered only a training ground for Hitler's and Mussolini's armies. It was a country for bombing practice by fascist pilots, and the impending World War II would be everywhere.

When Jacques Roumain claimed the world would end, Hughes quipped, "I doubt it . . . and if it does, I intend to live to see what happens."

Hughes's work continued to earn public recognition from 1938 to 1967, the year of his death. The poems in *A New Song* (1938) are politically sensitive and direct, yet replete with social irony and personal determination. "Let America Be America Again" shows the loss of an ideal, yet invokes the reappearance of it. Through the images of eye sores, the satirical poem "Justice" emphasizes social blindness.

After founding the New Negro Theater in Los Angeles during 1939, Hughes wrote a script for the Hollywood film *Way Down South*. From May through September he completed *The Big Sea*, the first segment of his autobiography, and when the book came out the next year (1940), he received a Rosenwald fellowship to write historical plays. In 1941 he founded the Skyloft Players, who produced his musical *The Sun Do Move* in Chicago in 1942. Whatever his claims for poetry, his imprint on Afro-American drama was certain.

Shakespeare in Harlem (1942), his next book of poems, was well crafted. In the blues monologue "Southern Mammy Sings," a poor black narrator opposes a white socialite. In biblical overtones the speaker criticizes present and past war as well as the failure of interracial democracy. "Ballad of the Fortune Teller" presents humorously and colloquially the situational irony of a woman who allegedly foretells the future of others but fails to prophesy her lover's desertion of her. In the deceptively simple "Black Maria," an enthusiastic urbanite focuses, almost allegorically, upon the music playing in a tenement upstairs instead of on a hearse passing in the street below.

Such meanings escaped most of the critics. Saying that *Shakespeare in Harlem* was a "careless surface job," and that Hughes was "backing into the future looking at the past," Owen Dodson was unduly harsh. Alfred Kreymborg, however, was reminded of such "master singers of Vaudeville as Bert Williams and Eddie Leonard . . . a subtle blending of tragedy and comedy, which is a rare, difficult, and exquisite art." Edna Lou Walton, overlooking the poet's new growth in complexity and symbolic depth, wrote: "Hughes only writes as he always has. His poems, close to folk songs, indicate no awareness of the changed war world. . . . Easily listened to, they do not invoke sufficient thought."

When *Shakespeare in Harlem* had been published, Hughes returned to New York. For a

A 1965 Christmas card that Hughes created and sent to friends (courtesy of the Schomburg Center for Research in Black Culture, the New York Public Library, Astor, Lenox and Tilden Foundations)

while he shared a three-room apartment with Emerson and Toy Harper, two old family friends, and he wrote verses and slogans to help sell U.S. Defense Bonds. In a weekly column for the *Chicago Defender*, a black newspaper, he began to publish the tales of Jesse B. Semple—later called Jesse B. Simple—a folk philosopher who would capture the hearts of thousands of readers. In 1946 he won a medal and a prize of $1,000 from the American Academy of Arts and Letters. In the early months of 1947 he served as Visiting Professor of Creative Writing at Atlanta University. For a few weeks in 1949 he was poet in residence at the Laboratory School of the University of Chicago.

In *One-Way Ticket* (1949) Hughes infused humorous realism with satire and biblical irony. His well-known persona Alberta K. Johnson became the hilarious folk counterpart in poetry to his comic character Jesse B. Simple in prose. In one poem, Madam asserts her independence from the phone company as well as from a lover:

You say I O.K.ed
LONG DISTANCE?

O.K.ed it when?
My goodness, Central,
That was *then!*

I'm mad and disgusted
With that Negro now.
I don't pay no REVERSED
CHARGES nohow.

Madam blames society for her misfortunes in life
and love while she directs the criticism inward to
her own character. Her self-image is sometimes
overblown and superstitious. Possibly happiness
has eluded her because she doubts her worthi-
ness to be loved.

The critical reception to *One-Way Ticket* was
mixed. G. Lewis Chandler observed the humor,
irony, and tragedy, as well as the folksiness, subtlety, puckishness, and hope. The communal "I"
reminded him of Walt Whitman, and he praised
the poet's ability to deepen racial material into universal experience. Rolfe Humphries, who acknowledged Hughes's forbearance, praised the basic restraint of vocabulary, the simple rhymes, the
short lines, the absent violence, and the missing hyperbole. Hughes needed, he thought, to be more
elaborate, involved, and complex; to exploit
more fully education, travel, reading, and music
other than the blues.

However modern he was, Langston Hughes
would never abandon black folk life for Western
imagism. In *Montage of a Dream Deferred* (1951),
his first book-length poem, dramatic and colloquial effects challenged his lyricism. Numerous
projects in the writing of history and short fiction, such as *The First Book of Negroes* (1952) and
Simple Takes a Wife (1953), drained his poetic energies. His style became more sophisticated.
Through monologue and free verse, he stressed
dramatic situations and mastered the apostrophe.
In blending content with form, he fused narrative with sound effects.

The critics overlooked such skill. Rolfe
Humphries, who commented that the poems in
Montage of a Dream Deferred confused him, as
work by Hughes often did, saw an irreconcilable
split between Hughes the spokesman and the individual. The statement, he said, was oversimplified and theatrical. Babette Deutsch believed that
the verses, which invited approval, "lapsed into a
sentimentality that stifles real feeling." Conscious
of the limitations of folk art, she asserted that
Hughes should resemble more his French contemporaries. Saunders Redding said Hughes offered
nothing new; he called his idiom constant and his

rhythms more be-bop than jazz. Despite a sophisticated ear, according to Redding, Hughes was too
concerned with personal reputation and innovation.

After testifying in 1953 before the Senate
subcommittee chaired by Joseph McCarthy investigating the purchase of books by subversive writers for American libraries abroad, Hughes received fewer offers to read poems over the next
several years but enhanced the craft of his fiction. When *The Best of Simple* (1961) appeared he
had developed a comic veneer and lightness
which artfully concealed complex symbolism.
Through urban dialect he had juxtaposed the seriousness of the Great Migration in Simple's past
with the humorous tone of the moment. Simple's
folk imagination struck a balance with the polished reason of Boyd, his bar buddy.

In "Feet Live Their Own Life," Simple's
comic discourse suggests an awareness of the present and the past. Through the caricatured figure
of the former Virginian, Hughes helps the
reader to laugh at himself and at American society. In "There Ought to be a Law," Simple calls
for a game preserve for "Negroes." Another tale,
"They Come and They Go," is a narration about
Simple's eighteen-year-old second cousin,
Franklin D. Roosevelt Brown, coming North.
The youngster's stepfather has whipped him,
and the mother has predicted the same failure
for the youth as that which beset his "no-good" father. But Hughes's narrator manages a sympathetic tone for all involved.

In 1960 Hughes visited Paris for the first
time in twenty-two years, and he would from
then on make many trips on cultural grants from
the state department—an irony indeed, since until
1959 he was on the "security index" of the FBI's
New York office. He would visit Africa again and
revisit Europe also. The year 1961 saw the publication of Hughes's crowning achievement. *Ask Your
Mama* is as much Juvenalian as Horatian in its satiric response to the rising anger of the 1960s. Fus-
ing poetry with jazz, Hughes interweaves myth
and history. He moves now into the child's mind
and then into the man's; he reverses himself and
begins afresh. Through fantasy, travesty, allusion, and irony, he depicts singers, actors, writers, politicians, and musicians. With a deepened
imagination, he draws upon the rich themes of
his entire career, such as humanism, free speech,
transitoriness, and assimilation; nationalism, racism, integration, and poverty. He speculates
about Pan-Africanism and personal integrity.

Praising Hughes's commitment to universal freedom, Rudi Blesh called *Ask Your Mama* "a half angry and half derisive retort to the bigoted, smug, stupid, selfish, and blind." Dudley Fitts, who compared it to Vachel Lindsay's *Congo* (1914), drew parallels between Hughes and the Cuban poet Guillén, as well as between Hughes and the Puerto Rican Luis Matos.

Though many white Americans believed blacks had moved too fast, Hughes complained about slowness and regression. The last poem he is said to have submitted for publication before his death in New York City's Polyclinic Hospital on 22 May 1967 was "Backlash Blues." Yet other poems are more optimistic. In "Frederick Douglass" his narrator anticipates the return of good, despite a period of regression, like that which began in 1895, the year of Douglass's death, with Booker T. Washington's Atlanta Compromise speech in which he spoke of the races as being "separate as the five fingers." Douglass is one of the many complex heroes whom Hughes had portrayed, including such memorable figures as Roy Williams, Oceola Jones, or Bert Norwood (all in *The Ways of White Folks*). Creative and good people reinforce one another in human history, and they come again.

Following Hughes's death critical commentary was respectful. Reviewing *The Panther & The Lash* (1967), Bill Katz praised the writer's commitment to diverge from both liberal and reactionary views of race. Lamine Diakhaté called Hughes a "pilgrim who affirmed the identity of man in the face of the absurd . . . showed the problems of blacks in a democratic society, restored the rhythmical language of Africa introduced by jazz in America, and demonstrated inextinguishable hope." Francois Dodat noted Hughes's humanistic faith. Most celebrators mention the writer's great generosity.

The 1980s have marked a timely renaissance in Hughes's reputation. A Langston Hughes Study conference in March 1981 at Joplin, Missouri, helped inspire the founding of the Langston Hughes Society in Baltimore, Maryland, on 26 June of the same year. After a joint meeting with the College Language Society in April, 1982, the Society became in 1984 the first group on a black author ever to be an allied affiliation of the Modern Language Association. In the fall of 1988, Raymond R. Patterson directed, at the City College of the City University of New York, "Langston Hughes: An International Interdisciplinary Conference," one of the most brilliant tributes ever paid to the author. There, more than a dozen renowned scholars and artists reassessed the contributions of Hughes to the reshaping of American voices and visions, shortly after a public television release, so similarly titled, had reaffirmed the high place of Hughes among the most celebrated national poets.

But Hughes's technical and visionary reach, his dream, superseded any one genre or even the process of literary form itself. His effort extended to drama, to rituals of good and evil, to politics, to international relations, to women, and, inclusively, to the human imagination at large. Langston Hughes promises to exert this creative influence, this powerful authenticity, so stirring within the literary forms of Afro-American memory and celebration, possibly well beyond the twenty-first century.

Letters:

Arna Bontemps-Langston Hughes Letters, 1925-1967, edited by Charles H. Nichols (New York: Dodd, Mead, 1980).
Five hundred of the most important and interesting letters, selected from the twenty-three hundred exchanged between Hughes and Bontemps between 1925 and 1967.

Bibliographies:

Donald C. Dickinson, *A Bio-Bibliography of Langston Hughes, 1902-1967* (Hamden, Conn.: Shoe String Press, 1967).
Presents a literary biography of Hughes, an appendix entitled "Foreign Reception of Langston Hughes," and an epilogue which lists Hughes's posthumously published works and the most current Hughes biographies; includes a bibliographical listing ending with 1965 publications by and about Hughes.

R. Baxter Miller, *Langston Hughes and Gwendolyn Brooks: A Reference Guide* (Boston: G. K. Hall, 1978).
Comprises an annotated bibliography of Hughes scholarship from 1924 to 1977, arranged chronologically, a detailed introduction on how to use the guide, a table listing major works, and an index of titles and names.

Biographies:

Faith Berry, *Langston Hughes: Before and Beyond Harlem* (Westport, Conn.: Lawrence Hill, 1983).
  This critical biography focuses on the period in the Hughes's life before he moved to Harlem and catalogues the events and people who influenced his life and literary career.

Arnold Rampersad, *The Life of Langston Hughes; Volume 1: 1902-1941. I, Too, Sing America* (New York: Oxford University Press, 1986).
  This literary biography and social history chronicles the first forty years of Hughes's life; Hughes's family life, his literary development, his travels, his involvement with socialism, and the question of his sexuality make for interesting reading.

Rampersad, *The Life of Langston Hughes; Volume 2: 1941-1967. I Dream a World* (New York: Oxford University Press, 1988).
  In a scholarly and meticulous fashion Rampersad chronicles Hughes's life from 1941 to his death in 1967, by which time he was perhaps the leading Afro-American writer and a world-renowned artist who had sown profound seeds of influence throughout the African diaspora.

References:

Richard K. Barksdale, "Langston Hughes: His Times and His Humanistic Techniques," in *Black American Literature and Humanism,* edited by R. Baxter Miller (Lexington: University Press of Kentucky, 1981), pp. 11-26.
  Explains how Hughes, in his folk poetry, sought to sever some of the ties of tradition in Afro-American literature; and how he used humanistic techniques to present the richness of the folk culture of black people.

Barksdale, *Langston Hughes: The Poet and His Critics* (Chicago: American Library Association, 1977).
  Contains six essays discussing the critical reactions to those poems by Hughes which received a great deal of critical response; various critical approaches are represented.

George Houston Bass, "Five Stories about a Man Named Hughes: A Critical Reflection," *Langston Hughes Review,* 1 (Spring 1982): 1-12.

Hughes's secretary and literary assistant from 1959 through 1964 recounts five stories from the author's personal life and connects what they reveal about his aesthetic beliefs and values to the literary work which expresses these same beliefs.

Black American Literature Forum, special Hughes issue, edited by Miller, 15 (Fall 1981).
  Diverse collection of critical essays on Hughes and his work since 1968; includes historical, psychological, rhetorical, textual, and biographical assessments.

Arthur P. Davis, "Langston Hughes: Cool Poet," *CLA Journal,* 11 (June 1968): 280-296.
  Discusses four major themes that appear in Hughes's poetry: Harlem, the African heritage of the American Negro, protest and social commentary, and folk material, as well as miscellaneous minor themes; asserts that Hughes is more a poet of statement than one of symbol and that critics fail to see the different levels of meaning in his work.

Davis, "The Tragic Mulatto Theme in Six Works by Langston Hughes," *Phylon,* 16 (Winter 1955): 195-204; republished in *Five Black Writers,* edited by Donald B. Gibson (New York: New York University Press, 1970), pp. 167-177.
  Traces the treatment of this theme in six works written between 1925 and 1952 and asserts that through writing about the mulatto Hughes was able to work out his own disappointment at being rejected by his father.

James Emanuel, *Langston Hughes* (New York: Twayne, 1967).
  One of the earliest attempts to analyze the life and works of Hughes, this thematic overview surveys the author's life and examines the short stories and poems in which the major themes appear; includes a detailed chronology, notes and references, a bibliography, and an index of titles and persons.

Emanuel, "The Literary Experiments of Langston Hughes," *CLA Journal,* 11 (June 1967): 335-344.
  Examines Hughes's stylistic experiments in his dramas, short stories, and poetry; analyzes his innovative techniques, his use of in-

terior monologue, and the use of typology and emblems in the poetry.

Nathan Huggins, *Harlem Renaissance* (New York: Oxford University Press, 1971).
An account of black life in Harlem during the 1920s demonstrating how interaction between blacks and whites shaped "American character and culture"; compares Hughes to other political and literary figures of the time and details Hughes's theory of art while giving broadly thematic illustrations of the poetry.

Blyden Jackson, "A Word About Simple," *CLA Journal,* 11 (June 1968): 310-318.
Portrays Hughes's fictional character, Jessie B. Semple, as a "Negro Everyman," "a valuable specimen to Americana" who transcends racial stereotypes by displaying the attitudes and desires that are typical of all common Americans.

David Levering Lewis, *When Harlem Was in Vogue* (New York: Knopf, 1981).
Chronicles the social, cultural, and political history of Harlem; the account of Hughes includes the author's early family life, his travels, and his relationships with other writers of the Harlem Renaissance as well as explications of some poetry and prose.

Peter Mandelik and Stanley Schatt, *Concordance to Langston Hughes* (Detroit: Gale Research, 1975).
Provides the Hughes scholar with a vehicle to study the linguistic and imagistic features of Hughes's poetry; the concordance contains a short introduction that explains how to use the volume, a table of abbreviations, an index of titles of poems, a statistical summary table of word frequencies in rank order, and a table of words omitted from the concordance.

R. Baxter Miller. *The Art and Imagination of Langston Hughes* (Lexington: University Press of Kentucky, 1989).
Explores Hughes's life and art in order to demonstrate the formal and philosophical range of his autobiographical imagination, the apocalyptic imagination signified by black women, his lyrical imagination, his political imagination, and his tragi-comic imagi-

nation; one of the unique characteristics of the study is the use of recent approaches such as formalism, structuralism, and semiotics, as black American heritage informs and transforms them.

Miller, " 'For a Moment I Wondered': Theory and Form in the Autobiographies of Langston Hughes," *Langston Hughes Review,* 3 (Fall 1984): 1-6.
Contends that Hughes's autobiographies, *The Big Sea* and *I Wonder as I Wander,* are more than the author's personal recollections of life's events and that Hughes's recounting is instead an artistic exercise in which he demonstrates his own development and elevates events to metaphorical and symbolic levels of literary art.

Therman B. O'Daniel, ed., *Langston Hughes: Black Genius* (New York: Morrow, 1971).
Fourteen critical essays by twelve literary scholars examine Hughes the poet, novelist, playwright, and translator; includes an account of Hughes's life and an extensive bibliography listing works by and about Hughes as well as explorations of such subjects as Hughes' thematic concern with the common man, his use of folklore, his Jesse B. Semple character, his literary experimentations, and his similarity to Walt Whitman.

Stanley Schatt, "Langston Hughes: The Minstrel as Artificer," *Journal of Modern Literature,* 4 (September 1974): 115-120.
Demonstrates how and why Hughes made changes in his works by comparing a sample of the author's original texts to the revised ones; some revisions eliminating black dialect from the early poems were motivated by changes in the author's own philosophical beliefs and his desire to present a more universal meaning in his poetry.

Amritjit Singh, "Beyond the Mountain: Langston Hughes on Race/Class and Art," *Langston Hughes Review,* 6 (Spring 1987):37-43.
Claims that Hughes addresses himself to the interplay between the processes of writing and the lived existence of being "different," that he discusses these issues not in the "idiom of modern theory" but "as a practicing artist—out of his lived experience," and that his artistic skill was rooted in the cre-

ative intelligence that allowed him to recognize the dialectic of "difference" and "equality," thereby expressing, through various genres, its revelation.

Steven C. Tracy, *Langston Hughes & the Blues* (Urbana & Chicago: University of Illionis Press, 1988).
Traces the influence of the oral blues tradition on Hughes's blues poems, demonstrating how Hughes merged the African-American oral and written traditions by exploiting conventions, techniques, and the goals of both to achieve a poetry that is intellectually stimulating, sociopolitically responsible, and aesthetically pleasing both as folk poetry and literature; chapters include "Folklore and the Harlem Renaissance," "Defining the Blues," and "Creating the Blues."

Darwin T. Turner, "Langston Hughes as Playwright," *CLA Journal* (June 1968): 297-309.
Explores the reasons for Hughes's lack of literary success as a dramatist by examining the strengths and weaknesses in seven of the author's plays.

Jean Wagner, "Langston Hughes," in *Black Poets of the United States,* translated by Kenneth Douglas (Urbana: University of Illinois Press, 1973), pp. 385-474.
A literary history of black American poets who published from 1890 through 1940, encompassing the social and historical context in which they lived and wrote; also includes analytical interpretations of selected works.

Papers:
The James Weldon Johnson Memorial Collection, Beinecke Library, Yale University, includes letters, manuscripts and typescripts of published and unpublished work, lecture notes, and various magazine and newspaper clippings and pamphlets. Additional materials are in the Schomburg Collection of the New York Public Library, the library of Lincoln University in Pennsylvania, and the Fisk University Library.

Henry Miller

This entry was updated by Wallace Fowlie (Duke University) from his entry in DLB 9,
American Novelists, 1910-1945.

Places	Brooklyn Big Sur, Cal.	Paris	Greece
Influences and Relationships	Alfred Perlès Lawrence Durrell Anaïs Nin	Otto Rank Arthur Rimbaud D. H. Lawrence	Maurice Girodias George Katsimbalis George Seferides
Literary Movements and Forms	Postmodernism Surrealism	French Symbolism Romanticism	Satire

Major Themes	Individual Freedom
	Spirituality via
	   Eroticism
		The "Noble Savage"
		"America the
		   Unbeautiful"
			Alienation
			Sexuality

Cultural and Artistic Influences	The Beat Movement	Bohemianism	Psychoanalysis
Social and Economic Influences	Expatriation	Censorship	

See also the Miller entries in DLB 4, American Writers in Paris, 1920-1939 *and* DLB Yearbook 1980.

BIRTH: New York, New York, 26 December 1891, to Heinrich and Louise Marie Nieting Miller.

EDUCATION: City College of New York, 1909.

MARRIAGES: 1917 to Beatrice Sylvas Wickens (divorced); child: Barbara. 1 June 1924 to June Edith Smith Mansfield (divorced). 18 December 1944 to Janina Martha Lepska (divorced); children: Valentine, Tony. 29 December 1953 to Eve McClure (divorced). 10 September 1967 to Hiroko Tokuda.

AWARDS AND HONORS: Elected to the National Institute of Arts and Letters, 1958; Legion of Honor, 1975.

DEATH: Pacific Palisades, California, 7 June 1980.

SELECTED BOOKS: *Tropic of Cancer* (Paris: Obelisk Press, 1934; New York: Medusa, 1940; New York: Grove, 1961; London: Calder, 1963);

What Are You Going to Do About Alf ? (Paris: Lecram-Servant, 1935; Berkeley, Cal.: Porter, 1944; London: Turret, 1971);

Aller Retour New York (Paris: Obelisk Press, 1935);

Black Spring (Paris: Obelisk Press, 1936; New York: Grove, 1963; London: Calder, 1965);

Money and How It Gets That Way (Paris: Booster Publications, 1938; Berkeley, Cal.: Porter, 1945);

Max and the White Phagocytes (Paris: Obelisk Press, 1938);

Hamlet, by Miller and Michael Fraenkel, volume 1 (Santurce, Puerto Rico: Carrefour, 1939; enlarged edition, New York: Carrefour, 1943); volume 2 (New York: Carrefour, 1941); volumes 1 and 2 enlarged again as *The Michael Fraenkel-Henry Miller Correspondence Called Hamlet* (London: Edition du Laurier/Carrefour, 1962);

Tropic of Capricorn (Paris: Obelisk Press, 1939; New York: Grove, 1961; London: Calder, 1964);

The Cosmological Eye (Norfolk, Conn.: New Directions, 1939; London: Editions Poetry, 1945);

Henry Miller (The Humanities Research Center, University of Texas at Austin)

The World of Sex (Chicago: Argus Book Shop, 1940; revised edition, Paris: Olympia, 1957; New York: Grove, 1965);

The Colossus of Maroussi (San Francisco: Colt Press, 1941; London: Secker & Warburg, 1942);

Wisdom of the Heart (Norfolk, Conn.: New Directions, 1941; London: Editions Poetry, 1947);

Sunday after the War (Norfolk, Conn.: New Directions, 1944; London: Editions Poetry, 1945);

Why Abstract?, by Miller, Hilaire Hiler, and William Saroyan (Norfolk, Conn.: New Directions, 1945);

The Air-Conditioned Nightmare (New York: New Directions, 1945; London: Secker & Warburg, 1947);

Remember to Remember (New York: New Directions, 1947; London: Grey Walls, 1952);

The Smile at the Foot of the Ladder (New York: Duell, Sloan & Pearce, 1948);

Sexus, book 1 of *The Rosy Crucifixion* (Paris: Obelisk Press, 1949; New York: Grove, 1965; London: Calder & Boyars, 1969);

The Books in My Life (Norfolk, Conn.: New Directions, 1952; London: Owen, 1952);

Plexus, book 2 of *The Rosy Crucifixion* (Paris: Olympia, 1953; London: Weidenfeld & Nicolson, 1963; New York: Grove, 1965);

Quiet Days in Clichy (Paris: Olympia, 1956; New York: Grove, 1965; London: Calder & Boyars, 1966);

The Time of Assassins: A Study of Rimbaud (Norfolk, Conn.: New Directions, 1956; London: Spearman, 1956);

Big Sur and the Oranges of Hieronymus Bosch (New York: New Directions, 1957; London: Heinemann, 1958);

The Intimate Henry Miller (New York: New American Library, 1959);

The Henry Miller Reader, edited by Lawrence Durrell (New York: New Directions, 1959); republished as *The Best of Henry Miller* (London: Heinemann, 1960);

Art and Outrage, by Miller, Durrell, and Alfred Perlès (London: Putnam's, 1959; New York: Dutton, 1961);

Nexus, book 3 of *The Rosy Crucifixion* (Paris: Obelisk Press, 1960; London: Weidenfeld & Nicolson, 1964; New York: Grove, 1965);

Henry Miller: Watercolors, Drawings, and His Essay, The Angel Is My Watermark (New York: Abrams, 1962; London: Thames & Hudson, 1962);

Just Wild About Harry: A Melo-Melo in Seven Scenes (New York: New Directions, 1963; London: MacGibbon & Kee, 1964);

Greece, text by Miller and drawings by Anne Poor (New York: Viking, 1964; London: Thames & Hudson, 1964);

Henry Miller on Writing, edited by Thomas H. Moore (New York: New Directions, 1964);

My Life and Times (Chicago: Playboy Press, 1971);

On Turning Eighty (Santa Barbara, Cal.: Capra, 1972);

Reflections on the Death of Mishima (Santa Barbara, Cal.: Capra, 1972);

First Impressions of Greece (Santa Barbara, Cal.: Capra, 1973);

The Nightmare Notebook (New York: New Directions, 1975);

Henry Miller's Book of Friends (Santa Barbara, Cal.: Capra, 1976; London: Allen, 1978);

Gliding Into the Everglades and Other Essays (Lake Oswego, Oreg.: Lost Pleiade Press, 1977);

Mother, China, and the World Beyond (Santa Barbara, Cal.: Capra, 1977);

My Bike and Other Friends (Santa Barbara, Cal.: Capra, 1978);

The World of Lawrence: A Passionate Appreciation (Santa Barbara, Cal.: Capra, 1980);

Opus Pisto Rum (New York: Grove, 1983).

Henry Miller was a leading example of a special kind of writer who is essentially seer and prophet, whose immediate ancestor was Rimbaud, and whose leading exponent was D. H. Lawrence. This kind of writer is characterized by his vulnerability to experiences. He exposes himself to them all in a propitiatory frenzy. He relives all the incarnations of the hero, which he calls, in his more modest language, his masks. Miller was fascinated by the names Rimbaud used for himself in *A Season in Hell* (1873): "acrobat, beggar, artist, bandit, priest."

Beginning with *Tropic of Cancer* in 1934, and continuing in all of his subsequent writings, Henry Miller wrote his autobiography and at the same time the history of our age. "And always am I hungry," he wrote in *Wisdom of the Heart* (1941). Alimentary and sexual hungers are one kind, and spiritual hunger is another. Both are centrally analyzed in Miller's books. He knew that there is no solution to the problem of man's sexual hunger. In *The World of Sex* (1940) he said, "I am essentially a religious person, and always have been."

Older than Dos Passos, Hemingway, and Fitzgerald, he was not a member of the "lost generation," hesitating between exile in Montparnasse and commitment to social improvement at home. He was always the pure singer of individual freedom who was apolitical because he believed that to give up a capitalist regime for a socialist regime was simply to change masters. His personal creed may be attached in part to the European utopian concept of the "noble savage," and in part to the American tradition of the return to nature as in Thoreau and Whitman. His sense of anarchy is partly that of Thoreau and partly that of the Beat Generation and the flower children of the 1960s.

How can one even sketch a biography of Henry Miller after his many claims that no one could write his biography? His books are his autobiography, but they are also the legend of his life and nowise do they form a biography. He often said that he told lies to fool any future biographers and lead them off his tracks. In 1978 Jay Martin's long, carefully documented biography was published. Miller had given permission for the

Henry Miller at age three

fulness, and other traits that have tended to be more noticed: lustiness and obscenity.

He was born Henry Valentine Miller on 26 December 1891 in Manhattan, at 450 East Eighty-fifth Street, of German ancestry (the name Henry came from grandfather Heinrich Müller and Valentine came from grandfather Valentin Nieting). Within a year the family moved to Brooklyn, first to 662 Driggs Avenue in the Williamsburg section, and then in late 1900 to 1063 Decatur Street in the Bushwick section, where Heinrich Miller, his father, an affable, easy-going man, kept a tailor shop. His relationship with his mother was difficult. She was nagging, perfection-demanding, and impossible to please. His feelings for her were ambivalent, involving both love and hate. She was undoubtedly responsible for Miller's failure to secure a lasting relationship with a woman. At the heart of Miller's legend, and at the heart of most of his books, is the semitragic story of his relations with women.

His intermediate school was Public School Number 85 in Brooklyn. There he made friends with a boy his own age whom he watched one day covering a large blackboard with murals in colored chalk. Emil Schnellock, who was to become an advertising artist, has written movingly of Miller as "Just a Brooklyn boy," and of the quality of Henry's interests and intense enthusiasms even at the age of fourteen. He was always ready for pranks and clowning in school, but he graduated in 1909 second in his class.

Twelve years elapsed between that graduation and the next meeting between Miller and Schnellock. They had been hard years for Miller: dreary jobs of many kinds as dishwasher, typist, bartender, dockworker, gymnasium instructor, gasman; periods of unemployment, an attempt to study at City College, where he found the atmosphere intolerable and left it almost immediately. He read omnivorously all kinds of books, and they filled his dreams: Balzac, Rabelais, Petronius, Maeterlinck. He spent time in beer halls and drugstores. In 1915 he took piano lessons with Beatrice Wickens, fell in love with her, and married her in 1917. A daughter, Barbara, was born in September 1919.

Miller was nearly twenty-eight and considered himself a failure in every way. He applied, with a sense of humiliation, for a job as messenger boy at Western Union Telegraph Company and was refused. He complained about this rejection to the general manager and, to his surprise, was hired to investigate the inefficiency of the mes-

work while reminding Martin of how suspicious he was of biographies as well as of historical records and events, and Martin acknowledges that neither he nor Miller is satisfied with *Always Merry and Bright.* Any man is justified in protecting his legend and his life, and if the man is a writer, one has to accept the fact that the writer's existence and his books are inseparable.

Each of the many semibiographical books and articles that appeared before Martin's "definitive" biography were based upon intimate knowledge of Miller during a short or limited amount of time: the accounts of Alfred Perlès, Anaïs Nin, and Lawrence Durrell, for example. Never pretending to give complete truth about himself, Henry Miller often reiterated to friends that he saw everything, especially himself, as metamorphosis. The faces he has shown to the world are multiple, but all of them are geniune. All of his qualities are genuine, and yet there are endless contradictions among them because Miller has shown traits of confusion, negligence, recklessness, as well as thoughtfulness, scrupulosity, truth-

Anaïs Nin, whom Miller once hoped to marry (photo by Sunami, New York)

senger service. After a few months he was made employment manager. This job, which he held for five years, gave him exceptional insight into many of life's problems. People from every walk of life, every country, almost every race, came to him for help. He celebrated this job in *Tropic of Capricorn* (1939), in the passage on the "Cosmodemonic-Cosmococcic Telegraph Company," where he appears in his role of employment manager and father confessor to a variety of types of men. Long before *Tropic of Capricorn*, he wrote about Western Union messengers in an early unpublished work called "Clipped Wings." The title indicates his theory that messenger boys are murdered angels.

Miller used to visit Schnellock at his friend's studio at 60 West Fiftieth Street (now swallowed up by Radio City). They played chess, and they used to paint watercolors together. The act of painting always aroused Miller to a state of excitement. He would go at it in a frenzy, jumping up and down, singing, shouting.

One evening in the summer of 1923 he went to a dime-a-dance hall on Broadway, bought a string of tickets, and there met a taxi dancer who called herself June Mansfield; she was destined to become the most important woman in his life, the second of his five wives. Miller became attached to her in an almost masochistic way. The story of their love is related in part in *Tropic of Cancer,* in which June is called Mona. When Beatrice Miller divorced him, Miller believed a new life had begun for him. He married June in 1924 and, unwisely, because he had no funds, rented an apartment at 91 Remsen Street, in Columbia Heights, Brooklyn. For a while he enjoyed playing the role of writer and tried not to think of the various ways, the various rackets employed by June Miller to support herself and her husband.

Between 1924 and 1925 June Miller moved from nightclub to nightclub, and the couple moved from apartment to apartment. In late 1926 June Miller began her most serious betrayal of her husband with a new friend, Jean Kronski, who became almost her double. Miller, forced to live with both of them, accused them of lesbianism and, in excessive fits of jealousy, threatened suicide. In April 1927 the two women left for Paris, after making puppets and selling them in order to provide funds for their trip. These were months of grief and despair for Miller. As soon as the two young women returned to New York, June and Henry Miller began making plans for their own trip to Europe. They left in April 1928 and returned nine months later after their money had run out. During those nine months they went to London, Paris, Belgium, Germany, Romania, and back to Paris, where they had a few favorite spots: le Café Select, the American Express on the rue Scribe, Les Deux Magots, Ossip Zadkine's studio (the sculptor was attracted to June), the Dome and the Rotonde in Montparnasse. June Miller introduced her husband to Alfred Perlès, an Austrian writer who in time became a good friend.

Soon after their return trip to New York in January 1929 June Miller learned that Jean Kronski had killed herself. Miller continued with his writing and was fast developing a mania for painting watercolors. His friend Emil Schnellock had talked to him about Italian art and had introduced him to Walter Pater's *Studies in the History of the Renaissance* (1873), which had led to Miller's reading of Elie Faure's *History of Art.* Painting may have helped to preserve his sanity during

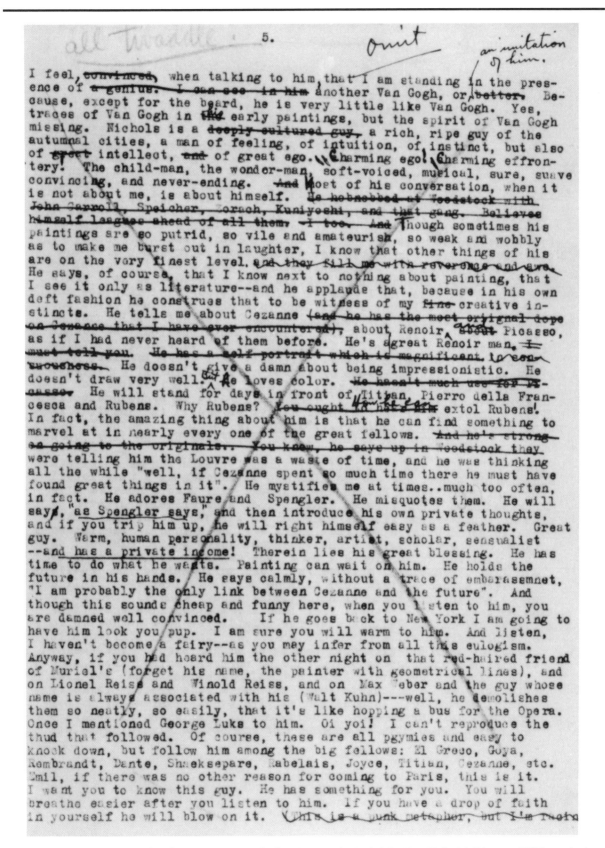

Manuscript page for Tropic of Cancer *(postcard advertisement for Sotheby's, New York, 14 February 1986 auction)*

this trying period. June Miller herself introduced the possibility of Miller's returning to Paris alone, and in late February 1930 he sailed on the *American Banker,* stopping briefly in London before going on to Paris.

Miller was lonely and depressed during his first days in Paris. At the age of thirty-eight he was poor and unknown. Had he come to Paris at twenty-one, Miller observed, he possibly would have met such kindred spirits as Max Jacob, Picabia, Apollinaire, and Gauguin. With him he had brought a copy of Whitman's *Leaves of Grass* (1855), a completed manuscript of a novel, and the draft of another novel, about June Miller. For about a month he stayed in the Hôtel Saint Germain-des-Prés on the rue Bonaparte; then lack of money caused him to move on. In the many galleries of the rue Bonaparte he could see paintings by Miró, gouaches by Max Jacob, watercolors by Marie Laurencin. He fervently read Francis Carco on Parisian bohemianism. At the end of the first Sunday he wrote in a letter to Emil Schnellock: "I will write here. I will live quietly and quite alone."

After four months in Paris, in the summer of 1930, the fear of starving became very real to Miller as he moved from place to place with no fixed domicile. At one point he was eating oatmeal three times a day in an effort to survive on as little money as possible. At critical moments friends would help him with small gifts and free meals, or sometimes June Miller would cable him money. Through Perlès he met Brassai, the Hungarian photographer who became an enthusiastic companion and pointed out to Miller the seamier aspects of Pigalle and the brothels on the rue Blondel.

Help, in a very direct way, came from two new friends in the latter part of 1930: the painter John Nichols and the writer Richard Osborn, a graduate of Yale University and Yale Law School, who was working in the Paris branch of the National City Bank. Osborn was unmarried and lived alone in the seventh floor apartment at 2, rue Auguste Bartholdi, not far from the Ecole militaire. He looked upon Miller as a genius and offered him lodging in his apartment if he would take care of the apartment and keep the fire in the coal stove burning as the cold of winter settled over Paris. On leaving the apartment each morning, he gave Miller a ten franc note for daily expenses. Miller worked hard at his typewriter on his novel about June, which he was then calling "Crazy Cock," and after he finished

this novel, he began writing various sketches of his life in Paris.

Osborn seemed happy to have him in the apartment, although the two men had opposing temperaments and habits. Miller, more orderly and methodical, kept the house clean and often cooked dinner. Osborn was more careless and heedless in his behavior, but he seemed to enjoy on his return home each night finding Miller at his typewriter, typing at great speed the words that poured forth so easily. Miller felt somewhat humiliated in his role of quasi servant and envied Osborn's good salary and security. Osborn, who wanted to be a writer, envied Miller's freedom and long hours for writing. Encouragement came when Samuel Putnam accepted for publication in the *New Review* Miller's article on Buñuel's film *L'Age d'Or* and his short story "Mademoiselle Claude." About the same time, Perlès secured commissions for Miller to write articles for the European edition of the *Chicago Tribune,* often called the Paris *Tribune.*

Walter Lowenfels was a serious writer, a poet who was working on elegies for D. H. Lawrence and Hart Crane when Miller met him in April 1931. He befriended Miller, helped him in many ways, and introduced him to Michael Fraenkel, a naturalized American of Lithuanian extraction and the author of *Werther's Younger Brother* (1930), a book that appealed strongly to Miller because of its theme of death. Whereas for Lowenfels death was just a physical experience, Fraenkel's main concern was spiritual death of the world. Fraenkel read and severely criticized "Crazy Cock" and urged Miller to tear it up and begin again. Miller was now in his fortieth year, and when he began the writing of *Tropic of Cancer,* he knew he had found his own voice.

Having moved out of Osborn's apartment earlier that spring, Miller moved in with Fraenkel at 18, rue Villa Seurat, in June 1931 and stayed until Fraenkel sublet his apartment and moved out in July 1931. He worked steadily on the new book which was in many ways the autobiography of his first year in Paris. Villa Seurat was an impasse in the fourteenth arrondissement, close to the Métro Alésia and the Café Zeyer frequented by Miller and his friends. Perlès, in his memoir of Miller, always stressed the gentleness of the man and his humility.

At this time another very important encounter took place which was to alter Miller's life considerably. Richard Osborn's chief at the bank was Hugh Guiler. He was married to a young woman named Anaïs Nin, who was born in Paris in 1903. Her father was the Spanish pianist and composer Joaquin Nin, and the family had traveled over a good part of Europe. When Anaïs Nin was eleven, her parents separated and her mother took the children to the United States. When Miller met her, he was instantly attracted in many ways: by her beauty, by her Greek name of Anaïs, by her book on D. H. Lawrence, and by the diary she talked to him about and which she ultimately gave him to read. The Guilers' house at Louveciennes, a town west of Paris, by train a forty-five minute ride, became a refuge for Miller. When June Miller turned up in Paris in September 1931 and was introduced to Nin, Miller's feelings for his wife were lessening and he worried that Nin was strongly attracted to June Miller.

June Miller left for New York in January of 1932, and Miller, desperate for some kind of reliable income, accepted the post of *repétitéur d'anglais* in the Lycée Carnot in Dijon. He was depressed by the fog and snow of Dijon, by the lack of courtesy in the lycée staff, and by the discovery that he would have only bed and board and no stipend for his work as teacher. Anaïs Nin and her husband helped him with money and books (notably some volumes of Proust in which the character of Albertine fascinated him). He was able to stand Dijon only a short time and returned to Paris.

Urged by Fraenkel and Nin, he decided to write his autobiography in the form of a diary. In this writing, which ultimately became *Tropic of Cancer*, a reader can discover several of the friends and presences in Miller's life in Paris, including Perlès, Fraenkel, and the sculptor Ossip Zadkine. With considerable humor he related the Dijon episode. As the work was nearing completion, Richard Osborn fell ill with a serious mental breakdown and left Paris for America.

The problem of finding a publisher for *Tropic of Cancer* was solved by a contract offered Miller by Jack Kahane, owner of the Obelisk Press. By that time Miller had already written several pages of *Tropic of Capricorn* and was working with great joy on a manuscript that was to be called *Black Spring* (1936). He was sustained throughout 1932 and 1933 by Anaïs Nin's belief in him, by her giving nature, and by his visits to Louveciennes. She was the one woman who made him happy, and his love for her grew. In his personal correspondence he expressed the

South Hope no. 2 or 3, *watercolor by Miller*

hope of marrying her, but Nin was to remain married to Guiler.

During 1933 while he lived in an apartment in Clichy with Alfred Perlès, he was working for a while on three projects: a revision of *Tropic of Cancer*, the future *Tropic of Capricorn*, and the outline of a book on D. H. Lawrence which the Obelisk Press wanted to publish in advance of *Tropic of Cancer* in order to offset by a critical work the possible accusation that the novel was pornography. The book on Lawrence was never completed, but parts of the manuscript were published in 1980 as *The World of Lawrence*.

Tropic of Cancer was published 1 September 1934 in Paris by the Obelisk Press. The cover was designed by the sixteen-year-old son of the owner, Maurice Kahane, who was to change his name to Maurice Girodias after World War II. On the day of the publication Miller moved into an apartment at 18, rue Villa Seurat, and it was there he received the earliest praise for his work. It came first from two Frenchmen: Marcel Duchamp and Blaise Cendrars, and then in letters from Ezra Pound, Havelock Ellis, and T. S. Eliot.

In the form of a first-person narrative, *Tropic of Cancer* is the monologue of a man who tells the story of an American expatriate in Paris, a Left Bank vagabond who often depends on his friends for meals. His frequent erotic adventures with every type of woman are graphically described. The narrator falls in love with an American girl whom he calls Mona; he marries her but she remains elusive. Lyric evocations of Paris and the Seine are as frequent as the sexual scenes. The Dijon sequence, based on Miller's stay there, is a brilliant example of Miller's humor.

In the deeper sense this is a novel of protest against all that stifles the life impulse. The hero has the dignity of a man who welcomes poverty, hunger, and ostracism in praise of his soul's freedom. In speaking of *Tropic of Cancer*, Lawrence Durrell said: "American literature today begins and ends with the meaning of what [Miller] has done." Horace Gregory said: "This book is Huck Finn in Paris, a living twentieth century Huck Finn."

Miller was divorced from June Miller by proxy in Mexico City in December 1934. This liberated him for what he had been hoping for for some time: marriage to Anaïs Nin. At this time Nin was deeply involved with the practice and technique of psychoanalysis. She had undergone analysis with Dr. René Allendy and Otto Rank in Paris and had been assisting Rank with some of his patients. More and more both Allendy and Rank were referring patients to her. Miller had never undergone analysis, but Nin had begun to teach him the technique of psychoanalytic counseling, and he had been able to foresee a very profitable career as therapist in Paris.

But suddenly Rank moved his practice to New York and urged Nin to accompany him. She too left Paris, and Miller, without much hesitation, followed her back to New York at the end of December 1934, after five years absence from the city. He was hoping for a more cordial reception from American writers and publishers than he received in that year of 1935. He had no luck with publishers, and only a few writers showed interest in his work and in him: William Carlos Williams, Nathanael West, James T. Farrell, and William Saroyan.

In his practice of psychoanalysis Rank was highly successful in New York. He referred patients to Nin, and she, in turn, referred some of these patients to Miller. The intimacy he had hoped to reach with Nin did not develop. In May 1935 she returned to Paris and to her husband. In October Miller too returned to Paris.

Miller's increasing fame had forced him into a huge correspondence. Two very long letters written at this time became his second and third published works. The first of these letters was an appeal for funds to help support his friend Alfred Perlès: *What Are You Going to Do About Alf?*, a twenty-page pamphlet printed at the author's expense in 1935. The second letter, addressed to Perlès, *Aller Retour New York* (1935), is a book of 147 pages on how an artist responds to the experience of returning to his native land.

In the heat of this epistolary activity, Miller began with Michael Fraenkel a very curious artistic collaboration: a series of letters exchanged between the two men on the varieties of death. Volume 1, called *Hamlet*, was not published until June 1939. Volume 2 came out in May 1941. Much of the discussion about death in this correspondence centers on the character of Shakespeare's Hamlet and his soliloquies.

More and more attention was paid to Miller in 1935 and 1936. Cyril Connolly, for example, wrote to him from London. James Laughlin, destined to be the founder of New Directions and publisher of Miller's works, wrote to him from Harvard requesting permission to publish *Aller Retour New York* in the *Harvard Advocate*. The Boston police destroyed the edition of the *Advocate* in which Miller's piece appeared and jailed the editors. From Corfu, Greece, the very young Lawrence Durrell wrote a moving letter of homage to Miller and in 1937 came to Paris, principally to talk to Miller and Nin. Abe Rattner, the American painter, visited him briefly at that time. Anaïs Nin saw him regularly and introduced him to the Swiss-French astrologer Conrad Moricand (who had known Max Jacob and who cast Miller's horoscope). Moricand interested him in astrology and recommended that he read Balzac, especially *Seraphita* and *Louis Lambert*. Raymond Queneau reviewed both *Tropic of Cancer* and *Black Spring* in the *Nouvelle Revue Française*. Alfred and Blanche Knopf in New York and T. S. Eliot of Faber and Faber in London showed interest in publishing Miller but did not offer definitive contracts. At Dartmouth College Prof. Herbert West spoke glowingly of Miller to his classes, and Huntington Cairns, a Washington attorney, praised the literary merits of *Tropic of Cancer*.

Encouraged by a reading of Peter Abelard's *Historia Calamitatum* (c. 1134), Miller began a re-

Henry and Eve Miller in their home in Big Sur, California. Pictured in the lower left corner are Miller's children by Janina Martha Lepska, Tony and Valentine (photo by Wynn Bullock).

writing of *Tropic of Capricorn* in 1936, the year that *Black Spring* was published by Kahane and the Obelisk Press in Paris. In this second installment of his life story (the first being *Tropic of Cancer*) scenes of his Brooklyn childhood alternate with episodes of his Paris experiences. "A Saturday Afternoon," for example, is a chapter on a tour of French urinals, and "The Tailor Shop" is a chapter on Brooklyn sidewalks. Of these three major works, *Tropic of Capricorn,* not to be published until February 1939 by the Obelisk Press, is perhaps his best book. It is largely concerned with the physiological and psychic aspects of sexuality. The sexual drive in man is, for Miller, a means of self-expression. This drive becomes uppermost when man is enslaved to a mechanistic society. This is the theme of the long episode on the Cosmodemonic Telegraph Company. In *Tropic of Capricorn* Miller leads a lusty sexual odyssey. Physical ecstasy keeps the hero from dying. He dedicated the book to June Miller (to "Her") and looked upon it as the first part of a series of

books that would attempt to depict his complete life with her.

Black Spring, the third part of the trilogy including *Tropic of Cancer* and *Tropic of Capricorn,* is the story of Miller's earliest years, his home life, his childhood and adolescence. It moves from his father's tailor shop in Brooklyn to literary scenes in Paris, and then back to scenes in Brooklyn. He felt himself an outcast from his moralistic German family and preferred the scenes he watched on Delancy Street and in the Fourteenth Ward of Brooklyn.

The passage called "The Angel is My Watermark" has become justly famous. In it Miller describes himself painting a watercolor. He begins by drawing a horse. (He has vaguely in mind the Etruscan horses he had seen in the Louvre.) At one moment the horse resembles a hammock, and then when he adds stripes, it becomes a zebra. He adds a tree, a mountain, an angel, cemetery gates. Finally it is done: a masterpiece that has come about by accident. But then Miller

Henry and Eve Miller, 1953 (Photo Interpress, Paris)

writes that the Twenty-third Psalm was another accident. Every work of art has to be credited, in some mysterious way, to every artist. So Miller credits Dante, Spinoza, and Hieronymus Bosch for his little watercolor.

In December 1937 Miller announced the Villa Seurat Series of publications. With money guaranteed by Nancy Durrell (wife of Lawrence Durrell) three books were printed in the series and distributed by Obelisk: Miller's collection of stories and essays, *Max and the White Phagocytes* (1938), Anaïs Nin's *Winter of Artifice* (1939), and Durrell's *The Black Book* (1939). When Nancy Durrell's money gave out, the series stopped.

Soon after the publication of *Tropic of Capricorn* on 10 May 1939, Miller began preparing to leave Villa Seurat forever. He sold or gave away most of his possessions. On the advice of Durrell, he decided to go home by way of Greece. After spending the month of June in Rocamadour, in the department of the Lot near Bordeaux, he boarded the *Théophile Gautier* in Marseilles on 14 July. He felt despondently alone at this time in his life. Nin had been with him briefly in southern France and then had returned to her husband in Paris.

The boat made a brief stop at Athens and then went to Corfu where Lawrence Durrell met him. Late that summer in Athens, Miller met two Greek men of letters to whom he felt strongly drawn: George Katsimbalis (whom he was to call the "colossus" in *The Colossus of Maroussi*) and the poet-translator of Eliot, George Seferides, who used the pen name Seferis. He enjoyed with these men the kind of lusty comradeship he liked the most.

His financial status was confused. Jack Kahane of the Obelisk Press died in September 1939. His son Maurice promised royalties to Miller, but France was soon in the turmoil of war, and there was no communication from the press during the war years. James Laughlin of New Directions published in 1939 a collection of essays: *The Cosmological Eye*. It was the only book by Miller that had appeared in the United States when he reached New York in March 1940, after a long dreary crossing on an American cargo boat.

Soon after Miller arrived in New York, Caresse Crosby gave him lodging in her apartment house at 137 East Fifty-fourth Street. He began work almost immediately on an essay, *The World of Sex* (1940), somewhat related to his essay *Quiet Days in Clichy* (1956), also written that spring, because both of them deal directly with the problems of sex and pornography. But his principal writing, *The Colossus of Maroussi*, not to be published until 1941, was about his Greek experience. This is the account of what happened to him between July and December 1939 and his impressions of Katsimbalis. He was moved by the generous Mediterranean people and often wrote about them in a rhapsodic strain. Karl Shapiro calls *The Colossus of Maroussi* "one of the best travel books on Greece ever done," but other critics have found it too strident, too sentimental.

Urged by publishers to write a book about his own country, Miller undertook a year of traveling throughout America (October 1940-October 1941), which on the whole was a disaster. His friend the painter Abraham Rattner traveled part of the way with him, but most of the time he was alone. The book, finished in 1941 but not published until 1945, was called *The Air-Conditioned Nightmare*. This anti-American travelogue is decidedly one of Miller's weakest books.

In January 1942 Miller resumed work on *The Rosy Crucifixion*, the projected long work on his "calamities" with June Miller, which ultimately appeared in three volumes. By June 1942 he had decided to live in California, first in Beverly Glen in west Los Angeles and then eventually in Big Sur, where he moved in 1944. He found in California a community of friends: the librarian at UCLA, Lawrence Clark Powell, whom Miller had met in Dijon ten years earlier, the painter Jean Varda, Emil White, George Leite, Bern Porter, and others.

In the summer of 1943 Miller read Rimbaud's *A Season in Hell*. He had first heard of Rimbaud when he was thirty-six and living in Brooklyn. Six or seven years later, at Anaïs Nin's house outside of Paris, he looked at the texts of Rimbaud, but not too attentively. At Beverly Glen he began reading about Rimbaud and was struck in his first contact with the poet's biography by the many parallels between Rimbaud's life and his own. He has carefully explained that the original of his study of Rimbaud, *The Time of Assassins* (1956), came from his dissatisfaction with an attempt to translate the book into English. This detailed study of French words brought him into the closest possible contact with a text that stimulated and held him more firmly than any other single text. Every line of Rimbaud seemed to awaken in him echoes and reminiscences of his own life and his own thoughts. As Baudelaire found in Poe, so Miller found in Rimbaud confirmation and emotions and illuminations.

He began writing out phrases from Rimbaud on the walls of rooms where he lived. Thanks to the study of Rimbaud, the word *poet* took on a fuller meaning, as representing the man who dwells in the spirit and the imagination. He saw the poet Arthur Rimbaud also as the pariah, as the anomaly, as the symbol of the disruptive forces now making themselves felt in the world. In Rimbaud, Miller rediscovered his own plight in the world. He acknowledged that the French poet heads the list of those rebels and failures he loved and identified with. The very life of the rebel-failure is the proving ground of the spirit. In no other writer had Miller seen himself so clearly as in Rimbaud. Despite the difficulties of a language he never totally mastered, Miller claimed that Rimbaud articulated nothing that was alien to him.

Frequently in writing of Rimbaud, Miller returned to the letters Rimbaud wrote to his mother and sister when he was traveling at a great distance from his native Charleville and seeking some form of employment. A genius such as Rimbaud looking for employment was for Miller the saddest thought in the world. Miller called

the poet's voyages through various countries of Europe and through Ethiopia and Arabia Rimbaud's "*tour du monde . . . on an empty stomach.*" And he pointed out the "sheer dementia" that voyage must represent to most Frenchmen cultivating their gardens. Every time he picked up Rimbaud's book, or every time he reread the haunting passages he copied out on the walls, Miller was touched by the poet's purity. The future belongs to the poet, he believed, as once the future belonged to Christ's acceptance of the cross, or to Joan of Arc's mission. Miller also wrote that the Rimbaud type would replace the Hamlet and the Faust type.

As prophet and mystic for Miller, Rimbaud was the poet exalting the created universe where everything is a sign. Miller found in Rimbaud that paradox or paradoxes which both distressed and inflamed him: *le maudit*, the poet cursed by his world because he was angelic, the innocent walking in the midst of the world's corruption. Of all the arts, poetry is the one in which the power of man's spirit is best measured. This is exactly the confirmation that Miller discovered on the pages of Rimbaud in the passages that seemed to him pure, autonomous, liberated from all traces of vulgarity and compromise.

In the fall of 1944 Miller visited Wallace Fowlie at Yale, talked with groups of students, exhibited some of his watercolors, and courted a young graduate student in philosophy, Janina Martha Lepska, whom he married in December in Boulder, Colorado. Life at Big Sur was not easy for them, and the early happiness in their marriage soon faded. A daughter was born in November 1945 and given Miller's middle name: Valentine.

The years between 1945 and 1949 were troubled by personal tensions. The New Directions editions of Miller's books were selling poorly. In Paris the accumulation of royalties had reached forty thousand dollars, but postwar regulations forbade the exportation of such a sum. Miller's success in France had brought him fame there, and in America he was receiving attention from such critics as Edmund Wilson, Frederick Hoffman, Philip Rahv, and John Cowper Powys.

Those years at Big Sur prior to 1950 are best described by Miller in his book *Big Sur and the Oranges of Hieronymus Bosch* (1957). To the real oranges of California he preferred the ones painted by Bosch in his famed *Millennium*. Big Sur had become almost an artists' colony with Henry Miller as its leading prophet. Many pages

Henry Miller, 1962, during preparations for the obscenity hearings for Tropic of Cancer *(Edward P. Schwartz)*

of the book are purely autobiographical: accounts of Miller at home with Lepska Miller and their children (a son, Tony, was born in August 1948) and the many visitors who made their way to Big Sur to see its prophet. A passage of one hundred pages in the book, called "Paradise Lost," concerns Conrad Moricand, the astrologer-writer whom Miller had known in Paris and who made a haven for himself in Miller's home in Big Sur. His presence there plunged the family into great discomfort. Miller in fact recognized Moricand as the Devil Incarnate type. Despite the Moricand episode, the book is an account of a utopian colony, and the message that Miller was preaching in it was soon to be known as "togetherness."

By late 1949 Miller completed *Plexus*, the second of three volumes of *The Rosy Crucifixion*. Rather than continuing with the third, *Nexus*, he wrote a history of his readings, *The Books in My Life* (1952), a suggestion made to him by Lawrence Clark Powell. By this time Powell had founded the Henry Miller Archives in the UCLA Special Collections Library.

When Lepska Miller finally left Miller in July 1951, he tried for a while to take care of Val and Tony and to continue alone with his work.

This became too difficult for him, and he asked Lepska Miller to take the children. In March 1952 he met Eve McClure, a beautiful young woman who was to become his fourth wife. She lived with him in Big Sur where she made it possible for Miller to have Val and Tony with him often. There were three happy years then which included a return to Europe with Eve (in 1952 for seven months). There he saw old friends and admirers: Maurice Nadeau, Georges Belmont, Brassai, the actor Michel Simon, and Joseph and Caroline Delteil. By August 1953 Henry and Eve Miller were back in Big Sur, which seemed to them the real paradise.

The publication in 1957 of *Big Sur and the Oranges of Hieronymus Bosch* encouraged more pilgrims than ever to call on Miller. They saw him now as a kind of guru and often made impossible demands. An important recognition came to him in 1958 when he was made a member of the National Institute of Arts and Letters.

In 1959 Barney Rosset, the owner of Grove Press, was about to publish D. H. Lawrence's *Lady Chatterley's Lover* and preparing to fight through the courts for the freedom to sell it. He met Henry Miller that summer in Paris and, with

Maurice Girodias, urged him to give Grove Press the American rights to publish *Tropic of Cancer* and *Tropic of Capricorn*. At first Miller hesitated for personal reasons and for fear of excessive publicity. He was having serious trouble with his hip, which was to result in a series of operations beginning in 1960. His marriage with Eve Miller was deteriorating, and there were financial problems because of alimony.

Miller finally did sign contracts with Grove Press, and on 24 June 1961 *Tropic of Cancer* was published in the United States and soon was on sale in every bookstore in New York City. It quickly became a best-selling book. In one year one hundred thousand hardbound copies were sold, and over a million paperback copies. Bradley Smith in Los Angeles was arrested for selling the book. He was convicted and litigation began. Many American writers signed a statement supporting Miller and condemning censorship. Among these signers were Saul Bellow, John Dos Passos, Lillian Hellman, Alfred Kazin, Norman Mailer, Bernard Malamud, William Styron, Robert Penn Warren, and Edmund Wilson. During the first year after the publication of *Tropic of Cancer*, Grove Press fought sixty cases and spent over one hundred thousand dollars in legal fees. Miller finally wrote an open letter to the U.S. Supreme Court. This letter unquestionably helped him win his case.

After his divorce from Eve Miller in April 1961 Miller moved about often during the rest of that year and during 1962. He was anxious to be as close as possible to his children and, largely for their sake, moved into a large house on Ocampo Drive in Pacific Palisades in February 1963. Lepska Miller and the two children joined him there. He was happy with this situation, despite the ever-increasing harassments in his life: requests to publish new editions of his books, permissions to translate his books, film adaptations (an extremely poor film was made of *Tropic of Cancer* in 1969), radio productions, and tedious meetings with lawyers and tax accountants.

Val was married in 1964, and Lepska Miller remarried and moved out of the house on Ocampo Drive. Tony returned home from a military academy he had been attending. When Val and her husband moved in with Miller, he enjoyed a brief period of contentment, save for worry over *Sexus*. Its publication in Paris had caused considerable turmoil, and Maurice Girodias was sentenced to a year in prison. When in 1965 Grove Press published in America *The*

Rosy Crucifixion (composed of *Sexus*, *Nexus*, *Plexus*), there was little opposition.

In September 1967 Miller married a Japanese jazz singer, Hiroko Tokuda, called Hoki, forty years younger than himself; but after two years of marriage, Hoki left the house in Pacific Palisades. Miller, close to eighty, was feeling his age. Both painting and his favorite game of Ping-Pong had become difficult for him. Val was then living in the house at Big Sur, and Tony moved back into the Pacific Palisades house in order to take care of his father.

Despite his fame today, despite the notable success of his books throughout the world, Henry Miller still tended to think of himself as a failure, *un raté*, as he said to Georges Belmont in a television interview. In another age he would have been a gnostic or a monk, leading that kind of life in which all the contradictions of his nature would be explained and harmonized. Those friends who have perhaps understood him best–Lawrence Durrell, Anaïs Nin, Brassai, Perlès–in their praise have always spoken of the good influence he has been in the world, of his simplicity and honesty, of his ability to find himself the same man in his role of clown and angel, the same man wherever he is living: Brooklyn, Dijon, Big Sur, Paris, or Pacific Palisades. He knew suffering and upheavals in his personal life, anguish that at times brought him close to suicide, but more than most men, he was able to be at peace with himself in the midst of his conflicts.

Henry Miller was always surprised at his reputation as a writer about sex, and through the years he grew weary of the same question always asked him: "If you consider yourself a religious man, why do you write about sex as you do?" The answer is simple, and Miller repeated it on many occasions: In Western civilization Christianity has created a conflict between the body and the spirit which Miller did not feel. The facades of some of the great temples of India are covered with sculptured bodies of men and women in extremely erotic postures. For Miller they were the works of religious spirits for whom sexuality, the worship of the human body, is the way leading to God. He wrote directly about sexual adventures which other men conceal under the words they use. A close reading of Miller's books will show that actually he was timid in the presence of women. It is they who seduced him. We may never learn what demon inhabited Henry Miller, what spirit made him into the honest writer that he was. But we do know beyond any doubt that

Henry Miller playing Ping-Pong (Robert Fink)

he remained totally faithful to his demon. He was incorruptible. He could not be bought by fame or money. He was more honest than most intellectuals. He had the integrity of a primitive living in a decadent world. He was not an exile from that world but he was its critic. He should be compared not so much to Rabelais, as many critics have done, but to Saint Francis. *Black Spring* is our contemporary "Hymn to the Sun."

Letters:

Lawrence Durrell/Henry Miller: A Private Correspondence, edited by George Wickes (New York: Dutton, 1963).
An incomplete and heavily edited compilation selected from the voluminous correspondence of Miller and Durrell between 1935 and 1959; both writers objected to the project.

Writer and Critic: A Correspondence with Henry Miller, edited by William A. Gordon (Baton Rouge: Louisiana State University Press, 1967).

Reprints the correspondence between Miller and Gordon concerning Gordon's book *The Mind and Art of Henry Miller;* these fifteen letters trace Miller's reactions to and comments on the book and Gordon's compromises.

Collector's Quest: The Correspondence of Henry Miller and J. Rives Childs, 1947-1965 (Charlottesville: University Press of Virginia, 1968).
Traces the relationship, from 1947 to 1965, between Miller and bibliophile J. Rives Childs; an interesting account of an epistolary friendship that thrived for nearly fifteen years before the two men met in 1961; includes a listing of works by Miller and selected criticism.

Letters of Henry Miller and Wallace Fowlie, 1943-1972, edited by Wallace Fowlie (New York: Grove, 1975).
A remarkable chronicle of the warm personal and literary friendship that grew out of the two men's admiration for one

another's writings; provides interesting glimpses into Miller's personal life as well as his ideas about life and literature.

Henry Miller: Years of Trial and Triumph, 1962-1964: The Correspondence of Henry Miller and Elmer Gertz, edited by Elmer Gertz and Felice F. Lewis (Carbondale & Edwardsville: Southern Illinois University Press, 1978).

Reprints the voluminous correspondence– 265 letters, notes, postcards, and telegrams– between Miller and his lawyer, Elmer Gertz, who defended *Tropic of Cancer* against charges of obscenity.

A Literate Passion: Letters of Anaïs Nin and Henry Miller, edited by Gunther Stuhlmann (San Diego, New York & London: Harcourt Brace Jovanovich, 1987).

Chronicles the lifelong closeness between Miller and Nin–their failed romance and temporary estrangement, their ultimately enduring friendship, and their literary interdependence upon one another; presents intimate correspondence written between 1932 and 1953. Supercedes Stuhlmann's *Henry Miller's Letters to Anaïs Nin*, 1965.

Interview:

Robert Snyder, *This Is Henry Miller from Brooklyn: Conversations with the Author* (Los Angeles: Nash, 1974).

A copiously illustrated miscellany of letters, interviews, memoirs, and excerpts compiled by filmmaker Robert Snyder in connection with the making of his documentary *The Henry Miller Odyssey*.

Bibliographies:

Thomas H. Moore, *Bibliography of Henry Miller* (Minneapolis: Henry Miller Literary Society, 1961).

Contains listings of primary and secondary materials up to 1961; useful but dated.

Lawrence J. Shifreen, *Henry Miller: A Bibliography of Secondary Sources* (Metuchen, N.J. & London: Scarecrow, 1979).

Annotated listing of materials about Miller.

Biographies:

Alfred Perlès, *My Friend Henry Miller: An Intimate Biography* (London: Spearman, 1955).

This subjective and illuminating anecdotal account, described by Miller as "this droll piece of non-fiction," covers the writer's life from his residence in Paris in the 1930s to the mid 1950s in Big Sur, California.

Annette Kar Baxter, *Henry Miller, Expatriate* (Pittsburgh: University of Pittsburgh Press, 1961).

Approaches Miller as a writer in exile and discusses his alienation from and initial rejection by his compatriots, his affinity for Paris, and the theme of "America the Unbeautiful" in his works.

Jay Martin, *Always Merry and Bright: The Life of Henry Miller* (Santa Barbara, Cal.: Capra, 1978).

The most complete biography of Miller to date; Martin is particularly good at explaining Miller's relationships with women: especially his second wife, June, and Anaïs Nin.

J. D. Brown, *Henry Miller* (New York: Ungar, 1986).

Sees Miller as a literary pioneer and "desperado," but primarily as a master of the autobiographical form, using fictional strategies, surrealism, and black humor to fuse art and life.

Kathleen Winslow, *Henry Miller: Full of Life* (Los Angeles: Jeremy P. Tarcher, 1986).

Intimate memoir of Miller by a friend who knew him for forty years; reconstructs his boyhood in Brooklyn, his Paris years, his move to Big Sur, and the establishment of the Chicago art gallery and bookstore M, THE STUDIO FOR HENRY MILLER; especially good on Miller in Chicago.

References:

Wallace Fowlie, *Aubade: A Teacher's Notebook* (Durham, N.C.: Duke University Press, 1983).

Described by Fowlie as "a reconstruction of events and thoughts that have framed me"– provides useful insights into Fowlie's three-decade correspondence with Miller.

Maurice Girodias, *The Frog Prince: An Autobiography* (New York: Crown Publishers, 1980).

Girodias, co-founder of Editions du Chêne, was well acquainted with Miller, Nin, and

Durrell; an interesting account of their years in Paris.

William A. Gordon, *The Mind and Art of Henry Miller* (Baton Rouge: Louisiana State University Press, 1967).
Sees Miller as a writer in the Romantic tradition of Keats, Wordsworth, and Coleridge, whose true subjects are the complexity of the human mind and the individual's quest for self-discovery; defends his works against charges of dullness and gratuitous obscenity; and explores his use of the psychological theories of Freud, Jung, and Otto Rank.

Ihab Habib Hassan, *The Literature of Silence: Henry Miller and Samuel Beckett* (New York: Knopf, 1967).
Discusses Miller's outrage toward and revolt against human civilization in general and American culture in particular, his obscenity, his role as prophet, his use of the theme of death and resurrection of the ego, and his comic vision.

Jack Kahane, *Memoirs of a Booklegger* (London: Joseph, 1939).
Wondrous account of the life and controversy of Obelisk Press publisher who was responsible for bringing *Tropic of Cancer* to the firm; documents problems with the censorship and exportation of English-language "avant-garde" publications in the early twentieth century.

Edward B. Mitchell, ed., *Henry Miller: Three Decades of Criticism* (New York: New York University Press, 1971).
Presents selected criticism of Miller's works from the 1940s through the 1960s; includes essays by George Orwell, Aldous Huxley, Wallace Fowlie, Karl Shapiro, Frank Kermode, and William Gordon.

Bern Porter, ed., *The Happy Rock: A Book About Henry Miller* (Berkeley, Cal.: Porter, 1945).

A collection presenting a critical overview of the first decade of Miller's career; contains essays by Lawrence Durrell, Alfred Perlès, William Carlos Williams, Wallace Fowlie, and others, as well as several short pieces by Miller.

George Wickes, *Americans in Paris* (Garden City, N.Y.: Doubleday, 1969), pp. 234-276.
Discusses Miller's reasons for leaving the United States, his life in Paris, his friendships with Anaïs Nin and Alfred Perlès, and his climb to success.

Wickes, ed., *Henry Miller and the Critics* (Carbondale: Southern Illinois University Press, 1963).
Collects essays on Miller's life in Paris, his return to America, and the censorship of *Tropic of Cancer;* includes writings by Blaise Cendrars, George Orwell, Lawrence Durrell, Kenneth Rexroth, Aldous Huxley, and others, statements by Miller, and transcripts from the *Tropic of Cancer* obscenity hearings.

Kingsley Widmer, *Henry Miller* (New York: Twayne, 1963).
Sees Miller as a minor writer and as a "comic buffoon" whose grotesque humor dilutes the gravity of his apocalyptic vision.

Papers:
The Henry Miller Archives at the Library of the University of California, Los Angeles, is the major repository of the author's manuscripts, letters, photographs, and publications. Other important manuscript and correspondence holdings are at the Humanities Research Center Library, University of Texas; Randolph-Macon College; the Barrett Collection, University of Virginia; the Library of Congress; the Brooklyn Public Library; Columbia University; Dartmouth College; Southern Illinois University; Harvard University; Princeton University; and the New York Public Library.

Marianne Moore

This entry was updated by Elizabeth Phillips (Wake Forest University) from her entry in
DLB 45, American Poets, 1880-1945, First Series.

Places	Bryn Mawr College	New York City	Pennsylvania
Influences and Relationships	William Blake Elizabeth Bishop Ezra Pound	Leonardo da Vinci Henry James T. S. Eliot	Pablo Picasso William Carlos Williams
Literary Movements and Forms	Modernism The Verbal Collage	Imagism The Fable	Metaphysical Poetry
Major Themes	Ethics: Justice and *Caritas* (Charity) The Mind's Response to the Life of Things	The Influence of the Past on the Present Relationship between Science and Art Biology	Science vs. Christian Myth Natural History Human History War
Cultural and Artistic Influences	Presbyterianism Cubism	The Bible (Old Testament) Linguistics	Darwinian Theory of Evolution Christian Hymns
Social and Economic Influences	The Great Depression World War II	Racism The Cold War	Ecological Issues

BIRTH: Kirkwood, Missouri, 15 November 1887, to John Milton and Mary Warner Moore.

EDUCATION: A.B., Bryn Mawr College, 1909; diploma, Carlisle Commercial College, 1910.

AWARDS AND HONORS: *Dial* award, 1924; Levinson Prize (*Poetry* magazine), 1933; Earnest Hartsook Memorial Prize, 1935; Shelley Memorial Award, 1941; Contemporary Poetry Patrons' Prize, 1944; Harriet Monroe Poetry Award, 1944; Guggenheim Fellowship, 1945; American Academy of Arts and Letters and National Institute of Arts and Letters Award in Literature, 1946; elected to the National Institute of Arts and Letters, 1947; Litt.D., Wilson College, 1949; Litt.D., Mount Holyoke College, 1950; L.H.D., Smith College, 1950; Litt.D., University of Rochester, 1951; Litt.D., Dickinson College, 1952; Pulitzer Prize for *Collected Poems*, 1952; National Book Award for *Collected Poems*, 1952; Youth Oscar (Brooklyn's Youth United for a Better Tomorrow), 1952; Bollingen Prize in Poetry, 1953; M. Carey Thomas Award (Bryn Mawr College), 1953; Gold Medal (National Institute of Arts and Letters), 1953; "One of Six Most Successful Women of Year" (*Woman's Home Companion*), 1953; elected to the American Academy of Arts and Letters, 1955; Litt.D., Rutgers University, 1955; L.H.D., Pratt Institute, 1958; Boston Arts Festival Poetry Award, 1958; Gold Medal (Poetry Society of America's Gold Medal), 1960; Brandeis University Creative Arts medal, 1963; Academy of American Poets Fellowship, 1965; MacDowell Medal, 1967; Gold Medal for Distinguished Achievement (Poetry Society of America), 1967; Litt.D., New York University, 1967; *Croix de Chevalier des Arts et Lettres*, 1968; National Medal for Literature, 1968; Litt.D., St. John's University, 1968; Litt.D., Princeton University, 1968; "Senior Citizen of the Year" (New York Governor's Conference on the Aging), 1969; Litt.D., Harvard University, 1969.

DEATH: New York, New York, 5 February 1972.

BOOKS: *Poems* (London: Egoist Press, 1921);
Marriage, Manikin, no. 3 (New York: Monroe Wheeler, 1923);
Observations (New York: Dial Press, 1924; revised, 1925);
Selected Poems (New York: Macmillan, 1935; London: Faber & Faber, 1935);

The Pangolin and Other Verse (London: Brendin, 1936);
What Are Years (New York: Macmillan, 1941);
Nevertheless (New York: Macmillan, 1944);
A Face (Cummington, Mass.: Cummington Press for The New Colophon, 1949);
Collected Poems (London: Faber & Faber, 1951; New York: Macmillan, 1951);
Predilections (New York: Viking, 1955; London: Faber & Faber, 1955);
Like a Bulwark (New York: Viking, 1956; London: Faber & Faber, 1957);
Idiosyncrasy & Technique (Berkeley & Los Angeles: University of California Press, 1958);
O To Be a Dragon (New York: Viking, 1959);
A Marianne Moore Reader (New York: Viking, 1961);
The Absentee, dramatic adaptation by Moore of Maria Edgeworth's novel (New York: House of Books, 1962);
Eight Poems (New York: Museum of Modern Art, 1963);
Occasionem Cognosce (Cambridge, Mass.: Lowell House, 1963);
Puss in Boots, The Sleeping Beauty & Cinderella: A Retelling of Three Classic Fairy Tales, Based on the French of Charles Perrault (New York: Macmillan/London: Collier-Macmillan, 1963);
The Arctic Ox (London: Faber & Faber, 1964);
Poetry and Criticism (Cambridge, Mass.: Adams House & Lowell House Printers, 1965);
Dress and Kindred Subjects (New York: Ibex Press, 1965);
A Talisman (Cambridge, Mass.: Adams House & Lowell House Press, 1965);
Silence (Cambridge, Mass.: Laurence H. Scott, 1965);
Tell Me, Tell Me: Granite, Steele, and Other Topics (New York: Viking, 1966);
Tipoo's Tiger (New York: Phoenix Book Shop, 1967);
The Complete Poems of Marianne Moore (New York: Macmillan/Viking, 1967; London: Faber & Faber, 1968);
Selected Poems (London: Faber & Faber, 1969);
The Accented Syllable (New York: Albondocani Press, 1969);
Prevalent at One Time (Philadelphia: Cypher Press, 1970);
The Complete Poems of Marianne Moore, edited by Clive E. Driver (New York: Macmillan/Viking, 1981);

Marianne Moore, 1935 (photo by George Platt Lynes; by permission of the Estate of Marianne C. Moore, courtesy of the Rosenbach Museum and Library)

The Complete Prose of Marianne Moore, edited, with an introduction, by Patricia C. Willis (New York: Viking, 1986).

OTHER: Adalbert Stifter, *Rock Crystal, A Christmas Tale*, translated by Moore and Elizabeth Mayer (New York: Pantheon, 1945; revised, 1965);

The Fables of La Fontaine, translated by Moore (New York: Viking, 1954); republished as *Selected Fables of La Fontaine* (London: Faber & Faber, 1955).

Marianne Moore made a new kind of verse, yet she denied that she was a poet. She worked with words: they were her trade. What she wrote was called poetry, she said, because there was no other category in which to put it. There are, in fact, no commonly accepted terms for describing the whole of her work and few accurate tags for designating the most radical forms she perfected. The verse received attention from the avant-garde poets and critics who were her contemporaries and from the generation of poets that followed them. She also became well known, in the later years of her life, as an American eccentric

who made "good copy," but her accomplished work baffled many readers. She continues, over a decade after her death, to be more highly regarded than widely read.

Moore's vision, a word that she would have thought too grand for the singular modes of perception embodied in her work, is simultaneously aesthetic and religious. For her, as she wrote in her poem "When I Buy Pictures" (1921), art "must be 'lit with piercing glances into the life of things' [a phrase she excised from A. R. Gordon's *The Poets of the Old Testament*, 1912]; it must acknowledge the spiritual forces which have made it." For example, Glenway Wescott (*Partisan Review*, 50, no. 3 [1983]) recalled, "she voyaged to Italy, and what did she notice in the Cathedral of Saint Pantaloon, one of the physician saints, in Ravillo? That all six of the lions guarding the pulpit were equally bowlegged but that each had a different face, and that their sexes were evenly matched, three and three." The pleasure of seeing the modest work of an anonymous sculptor with whom she felt an affinity is characteristic of Moore. The artist's comic particulars or imperfections, his respect for the individuality of the beasts even though they were conventional symbols, his democratic pairing of the sexes, and the sense of harmony within which the enlivened variations are delineated–all serve the function that art, in Moore's view, ideally served: the presentation of a moment of perception that renewed one's consciousness of the communal sacrament.

There is, as yet, no biography of Moore. Early conversation notebooks, reading diaries, poetry workbooks, drawings, and a voluminous correspondence are collected but unpublished. There are on public record, however, interviews she gave, brief autobiographical essays, reminiscences of friends, and articles written about her life. While they do not provide an intimate view of a long and resilient career, gleanings from them indicate the dedication, the exuberance, and the equanimity with which she went her own way in order to write as she pleased. She might be prudent or she might take risks, but she had sufficient confidence to claim the need to be fallible; and the dynamic equilibrium she sought to create in the activities of the imagination corresponds to a strong belief in life's faulty excellence.

As a child, Marianne Moore learned much about "flawed existence" and contingencies. Her family experienced frequent changes of fortune and loss. Her mother, Mary Warner, had married John Milton Moore, an engineer and inventor, in 1885. Suffering a nervous breakdown in 1887 after the failure of a business he had set up in Newton, Massachusetts, to manufacture a smokeless furnace that he had designed, he returned with his wife and son to his family in Portsmouth, Ohio, where they had settled after the American Revolution. William Moore, his father, a river pilot and ship owner before the Civil War, sank his steamer so that it would not be taken by the Confederacy but survived the loss and was a well-to-do iron founder. John Milton Moore, however, was committed to an institution for the mentally ill and never recovered from the collapse of his career. Mary Warner Moore and their young son went to live with her father, the Reverend Dr. John Riddle Warner, pastor of the First Presbyterian Church in Kirkwood, Missouri. He had moved to the town outside St. Louis in 1867 from Gettysburg, Pennsylvania, where he had served churches during the Civil War. His wife, Jennie Craig Warner, had died three months after the Battle of Gettysburg. Mary Moore, having named her son John Warner, named her daughter in memory of her mother. Marianne Craig Moore, who was born in the house of her maternal grandfather, never knew her father. After this grandfather died in 1894 when she was seven, her mother took the children to live in Carlisle, Pennsylvania, because she had a good friend there. Living on a small inheritance, the family was often in strained circumstances, and Mary Moore took a job as a teacher of English at Metzger Institute for Girls, at which the daughter had begun preparatory work in 1896. Though the poet thought that she herself was too young for the vicissitudes in her life to have been very upsetting, she never married, and, except for the four years that she was a student at Bryn Mawr College, she lived with her mother until her death in 1947. "She advantaged me," the daughter said of her, "when she remarked under crushing disappointment, *Sursum corda:* I will rejoice evermore."

Her family also influenced Moore's literary disposition. Her paternal grandfather, William Moore, was a "bookish man" who owned a large library and during the last years of life read the *Encyclopaedia Britannica* from A through Z. He was also the brother of "Captain Bixby," the steamboat pilot under whom Samuel Clemens was an apprentice on the Mississippi River. The Reverend

Dr. Warner had a regard for "serious books," played the flageolet for his daughter to dance to when she was a child, and was remembered by his granddaughter as "a most affectionate person." Believing in the education of women and tolerance for sectarian differences, he had sent Mary Warner to study at the Mary Institute, which was endowed by T. S. Eliot's Unitarian grandfather, Dr. William Eliot, in memory of his daughter. "My mother," Marianne Moore said, "first instructed us–my brother and me–in French and music (the piano) when we were very small" and had "a passion for books." From her, the poet learned verbal decorum, impatience with imprecision, and dislike, if not avoidance, of "the wish for the deed." Describing Mary Moore's sentences as "Johnsonian in weight and balance," Elizabeth Bishop thought she could detect echoes of the poet's own style–"the lighter and wittier ironies"–in the mother's enviable, extreme precision which provided "a sort of ground base for them." Of her education as a poet, Moore wrote that the most important influence on her style was ethical, and she linked the statement with the advice of her brother, Warner, who "once said of a florid piece of description, 'Starve it down and make it run.' "

Moore, who majored in biology and histology at Bryn Mawr College, where she received an A.B. degree in 1909, told Donald Hall in a 1961 interview that she was sure laboratory studies affected her poetry: "Precision, economy of statement, logic employed to ends that are disinterested, drawing and identifying, liberate–at least have some bearing on–the imagination." She thought seriously of studying medicine.

She was interested in the Bryn Mawr literary magazine and, to her "surprise," wrote "one or two little things for it." Two, appearing in 1907, were entitled "To Come After a Sonnet" and "Under a Patched Sail." There was also, among five others printed in the next two years, a simple, old-fashioned quatrain originally titled "Progress" when it was published in 1909. "They tell me, at college," Moore told Grace Schulman sixty years later, "it was the first thing I wrote," but she did not republish it till 1959, when it appeared in *O To Be a Dragon* as "I May, I Must, I Might." Moore defended it as a poem in which she deliberately broke up a cadence that was also continuous:

> If you tell me why the fen
> appears impassible, I then

will tell you why I think that I
can get across it if I try.

"There," she said, "everything comes in straight order, just as if I had not thought it before, and were talking to you. Unrestrained and natural." She added, "Well, that's an extreme example, too. I don't do that well. I'd *like* to."

The verse is hardly notable, but the comments Moore made about it suggest that she discovered for herself the effect of the run-on line and a colloquial manner. As a college student, she had been, she once remarked, "too immature" for English. She liked to tell that she could elect nothing but courses in biology: "the professors in that department were very humane and also exacting, detailed and pertinacious"; they "made biology and its toil, a pleasure and like poetry 'a quest.'" Moore did "fairly well" in Latin but twice failed the Italian course she had taken so that she could read Dante in the original; she chose a class in torts with a visiting law professor because "he was compassion itself" and praised another professor who created "an appetite for philosophy and dialectic." The work she remembered appreciating in English was "imitative writing" based on prose texts by Bishop Lancelot Andrewes, Francis Bacon, Jeremy Taylor, John Milton, and others. "People say, 'How terrible.' It wasn't at all, the very thing for me," Moore insisted. "I was really fond of those sermons and the antique sentence structure."

Equally significant, perhaps, was the fact that the course was taught by Georgiana Goddard King, a lecturer in comparative literature and the history of art, an acquaintance of Gertrude Stein's since the 1890s, and, as Laurence Stapleton observes, "one of the first art historians in America to recognize the importance of Picasso and other modern French painters" as well as the original work being done by Alfred Stieglitz, the New York photographer. Alerted to the controversially "new" developments in literature and art, the young Marianne Moore was as receptive to them as she was to the "antique" structures and sermonics she imitated in the "terrible" writing course. She once said during those years that she would like to be a painter: "I believe I was more interested in painting than poetry." Because she could visualize scenes and enjoyed stories, she also liked fiction: "And–this sounds rather pathetic and bizarre–I think my verse is perhaps the next best thing to it." All of these

predilections were seminal in Moore's finding her own voice and topics for a kind of poem of which no one had seen the like before. "I May, I Must, I Might" (or "Progress") certainly does not foretell it.

"Moore's work," as Bonnie Costello has pointed out, "does not conform to a strict chronological development." Each book she brought out not only published or republished earlier poems, sometimes reworked, sometimes resurrected in a revised form from her very early output (as with "I May, I Must, I Might"), but also included a variety of poems in very different styles and on very different themes. In her books she assembled her verse in groups that represent a variety of modes from different periods regardless of chronology of composition. "The past," she states in the title of a poem published in 1917, "is the present," and, for her, poetry, like science, was "never finished." She was not averse to changing her mind.

The Complete Poems of Marianne Moore, published in 1981, sixty years after her first book, *Poems,* in 1921, is appropriately both definitive and incomplete. The volume includes 125 poems that Moore chose from eleven books and uncollected work, translations of four of the *Fables of La Fontaine,* snippets she appended as notes from her heterogeneous learning, and authorized corrections of the first *Complete Poems* (1967). Containing all the verse she "wished to preserve" and conforming "as closely as possible to the author's final intentions," the posthumously published text does not satisfy the scholar's need for a variorum edition. Since Moore continued throughout her life to amend, to cull out, to pare down, and to "perfect" the work according to rules or whims of her own, however, the revised edition is representative of her habits and, in that sense, canonical.

The poet's development is a matter of current debate. Is the work a record of an advancement that was relatively steady over a period of more than fifty years, or was there a high mark with the publication of *Observations* in 1924 and *Selected Poems* in 1935, followed by a decline during the later decades? On the basis of the publication history of individual poems–many of which are excluded from her canon–it is possible to say that the earliest verse has the look of makeshift, not because of indifference but because of an urgent need to use one's frugal resources. Moore was like a girl learning to sew; if the garment was rather plain and not altogether comparable to

Marianne Moore at Bryn Mawr College, May Day 1906 (by permission of the Estate of Marianne C. Moore, courtesy of the Rosenbach Museum and Library)

the work of a modiste, it was lovingly made at home and would suffice for lack of anything better. At least she made it herself, and that was a pleasure. With diligence she would become more expert. Moore's "authority with language," as Jean Garrigue said, was "gained by an insistent kind of self-schooling." When a few early poems began to look less and less homemade, she attempted more intricate and complex work which she almost never botched. The successes also extend beyond the early *Observations* or the great middle period; and while there are fewer major poems after the *Collected Poems* of 1951, a small number of the last ones are as fine as anything she ever wrote. She once said that her progress was jerky.

Upon graduating from Bryn Mawr, Moore took a business course at Carlisle Commercial College in 1909-1910, went with her mother for the first time to England and Paris in the summer of 1911, and thereafter taught typing, stenography,

bookkeeping, commercial law, and commercial English, fixed the typewriters, and coached the boys in field sports at the United States Industrial Indian School in Carlisle. Continuing to write, she contributed ten poems to the Bryn Mawr alumnae magazine during the years 1910-1915. Then she burst onto the literary scene.

Two poems, "To the Soul of Military Progress" (later titled "To Military Progress") and "To a Man Working His Way Through a Crowd," appeared in the April 1915 issue of the *Egoist,* the London magazine which was then serializing James Joyce's *A Portrait of the Artist as a Young Man* (1916). During the same year, the *Egoist* published five additional poems; *Others,* edited in New York by Alfred Kreymborg, included five of Moore's poems in its December issue (in which there was also work by Man Ray and Carl Sandburg); and *Poetry,* in Chicago, printed four poems. The next year saw the publication of fifteen additional pieces. Twelve of these thirty-one poems survived Moore's sifting of her work over the years. As she wrote awkwardly in "To a Man Working His Way Through a Crowd," a poem in praise of the lynx eye of Gordon Craig, critic and revolutionary theorist of theatrical design, "The most propulsive thing you say,/Is that one need not know the way,/To be arriving."

The 1915-1916 poems are a disparate lot, but they set Moore's directions. Some of the titles suggest a determined originality: "In This Age of Hard Trying, Nonchalance is Good and," "That Harp You Played So Well," "Holes Bored by Scissors in a Work Bag," "In 'Designing a Cloak to Cloak His Designs,' You Wrested from Oblivion, a Coat of Immortality for Your Own Use," or "To Be Liked by You Would Be a Calamity." Several of the poems are addressed to writers: William Blake, Robert Browning, George Bernard Shaw, George Moore, Benjamin Disraeli, and William Butler Yeats (on Tagore)–with whom she had imaginary conversations as if her opinion mattered. "Counseil to a Bachelor [*sic*]" is Moore's first *verse trouvé,* an Elizabethan trencher motto (with her own title and a slight change), anticipating her use of lines from either unlikely or familiar sources in verbal collages to follow. " 'He wrote the History Book' " is an amusing play on the word *the* in a child's remark about the importance of his professorial father. Among the poems are also the earliest of what Helen Vendler calls portraits of "self-incriminating fools": "a moribund politician" in "To Statecraft Embalmed"; the obtuse and destructive critic in

"To a Steam Roller"; and the wooden obstructionist to learning in "The Pedantic Literalist." Vendler says the "deadly anatomies, so impossible in well-bred life, are unsparingly uttered in print," and Moore's "annihilating metaphors" remind her of "the aggression of the silent, well-brought-up girl who thinks up mute rejoinders during every parlor conversation." Although Moore is stringent on the subject of poetry vis-à-vis conscious and unconscious fastidiousness, determination, ambition, and understanding in "Critics and Connoisseurs," the observations are becoming more tempered and speculative. An easy confluence of images and commentary, fine distinctions, and subtle discriminations moves the poem beyond the acerbic tones of the other satirical sketches into a new freedom and openness.

Two additional early poems serve as examples of Moore's later willingness to return to old work she was not satisfied with and to salvage it when she found what seemed right for it. The humorous title "You Are Like the Realistic Product of an Idealistic Search for Gold at the End of the Rainbow" (1916) was sacrificed for the simple "To a Chameleon" when the poem appeared in *Observations* (1924); "Sun" (1916) was changed to "Fear Is Hope" in *Observations,* but that title became the epigraph when the poem was revised and republished as "Sun" in *A Marianne Moore Reader* (1961). "To a Chameleon" is appropriately printed as a calligram in *O To Be a Dragon;* and though it was written early, "Sun" is the concluding poem for *Tell Me, Tell Me* (1966). These two poems are not only examples of the fact that neither text nor chronology was immutable to her but also are significant in tracing Moore's orientations. "To a Chameleon" is her first description of a living animal observed in its own right. The visual sensation, the light and color of this resilient creature, twined "round the pruned and polished stem" of a grapevine, may have symbolic import, but it is the literal and factual that receive primary attention. "Sun" is a magnificent poem celebrating the "multiplied flames" of the resurrected Christ, and the splendid image of light-on-light partakes more irreducibly of the realities of Christian faith than of the phenomenal world. Whatever changes, returns, or advances one can chronicle in Moore's writing, she remained alert to both the natural and spiritual realms of being throughout her life.

The first appearance of Moore's work in little magazines coincided with other important events in her career. Warner Moore had com-

pleted studies at Yale Divinity School, had been ordained as a Presbyterian minister, and was appointed the pastor of Ogden Memorial Church in Chatham, New Jersey, where his sister and mother—"two chameleons"—joined him as housekeepers in 1916. The next year, after his training as a reserve officer, he joined the navy and went immediately on a convoy duty. He also became engaged to be married. Marianne Moore, who had gone on a five-day visit to New York in the winter of 1915 and made other visits to the city during the stay in Chatham, moved with her mother in 1918 to a basement apartment at St. Luke's Place in Greenwich Village, where they lived until 1929. And, "trapped by fortuities" (as she phrased it), she was where she wanted to be.

She had tried earlier without success to get work on Philadelphia and Boston newspapers (though she may have been joking when she mentioned that one of them was the *Boston Evening Transcript*—whose readers the young T. S. Eliot, in a 1915 poem, had ridiculed by comparing them to "some" people "with appetites for life"). But "New York/the savage's romance," Moore would say in a 1921 poem, provided (and she borrowed a phrase from Henry James) "accessibility to experience." No matter that it was "the center of the wholesale fur trade" and "a far cry from . . . // . . . the scholastic philosophy of the wilderness." At first she worked as a secretary and private tutor in a girls' school.

Having come of age during the period of modernism when writers, following the example of European artists, were incorrigibly experimental, Moore, as she wrote later of Elizabeth Bishop, was "archaically new." She made friends with other young writers, artists, and fledgling critics who gathered at the bohemian parties she attended; she visited museums, galleries, and exhibitions; she read the *New York Times* every day, and the Bible almost every day. As different as she was from the fashionably au courant, she was encouraged by her friends' romantic but common insistence on the right to be oneself, while at the same time she was given to distrusting the self.

There were fewer poems by Marianne Moore published in the years 1917-1918, but among those she collected are four that display the energy of a young moralist whose outrage stimulated the satirical voice she had already learned to use. "My Apish Cousins" (the title had been changed to "The Monkeys" by 1935 when it appeared in *Selected Poems*) caricatures the social scene as a zoo and ends with a contrast between patronizing snobs, who pretend to understand "difficult" art, and a cat, who genuinely appreciates that it is "strict with tension, malignant/in its power over us." "Those Various Scalpels" is a scathing condemnation of a woman, dazzlingly bejeweled, "Whetted to brilliance/by the hard majesty of that sophistication which is superior to opportunity," and dressed to kill with a bundle of lances: words. An equally spectacular description, "To the Peacock of France," on the other hand, glories in the color and display, the jewelry of sense—not license—in the art of Molière, who "hated sham" and "ranted up/and down through the conventions of excess." Criticizing British condescension toward Ireland, Moore's "Sojourn in the Whale" is the wittiest of the early poems. Ireland tries to open locked doors with a sword, threads the points of needles, plants shade trees upside down, has lived with every kind of shortage, and has been compelled by hags to spin gold thread from straw. "There is a feminine temperament," "Circumscribed by a/heritage of blindness and native incompetence" that "makes her do these things," but "she will become wise," "give in," and "turn back." At least, that is what "she" (Ireland) has heard "men say." Moore writes as if she knew from experience what those men were talking about. "Sometimes," Warner Moore had told his sister, "you have to have paws and teeth and know when to use them." The early poems confirm that she took the advice. Writing, for her, was an act of intellectual self-preservation. She understood combat and rebellion. Otherwise, she would never have become a person to reckon with in modern poetry.

Of the four poems published in 1918, the only one Moore chose to include in the definitive text is "The Fish." It seems to signal a turning point in the poet's development as, in Elizabeth Bishop's words, "the world's greatest living observer" of natural phenomena. While it is like "To a Chameleon" in the nuances of its images, it is not typographically mimetic. "The Fish," however, uses line breaks and stanzaic arrangements to prevent one from darting through the description, while the visual and aural modulations in the poem emphasize the sentience of the poet's response to the seascape, in which there is continual change, and quicken the reader's awareness. The ocean is both beautiful and treacherous, a source of life as well as a place of conflict, danger, and destruction: the final image of the poem is of a "defiant edifice"—a wrecked ship that, damaged as it is, "can live/on what can not

revive/its youth. The sea grows old in it." The curious paradox of dying life within the sea, and of the sea dying within what thrives on it, is emphasized in the third and fourth lines of the poem, where a mussel "keeps/adjusting the ash-heaps"—a startling image which tells the reader that this is a world of detritus as well as of edifice. The sense of life dying (and growing) within the sea and of the sea aging (and perhaps renewing) hovers over the poem in much the same way that a theme hovers over a Picasso painting without being obviously articulated, and the poem stimulates a meditation on time that the dissolving images express. It is perhaps significant that the poem is arranged by syllable count (a device Moore often used, though—contrary to the views of some early critics—she was by no means tied to it) in a period of "free" or "cadenced" verse: she eschews the vaguely intuitive and adopts the mathematical. She is very much a formalist and is unafraid of the arbitrary. Moore was never to write a better poem. There would be others as good, but they would be different.

During the next two years, 1919-1920, she published only six poems, but four of them appear in the final volume: "In the Days of Prismatic Color," "Poetry," "England," and "Picking and Choosing." The best known of them, and perhaps of all Moore's works, is "Poetry" (first published in 1919); by 1967 she had reduced it from thirty strict syllabic lines to a truncation of the first three, thus disconcerting readers familiar with the original. The notorious opening statement, "I, too, dislike it," had been followed in the original by the comment, "there are things that are important beyond all this fiddle," and the poem had set up and then explored a dialectic in which, "Reading it [poetry] . . . with a perfect contempt for it, one discovers in/it, after all, a place for the genuine." Readers used to the earlier version lamented the loss of her memorable phrase, often cited as a figure for poetry: "imaginary gardens with real toads in them" (which she herself placed in quotation marks, although the source has not been found), and of the quotation from W. B. Yeats identifying poets as "literalists of the imagination," with which phrase the dialectical contraries in the poem found resolution. The complete earlier version is reprinted in the "Notes" to the *Complete Poems*, but Moore nevertheless came to repudiate, in the 1960s, the syllabic verse that was, after the first publication of "Poetry," the form she used most often for years. If, when she cut "Poetry" and changed verse techniques, she wished to provoke impatience among admirers, she succeeded. She became known, probably to her delight, as a virtuoso who fiddled.

Moore's humor is irrepressible and occurs at surprising moments in some of the most serious of her poems. The opening of "In the Days of Prismatic Color," for instance, talks nostalgically of pure, original clarity, "when there was no smoke and color was/fine," and (ironically, since the poem is by a woman) locates those days when "obliqueness was a variation/of the perpendicular, plain to see" (itself a humorous rather than a whimsical conceit) in the time before Eve, "when Adam was alone." The poem comically (and to some readers cryptically) says that sophistication is "principally throat," and, in attacking complexity which refuses to recognize itself as "the pestilence that it is" and which is instead "murky," the poem affirms with disciplined passion that "the initial great truths" will "be there when the wave has gone by." It is a highly serious poem, but at moments the reader laughs out loud. In "Picking and Choosing" the patient and discursive tone is at odds with the rueful and comic assertions, and underlying the poem's humor is the poet's anger and *im*patience at a habit of reading (and of literary critical discourse) which *is* perhaps "daft about meaning." It is the "familiarity with wrong meanings" that puzzles one: *"Summa diligentia . . .* Caesar crossed the Alps/on top of a *'diligence'!"* "England" praises England and several other countries, but actually is about America and "plain American which dogs and cats can read!" She knew, too, that in America real toads did not turn into Prince Charmings but Mark Twains.

Moore's first book, *Poems* (1921), was published in England. Twenty-four of her early poems had been collected and arranged without Moore's knowledge by Hilda Doolittle (H. D.), Winifred Ellerman McAlmon (Bryher), and Robert McAlmon for the Egoist Press. Among the reviews was one by Edith Sitwell, who thought the verse "strange and interesting, 'thick and uncouth,' a product of life rather than art." An unsigned review in the *London Times* said that Moore wrote "clumsy prose," had not much to say, and disguised "lack of inspiration by means of superficial unconventionality." Mark Van Doren, in the *Nation*, said she had "wedded wit" but forsaken beauty and sense.

The title and the fifty-three poems assembled for Moore's 1924 book, *Observations*, were her own choice, and the impressive variety of her

work is evident. In addition to the early verse, there are three long poems that affirm her maturity: *Marriage,* "An Octopus," and "Sea Unicorns and Land Unicorns."

Marriage, which had been published as a single work in 1923 by Monroe Wheeler, is the longest of all of Moore's experimental compositions: collagelike assemblage in free verse of divergent fragments, quotations without regard to either narrative order or contextual relations as principles of design, it exemplifies the art of quotation at its wittiest. It is a precarious contrivance. The play between the opposing voices and divers texts Moore brings to bear on the subject of marriage is appropriate to the tensions, disharmonies, and imperiled happiness of the marital state. Because the conflicting elements of the poem tend to carry on a sort of guerrilla warfare with one another, the arrangement incurs the risk of seeming impenetrably chaotic or of being arbitrary rather than unified; but the discordant words of Adam, Eve, and their descendants are reconciled by a comment on "the statesmanship/of an archaic Daniel Webster" that "persists to their simplicity of temper/as the essence of the matter: 'Liberty and union/now and forever.' " Moore leaves unstated the fact that these words, later inscribed on the statue of Webster in Central Park, only temporarily resolved the conflict between the states, whose refusal to act on a fundamental issue of human rights resulted in a Civil War that destroyed a union but emancipated a people in bondage. Comparable as an experiment to T. S. Eliot's collagelike *The Waste Land* (1922), *Marriage* is more high-spirited. It is independently indebted to Picasso and the originators of synthetic cubism in 1912-1914 for both the contiguities of the angles within the form and the general action without a center of gravity. Amused that she was "diagnosed as 'a case of arrested emotional development,' " Moore well knew that the *plaisanterie* dared misreading also in relation to the fact that she never married. Having ridiculed an experience that she later said was "the proper thing for everybody but *me,"* she later volunteered the quixotic comment that "you don't marry for practical reasons but for *im*practical reasons." These attitudes underlie the bantering tones and good humor, the high and low comedy, the wit and satire of *Marriage.* It is one of Moore's triumphs.

Writing "An Octopus" was for Moore a vital matter. Its subject is the landscape of the spectacular lofty volcano, Mount Rainier, which she identifies by the Indian name, Tacoma. The work has

On Mount Rainier, 1922: Marianne Moore is third from right with her brother, John Warner Moore, standing behind her (by permission of the Estate of Marianne C. Moore, courtesy of the Rosenbach Museum and Library)

its antecedents in the romantic ode and the traditions of the sublime: the landscape of the soul. She begins the poem with a description of the "deceptively reserved" octopus of ice lying " 'in grandeur and in mass'/beneath a sea of shifting snow-dunes." She is spurred by this sight to move to insight and returns in the end to renewed understanding of the awesome "unegoistic action of the glaciers" of Tacoma. Moore and her brother climbed on the mountain when she visited Bremerton, Washington, in 1922 and again in 1923, and a map showing the octopus pattern of its glaciers is in the collection of her papers at the Rosenbach Museum. The description of Mount Rainier as an "Icy Octopus" is borrowed from Robert Sterling Yard, author of *The National Parks Portfolio* (1916) and *The Book of National Parks* (1919). Moore's poem is most certainly not set in an "imaginary garden." The accuracy with which the poet describes what she saw on Mount Rainier makes it possible for a reader who checks guidebooks to identify the trails she took and even the heights to which she ascended: her observation is scrupulous. She creates an extraordinary visual sense of the flora and fauna, the delicate beauty, and the ecology of the park; but she is not the romantic poet looking into nature to find her own image

everywhere. She is the self-effacing and invisible observer. At one point, as if by legerdemain, she quickly directs attention from an image of a marmot, "the victim on some slight observatory,/of 'a struggle between curiosity and caution,'/inquiring what has scared it" to a cavalcade of calico ponies instructed "to climb the mountain,/by businessmen who require for recreation/three hundred and sixty-five holidays in the year." The spotted ponies and the businessmen are the first "tame" creatures in the poem. After their appearance, she parodies the platitudes about the "advantage of invigorating pleasures," the "essentially humane" influence, and the stimulation of "moral vigor" for which the American wilderness is praised. But, she says, the laxity and excesses of the children of Adam threaten the "preserve" and its maintenance; one hears "the main peak of Mount Tacoma/ . . . damned for its sacrosanct remoteness"; "it is the love of doing hard things" that has rebuffed the public and worn them out.

Then fact takes over. The ode concludes in explosive cadences depicting an avalanche that cuts the claws of the glacier. Humanity is at the mercy of a fatal, sovereign power. The vital affirmation, through the whole poem, is that nature's sovereign power is indeed fatal, must never be forgotten or ignored, and must be *imaginatively* regarded and respected. Couched almost in the language and form of the discursive essay as well as of the romantic ode, the collagelike technique of the poem poses the absurdities and inadequacies of the language of everyday speech, of journalism, of the guidebook, and of the bureaucrat, against the sheer grandeur and delicate exactitude of a place the beauty of which "the visitor dare never fully speak at home/for fear of being stoned as an impostor." Those words are from the Department of the Interior Rules and Regulations, *The National Parks Portfolio* (1922) by the "aesthetic conservationist" Robert Sterling Yard, and the sheer variety in his language (comic in its hyperbole and in its context, a context which makes its extravagances sympathetic and insightful while at the same time accurate as a descriptive register of the park) reinforces the reader's sense of the indifferent arrogance of the state and of commerce, confronting nature, seeking to use or control it, seeking to appropriate it to its recreational or commercial ends. Affirming the essential vitality of the world of matter, "An Octopus" is one of the great twentieth-century poems of the planet earth.

Moore draws two word maps–terrestrial and celestial–in "Sea Unicorns and Land Unicorns." The natural world, real as it was for her, was not the totality of existence, and the view that rapid but pervasive changes in Western civilization deprive many people of "the sense of the wholeness of life" illuminates the poem. Within a geographic-mythographic context she deliberately chooses for developing the subject of spiritual poise, the poet brings together the emblematic unicorn (which she says amusingly she has not seen) and the lady, the exemplar of mysterious, irresistible grace, "curiously wild and gentle," by which one is qualified for the vocation of blessing the haughtiest, most elusive of beings: the unicorn is "impossible to take alive," but it can be "tamed only by a lady inoffensive like itself"–the Virgin Mary. The "unicorn 'with pavon high' "–signifying poise–is willingly submissive to a power that is the equal of its own but paradoxically superior; and the peaceful surrender of the proudhearted animal quietly dramatizes a reverence for mystery beyond human reason. The "matter" is again vital.

Had Moore written no more verse after these three major poems in *Observations*, she would have established the range and versatility of which she was capable. If she rejected the old

formalities in the poems, they are hardly prosaic but rather integrate characteristics of different types of writing in a revolutionary way. In 1924 the Dial Press awarded her two thousand dollars in recognition of "distinguished service to American letters," and Moore, who had become an assistant at the Hudson Park branch of the New York Public Library, benefited from the controversy that the award provoked among readers of new verse. The press brought out a revised printing of the book in 1925.

It contains one additional poem, "The Monkey Puzzler," which had become "The Monkey Puzzle" by the time it appeared in *Selected Poems* (1935). Moore's knowledge of biology and her interest in curios contribute the images in the verse, but it is particularly informed by the historical moment to which it belongs: the time of the Scopes trial (1925) when Americans were engaged in ugly debates over the challenges from the Darwinian theory of evolution and the origin of the species to the biblical account of the creation of man. Like the intertwined monkey-puzzle tree (of rare value to the evolutionary biologist because it is one of a family of conifers that provides a nearly unbroken record of the past), the poem is intricately articulated but has, nonetheless, "a certain proportion in the skeleton." The proportion is evident in the lighthearted attitude toward the many hindrances in the path of human efforts to apprehend the relationships between the past and the present, an appreciative acceptance of the discoveries attributable to that endeavor, and the acknowledgment of the magnitude of human unknowing. The poem's reconciliation of the conflict between scientific fact and Christian faith is ultimately simple and poignant: "but we prove, we do not explain our birth."

The ambitious modesty of these poems, beginning with "The Fish" and culminating with "The Monkey Puzzle," may be lost, as John Ashbery (*New York Times Book Review,* 26 November 1967) has pointed out, "in the welter of minutiae" that "people" some of them. Ashbery also notes an "unassuming but also rather unglamorous wisdom that flashes out between descriptions of bizarre fauna and rare artifacts" that is also evident in the work that would follow. The small detail and the monumental are held together conditionally and depend on each other; integrity does not deny the desire for either facts or the elusive truth which, as Moore put it in "An Octopus," lies "back/of what could not be clearly seen," but finds language itself to serve the need

Marianne Moore, circa 1921 (by permission of the Estate of Marianne C. Moore, courtesy of the Rosenbach Museum and Library)

Lawrence, Hart Crane, Ezra Pound, George Saintsbury, José Ortega y Gasset, Thomas Mann, Hugo von Hofmannsthal, Maxim Gorki, Paul Morand, Padraic Colum, William Carlos Williams, E. E. Cummings, Melville Crane, Paul Rosenfeld, Malcolm Cowley, and Archibald MacLeish. The artists whose work was represented were equally significant: John Marin, Charles Sheeler, Georgia O'Keefe, Max Weber, Kuniyoshi, Stuart Davis, Wyndham Lewis, *le douanier* Rousseau, Brancusi, Gaston Lachaise, Picasso, Cocteau, Seurat, Chirico, and American Indians. Moore not only scrupulously edited manuscripts and wrote editorial comments and more than a hundred "Briefer Mention" reviews but also assisted Dr. James Sibley Watson and Hildegaard Watson in the selection of the art to be included. The work was, Moore said, "a revel," even though she had to contend with the grudges and griefs of contributors. To her discredit, she rejected a section of James Joyce's *Work in Progress* (*Finnegans Wake*, 1939) but she was generally clear-sighted and prescient. The editing helped her to win her first international recognition, and, after the magazine was discontinued, she was able to support herself and her mother by writing verse and independent reviews or occasional essays.

She and her mother moved in 1929 to Brooklyn, where Warner Moore, who was stationed at the Brooklyn Naval Yard, lived with his family. Remaining there until she felt that the neighborhood was no longer safe for her, Moore returned to Manhattan in 1966; and except for brief periods of teaching at the Cummington School in Massachusetts (1942) and at Bryn Mawr (1953), she continued to work as a freelance writer until she became a semi-invalid in 1970.

In 1935, urged by friends, especially by T. S. Eliot, she brought out *Selected Poems*, for which Eliot wrote an introduction. The book is dedicated to her mother. By 1942 only 864 copies of the American edition had been sold, and in 1940 nearly 500 remainder copies were sold to Gotham Book Mart for thirty cents apiece. Yet Moore was philosophical about the book's fate. "To have had the book printed," Moore wrote at the time she learned accidentally of the sale to the Gotham Book Mart, "is the main thing, and all will be well if I can manage to produce some first rate stuff." She would say in 1958 that "Discouragement is a form of temptation."

Selected Poems includes forty-two poems from *Observations* and nine poems that had been

of coping with the problematics. Among the first critics to recognize Moore's objectives in 1925 was Yvor Winters, who wrote that their basis is "the transference of the metaphysical into physical terms." "I am," he said, "sure of her genius."

The year 1925 was pivotal for Moore, who moved from the job of charging out books at the library to that of editor of the *Dial* magazine, where she worked until it ceased publication in July 1929. She remembered later that "those were days when . . . things were opening out, not closing in." The *Dial*, which had a reputation for esotericism in "the other 'école de Paris,'" concentrated on the arts and sought to connect high culture with all aspects of national life. Critical essays by I. A. Richards, T. S. Eliot, Paul Valéry, Conrad Aiken, Kenneth Burke, and Winters aimed to define literary value, the nature of poetry, and their relation to science and civilization. Other contributors included W. B. Yeats, D. H.

published in the years 1932-1934. She later retained all of the new verse in her canon and placed the group at the beginning of *Collected Poems* (1951) and *The Complete Poems* (1967), in the same order she had established in the 1935 volume: "The Steeple-Jack," "The Hero," "The Jerboa," "Camellia Sabina," "No Swan So Fine," "The Plumet Basilisk," "The Frigate Pelican," "The Buffalo," and "Nine Nectarines" (the original title was "Nine Nectarines and Other Porcelain"). All of them are superbly realized.

"The Steeple-Jack," which has the precision of a Dürer etching and the ambience of an old-fashioned genre painting, describes "the tame excitement," the confusion brought on by a storm, and the peace after its passing on a summer day in a New England coastal town. This setting, Jean Garrigue observed, has "the gusto of a very idiomatic, very home-grown paradise, . . . the one that's found, when it is found, on earth, when 'there is nothing ambition can buy or take away.'" "The Hero," without self-importance, transcends personal likes and dislikes, fears and exigencies, that limit action: "He's not out/seeing a sight but the rock/crystal thing to see–the startling El Greco/brimming with inner light–that/covets nothing that it has let go." The understated themes of these two poems are the virtues of hope and courage.

"The Jerboa" has antecedents in the economic crisis of the 1930s and in the Roman Empire, as it is portrayed in Gibbon's *Decline and Fall of the Roman Empire* (1776-1788). The poem is divided into two unequal parts: "Too Much" and "Abundance." The first and necessarily longer part delineates the conspicuous consumption of the Pompeys, popes, pharaohs, princes, queens, and royal households. Describing their good and bad taste, it also points out the servitude of labor and of artists necessary to create the luxuries that such privilege commanded. "Abundance" ironically celebrates the free and vulnerable jerboa. But the complexities of the poem are not resolved by an obvious satirical contrast between "all those things" in "Too Much" and a minimal existence in "Abundance." The jerboa is a resourceful creature living in harmony with its surroundings. "It/honors the sand by assuming its color"; it is self-sufficient, amazingly fast, yet delicate: "it stops its gleaning/ . . . and makes fern-seed/footprints with kangaroo speed" (that "fern-seed" and the rhyme it then provides for "speed" are both characteristic and astonishing). But still, "Course//the jerboa, or/plunder its food store,/

and you will be cursed." The tone is hardly one of sanguine acceptance of threats to the life of the adaptable little animal. And when, at the end of the poem, with characteristically startling humor, Moore says, "Its leaps should be set/to the flageolet," she is not simply affirming that the jerboa should be the subject of art and the source of music, albeit a desert music, haunting, delicate and clear; she is also reaffirming what has been implicit in her description of the animal all along, that it embodies, in itself, those qualities associated (in the first section, "Too Much") with art and music; it is painterly in assuming the color of the sand; in leaping "By fifths and sevenths" it is a musician.

The strains of hunger are also clear in "Camellia Sabina," with its evocative images of food, vintage wines, exotic flowers, circus entertainment, and holiday, all real enough in juxtaposition to the surreality of hallucination and mirage or far-fetched allusions to horticulture, French cuisine, the Spanish Order of the Golden Fleece, the children's story of Tom Thumb, and Jean François Millet's well-known painting *The Gleaners*–in which peasants are stooped over to pick up the leavings of grain after the reapers. "I have been finishing a new poem about the camellia and the prune," Moore wrote on 6 February 1933. "Sounds like Will Rogers but it is serious." Rogers, who repeatedly said all he knew was just what he read in the papers, commented during the worst time of the Great Depression that the Senate had "passed a bill appropriating $15 million for food, but the House of Representatives has not approved it. They must think it would encourage hunger."

A mélange of sources and modes serves many purposes in Moore's work. Expressing both religious and aesthetic concepts, her poetry is not without political implications and social criticism. Its moral fervor, furthermore, is inseparable from her close attention to language. "To speak of 'Christ, the beggar,' is inexact," she wrote summarily of Vachel Lindsay's carelessness with words, "since it has never been said of Christ that he begged; he did without." Moore's strategy in the sonnet "No Swan So Fine" points up the difference between an imprecise and a precise use of the word *dead*. Quoting Percy Phillip, who had written in the *New York Times Magazine* (10 May 1931) that there was "No water so still as the/dead fountains of Versailles," the poet then contrasts a live swan to a fine china swan perched among "cockscomb-/tinted buttons, dahlias,/sea-urchins, and everlastings" in a rococo candelabrum, and boldly concludes with the statement "The king is dead." In counterpoint to the still water in fountains that are not dead but inactive is the dead king who commissioned their construction. The witty use of the word *fine* to describe a static art object rather than the living but mortal bird also underscores the poet's interest in the accurate use of the right word. And her use of a strict, traditional form–the sonnet–to show without telling the reader that language deserves disciplined regard and care epitomizes the adroitness with which Moore worked.

"The Buffalo" is an original and expressive poem involving the reader in a mental exercise much like that demanded by seeing a face emerge from the overlapping and contrary planes in which it is embedded in Picasso's cubist portraits of Reine Isabeau (1909), Daniel-Henry Kahnweiler (1910), or Ambroise Vollard (1910). After thirty-four lines–"little grids of visual symmetry," as Hugh Kenner called them–the water buffalo comes into focus. The poem's coherence resides in its unstated theme, for which the pretext is Gerard Manley Hopkins's "Pied Beauty" (1910), with its praise of God for "All things counter, original, spare, strange."

Moore's penchant for employing animals as a subject for art is pronounced in the decade of the 1930s. *The Pangolin and Other Verse* (1936) continues the interest. Two of the five poems in that volume, "The Pangolin" and "Bird-Witted," show how rarely she repeated herself. The pangolin is initially in the foreground of the poem that bears its name and is described for its own sake: a "model of exactness, on four legs; on hind feet plantigrade,/with certain postures of a man." Yet pangolins "are not aggressive animals," and, since man "in all his vileness"–his aggressiveness?–has never been long absent from the scene, he inevitably assumes the foreground. (The structure of the poem, rather than narrative, makes this fact apparent. William Carlos Williams said the only help Moore ever gave him in understanding her poems was to tell him she despised connectives.) Whatever similarities or differences between pangolin and man, the two creatures are not yoked together by oversimplified contrasts. They are seen through and contained in Moore's comic vision, which has room for grace in its devotion to incongruities and absurdities. The poem, indeed, is a meditation on grace: the pangolin ("mechanicked") has "the frictionless creep of a thing/made graceful by adversities, con-//versities." The

natural ease of its movements, however, is only one kind of grace, rather a cautious kind. "To explain grace requires/a curious hand," the poet comments. And Moore is nothing if not curious. Who else would choose a pangolin as the embodiment of grace in a bestiary? She considers with seeming ease the manifestations of grace in social behavior, business dealings, "the cure for sins," architecture, and sculpture, but also in the act of writing–the cogent moment: "Bedizened or stark/naked, man, the self, the being we call human, writing-/master to this world, griffons [scrawls, scribbles] a dark/'Like does not like like that is obnoxious'; and writes error/with four/r's. Among animals, *one* has a sense of humor." The poet who was so fierce when she was young has, like the pangolin, been tempered by adversities and conversities; she has learned tact; she has grace; she has humor. Not surprisingly, she concludes in "The Pangolin" that yahoo man has "power to grow." If the verse turns on whether one can think well of such an aggressive "animal," Moore prefers to give him the benefit of the doubt.

Although "The Pangolin" is one of the most relaxed and discursive of Moore's poems, "Bird-Witted" is fraught with tension and is narratively straightforward. The poet as bird-watcher writes a discordant song of innocence and experience in the face of danger from an "intellectual cautious-/ly creeping cat." The scene is a pussy willow tree where three wide-eyed, open-mouthed young mockingbirds as large as their mother wait for her to bring something that "will partially/feed one of them." Ignoramuses that they are, the fledglings make room on their twig of the tree for the cat, and their tired mother "with bayonet beak and/cruel wings" must save them. No poem that Moore ever wrote is as relentlessly clear. For all her good will and politesse, she had her nerve and she knew what it was to be imperiled.

What Are Years, dedicated to John Warner Moore, came out in 1941. The book includes four of the five poems in *The Pangolin*, of which only one hundred and twenty copies had been printed, as well as ten new poems. The first of them, "What Are Years?," is a wisdom psalm in which the poet meditates on the subjects of fallibility and strength, imprisonment, resolute doubt and mighty singing, mortality and eternity. The syllabic verse has the formality, order, and perfection of ritual; the strophic structure with its questions ("What is our innocence,/what is our guilt? All are/naked, none is safe") and affirmations ("satisfaction is a lowly/thing, how pure a thing is joy") is faithful in form to the antiphonal reading of scriptures at religious services, but the disciplined and subtle rhythms are the poet's own. The poem, she said, was partly written in 1931 and finished in 1939. "The depression attendant on moral fallibility is mitigated for me," she wrote, "by admitting that the most willed and resolute vigilance may lapse . . . ; but that failure, disgrace, and even death have now and again been redeemed into inviolateness by a sufficiently transfigured courage."

Among the other memorable poems in *What Are Years*, "He 'Digesteth Harde Yron'" continues the moral and aesthetic preoccupations, and draws on and amplifies the moral and aesthetic energies, the lines of force that began with Moore's regard for natural history. She writes about extinct birds–the roc known only from its remains and legend, the flightless moa, the great auk–and the flightless ostrich, exploited, threatened, and nearly extinct. The ostrich–a "camel-sparrow"–"was and is/a symbol of justice." The poem, like that on the emblematic jerboa, fuses observation with interpretations. Citing records ("Six hundred ostrich-brains served/at one banquet," the use of the birds' eggshells as goblets and the plumes for decorative purposes, or eight pairs of the birds harnessed to draw carts), she says the facts "dramatize a meaning/always missed by the externalist." The poem continues:

> The power of the visible
> is the invisible; as even where
> no tree of freedom grows,
> so-called brute courage knows.
> Heroism is exhausting, . . .

The revulsion apparent in her account of an endangered species joined with themes that are essentially religious and political is hardly an accident. Among the agonies the poet experienced as she witnessed the menace of totalitarianism to human freedom was the effort to exterminate the Jews of Europe. In an essay on "Feeling and Precision" (1944), Moore wrote that Jacques Maritain, the French moral philosopher, "when lecturing on scholasticism and immortality, spoke of those suffering in concentration camps, 'unseen by any star, unheard by any ear,' and the almost terrifying solicitude with which he spoke made one know that belief is stronger even than the struggle to survive. And what he said so unconsciously was poetry." Moore did not write directly about the atrocities of the holocaust, but "He

'Digesteth Harde Yron'" commends heroism for contradicting

> a greed that did not wisely spare
> the harmless solitaire
>
> or great auk in its grandeur;
> unsolicitude having swallowed up
> all giant birds but an alert gargantuan
> little-winged, magnificently speedy running-bird.
> This one remaining rebel
> is the sparrow-camel.

The parallels between birds and a people, whose concepts of justice and faith in the power of the invisible are basic in Moore's education, are unspoken in the poem, but the awareness of human suffering because of injustice, intolerance, hatred, greed, and unsolicitude is integral with the work. She had written, in a letter of 1939, of "the wrongful tyranny" of the Germans "in persecuting and being subject to Hitler." She was a student of both natural and human history.

"Rigorists," another of the poems in *What Are Years*, is a tribute to a quiet man, Seldon Jackson, general agent for the U.S. Education Bureau in Alaska, remembered for actions that prevented "the extinction/of the Eskimo." In "The Labors of Hercules," first published in the *Dial* in 1921 during a postwar period of hysteria and "know nothingism" in the United States, she had protested "age-old toadyism,/kissing the feet of the man above,/kicking the face of the man below," and impatiently asserted

> that one keeps on knowing
> "that the Negro is not brutal,
> that the Jew is not greedy,
> that the Oriental is not immoral,
> that the German is not a Hun."

In that poem she also stated a principle that motivated the judgments which are pervasive in her writing: "one detects creative power by its capacity to conquer one's detachment," and "while it may have more elasticity than logic,/it flies along in a straight line like electricity." "Light Is Speech," also in *What Are Years*, is for the French people at the time of the Nazi occupation, of the acceptance of fascism by the French radical right, and of the resistance to collaboration with the enemy. The poet's play with words–"free," "frank," "enfranchisement," "France"; "liberty," "fraternity," "generosity," "sincerity,"–*lux et veritas* which animate the poem–prove her sympathy for a people to whom she paid the compliment of light speech, that is, speech which is light in tone but enlightening.

"Virginia Britannia" is the poem for Americans in *What Are Years.* The theme, again unspoken, as Marie Borroff has said succinctly, is "E pluribus unum." Moore, Borroff says, "made her country's aspiring motto come true imaginatively in her vision of genuineness: the perceived authenticity of aspect or action that can 'unite' the deer-fur crown of the Indian chief with the coat of arms of the English colonist, and the singing of the hedge-sparrow with the affirmation of human rights in the Preamble to the Declaration of Independence." Moore did not overlook the Irish either. Having written in "The Labors of Hercules" "that we are sick of the earth,/sick of the pigsty, wild geese and wild men," Moore returned in "Spenser's Ireland," also in *What Are Years,* to "the greenest place I've never seen." It is tempting but mistaken to read the poem as autobiographical:

> a match not a marriage was made
> when my great great grandmother'd said
> with native genius for
> disunion, "Although your suitor be
> perfection, one objection
> is enough; he is not
> Irish."

The Irish, who can "play the harp backward at need," "say your trouble is their/trouble and your/joy their joy? I wish/I could believe it;/I am troubled, I'm dissatisfied, I'm Irish." No poet since Whitman has attempted to give Americans as large an overview of themselves and their relations to humankind as Moore.

Royalty slips record the sale of 1,251 copies of *What Are Years* between 1941 and 1948. The author was beginning to receive serious and praiseworthy attention in academic journals, but she was also damned (by Elizabeth Drew and John L. Sweeney) for "aristocratic quietism," for not speaking "directly to 'general humanity' "; (in the *Christian Century*) for being "a poet's poet" and "sometimes unintelligible"; or (in Clement Greenberg's words) "deficient in energy" and lacking "cultural capital." She was even said (by Randall Jarrell) to represent "a morality divorced from both religion and economics." Ruth Lechlitner (*New York Herald Tribune Books,* 23 November 1941), however, remarked on Moore's "comparatively restricted audience" and observed that her gifts "make her a major poet of our time."

Nevertheless (1944) attracted a slightly larger number of readers and went through three printings–a total of four thousand copies, a figure that probably includes all impressions of the first edition. The war poem "In Distrust of Merits" became one of Moore's most popular poems (indeed Oscar Williams called it "one of the finest poems" of World War II) and the subject of critical debate. Asked about the work in 1961, she said she thought it sincere and truthful, "a testimony–to the fact that war is intolerable, and unjust." But the poem was "haphazard." "As to form," she continued, "What has it? It is just a protest, disjointed, exclamatory. Emotion overpowered me." Yet, honestly critical as she was, she allowed the evidence against her to remain in the canon.

She also retained all of the other poems that make up *Nevertheless.* Among them, "Elephants" is a dream of peace; "A Carriage from Sweden" suggests a travel poster but is a work of deft ironies directed at that country's neutrality during World War II and its belated decision in March 1944 to receive Jewish refugees who had found sanctuary in Denmark. Toward the end of the poem Moore asks, "Sweden,/what makes . . . / . . . those who see you wish to stay?" The images throughout the poem suggest the answer: "sun-right gable-/ends due east and west, the table/ spread as for a banquet," a "Dalén/light-house, self-lit," "moated white castles," or a "bed/of white flowers densely grown in an S/meaning Sweden and stalwartness"–all signify safety and relief.

The two finest pieces in *Nevertheless* are the title poem and "The Mind Is an Enchanting Thing." In "Nevertheless," Moore looks at a strawberry "that's had a struggle" as if she were an analytical cubist. All the poem's fragmented images from hedgehog and starfish to apple seeds and "counter-curved twin/hazel nuts" (split open), from rubber plant and prickly pear leaf to grape tendril and carrots which form mandrakes or ram's horn-roots define qualities of the strawberry. Having taken it apart and looked at it from the varied angles that constitute what is known about the fruit, the plant, and its hardiness, the cubist poet evokes the world's garden and a moral universe: "What is there//like fortitude! What sap/went through that little thread/to make the cherry red!" With the red cherry, the perception not simply of unity but of an identity which runs through seemingly disparate images is complete, and the composition is whole. The

Moore's notes on lizards with a drawing of a Malay dragon, circa 1924-1930, and her 1932 drawing of a plumet basilisk. Both lizards appear in "The Plumet Basilisk," completed in late 1932 (by permission of the Estate of Marianne C. Moore, courtesy of the Rosenbach Museum and Library).

poem itself begins by focusing on seeds contained within the fruit, and proceeds–via the leaves–to the roots: the tendril of the prickly pear leaf rooting itself through two feet of air to the ground beneath is echoed in the grape tendril which ties itself in a knot made out of knots (and points the alert reader, perhaps, toward thoughts of those strawberry tendrils called runners, which take root in the ground). The delicacy of the poet's precise attention threads through the complexities of the poem as the sap delicately threads from root to branch to fruit to make the cherry, with its fragile hold upon the tree, so red. The quiet persistence which, the poem tells the reader, enables "the weak" to overcome "its menace" is one manifestation of the force which makes "the strong" overcome "itself "– and which enables the poet to write the poem, and the reader to read it. There is always in Moore's best poems this coherence which is at one with the form: the language itself acts out the theme.

In "The Mind Is an Enchanting Thing," there is a change of a single syllable between title and first line, as the verse begins:

is an enchanted thing
like the glaze on a
katydid-wing
subdivided by sun
till the nettings are legion.

"The speculative, self-correcting attempt to 'define' the mind, advanced through an imagery of light refracted from a smoothly shining yet living, active surface," M. L. Rosenthal (*The Modern Poets*, 1960) has noted, "is true Marianne Moore in both its quiet abstractness and its detailed excitement." The poem becomes, he says, "even more characteristically Moore as it advances through a series of similes ('like Gieseking playing Scarlatti,' 'like the apteryx-awl,' like 'the kiwi's rain-shawl,' 'like the gyroscope's fall') for the mind in action," and nears completion of the figurative network of qualities "through a series of metaphors that gather the intensities of its dominant conception into one last concentrated statement"–"it's/not a Herod's oath that cannot change." The poem itself might be taken as the central piece in all Moore's work: its nettings are legion, its surfaces are often brilliant, its utterances quick and to the point, and its openness to change almost as quick. In the obvious matter of how the poems look on the page, no two are exactly the same. Poetry was, to her, the art of singular forms.

There was a significant change in Moore's life and work after *Nevertheless*. The final illness and death of her eighty-five-year-old mother in 1947 was an ordeal, perhaps the greatest of many in her life, for the poet. Her grief was intense: "The thing must be admitted, I don't care for books that weren't worked on by her." When *Collected Poems* came out in 1951, the dedication was simply: "To/MARY WARNER MOORE/ 1862-1947." Among the nine new poems, there is a brief elegy, "By Disposition of Angels." It is one of the two sonnets in *The Complete Poems* and is the most lyrical verse Moore ever wrote. In a solitary meditation on death and loss and darkness, a high cold star shines steadfastly and inviolate. The star's divine fire is a ministering spirit beyond human reason or mortal grief.

Another short verse, "At Rest in the Blast," was first published in 1948 and became "Like a Bulwark," the title poem for a small volume of new poems published in 1956. Addressed to an unidentified "you," it alludes to two well-known Protestant hymns, "O God, Our Help in Ages Past" (1719) by Isaac Watts and "A Mighty Fortress is Our God" (1529) by Martin Luther. It is a poem to God, while it is the validation of a person: "Affirmed. . . . Pent. Hard pressed,/you take the blame and are inviolate." This individual is not abased but "firmed by the thrust of the blast/ till compact, like a bulwark against fate;/lead saluted,/saluted by lead?/As though flying Old Glory full mast." Full military honors–a twenty-one-gun salute, as Donald Hall put it–for a heroic person. This fusion of language from religious, military, and secular life is so vigorous that it is difficult to remember the original title was "At Rest in the Blast." Like "By Disposition of Angels," the poem has no explicit dedication; but the first title, the imagery, the new title, the life and character of Mary Warner Moore all suggest that it also expresses the poet's devotion to her. Another impressive poem in *Like a Bulwark* (1956) is "Apparition of Splendor," set in a dark wood, where the poet finds a resister, "the double-embattled thistle of jet," the porcupine. The poem might have been entitled "How To Look at a Porcupine or Anything Else": it displays Moore's capacity for enchantment, imaginative appreciation, informed intelligence, sensitivity, and keen eyes.

During the years between the publication of *Nevertheless* and the appearance of *Like a Bulwark*, Moore devoted much of her energy to translation. She and Elizabeth Mayer brought out a version of Adalbert Stifter's *Rock Crystal* ("A Christmas Tale") in 1945. *The Fables of La Fontaine* (on which Moore, doing "the whole thing over four times," spent nine years) came out in 1954. The "glacial style" of the prose for the German story was said to read like the original, but Moore's verse translation of the *Fables* was a subject of dispute among admirers of La Fontaine. Some readers, in comparing it to the original French, thought her verse had lost La Fontaine's music; others commended her success in finding an equivalent to the French in "common American speech" without having betrayed the humor, spontaneity, and intelligence of the original. The French awarded her the *Croix de Chevalier des Arts et Lettres* for the work. The only additional translating she undertook was a "retelling" of Charles Perrault's *Puss in Boots, The Sleeping Beauty & Cinderella* which appeared in 1963. The translation was well received.

In 1955 she brought out *Predilections,* twenty-two essays and reviews selected from nearly four hundred pieces that she had written over a period of four decades, beginning in 1916. The prose is critical, intelligent, penetrating; never hostile, it avoids pedantry and is never assertive. It reveals much of what she valued in life. The book begins with two essays on language ("Feeling and Precision" and "Humility, Concentration, and Gusto") and includes what Moore called "observations" on Henry James, Sir Francis Bacon, George Saintsbury, Wallace Stevens, T. S. Eliot, Ezra Pound, W. H. Auden, Louis Bogan, D. H. Lawrence, Jean Cocteau, E. E. Cummings, Anna Pavlova, and other contemporaries. Like Moore's poems, the essays—to use her own borrowing from Cicero's *Orator* and St. Augustine's analysis of Christian persuasion in *De Doctrina Christiana*—"teach, stir the mind, afford enjoyment."

Moore's zest for learning, her resoluteness, her continuing lively responses to what pleased or troubled her became a matter of public interest. She knew how to grow old without ceasing to grow. During 1955 and 1956, when she was approaching seventy, for instance, she attended poetry workshops given by W. H. Auden and Louise Bogan at the New York YMHA. Having won the triple crown of the National Book Award, the Pulitzer Prize, and Bollingen Prize in Poetry for the *Collected Poems* that appeared in 1951, Moore could well have conducted the classes herself. Instead, the doyenne of American poets, as Elizabeth Bishop recounts, "took notes constantly, asked many questions, and entered into the discussions with enthusiasm." The other students were timid and nonplussed in the presence of Moore, who said she "was learning a great deal, things she had never known before."

Because she liked the tango, she had a decade earlier taken lessons at a Brooklyn dance school. "The young dancers, male and female, may have been a little surprised," Bishop writes, "but soon they were competing with each other to dance with her"; all of them, Moore insisted, had enjoyed the experience thoroughly, and she was taught "a modified version of the tango" as well as several new steps. At seventy she learned to drive a car, although she never owned one; she thought the "policeman," who gave her the test for the license, "a little overlenient." Or, famous for liking baseball–"a game of precision" and grace under pressure–she was asked to throw out the first ball for the opening day at Yankee Stadium in 1968 and showed up in mid season of 1967 to practice. She threw "a sinking slider." Among the things she said she would have liked to have invented were "that eight-shaped stitch with which the outer leather is drawn tight on a baseball," epoxy glue, the zipper fastener, and the collapsible dustpan. She enjoyed being a writer, but, asked when she was seventy-two at what point poetry "had become world-shaking to her," she replied, "Never!"

Critics tend toward the view that as recognition of Moore's achievement increased, the quality of her verse diminished. During the years 1956-1970 she contributed forty-five poems to various magazines, principally to the *New Yorker,* but also to publications as different as *Shenandoah, Sequoia, Sports Illustrated,* the *Ladies' Home Journal, Harper's Bazaar,* the *Philadelphia Inquirer, It's Pencil Week, Art News,* the *Nation,* and the *Paris Review.* Many of the poems seem the work of a writer enjoying success and interested in reaching a wider audience. If they are not all equally impressive, they confirm the amplitude of her imagination and are not to be written off entirely. She chose thirty-five of them for the canonical text.

Some of the poems are for holidays: "Saint Nicholas" (1958), "For February 14th" (1959), and "Saint Valentine" (1960). Among those that speak to a cause, "Carnegie Hall: Rescued" (1960) is simply bad; "Rescue with Yul Brynner" (1961) is better but prosaic in its commendation of the actor's work with the United Nations Commission for Refugees ("There were thirty million; there are thirteen still–/healthy to begin with, kept waiting till they're ill"). "Combat Cultural"

(1959) is an appreciation of the performance, at the time of the cold war, of the Moiseyev Dance Company during its first successful American season–the troupe came to the United States after "the door had been shut" to artists from the U.S.S.R. for forty years. The poem is a jeu d'esprit on seeing and seeming; it is "great fun."

Tipoo's Tiger (1967), which Moore calls a ballad, is the trenchant antiwar poem she had never quite succeeded in writing earlier. Sultan Tipoo's tiger is no paper tiger but a monstrous "toy," a cruel man-eating machine, and the poem is an expression of the poet's genuine need to find effective words–symbols–for the self-defeating arrogance of the will to power, the exercise of brutal force, and the blood-dimmed tide that is loosed upon the world. It is one of her great but not one of her popular poems.

Moore's fury and indignation–which her humor, sense of decorum, and humility helped her to moderate–are reasserted in some of the late poems. "Tell Me, Tell Me" (1960) is a plea for refuge from the egocentric people who impose on the weary writer, and it is with some difficulty that she restrains her rancor. She is glad to give her approval to "W. S. Landor" (1964), "who could/throw/a man through a window,/yet 'tender toward plants,' say 'Good God, the violets!' (below)." In "Charity Overcoming Envy" (1963) the allegorical figures enact the age-old problem of the relation between justice and *caritas.* "An Expedient–Leonardo da Vinci's–and a Query" (1964) is Moore's troubled sketch of the historical personage she most admired, the artist-scientist who inaugurated a radical new style that marked the beginning of the modern imagination. Although "great wrongs were powerless to vex" him, Leonardo's dejection and his inability to say "proof refutes me" when he was in error or to take consolation from what he had accomplished perplex the poet. All of these poems, revealing the restlessness of Moore's inquisitive mind, are as good as the best of the early work and are often as significant as any of her spiritual exercises.

Several of the late poems were written for occasions or upon request. "Hometown Piece for Messrs. Alston and Reese," a poem for the Brooklyn Dodgers, appeared on the front page of the *New York Herald Tribune* during the World Series of 1956. "Enough: Jamestown, 1607-1957" was commissioned for the tercentenary of the first permanent English settlement in America. "In the Public Garden" was written for the 1958 Boston

Arts Festival, where she read the poem to a crowd of five thousand people. "To a Giraffe" was written for *Poetry in Crystal,* published by Steuben Glass in 1963. "Occasionem Cognosce" ("I've Been Thinking") was read in 1963 at Lowell House, Harvard, and first published "in honor of Elliott and Mary Perkins," who were long associated with the house. "In Lieu of the Lyre" was a response to a 1965 request for a poem from the president of the *Harvard Advocate.* "The Camperdown Elm" (1967) commemorates the need for saving the massive old tree in Prospect Park, Brooklyn.

Many of these poems tease if they do not profoundly engage the imagination, and they often experiment with rhythms or rhyme. "I don't see how anyone," Donald Hall said of "Hometown Piece for Messrs. Alston and Reese," "can fail to be delighted by this funny, happy poem. It is meant to be sung, one gathers, but I wouldn't try it." "In the Public Garden" is graver in tone and theme, but the variations on a single rhyme, which recurs forty times, beginning with "festival" and ending with "personal," suggest a prolonged pealing of bells in gratitude for artistic, intellectual, religious, and political freedom. The final version of "Occasionem Cognosce" is titled "Avec Ardeur" and inscribed to "Dear Ezra [Pound] who knows what cadence is." Moore frolics with language about language in short-lined rhymed couplets: "I'm annoyed?/Yes; am. I avoid/ 'adore'/and 'bore';/am, I/say, by/the word/(bore) bored./I refuse/to use/'divine'/to mean/something/ pleasing." The verse concludes: "Without pauses,/ the phrases/lack lyric/force, unlike/Attic/Alcaic,/or freak/calico-Greek./This is not verse/of course./ I'm sure of this;/Nothing mundane is divine;/ Nothing divine is mundane." This seriocomic tirade against the banal secularizing of the sacred is as close as Moore ever came to showing off. The poet, willing to act as counterpoet, finally succumbs to a facile pedagogic pronouncement by which she gains an equilibrium she really had not lost. It is a pleasure to see that she reveled in whimsy and allowed herself to improvise with words. She could do anything she wanted with them.

She even dared write "To Victor Hugo of My Crow Pluto" (1961) in what she called esperanto *madinusa* ("pidgin Italian") and "My Crow, Pluto–a Fantasy" (in plain American prose), which are parodies of the best-known–and most notorious–of Poe's poems, "The Raven," and his companion essay, "The Philosophy of Composition." She was, like their author, crazy about

Marianne Moore (photo by Esther Bubley; by permission of the Estate of Marianne C. Moore, courtesy of the Rosenbach Museum and Library)

words. "Dream" (1965) is a jubilant satire on "academic appointments for artists": "Bach and his family/'to Northwestern'" and "Haydn, when he had heard of Bach's billowing sail,/begged Prince Esterházy to lend him to Yale." Bach "would not leave home" without his five harpsichords, but all is arranged, and in the poet's dream "BACH PLAYS BACH!" The last verse in *The Complete Poems* (1981) is a finger exercise, "Prevalent at One Time": "I've always wanted a gig/semicircular like a fig/for a very fast horse with long tail/for one person, of course...." The pre-text is Emily Dickinson's "Because I could not stop for Death–/He kindly stopped for me–/The Carriage held but just Ourselves–/And Immortality."

James Dickey has written that, if he had to choose a poet to construct heaven "out of the things we already have," he would choose Moore. Her heaven, he said, would be "Much, most probably, like the earth as it is, but refined by responsiveness and intellect into a state very far from the present one; a state of utter consequentiality." He explained that she "spent her life in remaking– or making–our world from particulars that we

have never adequately understood on our own," but that the creative person open to experience can "endow ... with joyous conjunctions" and reach "conclusions unforeseeable until they were made."

Moore did not, however, presume to an extraordinary vision. Hers is a postlapsarian world that is, nevertheless, rich and manifold; her love of being in the world is realized in an art attentive to one's obligations toward the commonweal and mindful that "After all/consolations of the metaphysical/can be profound. In Homer, existence/is flawed; transcendence, conditional; 'the journey from sin to redemption, perpetual.'"

Despite "the obvious grandeur of Moore's chief competitors," including William Carlos Williams and Wallace Stevens, John Ashbery has said, "I am tempted to call her our greatest modern poet."

Letters:

Letters From and To The Ford Motor Company, by Moore and David Wallace (New York: Pierpont Morgan Library, 1958).

Interviews:

Donald Hall, "The Art of Poetry IV: Marianne Moore," *Paris Review*, 7 (Summer/Fall 1961): 41-66.

Hall, "An Interview with Marianne Moore," *McCall's*, 93 (December 1965): 74, 182-190.

Grace Schulman, "Conversation with Marianne Moore," *Quarterly Review of Literature*, 16 (1969): 1-2, 155-162.

Bibliographies:

Eugene P. Sheehy and Kenneth A. Lohf, *The Achievement of Marianne Moore: A Bibliography 1907-1957* (New York: New York Public Library, 1958).

Craig S. Abbott, *Marianne Moore: A Descriptive Bibliography* (Pittsburgh: University of Pittsburgh Press, 1977).

References:

Craig S. Abbott, *Marianne Moore: A Reference Guide* (Boston: G. K. Hall, 1978).
Useful, although incomplete, list and abstracts of 818 writings about Moore in newspapers, periodicals, and books from 1916 through 1976.

Elizabeth Bishop, "Efforts of Affection: A Memoir of Marianne Moore," in *The Collected*

Prose of Elizabeth Bishop, edited by Robert Giroux (New York: Farrar, Straus & Giroux, 1984), pp. 121-156.
Reminiscences of the character and personality of Bishop's mentor, friend, and fellow poet—"at her best when she made up her own rules and when they were strictest."

Louise Bogan, *A Poet's Alphabet: Reflections on the Literary Art and Vocation*, edited by Robert Phelps and Ruth Limmer (New York: McGraw-Hill, 1970), pp. 303-308.
Praises Moore's fifth book of poetry, *Nevertheless* (1944), as her best and commends the translation of *The Fables of La Fontaine* (1954).

Marie Borroff, *Language and the Poet: Verbal Artistry in Frost, Stevens, and Moore* (Chicago & London: University of Chicago Press, 1979), pp. 80-135, 174-186.
Analyzes resemblances between Moore's style and journalistic-technical prose, advertising, and photography, and relates the style to her moral vision.

Bonnie Costello, "The 'Feminine' Language of Marianne Moore," in *Women and Language in Literature and Society*, edited by Sally McConnell-Ginet, Ruth Borker, and Nelly Furman (New York: Praeger, 1980), pp. 222-238.
Discusses Moore's transformation of the "feminine" virtues—humility, affection, and reserve—into virtues of style as well as a means of vital contact between herself and her surroundings.

Costello, *Marianne Moore: Imaginary Possessions* (Cambridge & London: Harvard University Press, 1981).
Investigates Moore's consciousness of the way the creative mind shapes the world and her desire to "expand the domain of the self" but narrow the world.

Guy Davenport, "Marianne Moore," in his *The Geography of the Imagination* (San Francisco: North Point Press, 1981), pp. 114-122.
Claims that each of Moore's poems is a unique complex of experiences.

James Dickey, *Babel to Byzantium: Poets and Poetry Now* (New York: Farrar, Straus & Giroux, 1968), pp. 156-164.
Praises *A Marianne Moore Reader* (1961) and *Tell Me, Tell Me* (1966) as examples of the "unlimited number of fashions" and "unlimited number of reasons" Moore finds for loving the things of "this earth."

Bernard Engel, *Marianne Moore* (New York: Twayne, 1964).
First overview of the poet's work from the early period ending with *Selected Poems* (1935) to the middle period culminating in *Collected Poems* (1951) and *The Fables* (1954) vis-à-vis her ethical bearings, recognition of the unity of spiritual forces with appearances, and a Christian aesthetic.

Jean Garrigue, *Marianne Moore* (Minneapolis: University of Minnesota Press, 1965).
Views Moore as a poet characterized by irony, humor, rich indigenous honesty, and the wish to please herself.

Pamela White Hadas, *Marianne Moore: Poet of Affection* (Syracuse, N.Y.: Syracuse University Press, 1977).
Suggests that Moore "may be seen as a knight set upon finding the Grail," which enables the poet to speak "in the wasteland of letters."

Donald Hall, *Marianne Moore: The Cage and the Animal* (New York: Pegasus, 1970).
Argues, in an account of Moore's life and career, that the surface brilliance and technical precision of her work restrain "the dark music of feeling," the underlying emotions and the vulnerability to metaphysical dangers that inform her art.

Hugh Kenner, *A Homemade World: The American Modernist Writers* (New York: Knopf, 1975), pp. 91-118.
Emphasizes the mind's response to the visual aspect of a Moore poem—"a thing made"; also sketches the history of attitudes toward description in verse and the significance of what Moore discovered for a twentieth-century American poetic.

George W. Nitchie, *Marianne Moore: An Introduction to the Poetry* (New York & London: Columbia University Press, 1969).
Searches for principles that will explain the revision, the grouping, and the regrouping of the poems in successive stages of Moore's life.

Elizabeth Phillips, *Marianne Moore* (New York: Ungar, 1982).
Reads Moore's singular, innovative verse in the context of a turbulent age to which the poet speaks from Christian conviction for the values of the common good threatened by violent change.

Winthrop Sargeant, "Humility, Concentration, and Gusto," *New Yorker*, 32 (16 February 1957): 38-77.
Profile, based on conversations with Moore at age seventy; striking for the examples of the manner in which she integrated seemingly unconnected points clearly unified by an unstated idea.

John M. Slatin, *The Savage's Romance: The Poetry of Marianne Moore* (University Park & London: Pennsylvania State University Press, 1986).
Analyzes Moore's procedures for resolving the conflict between an "obsession with originality" and the desire to overcome it in relation to the rest of the American literary tradition.

Laurence Stapleton, *Marianne Moore, The Poet's Advance* (Princeton: Princeton University Press, 1978).
Studies—with access for the first time to Moore's workbooks, manuscripts, diaries, and correspondence at the Rosenbach Museum and Library—the sources of her originality, her experiments in verse, her emergence as a professional writer, and the full range of her achievement.

Sister Mary Therese, *Marianne Moore: A Critical Essay* (Grand Rapids, Mich.: Eerdmans, 1969).
Claims that Moore is a poet who celebrated *all* life and never deviated from the Christian perspective central to the inner structure of the poetry.

Charles Tomlinson, *Some Americans: A Personal Record* (Berkeley, Los Angeles & London: University of California Press, 1981), pp. 1-43.
Recalls a young Englishman's initial encounters with the new "unEnglish" American poets–including Marianne Moore–at mid century as well as the cordial exchanges and brief meetings with her in later years.

Tomlinson, ed., *Marianne Moore: A Collection of Critical Essays* (Englewood Cliffs, N.J.: Prentice-Hall, 1969).
Represents early and later views of Moore's poetry, as well as judgments of the La Fontaine translations and an apologia for her "idiosyncratic" prose.

Twentieth Century Literature, Marianne Moore issue, edited by Andrew J. Kappel, 30 (Summer/Fall 1984).
Includes fourteen original essays on Moore's Presbyterian faith; her relationships with Elizabeth Bishop, William Carlos Williams, E. McKnight Kauffer (a graphic artist), and Arthur Gregor (an editor at one of her publishers); working notes for "An Octopus"; syllabic verse; her fables and the influence of her translation of La Fontaine on the later poetry; her attitudes toward modern America and her modernism; a psychoanalytic paradigm for the dissociated image in the poetry; and her achievement.

Helen Vendler, *Part of Nature, Part of Us* (Cambridge & London: Harvard University Press, 1980), pp. 59-76.
Comments primarily on the poems of the young Marianne Moore and the changes the poet underwent as she lost the sense of being isolated from literary society.

A. Kingsley Weatherhead, *The Edge of the Image: Marianne Moore, William Carlos Williams, and Some Other Poets* (Seattle & London: University of Washington Press, 1967), pp. 1-95.
Explores whether Moore's use of carefully delineated, discrete images are linked by an associative process that avoids grand gestures or subordinated to an overpowering idea that risks sentimentality and loss of the integrity of the images.

William Carlos Williams, "Marianne Moore: A Novelette and Other Prose, 1921-1931," in *Selected Essays of William Carlos Williams* (New York: Random House, 1954), pp. 121-131. These brief but seminal remarks are points of references for critics' later discussion of the language, imagery, and structure of Moore's poems.

Papers:

Moore's notebooks, the bulk of her correspondence, her manuscripts, and her library are at the Museum of the Philip H. and A. S. W. Rosenbach Foundation in Philadelphia, where her Manhattan living room is also re-created.

John O'Hara

This entry was updated by Charles W. Bassett (Colby College) from his entry in
DLB 9, American Novelists, 1910-1945.

Places	Pennsylvania Anthracite Region	New York City Ivy League Colleges	Hollywood
Influences and Relationships	Ernest Hemingway F. Scott Fitzgerald	Dorothy Parker Ring Lardner	Sinclair Lewis John Steinbeck
Literary Movements and Forms	Realism and Naturalism	Epistolary Fiction Novel of Manners	The Novella Journalism
Major Themes	Dangers of Sexual Passion	Emotional Atrophy Misogyny	American Class System
Cultural and Artistic Influences	Freudian Psychology Irish-Catholic Heritage	American Social History	Popular Music and Jazz
Social and Economic Influences	Franklin D. Roosevelt's New Deal	World War II The Great Depression	Prohibition

See also the O'Hara entry in DLB: Documentary Series 2.

BIRTH: Pottsville, Pennsylvania, 31 January 1905, to Patrick Henry and Katharine Delaney O'Hara.

MARRIAGES: 28 February 1931 to Helen Ritchie Petit (divorced). 3 December 1937 to Belle Mulford Wylie (deceased); child: Wylie. 31 January 1955 to Katharine Barnes Bryan.

AWARDS AND HONORS: Donaldson Award and New York Drama Critics' Circle Award for *Pal Joey* (libretto), 1952; National Book Award for *Ten North Frederick,* 1956; Award of Merit for the Novel, American Academy of Arts and Letters, 1964.

DEATH: Princeton, New Jersey, 11 April 1970.

BOOKS: *Appointment in Samarra* (New York: Harcourt, Brace, 1934; London: Faber & Faber, 1935);
The Doctor's Son and Other Stories (New York: Harcourt, Brace, 1935);
Butterfield 8 (New York: Harcourt, Brace, 1935; London: Cresset, 1951);
Hope of Heaven (New York: Harcourt, Brace, 1938; London: Faber & Faber, 1939);
Files on Parade (New York: Harcourt, Brace, 1939);
Pal Joey (New York: Duell, Sloan & Pearce, 1940; London: Cresset, 1952);
Pipe Night (New York: Duell, Sloan & Pearce, 1945; London: Faber & Faber, 1946);
Hellbox (New York: Random House, 1947; London: Faber & Faber, 1952);
A Rage to Live (New York: Random House, 1949; London: Cresset, 1950);
The Farmers Hotel (New York: Random House, 1951; London: Cresset, 1953);
Pal Joey: The Libretto and Lyrics, libretto by O'Hara and lyrics by Lorenz Hart (New York: Random House, 1952);
Sweet and Sour (New York: Random House, 1954; London: Cresset, 1955);
Ten North Frederick (New York: Random House, 1955; London: Cresset, 1956);
A Family Party (New York: Random House, 1956; London: Cresset, 1957);
From the Terrace (New York: Random House, 1958; London: Cresset, 1959);

John O'Hara

Ourselves to Know (New York: Random House, 1960; London: Cresset, 1960);
Sermons and Soda-Water, 3 volumes–*The Girl on the Baggage Truck, Imagine Kissing Pete,* and *We're Friends Again* (New York: Random House, 1960; London: Cresset, 1961);
Five Plays (New York: Random House, 1961; London: Cresset, 1962);
Assembly (New York: Random House, 1961; London: Cresset, 1962);
The Big Laugh (New York: Random House, 1962; London: Cresset, 1962);
The Cape Cod Lighter (New York: Random House, 1962; London: Cresset, 1963);
Elizabeth Appleton (New York: Random House, 1963; London: Cresset, 1963);
The Hat on the Bed (New York: Random House, 1963; London: Cresset, 1964);
The Horse Knows the Way (New York: Random House, 1964; London: Cresset, 1965);
The Lockwood Concern (New York: Random House, 1965; London: Hodder & Stoughton, 1966);
My Turn (New York: Random House, 1966);

215

Waiting for Winter (New York: Random House, 1966; London: Hodder & Stoughton, 1967);

The Instrument (New York: Random House, 1967; London: Hodder & Stoughton, 1968);

And Other Stories (New York: Random House, 1968; London: Hodder & Stoughton, 1968);

Lovey Childs: A Philadelphian's Story (New York: Random House, 1969; London: Hodder & Stoughton, 1970);

The Ewings (New York: Random House, 1972; London, Sydney, Auckland & Toronto: Hodder & Stoughton, 1972);

The Time Element and Other Stories (New York: Random House, 1972; London, Sydney, Auckland & Toronto: Hodder & Stoughton, 1973);

A Cub Tells His Story (Iowa City: Windhover Press/ Bruccoli Clark, 1974);

Good Samaritan and Other Stories (New York: Random House, 1974; London, Sydney, Auckland & Toronto: Hodder & Stoughton, 1976);

"An Artist Is His Own Fault," edited by Matthew J. Bruccoli (Carbondale & Edwardsville: Southern Illinois University Press, 1977);

The Second Ewings (Bloomfield Hills, Mich. & Columbia, S.C.: Bruccoli Clark, 1977);

Two by O'Hara (New York & London: Harcourt Brace Jovanovich/Bruccoli Clark, 1979);

Collected Stories by John O'Hara, edited by Frank MacShane (New York: Random House, 1984).

PLAY PRODUCTION: *Pal Joey,* New York, Ethel Barrymore Theatre, 25 December 1940.

SCREENPLAYS: *Moontide,* Twentieth Century-Fox, 1942;

The Best Things in Life Are Free, screen story by O'Hara, Twentieth Century-Fox, 1956.

OTHER: *Remarks on the Novel,* tape recording of O'Hara's 1957 Gertrude Clark Whittal Lecture at the Library of Congress (Bloomfield Hills, Mich. & Columbia, S.C.: Bruccoli Clark, 1977).

John O'Hara claimed to be the hardest working author in the United States, and one of his biographers, Matthew J. Bruccoli, believes that "O'Hara published more words than any other major writer of the century." In fact, few–even

those who denigrated his achievements as an artist–disputed his status as the most popular *serious* writer of his time. In O'Hara's prime, the books appeared with metronomic regularity: novels, collections of short stories, collections of plays, collections of essays. Every Thanksgiving of the 1960s saw the publication of an O'Hara book, and five more made print without the benefit of the pre-Christmas rush to the bookstores. And despite the critics' animadversions on the quality of this burst of creative energy, almost unprecedented among major American authors, O'Hara's work sold extremely well.

The contradiction between John O'Hara's low critical reputation and his enormous popular success must be analyzed in any estimate of his accomplishment as a writer. From the appearance of his first novel, *Appointment in Samarra,* in 1934, reviewers and critics had never been easy with or on O'Hara, but their negative litany increased in intensity in the later years of O'Hara's career. In time, the semiannual skirmish between O'Hara's critical contractors and his avid audience took on the rigidity of ritual: one deplored, the other adored. Since O'Hara refused to change his style, his subject matter, and his vision, his readers were delighted, and the critics could only shake their heads over their failure to disturb a relationship that was one of the most profitable and enduring in recent American literary history.

On the other hand, O'Hara's most virulent critical abusers refused to class him with writers such as Mickey Spillane or Ian Fleming; no one called him a hack. Some even expressed grudging admiration for his stubborn dedication to his old-fashioned realist's principles, his plain style, and his scorn for fictive actions consciously echoing archetypal or mythic patterns. O'Hara's skill with dialogue, his verisimilitude, and his handling of detail impressed even his detractors. Indeed, the popularity of John O'Hara's work stands as the most obvious refutation of those literary tastemakers who anathematized as obsolete and unconvincing the methods and insights of the realist writer.

For John O'Hara was indisputably a realist-naturalist, his fiction embodying the achievements and limitations of that genre, style, and sensibility. His fiction was mimetic, its primary emphasis focused on the actuality imitated. Critic Malcolm Bradbury has called O'Hara "the best modern case of the writer as social historian," and Irving Howe concluded that "in his own stolid way [O'Hara] seems driven to the consecration to art we associate with a Flaubert or a James ... diagramming all the hidden channels of our social arrangements." O'Hara himself described his mission in a foreword to *Sermons and Soda-Water* (1960): "I want to get it all down on paper while I can.... The United States in this Century is what I know, and it is my business to write about it to the best of my ability, with the sometimes special knowledge that I have. The Twenties, the Thirties, and the Forties are already history, but I cannot be content to leave their story in the hands of the historians and the editors of picture books. I want to record the way people talked and thought and felt, and do it with complete honesty and variety."

Certainly O'Hara felt the realist's compunction to be historically accurate, but his depiction of men and women forsook political, economic, and ideological explanations of human behavior in favor of a perpetual search for reality among the class and status anxieties of a materialistic American society. O'Hara's great subject was the illusions that snobbery generates and the pathetic waste of potentially valuable American lives in the quest for respect and security. What Lionel Trilling called John O'Hara's "exacerbated social awareness" struck a responsive chord in his readers, who shared O'Hara's belief in the solidity of social forms, the symbolic value of *things,* and the awesome power of established wealth. At the same time O'Hara's failure to win acclaim from the critics stemmed from their rejection of his basic premise about the importance of society. Few critics agreed with John Brooks's statement that "Not the least of the jobs of the contemporary novelist is that of rescuing American society from the charge that it doesn't exist."

Given the basic disagreement between John O'Hara and most of the critics, the fact that his work was savaged so often is no surprise. O'Hara, however, aided his own cause little by taking a relentlessly anti-intellectual stance in his estimates of his role as writer: "I'm not some hairy philosopher. I'm just an ordinary guy who happens to write well." This disingenuousness may have been intended to confound the symbol-mongers, but O'Hara was convinced that he was not ordinary.

More usually O'Hara styled himself as a "pro," a lonely and dedicated toiler whose life was his craft. "If you're a pro you keep going; if you're not a pro, you get the hell out." A pro is sustained by "sensitivity, alertness, active intelligence, and work." He felt that his talent was "God-given" and that he owed total consecration to it: "The way I feel about writing, which is practically a religious feeling, would not permit me to 'dash off ' a story." And though he found writing one of his "natural" talents, it was not until the last two decades of his career that he developed the Trollopian sense of commitment that sent him each night to his Remington Noiseless to type until dawn.

Such puritan rigor had not distinguished John O'Hara's early life. Eldest of eight children of a prominent Pottsville physician, John spent his childhood and adolescence alternatively rebelling against the austere expectations of his hard-driving, nonsmoking, teetotaling father and striving to find his place in the social aristocracy of his conservative little native city in Pennsylvania's anthracite region. Well educated and relatively sophisticated, the O'Haras were still Irish and Roman Catholic in a town dominated by a Protestant elite. Only thirty years before John's birth, Pottsville had applauded the hanging of nine members of the Molly Maguires, the secret Irish terrorist society whose violence in support of the unionization of miners had exacerbated ethnic hatred in the coal fields.

However, Dr. O'Hara was dedicated to "going first-class," and his lucrative surgical practice furnished his family with five automobiles, a house on Pottsville's "best" street, riding and dancing lessons for the children, and membership in the country club. Still, John O'Hara early noted the homes where Irish were not welcome, the impressive chauffeur-driven Loziers of the local coal magnates, and the well-mannered contempt of the Episcopalian establishment for the communicants of St. Patrick's, the "Irish church." Though his devout mother saw to it that he served Mass and took his lessons from the nuns, O'Hara's Catholic faith declined in the face of Pottsville's elaborate social demarcations according to wealth, class, and religion. Father and son fought constantly, and John knew that he could never succeed if he allowed his father's values to define him.

Not unexpectedly, then, O'Hara's scholastic career was an unmitigated disaster. First he was "honorably dismissed" by the Jesuits at Fordham Preparatory School in New York City for poor discipline, then expelled from the college-preparatory department of the Keystone State Normal School near Pottsville for romancing a trustee's daughter. His angry father interspersed these scholastic calamities with bouts of hard

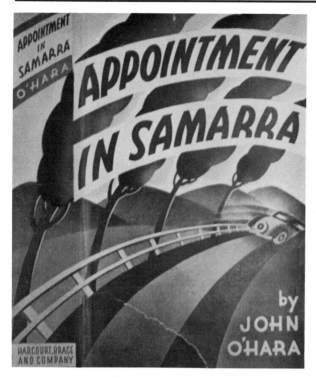

Dust jacket for O'Hara's first novel

labor, placing the fractious boy with steelworkers, locomotive greasers, and surveying crews. Finally, when he threatened to fulfill his intellectual promise as valedictorian of the class of 1924 at Niagara Preparatory School, he failed to graduate because of a drunken spree.

Still impressed by the Ivy League panache of Pottsville's Protestant aristocracy, O'Hara had hoped to matriculate at Yale in the fall of 1924. Dr. O'Hara balked, decreeing an entire year of good conduct and faithful work before John might think of New Haven. The boy began as an unsalaried cub reporter on the *Pottsville Journal*, where sporadic and irresolute performance kept his status in jeopardy. His life was made more chaotic by his stormy love affair with the daughter of one of the town's distinguished families. Several years older than O'Hara, this bright and attractive Bryn Mawr graduate remained the central figure of his life for another decade. Their plans for the future, nevertheless, always fell apart in the face of O'Hara's drinking and barren prospects for a career.

Life seemed to reach absolute bottom with the unexpected death of Dr. O'Hara in 1925. John's father died intestate and his investments proved valueless, plunging the family into instant genteel poverty. Dismissing any prospect of Yale, O'Hara stayed with the *Journal,* but his irresponsi-

bility about routine assignments and frequent debilitating hangovers lost him the first of two newspaper jobs in Schuylkill County (or "The Region" as natives know the anthracite fields). He tried flight, shipping out as a waiter on a liner to Europe, then hitchhiking west in an unsuccessful quest for a reporter's job. Down and out in Bremerhaven and Chicago, John learned about the seamy side of life firsthand, and, still lacerated by his hopeless love affair, he considered suicide.

Success in placing items in F. P. Adams's famous "Conning Tower" column in the *New York World* lured O'Hara to New York City where he began an equally feckless career on a succession of metropolitan newspapers and magazines: the *Herald Tribune, Time, Editor & Publisher,* the *Daily Mirror,* the *Morning Telegraph.* As a night rewrite man, he developed his lifelong habit of writing in the hours after midnight, but he was hardly a distinguished reporter. Fired with monotonous regularity, he did manage to sell pieces to the *New Yorker* beginning in May 1928.

Forty years later, John O'Hara took pride in having published more fiction in the *New Yorker* than any other author, but in the 1920s, Harold Ross's magazine paid O'Hara less than a living wage. He made friends with the magazine's stable of luminaries–Dorothy Parker, Robert Benchley, Wolcott Gibbs–but he could not keep himself on his *New Yorker* reputation in the early 1930s.

Complicating his life still more was his brief, tension-filled marriage to Helen R. Petit, an unhappy adventure that ended in 1933. A wretched stint as the editor of a magazine in Pittsburgh brought him to the edge of despair. Finally resolving to concentrate only on fiction, O'Hara holed up in a Manhattan hotel to write a series of integrated short stories; emerging from this isolation was *Appointment in Samarra,* his first novel, published by Harcourt, Brace in 1934.

The success of *Appointment in Samarra* (five printings in 1934-1935) made O'Hara attractive to Paramount Studios in Hollywood as a screenwriter, and he began the first of a sequence of jobs with major film studios that continued into the 1950s. O'Hara was never an outstanding screenwriter–his best efforts were devoted to polishing dialogue–but he earned respectable salaries, enjoyed the reckless life of the movie colony, and soaked up information that later proved useful in his fiction.

The 1930s were restless years for O'Hara, though a solid marriage to Belle M. Wylie in 1937 stabilized his life. From an excellent New

York family, Belle O'Hara nursed her husband through both his titanic hangovers and bouts of writing. And O'Hara's fame was growing: *Butterfield 8* (1935) was a best-seller if not a critical success, and his short stories–nearly all of them originally in the *New Yorker*–appeared in two published collections. A novel set in Hollywood, *Hope of Heaven* (1938), won less attention.

O'Hara conquered the Broadway stage in 1940 when he wrote the libretto for Rogers and Hart's musical adaptation of his *Pal Joey* stories. When the play was a hit, O'Hara basked in its glory, yet he continued to test his nondramatic skills by writing a column of media chitchat ("Entertainment Week") for *Newsweek,* to toil away on his *New Yorker* stories, and to receive sole screen credit for *Moontide,* a 1940 film nominated for an Academy Award. Foiled in his attempts to enter military service during World War II by ulcers and bad teeth, O'Hara fretted guiltily and wrote little, though he did get to the South Pacific as a correspondent in 1944. O'Hara was delighted by the birth of his only child, a daughter, Wylie, in 1945, but he was restive under the widely held critical estimate that he was the master only of the stereotypically oblique *New Yorker* short story.

He shattered that judgment with *A Rage to Live* (1949), his first novel in eleven years and a huge popular success (eight Random House printings, three printings by book clubs, and thirty-three paperback edition printings). Reviews of O'Hara's novel of small-town Pennsylvania society were mixed, but its publication inaugurated the major phase of his career. Moving his family from the distractions of New York City to the donnish quiet of Princeton, O'Hara began the sincere devotion to his art that continued for the next twenty years. Sealing this dedication was his ulcer-induced abstinence from alcohol after his brush with death in 1953.

O'Hara had become a literary force to be reckoned with in the 1950s. Though reviewers continued to denigrate his work, his fiction almost always made the best-seller lists and even carried off an occasional prize: the National Book Award for fiction for *Ten North Frederick* in 1956. O'Hara loved the symbols and badges of success, and he pursued awards with relentless avidity. A revival of *Pal Joey* in 1952 won him a gold key from the Donaldson Award Committee as the year's best librettist; the revival also took the New York Drama Critics' Circle Award as the best musical of 1952. An indefatigable O'Hara embarrassed his friends by touting his superior qualifica-

tions for (and his ill-natured disappointment at not receiving) the Pulitzer and other literary prizes in two columns that he wrote in the mid 1950s: "Sweet and Sour" for the *Trenton* [New Jersey] *Sunday Times-Advertiser,* and "Appointment With O'Hara" for *Collier's.*

O'Hara later asserted that only the pressure of completing these two weekly columns and his contract deadlines at Random House kept him from collapse when Belle O'Hara died of heart disease in 1954. However, his marriage to Katharine B. Bryan a year later was another strong and satisfying one, and order returned to the O'Hara house. "Sister," as she was called, came from an even more socially prominent family than had Belle Wylie, and moved easily through the world of the rich and powerful that O'Hara himself found so magnetically attractive. Decades had passed since his Pottsville disappointments, but he still sought to "fit in."

Moreover, by now O'Hara–the former "straight-ticket Democrat" and FDR devotee–had become both personally and politically conservative, some said reactionary. Never an advocate of revolutionary solutions to the conflicts of social class raised in his fiction, he likewise resented the taxes levied on his ever-more-substantial royalties by a liberal political establishment dedicated to faddish social engineering.

Sharpening his disgust was O'Hara's perception that the critical-academic liberals who reviled his work as shallow and old-fashioned worshiped the same false gods as their political counterparts. In a weekly syndicated column that he wrote for *Newsday,* a Long Island newspaper, in the mid 1960s, O'Hara heaped scorn on longhairs and rebels. "The total rejection of the standards and principles that we know were good," he asserted, "will make it extremely unlikely that honesty and decency will be revived." Only the continuously soaring sales of his books reassured O'Hara that the American public still cared about some of the old values.

Increasingly, O'Hara appeared as a pillar of the Princeton squirearchy, building an attractive house, Linebrook, on the town's wooded outskirts and exchanging dinners with selected prominent neighbors. Exultant at his success in joining several exclusive men's clubs (at various times, his *Who's Who in America* entry listed as many as sixteen clubs), he deeply resented being blackballed at two of New York's most restrictive. He summered at Quogue in the fashionable Southampton area of Long Island, gloried in his Rolls-

Royce, and visited England regularly. In tweeds, flannels, and cap, he had come a long way from his days as the Irish-Catholic outsider and wastrel in Pottsville.

That all of his success never quenched O'Hara's rage to write can be attributed to his eventual understanding that his father's dedication to surgery would only be matched by his own equal consecration to his art. His father's high and austere standards had become his own. Moreover, O'Hara's failure to win favor with the arbiters of American literary culture honed his sense of unfair treatment and his desire to garner honors in spite of his detractors. Little wonder that O'Hara wept when the American Academy of Arts and Letters presented him with its Award of Merit for the Novel in 1964. He was not humble in his acceptance speech, which concluded: "We all know how good we are, but it's nice to hear it from someone else."

He kept at his writing despite his progressive physical deterioration–constant lower back pain, a neuralgic jaw, a hiatus hernia, diabetes, hypertension, and vascular disease. The length of his nightly writing sessions had to be reduced, but the words still flowed. "It is pretty hard," he wrote his daughter, "for most writers not to be jealous of me, because I made it look easy and they know it is not." O'Hara the pro, whose fatalistic predictions of his imminent death had been a joke among his friends for decades, called on all of his resources to "get it all down" as he began his eighth novel since 1960. John O'Hara was seventy-four pages into *The Second Ewings* when a heart attack took him in his sleep in April 1970. He was sixty-five.

The obituaries and literary assessments of the next few months were respectful, dwelling on O'Hara's enormous popularity (twenty million copies of his books were sold, according to publishers' estimates) and his meticulous anatomies of American society. However, O'Hara's old critical enemies refused to retract their reservations; in 1973, Alfred Kazin once again spoke for his colleagues: "O'Hara was a novelist of manners crushingly interested *only* in manners, a documentarian whose characters were equivalents for the same social process." John O'Hara's somewhat wistful expectation that the professors and critics would finally acknowledge his importance and elevate him to his deserved place in the American literary pantheon beside Hemingway, Fitzgerald, and Faulkner proved as baseless in the 1970s and 1980s as it was when O'Hara was alive. Recent critics have been no less harsh: "O'Hara's reputation is lower, if anything, than it was at his death eight years ago" (Nicholas Lemann, the *New Republic,* 1978). Even the appearance in 1979 of a scholarly periodical dedicated to analyses of his work, the *John O'Hara Journal,* promised only slightly to awaken new interest among academicians.

O'Hara's fiction, therefore, constitutes an outstanding case in the continuing trial of realism-naturalism as an appropriate mode for the embodiment of imaginative truth in literature. When the greatest preponderance of his critics found against O'Hara, they were rejecting as futile and empty his attempts to find meaning through mimetic fidelity to the search for order in bourgeois society. Perhaps those critics would have been more sympathetic had the characters in O'Hara's work been more successful in their moral quests, but the typical configuration of an O'Hara novel or story features a protagonist whose life founders amid a series of forces over which he or she has no control. O'Hara's fictional world is an essentially deterministic one where waste is more common than success, or even endurance.

Nowhere in O'Hara's entire canon are these principles better personified than in his first novel, *Appointment in Samarra.* Still regarded by many as his most successful work, this naturalistic depiction of the last three days in the life of Julian English traces the major themes which O'Hara evoked consistently throughout his career: the power of a stratified social order to exclude (and therefore to destroy) misfits; the chaotic predominance of lust over love in human relationships; the failures of parental (most often paternal) sympathy; the ubiquity of "bad luck"; and the ironic discontinuity between public appearance and private reality.

Appointment in Samarra takes place at Christmastime, 1930, in Gibbsville, a street-by-street re-creation of O'Hara's native Pottsville. O'Hara was to return to the region and its Pennsylvania environs again and again for background in eight novels, several novellas, and at least sixty short stories. So familiar was this area to become to his readers that it was dubbed O'Hara Country, an eastern variation of Faulkner's Yoknapatawpha County.

The novel's title invokes the legend of the man who seeks to escape death only to find that in his very flight he keeps his appointment with it. The inescapability of Julian English's destruction, however, owes as much to the inadequacies of his own character as to cosmic irony. A revenge-

Chapter 1

Our story opens in the mind of Luther L. (L for
LeRoy) Fliegler, who is lying in his bed, not thinking of anything, but
just aware of sounds, conscious of his own breathing, and sensitive to
his own heartbeats. Lying beside him is his wife, lying on her right
side and enjoying her sleep. She has earned her sleep, for it is
Christmas morning, strictly speaking, and all the day before she has
worked like a dog, cleaning the turkey and baking things, and, until
a few hours ago, trimming the tree. The awful proximity of his heartbeats makes Luther Fliegler begin to want his wife a little, but Irma
can say no when she is tired. It is too much trouble, she says when
she is tired, and she won't take any chances. Three children is enough;
three children in ten years. So Luther Fliegler does not reach out for
her. It is Christmas morning, and he will do her the favor of letting
her enjoy her sleep; a favor which she will never know he did for her.
And it is a favor, all right, because Irma likes Christmas too, and on

First page of the typescript for Appointment in Samarra *(Pennsylvania State University Libraries)*

ful, status-jealous social order and the misfortunes of chance contribute to Julian's drunken decision to end his life with the carbon monoxide of his own Cadillac, but he reveals himself to be an insecure and reckless child-man whose sexual attractiveness, superficial charm, and inherited social status have given him an unwarranted and self-deceiving sense of freedom from retribution. When Julian throws a drink in the eye of Harry Reilly, an Irish parvenu to whom he owes twenty thousand dollars and to whom he fears his wife Carolyn, will become attracted, Julian begins the chain of events that lead to his inevitable disintegration.

Julian's failure derives as well from his own lack of will; escape from the vicious cohesiveness of Gibbsville's threatened dignity depends upon nerve. Julian, however, lacks the resources to accept responsibility for his actions and the courage to accept social ostracism. *Appointment in Samarra* makes clear some of the causes of his spinelessness—his physician father's coldness has denied Julian a stable identity; his mother is an ineffectual shadow; his wife controls him by indulging his immaturity and using her sexual favors to keep him "proper." Weakly, Julian drinks to excess, enjoying the chimerical sense of license that alcohol lends to his heedlessness. Finally, alienating Carolyn, Gibbsville's middle class, and the local mobsters by a drunken public tryst with a bootlegger's mistress, he seals his own doom: "Julian, lost in the coonskins, felt the tremendous excitement, the great thrilling lump in the chest and abdomen that comes before the administering of an unknown, well deserved punishment. He knew he was in for it."

In *Appointment in Samarra,* John O'Hara managed to unify the spirit of an age, the latent violence and envy that characterize social stratification, and the neurotic self-pity of a hypersensitive hero. The result was a powerful novel that chronicled the insecurities of Americans just entering the Depression, that anatomized the effects of impulsive sexual appetite, and that made victimization credible if not rational. O'Hara buttressed his study with endless documentary detail: menus for the $2.50 dinner at the country club (filet mignon), Reo Speed-wagons, Condax Cigarettes, Delta Kappa Epsilon, "Is it a real Foujita or a copy?" All of these *things*—the badges of status in Gibbsville—have enormous relevance for an understanding of Julian's world. O'Hara's ear for dialogue—acknowledged by critics as flawless—produced an ungrammatical verisi-

militude, the authentically reproduced accents marking the speakers as belonging to a specific social class. And despite O'Hara's objective tone, irony intruded often enough to demonstrate the author's opinion of the hypocrites and fools of Gibbsville.

The success of *Appointment in Samarra* encouraged Harcourt, Brace to publish a collection of O'Hara's short fiction, *The Doctor's Son and Other Stories,* early in 1935. Notable primarily for its long title story, the book also included a number of briefer vignettes of New York and Hollywood life that had been published in the *New Yorker.* Slender as most of these stories seem now, one is particularly ironic in its depiction of mistaken intentions. "Over the River and Through the Wood" features an aging, once-rich roué visiting a house that he once owned. His libidinousness now dormant, he is still attracted by the vitality of one of his granddaughter's guests, and, mishearing her "Come in," enters her room to find the girl naked and glaring at him with suspicious hatred: "Mr. Winfield knew that this was the end of any worthwhile life he had left. . . . For a while he would just sit there and plan his own terror."

The novella-length story "The Doctor's Son" is the center of this collection. In it, O'Hara introduces an autobiographical persona, James Malloy, who will reappear frequently in the later fiction—prominently in two novels, three novellas, and fourteen stories. Malloy is the rebellious son of an Irish-Catholic surgeon in Gibbsville, fifteen years old in "The Doctor's Son," which takes place at the height of the influenza epidemic ravaging the anthracite region in 1918. O'Hara recreates his adolescent admiration for and quarrel with his own father in Malloy's estrangement from Dr. Malloy, who cannot understand his son's preference for journalism over medicine. The story is most meaningful in its depiction of Jimmy Malloy's initiation into the meaninglessness of death and the cruelty of adultery. He is shorn of romantic illusion by the violence of disease and lust.

Violence, only thinly veneered by the conventions of society, always preoccupied O'Hara. Perhaps his own personality—vain, argumentative, emotional, rebellious, cynical, pessimistic—led him to focus on the physical ferocity of human relationships, but readers of O'Hara's fiction soon realize that violence is man's fate. Too young to have fought in World War I himself, O'Hara nevertheless shows the influence of writers like Hemingway who taught a generation of Americans to think of war as a metaphor for the human condition. War rages in Gibbsville, violent and deadly, and O'Hara's characters must learn to recognize that beneath the surface of society's reactions to apparently inconsequential gaffes hide envy and revenge and mayhem. "The war's over," Julian English tells an opponent in *Appointment in Samarra*. The reply—"Yeah, that's what you think"—underscores the permanence of the latent violence informing all social relations in O'Hara's world.

Butterfield 8 (1935), O'Hara's next novel, accentuates the motif of violence, coupling the strategic hostilities of social humiliation with the tactical savageries of sexual violation. As O'Hara's only roman à clef, *Butterfield 8* took for its basis the notorious Starr Faithfull drowning which filled New York City tabloids in 1931. Starr Faithfull was a highly visible demimondaine in the speakeasy society of New York; her sexually explicit diaries implicated men from various levels of that society, and the cause of her death (murder? suicide?) was never determined.

O'Hara's doomed heroine, Gloria Wandrous, lives the same promiscuous and self-destructive life as her prototype, but O'Hara sees Gloria, as he earlier had seen Julian English, as a victim of her environment. Because she was sexually molested in her youth, she has engaged in an endless series of unsatisfactory, even pathetic attempts to win love through sex. Yet the unlawful, hedonistic, and exploitive milieu in which she must search for mature love dooms her quest utterly. O'Hara's picture of the depravity of speakeasy life—American democratic society gone manic and cruel—reveals no real exit for Gloria. As in *Appointment in Samarra*, the Depression has added economic insecurity to animalistic aggression; consequently, the reader is a spectator at a perverted peep show, glittering but terrifying.

Two men might have had the potential to rescue Gloria from this immoral morass—Eddie Brunner, innocent and virtuous, and Weston Liggett, a married and monied aristocrat from Yale. But Eddie cannot overcome his repugnance at Gloria's promiscuity, and Liggett is too driven by his selfish passion to offer stable love. Accordingly, though Gloria realizes the futility of her debauched life—one-night stands, booze, drugs, theft—her men let her down. On purpose or by accident, she falls into the paddle wheel of an excursion boat; as with Julian English, "it was time for her to die."

Several other themes make *Butterfield 8* significant for O'Hara's readers. In spite of Gloria's pathos as a victim, she also represents the promise of unexampled sexual pleasure unhindered by social convention which is often the source of disorder in O'Hara's fictional world. In *Butterfield 8*, Liggett's self-seeking egocentricity undercuts any sympathy that he might attract as a captive of the fatal allure of a Gloria Wandrous, but rampant carnality like hers will lay waste dozens of other men in O'Hara's novels and stories. These femmes fatales zero in on the weak spot in the moral armor of O'Hara's men, the innate rebelliousness of sex, and no one is proof against them. Furthermore, nothing seems more frightening and reprehensible to John O'Hara than an unbridled female sexual appetite.

Stylistically, *Butterfield 8* offers a defense of O'Hara's loyalty to simple and direct prose and the unreliability of metaphors: "(Shakespeare . . . said it just as badly as anyone ever said it. 'All the perfumes of Arabia' makes you think of all the perfumes of Arabia and nothing more. It is the trouble with all metaphors where human behavior is concerned. People are not ships, chessmen, flowers, race, horses, oil paintings, bottles of champagne, excrement, musical instruments, or anything else except people. Metaphors are all right to give you an idea.)" This manifesto made O'Hara's style flat, prosaic, exact, and authoritative—an achievement wrought from scrupulous attention to traditional language and a desire to make that language embody a reality that is irrefragably physical. No solipsistic wordplay or interposition of internal values for O'Hara. If other authors would use a rhetorically complex style calling attention to itself as the principal meaning of their works, O'Hara wanted his words to stand for things—precise, familiar, "ordinary" things.

Finally, *Butterfield 8* features a cameo appearance by the autobiographical Jimmy Malloy, at this time a journeyman reporter selling his "real" work to the *New Yorker*. In several scenes with his girlfriend, a former Gibbsville aristocrat, he reveals his defensive sensitivity about his ethnic background: "I'm pretty God damn American, and therefore my brothers and sisters are, and yet we're not Americans. We're Micks, we're non-assimilable, we Micks. . . . What I started out to explain was why I said 'you people, you members of the upper crust,' and so on, implying that I'm not a member of it. Well, I'm *not* a member of it, and now I never will be." Malloy never meets Gloria Wandrous in the novel; we assume that he is present primarily for his cynical observations on her world and to voice O'Hara's bile at discriminatory hypocrisy.

In O'Hara's next novel, *Hope of Heaven* (1938), Malloy takes over the protagonist's role and, like his creator, has become a moderately successful screenwriter in Hollywood. O'Hara is able to manage a number of wry observations on West Coast vulgarity, while at the same time demonstrating his cynical "insider's" knowledge of the film industry. But *Hope of Heaven* is a slender and forgettable failure. Malloy, in love with Peggy Henderson, a left-leaning, intellectual bookstore clerk, becomes involved with Don Miller, whose origins in the anthracite region stir Malloy's old loyalties. Miller, however, has been passing stolen traveler's checks, bringing into the plot Peggy's estranged father, an investigator. The father accidentally kills his son, Peggy's much-loved younger brother, and Peggy, in despair, breaks off with Malloy. All of this rather complicated coincidence and accident is supposed to induce ironic headshaking at the operation of a malevolent fate, but few save O'Hara himself liked the novel. He had slaved over it—uncharacteristically making major revisions and missing publisher's deadlines—and called it his best for a decade thereafter.

Reviewers, however, found *Hope of Heaven* diffuse and undisciplined. Edmund Wilson called attention to a "Freudian behavior-pattern" in Peggy's relationship with one of O'Hara's typically cold and loveless fathers, but the traveler's check theft seemed nugatory. This last objection to the structure of O'Hara's novels was to become a shibboleth of negative critical commentary. Already in *Appointment in Samarra* and *Butterfield 8*, reviewers had scored the irrelevance of characters and episodes whose presence seemed to contribute little to theme or action. As a realist, however, O'Hara defended his inclusion of apparently trivial materials on the grounds that actuality itself, the object of his mimetic art, lacked symmetry and "discipline." Accordingly, he packed his novels with characters and data from which the reader is expected to derive connections, obscure and inappropriate though they may seem to aestheticians. Because O'Hara correlated his characters so closely with their milieu and its values, he expected his readers to *want* to understand that milieu as thoroughly as possible—hence, the "irrelevancies."

Moreover, again as a realist, O'Hara sought to capture the spirit of the age that he was depicting, "those facts which sometimes help to give truth to fiction." Praising the fiction of Arthur Conan Doyle for its authenticity, he wrote: "It is literature of a high order. The sights, sounds, smells, social customs, conversation—all so right and good that you don't have to read anything else to get the feeling of a period." Albeit the novelist was first of all an artist, the rigors of realist art involved him in other functions as well: "It is probably safe to say that every writer of fiction was a social historian." O'Hara scorned abstract messages in fiction, praising Booth Tarkington's Penrod stories and Sherwood Anderson's *Winesburg, Ohio* as exemplary: "Their message—which will be news to a lot of people is: That's how it was."

As literal precision was important to O'Hara's style, so absolute accuracy was the keystone of his function as social historian. Errors in fact were not simply sloppy, they were illusion-shattering lies: "I am extremely critical, and I have never been able to get beyond the first page of one of the most famous novels of our time because the author has made a 'weather' mistake (something about snow on the ground) that proves to me that he isn't a good writer." Accordingly, O'Hara would combine the historian's remorseless quest for the factual with the artist's mission to render "the way it was" meaningful. That goal involved him in depicting the social construction of reality in America, in the process of socialization by which American society confers identity on its members and struggles to maintain some semblance of social continuity.

Not surprisingly, therefore, John O'Hara admired writers whose work reflected his own conceptions of the author's mission. In a foreword to his collection of short stories *Files on Parade* (1939), he listed some of his favorites: Hemingway, Fitzgerald, Faulkner, Ring Lardner, Dorothy Parker, H. H. Munro (Saki), William Saroyan, Maupassant. On another occasion, he cited Owen Johnson, Tarkington, John Galsworthy, but chiefly Fitzgerald and Sinclair Lewis, as influences on his writing. Yet O'Hara had not, since his adolescence, been a ferocious reader of other writers' fiction. "I should admit," he told an audience, "or confess, or simply state, that there is no one in this room who is more than thirty years old, who has not read more novels than I have." Determinedly his own man, he claimed: "I have not read any current fiction . . . because I have

Belle, John, and Wylie O'Hara at Quogue, Long Island

been at work on my own novel. The reason is not only that I have wanted to avoid being influenced, however slightly or subtly, but because I am an extremely slow reader of fiction. . . ."

If most of the thirty-five stories in *Files on Parade* have any literary source, as one reviewer pointed out, it would have to be Chekhov: "O'Hara writes of *treachery*. Chekhov says it is important that a human being never be humiliated—that is the main thing. O'Hara knows it happens just the same, and this is what makes his stories so true and good." An outstanding example is "Price's Always Open," a brief picture of the snobbery of a WASP New England summer crowd toward a local Irish boy who goes to Holy Cross. When their disdain turns to violence, Price, owner of the diner where the action takes place, takes the local boy's side. Edmund Wilson thought that the forces of democracy triumphed, but O'Hara is more ironic: "Mr. Price agreed with himself that those would be the last sounds he ever expected to hear from the summer crowd."

Four of the stories in *Files on Parade* began

the series which was to bring John O'Hara great public notice. Adding ten more to the integrated series, O'Hara brought out *Pal Joey* in 1940, and his bush-league nightclub sharpie became a part of American folklore. The *Pal Joey* stories are epistolary in form, their egotistical hero recounting his triumphs and tragedies to his correspondent Ted. O'Hara had frequently featured Broadway and Hollywood types in other stories, but no other character simultaneously so attractive and so repellent had emerged. O'Hara's other show-business people are almost purely exploitive and revengeful, but Joey Evans—for all of his apparent wiseacre sophistication—is innocent, sentimental, occasionally good-hearted, and often a loser. Moreover, Joey's letters are gems of the vernacular, a tribute to O'Hara's perfect ear, and full of the irony of the satirical monologue. Ring Lardner and Sinclair Lewis may have furnished O'Hara with models of straight-faced ironic monologues, but *Pal Joey* is his own authentic triumph.

In a way, Joey shares the upwardly mobile instincts of O'Hara's more serious characters: in

"Pal Joey," he plans to marry the banker's daughter, join the country club, and settle down with children and golf clubs. But he reckons not with the vindictiveness of an old girlfriend, who reveals Joey's false respectability. Joey's success with women depends upon their lack of intelligence: he does well with the dull and unsophisticated (in "Bow Wow"), but the experienced ones defeat him utterly (in "Joey and Marvis" and "A Bit of a Shock"). As a fast-talking rogue, Joey can cadge a few extra dollars, but he is just not shrewd enough to deal with real power (in "Joey on Herta") or false appearances (in "The Erloff"). Joey frequently reveals himself as a heel, but his optimism, his perseverance, his resiliency make him very nearly likeable in spite of all his petty deviousness. Only in the last story, "Reminiss?," does his improvident con man's life lead him to bitterness and envy, revealing him finally as another of O'Hara's lost love seekers: "Mostly at that time of the nite I want it for free and with love too at that."

Pal Joey hit the big time in a way that would have pleased its egocentric protagonist when, in December 1940, O'Hara converted his Joey material into the libretto for a musical comedy with lyrics by Lorenz Hart and music by Richard Rodgers. The show was a success despite those reviewers who were shocked by the sexual innuendo of the songs and dialogue. Only "Bow Wow" and "A Bit of a Shock" remained from the stories; O'Hara involved Joey in an entirely original set of complications on stage. Still a second-rate nightclub personality, Joey becomes a star when Vera Simpson, rich wife of a Chicago bakery tycoon, bankrolls Chez Joey for him in return for his sexual favors ("In Our Little Den of Iniquity" was considered a rather explicit song in the 1940s). When the evil actor's agent Lowell attempts to blackmail the pair, Vera shows her muscle by having the police run Lowell out of town. But Vera is tired of Joey, and—having chosen Vera over the "pure" Linda earlier—Joey is alone at the final curtain. The play made O'Hara a good deal of money, running for 374 performances. It was an even greater hit later; in its 1952 revival, *Pal Joey* ran for 540 performances, the longest Broadway run a musical revival has ever had.

O'Hara's success with *Pal Joey* and an Academy Award nomination for the film *Moontide*, for whose script he received sole credit, convinced O'Hara that he might well abandon fiction for the theater, but he continued to write short sto-

ries in the 1940s, although at a somewhat diminished rate. Not until 1945 did another collection appear, and *Pipe Night* sold well (five printings in 1945). It also contains some of O'Hara's best stories to this time, including the memorable "Graven Image." A highly placed Washington official is interviewing a Harvard classmate for a wartime job. The job seems won until the aristocratic applicant expresses relief that the undersecretary bears no grudges at not having been elected to Porcellian years ago. But of course the undersecretary has never forgotten the undergraduate snub, and the job will not go to the Porcellian man. Both characters come off badly—one still a snob, the other a hypersensitive parvenu. "Where's the Game" concerns the cruel exclusion of a lonely salesman from a poker game. "Bread Alone" is O'Hara's only story about blacks: a shy father and son are brought closer together when the boy presents the father with a baseball fouled into the Yankee Stadium bleachers. And "Too Young" is another effective initiation story: a teenage boy learns that the older college girl he admires is having an affair with a tough cop.

Hellbox (1947), O'Hara's first book for Random House, was an attempt to energize a flagging career. However, the collection of twenty-six stories marks a falling off in O'Hara's mastery of the form; only "The Decision" is vintage John O'Hara. After graduation from medical school, Dr. Townsend learns his family's secret from his uncle: both his parents died insane, and the young man can neither marry nor practice medicine. Devastated, Townsend spends the rest of his life drinking and waiting for his "beast in the jungle." O'Hara's irony, like Henry James's, is that insanity never comes, and Dr. Townsend's life is wasted. James Malloy, the autobiographical persona, reappears in *Hellbox* in four stories, but only one, "Transaction," is noteworthy. There Malloy eases his status anxiety by paying some temporarily strapped aristocrats extra for their Duesenberg, thus demonstrating his own rise in the world while at the same time showing the patricians that he shares their appreciation for the symbols of elegant living.

For several years reviewers had been damning O'Hara's collections of stories as "finger exercises" and lamenting his failure to live up to his "early promise." Eleven years was a long time to wait for an O'Hara novel, but *A Rage to Live* (1949) was a blockbuster. Nearly six hundred pages long, minutely documented, historically dense, O'Hara's chronicle of upper-class power, values, and style in Fort Penn (very like Harrisburg, Pennsylvania) had a huge sale–eight hardcover printings, four book club reprintings, and thirty-three paperback printings. Over one hundred thousand copies were sold in its first two months, eight thousand in one day.

A Rage to Live succeeded in spite of some of the most vituperative reviews that O'Hara had received to date, particularly those in the *New York Times* and the *New Yorker*. "Sprawling" and "prolix" were mild adjectives; "meretricious, dull, and pointless" were more typical. O'Hara's characters "weren't worth writing about." This drumfire of objections hurt the author, who was particularly bitter at the *New Yorker*'s disloyalty to its longtime contributor.

The novel *is* overcrowded with the historical artifacts of aristocratic life in a Pennsylvania city, with family annals, with things in rich variety. *A Rage to Live* was the first novel really to fulfill O'Hara's mission: "Everything I have written since 1948," he asserted, "has had a secondary purpose; I have deliberately attempted to record the first half of the century in fictional forms but with the quasi-historical effect that, say, Dickens achieved." *A Rage to Live* does not rival Dickens, and its social history–lucid and lively though it is–tends to overshadow the primary action, the rise and fall of the marriage of Sidney and Grace Tate.

On the other hand, in Grace, O'Hara has created one of his most memorable predatory females, irresistibly alluring, almost amoral. She is heedlessly passionate: "It has to be love with me, Paul. Or the other so much that I don't know where it comes from, and can't help it." Grace is no pathetic love seeker like Gloria Wandrous; Grace gives in to "the other" without fear because she can, as the libidinous princess of the Caldwell family's Pennsylvania kingdom, break the sexual rules at her whim. The Caldwells need only keep their dignity in public; what they do privately will seemingly never harm them.

But of course, in O'Hara's world harm assumes various guises. Sidney Tate, Grace's victimized husband, is a quintessential O'Hara nobleman, Yale '00, from a fine New York family. He has the ability to succeed at almost anything, but he is most content as a gentleman farmer. After Sidney and Grace marry and the three children are born, all seems placid and orderly until Grace sleeps with a boorish Irish contractor. Stricken and outraged, Sidney voices O'Hara's clearest statement of the code of the aristocrat:

"in this world you learn a set of rules, or you *don't* learn them. But assuming you learn them, you stick by them. They may be no damn good, but you're who you are and what you are because they're your rules and you stick by them. And of course when it's easy to stick by them, that's no test. It's when it's hard to obey rules, that's when they mean something. That's what I believe, and I always thought you did too. . . . But you obeyed the rules, the same rules I obeyed. But then you said the hell with my rules, and the hell with me." Critics saw this code as platitudinous, but O'Hara's world struggles to keep faith with this traditional secular morality, this set of commitments on which any human relationship must be based. The Tate code demands total identification of person with vow; the rules are not abstract, but part of the people who live them. In her adultery, Grace has destroyed her husband.

And the destruction becomes irredeemable when the familiar O'Hara nemesis, chance, compounds Grace's transgression. Polio kills Sidney Tate, then their son, Billy. Grace must live on in the ironic light of the novels' epigraph: "You purchase Pain with all that Joy can give,/And die of nothing but a Rage to live." O'Hara would have been well advised to end the novel with the deaths of Sidney and Billy, but as always, he was too much the realist-historian to close so neatly. Grace survives her tragedy with patrician stoicism, and O'Hara follows her through still another messy affair with a newspaper reporter. He ends the novel with a postlude which reveals Grace, now in her sixties, involved with another married man. As he did Julian English, O'Hara draws Grace as charming, heedless, and handsome. Yet Julian lacks the nerve to match his attractiveness, the will to face down his mistakes. Grace, as a female, the deadlier of the species, lives on to sin again, even though O'Hara, the lapsed Catholic, understands that Grace's "grace" has made her life empty.

O'Hara's next book, *Sweet and Sour* (1954), was a collection of columns that he wrote for a New Jersey newspaper. Along with *My Turn* (1966), another such collection, these essays amount to little more than journalistic ephemera. Useful only to a thorough biographer, *Sweet and Sour* and *My Turn* add nothing to O'Hara's stature as an important writer. Indeed, his ill-tempered and injudicious growls at his critics and his reactionary politics furnished his enemies with ammunition.

Equally slender was *The Farmers Hotel* (1951), a novella which had originally been written as a play in 1946-1947. O'Hara saw it as an allegorical piece, though the references are murky. The scene is a small inn where show-business people, two O'Hara aristocrats, some sensible Pennsylvania common folk, and an ominous truck driver are trapped by a snowstorm. Amity blooms among this ill-assorted group until the innate aggressiveness of Rogg, the truck driver, brings an end to the democratic idyll. Ejected, Rogg rams his truck into the car carrying the aristocrats, killing them both. Rogg is clearly an animal whose destructive aggression disturbs any orderly society, but O'Hara meant him to stand for Stalin and the Russian threat to world security. Readers are supposed to conclude that only equal ruthlessness can be used to deal with the Roggs, that they deserve killing before they can kill. *The Farmers Hotel*, in spite of its deft dialogue and clever dramatic structure, turns out to be a rather simplistic McCarthy-era morality play.

Neither slender nor simplistic was John O'Hara's *Ten North Frederick* (1955), a major novel that won a National Book Award. Returning to Gibbsville, O'Hara chooses another Pennsylvania aristocrat, Joseph B. Chapin, for his protagonist. Uncharacteristically, O'Hara reverses his normal chronological structure by opening the novel with Chapin's funeral, a notable event in Gibbsville, attended by influential power brokers from New York to Philadelphia. This ceremonial occasion prefigures the theme of *Ten North Frederick*: the ironic contrast between the "public" Joe Chapin and the private hell which he lives. The public regards Joe as Richard Cory is regarded in Edwin Arlington Robinson's poem—"he glittered when he walked." Wealthy, a successful attorney, well educated (Yale '04), son of a prominent local family, husband of a wellborn Gibbsville woman, father of two attractive children, Chapin seems to have all he needs for the good life.

In his usual technique of delayed revelation, however, O'Hara consumes the remainder of this long novel with the story of the "real" Joseph B. Chapin, who turns out to be as pathetic a victim as any of O'Hara's star-crossed love seekers. Chapin's flaws stem from his innate malleability; from infancy he is made the instrument of the desires of others, particularly of the women close to him. O'Hara's misogyny was never far from the surface, even as far back as the early stories and *Appointment in Samarra*, but the power and utter ruthlessness of his strong women become increasingly evident as the body of his fiction grows in the 1950s and 1960s. Evil males are never absent in this fictional world; still, O'Hara's vision of the mantislike female, ever ready to pounce on her sex-bewitched mate, waxes in the later fiction.

In previous novels, cold fathers are instrumental in the neurotic tragedies of their children; in *Ten North Frederick*, paternal neglect becomes maternal domination. Quite obviously Joe Chapin's life would have been different had his father exercised paternal control, but Ben Chapin turns the boy's rearing over to Charlotte, and Joe grows up smothered in a combination of his mother's ambitions for him and an exalted sense of his own importance. Moreover, Chapin's subservience to his own mother has a good deal to do with his choice of a wife: Edith Stokes—ambitious, cold, shrewd, tough, selfish—whose mission is to "own" Joe completely. Edith's penchant for egocentric domination stems in part from the perverse nature of her early experiments in lesbian sexuality, and O'Hara's later fiction abounds with the sterile exploitiveness of lesbianism. In any event, Joe becomes the object of the obsessions of two formidable females; conjointly, mother and wife domesticate and ultimately dispirit Chapin.

Nevertheless, Joe Chapin is not "simply" victimized, as Julian English was by socioeconomic insecurity, or Grace Tate by sexual passion. Chapin is a man of some intelligence, great charm, and inherited wealth (he loses two million in the Crash of 1929, but has a million left), but his judgment is warped by the parochialism of his aristocratic social identity. Such a monied naif is ripe for plucking by the shrewder pragmatists of the "real" world. And plucked he is when his sense of noblesse oblige stirs in him an ambition to be president of the United States; Mike Slattery, cynical and acute boss of the Gibbsville Republican machine, takes his money but denies Joe nomination for any political office. Irish Catholics can revenge themselves on Gibbsville's patricians when the fight is outside the orderly circle of the wealthy.

In *Ten North Frederick*, O'Hara is dramatizing the ironic dark side of the code of the gentleman. If Sidney Tate showed the code to be morally right, Joe Chapin reveals it to be a kind of emotional straitjacket. Joe's father made the money that allowed Joe to develop properly, respectably, even admirably. O'Hara clearly sees Joe as juiceless, lacking vitality and intensity. As a prisoner of his own idealist egocentricity, he can ruin his daughter's marriage to a likable Italian

OTHER BOOKS BY JOHN O'HARA

Appointment in Samarra

DOROTHY PARKER: "*Appointment in Samarra* is a fine and serious American novel, of shrewd and inevitable pattern and almost unbelievable pace. This swift, savage story of Julian English's life and the lives of those who crowd his way, set down as sharp and deep as if the author had used steel for paper, is, it seems to me, of high importance both as a work of American letters and a document of American history. The novelist has included, in his telling of English's short years, a record of the ways and mores of English's times—our times. Mr. O'Hara's eyes and ears have been spared nothing; but he has kept in his heart a curious, bitter mercy."

CLIFTON FADIMAN, *The New Yorker:* "The most sheerly readable novel within miles . . . it is something we cannot lay down."

JOHN CHAMBERLAIN, *The New York Times:* "There is no doubt about it, Mr. O'Hara is possessed by the America he has known, and he is able to communicate that possession amply and remarkably."

ERNEST HEMINGWAY, *Esquire:* "If you want to read a book by a man who knows what he is writing about and has written it marvellously well, read *Appointment in Samarra* by John O'Hara."

$2.50

The Doctor's Son and Other Stories

Time Newsmagazine: "As straight a reporter of U. S. dialect as the late great Ring Lardner and straighter than Hemingway, O'Hara writes without bitterness, without pity."

EDITH H. WALTON, *New York Times:* "O'Hara is a superbly gifted observer, shrewd, savage, merciless and apparently fertile in ideas. . . . Trenchant all of these stories, usually ironic, often a little cruel, they display precisely the same qualities as 'Appointment in Samarra.'"

LEWIS GANNETT, *New York Herald Tribune:* "O'Hara has the Hemingway touch with the American language and the O. Henry gift of the sharp ending."

$2.50

Harcourt, Brace and Company
383 MADISON AVENUE, NEW YORK

BUTTERFIELD 8

JOHN O'HARA
AUTHOR OF
APPOINTMENT
IN SAMARRA

HARCOURT, BRACE
AND COMPANY

Dust jacket for O'Hara's second novel, which depicts New York society in the early 1930s

musician and thwart his son's only love, jazz piano. He loves his children, but his vision has the opaque narrowness of inexperience and aristocratic conventionality.

Chapin's last attempt to break out of this deadening world does afford him some passion. In his middle fifties, Joe has an affair with a beautiful friend of his daughter's, but the iron rules of convention vitiate even this idyllic December-May love match. Knowing that society will see their love as absurd, Joe gives up Kate Drummond for *her* sake, only to spend the remaining ten years of his life quietly drinking himself to death in his library at Ten North Frederick Street in Gibbsville.

Ten North Frederick is not as vivid and intense a novel as *Appointment in Samarra*, but it is just as powerful in its less spectacular, more complex narrative scope. O'Hara constantly changes focus and shifts perspective, vivifying legions of minor characters in the process, and he is able to probe the wellsprings of futility with a more serene yet absorbing tone. *Ten North Frederick* is probably his most successful "big" novel.

Another "big" novel, the nearly nine-hundred-page *From the Terrace*, was in O'Hara's typewriter when a minor novella, *A Family Party*, was published, first in *Collier's*, then in a Random House edition in 1956. In a dramatic monologue in the form of a testimonial speech, the narrator pays tribute to the virtues of Sam Merritt, small-town physician (Dr. O'Hara became more admirable as his son aged). The book is nostalgic, its pleasantries leavened by O'Hara's revelations of Merritt's failure to achieve his ambitions and Mrs. Merritt's insanity.

Until his death, John O'Hara considered *From the Terrace* (1958) his greatest achievement as a writer. As his biggest, most expensive book ($6.95, a high price in 1958), *From the Terrace* sold one hundred thousand copies in the hardcover edition, but it was O'Hara's greatest success in paperback: well over two and a half million copies at ninety-five cents sold in eight years. Despite all of O'Hara's enthusiasm for this novel, a particularly tangled mixture of history, fiction, and panorama makes *From the Terrace* less than satisfactory as the "chronicle" of O'Hara's intention. The book traces the life of its protagonist, Alfred Eaton, from 1897 until 1946 (that "first half of the Century" which O'Hara regarded as his special province and responsibility). Alfred's life, from his birth into an iron- and steel-rich Pennsylvania family, through adolescent love affairs, preparatory school and Princeton, service in the navy in World War I, then on to wealth and power in aviation and banking, is an eventful one. If Alfred's first marriage to Mary St. John goes awry, he does find love with the beautiful Natalie Benziger. In World War II, he becomes assistant secretary of the navy and a toughminded civilian warrior. Eaton, unlike the parochial and less active Joe Chapin of *Ten North Frederick,* pursues his goals pragmatically and single-mindedly. He works at his luck, and he has many admirable qualities–loyalty, conscience, and responsibility.

O'Hara would have had his readers understand, however, that Alfred Eaton's almost frenetic drive to the top carries with it the seeds of its own destruction. As is so often the case in O'Hara's world, Alfred is emotionally stunted by his father's cold refusal to love him after the death of Alfred's older brother. Driven by a desire to win approval from his distant father, Alfred himself becomes what he hates in his father: personally indifferent to human relationships, Alfred seems to become a glacial competitor whose passion is spent in capitalistic aggression. That Eaton's mother is weak, her potential for balancing Alfred's emotional starvation drowned in alcohol and affairs, compounds this interpretation.

Nevertheless, Alfred is capable of evading this fate. He has a capacity for intense passion, his deepening love for Natalie, even though adulterous, giving the lie to his putative frigidity. He loves his children, even though he might have repeated the family pattern when his eldest son is killed in a wartime plane crash. And despite working very hard, he finds time to carry on loyal friendships with at least three men. Even his business affairs are scrupulously fair. Finally, though no match for Sidney Tate in his sexual morality, Eaton bears some of the hallmarks of the gentleman–rationality, common sense, honesty.

O'Hara's depiction of Alfred's decline into emptiness and futility is, therefore, not as convincing as it should be. Venal rivals at his banking house force his resignation; his best friend is killed in an accident; he nearly dies from bleeding gastric ulcers; his plans for future business activity fall through; Natalie, now his wife, delivers a stillborn child. Still wealthy, Alfred is reduced to an aimless and hollow uselessness. Yet the real cause of this pathetic ending, a fate worse than death for one formerly so vital, is ultimately unclear.

Several other aspects of *From the Terrace* deserve mention: O'Hara creates another devious

Irish Catholic in Creighton Duffy, a less shrewd but more socially presentable Mike Slattery; Duffy, whose child Alfred rescues from drowning, repays him by forcing him out of the banking house where both are partners. O'Hara's portrayal of the steel-mill town of Alfred's birth is as graphic and acute as were his anatomies of Gibbsville earlier. Eaton's Princeton experience lacks intellectual bite; one surmises that Alfred never read a book, so relentlessly nonintellectual is O'Hara's account of his college career. And finally, in Mary, Eaton's first wife, O'Hara has created perhaps his most frightening portrait of female sexuality gone wild. Grace Tate's lubriciousness pales beside Mary's orgiastic decadence. *Why* she becomes such a nightmarish figure of debauched lust is not obvious, but Mary Eaton seems to be able to get away with anything in ways that O'Hara's men never can.

The insatiable Mary has her counterpart in Hedda, the amoral nymphet bride of Robert Millhouser in O'Hara's next novel, *Ourselves to Know* (1960). Hedda is pure sensation, a beautiful captive of her sexual urgency. This time, however, the O'Hara succubus fails to escape retribution: Millhouser–cuckolded, taunted, rendered impotent by Hedda's cold-blooded humiliation–murders his wife. O'Hara reveals the murder early in the novel; readers continue in an effort to learn why Robert did it and what happens to his life after his violent crime.

Ourselves to Know is perhaps the most technically difficult of O'Hara's novels. In it, he tries a more complex narrative structure, using his usual omniscient narrative voice and that of a first-person narrator, Gerald Higgins, whose interest in the Millhouser case rather improbably gets its justification as material for a Princeton M.A. thesis. That premise might give Higgins's curiosity and Millhouser's willingness to respond a "respectable" academic grounding, but the title of the novel, drawn from Pope's *Essay on Man* ("And all our Knowledge is, ourselves to know"), indicates that self-knowledge is man's most significant and unavoidable quest. Robert Millhouser must understand himself, then learn to live with that bleak knowledge; Gerald Higgins will find that by understanding Millhouser, he may come to know himself.

Emotions atrophied by rejection had become a pattern in O'Hara's protagonists. Like Julian English, Joe Chapin, and Alfred Eaton, Robert Millhouser is the victim of his parents' (particularly his mother's) refusal to forge any emotional links between themselves and their only child. Exacerbating this perversion of parental love is Robert's discovery that his worldly, talented, and sensitive best friend is a homosexual whose love is also distorted. All of Millhouser's efforts to escape from his ingrown and solitary existence fall prey to bad luck, and he seems destined to die an arid death in a rural Pennsylvania farming community.

Critics objected to Millhouser's seemingly senseless choice of the wanton, rebellious, neurotic, supersensual Hedda as the bride of his middle age; a semiadolescent strumpet, they claimed, would never have appealed to the austere and conservative Robert. These doubters fail to recognize O'Hara's clear demonstration of Millhouser's desperate need for Hedda's emotional vitality, lacerating as this need turns out to be. Millhouser realizes that he can enjoy Hedda's passion for only a short time, but he is prepared to let her go, his life brighter for her revivification and hers more comfortable for a share of his wealth. Robert kills Hedda only when her scandalous infidelities unman him completely, foreclosing all hope even of the possibilities for rejuvenation through sensual pleasure. In a rhetorical question, Millhouser provides the reason for the murder: "Did I kill Hedda because I was secretly afraid that I wasn't losing only her, I was losing the beautiful and passionate side of myself?" Robert's hope for an emotional life is blasted by his violent act, but he must live on for thirty-six more years in a stoic attempt to come to terms with his crime.

Millhouser's readiness to relate his story to Gerald Higgins indicates that he has fallen neither into self-justification nor into emotional catalepsy. He recognizes in Higgins his own symptoms, and Millhouser votes for life by using his sorry condition as a cautionary tale. Higgins's wife is an adulteress, but Gerald will not become an emotional zombie by reenacting Millhouser's crime. Higgins has learned more about feeling and passion from this seemingly reserved and solitary old man than from his own ill-considered experiences. With the Millhouser example constantly before him, Gerald Higgins will learn the importance of forgiveness and love.

The qualified optimism of Millhouser's stoic example is reflected in *Imagine Kissing Pete,* one of the three novellas comprising the three-volume collection *Sermons and Soda-Water* (1960). Using James Malloy as his narrator, O'Hara returns the scene to Gibbsville to recount the details of the drunken and infidelity-filled marriage of upper-class Bobbie McCrea and her feckless husband, Pete. Theirs is a marriage based on his envy and resentment, her disappointment and snobbery. Yet after poverty, illness, and recrimination have reduced Bobbie and Pete to despair, they manage to stay together, bound by their pride in and love for a brilliant son. Malloy, who, like his aging creator, had always masked a certain sentimentality with his tough-guy exterior, cries at the ceremony of the son's graduation, knowing that Pete and Bobbie's resignation is a prelude to the restoration of order.

The other two novellas in *Sermons and Soda-Water* also employ Malloy as narrator, but the scene shifts from Gibbsville to the estates of the very rich outside New York City. *The Girl on the Baggage Truck* concerns Charlotte Sears, a Hollywood actress, whose insecurity in the Darwinian world of films forces her to use her body off as well as on camera. But if Hollywood is exploitive, Long Island's rich use Charlotte as brazenly in their pursuit of titillation. Disfigured in a fateful accident, Charlotte is forced out of films, retires, raises flowers, finds a good man, and achieves a measure of happiness. *We're Friends Again* is the least successful of the three novellas, although it does highlight a particularly repellent O'Hara spider-woman, Nancy Preswell Ellis, who is a living catalogue of social and political evils (though, strangely, she is not promiscuous). Malloy shakes his head over the marriages, infidelities, and divorces of a rather dull set of wealthy New Yorkers, but his two favorites–cousins estranged by the vindictive Nancy–become "friends again" as age quiets lust.

The principal theme in *Sermons and Soda-Water* is loneliness, its ubiquity, and the struggles of O'Hara's characters to overcome it. Malloy has used his own "old frenetic loneliness that none of us admit to, but that governed our habits and our lives." A friend calls him "the lonesomest son of a bitch I knew." But in the increasing serenity of age, Malloy finds a reason for loneliness: "What, really, can any of us know about any of us, and why must we make such a thing of loneliness when it is the final condition of us all? And where would love be without it?" This careful combination of human frailty and hope fans the spark of optimism that O'Hara had kindled in *Ourselves to Know.*

A more mundane optimism marked John O'Hara's attitudes toward his chances for fame as a playwright. Ever since *Pal Joey* had succeeded, O'Hara felt that he had the right stuff for the stage, particularly the musical drama. Potential directors and collaborators disagreed, unwilling to test O'Hara's plays on stage without extensive revision. A wealthy and famous novelist by now, and one unused to editorial interference, O'Hara refused to change anything. Probably out of deference to his best-selling novels, Random House brought out O'Hara's *Five Plays* in 1961, and the kindest comment on these efforts is that his wary collaborators were right. O'Hara never pandered to formulas for successful fiction in his novels, but these plays are designed to fulfill what O'Hara conceived of as the conventions of popular success on Broadway. They are alternately talky and dull, or melodramatic and incredible. *Five Plays* sold badly, its only achievement the dramatic prototype for *The Farmers Hotel*, which had already achieved its success as a novella. O'Hara believed that only a conspiracy of jealous directors could block the success of his efforts, but a play like *Veronique* is so bad that it makes one doubt that John O'Hara wrote it. That he was proud of it convinces no one of his critical acuity as a dramatist.

Much more successful, and justifiably so, was the volume of twenty-six stories published in 1961. *Assembly* has several first-rate stories in the finest O'Hara tradition and, in fact, constitutes the first volume of short fiction that he had published in fourteen years. O'Hara felt some joy in returning to the short story: "I had an apparently inexhaustible urge to express an unlimited supply of short story ideas." As had been the case in the past, several of the stories in *Assembly* had originally appeared in the *New Yorker* and had the familiar O'Hara touch and themes—the failures of love, the nastiness of infidelity, the potential (sometimes real) violence of a sexual encounter, and the defeats of social snobbery. A particularly gruesome tale involves a murderous ex-Hollywood producer, in the desert after failing in movies, who cajoles an old associate into bed with his wife, then kills them both. "In a Grove" is more sensational than the "normal" O'Hara story, but it is a carefully constructed portrait of revenge and depravity.

Other stories in *Assembly* combine aging with love, death with devotion, in far less violent terms. The protagonists, now beyond the youthful impetuosities of the earlier stories, will even forego their desires (in "The Lighter When Needed" and "You Can Always Tell Newark") in favor of preserving the order of marriage and decency. For every promiscuous wife or lustful hus-

band in the collection, O'Hara creates a balance with a loving mother (in "Mrs. Stratton of Oak Knoll") or a forebearing friend (in "The Compliment").

The best story in *Assembly* is "The Cellar Domain," a tight and ironic account of the failure of democracy in a Gibbsville barbershop. Peter Durant runs the best shop in town, catering to Gibbsville's elite, but he tries to make a place for the vulgar, Babbitt-like Andy Keever among his aristocrats. Their disdain keys Peter's defensive anger, and the social tension, which is always just beneath the surface in O'Hara's stories, flares into anger, accusations, and eventually alienation. Peter Durant has shown his integrity by "running his own shop," but the aristocrats will soon be patronizing another barber.

Several of the stories in *Assembly* concern Hollywood figures, some of them bitches and cheats, some of them not so bad after all. Film people had been the subjects of O'Hara's inspections as far back as *The Doctor's Son*, when the title character of "Mr. Sidney Gainsborough: Quality Pictures" turned out to be a philandering slob and petty tyrant. O'Hara's next novel was *The Big Laugh* (1962), a full-length treatment of an unredeemably rotten movie actor, Hubert Ward. The book was not particularly popular in hardcover, but eleven paperback printings kept it in circulation. Despite O'Hara's solid knowledge of the competition and exploitive venery of Hollywood, few readers would consider *The Big Laugh* a solid piece of fiction. The plot recounts the stallionlike career of Hubert Ward from his youth as a thief and despoiler of virgins to his rise to prominence as a star in motion pictures. Ward is one of O'Hara's nastiest villains, an amoral stud whose roles as a "clean-cut heavy" mirror his actual nature.

Yet, as critics of the novel point out, Ward is never really adequately motivated; O'Hara's Hollywood hypocrite and sexual athlete becomes a boring and respectable film-colony pillar after his marriage to Nina Stevens, a Chicago aristocrat. So boring does he become that he drives Nina into an affair, divorce, and departure. This "change" in Hubert Ward is supposedly an image-building ploy, but, again supposedly, Ward so deeply immerses himself in his new image that he *becomes* respectable. Similarly flimsy is the motivation behind Ward's affair with the wife of an important movie executive: Mildred Simmons blows up her marriage on the weakest of pretenses. And O'Hara can only follow Ward down the

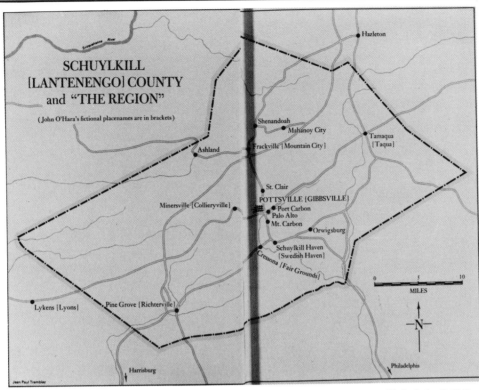

*O'Hara's fictional Gibbsville in Lantenengo County, Pennsylvania, which closely resembles Pottsville in Schuylkill County, Pennsylvania (*The O'Hara Concern, *courtesy of Random House)*

path to a lonely middle age, full of broken promises, sensual gratification, and self-aggrandizement. The hypocrite has come full circle; the path, however, is not a particularly interesting one. Ward has some of the exploitive qualities of his fictional ancestor, Joey Evans, but he lacks Joey's verve, innocence, and enthusiasm. As O'Hara's slice of the reptile-garden world of Hollywood, *The Big Laugh* is thin.

For the next several years John O'Hara produced dozens of short stories–too many, his critics chorused–from his self-proclaimed "unlimited supply." *The Cape Cod Lighter* (1962; twenty-three stories), *The Hat on the Bed* (1963; twenty-four stories), and *The Horse Knows the Way* (1964; twenty-eight stories) show his ease with the form, and if O'Hara could not produce winners every time, the quality of all three of these collections is higher than the achievement of his novels of the same era. The Gibbsville stories in *The Cape Cod Lighter* are first-rate, the best probably "Pat Collins," about a man whose wife destroys his relationship with his closest friend by sleeping with him. Pat will have another friend, but Madge will never learn of it, her dangerous sexuality being the source of misery and disruption in their marriage. "Winter Dance" echoes O'Hara's own infatu-

ation with an older girl, as Ted risks embarrassment and failure in his hopeless love for the glamorous Natalie. And "The First Day" makes real the chill felt by a once-famous foreign correspondent now so down on his luck that he must take a job on his provincial hometown newspaper.

"Exterior: With Figure" (*The Hat on the Bed*) reinforces a theme that O'Hara had used so effectively thirty years earlier in *Appointment in Samarra:* "There are, most definitely, such things as hard-luck people, hard-luck families; . . . we hesitate to bring up the family name for fear of hearing one more bit of evidence that bad luck begets bad luck, that we too, once started on a run of bad luck, may have to endure not a single disaster but a lifetime of it." This foreboding fatalism is offered by James Malloy, O'Hara's familiar autobiographical persona. The Armour family, the subject of Malloy's rumination here, fall from upper-middle-class rectitude to poverty, madness, and despair in Gibbsville. Their descent is triggered by ubiquitous mischance, but its effect on Malloy, now older and more "philosophical," is not his previous anger at the unfairness of it all; now he can only shrug over the fate of Mr. Armour, a nice pathetic man. "I do not know. I wish I knew. I want to know, and I never can know. I wish, I wish I knew."

"Exterior: With Figure" and Malloy's puzzlement at the inexplicable operations of bad luck are reflected in the title of the collection itself, *The Hat on the Bed*. O'Hara is recalling the old superstition that a hat placed on a bed will bring bad luck, but the short stories in this volume continue the recurrent theme of aging and death already noted in *Assembly*. Death is not bad luck for most of the characters in the stories in *The Hat on the Bed;* they have lived full lives, they are not cut off in their youth like Julian English or Sidney Tate. Rather, O'Hara's protagonists, like Malloy, approach the end of their lives gradually, naturally. And though some fear death ("Agatha"), others are reasonably content, even nostalgic. A character in "The Man on the Tractor" (*The Hat on the Bed*) expresses the new equanimity well: "Life has been awful to them, Pam, the town and the people, and it hasn't been nearly as bad to you and me. Not yet, anyway. But our luck will start running out. We're getting there. And I wanted to bring you here and tell you that I've always loved you. Here where I told you the first time."

Some critics used stories like "The Man on the Tractor" to claim that O'Hara was getting sentimental. Such a judgment might have had some validity if stories like "Justice" (*The Cape Cod Lighter*) or "How Can I Tell You?" (*The Hat on the Bed*) or "Zero" (*The Horse Knows the Way*) are ignored. But this last story exemplifies the quintessential O'Hara trap: a hopeless man caught in a joyless adultery. He has paid off his mistress, at least temporarily, with an abortion and cash. Yet his wife knows, and when he slaps her, she threatens to kill him: "Go ahead, you'd be doing me a favor,' he said. The strange simple words shocked her. Whatever else he said to her, those words she recognized as the truth; at this moment he wished to be dead and free, but not only free of her. More than to be free of her, he wished to be free of the other woman.... She was looking at destruction and she had had no part in it."

John O'Hara, whose own experience with higher education had been spotty and secondhand, could hardly be expected to feature academic heroes in his fiction. He used two aging faculty antagonists in "The Professors" (*The Cape Cod Lighter*), but the good-heartedness of the university is undercut by O'Hara's ironic awareness that its faculty are close to poverty unless they have "their own" money. Few, therefore, antici-

pated *Elizabeth Appleton* (1963), a novel at least ostensibly about John Appleton's failure to attain the presidency of Spring Valley College. O'Hara understands the political infighting consequent to a presidential search, and his irony is almost gleeful when, early in the novel, he reveals that John will be rejected in favor of a less talented candidate because the trustees exercise their power arbitrarily.

Still, Appleton's loss of the office is not especially damaging to him psychologically or professionally. Much more disappointed is Elizabeth Appleton, the real center of the book. As was the case with his portrait of Princeton in *From the Terrace*, O'Hara is not really concerned with the life of the mind. More important is another side of life in a college town, the combination of social ambition and rampant sensuality that constitutes the essential nature of Elizabeth Appleton. Born into a family of wealth and power, she marries beneath her when she accepts John Appleton, but she seems willing to carry on gamely enough if extra money continues to arrive from her mother. It is Elizabeth, not John, who aspires to the leadership of Spring Valley College, and she expects it because she has always gotten what she has set out to get.

In Elizabeth, O'Hara has created another of his rapacious Lilith-figures, confident, secure in her money-induced snobbery, beautiful, lubricious, and heartless. Perhaps she is not the equal of Grace Caldwell Tate or Mary St. John Eaton, but her infidelity to John in her affair with a local aristocrat, Porter Ditson, awakens no remorse in her when she cuts it off. Ditson may have been devastated, but Elizabeth has used him for her pleasure, then discarded him at her convenience. Her rationalization for adultery arises from her contempt for her husband (who should have known of her affair if he were not so self-deceiving), but O'Hara's sympathies lie with the cast-aside Ditson and the cuckolded Appleton, not with Elizabeth. Both men are nearer the moral center of O'Hara's fiction, Sidney Tate of *A Rage to Live;* however, as Sheldon Grebstein has pointed out; "The men in O'Hara's work think morally about what should be; the women think about what they want."

As if to prove the critics wrong about the stereotypical sex roles in his fiction, John O'Hara created a gaggle of scheming and ambitious men in his next novel, *The Lockwood Corners* (1965). Another "big" novel, O'Hara's panorama this time encompasses four generations of the Lockwood fam-

"I think it a remarkably able novel, readable from first word to last, written with extraordinary crispness and honesty. I know of no finer presentation in our recent fiction of the culture of the rich Americans of our medium-sized towns. Mr. O'Hara's eyes and ears have never worked with such merciless accuracy."
— Clifton Fadiman

A RAGE TO LIVE

JOHN O'HARA

A RAGE to LIVE

A NOVEL BY JOHN O'HARA

RANDOM HOUSE

Dust jacket for O'Hara's 1949 novel

ily from the birth of Moses in 1811 to the death of George in 1926. The "concern" of this family is dynastic obsession, the schemes of several generations of money-makers and women chasers to found an American aristocracy in Swedish Haven, Pennsylvania, not far from Gibbsville.

Webster Schott, reviewing *The Lockwood Concern,* called O'Hara "America's most distinguished out-of-date novelist." Schott's reservations, and grudging praise, were based on the multi-generational scope of the novel, its unresolved subplots, its jam-packed catalogues of details chiefly interesting to social historians. In fact, *The Lockwood Concern* is only half the length of *From the Terrace,* and O'Hara creates a marvelously obsessed character in Abraham Lockwood. The "concern" is really his, an intense commitment to a ruling family worthy of analysis. Abraham is almost a "pure" O'Hara character, motivated solely by drives for money, power, and—oddly—immortality through the dynastic impulse. Yet like all of the Lockwoods, Abraham can take time out from empire building for the wayward sexual activity of the sensualist.

Abraham's dream turns to dust in the hands of his son, George, a complete snob yet almost as ambitious as his father. George realizes,

however, that he will never really rank among the American aristocrats, despite his money, and George's son, Bing, hates his father and deserts Swedish Haven for fast oil money in the West. Ernestine, George's daughter, is sterile, and the Lockwoods will vanish soon. In a heavily symbolic ending, George falls on the secret stairway in his house and dies, isolated and forgotten by the world that he walled out and sought to conquer.

The Lockwood Concern is not one of John O'Hara's major novels. O'Hara wrote of status-hungry Americans in more vivid terms in *Appointment in Samarra* and *Ten North Frederick,* and, as a study in obsessions, *The Lockwood Concern* is surpassed by *A Rage to Live* and *Ourselves to Know.* The social history is still insightful and interesting, but critics of the novel have a sound basis for slighting O'Hara's powers of characterization in this novel. The death of the Lockwood dream simply does not create the emotional effects of other, and better, O'Hara portrayals.

By the mid 1960s, O'Hara's writing habits were so fixed that the title of his next collection of stories was purely autobiographical. *Waiting for Winter* (1966) reflected his established pattern of giving his summers to short stories, his winters to his novels. Yet if the decline in the effectiveness of the novels might be associated with a wintry quality in O'Hara's own creativity, the stories in *Waiting for Winter* show no evidence of deterioration. In his own mind O'Hara might have regarded his stories as secondary to the longer fictions, but his readers knew better. Like the other story collections of the 1960s *Waiting for Winter* was popular.

Several stories in this collection are among O'Hara's best. "Flight" is a tight and perceptive tale of an aging playwright who falls on the ice, returns to go over his life with his wife in a clear-headed and rational way, then drifts into a dream of the past. Charles Kinsmith is frightened, but muses: "I'm convinced that most people really know just about how long they're going to last, and they guide their lives and expend their resources accordingly. . . . If you ask a man when he's going to die, he won't be able to tell you, but he knows. I know when I'm going to die, but it isn't going to be from this fall." Then, ironically, Kinsmith dies. A summary, however, does little justice to the mutual devotion that has kept Kinsmith and his wife together for forty years, yet that love is counterbalanced by "The Pomeranian," a cool description of a marriage held together by fear, weakness, and petty tyrannies. More violent is the suicide that ends the long-standing affair of two people who will not give themselves to love (in "Andrea"), and a peep into the sexual jealousy of working-class Gibbsville where James Malloy's unhappy genteel poverty is contrasted to a brutal murder (in "Fatimas and Kisses"). One Hollywood story, "Natica Jackson," echoes the Medea myth when a betrayed wife, her husband bewitched by the easy sexuality of a Hollywood actress, drowns their two children in revenge. O'Hara's disgust is directed not only toward the married pair but also toward Natica, the shallow actress, whose career demands that she dissociate herself from the situation. She is a coward and a fool.

O'Hara's next novel, one of the weakest in his long career, carries on the contempt for show-business people that had always characterized the fiction featuring Broadway and Hollywood. *The Instrument* (1967) focuses on a malefic theatrical monster, playwright Yancey "Yank" Lucas. Though Lucas's conversation shows scant traces of intellect, he is supposedly a gifted author whose play has captivated New York. Yank's more apparent attitudes show up in bed, into which tumble a variety of compliant young women.

O'Hara in his study at Linebrook (photo by Martin D'Arcy)

The upshot of Lucas's couplings is unrelieved misery for his partners. In novels like *Ourselves to Know* and *From the Terrace*, O'Hara's created loveless and cold men whose social and psychological credibility made their plights significant, but *The Instrument* fails to make Yank Lucas come alive. He cannot love because he "uses" women in his art, thus reifying them into "material." However, such emotional deadness in the service of his art is unmotivated and unbelievable, particularly since the nature of Yank's appeal to women remains mysterious. O'Hara's attractive theatrical heels, particularly Pal Joey, make Yank Lucas a pale, if "serious," imitation.

Critics claimed that O'Hara was running out of titles when *And Other Stories* appeared in 1968. The collection is built around a James Malloy story of novelette length, "A Few Trips and Some Poetry." Malloy's long and sporadic affair with Isabel Barley proves mainly that neither is right for the other; more significant for O'Hara's readers is the prominence in this story of an egregious lesbianism which, in these last books, becomes the most grievous sin in the canon of morality for his characters. However, O'Hara can use just a soupçon of lesbianism very effectively, as in

"We'll Have Fun." Here a pretty girl's loneliness is tempered by the sensitivity and competence of an apparently feckless Irish stableman. More typical of the lesbian villain is the brutal and vulgar Margo, whose seduction of the aristocratic Mary Brewer in "The Broken Giraffe" bodes disaster for all.

Such disaster lays waste most of the unhappy crew of *Lovey Childs: A Philadelphian's Story* (1969), a novel that vies with *The Instrument* for last place on O'Hara's achievement list. Once again the scene is the bedrooms of the rich, but by now what John Cheever called "O'Hara's vision of things, the premise of irony, generated by a ceremonial society and an improvisational erotic life," has become almost purely erotic. The irony is gone, in much the way it had been gone from *The Instrument,* because O'Hara can generate little enthusiasm for the plight of his characters. Other O'Hara sirens may have been greedy wantons, but at least they existed in a framework of carefully observed norms. Lovey Childs has none of Gloria Wandrous's pathos, little of Grace Tate's charm, even a short measure of the evil decadence of Mary Eaton and Hedda Millhouser. Connoisseurs of O'Hara's harpies might object that Lovey is the first to drive a Roman Catholic priest to suicide by means of seduction, but this incredible triumph fails to make her a fully realized character. And female homosexuality is hardly an adequate explanation of her contradictions.

O'Hara's rich had always been able to indulge their sexual peculiarities with relative freedom, and in the world of Philadelphia's rich, lesbianism flourishes. Dorothy Lewis, Lovey's mother, introduced to the deviation by her daughter's schoolmate, becomes brazen and is put away in a sanatorium. Lovey, whose proclivities are nominally heterosexual, can take intense pleasure from the ministrations of a woman reporter. She can marry a playboy and divorce him quickly, and she can marry one of her Philadelphia cousins and settle down to a placid monogamy. For all that, O'Hara ends the novel so abruptly that Lovey's life remains murky.

In the posthumously published *The Ewings* (1972), O'Hara returned to the social history that often makes his novels valuable and credible despite the lubriciousness of the characters. If *Lovey Childs* hovered on the thin edge of deviant scatology, *The Ewings* returns us to the world of big business and corporate infighting, the like of which O'Hara had not featured since *From the Terrace.*

Bill Ewing, a Clevelander in the boom days of World War I, marries his college sweetheart and begins his rise to the top. Edna Ewing is as shrewd and ambitious as he, and the manipulations, adaptations, and calculations of financial success are meticulously catalogued by O'Hara. Neither Bill nor Edna is a memorable creation but–save for the sensationalism of Bill's mother's lesbianism–the novel deserves good marks.

When he died, O'Hara left some fifty unpublished stories, some of which when combined with several previously published but uncollected stories allowed Random House to bring out *The Time Element and Other Stories* (1972) and *Good Samaritan and Other Stories* (1974). The majority of the stories in *The Time Element* date from the 1940s; they are shorter, more anecdotal than the developed forms that O'Hara adopted in the 1960s, when the longer stories in *Good Samaritan* were written. The two collections were not extensively reviewed, and neither sold in the fashion of the short stories published earlier.

Nevertheless, for O'Hara fans these stories have a masterful touch. A taut story of Jimmy Malloy's sexual initiation by an older woman, "A Man to be Trusted" (*Good Samaritan*), is made suspenseful by latent violence. And that honored O'Hara theme, social inferiority, is nicely dramatized in Mr. Langley's recognition that his wife has remade him in her image in "Not Always" (*The Time Element*). These stories for the most part are tenser than O'Hara's work in the later collections, but *Good Samaritan* ends with a sentimental, nostalgic return to the 1920s in "Christmas Poem." Echoing O'Hara's own Christmases in Pottsville, "Christmas Poem" concerns Billy Warden's desire to escape home for a gala house party being thrown by the wealthy Coopers. Billy considers his family hopelessly middle-class and dull until he finds that his father secretly writes a poem for his mother for Christmas and has for twenty-six years. "He wondered if Henrietta Cooper's father had ever written a poem to her mother. But he knew the answer to that." The triteness of this "home's best" sentimentality is washed away by the realistic portrayal of Billy's social ambitiousness and his parents' very obvious shortcomings. Yet they love him, and he discovers that he loves them.

Left unfinished at John O'Hara's death was *The Second Ewings,* some seventy pages of a sequel to *The Ewings.* Published as a facsimile of the typescript in 1977, this fragment carries the rising Bill Ewing to more responsible and remunerative executive positions in Cuyahoga Iron & Steel, but Bill's affair with Alicia Cott casts a menacing shadow over the unfinished sequel.

The last O'Hara book to be published was *Two by O'Hara* (1979): an unproduced play written in 1962, *Far from Heaven;* and *The Man Who Could Not Lose,* an unproduced screen story. The play is better than several of those in *Five Plays*, and its politician hero, fighting to regain power after a prison term, is an interesting man. The screen story, imaginative but forgettable, concerns an expatriate crooked financier. That these two fugitive O'Hara works saw print stems from the diligence of O'Hara's biographer Matthew J. Bruccoli, whose interest in O'Hara also made possible the publication of *The Second Ewings.*

Bruccoli concluded his biography, *The O'Hara Concern*, with an estimate of his subject far more generous than the critical consensus. To Bruccoli, O'Hara was "one or our best novelists, our best novella-ist, and our greatest writer of short stories." To Stanley Kauffmann, O'Hara was "in effect merely an aggrandized stenographer with narrative skills, an enervated tag-end of naturalism being maintained for its own exploitive sake." Nevertheless, both of these critics admit to weaknesses and strengths in John O'Hara, and the final judgment rests somewhere between the extremes.

Any good novelist is concerned with accurate observation and credible ordering of social facts. The novelist uses this data to dramatize a new imaginative explication of human experience. John O'Hara's fiction, like that of other realist-naturalist writers, is heavily tilted toward accuracy and credibility; his imaginative side is less apparent, but only a solidly creative imagination could have generated memorable characters like Julian English, Sidney Tate, Joey Evans, and James Malloy. If O'Hara's work is laden with social history, with cultural data, with sexual mores, this material is–in his best novels–integral to an understanding of his characters' concerns.

Perhaps the most serious charge leveled at O'Hara is that his characters are not adequately motivated, a claim that even his most ardent supporters must occasionally acknowledge when faced with the love-at-first-sight clichés that are apparently a part of O'Hara's system of belief. O'Hara himself echoed this critical reservation by confessing that he did not know how his characters thought ("I wish I knew"). The character-as-fate which moves his men and women is often left unexplained. Yet for an author so consciously committed to explanations, this failure to "see" constitutes a significant flaw, particularly in the weakest novels like *Lovey Childs* and *The Instrument.*

In O'Hara's successes, however, the characters live clearly and credibly, and, often, tragically. Julian English and Joe Chapin never grow up, never escape the suffocating rigidity of caste and status. The necessary patterns of denial in American society war against the expressions of instinct, and only those whose social power is almost absolute (Grace Tate, Elizabeth Appleton) escape frustration, even disintegration. Finally, even the aristocracy can waste away under the blows of bad luck.

Many of O'Hara's less perceptive critics interpreted the incessant sexual encounters in his fiction to be approval of license. No modern writer, however, was more committed to love and loyalty and forgiveness than John O'Hara. His was a conservative ethic, often expressed in his grudging admiration for the decent values of the elite. That he could admire these values while dissecting the hypocrites who professed to hold them is at the core of his achievement as a writer. And his fiction is stronger because O'Hara lets his vast audience know what he *does* know: honest compassion is the rarest and most necessary of human emotions. His observations of Pennsylvania, New York, Hollywood, and dozens of other locales taught him that most Americans–rich or the would-be-rich–don't have time for compassion, thus the tragedy of their existence.

Furthermore, he accomplished his thematic mission in a professionally skillful way, his prose pellucid, his structures (at their best in the stories) tight and inevitable. O'Hara used point of view brilliantly, shifting from objective narration to flawless dialogue easily and naturally. In stories like "The Doctor's Son" or "Price's Always Open," he selects scene and focus unerringly, pares the prose of extras (including the famous avoidance of metaphor), and achieves a rhythmic alteration of narrative techniques that keeps everything moving. He may have "made it look easy," but consistent readability is no mean achievement, especially when O'Hara is cataloguing the many components of a social value system removed by fifty years from readers' experience.

These achievements were not enough to keep the vast majority of literary critics from rejecting O'Hara's work. He was indeed out of step with fashionable writing, particularly during the 1960s, when book after book brought negative critical response yet huge sales to the reading public. Lionel Trilling had once praised O'Hara's "sense of the startling anomaly of man's life in society, his consciousness of social life as an absurd and inescapable fate, as the degrading condition to which the human spirit submits if it is to exist at all." American readers from 1928 to 1970 recognized this strength in O'Hara, for it was a very American concern. In an earlier age Nathaniel Hawthorne had expressed the same anomaly in *The House of the Seven Gables* (1851): "In this republican country, amid the fluctuating tides of our social life, somebody is always at the drowning point." John O'Hara made it his mission to chronicle these drownings.

However, O'Hara–for all of the determinism of his fictional world and the cool irony of his tone–kept his readers aware of the lifelines available to those struggling in the destructive element of society. O'Hara continued to believe in decency, forbearance, and the fundamental strength of American capitalist democracy. He found that American society did waste lives and spirits in the most profligate ways, but he saw as well that the strivers, the seekers, the outsiders knew what they were about when they sought a place in the American system. O'Hara's own achievements showed him that the place was worth fighting for, and his millions of readers honored his vision of this goal. In the huge body of his work, John O'Hara staked out his territory and marked it with his unmistakably personal stamp. Some of his contemporaries may have had grander visions, but John O'Hara's was powerful and will endure.

Letters:

Selected Letters of John O'Hara, edited by Matthew J. Bruccoli (New York: Random House, 1978).
Contains 450 letters with footnotes.

Bibliography:

Matthew J. Bruccoli, *John O'Hara: A Descriptive Bibliography* (Pittsburgh: University of Pittsburgh Press, 1978).
Comprehensive listing of all materials published by O'Hara, including articles, reviews, letters, statements, and interviews.

Biographies:

Finis Farr, *O'Hara: A Biography* (Boston: Little, Brown, 1972).

Indulgent treatment of O'Hara by a friend and fellow journalist, best on the psychology of the American Irish.

Matthew J. Bruccoli, *The O'Hara Concern: A Biography of John O'Hara* (New York: Random House, 1975).
Comprehensive and authoritative account, strongly supportive of O'Hara's literary achievements.

Frank MacShane, *The Life of John O'Hara* (New York: Dutton, 1980).
Gracefully written biography, probably the most balanced evaluation of O'Hara's fiction.

References:

Charles Bassett, "John O'Hara: Irishman and American," *John O'Hara Journal,* 1 (Summer 1979): 1-81.
Analysis of ethnic tensions influencing O'Hara's life and literary production.

Bassett, "Naturalism Revisited: The Case of John O'Hara," *Colby Library Quarterly,* 11 (December 1975): 198-218.
Treats determinism as a central theme in O'Hara's work, particularly *Appointment in Samarra.*

E. Russell Carson, *The Fiction of John O'Hara* (Pittsburgh: University of Pittsburgh Press, 1961).
Extended pamphlet, earnest and workmanlike.

John Cobbs, "Caste and Class War: The Society of John O'Hara's *A Rage to Live,*" *John O'Hara Journal,* 2 (Winter 1979-1980): 24-34.
Analysis of the social tensions behind a popular novel.

Beverly Gary, "A Post Portrait: John O'Hara," *New York Post,* 24 May 1959, pp. 18-22.
Unflattering profile typical of the views of O'Hara in his prime.

Sheldon Grebstein, *John O'Hara* (New York: Twayne, 1966).
Eminently sensible criticism of O'Hara, notably on themes that pervade the entire canon.

John O'Hara Journal, 1978-1983.
Only five issues of this journal, "devoted to the life and writings of John O'Hara," appeared during the six years of its existence.

Robert Emmet Long, *John O'Hara* (New York: Ungar, 1983).
Excellent critical analysis of O'Hara's work, especially acute on the theme of isolation and loneliness.

Bernard McCormick, "A John O'Hara Geography," *Journal of Modern Literature*, 1 (1970-1971): 151-158.
An account of the reception of O'Hara's work and reputation in his hometown, Pottsville, Pennsylvania.

Don Schanche, "John O'Hara Is Alive and Well in the First Half of the Twentieth Century," *Esquire*, 72 (August 1969): 84-86, 142, 144-149.
A biographical essay by a journalist who had O'Hara's trust.

Lee Sigelman, "Politics and the Social Order in the Work of John O'Hara," *Journal of American Studies*, 20 (August 1986): 233-257.
Finds O'Hara to be far more politically astute than suspected, particularly in *Ten North Frederick*.

Lionel Trilling, Introduction to *Selected Short Stories of John O'Hara* (New York: Modern Library, 1956).
Perhaps the most influential estimate of O'Hara's social vision; Trilling believes that O'Hara is an American Kafka portraying social absurdities.

Charles Walcutt, *John O'Hara* (Minneapolis: University of Minnesota Press, 1969).
Scorn for O'Hara's novels is counterbalanced by his insights on the stories in this pamphlet.

Eugene O'Neill

This entry was updated by Laura Ingram from the entry by George H. Jensen (Chicago, Illinois) in DLB 7, Twentieth-Century American Dramatists.

Places	Provincetown, Mass.	Broadway	Greenwich Village
Influences and Relationships	August Strindberg Friedrich Nietzsche Joseph Conrad Henrik Ibsen	George Pierce Baker Classical Greek Dramatists	George Jean Nathan James O'Neill (Melodrama)
Literary Movements and Forms	Supernaturalism Satire	Experimental Drama	Realism
Major Themes	Madness Disintegration of the Self-Image Alcohol and Drug Addiction	Sacrifice as an Expression of Love Abandonment Alienation The Mask	Adventure Sexual Passion Rejection of Patriarchal God
Cultural and Artistic Influences	Rejection of Philistinism in the American Theater	Seafaring Life Freudian Psychology	Catholicism
Social and Economic Influences	Latin American Revolutions	Miscegenation	Racism

BIRTH: New York, New York, 16 October 1888, to James and Ellen Quinlan O'Neill.

EDUCATION: Princeton University, 1906-1907; Harvard University, 1914-1915.

MARRIAGE: 2 October 1909 to Kathleen Jenkins (divorced); child: Eugene Gladstone, Jr.; 12 April 1918 to Agnes Boulton (divorced); children: Shane, Oona; 22 July 1929 to Carlotta Monterey.

AWARDS: Pulitzer Prize for *Beyond the Horizon*, 1920; Pulitzer Prize for *Anna Christie*, 1922; National Institute of Arts and Letters Gold Medal Award for Drama, 1923; election to the National Institute of Arts and Letters, 1923; Litt.D., Yale University, 1926; Pulitzer Prize for *Strange Interlude*, 1928; Nobel Prize for Literature, 1936; Pulitzer Prize and New York Drama Critics Circle Award for *Long Day's Journey into Night*, 1957.

DEATH: Boston, Massachusetts, 27 November 1953.

Eugene O'Neill (Gale International Portrait Gallery)

PLAY PRODUCTIONS: *Bound East for Cardiff*, 28 July 1916, Wharf Theatre, Provincetown, Mass.; 3 November 1916, Provincetown Playhouse, New York;

Thirst, Summer 1916, Wharf Theatre, Provincetown, Mass.;

Before Breakfast, 1 December 1916, Provincetown Playhouse, New York;

Fog, January 1917, Provincetown Playhouse, New York;

The Sniper, 16 February 1917, Provincetown Playhouse, New York;

In the Zone, 31 October 1917, Comedy Theatre, New York;

The Long Voyage Home, 2 November 1917, Provincetown Playhouse, New York;

Ile, 30 November 1917, Provincetown Playhouse, New York;

The Rope, 26 April 1918, Provincetown Playhouse, New York;

Where the Cross Is Made, 22 November 1918, Provincetown Playhouse, New York;

The Moon of the Caribbees, 20 December 1918, Provincetown Playhouse, New York;

The Dreamy Kid, 31 October 1919, Provincetown Playhouse, New York;

Beyond the Horizon, 2 February 1920, Morosco Theatre, New York, 111 [performances];

Chris, 8 March 1920, Atlantic City, N.J.; revised as *Anna Christie*, 2 November 1921, Vanderbilt Theatre, New York, 177;

Exorcism, 26 March 1920, Provincetown Playhouse, New York;

The Emperor Jones, 1 November 1920, Provincetown Playhouse (transferred to Selwyn Theatre), New York, 204;

Diff'rent, 27 December 1920, Provincetown Playhouse, New York, 100;

Gold, 1 June 1921, Frazee Theatre, New York, 13;

The Straw, 10 November 1921, Greenwich Village Theatre, New York, 20;

The First Man, 4 March 1922, Neighborhood Playhouse, New York, 27;

The Hairy Ape, 9 March 1922, Provincetown Playhouse, New York, 127;

Welded, 17 March 1924, Thirty-ninth Street Theatre, New York, 24;

The Ancient Mariner: A Dramatic Arrangement of Coleridge's Poem, 6 April 1924, Provincetown Playhouse, New York, 29;

All God's Chillun Got Wings, 15 May 1924, Provincetown Playhouse (transferred to Greenwich Village Theatre), New York, 100;

S.S. Glencairn, 14 August 1924, Barnstormer's Barn, Provincetown, Mass.; 3 November

1924, Provincetown Playhouse, New York, 99;

Desire Under the Elms, 11 November 1924, Greenwich Village Theatre, New York, 208;

The Fountain, 10 December 1925, Greenwich Village Theatre, New York, 24;

The Great God Brown, 23 January 1926, Greenwich Village Theatre, New York, 283;

Marco Millions, 9 January 1928, Guild Theatre, New York, 92;

Strange Interlude, 30 January 1928, John Golden Theatre, New York, 426;

Lazarus Laughed, 9 April 1928, Community Playhouse, Pasadena, Cal., 28;

Dynamo, 11 February 1929, Martin Beck Theatre, New York, 50;

Mourning Becomes Electra (Homecoming, The Hunted, and *The Haunted*), 26 October 1931, Guild Theatre, New York, 150;

Ah, Wilderness!, 25 September 1933, Nixon Theatre, Pittsburgh; 2 October 1933, Guild Theatre, New York, 289;

Days Without End, 8 January 1934, Henry Miller's Theatre, New York, 57;

The Iceman Cometh, 9 October 1946, Martin Beck Theatre, New York, 136;

A Moon for the Misbegotten, 20 February 1947, Hartman Theatre, Columbus, Ohio; 2 May 1957, Bijou Theatre, New York, 68;

Long Day's Journey Into Night, 10 February 1956, Kungl. Dramastika Teatern, Stockholm; 7 November 1956, Helen Hayes Theatre, New York, 390;

A Touch of the Poet, 29 March 1957, Kungl. Dramastika Teatern, Stockholm; 2 October 1958, Helen Hayes Theatre, New York, 284;

Hughie, 18 September 1958, Kungl. Dramastika Teatern, Stockholm; 22 December 1964, Royale Theatre, New York, 51;

More Stately Mansions, 11 September 1962, Kungl. Dramastika Teatern, Stockholm; 31 October 1967, Broadhurst Theatre, New York, 142.

BOOKS: *Thirst and Other One Act Plays* (Boston: Gorham Press, 1914);

Before Breakfast (New York: Shay, 1916);

The Moon of the Caribbees and Six Other Plays of the Sea (New York: Boni & Liveright, 1919; London: Cape, 1923);

Beyond the Horizon (New York: Boni & Liveright, 1920);

The Emperor Jones, Diff'rent, The Straw (New York: Boni & Liveright, 1921); republished as

Eugene O'Neill as an infant (Yale University Library)

Plays: First Series, The Straw, The Emperor Jones, and *Diff'rent* (London: Cape, 1922);

Gold (New York: Boni & Liveright, 1921);

The Hairy Ape, Anna Christie, The First Man (New York: Boni & Liveright, 1922);

The Hairy Ape and Other Plays (London: Cape, 1923);

Beyond the Horizon and Gold (London: Cape, 1924);

All God's Chillun Got Wings and Welded (New York: Boni & Liveright, 1924);

The Complete Works of Eugene O'Neill, 2 volumes (New York: Boni & Liveright, 1924);

Desire Under the Elms (New York: Boni & Liveright, 1925);

All God's Chillun Got Wings, Desire Under the Elms, and *Welded* (London: Cape, 1925);

The Great God Brown, The Fountain, The Moon of the Caribbees and Other Plays (New York: Boni & Liveright, 1926); republished as *The Great God Brown Including The Fountain, The Dreamy Kid,* and *Before Breakfast* (London: Cape, 1926);

Marco Millions (New York: Boni & Liveright, 1927; London: Cape, 1927);

Lazarus Laughed (New York: Boni & Liveright, 1927);

Strange Interlude (New York: Boni & Liveright, 1928; London: Cape, 1928);

Dynamo (New York: Liveright, 1929);

Lazarus Laughed and Dynamo (London: Cape, 1929);

Mourning Becomes Electra (New York: Liveright, 1931; London: Cape, 1932);

Ah, Wilderness! (New York: Random House, 1933);

Days Without End (New York: Random House, 1934);

Ah, Wilderness! and Days Without End (London: Cape, 1934);

The Iceman Cometh (New York: Random House, 1946; London: Cape, 1947);

Lost Plays of Eugene O'Neill (New York: New Fathoms, 1950)–includes *Abortion, The Movie Man, The Sniper, Servitude,* and *A Wife for a Life;*

A Moon for the Misbegotten (New York: Random House, 1952; London: Cape, 1953);

Long Day's Journey Into Night (New Haven: Yale University Press, 1956; London: Cape, 1956);

A Touch of the Poet (New Haven: Yale University Press, 1957; London: Cape, 1957);

Hughie (New Haven: Yale University Press, 1959; London: Cape, 1962);

More Stately Mansions (New Haven & London: Yale University Press, 1964; London: Cape, 1965);

Ten "Lost" Plays (New York: Random House, 1964; London: Cape, 1965)–includes *Thirst, The Web, Warnings, Fog, Recklessness,* and *Abortion;*

"Children of the Sea" and Three Other Unpublished Plays (Washington, D.C.: Microcard Editions, 1972)–includes *Bread and Butter, Now I Ask You,* and *Shell Shock;*

Poems 1912-1944, edited by Donald C. Gallup (Boston: Ticknor & Fields, 1980);

The Unknown O'Neill: Unpublished or Unfamiliar Writings of Eugene O'Neill, edited by Travis Bogard (New Haven & London: Yale University Press, 1988).

OTHER: *Bound East for Cardiff,* in *The Provincetown Plays, First Series* (New York: Shay, 1916);

Before Breakfast, in *The Provincetown Plays, Third Series* (New York: Shay, 1916);

The Dreamy Kid, in *Contemporary One-Act Plays,* edited by Frank Shay (Cincinnati: Kidd, 1922).

PERIODICAL PUBLICATIONS: "Tomorrow," *Seven Arts* (June 1917): 147-170;

"Strindberg and Our Theatre," *Provincetown Playbill,* no. 1 (1923-1924): 1,3;

"The Playwright Explains," *New York Times,* 14 February 1926, VIII: 2;

"Memoranda on Masks," *American Spectator* (November 1932): 3;

"Second Thoughts," *American Spectator* (December 1932): 2;

"A Dramatist's Notebook," *American Spectator* (January 1933): 2;

"Prof. George Pierce Baker," *New York Times,* 13 January 1935, IX: 1;

The Ancient Mariner, Yale University Library Gazette, 35 (October 1960): 61-86.

In the 1910s the American theater, long dominated by melodramas, dictatorial producers (most of whom were artless magnates), and an audience more drawn by stars–preferably British–than good scripts, was finally ready to establish its own identity. The change had begun in the late nineteenth century with a generation of earnest though ultimately ineffective playwrights: James A. Herne, Bronson Howard, David Belasco, Augustus Thomas, Clyde Fitch, and William Vaughn Moody. Belasco's experiments with lighting, set construction, and special effects made the American theater equal and, in some ways, superior to the European theater. The American innovations of the nineteenth century and the dramas of Henrik Ibsen, August Strindberg, and George Bernard Shaw brought more of the next generation's talent to the theater. George Jean Nathan, Barrett H. Clark, Joseph Wood Krutch, Alexander Woollcott, Kenneth Macgowan, Heywood Broun, and Burns Mantle formed a critical battery willing to demand and capable of appreciating good drama. Robert Edmond Jones, Lee Simonson, and Cleon Throckmorton added to Belasco's developments in scenic design. Young energetic intellectuals began forming experimental theater groups to encourage good productions and good playwrights. Lawrence Langner, Helen Westley, Philip Moeller, and Edward Goodman formed the Washington Square Players in 1914 in New York; George "Jig" Cook, Susan Glaspell, and friends formed the Provincetown Players in 1915. The catalyst and symbol of this collection of talent, the rejection of melodrama, and the establishment of American drama became Eugene Gladstone O'Neill, America's first great playwright. His career, so tied to this generation of theatrical personnel, should be judged within its historical context, as a reaction against melodrama and a search for a theatrical aesthetic to replace it.

Eugene O'Neill, age five (Carlotta Monterey O'Neill)

O'Neill was born into the very theatrical world he would help to displace. He was born in a New York hotel on Forty-third and Broadway on 16 October 1888. His father, James O'Neill, Sr., who had worked with James A. Herne and David Belasco in the early 1880s, was then on tour. O'Neill, Sr., spent most of his career playing the title role in *The Count of Monte Cristo* (1846), a melodrama adapted from Alexandre Dumas's novel. Eugene, since he grew up with melodrama, knew its dangers and limitations. Also crucial to his development as a playwright was the nature of his family life, which was structured on guilt, betrayal, and accusations. These themes, implicitly or explicitly, appear in most of his plays. Ellen Quinlan O'Neill, his mother, felt betrayed when, three months after her marriage, her husband was sued by Nettie Walsh, who claimed James O'Neill, Sr., was married to her and was the father of her child. Jamie, Ellen's firstborn, passed measles on to Edmund, her secondborn, who died soon afterward. Ellen became a drug addict after a doctor administered morphine while she was recovering from Eugene's birth. She later blamed her addiction on her husband, claiming that he was too miserly to pay for a competent doctor.

For the first seven years of his life O'Neill traveled with his parents. He was educated first in authoritarian Catholic schools–St. Aloysius

Academy for Boys in Riverdale, New York, from 1895 to 1900, and De La Salle Institute in New York City, from 1900 to 1902–and later at Betts Academy, a nonsectarian preparatory school in Stamford, Connecticut. In 1906-1907 he spent less than a year at Princeton. He was suspended in April for breaking a window in a railroad stationmaster's house and did not return.

After leaving Princeton, O'Neill perfunctorily worked at a few jobs, but his life was for the most part aimless and dissipated. In 1907-1908 he worked at the New York-Chicago Supply Company. In the following year he met and married Kathleen Jenkins. His father, who disapproved of the marriage, arranged for him to prospect for gold in Honduras. After contracting malaria, O'Neill returned to New York but did not live with his wife. On 5 May 1910 Kathleen gave birth to O'Neill's first son, Eugene Gladstone, Jr. O'Neill and Kathleen were divorced in 1912.

One month after the birth of his son O'Neill sailed as a seaman on the *Charles Racine*, a Norwegian square-rigger. He jumped ship in Buenos Aires, where he worked a few jobs but generally lived hand-to-mouth, begging for food along the waterfront. In spring 1911 he returned to New York on the *Ikala*, a freighter which would, with his other sea voyages, inspire the *S.S. Glencairn* series of one-act plays. After living at Jimmy-the-Priest's, a waterfront dive, for a few months, he shipped out on the *New Yorker* and returned on the *Philadelphia*, both luxury liners. The voyages provided material for *The Hairy Ape* (1922). He returned to Jimmy-the-Priest's, where he attempted suicide by taking an overdose of Veronal. He was then reunited with his family and toured with his father's *Monte Cristo* company.

At the end of 1912, after a short career as a journalist with the *New London Telegraph*, O'Neill entered Gaylord Farm Sanitarium to be treated for tuberculosis. During his six months in the sanitarium, probably feeling, at times, close to death (his maternal grandfather died from tuberculosis), O'Neill reassessed his life. He entered the sanitarium a dabbler in poetry; he left resolved to become a serious writer.

In the fall and winter of 1913-1914, while living with the Rippin family in New London, O'Neill began his apprenticeship. Having grown up with *The Count of Monte Cristo*, O'Neill had little choice but to begin by writing melodramas. Though he had read Ibsen, Strindberg, and Shaw (authors who had evolved from but transcended nineteenth-century melodramas), these models were less accessible, except in printed form, than American melodramas. In the early twentieth century, theatrical experiments in Europe were not easily transplanted to America. The unavoidable model, then, was the melodrama, in which plot was more important than characterization. O'Neill eventually broke from the tradition of melodrama by making characterization more important than plot.

A Wife for a Life (1950), O'Neill's first play, written in the spring of 1913 and not produced in his lifetime, is characteristic of his early works. It is a melodrama in which a great deal of stage time is devoted to exposition and action, little to the development of character. In the one-act play two miners share the same claim. They had become partners after Jack, in his thirties, saves the Older Man, in his fifties, from drowning. The Older Man was searching for a man he suspected of being his wife's lover. Through Jack's reminiscences, the Older Man learns that it was Jack who was in love with his wife and that his wife, despite her love for Jack, had remained true to her wedding vows. The Older Man is tempted first to kill Jack, half-drawing his gun, and later to destroy a telegram from his wife to Jack. In an inexplicable reversal, he decides instead to accept all responsibility: "In this affair I alone am to blame." He sends Jack off to his wife and ends the play with a modified version of John 15:13: "Greater love hath no man than this, that he giveth his wife for his friend."

The two-dimensional characters, the movement of the plot toward disaster, with a quick reversal toward a happy ending, and the simple moral are characteristic of melodramas. Yet within this short play, which O'Neill later referred to as a "vaudeville skit," are some embryonic themes of the mature playwright. Even in this early play O'Neill used the set for more than decoration: "On the horizon a lonely butte is outlined, black and sinister against the lighter darkness of a sky with stars." The butte, like the elms in *Desire Under the Elms* (1924), is the play's inanimate character influencing the actions of the animate characters. It is a scenic image of O'Neill's determinism. The Older Man, a cynic, self-isolated from civilization, is the prototype of characters in *The Iceman Cometh* (1946). He also makes reference to the ghosts that will haunt the characters of *Mourning Becomes Electra* (1931): "I cannot be a ghost at their feasts." These undeveloped themes, all of which are incompatible with the aesthetic of melodrama, reveal that the germinating

impulse of the play is tragic; it strains against the seams of its melodramatic framework.

After *A Wife for a Life* O'Neill began to write steadily, completing some twenty-four plays in the next four years. His next play, written in fall 1913, but not produced in his lifetime, was *The Web* (1964). Rose, who has recently become a mother, is a prostitute who, pathetically, has tuberculosis, a communicable disease. Steve, her pimp, still forces her to walk the streets to support his drug and drinking habits. When Steve gives Rose one week to abandon her child, they argue. Tim, a neighbor, bursts in with a gun drawn and orders Steve out. As Tim and Rose talk, they discover a common history. Rose is trapped in prostitution, and Tim is trapped in a life of crime, his most recent felonies being a jailbreak and a bank robbery. They begin to feel that there is hope for a better life with each other. Rose agrees to help Tim elude the police, and Tim gives Rose money. Steve, who has listened from the fire escape, shoots Tim, throws the gun into the room, closes the window, and flees. The police, who have been closing in on Tim, enter and accuse Rose of murder. The turn of events is as sensational and improbable as any in melodrama, but the play, as *A Wife for a Life*, has characteristics antithetical to melodrama. It does not end happily, and O'Neill adds a third dimension to the characters. Rose is a prostitute, but her concern for her child, her despair, her pathetic grasping for a new life with Tim, and O'Neill's already acute ear for dialect make her more than a prostitute.

In *The Web* O'Neill explored realism; in *Thirst*, written in fall 1913 and produced in summer 1916, he explored, as he would in *The Hairy Ape*, what he would later refer to as supernaturalism, which to O'Neill meant going beyond realism by using symbolism in a basically realistic play. In *The Hairy Ape*, where his supernaturalism is more developed, O'Neill felt that Yank was a particular character and yet a representation of mankind. The three characters of *Thirst*—a gentleman, a dancer, and a West Indian mulatto sailor—are nameless, as much representations of a class or type of character as individuals, and the dialogue is stylized rather than dialectal. They are on a life raft on "fantastic heat waves," surrounded by sharks. The dancer, consumed by the "mad fixed idea" that the sailor has water, offers a necklace, then herself, for a drink. When the sailor rejects her, she dances: "She is like some ghastly marionette jerked by invisible wires." She dies after the exhausting dance, and

Ella Quinlan O'Neill, the playwright's mother, in the early 1880s (Yale University Library)

the sailor, telling the gentleman that they will now eat and drink, begins to sharpen his knife. Attempting to preserve his values, the gentleman tries to stop the sailor. They both fall overboard, leaving only the necklace on the raft. The theme of what should be regarded as O'Neill's first experimental play is confused. The dancer abandons her moral values, the gentleman tries desperately to maintain his, and the sailor, like Melville's Queequeg, seems to be a pragmatic savage. Yet, they all die.

Recklessness (1964), a parlor melodrama written in fall 1913 but not produced in his lifetime, is uncharacteristic of O'Neill's later work. Mildred Baldwin, whose parents forced her into a loveless but lucrative marriage, is having an affair with Fred, her chauffeur. After learning of the affair, Baldwin tells Fred that Mildred is ill and sends him for a doctor in an unsafe racing car. The second scene focuses on Baldwin's maliciousness. Knowing that Fred has died in an auto accident, Baldwin questions his wife about the af-

fair and promises to grant her a divorce. As Mildred is thanking him, some men carry in Fred's body. Mildred shoots herself, and Baldwin calmly lights a cigar. Because of the play's provocative story line, it was sold to Hollywood and provided the plot for two B-movies.

Warnings (1964), written in fall 1913 but never produced, was an advancement for the young playwright in one important sense: it was his first attempt to move beyond the limited scope of one-act plays. Though *Warnings* is in one act, it has ten characters, two scenes, and a change of sets. The first scene presents Knapp, a wireless operator for the SS *Empress,* and his family in their Bronx flat. O'Neill is able to create sympathy for Knapp as one who has been beaten by fate through his inability to raise himself and his family from their minimal subsistence. The set adroitly reveals the family's life-style: "Several gaudy Sunday-supplement pictures in cheap gilt frames are hung at spaced intervals around the walls. . . . On the wall above the table is a mantelpiece on the middle of which a black marble clock ticks mournfully." In the scene Knapp, who has just learned that he is going deaf, is convinced by his wife, made "prematurely old by the thousand worries of a pennypinching existence," to work for one more voyage. The second scene shows the repercussions of Knapp's decision. Because Knapp was unable to hear a warning, the SS *Empress* struck a derelict and is sinking. When Knapp learns that he is responsible, he shoots himself. The first scene is a vivid and rich portrait of the Knapp family, similar to that of Robert Mayo's family in *Beyond the Horizon* (1920), and it presents the dramatic conflict of Knapp's having to choose between providing for his family and endangering the SS *Empress.* The second scene, however, is barren and reaches a premature climax.

The action of *Fog,* written in winter 1914 and produced in 1917 by the Provincetown Players, occurs after a shipwreck. A man of business, a poet, a Polish peasant woman, and her dead child are drifting in a lifeboat without oars. The lifeboat, shrouded by a slowly dissipating fog, is the forum for a debate between the man of business, who is materialistic, optimistic, and self-serving, and the poet, who is spiritualistic, melancholic, and altruistic. The man of business, who had to swim to reach the lifeboat, thinks that the child's death is a tragedy. The poet, who is weary of life and planned to go down with the ship, feels that the child is much better off dead. After the lifeboat drifts next to an iceberg, a steamer's whistle is heard. The poet insists that they not call out, for that would draw the ship into the iceberg. A lifeboat from the ship, however, returns for them, someone claiming to have heard a child crying. The play is, ultimately, an odd mixture. The first part is a philosophical debate between the man of business and the poet. The dichotomy, similar to that of Apollo and Dionysus in Nietzsche's *The Birth of Tragedy* (1872), is developed in later O'Neill plays, especially in *The Great God Brown* (1926). The end of the play, a rescue precipitated by the cries of a child, is pure sensationalism.

In 1914, after finishing *Fog,* O'Neill collected his plays in *Thirst and Other One Act Plays,* the printing costs of which were deferred to his father. Critic Clayton Hamilton, who suggested the publication, reviewed it for *Bookman,* but O'Neill remained a struggling, developing playwright, unproduced and relatively unread.

In spring 1914 O'Neill wrote his first full-length play, *Bread and Butter* (1972). The play, not produced in his lifetime, expanded the major conflict of *Fog,* that between the man of business and the poet. Edward Brown, Sr., a self-made hardware merchant in Bridgetown, Connecticut, and his effacing wife are, as their home indicates, hopelessly middle-class and artless. Edward Brown, Jr., the eldest son, an alderman as well as manager of the family business, is equally philistine. Harry, the second son, is working in the family business, but his drinking, cynicism, and wit (he is drawn from Jamie, O'Neill's older brother) set him apart from his family. John, the youngest son, is the artist. The conflict of the play is between John and his family. John wants to study art in New York, but his father wants him to study law. With the support of Maud Steele, his fiancée, and her father, both of whom want John to become a commercial artist, he is able to convince his father to subsidize his art education. After studying in New York for a few years, John reluctantly returns to Bridgetown, marries Maud, works in her father's business, and begins to drink heavily. Maud, who abandons even her superficial appreciation of art, grows closer to Edward. The marriage becomes like "two corpses chained together." Maud feels that John has no sense of propriety and is a failure in her father's business. John, who overhears Edward offering to take care of Maud, resents having given up art for his marriage. Each accuses the other of infidelity, and John escapes the marriage through suicide. The theme, the tragedy that evolves from

James O'Neill as the Count of Monte Cristo (The Players, Walter Hampden Memorial Library)

subverting temperament, is repeated in *Beyond the Horizon.*

Bound East for Cardiff, written in spring 1914 and produced in 1916, is the first play in a series involving the crew of the SS *Glencairn.* The plays all deal with the friendships that bind the crew and bring meaning to their lives and with the emotions that drive them apart. The major literary influence on the play is Joseph Conrad's *The Nigger of The 'Narcissus'* (1897). The title of the first American edition of Conrad's novel was *Children of the Sea,* which was also the original title for *Bound East for Cardiff.* Both works portray a crew's reactions to a dying shipmate. In *Bound East for Cardiff* Yank is dying; Driscoll, his best friend, and the rest of the crew are nursing him. Yank goes through stages as he prepares to die. At first he cannot accept his own death: "I'm goin' to—"; he regrets having spent his life as a seaman and wishes that he had settled down on a farm. As he and Driscoll reminisce about their voyages, Yank seems to find some validation of his life in his adventures with his friend. Finally, Yank begins to prepare for death by setting his life in order. He asks Driscoll if he was wrong to stab a man in Cape Town, and Driscoll reassures him that it was self-defense. He also asks Driscoll to divide his pay among the crew and to buy some candy for a barmaid who was kind to him. Before he dies, Yank sees a pretty woman dressed in black. Shortly after he dies, a fog surrounding the ship lifts. *Bound East for Cardiff,* with relatively little plot but strong characters, is one of the best plays of O'Neill's early career. It was the first of his plays to be produced and one of the first to be performed by the Provincetown Players.

In *Abortion,* written in spring 1914 but not produced until 1959, O'Neill returned to the theme of determinism. As the one-act play opens, Jack Townsend has just won the championship for his college baseball team by pitching a three-hitter. In the study of his dorm room his family, roommate, and fiancée praise his character and athleticism. The irony of the praise becomes apparent when, left alone with his father, Jack confesses that during the past year, he seduced a town girl and paid for her to have an abortion. Jack explains his actions by saying that he was like "the male beast who ran gibbering through the forest after its female thousands of years ago." He was doomed by his own biological urges. Joe Murray, the tubercular brother of the seduced girl, enters and is left alone with Jack. He tells Jack that his sister died after the shoddy abortion and attempts to shoot Jack, but Jack takes the gun from him. As students cheer Jack outside his window, he puts the revolver to his head and pulls the trigger.

The Movie Man, written in spring 1914 but not produced until 1959, is one of O'Neill's few comedies. It is both a satire on filmmakers and Latin-American revolutions and a parable of the selfish motives behind apparent altruism. Henry Rogers and Al Devlin, filming a real Mexican revolution for Earth Motion Picture Company, are awaiting the next two events in their filming schedule: the storming of a nearby town, brought nearer as the generals become drunker, and the execution of Ernesto Fernandez, who must be killed because he is the enemy of one of the revolu-

tionary generals. Anita Fernandez, daughter of the condemned man, solicits the aid of Rogers. When Gomez, the commander in chief, decides to storm the town at midnight, Rogers reminds Gomez that they have a contract which forbids night attacks—because the crew needs light to film—and that, if the contract is broken, the film company will cease to finance the revolution. Rogers eventually agrees to allow the night attack providing Gomez releases Fernandez. Anita, thanking Rogers, tells him that she and her father will regard him as a brother. Rogers questions, "Only—a brother?" Retreating in confusion, Anita tells him, "Who knows?"

David Roylston, the protagonist of *Servitude,* written in summer 1914 and published in 1950, is a novelist and playwright whose major theme is the influence of "the narrowing environment of the conventional home" on the individual and the need for the individual to become a Nietzschean superman and overcome his environment (that is, to break from the constrictions of marriage). In act 1 Ethel Frazer visits Roylston late in the evening and tells him that after being exposed to his works, she became disillusioned with her stockbroker husband and set out to begin a life of her own. She claims to be Roylston's creation because she changed after reading his fiction. Roylston, once he realizes that she has missed her train, asks her to stay the night. In act 2, the next morning, Mrs. Roylston returns home to discover Mrs. Frazer. Because Roylston has received many love letters from readers, Mrs. Roylston assumes that Mrs. Frazer is her husband's mistress. She then begins a confession—one of O'Neill's favorite techniques for exposition. She reveals her husband married her because he felt duty-bound. She was his father's stenographer. When Roylston's father found out that they were in love, he fired her. Roylston, feeling responsible, proposed. Mrs. Roylston, who believes that love is servitude, says that during the first years of their marriage, she supported the family, shielding and protecting her husband so that he could write. In act 3 Mrs. Frazer, who is now disillusioned with the egotistical Roylston, dispels his sense of self-importance with criticism. Roylston admits that he is not a "brilliant genius" tied to a "poor ignorant creature" of a wife: "Whatever I am she has made me." He resolves to be a man worthy of his wife's love. The relationship between Roylston and his wife is similar to the relationship between Cornelius Melody and his wife, Nora, in *A Touch of the Poet* (1957). Melody is an egotist whose self-concept is destroyed by humiliation; Nora is the wife whose happiness is in serving her husband. The major difference between the two plays is that Melody, unlike Roylston, is unable to accept the disintegration of his self-image.

In September 1914 O'Neill took George Pierce Baker's English 47 course on play writing at Harvard. Baker, considered the father of American drama, taught some of the most important writers and theatrical artists of the early twentieth century, including Sidney Howard, George Abbott, Thomas Wolfe, Lee Simonson, and Theresa Helburn. While at Harvard O'Neill collaborated with Colin Ford on "Belshazzar," a biblical adaptation (later destroyed); "Dear Doctor," an adaptation from a magazine story (also destroyed); *The Sniper*, a one-act; and "The Personal Equation," an unpublished full-length play.

The Sniper, produced in 1917 by the Provincetown Players, is a simple story of revenge. Rougon is a Belgian peasant whose farm has been demolished and son killed by the invading Prussians. He enters carrying his son's body. A priest is able to calm him temporarily, but when Rougon learns that his wife has also been killed, he begins shooting at Prussian soldiers. Rougon is captured and shot.

In "The Personal Equation" Tom Perkins, a merchant marine, joins the International Workers Union to rebel against his father, a loyal worker for Ocean Steamship Company, and because he loves Olga Tarnoff, a second-generation socialist. The play touches on several social issues, including free love and the labor movement, but the climax is reached when Tom and a few crew members try to sabotage the engines of the SS *San Francisco*. Tom's father, who works on the engines and feels that they are his friends, "accidentally" shoots his son to prevent the sabotage. The final scene is set in Tom's hospital room. Perkins and Olga meet in the room and agree to nurse Tom, now deranged as a result of the wound. They have found the personal equation that transcends political differences.

Baker, who found promise in the works that O'Neill wrote at Harvard, invited him to return for a second year of study. O'Neill, though he later said the experience was valuable, declined the offer. After living for almost a year in Greenwich Village, spending much of his time in a bar known as the Hell Hole, O'Neill moved to Provincetown, Massachusetts. He became involved with the Provincetown Players, who on 28 July 1916 produced his *Bound East for Cardiff*. Stimu-

Kathleen Jenkins, whom O'Neill married in 1909 (New York World, 11 May 1910)

lated, he began to write again. During the summer he wrote "Atrocity," "The G.A.M." (both destroyed), and *Before Breakfast* (1916). *Before Breakfast*, like Strindberg's *The Stronger*, is a short dialogue dominated by one character. Mrs. Rowland's only solace in her disappointing life is in taunting Alfred, her husband. As she prepares breakfast, she criticizes her husband, who remains offstage, for his laziness, lack of character, inability to find a job, and even his inability to hold his liquor: "You'd better give up drinking. You can't stand it. It's just your kind that get the D.T.'s *That would be* the last straw!" Finally, Mrs. Rowland, who married her husband after becoming pregnant, criticizes him for impregnating a girl named Helen. The play ends as Mrs. Rowland discovers that Alfred has slit his wrists.

Although he was still primarily a writer of one-act plays, O'Neill was beginning to develop a reputation in the theater. In November 1916 the Provincetown Players moved their theater to New York and in their first season produced *Bound East for Cardiff* (O'Neill had one line as the mate), *Before Breakfast* (O'Neill played the role of Alfred), *Fog*, and *The Sniper*. A year later the Washington Square Players produced *In the Zone.*

During the winter of 1917 O'Neill and Agnes Boulton lived together in Provincetown. It was a productive period during which O'Neill completed five plays, one of which was *Now I Ask You* (1972). This play satirizes the Greenwich Village bohemians of the 1910s and the melodramatic elements of the Ibsen dramas that influenced O'Neill's early plays. In the prologue, a flash-forward to the play's end, Lucy Ashleigh puts a revolver to her head. As the curtain drops, a shot is heard. In act 1, the day before Lucy's wedding, Mrs. Ashleigh advises her future son-in-law Tom to agree with Lucy's avant-garde ideas. When Lucy enters, she tells Tom that she does not want to marry and would prefer a "free love" relationship. Far more conventional than she pretends to be, Lucy is surprised and frightened when Tom agrees with her. Mrs. Ashleigh achieves a compromise by suggesting that they go through with the ceremony but draw up their own wedding contract, which could include clauses on free love. In act 2 Lucy, who has recently seen Ibsen's *Hedda Gabler,* is suffering from the ennui of married life. Her only relief is flirtation with Gabriel, who is living with her artist friend Leonora Barnes. In act 3 Tom unhappily flirts with Leonora to make Lucy jealous. The bohemians' underlying conventionality becomes more evident as Gabriel and Lucy are shocked by the possibility that Tom and Leonora are having an affair. Gabriel even confesses that he and Leonora have been secretly married for two years. As Tom and Leonora are preparing to leave for the evening, Lucy repeats the action of the prologue. She puts a revolver to her temple, and a shot is heard. In the epilogue the others discover Lucy sprawled on the floor and think that she is dead. Then Tom remembers that the gun was not loaded; the shot sound came from a tire blowout.

In the Zone is the second of the *S.S. Glencairn* series. In *Bound East for Cardiff* the death of Yank brings harmony to the crew; in *In the Zone* suspicion divides them. The play is set in 1915 in the forecastle of the *S.S. Glencairn,* which is transporting dynamite through the war zone. The crew's fear of submarines and saboteurs makes them suspicious of Smitty, who is more refined and aloof than the others. Several of the crew members, who have seen Smitty hiding a black box, convince themselves that he is a spy. They first submerge the box in water, thinking that it is a bomb, and then, after Smitty enters

and is restrained, open it–breaking the unwritten seaman's code of respecting each other's privacy. They find a package of love letters. By reading the letters, they learn that Smitty's real name is Sidney Davidson and that his girlfriend, unable to tolerate his drinking, ended their relationship. The crew, satisfied that Smitty is not a spy, crawl into their bunks and roll over to face the wall.

The Long Voyage Home, which premiered in November 1917, is the third of the *S.S. Glencairn* series. In it, alcohol disrupts the crew's unity. While on shore leave Driscoll, Cocky, and Ivan are escorting Olson to a ship that will take him home to Sweden. On the way they stop at a disreputable waterfront bar. Olson, who does not want to miss his ship or lose his money, drinks ginger beer, but the others drink heavily. When Ivan passes out, Driscoll and Cocky carry him to a boardinghouse. The bartender drugs Olson's ginger beer, steals his money, and then delivers him to the *Amindra,* a tramp steamer in need of an extra hand. Olson, whose drinking prevented him from returning home earlier, is let down by the drinking of his crewmates.

Ile, also produced in November 1917, is a one-act play set in Captain and Mrs. Keeney's cabin on board the *Atlantic Queen,* a whaling ship. The ship is locked in ice. Though the ice has broken to the south and the crew is considering mutiny, Keeney refuses to turn toward home. He is obsessed with the idea of always returning with a full hull of whale oil (or *ile*). Mrs. Keeney is the victim of her own fixed idea. Her storybook idea of sailing life as free, adventurous, and romantic enticed her to sail with her husband. Because of the severity and boredom of the voyage, she begs her husband to return home immediately. He agrees, but when the ice breaks to the north, he changes his mind and continues. Mrs. Keeney, losing her sanity, begins to play an organ wildly. The relationship presented is found in many of O'Neill's plays, including *Long Day's Journey Into Night* (1956). The husband, obsessed with his career or some other fixed idea, neglects his wife; the wife, unable to reconcile her romantic notions with the reality of her marriage, is driven insane.

The Moon of the Caribbees, which was produced in 1918, the final play of the *S.S. Glencairn* series, continues the theme of harmony and chaos. The *Glencairn* is anchored off a West Indies island. The crew, waiting for native women to bring them fruit and–without the captain's knowledge–rum, listen to a "melancholy Negro

O'Neill at the time his play Beyond the Horizon *had been awarded the Pulitzer Prize (Agnes Boulton Collection; Beinecke Rare Book and Manuscript Library, Yale University)*

chant." Since the chant depresses some of the crew and makes Smitty remember things that he became a sailor to forget, Driscoll sings "Blow the Man Down." Though the chantey brings unity to the crew, dissension arises almost as soon as the native women climb on board. After drinking the rum, the crew fight each other and a man is knifed. The play ends with the brooding native music which is "faint and far-off, like the mood of the moonlight made audible."

In *The Rope,* written in winter 1918 and produced in April 1918, Abraham Bentley, the prototype for Cabot in *Desire Under the Elms,* is a stingy, senile, Bible-quoting monomaniac. When his son Luke stole one hundred dollars from him, Bentley hung a noose in the barn. Before Luke ran off to sea, Bentley told him to hang himself with the noose if he ever returned. All of the characters, except for Bentley's granddaughter, are motivated by money. Bentley's daughter, Annie, and son-in-law, Sweeney, are trying to take the farm from him. Bentley's stinginess, according to his daughter, killed his first wife, and he mortgaged the farm for his second wife. When Luke returns, he and Sweeney agree to hunt for and divide the mortgage money they feel that Bentley must have hidden. The play ends ironically. As the idiotic granddaughter plays by swinging on the noose, a bag of gold

coins falls. The child uses the coins to play "skip-rock."

The theme of *Beyond the Horizon* is simple: be true to your nature. The play, written in winter 1918, contrasts the two Mayo brothers: Robert, sickly and poetic, and Andrew, practical and a born farmer. In act 1 Robert is about to ship out with his uncle to seek freedom, mystery, and beauty. After he discovers that Ruth, with whom he and his brother grew up, loves him, he decides to stay and become a farmer. Andrew, who also loves Ruth, decides to sail in Robert's place. Both brothers go against their nature, and both suffer. In act 2 Robert, though he works hard, is unable to manage the farm effectively. His marriage and his health deteriorate. Andrew, who returns for a short visit, finds sea life dissatisfying. In act 3 the farm and Robert's health and marriage have further deteriorated. Andrew, who has lost his money speculating, returns with a doctor but is too late. Robert dies of consumption. The play was an important watershed in O'Neill's career. With it he moved from little theaters in Greenwich Village to prominent producers on Broadway. It was first produced experimentally by John Williams as a matinee feature. Because of critical praise, it was brought to the Morosco Theatre in 1920.

Written in the summer of 1918, shortly after O'Neill married Agnes Boulton (on 12 April), and produced a year later, *The Dreamy Kid* is, perhaps, more important for what follows it than for itself. The simple one-act is about a young black gangster named Dreamy who visits his dying grandmother even though he is wanted for murder. As the play ends, Dreamy is holding his grandmother's hand in one hand, his gun in the other, and is waiting for the police to charge through the door. In the play O'Neill was experimenting with black characters and dialect; what he learned from writing *The Dreamy Kid* enabled him to write *The Emperor Jones* (1921) and *All God's Chillun Got Wings* (1924).

In *Where the Cross Is Made,* a one-act written and produced in fall 1918, O'Neill experimented with the relationship between the stage action and the audience. The play is set in Captain Bartlett's room, which is decorated as a cabin and built onto a seaside house where he lives with his son and daughter. Seven years ago, while shipwrecked on an island, Bartlett and three of his crew found what they believed to be lost treasure. They buried it, made a map, and after they returned to San Francisco, the three crew members went back for the treasure in the *Mary Allen*. Even though he received word that the *Mary Allen* had sunk, Bartlett has been waiting for the ship's return. His insane vigil places a strain on his son, Nat, who knows that the treasure is only paste, but nonetheless wants to believe in the treasure. On the night that Nat has asked a doctor to take his father to a sanatorium, more to preserve his own sanity than to restore his father's, Captain Bartlett shouts, "Sail-ho." Nat also sees the *Mary Allen*, but Sue, his sister, sees nothing. The ghosts of the crew, seen only by Nat and his father and the audience, enter and give a map to Bartlett. By having the ghosts onstage, O'Neill was attempting to make the audience believe in the treasure also.

In the fall of 1918 O'Neill also wrote *Shell Shock*. This one-act play, published in 1972 but not produced in his lifetime, is set in a New York bar during World War I. In it, he begins to develop his theme of pipe dreams: men cannot function if they face reality unbuffered. As the play opens, Herbert Roylston, just back from the front, tells Robert Wayne, who was sent to New York to treat shell-shock victims, how a mutual friend saved his life. After Roylston was wounded and left for dead in no-man's-land for three days, he screamed and briefly stood up. Then Jack Arnold, his major, rushed to him and carried him to safety. As Roylston is exiting to write some letters, Arnold, sent home to be treated for shell shock, enters. He tells Wayne about the horrors of war and how cigarettes, which he began to smoke to clear the stench of rotting bodies, became an obsession. He then confesses that—thinking Roylston was dead—he went out into no-man's-land and carried him back because he needed a cigarette and hoped that he could find one on the body. Wayne is able to convince Arnold that he saw Roylston stand up and that he did not carry the body back for cigarettes. Once Arnold believes in his pipe dream, or what Ibsen called a life-lie, Wayne pronounces him cured.

The Straw was written in 1918 and 1919 and produced in 1921. In act 1 Eileen, suffering from tuberculosis, learns that she will have to leave her family and go to Hill Farm Sanatorium. Since her mother died, Eileen has found meaning in serving her family. Now that she is ill, however, she finds little support. Her father is more worried about the expense than her health, and her boyfriend fears that he may contract the disease. At the sanatorium Eileen meets Steven Mur-

ray, a journalist with aspirations of becoming a fiction writer. Eileen encourages him to write and offers to type his stories. By act 2 Murray has sold a story, and Eileen has fallen in love with him. When the patients are weighed (a weight gain indicates an improvement) Eileen has lost three pounds and Murray has gained three. The sacrificing Eileen has symbolically given Murray, who is now healthy enough to leave, three pounds. At Eileen's request the two meet at a crossroads, and she confesses that she loves him. In act 3 Murray returns to the sanatorium for a checkup. A nurse tells Murray that Eileen is dying and that she would be happier in her last days if she believed that he loved her. Murray agrees, and while asking Eileen to marry him, he discovers that he actually does love her. The ending supports O'Neill's belief that love is best expressed through sacrifice. Only when Murray is acting in Eileen's behalf can he discover love. Critics were held by the play's interesting characters, but, largely because of poor direction and management, it closed after twenty performances.

In the summer of 1919 O'Neill and Agnes moved to an old Coast Guard station in Peaked Hill Bars, Massachusetts. They both drank heavily and argued frequently. On 30 October 1919 O'Neill's second son, Shane, was born. O'Neill, who was never close to any of his children, suggested to Agnes that they move Shane's crib into the basement, where the child would be less distracting. But, despite the changes in his family life, O'Neill continued to write steadily.

Gold, written in the winter of 1920 and produced in 1921, is a full-length version of *Where the Cross Is Made*. In act 1 Captain Bartlett and a few of his crew, shipwrecked on an island in the Malay Archipelago, find what they believe to be gold. Before they are rescued, Jimmy Kanaka, with Bartlett's passive permission, kills the cook and cabin boy, whom the other crew members do not trust. In act 2 Bartlett and the remainder of his crew are stocking a new ship to return for the gold. Mrs. Bartlett, who heard her husband talking of the murders in his sleep, refuses to christen the ship as she has always done. She finally agrees to christen it, but only after Bartlett threatens to take Nat, his son, on the voyage. Act 3 begins shortly after Mrs. Bartlett, despite being weak from an illness, has christened the ship. Bartlett, who is obsessed with the gold, is neglectful of her. Sue, Bartlett's daughter, who wants her father to remain with her mother, convinces her fiancé to sail in her father's place. In act 4 Bart-

Carlotta Monterey, whom O'Neill married in 1929
(Louis Sheaffer)

lett is waiting for the ship to return even though word has arrived that it has sunk. While a doctor is making arrangements to have Bartlett committed, Bartlett is able to infect Nat with his madness, but only temporarily. Nat is able to realize that the trinkets Bartlett brought back with him are just brass. Though *Gold* is technically a better play than *Where the Cross Is Made*, it takes four acts rather than one to develop the same themes: the effects of guilt on the individual and the effects of one person's insanity on his family. *Gold* closed after thirteen performances.

Anna Christie (produced in 1921), which went through several painful revisions between 1919 and 1920, was originally entitled "Chris Christopherson." During the revisions the emphasis shifted from Chris to Anna. In act 1 Chris, who is the captain of a coal barge, and Maggie, who lives with him, learn that his daughter, Anna, is to meet him at Johnny-the-Priest's saloon. After Maggie agrees to move out and Chris leaves to sober up, Anna enters. Maggie, a tough woman who has lived a hard life, realizes immedi-

ately that Anna has been a prostitute. Anna tells Maggie her life story. Her father left her to be raised by relatives on a farm in Minnesota; one of her cousins seduced her; she then worked as a nurse but soon turned to prostitution. In act 2, set on the fog-enshrouded barge, Anna feels clean because the fog hides her past. Mat Burke, a shipwrecked sailor, comes alongside and quickly attempts to seduce Anna, who reacts by hitting him. Mat respects her for her reaction and proposes. In act 3 Anna tells Mat that she will not marry him and relates her past. Both Chris and Mat leave to get drunk. In act 4 Mat returns to ask Anna's forgiveness. He has decided to ship out after they are married and will send Anna his money. When Chris enters, also to ask Anna's forgiveness, he announces that he has signed for a voyage on the same ship as Mat. The play was wrongly criticized for having a happy ending. Anna, who was once abandoned by her father, is about to be abandoned by her future husband and again by her father. Further, Chris's final words refer to the "ole davil sea," which has ruled and destroyed the men in his family for generations. Despite the mixed reviews, the play won a Pulitzer Prize and ran for 177 performances.

The Emperor Jones, written in fall 1920 and produced in November, is perhaps the most remarkable of O'Neill's early plays. Scene 1 is set in the emperor's palace on an island in the West Indies. All but a native woman stealing a few artifacts have deserted the court because the overtaxed islanders are about to rebel. They would have rebelled long before, but Brutus Jones, a black American who became emperor, convinced them that he could only be killed by a silver bullet. In the scene Smithers, a white trader who helped instate Jones and now vacillates between hatred and genuine admiration for him, tells Jones that he had better resign as emperor. Jones is not worried because he feels that the myth about the silver bullet, his religion (though he has "put it on the shelf"), and his escape plan will save him. During Jones's flight through the forest, the natives in pursuit beat a drum. The rate of the drumbeat is seventy-two beats per minute at first—corresponding to a normal heartbeat—but as Jones's flight becomes more frantic, the beat accelerates. In a series of scenes depicting his flight, Jones experiences events from his past and racial heritage. In scene 2 he encounters "formless creatures" that represent his fears; when he fires his revolver at them, they disappear. In scene 3 he encounters Jeff, a Pullman porter whom Jones killed during a dice game. Another bullet is used to dispel this ghost. In scene 4 Jones finds himself a member of a chain gang of blacks. He attempts to kill the white guard with his imaginary shovel, but, realizing that he does not have a shovel, he has to shoot the ghost again. In scene 5 Jones is placed on an auction block. He is about to be sold when he fires two shots, one at an auctioneer and one at a planter. In scene 6 Jones faces a Congo witch doctor who demands that he sacrifice himself to a god, represented by a crocodile head. Jones uses his last bullet, the silver one he was saving to kill himself if worse came to worst, to dispel the crocodile. In scene 8 Jones's body, stripped of its clothes as Jones is stripped of his pretensions, is brought before Smithers and Lem, the leader of the revolt. He is then killed by silver bullets made from melted money.

The play marks a turning point in O'Neill's career. In fact, Travis Bogard wrote of it, "Not only the literate American drama, but the American theater came of age with this play." *The Emperor Jones* was the first American play to adapt expressionistic techniques. The play, however, is more than an imitation of European plays. O'Neill effectively used the scenic design of the play (sets, lights, and sound) to bring the audience into Jones's psyche. The combination of techniques and their effects was revolutionary, but O'Neill, even though the play was successful and ran for 204 performances, did not write only in the mode of *The Emperor Jones.* In the 1920s he continued to experiment: with expressionistic techniques in *The Hairy Ape;* with masks in *The Great God Brown* and other plays; with spoken thoughts in *Strange Interlude* (1928) and *Dynamo* (1929); with a chorus in *Lazarus Laughed* (1927); with sets in *Desire Under the Elms;* and with lighting in *Welded* (1924). During this period he also wrote histories and traditional plays. It was a period during which O'Neill was certain of the kind of play he did not want to write but was not certain of the kind of play he did want to write. He was thoroughly divorcing himself from melodrama as he experimented with a variety of dramatic forms that might replace it.

Diff'rent, a more traditional play that was also written in fall 1920 and produced in December, illustrates the destruction that comes from trying to meet an impossible ideal. In act 1 Emma and Caleb are to be married in two days. Emma loves Caleb because she thinks he is different— better than other men, like the heroes in the ro-

mantic novels she has been reading. When Emma learns that the town is laughing about a South Sea island woman who, during Caleb's last voyage, seduced him, she breaks off the engagement. Her mother and Caleb's sister try to convince her that Caleb's actions were natural, but Emma vows never to marry. Caleb, equally idealistic, vows to wait until she changes her mind. In act 2 Emma, who has not matured emotionally, is an eighteen-year-old in the body of a forty-eight-year-old. She has redecorated her home and dressed as a 1920s flapper to attract the attention of Benny Rogers, Caleb's nephew. With Benny, Emma relives her aborted relationship with Caleb. The relationship with Caleb was different because Emma wanted it to fulfill her idea of love; the relationship with Benny is different because it is pathetically unnatural. The act reaches a melodramatic denouement as Benny, to revenge himself on Caleb, whom he resents for his stinginess, asks Emma to marry him. When Caleb learns of it, he hangs himself. As the play ends, Emma goes insane and begins marching to the barn to join Caleb. Even though the critical reception was tepid, the play ran for one hundred performances.

In *The First Man,* written in winter 1921 and produced in 1922, O'Neill depicts the two destructive forces to the family: the quest of a romantic ideal and the narrow-mindedness of a puritanical society. In act 1, set in Bridgetown, Connecticut (the same setting as *Bread and Butter*), Curtis Jayson, who was influenced by the stories of Bret Harte, is about to begin a five-year expedition in search of the first man, the missing link. Since their two daughters died, Curtis and his wife, Martha, have been nomadic, he working as an anthropologist and she as his assistant. While Curtis was writing a book in Bridgetown, Martha spent a great deal of time with Edward Bigelow, Curtis's college friend who has been marked by the town as an infidel. In act 2, the next day, Curtis tells Martha that he has arranged for her to accompany him on the expedition; Martha tells him that she cannot go because she is pregnant. The news destroys Curtis's romantic ideal of the two working together; he tells her, "You have blown my world to bits." The Jayson family, who disapprove of Martha's familiarity with Bigelow, assume that the child is not Curtis's. In act 3, while Martha is having a difficult childbirth, Curtis tells Bigelow that he hopes the child will be still-born and thus not separate him from Martha. The child, the first son in that generation of

Jaysons, is born healthy, but Martha dies in childbirth. In act 4, after Martha's funeral, Curtis has refused to see the child, whom he considers a murderer, and still plans to join his expedition. His family, concerned about forestalling a scandal, is finally so blunt in expressing their suspicions that Curtis learns what the rumors in Bridgetown have been. In an act of defiance, he claims his child, leaves him in the care of a kindly aunt, and then departs, vowing to take the child with him on later expeditions. O'Neill seems to imply that the child will somehow trigger a new step in the evolution of man, perhaps the evolution of a Nietzschean superman, but the point is not made clear. The play is also flawed by an overabundance of characters, allowing little stage time for any of them to develop, and obscure motives for the few character changes that do occur. *The First Man* closed after twenty-seven performances.

The Hairy Ape, written in fall 1921, is O'Neill's clearest treatment of one of his most important themes: modern man has lost his place in the universe; he is isolated from his history, his fellowmen, and his purpose. Yank, different from the Yank in *Bound East for Cardiff,* is a stoker on a transatlantic liner and feels that he is part of the engines. When Mildred Douglas, the daughter of a millionaire, descends into the forecastle, she is shocked at the sight of Yank and calls him a beast. The encounter destroys Yank's unity with the engines, and he then begins an odyssey to reestablish his self-esteem and regain his sense of belonging. On Fifth Avenue in New York, where the rich parade like marionettes, Yank fights a gentleman and is thrown in jail. After spending time in jail, where the cells "disappear in the dark background as if they ran on, numberless, into infinity," Yank attempts to revenge himself on Mildred by joining the Industrial Workers of the World. The socialists, who think that Yank must be a secret-service spy, refer to him as a "brainless ape." In the final scene Yank climbs into the ape cage at the zoo and is killed by the gorilla. The final stage direction reads: "And, perhaps, the Hairy Ape at last belongs." The short, compact play, which made use of expressionistic techniques, was so successful that it had to be moved from the small Provincetown Players' theater to a large one.

In *The Fountain,* written in 1921 and 1922 and produced in 1925, O'Neill used the story of Juan Ponce de Leon and his search for the fountain of youth to present, as he would with his other historical plays, his view of salvation. Juan,

O'Neill with his son Eugene, Jr. (Culver Pictures)

whose affair with Maria de Cordova and whose duel with her husband resulted in exile from the Spanish court, travels to Puerto Rico on Columbus's second voyage. Twenty years later, after Juan has become governor, Beatriz, Maria's daughter, the "personification of youthful vitality," travels to Puerto Rico to bring Juan a patent to find the western route to Cathay. Juan falls in love with Beatriz and becomes obsessed with finding the fountain of youth. Through torture and promises, Juan eventually convinces Nano, an Indian, to lead him to the fountain. Nano leads Juan to a spring where other Indians ambush him. While wounded, Juan sees figures arise from the stream, Beatriz wearing the mask of an old hag, then a Chinese poet, a Moorish minstrel, and others. Through the figures' expressionistic dances, during which Beatriz unmasks, Juan realizes, "All things dissolve, flow on eternally!" In the final scene, months later in a Cuban monastery, Beatriz and Juan's nephew arrive as Juan is dying. Juan discovers that his love for Maria has been reborn in his nephew's love for Beatriz. The theme of *The Fountain,* that immortality is found in the continuity of generations and nature, has filled out many great sonnets, but it makes for a simplistic, drawn-out play. It closed after twenty-four performances.

Welded, written in 1922 and 1923 and produced in 1924, is an experimental combination of a Strindbergian love-hate relationship and the expressionistic evolution of the superman. Through the play Michael Cape, a playwright, and Eleanor, his wife, who acts in his plays, are both encircled by spotlights, which are like "auras of egoism." They have an idealistic view of marriage that is disrupted by the strength of their egos. Michael says of the marriage, "Our marriage must be a consummation demanding and combining the best in each of us! Hard, difficult, guarded from the commonplace, kept sacred as the outward form of our inner harmony!" As the play opens, Michael has just arrived home and the two are about to spend an evening alone when John, a friend and the producer of Michael's plays, visits briefly. Michael is jealous of John and angry because Eleanor flees the apartment. They both–as a means of revenge–attempt to have an affair. Eleanor runs to John but is unable to consummate the affair because she thinks that she sees Michael standing before her. Michael visits a "bovine stolid type" prostitute, whom he sees as a symbol of "the tortures man inflicts on woman," but is also unable to consummate the affair. In the final act they are able to overcome the "vanity of personality" and are united in the desire to find a greater love. Michael says, "Our life is to bear together our burden which is our goal–on and up! Above the world, beyond its vision–our meaning!" There are many faults with the play. The experimental lighting, the stylized dialogue, and the symbolic acting seem contrived. The play, however, is important because in it O'Neill first began to experiment with the technique of spoken thoughts; in act 1 Michael and Eleanor sit side by side and, while remaining motionless, speak their thoughts. The technique is further developed in *Strange Interludes.*

All God's Chillun Got Wings, unlike *Welded,* concentrates on the destructiveness of love. Jim Harris, a black, and Ella Downey, a white, are children when the play begins. Despite their racial differences, a childhood romance develops. Ella outgrows her affection for Jim, becomes the girlfriend of a white boxer, and has a child by him, but Jim remains in love with her. After Ella is deserted by the boxer and her child dies, Jim becomes her protector. Even though Jim, studying to become a lawyer, has been unable to pass the bar exam because of the tension he feels while being examined by "white faces," he tells Ella

that he wants to be her "black slave." They are married and spend two years in France, where, despite the lack of prejudice, Ella leads an isolated life. Because the isolation also makes Jim feel that he is not a real man, the two return to New York so that Jim can retake the bar examination. In New York Ella, who is unable to isolate herself from the outside world even in her own home, begins to lose her sanity. She feels threatened by Jim's attempt to pass his exam and begins to vacillate from love for Jim to fear of his success. At one moment she tells Jim not to take the examination, the next she tells him that she wants him to pass. After failing the examination for the second time, Jim also loses mental balance. They both regress into childhood: Jim kneels before Ella and becomes her "black slave." The ending, showing O'Neill's maturation from the suicide finales of his early career, is fitting for a marriage based on unhealthy motives: Ella wanted someone to feel superior to and Jim wanted someone to make him feel inferior.

All God's Chillun Got Wings, because of its miscegenation theme, brought the play censorship and O'Neill a letter from the Ku Klux Klan. New York City government did not allow children to act in the opening scene, so it was read to the audience. Despite, or perhaps because of, the censorship, the play ran for one hundred performances.

Desire Under the Elms, written in the first half of 1924, is set in 1850 in and around the Cabot farm in New England. Over the farm hover the elms which seem to control the actions of the characters: "They appear to protect and at the same time subdue. There is a sinister maternity in their aspect, a crushing, jealous absorption. They have developed from their intimate contact with the life of man in the house an appalling humaneness. They brood oppressively over the house. They are like exhausted women resting their sagging breasts and hands and hair on its roof, and when it rains their tears trickle down monotonously and rot on the shingles." The characters in the play, like the crushing, jealous, oppressive elms, vie for possession of the farm; their possessiveness generates isolation and loneliness.

The play opens as Cabot is about to return with a new wife. Before he returns, Eben, Cabot's son by his second marriage, buys rights to the farm from Simeon and Peter, Cabot's sons by his first marriage, with money that the stingy Cabot had hidden. Eben feels that the farm is rightfully his because his mother's family sued

Cabot for the deed to the farm. Cabot, to end the suit, married Eben's mother. Once Cabot arrives with his new wife, Abbie, a three-way struggle develops for possession of the farm. Abbie and Eben eventually have an affair and a child. The lovers' motives are similar to those in *All God's Chillun Got Wings;* Eben wants to revenge himself on his father, and Abbie wants a child to secure her rights to the farm. The relationship, unlike that in *All God's Chillun Got Wings,* develops. When Cabot tells Eben that Abbie had a child in order to prevent him from inheriting the farm, Eben accuses her of betraying him and threatens to leave. To prove that she loves Eben, Abbie kills the child. Though initially shocked (he reports her to the sheriff), Eben later sees the significance of the murder and shares the blame. He says to Abbie, "If I'm sharin' with ye, I won't feel lonesome, leastways." Because of the explicit treatment of adultery and the rather bizarre means of expressing love, the play was banned in several cities, including London and Boston. But, as with *All God's Chillun Got Wings,* the play was successful, running for 208 performances.

Like O'Neill's other historical plays, *Marco Millions,* written between 1923 and 1925 and produced in 1928, is concerned with the salvation and destruction of the soul. In the prologue, as businessmen debate the religious significance of a sacred tree, each claiming it as a symbol of his own religion, the coffin of Kukachin, granddaughter of Kublai Kaan, is pulled onto the stage by slaves. Kukachin, who represents the triumph of the soul and love over death, rises and speaks to the Christian businessman: "Say this, I loved and died. Now I am love, and live. And living, have forgotten. And loving, can forgive." In the first act, set twenty-three years earlier, Marco Polo is a young man wooing Donata. The young Polo has a soul, but the materialism of his father and uncle soon destroy it. In the second scene, set in the papal palace, the Polos are waiting for a new pope to be chosen. Before returning to Cathay, they want to fulfill a request from Kublai Kaan, that the pope send him one hundred wise men from the West. Once the pope is chosen, he tells the Polo brothers to take Marco in place of the wise men. In the next scenes Marco begins to learn how to be a salesman and a trader and, in the process, loses his desire to write poetry. In the final scene of the act the Polos present themselves to Kublai, who, because he is amused with Marco's foolishness, appoints him to a government position. In act 2, fifteen years later,

Kukachin, who has since fallen in love with Marco, is about to be married to the Khan of Persia. Kublai Kaan, who is beginning to weary of Marco, says that the Venetian "has memorized everything and learned nothing." Since Marco is returning to Venice, Kukachin asks that he escort her to Persia. During the voyage Marco saves Kukachin's life several times but remains soulless. He returns to Venice and Donata, now overweight and the symbol of material greed. The epilogue occurs in and outside the theater as the audience exits. Marco Polo, discovered sitting in the first row, rises and walks out with the audience, obviously perplexed by the play's meaning. He enters a limousine and "resumes his life."

It was a few years before the play, an unusual blending of pageant, satire, and history, found a producer. The Provincetown Players had failed to grow with O'Neill and did not have the resources to produce it. David Belasco and other Broadway producers considered the play but were eventually frightened by the high production costs and the uncertainty of an audience. In 1928 the Theatre Guild, which had the resources of a large subscription audience and a desire to promote developing playwrights, finally agreed to produce it. The play ran for ninety-two performances in New York and was later even more popular on the road, but, more importantly, a relationship was established with the Theatre Guild that would last for the rest of O'Neill's career.

Though O'Neill used masks occasionally in earlier plays, *The Great God Brown* is the first play devoted to restoring masks to the theater. O'Neill felt that, with masks, the modern theater could "express those profound hidden conflicts of the mind which the probings of psychology continue to disclose to us." The mask is a defense, a pose, a lie that a character presents to the world to protect the vulnerable self beneath it. Only rarely can a character feel secure enough to unmask and reveal his true self. The mask, O'Neill felt, was an unfortunate necessity. It protects the self, but maintaining a mask (the strain of living a lie) dissipates, haunts, and isolates the self. In O'Neill's words, "One's outer life passes in a solitude haunted by the masks of oneself."

In *The Great God Brown* O'Neill combines his theory of masks with a theme developed in preceding plays: the conflict between a soulless, materialistic businessman and a poet-artist. William Brown is the materialist, an architect who designs buildings that look like tombs. Dion Anthony (whose name combines Dionysus and St. Anthony) is the artist and a boyhood friend of Brown's. Margaret shares the love of both men. At the beginning of the play Dion wears a mask of Pan; he is the artist who wants to immerse himself in life. As the play develops, his mask becomes a mocking, Mephistophelian shield to protect his "supersensitive" self. Dion can only unmask before Cybel, outwardly a prostitute, inwardly an earth goddess. She understands and accepts Dion's true self. He says of Cybel, "You're strong. You always give. You've given my weakness strength to live." At first, Margaret, who understands and accepts Dion's mask, wears a mask of her own features; after years of dealing with Dion's alcoholism, her mask becomes a pleasant pretense to hide her tortured self.

The plot of the technically complex play, similar to Ibsen's *The Master Builder* (1892), is simple. Brown, who needs Dion's creativity to enhance his staid designs and "to reassure him he's alive," hires Dion to work in his architectural firm. When Dion dies of a heart attack, a complication of his alcoholism, Brown assumes Dion's identity and creativity by wearing his mask, visiting Cybel, and being a husband to Margaret. Ironically, Brown—while wearing Dion's mask—is shot by the police for murdering Brown. When this simple plot is encased in poetic dialogue and the mask schema, it seems more complicated. Surprisingly, however, the play was accepted by critics and the public; it ran in New York in 1926 for 283 performances.

In *Lazarus Laughed,* written in 1925 and 1926 and produced in 1928, masks are used in a different way. O'Neill later wrote of the play, "I advocate masks for stage crowds, mobs—wherever a sense of impersonal, collective mob psychology is wanted." The play opens shortly after Lazarus has been revived by Jesus. Lazarus, who has already died and thus does not fear death, is the only character who does not wear a mask. The other characters, Lazarus's family, the Romans, and a chorus of forty-nine Greeks, legionnaires, and Roman senators, representing different periods of life, wear masks. The large chorus is an important element in the play. It reacts to and chants Lazarus's message from beyond death, that "death is dead," that men kill because they are afraid to die, and that man can revel in life through laughter. With Lazarus chanting his message and the chorus echoing it, the play almost becomes an opera. As with *The Great God Brown,* the techniques are complex, the plot and theme simple. Lazarus offers salvation, but the chorus,

Playbill for O'Neill's autobiographical drama

representing mankind, is ultimately unable to accept it. Lazarus is burnt alive by the Roman Caligula because he wants to prove that there is death. The play, produced in California by the Pasadena Community Playhouse, ran for twenty-eight performances.

In *Strange Interlude,* written in 1926 and 1927, O'Neill achieved a scope and depth not often found in modern realistic drama. The Theater Guild production began at 5:15 and ended at 11:00; the audience was allowed an hour break after act 5. Spoken thoughts—O'Neill's version of the aside—created a sensational effect. By presenting the characters' thoughts as well as what they actually say, O'Neill added depth to the characters and complexity to the dynamics between characters. In the production the spoken thoughts were differentiated from dialogue by a contrast between motion and stillness. While one character was speaking his thoughts, the other characters remained motionless. During the traditional dialogue, the characters moved about freely. Though the technique and the way it was staged seem awkward, the audience adjusted to it.

The action of the play evolved from Nina Leeds's relationships with the male characters. The play opens after her fiancé, Gordon, has been killed in World War I. Though her father convinced Gordon to delay the marriage, Nina feels guilty about never having slept with him. To punish herself, she leaves her father, works as a nurse, and sleeps with several maimed soldiers. After her father dies, she returns home only to have others control her life. Ned Darrell, the doctor for whom she worked at the clinic, and Charlie Marsden, a family friend and a writer of sexless novels who is emotionally crippled by ties to his mother, convince Nina to marry Sam Evans, one of Gordon's college friends, and have children. Her mother-in-law, after revealing that the Evans family suffers from genetic insanity, advises Nina to have an abortion and then have a child by a healthy man. Nina follows her advice and has a child by Ned Darrell. For the first time her life is complete. She is a wife, mother, and mistress. But the vitality she experiences from a fulfilled life, the strange interlude, is short-lived. Her husband dies, her lover returns to his work, and her son marries. Her life has come full circle as she is left with Charlie Marsden, a lifeless father figure. In the play Nina attempts to escape from the influence of what she calls "God the Father" (guilt, distance, and death) and seek out "God the Mother" (compassion, union, and life). She succeeds–but only briefly.

The play established O'Neill as a popular playwright and writer. The Theater Guild expected to lose five hundred thousand dollars on it, but, instead, it ran for 426 performances. It sold over one hundred thousand copies in hardback and earned O'Neill over $250,000. The play's popularity, however, also brought problems. It was banned in Boston, and in 1929 Georges Lewys, claiming similarities to her novel *The Temple of Pallas Athene*, sued for plagiarism. The suit, which Lewys lost, received nationwide press coverage.

Though the preliminary notes for *Dynamo* were made in 1924, the play was not finished until 1928. It was the first play of what O'Neill hoped would be a trilogy on religion in the modern world. The second play in the trilogy was *Days Without End*, not completed until 1933. The third play was never written. O'Neill wrote in the playbill of the trilogy's theme: "The playwright today must dig at the roots of the sickness of today as he feels it–the death of the Old God and the failure of science and materialism to give any satisfying new One for the surviving primitive religious instinct to find meaning for life in, and to comfort its fears of death with." The statement is more true of *Dynamo* than of *Days Without End*.

Reuben Light, the protagonist of *Dynamo*, is the son of a preacher. Their next-door neighbor, Ramsay Fife, an atheist who worships electricity, uses Reuben, who is in love with Fife's daughter, Ada, to bait Reverend Light. Fife invents the story that he is wanted for murder and tells Reuben to keep it secret. To avoid a beating, Reuben tells the secret to his father. When Reverend Light tells the police and the joke is revealed, Reuben and his father argue. Reuben rejects his father's god, a paternal god of guilt, and runs away from home. When Reuben returns fifteen months later, his father blames him for his mother's death. Like Nina Leeds in *Strange Interlude*, Reuben tries to escape the masculine god of guilt by seeking a feminine god of compassion. For Reuben the feminine god is the dynamo, to which he prays and from which he receives forgiveness. The guilt, however, returns. After Reuben and Ada make love in the dynamo room, he feels guilty. He then kills Ada and is electrocuted as he attempts to achieve spiritual union with the god of the dynamo. He is unable to find comfort in traditional religion or the new religion of science.

Dynamo closed after fifty performances and would have closed sooner if it were not one of the Theater Guild's subscription plays. O'Neill blamed the failure on his inability to attend rehearsals–he was living with Carlotta Monterey in France–and his marital problems–he was undergoing a divorce from Agnes Boulton during the play's composition. Almost as an act of atonement, O'Neill extensively revised the play before publication.

On 22 July 1929, after a protracted and bitter divorce from Agnes, O'Neill married Carlotta Monterey in Paris. Though they traveled, O'Neill and Carlotta lived mostly in France, where he wrote *Mourning Becomes Electra*. Carlotta valued her role as the writer's wife, guarding to an extreme O'Neill's privacy. She limited visits and isolated O'Neill from some of his friends. In May 1931 the O'Neills returned to New York for the production of *Mourning Becomes Electra*.

This trilogy is pivotal in O'Neill's career, for it was both a new experiment and an end to experiments. In the fall of 1928 he conceived a play that would be a "modern psychological approximation of Greek sense of fate." Written between 1929 and 1931, *Mourning Becomes Electra* was ostensibly structured on Aeschylus's *Oresteia* and went through a series of aborted experiments. O'Neill incorporated but later abandoned spoken

Carlotta and Eugene O'Neill (Billy Rose Theatre Collection, The New York Public Library of Lincoln Center, Astor, Lenox and Tilden Foundations)

thoughts (like those in *Strange Interlude*), half-masks, and stylized soliloquies (probably an attempt to develop a language for tragedy). The six drafts of false starts and abandoned experiments indicate that O'Neill was moving away from the avant-garde toward a simpler, more traditional theater. In the transition, however, his experiments were not lost; they were, instead, subtly incorporated into his later plays.

Homecoming, the first play in the trilogy, is set in the tomblike Mannon mansion shortly after the Civil War and centers on the competition between Christine Mannon and her daughter Lavinia. Lavinia is an Electra figure; she hates her mother and competes with her for the affection of her father, brother, and Adam Brant. Brant, whose father was the disgraced David Mannon (Lavinia's great uncle) and whose mother was a Mannon servant, blames his parents' harsh life on the Mannon family and seeks revenge by courting Lavinia and having an affair with Christine. The romance between Brant and Christine is, like the romance in *Desire Under the Elms*, founded on unnatural motives, but it evolves into

love. The play reaches a climax when Christine poisons her husband. In *The Hunted*, the second play, Lavinia, who knows that her father was murdered, convinces Orin, her brother, to help her kill Brant. Brant's murder precipitates Christine's suicide. In the final play, *The Haunted*, Orin and Lavinia are unable to escape their past. They travel to a South Sea island, which is Orin's ideal of a sinless paradise. Orin is unable to shed his puritan morality, but Lavinia, more like her mother than she realizes, has an affair with a native. After returning to the Mannon house, Orin commits suicide and Lavinia, whose guilt returns, resolves to entomb herself in the Mannon mansion.

Philip Moeller, who directed this play as well as *Strange Interlude*, criticized it for being "too big for its size." Even though it is as long as *Strange Interlude*, *Mourning Becomes Electra* does not have the earlier play's depth and complexity. Critics, however, welcomed the trilogy as one of O'Neill's best plays; some called it his masterpiece. It ran for 150 performances in 1931.

Days Without End, the second play of an unfinished trilogy, was begun in 1927; the difficult composition ended in 1933. In the last of his avant-garde plays O'Neill uses a mask to present John Loving, who becomes disillusioned with Catholicism after losing his parents. He wants to find a substitute for religion in his love for Elsa, his wife, but he is afraid of placing faith in his love and becomes cynical to protect himself from the possibility of his wife's death. The ambivalence is represented onstage by two actors: the first actor plays John, the seeker of faith; the second actor plays the other side of his personality, Loving, the cynic, and wears a tortured, mocking mask of John the seeker. John speaks most of the dialogue; Loving occasionally interrupts with cynical lines. The other characters react to John and Loving as one but are aware of the dissonance of Loving's cynical interruptions.

The complication of the plot evolves from an affair that John Loving has with his wife's best friend and his attempt to atone for his guilt. After telling Elsa the plot of a novel he is writing, which is a thinly disguised version of his own search for faith, his love for Elsa, and his adultery, John Loving asks her if she would forgive the character in the novel. Elsa says she could not, and she eventually realizes that the novel is her husband's story, that he has defiled their ideal marriage, their faith in each other. She then rushes out into the cold and contracts pneumonia. The play closes as John Loving leaves Elsa's bedside–just as she forgives him–to pray at the foot of a cross. As John prays to a god of love, Loving, his cynical self, dies at the foot of the cross "like a cured cripple's testimonial offering in a shrine," and word comes that Elsa's fever has broken. Critics, somewhat confused by the play, felt that O'Neill was now a reformed Catholic. In the final scene, however, John Loving accepts the love–not the dogma–of Christianity: "Life laughs with God's love again? Life laughs with love!" Audiences were as confused as the critics, and the play, which premiered in 1934, closed after fifty-seven performances.

In fall 1932, while living at Sea Island, Georgia, during the difficult composition of *Days Without End*, O'Neill dreamed the plot of *Ah, Wilderness!* (1933), which he called a "Nostalgic Comedy." He quickly wrote what he intended to be a light comedy of a childhood that he wished he had lived, yet, unintentionally, he wrote about Richard Miller's initiation into his family's use of guilt as a subtle means of dominance. Only in recent years have critics acknowledged the darker side of the Miller family.

As the play begins on 4 July 1912, Richard is naive, idealistic, and poetic. He is in love with Muriel McComber, but the romance is virtually ended in act 1. Muriel's father, after reading Richard's love poetry to her, orders her to cease seeing him. To console himself, and as an act of rebellion against his father, Nat, and his mother, Essie, Richard goes to a bar with one of his brother's classmates at Yale and two disreputable girls and becomes drunk for the first time. Richard's drunkenness is parallel to his Uncle Sid's drunkenness earlier in the day. Sid, Essie Miller's brother, has for years been in love with Lily, Nat Miller's sister. Lily refuses to marry Sid because of his drinking but still retains control over him by making him feel guilty for becoming drunk, then by graciously forgiving him. Sid is so relieved to be forgiven that he becomes totally servile. After Richard comes home drunk, his parents treat him as Lily treated Sid. After receiving a message from Muriel, Richard meets her at midnight on the following evening. During their talk Richard manages to make Muriel feel partially responsible for his drunkenness. He is beginning to learn the value of guilt. In the final scene Richard's father decides to punish him for his drinking by not letting him go to Yale. Richard is pleasantly surprised at his father's punishment. He had been planning to forego college and to get a job on his father's newspaper in order to marry Muriel much sooner. But Nat Miller's threat not to send his son to college was only a threat; "only half concealing an answering grin," he tells Richard that he must go to Yale and stay until he graduates, whether he likes it or not. The play concludes with a heartfelt reconciliation between Richard and his parents. As Richard leaves the room, he and his father hug each other and, much to his father's surprise, Richard kisses him. When the play opened in 1933 with George M. Cohan playing the role of Nat Miller, critics and audiences found it a pleasant comedy. It ran for 289 performances and would have run longer if Cohan had not decided to leave the cast.

After the production of *Ah, Wilderness!*, O'Neill became an exile from Broadway for twelve years. He and Carlotta moved to the West Coast. From afar, O'Neill was able to criticize the commercialism of the New York theater industry and begin work on what he hoped would be his magnum opus, a cycle of nine plays entitled "A Tale of Possessors Self-Dispossessed." Although O'Neill worked on the cycle into the 1940s, most of the plays were written or planned in late 1934 and 1935. The origins of the cycle can be traced back to "On to Betelgeuse," a play that he worked on in 1928 and 1929. It was revised into "The Life of Bessie Bowen" in 1932 and later into "Hair of the Dog." Though "On to Betelgeuse" was written much earlier, the cycle actually evolved from the "Calms of Capricorn" trilogy, which traced the history of Sara Harford and her sons. The action of "The Calms of Capricorn," which occurs in 1857, begins on a clipper ship docked in Boston harbor and follows a trip through the South Atlantic to San Francisco. In the play Sara Harford is fifty years old, and her sons are in their twenties. "The Earth's the Limit" is set in 1858 in a San Francisco hotel and on top of a pass in the Sierras. Sara and her sons apparently become involved in trade and, perhaps, privateering. The third play, "Nothing Is Lost Save Honor," covers the years 1862-1870. In it, the Harford brothers make a fortune from unethical railroad deals. The play is the moral culmination of the trilogy. Within the three plays, which move from the poetic clipper ship to steam-driven trains, is the theme that would be embodied in the cycle: the members of the Harford family gain the world but lose their souls. O'Neill expanded the cycle to nine plays: "The Greed of the Meek," "Or Give Us Death," "A Touch of the Poet," "More Stately Mansions," "The Calms of Capricorn," "The Earth's the Limit," "Nothing Is Lost Save Honor," "The Man on Iron Horseback," and "Hair of the Dog." The first two plays were so long, as long as *Strange Interlude*, that O'Neill considered splitting each into two plays, which would have expanded the cycle to eleven plays. The ambitious project eventually became unmanageable; it was too large and interconnections between plays made it too complicated. In June 1939 O'Neill shelved the cycle, after which he returned to it only periodically. In winter 1952-1953 he and Carlotta attempted to destroy all of the cycle except *A Touch of the Poet*, the only one he completed. The unfinished *More Stately Mansions* (1964) survived by accident.

In *A Touch of the Poet*, which was produced in Stockholm in 1957, then in New York in 1958, Sara Melody meets Simon Harford, her future husband. Although Sara's father, Cornelius Melody, maintains the pretensions of an Irish gentleman and an officer in the British army by keeping an expensive horse and his old uniform (more subtle forms of a mask), he is a poor innkeeper in New England. Sara's mother, Nora, is a self-sacrificing wife who understands Cornelius's

need to assume a Byronic superiority. Sara met Simon Harford, who remains offstage for the entire play, while he was living in a cottage near her father's inn. When he became ill, Sara brought the idealistic youth to the inn to nurse him and calculatingly seduce him into marriage. The Harfords reject the proposed marriage and attempt to bribe Sara into leaving New England. Cornelius, who feels that his family has been insulted, leaves in his uniform to duel with Simon's father. After brawling with the Harford servants and police, Cornelius returns in a tattered uniform, his pretensions dissolved, and shoots his horse, the symbol of his superiority. Sara, who had previously despised Cornelius's posing, tries to restore her father's self-esteem. The play had a successful run of 284 performances on Broadway.

More Stately Mansions, produced on Broadway in 1967, is set four years after the end of *A Touch of the Poet* and continues the story of Sara's relationship with Simon. Simon, now less idealistic, is a successful businessman living with his mother, Deborah, and his wife, Sara. Each character struggles to possess the others through love. As Horst Frenz says, love "is transformed into desire to possess . . . which never brings victory but only inner impoverishment and ultimately loss of identity." Deborah loses her sanity and any connection with reality, and Simon becomes his wife's child. Sara is left in control of the Harford business and her three sons. The two surviving plays are a strong indication of the cycle's direction; Sara and her sons will grow more materialistically successful, but any idealism in the two branches of the family—in Sara's mother and the young Simon—will be destroyed in the process.

In June 1939, when O'Neill decided to put the cycle aside, he began one of the most productive phases of his career. In the next few years, despite his failing health (he was suffering from a hereditary nervous disease that brought a loss of motor control), he would write *The Iceman Cometh, Long Day's Journey Into Night, Hughie* (1959), and *A Moon for the Misbegotten* (1952), four of his best plays.

The Iceman Cometh, written in the latter half of 1939, is set in Harry Hope's saloon and boardinghouse. In act 1 the characters, all of whom live on pipe dreams and lies that buffer the harshness of reality, are sleepily waiting for the arrival of Hickey, a traveling salesman. He visits once a year to drink, buy drinks for others, celebrate Harry's birthday, and tell jokes about his wife's affair with the iceman. Before Hickey arrives, Don Parritt rents a room. He knew Larry Slade, who lives at Harry's, when Don's mother and Larry were radicals in "the movement." Don tells Larry that he is trying to hide from the police, who have recently arrested his mother. When Hickey arrives, he is, to the surprise of all, sober. He claims to have overcome his reliance on whiskey and pipe dreams and wants to show the denizens of Harry Hope's how to do the same. In act 2, where the setting of Harry's birthday party evokes the Last Supper, Hickey disrupts the festivities by dispelling everyone's pipe dreams. Larry's dream is that he is in the grandstand, no longer interested in life; Hickey shows him that he is still a vulnerable idealist. In act 3, where the set almost becomes a circus with Hickey as a ringleader, the characters, stripped of their pipe dreams, attempt to leave the bar and do what they have been putting off until tomorrow for years. They all return, devastated failures. In the final act Hickey and Parritt confess in counterpoint: Hickey that he murdered his wife to end the suffering he had been causing her, and Parritt that he turned in his mother for money. Both men have a common motive; they were unable to live up to the ideals of the women in their lives. After the confessions, Harry Hope and his friends return to their pipe dreams and drink. Hickey and Parritt react to their sense of inadequacy by destroying the women who set unrealistically high standards for them; Harry Hope and his friends react to their sense of inadequacy by fabricating pipe dreams.

Because O'Neill felt that *The Iceman Cometh* would be ill received during the war, it was not produced until 1946. The press coverage of the first new O'Neill production in thirteen years briefly brought him back to the public. It was, however, also the last new play to be produced on Broadway in his lifetime, and, after the 136 performances, critical interest in O'Neill began to decline. A revival of *The Iceman Cometh* in 1956, which ran for 565 performances, initiated an O'Neill revival.

O'Neill made notes for *Long Day's Journey Into Night,* his masterpiece, in June 1939. He wrote it in 1940 and revised it in spring 1941. In many ways, *Long Day's Journey Into Night* is the play O'Neill had been trying to write all of his career. After twenty-seven years of play writing, he had finally broken from melodrama and perfected his own theatrical aesthetic.

The play, set in New London, Connecticut, in 1912, depicts the Tyrone family during a crisis. Mary, the convent-bred mother, is in the process of trying to overcome her drug addiction. The youngest son, Edmund (O'Neill gave the name of his brother who died as a child to his self-portrait), is a journalist and has what the family refers to as a "bad cold," later to be diagnosed as tuberculosis. James, the father, a successful actor, is land poor; he buys large tracts of real estate to alleviate his fears of dying in the poorhouse. Jamie, the older brother, an actor in his father's company, is a cynical alcoholic. As Timo Tiusanen states, there are a large number of unfinished statements in the play. With unfinished statements and other devices, O'Neill achieves subtly what he attempted to achieve in earlier plays with masks or spoken thoughts. He is able to hint at the characters' inner lives and show that the family, though dependent on each other, is afraid to face reality (that Edmund has tuberculosis), be honest with each other (Jamie adds water to the whiskey bottle after he drinks from it), and trust each other (Mary realizes, from suspicious stares, that the others fear her return to drugs). Their need for mutual support is in conflict with obsessive lying, betrayal, and destructiveness. Mary blames her addiction on her husband, who, she feels, was too miserly to pay for a good doctor when Edmund was born; Jamie, conscious of his own inadequacies, attempts to convince Edmund that he will never become a writer. Even though the men make some attempt to be more honest with each other in a long confessional scene, the honesty comes with the aid of alcohol and will probably pass. The play ends as Mary descends the stairs wearing her wedding dress, lost in drugs and the past. The structure of the Tyrone family will not allow one character to change until they all change, and that is unlikely.

Because of the autobiographical elements of the play, O'Neill did not want *Long Day's Journey Into Night* published or produced until twenty-five years after his death. O'Neill's widow, however, allowed it to be produced by the Royal Dramatic Theatre in Stockholm in February 1956, two and a half years after he died. A New York production followed in November and had a very successful run of 390 performances.

In November 1940 O'Neill decided to begin a series of one-act plays entitled "By Way of Obit." Originally, he planned five plays. Each play would have one character who would deliver a monologue to a life-sized marionette, represent-

O'Neill with his daughter, Oona (courtesy of the Beinecke Rare Book and Manuscript Library)

ing "The Good Listener." He later expanded the series to eight plays and added a second character to be the listener. Some of the plays that were planned were about a railroad man, a man in Jimmy-the-Priest's saloon who recited Homer, a character named Thompson who was connected to a "rat idea," and a minstrel. Only *Hughie*, written in the spring of 1941, was completed, and it was not published or produced during O'Neill's lifetime.

Hughie is set in a run-down New York hotel lobby in the summer of 1928. After the funeral of Hughie, to whom he felt close, Erie Smith, a gambler with pretensions of being a Broadway sport, went on a binge. The friendship, though both men valued it, was limited. Erie told Hughie embellished stories and outright lies about gambling and relationships with chorus girls. Hughie, trapped in a boring job and a static marriage, created his own fantasies from Erie's stories. When Erie returns to the hotel after his binge and asks for his key, he tries to re-create the friendship between him and Hughie with the new clerk. The clerk, who at first is too consumed in his own boredom and fantasies to listen, eventually responds

to Erie, and a new bond seems to be forming at the play's end. The friendship, however, will be, as was Erie and Hughie's, limited; it is really a relationship between Erie's stories and the clerk's fantasies. It does not improve the quality of their lives significantly; it only makes them a little less lonely and pathetic.

In fall 1941 O'Neill made the notes for *A Moon for the Misbegotten*, which would be his last play. Written in 1942 and 1943, it evolved from an episode in act 1 of *Long Day's Journey Into Night*, a story that Jamie tells about an Irishman who outwits a New England aristocrat. The play begins with an enactment of Phil Hogan's triumph over a New England oil tycoon. The oil tycoon rides to Hogan's house to complain about the Irishman's pigs wallowing in his ice pond. Before the tycoon leaves, Hogan drags him through the pigpen. The episode brings Jamie Tyrone, whose father leases the farm to Hogan, to the scene. Jamie, who faces the world with the "mask" of a hardened cynic, and Josie Hogan, a large woman who faces the world with the "mask" of the village slut, are brought together. They both understand the other's hidden self.

Jamie knows that Josie is actually virginal, and Josie is aware of Jamie's sensitivity. Through long confessions, the characters achieve a closeness missing in their lives. In 1947 the Theatre Guild produced the play, but casting and censorship problems caused it to close after playing in three cities. It was O'Neill's last contact with the theater.

After the failed production of *A Moon for the Misbegotten* he wrote no new plays. Though his nervous disorder, his loss of motor control, made it difficult to hold a pencil without trembling, he still could have written. He owned a crude dictating machine, a gift from the Theater Guild, but was unwilling to use the machine for composing. He claimed that he could not write without pencil and paper. Some of his friends felt that he was passively waiting for death. He died in 1953 apart from the theater that he had helped to reshape.

Before O'Neill began to write, most American plays were poor imitations or outright thefts of European works. By the 1920s he was hailed in America as the most promising of the young playwrights and was also gaining an international reputation. A few decades later he was the model for the American playwrights who followed. Tennessee Williams, Arthur Miller, Edward Albee, and others could begin their careers in a tradition which O'Neill, more than any other playwright, had established. This legacy to his successors is of incalculable value.

An epigrammatic evaluation of O'Neill's career might be that he wrote some of the very best and some of the worst plays of the twentieth century. *The Emperor Jones, The Hairy Ape, Desire Under the Elms, Strange Interlude, Mourning Becomes Electra, A Touch of the Poet, The Iceman Cometh, Hughie,* and *A Moon for the Misbegotten* are all great plays, and *Long Day's Journey Into Night* is one of the greatest plays of Western literature. *The Great God Brown, Lazarus Laughed,* and other failed experiments, though the products of a dramatic genius, are, in one way or another, embarrassingly bad. A fairer evaluation would incorporate an understanding of O'Neill's need for experimentation. The variety of modes in which he wrote, especially during the middle period of his career, was his way of discovering how the theater might be transformed into a medium for his thoughts. A still fairer evaluation of his career would include an appreciation for the magnitude of his accomplishments given the significant obstacles he encountered. He had to create American

drama as an art form before he could begin to write great American plays.

Letters:

"Love and Admiration and Respect": The O'Neill-Commins Correspondence, edited by Dorothy Commins (Durham, N.C.: Duke University Press, 1986).
Chronicles the friendship between O'Neill and Saxe Commins, "like that of two brothers rather than that of a writer and his editor," from 1920 until two years before O'Neill's death; also includes correspondence between Commins and some members of O'Neill's family after his death.

Selected Letters of Eugene O'Neill, edited by Travis Bogard and Jackson R. Bryer (New Haven & London: Yale University Press, 1988).
O'Neill's letters to his family, the women in his life, and his literary associates; provides a glimpse into his inner life and intimate relationships.

Bibliography:

Jennifer McCabe Atkinson, *Eugene O'Neill: A Descriptive Bibliography* (Pittsburgh: University of Pittsburgh Press, 1974).
The first descriptive bibliography since O'Neill's death, this volume provides listings of first and subsequent book publications, first appearances in periodicals, and various miscellaneous items of interest to the O'Neill scholar.

Biographies:

Arthur Gelb and Barbara Gelb, *O'Neill* (New York: Harper, 1962).
This lengthy and comprehensive account of O'Neill's life attempts to capture the "bizarre personal life . . . reflected in the dark mirror of his plays."

Louis Sheaffer, *O'Neill: Son and Playwright* (Boston: Little, Brown, 1968); *O'Neill: Son and Artist* (Boston: Little, Brown, 1973).
In addition to chronicling his life, these two volumes seek to explain the nature of O'Neill's creative impulse in relation to his childhood, his selective view of reality, and his preoccupation with insanity.

References:

Travis Bogard, *Contour in Time* (New York: Oxford University Press, 1972).
Analyzes the "intense subjectivity" of O'Neill's plays, his mythic vision, his manipulation of theatrical devices, and his innovative treatment of psychology and the feminine mind.

Oscar Cargil, N. Bryllion Fagin, and William J. Fisher, eds., *O'Neill and His Plays: Four Decades of Criticism* (New York: New York University Press, 1961).
Collects nearly one hundred essays, letters, and memoirs by and about O'Neill representing a wide range of critical response by critics in the United States and abroad.

Barrett H. Clark, *Eugene O'Neill: The Man and His Plays* (New York: McBride, 1929).
The first book to deal exclusively with O'Neill, written against his wishes; reflects the critical reception of his early plays during his lifetime.

Dorothy Commins, *What Is an Editor? Saxe Commins at Work* (Chicago: University of Chicago Press, 1978).
Correspondence to Saxe Commins from O'Neill, Auden, and Faulkner; editorial documents; and commentary from his wife, Dorothy.

Helen Deutsch and Stella Hanau, *The Provincetown: A Story of the Theatre* (New York: Farrar & Rinehart, 1931).
Re-creates the atmosphere and sense of the Provincetown Players through the conflicting anecdotes of many who were involved in the company, such as O'Neill, Bette Davis, Jig Cook, and Susan Glaspell; excellent illustrations–posters, playbills, photographs.

Edwin A. Engel, *The Haunted Heroes of Eugene O'Neill* (Cambridge: Harvard University Press, 1953).
Explores O'Neill's use of characterization and the recurring character types which form a consistent pattern throughout the body of his work.

Doris V. Falk, *Eugene O'Neill and the Tragic Tension* (New Brunswick: Rutgers University Press, 1958).
Treats the themes of hubris and the Fall, human suffering, and the ultimate tragedy of the human condition in the plays and O'Neill's use of psychoanalysis and Jungian psychology to relate ancient myth to twentieth-century life.

Virginia Floyd, *The Plays of Eugene O'Neill: A New Assessment* (New York: Ungar, 1985).
Aimed at the general reader, this analysis offers interpretations of each of the plays and reasserts O'Neill's place as America's most important playwright.

Winnifred Frazer, *Love as Death in 'The Iceman Cometh'* (Gainesville: University of Florida Press, 1967).
Asserts that the play's theme, "love as death," has its basis in the ecstasy of the saints and in the psychoanalytic theories of Freud, and draws upon "the warlike language of love."

Horst Frenz, *Eugene O'Neill* (New York: Ungar, 1971).
Originally published in German, this analysis of the achievement of Eugene O'Neill credits him with revolutionary American drama and discusses his rejection of the mediocrity of the American theater, partially as a revolt against his actor father.

Frenz and Susan Tuck, eds. *Eugene O'Neill's Critics: Voices from Abroad* (Carbondale: Southern Illinois University, 1984).
Collects essays on O'Neill and his works by critics from Great Britain, Eastern Europe, the Scandanavian countries, France, Spain, the Soviet Union, China, and Japan.

John Gassner, *Eugene O'Neill* (Minneapolis: University of Minnesota Press, 1965).
Pamphlet providing basic information on O'Neill's life and plays; brief but useful.

Virgil Geddes, *The Melodrama Madness of Eugene O'Neill* (Brookfield, Conn.: Brookfield Players, 1934).
A forty-eight-page pamphlet which briefly describes twelve of O'Neill's plays and examines his use of character as well as his roles for women.

Isaac Goldberg, *The Theatre of George Jean Nathan* (New York: Simon & Schuster, 1926).
Exploration of drama critic Nathan; contains letters from O'Neill outlining embryonic stages of *Anna Christie* (pp. 140-165).

Michael Manheim, *Eugene O'Neill's New Language of Kinship* (Syracuse: Syracuse University Press, 1982).
Claims that O'Neill's appeal lies in his personalization of "the struggle to come to grips with the mysteries of human emotion" and that his major characters are based upon members of his own family.

Jordan Y. Miller, *Eugene O'Neill and the American Critic* (Hamden, Conn.: Archon Books, 1973).
Discusses O'Neill's critical reception and lists critical works about O'Neill.

John Henry Raleigh, *The Plays of Eugene O'Neill* (Carbondale: Southern Illinois University Press, 1965).
This complex and detailed analysis proceeds from the premise that O'Neill was "a Strindbergian conglomeration" and that his plays are best understood by studying his body of work as a whole.

Margaret Loftus Ranald, *The Eugene O'Neill Companion* (Westport, Conn. & London: Greenwood Press, 1984).
Provides synopses of all the plays, including unproduced, unpublished, and incomplete works; brief sketches of the characters; and biographical pieces on persons associated with O'Neill (family and friends) or his plays (actors, directors, etc.).

James A. Robinson, *Eugene O'Neill and Oriental Thought: A Divided Vision* (Carbondale: Southern Illinois University Press, 1982).
Claims that O'Neill's western dualism is mitigated by his use of Oriental philosophy to reconcile "the breach between subject and object by emphasizing the unity of soul and cosmos in a sphere beyond moral categories."

Richard Dana Skinner, *Eugene O'Neill: A Poet's Quest* (New York: Longmans, Green, 1935).
Discusses the way in which O'Neill's poetic sense–which is both rooted in yet transcends his American heritage–explores universal questions of good, evil, and spiritual conflict.

Timo Tiusanen, *O'Neill's Scenic Image* (Princeton: Princeton University Press, 1968).
Asserts the importance of the "scenic image" (the visual impact of the stage and setting on the audience) in dramatic performance and analyzes the way in which O'Neill exploits this element of drama to underscore his thematic concerns.

Egil Törnqvist, *A Drama of Souls* (New Haven: Yale University Press, 1969).
Examines O'Neill's use of symbols, his psychological and spiritual concerns, the influence of his Catholic childhood, and his "supernaturalistic" technique.

Upton Sinclair

This entry was updated by William A. Bloodworth (East Carolina University) from his entry in DLB 9, American Novelists, 1910-1945.

Places	Chicago New York City	Baltimore Boston	California
Influences and Relationships	Friedrich Nietzsche	Percy Bysshe Shelley	Karl Marx
Literary Movements and Forms	Romanticism Formula Fiction	Muckraking Naturalism	Historical Novels Autobiography
Major Themes	Political and Financial Corruption	Failure of the American Dream	American History Political Corruption
Cultural and Artistic Influences	Bohemianism	Utopian Communities	
Social and Economic Influences	Socialism The Rise of Industrialism	The Great Depression Sacco & Vanzetti World War I	World War II Health Reform

BIRTH: Baltimore, Maryland, 20 September 1878, to Upton Beau and Priscilla Harden Sinclair.

EDUCATION: B.A., City College of New York, 1897; Columbia University, 1897-1900.

MARRIAGES: 1900 to Meta H. Fuller (divorced); child: David. 1913 to Mary Craig Kimbrough; 1962 to May Hard.

AWARDS AND HONORS: Pulitzer Prize for *Dragon's Teeth*, 1943.

DEATH: Washington, D.C., 25 November 1968.

SELECTED BOOKS: *Springtime and Harvest* (New York: Sinclair Press, 1901); republished as *King Midas* (New York & London: Funk & Wagnalls, 1901; London: Heinemann, 1906);

The Journal of Arthur Stirling (New York: Appleton, 1903; London: Heinemann, 1903);

Prince Hagen (Boston: Page, 1903; London: Chatto & Windus, 1903);

Manassas (New York & London: Macmillan, 1904);

The Toy and the Man (Westwood, Mass.: Ariel Press, 1904);

Our Bourgeois Literature: The Reason and the Remedy (Chicago: Kerr, 1905);

The Jungle (New York: Doubleday, Page/New York: Jungle Publishing 1906; London: Heinemann, 1906);

A Captain of Industry (Girard, Kans.: Appeal to Reason, 1906; London: Heinemann, 1906);

The Industrial Republic (New York: Doubleday, Page, 1907; London: Heinemann, 1907);

The Overman (New York: Doubleday, Page, 1907);

The Metropolis (New York: Moffat, Yard, 1908; London: Arnold, 1908);

The Moneychangers (New York: Dodge, 1908; London: Long, 1908);

Samuel the Seeker (New York: Dodge, 1910; London: Long, 1910);

Love's Pilgrimage (New York & London: Kennerley, 1911; London: Heinemann, 1912);

Sylvia (Philadelphia & Chicago: Winston, 1913; London: Long, 1914);

Sylvia's Marriage (Philadelphia & Chicago: Winston, 1914; London: Laurie, 1915);

Upton Sinclair

King Coal (New York: Macmillan, 1917; London: Laurie, 1917);

The Profits of Religion (Pasadena: Upton Sinclair, 1918; London: Laurie, 1936);

Jimmie Higgins (New York: Boni & Liveright; Pasadena: Upton Sinclair, 1919; London: Hutchinson, 1919);

The Brass Check (Pasadena: Upton Sinclair, 1920; London: Laurie, 1921);

100%: The Story of a Patriot (Pasadena: Upton Sinclair, 1920); republished as *The Spy* (London: Laurie, 1921);

They Call Me Carpenter (Pasadena: Upton Sinclair; Chicago: Paine/New York: Boni & Liveright, 1922; London: Laurie, 1922);

The Goose-Step (Pasadena: Upton Sinclair/Chicago: Economy, 1923; London: Laurie, 1923);

Mammonart (Pasadena: Upton Sinclair, 1925; London: Laurie, 1934);

Oil! (New York: Boni/Long Beach, Cal.: Upton Sinclair, 1927; London: Laurie, 1927);

Money Writes! (New York: Boni/Long Beach, Cal.: Upton Sinclair, 1927; London: Laurie, 1931);

Boston, 2 volumes (New York: Long Beach, Cal.: Upton Sinclair, 1928; London: Laurie, 1929);

Mountain City (New York: Boni/Long Beach, Cal.: Upton Sinclair, 1930; London: Laurie, 1930);

Mental Radio (New York: Boni/Pasadena: Upton Sinclair, 1930); republished as *Mental Radio: Does It Work, And How?* (London: Laurie, 1930);

Roman Holiday (New York: Farrar & Rinehart/ Pasadena: Upton Sinclair, 1931; London: Laurie, 1931);

The Wet Parade (New York: Farrar & Rinehart/ Pasadena: Upton Sinclair, 1931; London: Laurie, 1931);

American Outpost (New York: Farrar & Rinehart/ Pasadena: Upton Sinclair, 1932); republished as *Candid Reminiscences: My First Thirty Years* (London: Laurie, 1932);

I, Governor of California, and How I Ended Poverty (Los Angeles: Upton Sinclair, 1933; London: Laurie, 1933);

Co-Op (New York & Toronto: Farrar & Rinehart/ Pasadena: Upton Sinclair, 1936; London: Laurie, 1936);

What God Means to Me (New York: Farrar & Rinehart/Pasadena: Upton Sinclair, 1936; London: Laurie, 1936);

The Flivver King (Detroit: United Automobile Workers of America/Pasadena: Upton Sinclair, 1937; London: Laurie, 1938);

No Pasaran! (Pasadena: Upton Sinclair, 1937; London: Laurie, 1937);

Little Steel (New York & Toronto: Farrar & Rinehart/Pasadena: Upton Sinclair, 1938; London: Laurie, 1938);

World's End (New York: Viking/New York & Pasadena: Upton Sinclair, 1940; London: Laurie, 1940);

Between Two Worlds (New York: Viking/New York & Pasadena: Upton Sinclair, 1941; London: Laurie, 1941);

Dragon's Teeth (New York: Viking/New York & Pasadena: Upton Sinclair, 1942; London: Laurie, 1942);

Wide Is the Gate (New York: Viking/Monrovia, Cal.: Upton Sinclair, 1943; London: Laurie, 1944);

Presidential Agent (New York: Viking/New York & Monrovia, Cal.: Upton Sinclair, 1944; London: Laurie, 1945);

Dragon Harvest (New York: Viking/New York & Monrovia, Cal.: Upton Sinclair, 1945; London: Laurie, 1946);

A World to Win (New York: Viking/Monrovia, Cal.: Upton Sinclair, 1946; London: Laurie, 1947);

Presidential Mission (New York: Viking/Monrovia, Cal.: Upton Sinclair, 1947; London: Laurie, 1948);

One Clear Call (New York: Viking/Monrovia, Cal.: Upton Sinclair, 1948; London: Laurie, 1949);

O Shepherd, Speak! (New York: Viking/Monrovia, Cal.: Upton Sinclair, 1949; London: Laurie, 1950);

Another Pamela: or Virtue Still Rewarded (New York: Viking, 1950; London: Laurie, 1952);

The Return of Lanny Budd (New York: Viking, 1953; London: Laurie, 1953);

What Didymus Did (London: Wingate, 1954); republished as *It Happened to Didymus* (New York: Sagamore Press, 1958);

The Autobiography of Upton Sinclair (New York: Harcourt, Brace & World, 1962; London: Allen, 1963).

Upton Sinclair was a writer whose main concerns were politics and economics. His ideas about literature–his own, written over more than six decades, and that of others–were inseparable from his dreams of social justice. Consequently, the great majority of his books, fiction as well as nonfiction, were written as specific means to specific ends. Since the essential purpose of literature, for Sinclair, was the betterment of human conditions, he was a muckraker, a propagandist, an interpreter of socialism and a critic of capitalism, a novelist more concerned with content than form, a journalistic chronicler of his times rather than an enduring artist. Since World War II, his literary reputation has declined. Yet *The Jungle* (1906) is one of the best known and most historically significant of American novels, and Sinclair himself remains an important figure in American political and cultural history.

Although it is possible to do justice to several of Sinclair's novels by examining them as individual literary works–particularly in the cases of *The Jungle* (1906) and *Oil!* (1927)–there are equally significant things to be learned by studying Sinclair's entire career and noting in it the interrelationships among his life, his times, and his writings. His single-minded intensity is the unifying feature. Sinclair was always an idealist–and a visionary–who agreed with Percy Bysshe Shelley that writers are the unacknowledged legislators of the world, or at least should be, and who sel-

Upton Sinclair at age eight

only son of a ne'er-do-well salesman from a respected Virginia family. His mother was the daughter of a wealthy Baltimore family that presented a decided contrast to the usually shabby existence provided by his father. At the age of eighteen, while completing his studies at the City College of New York, Upton Beall Sinclair, Jr., began his writing career as the pseudonymous author of boys' adventure stories for Street and Smith, the leading American publisher of pulp fiction and dime novels. In embarking upon a career as a hack writer, Sinclair sought, with considerable success, to achieve economic independence from his alcoholic father. In four years he produced hundreds of stories whose techniques, especially deus ex machina plots and two-dimensional characterizations, seem to have periodically insinuated themselves into his later works. During the latter three years of this unusual apprenticeship, following his graduation from CCNY, he also took courses, but no degree, from Columbia University. Among the subjects he felt himself drawn to were music, contemporary politics, and Romantic poetry. In the Romantic poets, especially Shelley, whom he studied under George Edward Woodberry, Sinclair found sufficient inspiration to abandon his career as a pulp writer and begin writing serious literature.

Sinclair's first real literary efforts, between 1900 and 1904, were novels which took romantic idealism itself as their central subject. Read today, these works—*Springtime and Harvest* (1901), *Prince Hagen* (1903), *The Overman* (1907, written in 1902-1903), *The Journal of Arthur Stirling* (1903), and *A Captain of Industry* (1906, written in 1903)—seem immature and awkwardly pretentious. But they clearly show Sinclair groping toward a discovery of socialism. This discovery began with romantic idealism, passed through an exuberant fascination with Friedrich Nietzsche and the possibilities of self, and emerged in a recognition that spirit and idealism have few chances in a world of corruption and oppression.

Sinclair's essential step toward literary socialism was the writing of *Manassas* (1904), a novel of the Civil War in which a young Southerner, Alan Montague, the son of a plantation owner, becomes a proponent of abolition. Prior to writing this novel Sinclair had begun to learn about the socialist movement from prominent socialists in New York. His writing an abolitionist novel suggested that he had broken with his own Southern roots and was now prepared to adopt a radical stance toward social problems. Furthermore, the

dom doubted that his ideas and words would, if heeded, produce a better world. Beyond these surface attitudes, but never completely buried in his works, lie a number of contradictions and tensions. Sinclair was a person of essentially genteel and conservative upbringing who became a literary radical. Although he has often been seen as the champion of the oppressed, a novelist who wrote for and about the lowest working classes, many of his works have elitist tendencies. More than anything else, though, he was a nineteenth-century idealist of initially romantic and even Nietzschean traits who chose to confront the hard facts of twentieth-century industrial life. His sense of certainty led him astray at times and prevented him from creating complex modern works of fiction, but he probably had a larger and more concrete influence on American life than most other novelists of the twentieth century.

The origins of Sinclair's unique career lie in the circumstances of his childhood and adolescence: genteel poverty, idealism, ambition. He grew up in Baltimore and New York City as the

form of *Manassas*, in which Alan Montague is present at many important events and meets a wide
range of historical figures–including Jefferson
Davis, Abraham Lincoln, Frederick Douglass,
and John Brown–prefigures the structure of
many of Sinclair's later novels, particularly the
eleven-volume Lanny Budd series published between 1940 and 1953. *Manassas* is the best of his
early novels, and its theme of idealistic opposition to an unjust society is *the* theme of Upton Sinclair.

Manassas also led to the opportunity for *The
Jungle* (1906) when the editor of a radical paper
challenged Sinclair to write a novel treating the
"wage slaves" of industry in a manner similar to
the treatment of chattel slaves in *Manassas*. In the
fall of 1904 Sinclair spent two months in the
packing-plant district of Chicago, the scene of an
unsuccessful strike against the packers several
months earlier. He talked with workers and visited the packing plants both as an official tourist
and, in disguise, as a worker. He saw enough corruption, filth, and poverty to make *The Jungle* a
gripping, emotionally wrenching novel.

The Jungle lies somewhere between pure fiction and muckraking journalism on a formalistic
scale, and somewhere between determinism and
reform on an ideological scale. It is the story of oppressive industrial conditions as they affect a Lithuanian family that comes to Chicago expecting to
achieve the American dream. Instead, their life becomes a nightmare of toil, poverty, and death.
Jurgis Rudkus, the leader of the family and
Sinclair's version of a proletarian hero, not only
sees his father, wife, and son die, but he is also brutalized by working conditions in the Chicago packing houses and exploited by corrupt politics fashioned by the "Beef Trust." The grim details of
life in Packingtown, all drawn from Sinclair's
own firsthand knowledge, are communicated
with a raw energetic style quite appropriate to
Sinclair's equally raw and violent subject matter.

The structure of the novel is complicated by
Sinclair's attempt first to show how heartbreaking
life could be for the industrial proletariat and
then to depict socialism as the obvious way to improve that life. After Jurgis is reduced to extreme forms of degradation–becoming a hobo, a
criminal, and even a strike-breaking scab–he stum-
bles into a socialist lecture. The lecture transforms his view of the world; he is virtually born
again. But once this occurs, his role as protagonist in the narrative disappears, and the last few
chapters of the novel are given over to socialist ar-

*Meta H. Fuller, whom Sinclair married in 1900 (courtesy of
David Sinclair)*

gument and analysis which Jurgis hears but does
not generate. Instead, the statements, chiefly optimistic projections of a new world in the making,
come from the mouths of articulate, educated,
and even wealthy socialists. In the socialist ending
of *The Jungle*–in contrast to the naturalistic narrative proceeding it–the working class loses its
voice.

In spite of these problems, *The Jungle* had,
and still has, inestimable value as a powerful
story depicting conditions and people that do not
often appear in the pages of American literature.
It both questions the American dream of success
and demands that dream be more inclusive and
more rigorously transformed into economic reality.

For Sinclair himself, *The Jungle* virtually guaranteed that the rest of his career would be anticli-
mactic. The success of the novel, including its impact on legislation aimed at pure food and
sanitary meat processing, was an act which Sinclair found difficult to follow. Between 1906 and
1914, at which time Sinclair was again drawn to a
specific working-class problem, his career took sev-

eral directions. He organized a communal living experiment at Helicon Hall in New Jersey only to see the building burn down in March 1907. He wrote *The Industrial Republic* (1907), a nonfiction attempt to explain that socialism can be achieved by "a process as natural . . . as that by which a chick breaks out of its shell." The primary value of the book is its elucidation of the benevolent but naïve spirit of pre–World War I American socialism.

Seeking answers to personal problems, especially the breakup of his marriage, Sinclair began to live in several utopian communities. He wrote about diet and health, at times promoting fasting as a cure for a wide variety of diseases. All the while he continued to write novels. In 1908 he had *The Metropolis* and *The Moneychangers* published, the first a muckraking novel about upper-class New York society and the second an almost libelous story of high finance based rather obviously on the affairs of J. P. Morgan; both are poor novels of good intentions in which Sinclair's obsessive hatred of wealth, corruption, and loose morals triumphs over his narrative skills. In 1910 he produced *Samuel the Seeker*, the story of a young man who tries on various religious and ideological identities before settling on socialism. As a result of his socialist activities he is left unconscious and badly beaten at the end of the novel, a victim of police brutality.

While Sinclair was still in the midst of his physical and intellectual wandering, his strange autobiographical novel entitled *Love's Pilgrimage* (1911) appeared, describing the painful circumstances of his life with Meta Fuller, whom he married in 1900. Written as personal justification for the divorce which Sinclair would eventually get in 1913, *Love's Pilgrimage* is a neo-feminist work arguing for the personal and intellectual needs of married women and showing candidly how in one specific marriage an initially idealistic union had come apart under various pressures, including Sinclair's own confused and prudish attitudes toward sexuality. In 1913 Sinclair found himself interested in the subject of venereal disease, an interest which produced *Sylvia* (1913) and *Sylvia's Marriage* (1914), two novels detailing the life of a Virginia belle who marries for social status only to find that her upper-class husband is a carrier of gonorrhea.

Three events helped bring Sinclair back to the kind of novel that he wrote best. One was his successful marriage, in 1913, to Mary Craig Kimbrough, a Southern belle with socialist sympa-

Sinclair and David, his son, 1905

thies. Another was his permanent residence in southern California beginning around 1914. The third was an outbreak of industrial violence. Disturbed by the massacre of striking coal miners and their families in Ludlow, Colorado, Sinclair became involved in the labor and social problems of western miners. Following the pattern that produced *The Jungle*, he took a trip to Colorado, visited with miners, talked to union officials, and, in describing his impressions of Ludlow in an eloquent public letter to John D. Rockefeller (who owned many mines), said he felt "as if the air I breathed were full of the smoke of powder and the scent of human flesh; as if my ears were deafened with the screams of women and children." The end result, three years later, was *King Coal* (1917), his attempt to dramatize conditions in the coal fields of the West.

Unfortunately, *King Coal* did not meet the expectations set by *The Jungle*, nor did it fall upon particularly sympathetic ears in 1917, when, with the onset of World War I, the public had become more interested in submarines than coal mines. The novel tells the story of Hal Warner, a wealthy young man who poses as a coal miner to test social theories, becomes an advocate of unionization, and, at the end of the story, returns to upper-class society to fight for the miner's cause. Although many of the characters in the novel are well drawn, *King Coal* lacks the power of *The Jungle*. Part of the problem lies in Sinclair's choice of an upper-class protagonist instead of a coal field version of Jurgis Rudkus. Yet Sinclair himself was fond enough of this device (which he had used in both *Manassas* and *The Metropolis*) to reuse it in many of his later novels.

Following his work on *King Coal*, Sinclair was drawn into the controversy surrounding America's entrance into World War I. Feeling that German militarism represented a threat to world peace, Sinclair temporarily parted ways with the American Socialist party, which opposed intervention. His act suggests a more flexible ideological attitude than that typically demonstrated by American radicals in 1917. Sinclair's flexibility became just as evident in 1918 when he grew critical of American military attempts to suppress the Bolshevik revolution. The war itself, and the political dilemma of American socialists during the war, became the central concern of *Jimmie Higgins* (1919). The title character of the novel is a rank-and-file member of the Socialist party who, like Sinclair, decides that he must side against the German menace. He enlists in the army, fights valiantly, but is ultimately tortured into insanity when he speaks up against American intervention in Russia. Since the novel uses a member of the lower class as its hero, it represents a return to the techniques of *The Jungle*. It also resembles that earlier novel in its extensive depiction of violence, including not only death on the battlefields but also murder, industrial violence, castration, torture, and brainwashing. *Jimmie Higgins* lacks convincing psychological tension within its main character, however, and stands primarily as a literary document of American socialism in World War I.

In the 1920s Sinclair was one of the few prewar socialists who neither grew conservative nor became a member of the Communist party and an advocate of revolution. One of the main ways that he resisted the conservatism of the decade was by printing and distributing his own books, thus avoiding what he perceived as the unhealthy influence of big business on commercial publishing. Consequently, from 1917 to the early 1940s, Sinclair himself published virtually all of his books and pamphlets; many of his major works,

Sinclair with Mary Craig Kimbrough, whom he married in 1913

however, were also published simultaneously by New York publishers.

In the first years of the decade Sinclair wrote *100%* (1920) and *They Call Me Carpenter* (1922), novels of limited appeal that focus on false patriotism and violence among middle-class political reactionaries who, according to Sinclair, unwittingly acted out scenarios arranged by big business. These novels represent direct confrontation with the political atmosphere of the early 1920s, especially that associated with Attorney General Alexander Mitchell Palmer's "Red Raids" in 1919 and 1920. A similar confrontation occurs in a series of nonfiction analyses discussing the damaging influence of capitalism on various American institutions. These books, which Sinclair called his "Dead Hand" series–in contrast to Adam Smith's idea of a benevolent "Invisible Hand" at work in laissez-faire economics–include *The Profits of Religion* (1918); *The Brass Check* (1920), dealing with journalism; *The Goose-Step* (1923), dealing with education; and *Mammonart* (1925), dealing with art and literature. He also wrote tracts and plays, all critical of the normalcy which reigned in American politics in the 1920s.

That Sinclair was essentially a novelist, however, and a novelist of a particular kind, became abundantly clear at the end of the decade when he produced *Oil!* (1927) and *Boston* (1928).

Oil! is a long, expansive novel based loosely on the oil scandals of the Harding administration. Its central character is Bunny Ross, the son of an oilman, J. Arnold ("Dad") Ross. Dad Ross is a semiliterate entrepreneur who rises to wealth in the southern California oil fields. His son, Bunny, admires him until Bunny meets Paul Watkins, the intelligent son of a poor rancher, who is on his way to becoming a political radical. The psychological tension in the novel comes as a result of Bunny's being torn between his love for his father and his agreement with Paul Watkins's ideas. The tension increases when Bunny realizes that his father, by virtue of his capitalistic role rather than his intentions, is an agent of political oppression. By the end of the novel Dad Ross has died of a heart attack, and Paul Watkins, by joining the Communist party, has become an advocate of violence—and dies at the hands of a right-wing mob. Bunny himself struggles to work for social justice while maintaining a nonviolent position.

The strength of *Oil!* lies in Sinclair's depiction of Bunny Ross as a character who is genuinely divided in his attitudes and expectations. This depiction is strengthened by the sympathetic portrayal of Dad Ross as a three-dimensional character rather than a capitalist villain. Furthermore, the novel sweeps across southern California, dealing not only with oil fields but with Hollywood behavior and charlatanistic religion. Even though *Oil!* lacks the historical importance of *The Jungle*, it has been judged Sinclair's best novel and may well be his most readable one today.

Boston is a two-volume fictional account of the Sacco-Vanzetti case; the novel appeared one year after the execution of the two anarchists. It represents Sinclair's best effort at using the novel as a means to publicize and interpret contemporary events that he felt had not been adequately covered by the news media. The argument of the novel is suggested by its title: that the tragedy of Sacco and Vanzetti was the fault of Boston itself, particularly its social elite. To present this argument Sinclair chose to use as his central character an elderly Bostonian, Cornelia Thornwell, the ex-wife of a past governor of Massachusetts, who rebels against her own class, seeks experience among immigrant workers, but still retains family ties with the Boston elite. When Cornelia boards with an Italian family, she meets Vanzetti and becomes one of his most trusted friends; this fictitious relationship allows Sinclair to evaluate the Sacco-Vanzetti case through the reasonable mind of Cornelia, who has experience on several social levels. Cornelia does not affect the outcome of the case even though Sinclair creates a situation in which she turns down an opportunity to perjure herself before a jury and thus save the lives of Sacco and Vanzetti; her main role is to convey the sense of helplessness that real-life supporters of the anarchists felt. The main power of the novel, however, lies in its last two hundred pages, which describe the final, desperate months of Sacco's and Vanzetti's lives—and in its sympathetic portrayal of Bartolomeo Vanzetti as a person of great dignity and courage.

After his remarkable achievements in *Oil!* and *Boston*, Sinclair's career as a novelist faltered for some dozen years. Some of his literary failures in the early 1930s—especially *Mountain City* (1930) and *Roman Holiday* (1931)—resemble the weak muckraking fiction he produced immediately after *The Jungle*. Likewise, he again seemed to be sidetracked from the writing of genuinely realistic fiction focusing on class conflict and economic injustice; for instance, he wrote a book on telepathy entitled *Mental Radio* (1930) and a novel, *The Wet Parade* (1931), a moralistic plea for the retention of Prohibition.

But the chief reason for the decline of his career as a novelist in the 1930s was his involvement in electoral politics. In 1934, following the publication of a book entitled *I Governor of California, and How I Ended Poverty* (1933), Sinclair became the Democratic candidate for governor in California. His campaign became known as the EPIC (End Poverty in California) campaign. Although Sinclair was unsuccessful in his bid for election, his appeal may have influenced the Roosevelt administration to pay more heed to left-wing demands. His experience in California politics is reflected in his novel *Co-Op* (1936).

In the late 1930s Sinclair wrote his last novels about specific political situations. *The Flivver King* (1937) is a novelistic interpretation of Henry Ford; the book attacks Ford's employee practices and makes a case for the United Auto Workers. *No Pasaran!* (1937) is a short, quickly written story about the Spanish Civil War. *Little Steel* (1938) tells of an organization of steel companies determined to keep unions out of their industry.

Upton Sinclair (in wheelchair) and President Lyndon Johnson (far left) at the White House for the signing of a meatpacking reform bill in 1967 (Wide World)

At the end of the 1930s, with the world in turmoil, Sinclair looked backward to view the history of his times. Eventually he published eleven long, wide-ranging historical novels, all with the same central character, presenting the political history of the Western world from 1913 to 1950. The central character is Lanny Budd; the eleven novels are usually referred to as the Lanny Budd series. Lanny made his first appearance in 1940 in *World's End* at the age of thirteen, the son of an American munitions maker. Originally Sinclair did not intend to take the adventures of Lanny Budd beyond *World's End*, which culminates at the Paris Peace Conference following World War I. Apparently pleased by what he had started, however, Sinclair produced nine more Lanny Budd novels between 1941 and 1949. The third volume in the series, *Dragon's Teeth* (1942), dealing with Hitler's rise to power in Germany, won a Pulitzer Prize in 1943. In 1953 Sinclair revived his hero for service in *The Return of Lanny Budd*, the last of the series.

The Lanny Budd novels are interesting, well-paced, and diligently researched works of historical fiction. Much of the popularity that the series

created grew out of Sinclair's morally simple view of twentieth-century history. In the early novels Lanny observes a drama of grand historical forces: progress, represented by socialism and communism, in conflict with oppression, represented by fascism. As the series progresses, the mantle of progress is shifted to America; by *A World to Win* (1946), which presents America's entrance into World War II, Sinclair's allegiance has shifted away from the European socialist tradition and settled directly on FDR. By the time he wrote *The Return of Lanny Budd* in 1953 Sinclair had become an anti-Communist. Throughout the novels Sinclair's history lessons focus on conspiracy, whether that of international bankers or international communism.

By the 1950s Sinclair had entered his eighth decade and had written millions of words and dozens of books. The semiretirement that he entered in the 1950s was certainly deserved, but it did not prevent him from producing a few more novels and his complete autobiography. Among the novels *Another Pamela* (1950) stands out as a clever effort at writing a modern version of Samuel Richardson's *Pamela* (1740-1742); in Sinclair's version a rural California girl must resist and then reform the promiscuous nephew of her wealthy employer. Also, *What Didymus Did* (1954) is of some interest because its story, essentially a fantasy in which a divinely inspired reformer unsuccessfully tries to transform human nature in Los Angeles, suggests that Sinclair had finally grown skeptical about the limits of reform. *The Autobiography of Upton Sinclair* (1962), which adds several chapters to *American Outpost*, the autobiography which Sinclair had published in 1932, is an important source of information about the Progressive era as well as about Sinclair.

When Sinclair died in 1968 most of the obituaries were generous in their praise. Some of them noted one of the main ironies of his career: that such an essentially gentle person, a man who exuded genteel innocence and probity in his personal life and who dabbled in such quaint matters as spiritualism and vegetarianism, could have written some of the most socially combative works in American fiction.

Biographies:

Floyd Dell, *Upton Sinclair: A Study in Social Protest* (New York: Doran, 1927).

> The first book on the author, written at the midpoint of Sinclair's career by a fellow nov-

Upton Sinclair celebrating his eighty-ninth birthday

elist and offering a balanced, sympathetic view of his achievements.

Leon Harris, *Upton Sinclair: American Rebel* (New York: Crowell, 1975).
A well-researched, comprehensive biography of Sinclair.

William A. Bloodworth, Jr., *Upton Sinclair* (Boston: Twayne, 1977).
A study of Sinclair's works in the context of his life as a writer, reformer, and political figure; examines the frequent, autobiographical theme of an idealistic self in conflict with an unjust society.

William Brevda, "Love's Coming-of-Age: The Upton Sinclair-Harry Kemp Divorce Scandal," *North Dakota Review*, 51 (Spring 1983): 60-77.
A biographical account of Sinclair's relationship with Harry Kemp, famous before World War I as the "Boxcar Poet," whom Sinclair had befriended and supported.

References:
Van Wyck Brooks, *Emerson and Others* (New York: Dutton, 1927), pp. 209-217.

An early critical discussion of Sinclair claiming that his works, while representative of American traditions of protest, are rhetorically weak.

Robert Cantwell, "Upton Sinclair," in *After the Genteel Tradition*, edited by Malcolm Cowley (New York: Norton, 1937).
A sympathetic, leftist view of Sinclair, written during the Great Depression at a time of high political visibility for the author.

Timothy Cook, "Upton Sinclair's *The Jungle* and Orwell's *Animal Farm*: A Relationship Explored," *Modern Fiction Studies*, 30 (Winter 1984): 696-703.
Notes the similarity of animal imagery, especially of pigs, and their connections to political analyses in the two novels.

Judson A. Grenier, "Muckraking the Muckrakers: Upton Sinclair and His Peers," in *Reform and Reformers in the Progressive Era*, edited by David R. Colburn and George E. Pozzetta (Westport, Conn.: Greenwood Press, 1983), pp. 71-92.
Focuses on Sinclair's role as a muckraker who worked both in fiction and nonfiction.

Albert Mordell, *Haldeman-Julius and Upton Sinclair: The Amazing Record of a Long Collaboration* (Girard, Kan.: Haldeman-Julius, 1950).
A study of Sinclair's relationship with a populist publisher; provides some information about Sinclair's interest in psychic phenomena.

Harvey Swados, "The World of Upton Sinclair," *Atlantic Monthly* (December 1961): 96-102.
An appreciative essay on Sinclair; sees *The Jungle* as both an important historical document and as effective propaganda, in 1906, on behalf of American workers and consumers.

Jon Yoder, *Upton Sinclair* (New York: Ungar, 1975).
Provides a brief survey of Sinclair's career and his major works; argues that Sinclair's socialism was an appropriate response to sociopolitical conditions.

John Steinbeck

This entry was updated by Louis Owens (University of New Mexico) from the entry by Richard Astro (Northeastern University) in DLB 9, American Novelists, 1910-1945.

Places	Central California (Salinas Valley)	New York City	Russia

Influences and Relationships	Sir Thomas Malory (*Le Morte D'Arthur*)	Pascal Covici	Edward F. Ricketts

Literary Movements and Forms	Short Story Novel	Travel Narrative Allegory	Proletarian Fiction

Major Themes	Madmen and Idiots
	The Vanity of
	    Human Wishes
	The Search for
	    Meaning
	The "Phalanx"
		The Interrelationship
		    of All Life
		The "Tragic Miracle
		    of Consciousness"
		"Free Men" vs.
		    "Herd Men"
			The Cycle of
			    Birth and Death
			Human Self-Hatred
			The Emptiness of
			    Modern America

Cultural and Artistic Influences	Metaphysical Philosophy	Marine Biology Arthurian Legend	Materialism

Social and Economic Influences	The Plight of the Migrant Worker	Agrarian Reform World War II	The Great Depression Marxism

See also the Steinbeck entries in DLB 7, Twentieth-Century American Dramatists *and* DLB: Documentary Series 2.

BIRTH: Salinas, California, 27 February 1902, to John Ernst Steinbeck II and Olive Hamilton Steinbeck.

EDUCATION: Stanford University, 1919-1925.

MARRIAGES: 14 January 1930 to Carol Henning (divorced). 29 March 1943 to Gwyndolyn Conger (divorced); children: Thom, John. 28 December 1950 to Elaine Scott.

AWARDS: California Literature Gold Medals (Commonwealth Club of California) for *Tortilla Flat*, 1936, and *In Dubious Battle*, 1937; New York Drama Critics Circle Award for *Of Mice and Men*, 1938; elected to membership of the National Institute of Arts and Letters, 1939; Pulitzer Prize for *The Grapes of Wrath*, 1940; King Haakon Liberty Cross for *The Moon is Down*, 1946; elected to the American Academy of Arts and Letters, 1948; Nobel Prize for Literature, 1962; Presidential Medal of Freedom, 1964; Press Medal of Freedom, 1964.

DEATH: New York, New York, 20 December 1968.

SELECTED BOOKS: *Cup of Gold* (New York: McBride, 1929; London & Toronto: Heinemann, 1937);

The Pastures of Heaven (New York: Brewer, Warren & Putnam, 1932; London: Allan, 1933);

To a God Unknown (New York: Ballou, 1933; London & Toronto: Heinemann, 1935);

Tortilla Flat (New York: Covici Friede, 1935; London: Heinemann, 1935);

In Dubious Battle (New York: Covici Friede, 1936; London & Toronto: Heinemann, 1936);

Of Mice and Men (New York: Covici Friede, 1937; London & Toronto: Heinemann, 1937);

Of Mice and Men: A Play in Three Acts (New York: Covici Friede, 1937);

The Red Pony (New York: Covici Friede, 1937; enlarged edition, New York: Viking, 1945);

Their Blood Is Strong (San Francisco: Simon J. Lubin Society, 1938);

The Long Valley (New York: Viking, 1938; London & Toronto: Heinemann, 1939);

John Steinbeck (photo by Martha Cox; courtesy of the Steinbeck Research Center/San Jose State University)

The Grapes of Wrath (New York: Viking, 1939; London & Toronto: Heinemann, 1939);

Sea of Cortez: A Leisurely Journal of Travel and Research, by Steinbeck and Edward F. Ricketts (New York: Viking, 1941); republished in part as *The Log from the Sea of Cortez* (New York: Viking, 1951; London, Melbourne & Toronto: Heinemann, 1958)—adds "About Ed Ricketts," by Steinbeck;

The Moon Is Down (New York: Viking, 1942; London & Toronto: Heinemann, 1942);

The Moon is Down: A Play in Two Parts (New York: Dramatists Play Service, 1942; London: English Theatre Guild, 1943);

Bombs Away: The Story of a Bomber Team (New York: Viking, 1942);

Cannery Row (New York: Viking, 1945; London & Toronto: Heinemann, 1945);

The Wayward Bus (New York: Viking, 1947; London & Toronto: Heinemann, 1947);

The Pearl (New York: Viking, 1947; Melbourne, London & Toronto: Heinemann, 1948);

A Russian Journal (New York: Viking, 1948; London, Melbourne & Toronto: Heinemann, 1949);

Burning Bright (New York: Viking, 1950; Melbourne, London & Toronto: Heinemann, 1951);

Viva Zapata! (Rome: Edizioni Filmcritica, 1952); new edition, edited by Robert Morsberger (New York: Viking, 1975);

East of Eden (New York: Viking, 1952; Melbourne, London & Toronto: Heinemann, 1952);

Sweet Thursday (New York: Viking, 1954; Melbourne, London & Toronto: Heinemann, 1954);

The Short Reign of Pippin IV: A Fabrication (New York: Viking, 1957; Melbourne, London & Toronto: Heinemann, 1957);

Once There Was a War (New York: Viking, 1958; London, Melbourne & Toronto: Heinemann, 1959);

The Winter of Our Discontent (New York: Viking, 1961; London, Melbourne & Toronto: Heinemann, 1961);

Travels with Charley in Search of America (New York: Viking, 1962; London, Melbourne & Toronto: Heinemann, 1962);

Speech Accepting the Nobel Prize for Literature (New York: Viking, 1962);

America and Americans (New York: Viking, 1966; London: Heinemann, 1966);

The Acts of King Arthur and His Noble Knights, edited by Chase Horton (New York: Farrar, Straus & Giroux, 1976).

PLAY PRODUCTIONS: *Of Mice and Men*, New York, Music Box Theatre, 23 November 1937;

The Moon is Down, New York, Martin Beck Theatre, 7 April 1942;

Burning Bright, New York, Broadhurst Theatre, 18 October 1950.

MOTION PICTURES: *The Forgotten Village*, Arthur Mayer-Joseph Burstyn, 1941;

Lifeboat, screen story by Steinbeck, Twentieth Century-Fox, 1944;

A Medal for Benny, screen story by Steinbeck and Jack Wagner, Paramount, 1945;

The Pearl, by Steinbeck, Emilio Fernandez, and Wagner, RKO, 1948;

The Red Pony, Republic, 1949;

Viva Zapata!, Twentieth Century-Fox, 1952.

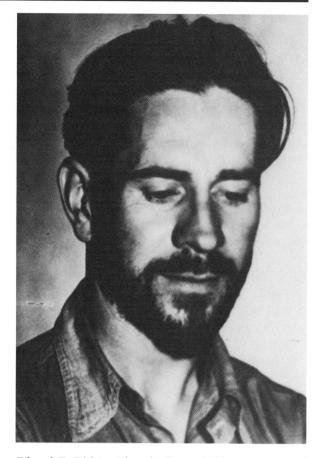

Edward F. Ricketts (photo by George Robinson; courtesy of the Steinbeck Research Center/San Jose State University)

PERIODICAL PUBLICATIONS:
FICTION
"Fingers of Cloud: A Satire on College Protervity," *Stanford Spectator*, 2 (February 1924): 149, 161-165;

"Adventures in Arcademy: A Journey into the Ridiculous," *Stanford Spectator*, 2 (June 1924): 279, 291;

"How Edith McGillicuddy Met Robert Louis Stevenson," *Harper's*, 183 (August 1941);

"Miracle of Tepayac," *Collier's*, 122 (25 December 1948): 22-23;

"His Father," *Reader's Digest*, 55 (September 1949): 19-21;

"Sons of Cyrus Trask," *Collier's*, 130 (12 July 1952): 14-15;

"How Mr. Hogan Robbed a Bank," *Atlantic*, 197 (March 1956): 58-61.

NONFICTION
"Dubious Battle in California," *Nation*, 143 (13 September 1936): 302-304;

"The Stars Point To Shafter," *Progressive Weekly* (24 December 1938);

"The Secret Weapon We Were Afraid to Use," *Collier's*, 131 (10 January 1953): 9-13;

"Jalopies I Cursed and Love," *Holiday*, 16 (July 1954): 44-45, 89-90;

"Fishing in Paris," *Punch*, 227 (25 August 1954): 248-249;

"How to Fish in French," *Reader's Digest*, 66 (January 1955): 59-61;

"Some Thoughts on Juvenile Delinquency," *Saturday Review*, 38 (28 May 1955): 22;

"Always Something to Do in Salinas," *Holiday*, 17 (June 1955): 58ff;

"Conversation at Sag Harbor," *Holiday*, 29 (March 1961): 60-61, 129-131, 133.

Carol Henning, whom Steinbeck married in 1930 (courtesy of the Steinbeck Research Center/San Jose State University)

Through a career which spanned four decades, John Steinbeck was a novelist of people. His best books are about ordinary men and women, simple souls who do battle against dehumanizing social forces or who struggle against their own inhumane tendencies and attempt, sometimes successfully, sometimes not, to forge lives of meaning and worth. At the center of Steinbeck's thematic vision is a dialectic between contrasting ways of life: between innocence and experience, between primitivism and progress, and between self-interest and commitment to the human community. His most interesting characters, George Milton and Lennie Small in *Of Mice and Men* (1937), the paisanos of *Tortilla Flat* (1935), Doc Burton of *In Dubious Battle* (1936), Mack and the boys in *Cannery Row* (1945), and the Joads of *The Grapes of Wrath* (1939), struggle to resolve this personal and social conflict in a world of human error and imperfection.

In much of his work Steinbeck championed what in *The Grapes of Wrath* he called "man's proven capacity for greatness of heart and spirit." Man, says Steinbeck, "grows beyond his work, walks up the stairs of his concepts, emerges ahead of his accomplishments." And yet, he was sensitive to "a strange duality in the human." In the narrative portion of *Sea of Cortez* (1941), he says that man "might be described fairly adequately, if simply, as a two-legged paradox. He has never become accustomed to the tragic miracle of consciousness. Perhaps, as has been suggested, his species is not set, has not jelled, but is still in a state of becoming, bound by his physical memories to a past of struggle and survival, limited in his futures by the uneasiness of thought and consciousness."

The "tragic miracle of consciousness" is, for Steinbeck, man's greatest burden and his greatest glory. And the way in which Steinbeck portrays this burden and this glory in his novels and short stories is the source of his greatest strength as a writer. It accounts for the feeling, the passion in his fiction, as well as that feeling's extreme— sentimentality. It was his most important thematic concern, from his depiction of Henry Morgan's drive for power and wealth in *Cup of Gold* (1929) to the concluding statement in his Nobel Prize speech, in which he paraphrased John the Apostle by noting that "in the end is the Word, and the Word is Man, and the Word is with Man."

Steinbeck was born and grew up in that long, narrow strip of agricultural land called the Salinas Valley, which is bordered on the east by the Gabilon Mountains, on the west by the Santa Lucia range, and then Monterey Bay. He was the third of four children, and the only son, of John Ernst Steinbeck II, manager of a flour mill and treasurer of Monterey County, and Olive Hamilton Steinbeck, a former teacher. Years later Steinbeck said of his youth, "We were poor people with a hell of a lot of land which made us think we were rich people, even when we couldn't buy food and were patched." As a boy he explored the valley, following the Salinas River to its mouth in Monterey Bay and visiting the towns along its shore: Monterey, Carmel, Seaside, and Pacific Grove. He loved the Corral de Tierra and was awed by Big Sur, with its sea cliffs and forests.

In the Salinas Valley, in the Corral de Tierra, and on the Monterey Peninsula and Big Sur, Steinbeck found much of the material for his fiction. *Of Mice and Men, In Dubious Battle,* and *The Grapes of Wrath,* as well as many of the stories in *The Long Valley* (1938), are set in California's agricultural valleys. The action in *Tortilla Flat, Cannery Row,* and *Sweet Thursday* (1954) takes place along the waterfront of Monterey Bay. *The Pastures of Heaven* (1932) is Steinbeck's name for the Corral de Tierra. And the mystic quality of *To a God Unknown* (1933) owes much to the strange, brooding nature of Big Sur. Later in life Steinbeck became a New Yorker, and he summered in Sag Harbor rather than in Pacific Grove. Still, central California remained to Steinbeck what Yoknapatawpha was to Faulkner. There is an acute consciousness of place in Steinbeck's California fiction, a way of seeing which informs the thematic design of his most successful work.

Graduating from Salinas High School in 1919, Steinbeck entered Stanford University, which he attended intermittently until 1925. He had to work to pay for his education and sometimes took off one quarter to earn enough money to pay for the next quarter. He clerked in stores, worked as a surveyor in Big Sur, and was a hand on a ranch near King City, which he later used as the setting for *Of Mice and Men.* Several times he worked for the Spreckels Sugar Company, gaining firsthand knowledge of the labor problems he would write about in his political novels, *In Dubious Battle* and *The Grapes of Wrath.*

During the summer of 1923, Steinbeck took the general biology course at the Hopkins Marine Station in Pacific Grove, following an interest in marine biology that would be further stimulated in 1931 when he met marine biologist Edward F. Ricketts, whose ideas about the interrelationship of all life were to have a major impact on Steinbeck's worldview, although Ricketts and Steinbeck had differing opinions on some points.

Photo-sketch of Steinbeck from a 1939 United Artists brochure promoting the film Of Mice and Men *(courtesy of the Steinbeck Research Center/San Jose State University)*

Steinbeck wrote fiction at Stanford, and in 1924 two of his stories appeared in the Stanford *Spectator.* After he left Stanford in June 1925, he worked his way to New York on a freighter through the Panama Canal. In New York he worked as a laborer until his uncle, Joseph Hamilton, found him a job on the *New York American.* Before long the newspaper fired him, and, discouraged by his inability to sell any of the stories he had been writing, he worked his way back to California on another freighter. He worked at a series of odd jobs in the Lake Tahoe area for the next two years and continued writing. In February 1928 he wrote to a friend that he had finished *Cup of Gold,* his first novel, but that he was already dissatisfied with it.

During the summer of 1928 Steinbeck met Carol Henning, whom he would marry in 1930, and later in 1928 he moved to San Francisco, where she had a job. Steinbeck shared an apartment with a friend and began work on a novel which, after it had been rewritten several times and had several title changes, was published in 1933 as *To a God Unknown*.

In January 1929 Steinbeck received a telegram from Amassa Miller, a friend in New York who had been acting as Steinbeck's unofficial agent, informing him that Robert M. McBride and Company had accepted *Cup of Gold*. It had previously been rejected by seven other publishers. Steinbeck's reaction to the book's publication was ambivalent. In late 1929 he wrote to a friend that the novel's sale "pays enough for me to live quietly and with a good deal of comfort. In that far it was worth selling," and to another friend he wrote, "the book was an immature experiment written for the purpose of getting all the wise cracks . . . and all the autobiographical material . . . out of my system. And I really did not intend to publish it. . . . I have not the slightest desire to step into Donn Byrne's shoes. I may not have his ability with the vernacular but I have twice his head. I think I have swept all the Cabellyo-Byrneish preciousness out for good." By 1932 he stated frankly, "I've outgrown it and it embarrasses me."

Even before *Cup of God*, Steinbeck's fictionalized biography of Henry Morgan, the seventeenth-century Welsh pirate, was published, Steinbeck had outgrown his early literary models. *Cup of Gold* reveals the influence of Donn Byrne, James Branch Cabell, and James Stephens, on whose *Creek of Gold* (1912) the novel is patterned; but Steinbeck had new literary interests by 1929. In *Cup of Gold*, which centers on Henry Morgan's efforts to become a great adventurer, the language is stilted, and Steinbeck's attempt to deal with universal problems in an eighteenth-century adventure saga by drawing analogies to the Faust theme and the Grail legend results in a weak novel in which the mythical substructure is poorly integrated with the main line of the narrative.

Henry Morgan's greatest achievement is his seizure of the city of Panama and his winning the beautiful woman known throughout the Indies as La Santa Rojo. Finding no lasting pleasure in such success, he deserts his companions, petitions for and gains a pardon as well as knighthood from the British king, marries a beautiful woman of high society, and retires to Jamaica. But Morgan's drive for wealth and power has separated him from humanity—the unforgivable sin. He has achieved power through the use of violence, and it does him little good. Cut off from his fellowmen, Morgan fails to find love and hap-

piness and dies a "lumpish man," a fool who wanted something and "was idiot enough to think he could get it."

It is Morgan's solipsistic worldview that enables him to realize his dreams, but at the same time renders those dreams worthless. Early in the novel the young Henry learns from Merlin, the strange mystic seer, that he who seeks material greatness can succeed only if he remains a child. Merlin tells Henry, "All the world's great have been little boys who wanted the moon; running and climbing, they sometimes caught a firefly. But if one grow to a man's mind, that mind must see that it cannot have the moon and would not want it if it could—and so, it catches no fireflies." Henry's is the self-oriented dream of wealth and empire which results in power but not in lasting happiness.

But while Steinbeck concludes in *Cup of Gold* that the pursuit of power lacks meaning or purpose, he poses no alternatives. When, for example, Henry asks Merlin if he ever wanted the moon, Merlin responds that he did, but failed and found a new gift in failure: "there is this gift for the failure; folk know he has failed, and they are sorry and kindly and gentle. He has the whole world with him; a bridge of contact with his own people; the cloth of mediocrity." Steinbeck seems to present in his tale of Morgan an account of the corrupting forces of greed, and then, through his portrayal of Merlin and the novel's other characters, to seek alternative paths of behavior. We learn from them that the kind of greatness which results from acquisitive self-interest is self-defeating, but the suggestion of a reassurance provided by the "cloth of mediocrity" is unfulfilling and reveals the underdeveloped state of the author's worldview.

Amassa Miller had convinced Mavis McIntosh and Elizabeth Otis to represent Steinbeck in 1931, and they continued as Steinbeck's agents throughout his career. They first convinced Robert O. Ballou of Cape and Ballou to sign a contract with Steinbeck for his collection of short stories *The Pastures of Heaven* and two subsequent novels. After the bankruptcy of this firm Ballou took the contracts with him when he went to work at Brewer, Warren, and Putnam, which published *The Pastures of Heaven* in 1932. After Ballou started his own firm, he agreed to publish *To a God Unknown*, which had been rejected by several publishers prior to his agreements with Steinbeck, if Steinbeck would further revise the novel.

New Start
Big Writing

I.

To the red country and part of the grey country of Oklahoma, the last rains came gently and they did not cut the scarred earth. The plows crossed and recrossed the rivulet marks. The last rains lifted the corn quickly and scattered weed colonies and grass along the sides of the roads so that the grey country and the dark red country began to disappear under a green cover. In the last part of May the sky grew pale and the clouds that had hung in high puffs for so long in the spring were dissipated. The sun flared down on the growing corn day after day until a line of brown spread along the edge of each green bayonet. The clouds appeared and went away and in a while they did not try any more. The weeds grew darker green to protect themselves and they did not spread any more. The surface of the earth crusted, a thin hard crust, and as the sky became pale so the earth became pale, pink in the red country and white in the grey country. In the water cut gulleys, the earth dusted down in dry little streams. Gophers and ant lions started small avalanches. And as the sharp sun struck day after day the leaves of the young corn became less stiff and erect; they bent in a curve at first and then as the central ribs of strength grew weak, each leaf tilted downward. Then it was June and the sun shone more fiercely. The brown lines on the corn leaves widened and moved in on the central ribs. The weeds frayed and moved back toward their roots. The air was thin and the sky more pale and every day the earth paled. In the roads where the teams moved, where the wheels milled the ground and the hooves of the horses beat the ground, the dirt crust broke and the dust formed. Every moving thing lifted the dust into the air; a walking man lifted a cloud as high as his waist, and a wagon lifted the dust as high as the fence tops, and an automobile boiled a cloud behind it. The dust was long in settling back again. When June was half gone, the big clouds moved up out of Texas and the gulf, high, heavy clouds, rain-heads. The men in the fields looked up at the clouds and sniffed at them and held wet fingers up to sense the wind. And the horses were nervous while the clouds were up. The rain heads dropped a little spattering rain and hurried on to some other country. Behind them the sky was pale again and the sun flared. In the dust there were drop craters where the rain had fallen, and there were clean splashes on the corn and that was all. A gentle wind followed the rain clouds, driving them on northward, a wind that caressed the drying corn softly. A day went by and the wind increased, steady, unbroken by gusts. The dust from the roads fluffed up and spread out and fell on the weeds beside the fields and fell into the fields a little way. Now the wind grew strong and hard, and worked at the rain crust in the corn fields. Little by little the sky was darkened by the mixing dust, and the wind felt over the earth, loosened the dust and carried it away. The wind was stronger. The rain crust broke and the dust lifted up out of the fields and drove grey plumes into the air like sluggish smoke. The corn threshed the air and made a dry rushing sound. The finest dust did not settle back to earth now but disappeared into the darkening sky. The wind grew stronger, whisked under stones, carried up straws and old leaves, and even little clods

First page of the manuscript for The Grapes of Wrath (*John Steinbeck Collection [#6239], Clifton Waller Barrett Library, Special Collections Department, Manuscripts Division, University of Virginia Library*)

On the surface, *To a God Unknown* is Steinbeck's strangest novel. The plot is unconventional, and Steinbeck's hero is most unusual. But this was by intention, and in 1931, after Steinbeck's first version was rejected by several publishers, primarily because of its obscure plot, he told Mavis McIntosh that he would rewrite it, but that he would not do what publishers seemed to want most: popularize the story. After he completed revising the novel for Ballou in February 1933, he sent the manuscript to Ballou with a letter of explanation: "The book was hellish hard to write. I had been making notes for it for about five years. It probably will be a hard book to sell. Its characters are not 'home folks.' They make no more attempt at being sincerely human than the people in the Iliad. Boileau . . . insisted that only gods, kings and heroes were worth writing about. I firmly believe that."

To a God Unknown contains a mythic delineation of Steinbeck's developing worldview, and he could not popularize such a story, nor could he create a flesh-and-blood hero out of a character who is more than flesh and blood. This hero is Joseph Wayne, who leaves his small farm in Vermont and comes to California, where he establishes a homestead. Later, he is joined by his three brothers, and the Wayne family lives together on adjacent parcels of land which they treat as a single property. When a severe drought threatens the Wayne ranch, Joseph emerges as Steinbeck's Fisher King, the mythic figure whose fate is linked to that of the land and who sacrifices himself to insure the renewal of the land and of the natural order.

In 1931 Steinbeck had met Edward F. Ricketts, who owned and operated the Pacific Biological Laboratory on the Monterey waterfront. At that time, Ricketts was already an accomplished scientist at work on the most complete and useful guide to the marine invertebrates of the central Pacific Coast ever written. He was an ecologist long before the study of interrelationships, of the mutuality of life forms, became a national interest. He was also a philosopher, a student of music and literature, and an essayist who studied not isolated things but the structure of relations. He dismissed as useless those "picklers of the field who see the pieces of life without its principle."

During the time that Steinbeck was revising *To a God Unknown*, he and Ricketts had lengthy discussions about Ricketts's doctrine of "breaking through," which Ricketts defined in an essay of the same name as "an inner coherency of feeling and thought" which leads man into a "deep participation" and enables him to tie together unrelated pictures and see that the whole is more than the sum of its parts: "to achieve that integrated moment of living" in which one understands things "which are not transient by means of things which are."

In a very real way *To a God Unknown* is Steinbeck's morphology of breaking through, and it is significant that Ricketts considered the novel one of the few modern works of literature which concerns itself almost exclusively with a "conscious expression" of this concept. In Joseph Wayne, Steinbeck created as his protagonist a man who is more than a man. One of the other characters says of Joseph, "Perhaps a godling lives on earth now and then. Joseph has strength beyond vision of shattering. . . . You cannot think of Joseph dying. He is eternal. . . . he is all men . . . a repository for a little piece of each man's soul, and more than that, a symbol of the earth's soul." Yet Steinbeck shared Ricketts's conviction that "the crust broken through" is not "entirely possible on this earth." In "The Philosophy of Breaking Through," Ricketts noted that "the symbolism of religion, knowledge of the 'deep thing behind the name,' of 'magic' and of the 'god within,' ultimately may illumine the whole scene." This is the subject of Steinbeck's novel. The desire for this knowledge is what concerns Joseph Wayne most, and his strange compulsion to engage in rituals and his interest in religious symbols are best explained as vehicles by which he seeks to arrive at the meaning of life. In portraying Joseph's growing awareness of the world's underlying order, Steinbeck fuses images from Christ's Passion with the myths and rituals of the dying king in Sir James Frazer's *The Golden Bough*. And he depicts Joseph as the archetypal hero who breaks through to an understanding of the cosmic whole and then acts purposefully to save the natural order.

To A God Unknown is not without flaws. There is some bad writing, and Steinbeck occasionally lapses into the kind of sentimentality so many of his critics have found disturbing. At the same time the book as a whole greatly surpasses *Cup of Gold* in characterization and in the sweep of Steinbeck's imagination. And it indicates that Steinbeck was developing the thematic materials which would account for the strength of his best fiction.

Dust jacket for Steinbeck's 1939 novel

And yet, while *To a God Unknown* is an important novel, it, like *Cup of Gold*, did not sell. Steinbeck anticipated as much when, before its publication, he wrote to Ballou that the characters in the novel would not be "home folks." "The detailed accounts of the lives of clerks don't interest me much," Steinbeck told his publishers, "unless, of course, the clerk breaks into heroism."

Steinbeck's third book, *The Pastures of Heaven*, his second to be published, is a book about "clerks" who try but fail to break into heroism. Indeed, what seems to interest Steinbeck most in his novel is not the lives of clerks as clerks, but the reasons why most clerks do not become heroes—why in fact so few become Joseph Waynes. *The Pastures of Heaven* is a group of loosely related stories about the inhabitants of Corral de Tierra, a lovely valley community located between Monterey and Salinas, which Steinbeck calls the Pastures of Heaven in his book. The characters are simply people who have sought the quiet life of the Pastures as a refuge from a complex urban society which limits their freedom. But because they are shrouded in personal illusions and self-deceptions which render them unable to adapt to the simple patterns of life of the

valley, they fail in their efforts to find meaningful lives. Dreamers whose fantasies are undermined by the hard facts of reality, they are frail people living on the edge of personal chaos, attached by slender threads to a reality they do not understand and with which they cannot cope.

Shark Wicks, a farmer, has his self-esteem destroyed when his neighbors find out that, contrary to the image he projects, he is not a wealthy man and an expert in all financial matters. Helen Van Deventer comes to the valley to escape a series of personal tragedies but deprives herself of the chance for personal fulfillment when she takes her mad daughter's life. Junius Maltby and his son Robbie have moved to the Pastures from San Francisco, where Junius worked as an accountant. In the valley, Junius spends his days happily sitting beside a stream near his house, and his life becomes "as unreal, as romantic and as unimportant as his thinking. He was content to sit in the sun and to dangle his feet in the stream." Steinbeck portrays Junius as a weak man, and when some valley residents give Robbie a package of clothing, Junius cannot face the fact of his own poverty. He and Robbie leave the valley and return to San Francisco. Two other residents of

Gwyndolyn Conger, whom Steinbeck married in 1943

the valley are the carefree Lopez sisters, who give themselves to customers who buy their enchiladas but refuse to accept money for sex alone. However, they are eventually driven from the valley to lives of prostitution in San Francisco. The half-wit Tularecito thinks he is a gnome and digs a hole because he wants to communicate with "earth people" below the ground. After someone fills in the hole, the generally placid Tularecito becomes violent, and because no one can understand why, they decide he is dangerous and have him committed to a state mental facility. Other stories tell of Molly Morgan, the valley schoolteacher, who cannot cope with the haunting memory of a father who deserted her, and of Pat Humbert, who engages in futile efforts to remodel his old house on the mistaken assumption that the daughter of a valley neighbor will marry him once work on the house is completed.

Throughout *The Pastures of Heaven*, Steinbeck shows compassion, even affection, for the plight of ordinary people who strive for but cannot achieve happiness. Steinbeck never condemns their innocence, their simplicity, from the stand-

point of middle-class values, but he portrays their self-destructive tendencies toward illusion and self-deception. *The Pastures of Heaven* is an ironic title because in it Steinbeck shows us that however lovely or however redemptive the pastures of heaven may seem, true heaven cannot be attained by men on this earth.

Among Steinbeck's finest fictional creations are his primitives or half-wits and his escapees or his dropouts. Tularecito is his first half-wit, Junius Maltby his first escapee. Many others would follow. These simple people are foils against which he can measure the excesses and eccentricities of material society. Steinbeck draws his primitives and his dropouts with great warmth. He admires their ability to live simply and easily, but he simultaneously depicts their inability to survive in the modern world. In diverse ways, they are either destroyed or driven back to the society from which they fled.

So interested was Steinbeck in man's unsuccessful efforts to flee acquisitive society that he wrote *Tortilla Flat* (1935) to explore the subject. *Tortilla Flat* is the first novel in which Steinbeck employs the Monterey Peninsula as setting and backdrop, and it was his first popular success; the book became a best-seller. The connecting metaphor for this series of episodes about the paisanos of old Monterey is King Arthur's Round Table. (Steinbeck began reading Malory's *Morte d'Arthur* early in his youth, and it remained among his favorite books.) Steinbeck's judgment of the efficacy of retreat and his rejection of "dropping out" as a means of coping with the problems of contemporary life are revealed through an examination of how the paisanos' court, like Arthur's Round Table, forms, flourishes, and dies. The story, says Steinbeck, "deals with the adventuring of Danny's friends, with the good they did, with their thoughts and their endeavors. In the end, this story tells how the talisman was lost and how the group disintegrated."

The main characters in *Tortilla Flat* are among the most interesting in Steinbeck's canon. Danny, the center of the paisano brotherhood, is related to everyone in Tortilla Flat by blood or romance. Pilon, philosopher and logician, is able to rationalize self-interest into altruism. There are also the Pirate, a lover of dogs, and Jesus Maria Corcoran, soft-hearted doer of good deeds. But while Danny and his followers live for several months in glorious indolence, they become increasingly listless; life begins to lose its meaning. Finally, a fire destroys Danny's house, and the

Steinbeck and Gwyndolyn Conger on their wedding day, 29 March 1943 (courtesy of the Steinbeck Research Center/San Jose State University)

brotherhood disintegrates. The paisanos go their separate ways. They realize the feeble basis of their escape ethic. There is, Steinbeck concludes in *Tortilla Flat*, no strength or fiber in the philosophic/moral system of Danny's group, nothing that will enable them to achieve and retain more than the most superficial of goals.

Tortilla Flat was the first of Steinbeck's books to be published by Covici Friede, beginning a lifelong association between Steinbeck and Pascal Covici. Ben Abramson, a book dealer in Chicago, had called Covici's attention to Steinbeck's work, and Covici was impressed enough to write to Steinbeck and Mavis McIntosh in 1935 about becoming Steinbeck's publisher. When Covici Friede went bankrupt in 1938 and Covici went to Viking Press as a senior editor, he took Steinbeck with him. Although Covici published *In Dubious Battle* (1936) before *The Red Pony* (1937) and *The Long Valley* (1938), Steinbeck had completed most of the stories in *The Long Valley*, and four in *The Red Pony* before he began writing *In Dubious Battle*.

The Long Valley is a collection of short stories, several of which were published separately in a number of small magazines earlier in the decade. Steinbeck always felt comfortable with the short-story form: the episodic nature of *The Pastures of Heaven* and *Tortilla Flat* makes the fact clear. But in each of those volumes, there is a unifying thematic threat or story line. Such a connection is lacking in *The Long Valley*.

Steinbeck's achievement in the short story can scarcely be compared with that of his major contemporaries–William Faulkner, F. Scott Fitzgerald, and Ernest Hemingway–all of whom have reputations based in part upon their success in that form. Steinbeck's short stories reveal the fact that he never really reached artistic maturity in the genre. Indeed, *The Long Valley* was written in various modes: stories of manners, sketches, a four-part novelette, and even a beast fable.

Two pieces ("The Raid" and "Breakfast") are preparatory sketches for Steinbeck's political novels, *In Dubious Battle* and *The Grapes of Wrath*. Another, "The Snake," is Steinbeck's first fictionalized portrait of Ricketts and is based upon an actual incident. It is a strange story about a woman who fulfills a morbid psychological need by watching Dr. Phillips, a thinly camouflaged Ricketts, feed white rats to a rattlesnake. A more skillfully told tale is "Flight," which chronicles a boy's growth from adolescence to maturity during the course of his nightmarish and unsuccessful effort to avoid pursuers in the mountains south of Carmel. This same growth to manhood is the theme of "The Raid," in which a neophyte political organizer matures after being savagely beaten by angry vigilantes.

Among the best stories in *The Long Valley* are "The Chrysanthemums" and "The White Quail," Steinbeck's tales of two women shrouded in self-illusion and self-deception. Rarely comfortable with female characters, Steinbeck creates in Eliza Allen of "The Chrysanthemums" a woman with deep-seated sexual frustrations whose search for meaning and fulfillment is self-defeating and leaves her "crying weakly–like an old woman." In "The White Quail," Mary Teller is a superb portrait of a narcissistic woman whose strange identification with her garden and with the white quail that comes to drink from its artificial ponds suggests her distorted vision of herself. "The Harness" recalls an episode from *The Pastures of Heaven*. Peter Randall's feeling of freedom and fulfillment after harvesting a bountiful crop is destroyed when he realizes that his dead wife still has him "in harness." The leading characters of "The Harness," "Chrysanthemums," and "The White Quail" are tormented souls, three more of Steinbeck's characters who fail to become accustomed to the "tragic miracle of consciousness."

"Saint Katy the Virgin" is what Sanford Marovitz calls "the odd thirteenth" in Steinbeck's "Baker's Dozen of Stories" in *The Long Valley*. Derived at least in part from the pig/maiden rescue episode in Mark Twain's *A Connecticut Yankee*, this story is a goliardic farce in which a sow is canonized. Though possessing allegorical possibilities, "Saint Katy the Virgin" is best read as a light-hearted fable, a happy interlude in a volume of short stories in which Steinbeck depicts man's often unsuccessful efforts to find meaning in a complex, turbulent world.

Without question, the most carefully developed and artfully constructed portions of *The Long Valley* are the four stories which comprise *The Red Pony* (the first three were published separately in 1937). This work, which is continually popular among young readers, also reflects Steinbeck's ability to endow the simplest of narratives with mature thematic significance. Steinbeck's four-part study of the development of a young boy, Jody Tiflin, from childhood to the threshold of maturity is a story of initiation comparable to Faulkner's *The Bear* and to a number of Hemingway's Nick Adams stories.

The education of Jody Tiflin begins in "The Gift." Given a colt by his father, Jody gains self-esteem as he trains and cares for his new charge. He then moves from grief to acceptance that death is an inevitable part of the life cycle as his beloved horse falls ill and dies. The major event in "The Great Mountain" is Jody's meeting with the old man Gitano, who symbolizes the inevitability of old age and death as he leaves the Tiflin ranch to die in the great mountains which separate the ranch from the Pacific. Jody learns from the seemingly useless old man, and as a result he becomes more mature. In "The Promise," the life of a mare must be sacrificed so that her colt can be born alive, and Jody's awareness of the life cycle is expanded as he learns to celebrate the glory of birth, while at the same time he deals with the pain of death. The last story of *The Red Pony* is "The Leader of the People," in which Steinbeck demonstrates youth's compassion toward age in Jody Tiflin's understanding and acceptance of his grandfather, who lives in the past with his tales of westering the great frontier. "The Leader of the People" is also signifi-

cant because it contains Steinbeck's theory of the group man, which he was to develop more fully in his important political novels.

The four parts of *The Red Pony* are among Steinbeck's most popular stories, and the characters are among Steinbeck's most interesting. Yet Steinbeck wrote no more volumes of short stories. Perhaps, as Brian Barbour points out, Steinbeck realized that despite occasional successes, the short-story form was not really congenial to his talent. Steinbeck seems to have realized that by writing short stories, even those in the episodically organized but thematically linked *Tortilla Flat* and *The Pastures of Heaven*, he was not giving his characters much of a chance for real growth. And so he set upon the task of designing a fictional vehicle sufficiently expansive to work out his developing metaphysic.

Steinbeck had experienced popular success with *Tortilla Flat* before *In Dubious Battle* was published, but many readers considered him a teller of pleasant, inconsequential tales. His shift into the arena of social and political controversy with *In Dubious Battle* forced a new appraisal of his work, particularly as that work dealt with the complex socioeconomic problems that plagued California agriculture during the 1930s.

As Jackson Benson has pointed out, Steinbeck's interest in the California farm-labor conflict was the result of both circumstance and accident. His background in Salinas and some of the jobs he took to pay his Stanford tuition helped him understand the issues. By 1935 Steinbeck had come to understand that the power and depth he wanted to achieve in his fiction would result only if his narratives were "true," if they resulted from things he knew or learned about through careful observation.

The background for Steinbeck's political fiction is documented in several important historical and sociological volumes: in the writings of Henry George, the champion of the single tax, in James Bryce's *The American Commonwealth* (1891), and most important, in Carey McWilliams's *Factories in the Fields* (1939). These volumes tell of California's powerful land monopolists who developed large empires such as Kern County Land, the Southern Pacific Railroad, and the Irvine Corporation, all of which ruthlessly and systematically exploited the small farmer and the migrant worker.

Agriculture in California's central valleys during the 1930s differed from that in most rural areas of the country in that California

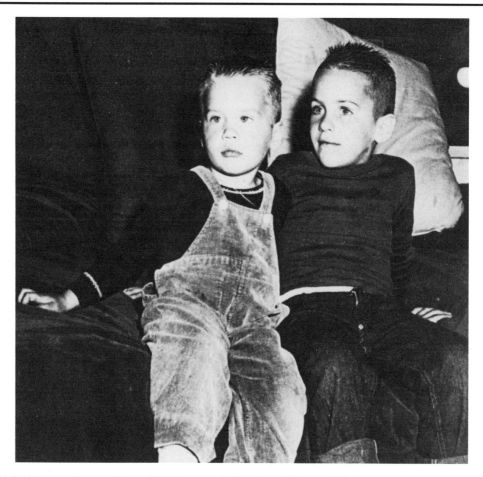

Steinbeck's sons, John and Thom, 1948 (courtesy of the Steinbeck Research Center/San Jose State University)

farms were large agribusinesses, farm factories operated by large corporations employing many hundreds of workers, mostly the migrant poor, who were paid low wages for picking fruit and vegetables. Steinbeck was deeply interested in the labor tactics of fugitive organizers in California during the 1930s, and he was determined to portray the facts about California agriculture as they actually were. Benson notes that during the winter of 1934 a friend named Sis Reamer told Steinbeck of two farm-labor organizers who were hiding in the attic of a house in Seaside. He visited them, and as a result of a series of long conversations, he acquired the material which was the basis for *In Dubious Battle*, a book about a strike in a California apple orchard. Completed in 1935, *In Dubious Battle* deals with the efforts of Mac, a seasoned party worker, and Jim Nolan, a zealous political neophyte, to organize a strike among migrant workers in the Torgas Valley. With the help of the key migrant leaders they organized, Doc Burton, a concerned observer but not a party member, helps them set up a camp that will meet public health standards on the land of a small apple grower named Anderson, whose son is sympathetic to the strikers. At first, Anderson is pleased because the strikers pick his apples while those of other growers rot on the trees; but the strike becomes increasingly violent, and after vigilantes burn down Anderson's barn, the outraged farmer calls the sheriff to evict the migrants, and the strike is doomed. In the final round of violence Jim is killed, and, as he had done before, Mac uses the death of a friend for political purpose.

In a February 1935 letter to Mavis McIntosh, Steinbeck acknowledged that *In Dubious Battle* "is a brutal book, more brutal because there is no author's moral point of view." *In Dubious Battle* is a tough, objective examination of diverse political opinions in which everything is learned from the actions and conversations of the characters. Taken as a whole, it is Steinbeck's statement of the wrong perspectives, the wrong approaches, and the wrong solutions. In using a small strike of apple pickers to symbolize what he called "man's eternal, bitter warfare with himself," Steinbeck seems to say that the battle is indeed dubious.

As Steinbeck explained to a friend in January 1935, the novel's title comes from Satan's speech in the first part of Milton's *Paradise Lost*, and he quoted these lines, which also appear as the book's epigraph:

> Innumerable force of Spirits armed,
> That durst dislike his reign, and, me
>   preferring,
> His utmost power with adverse power
>   opposed
> In dubious battle on the plains of
>   Heaven,
> And shook his throne. What though the
>   field be lost?
> All is not lost–the unconquerable will,
> And study of revenge, immortal hate,
> And courage never to submit or yield;
> And what is else not to be overcome?

The novel's mythic substructure is loosely tied to *Paradise Lost*. As Benson notes, the Torgas Valley may not be Milton's hell, but it is hell nevertheless. Rather than the story of Satan's hatred for God, *In Dubious Battle* is a parable of mankind's self-hatred. Unlike their real-life prototypes, Mac and Jim are satanic in their election of violence as a means of coping with labor problems in California. The value of any individual's life is what it contributes to their cause, and Steinbeck carefully balances a harsh condemnation of California agribusiness against the unsuccessful ideology of the Marxist organizers. *In Dubious Battle* is not, strictly speaking, a proletarian novel. It is a strike novel in which Steinbeck asserts that neither blind political activism nor frustrated detachment can solve the plight of the economically disinherited.

At about the time he was writing *In Dubious Battle*, Steinbeck wrote a two-page essay which he called "Argument of Phalanx." In it he noted that men are not final individuals, but parts of a greater beast he called the "phalanx," which controls its individual units and which can achieve ends beyond the reach of individual units. In times of crisis, Steinbeck says, man must "key into" the phalanx. And once man becomes part of a moving phalanx, he becomes more powerful than if he were acting as an individual man. "It is impossible," says Steinbeck, "for man to defy the phalanx without destroying himself. For if a man goes into a wilderness, his mind will dry up and

at last he will die of starvation for the sustenance he can only get from involvement in the phalanx." Doc Burton, who is unable and unwilling to key into the striking migrant phalanx and provide direction to its blind partisan leaders, grows lean and hungry and drifts away into the night.

That Doc Burton also voices some of Edward F. Ricketts's ideas illustrates the complexity of the intellectual relationship between the two men. In both *In Dubious Battle* and *The Grapes of Wrath*, Steinbeck analyzes Ricketts's precepts about man and the world, accepting some and rejecting others. While Ricketts's philosophy was undoubtedly a major influence on Steinbeck's thinking, there were other influences as well. While he was studying biology at the Hopkins Marine Station, Steinbeck discovered the ideas of William Emerson Ritter, whose doctrine of the organismal conception of life was then in vogue among West Coast naturalists. That notion, the idea that "the whole is more than the sum of its parts," is based upon Ritter's belief that "in all parts of nature and in nature itself as one gigantic whole, wholes are so related to their parts that not only does the existence of the whole depend upon the orderly cooperation and interdependence of its parts, but the whole exercises a measure of determinative control over its parts." The influence of this teleological view, in which the group is capable of moving toward some end or goal, is apparent in Steinbeck's concept of the phalanx, in which the individual may choose to be a part of the group in order to bring about changes that he could not bring about by himself.

In contrast, Rickett's philosophy–much influenced by the ideas of W. C. Allee, his mentor during his undergraduate days at the University of Chicago–was nonteleological. Allee was convinced that "The social medium is the condition necessary to the conservation and renewal of life." But he believed the principle of cooperation to be automatic, not the result of conscious decision making among organisms. Indeed, Allee concluded that even what we call altruistic drives in humans "apparently are the development of these innate tendencies toward cooperation, which find their early physiological expression in many simpler animals." Thus, for Ricketts the group has no conscious goal. The fact of relation, not its purpose, was what Ricketts gleaned from Allee's work on animal aggregations. For him the ultimate goal was breaking through to discover "the toto-picture," and in an essay entitled "A Spiritual Morphology of Poetry," Ricketts ex-

Elaine Scott, whom Steinbeck married in 1950 (courtesy of the Steinbeck Research Center/San Jose State University)

pressed the belief that when a great poet appears, "everything will be related and known, it will be recognized that's the way things really are." A creative synthesis will occur in which everything will be transformed into "an all-consciousness" in which it will be seen that because "all that lives is holy," there is no right or wrong, but rather "it's right, it's all right,' the 'good,' the 'bad' whatever is."

Steinbeck and Ricketts often argued the relative merits of Ritter's and Allee's philosophies, and from their discussions Steinbeck shaped his own philosophy, which incorporated the concept of "breaking through" that he had employed first in *To a God Unknown* and would use again in later novels, with the idea that the group could work together for its own betterment. For on the issue of social progress and reform, there is a fundamen-

tal discrepancy between Steinbeck's teleological belief of man's ability to "walk up the stairs of his concepts" and "emerge ahead of his accomplishments," which he affirmed in his next political novel, *The Grapes of Wrath*, and Ricketts's non-teleological pilgrimage toward breaking through to the "toto-picture." The failure of Doc Burton to join the "phalanx" and influence its direction in *In Dubious Battle* is Steinbeck's implicit criticism of Ricketts's philosophy. Like Ricketts he is a scientist by training but a philosopher by disposition who views life realistically and refuses "to put on the blinders of 'good' or 'bad' and limit my vision," and who strives "to see the whole picture . . . I want to be able to look at the whole thing." For Steinbeck, however, this aspiration was not enough, and for *The Grapes of Wrath* he created a character who shares Ricketts's holistic view of life but also comes to realize the importance of the group in bringing about social change.

Between Steinbeck's two great political novels he published his deepest exploration into what he later called the "tragic miracle of consciousness," *Of Mice and Men* (1937), his memorable parable about man's voluntary acceptance of responsibility for his fellowman. The novel was a Book-of-the-Month Club offering and Steinbeck's dramatic version was produced on the New York stage by George S. Kaufman. Both the novel and the play were immediate successes, and, as a result, Steinbeck became a national figure. Steinbeck's story is about two itinerant ranch hands, George Milton and Lennie Small, who travel from ranch to ranch and job to job, always dreaming of a little house and a couple of acres with rabbits where they will "live off the fatta the lan'." When at one point in the tale the dream almost seems plausible, Lennie, who cannot control his own physical strength, accidentally kills the wife of the boss's son, and the story ends when George mercifully kills Lennie to save him from an angry mob.

Of Mice and Men is one of Steinbeck's most impressive works of fiction because it is an artful rendering of the elemental conflict between the idealized landscape–where George and Lennie enjoy peace, leisure, and economic sufficiency–and the reality of modern life. George and Lennie are two simple souls who need each other and who want to live in that Arcadian garden which cannot exist in the contemporary world. Steinbeck portrays the beauty of the garden and even allows his characters a momentary glimpse of it, but he provides checks against such fantasies to show how the dream can never be realized. *Of Mice and Men* is Steinbeck's version of the pastoral, and it ends without reconciliation and with a mood of overwhelming sadness. George and Lennie's quest for their ideal fails because neither possesses the ability to bring that dream to life. Lennie is killed, and George is reduced to a life in a world he does not understand and with which he cannot cope. More poignantly than in any of his other novels, in *Of Mice and Men* Steinbeck asserts the superiority of the simple human virtues to the mean accumulation of wealth and power. At the same time, however, his pastoral design is decidedly ironic.

The original title for *Of Mice and Men* was "Something That Happened," and what is particularly impressive about Steinbeck's narrative is the way he tells what happened. The book is written from an unjudgmental, or what Steinbeck called a nonteleological, point of view. The log portion of *Sea of Cortez* says that the term *nonteleological* encompasses feeling as well as thinking: "*Modus Operandi* might be better–a method of handling data of any sort." Steinbeck employed this way of viewing things, which he had derived from the ideas of Ed Ricketts, as fictional method. He is at his best when, in a novel like *Of Mice and Men*, he achieves what T. K. Whipple calls "the middle distance," in which he places his characters "not too close nor too far away" so that "we can see their performances with greatest clarity and fullness." Thus, Steinbeck portrays his characters sympathetically and at the same time remains objective, not judging their actions.

The Grapes of Wrath (1939) is, without question, Steinbeck's most ambitious as well as his most successful novel. The epic scale of the book, which focuses on the struggles of the Joad family in their trek to California as part of a band of Oklahoma tenant farmers from the Oklahoma dust bowl, enabled Steinbeck to say virtually everything he knew and felt about man and the world in which he lives. And whereas the battle in *In Dubious Battle* ends in chaos, *The Grapes of Wrath* ends in triumph mainly because of the influence of Jim Casy, a visionary ex-preacher.

Casy expresses Rickett's holistic viewpoint in ignoring what he regards as superficial distinctions between right and wrong to arrive at a recognition of the unity of all life, which he defines as holy: "Maybe that's the Holy Sperit–the human sperit–the whole shebang," says Casy. Proceeding from a nonteleological belief like Ricketts's conviction that "no valid *a priori* evaluation can be put

on anything," Casy discards the codes of doctrinal Christianity and concludes, "There ain't no sin and there ain't no virtue. There's just stuff people do." But whereas the battle in *In Dubious Battle* is dubious, and whereas Doc Burton, despite the depth of his understanding, cannot communicate anything of value to the striking apple pickers, in time Casy comes to understand that "we got a job to do." And he applies the principles of the organismal conception of life to bring together "the folks that don't know which way to turn." Burton ends up a lonely man, "working all alone, toward nothing," but Casy, who affirms that "All that lives is holy," keys into the migrant phalanx and dedicates himself "to go where the folks is goin'." Finally giving his life to help end the oppression of the dispossessed, he becomes a Christ figure who directs his disciples (the Joad family) to action. His life and death serve as a catalyst which unites the Joads with the entire migrant family in the just struggle for human dignity and a decent way of life.

The Grapes of Wrath is surely underpinned by Steinbeck's working out the terms of his intellectual friendship with Ed Ricketts. But it also owes much to his friendship with Thomas Collins, to whom the book is dedicated and whose work as the manager of a migrant camp for the Farm Security Administration is chronicled in an important background piece to *The Grapes of Wrath* by Jackson J. Benson, and to a variety of other people associated with the problems of California agriculture at the time. In telling the story of the Joad family, Steinbeck fuses an agrarian idealism with the Ricketts doctrine of the unity of all life and with his personal gospel of social action. Throughout the course of the Joads's epic journey, Steinbeck chronicles the Joads's change from jealously regarding themselves as an isolated and self-important family unit to a recognition that they are part of one vast human family which, in Casy's words, "has one big soul ever'body's a part of." At the beginning of the novel the Joads are interested solely in themselves. Tom wants only to lay "his dogs down one at a time." And Ma, whom Steinbeck describes as the citadel of the family, regards the pilgrimage only in terms of the welfare of her own family. But gradually, under Casy's influence, Tom, Ma, and the rest of the Joad family shift their orientation from the family unit to the migrant community as a whole, an act which is symbolically portrayed at the novel's conclusion when Ma's daughter, Rose of Sharon, gives her own breast milk to save a starving migrant. The Joads have keyed into a moving phalanx so that "the fear went from their faces, and anger took its place, and the women sighed with relief for they knew it was all right–the break had not come; and the break would never come as long as fear could turn to wrath." Structurally, the novel is particularly interesting because of the way in which Steinbeck portrays microcosm and macrocosm by alternating sections of the Joad narrative with intercalary chapters which universalize the Joad story. These chapters depict the land and the social conditions that the Joads encounter on their trek westward and in California.

The Grapes of Wrath was an immediate bestseller. Published in April 1939, it reached the top of the best-seller list within two months and remained there throughout the rest of the year. The 1940 movie version, starring Henry Fonda and Jane Darwell, reinforced the book's popularity. It has been in print continuously and has been translated into a variety of foreign languages. It remains a classic and is on the reading lists in English classes throughout the world. Steinbeck, who had done some political writing, most notably in a pamphlet entitled *Their Blood is Strong* (1938), a nonfiction account of the migrant labor problem in California, was attacked by a variety of civic, agricultural, and political interest groups who claimed that *The Grapes of Wrath* grossly distorted agricultural conditions in Oklahoma and in California. A national controversy grew around the book, and it was banned by some libraries and school boards. An editorial in *Collier's* magazine branded it as Communist propaganda, and it was attacked on the floor of Congress. Though Steinbeck received as much acclaim for *The Grapes of Wrath* as he did condemnation (the *Saturday Review* poll in 1940 nominated *The Grapes of Wrath* as the most distinguished novel of the year, and Steinbeck received the Pulitzer Prize for it in 1940), the experience of writing the book and the controversy surrounding its reception took its toll on him. Feeling fatigue and needing a change of scene, he embarked with Ricketts on a zoological expedition, more for escape than anything else. They first considered collaborating on a handbook about the marine invertebrates of San Francisco Bay but abandoned that project in favor of a comprehensive study of the fauna of the Gulf of California, which was published in 1941 as *Sea of Cortez*.

Both men worked at organizing the expedition. Steinbeck chartered the boat and ordered

Steinbeck in Rome, 1954 (courtesy of the Steinbeck Research Center/San Jose State University)

the supplies while Ricketts arranged the collecting materials. Ricketts, Steinbeck, and a crew of five sailed from Monterey Harbor on 11 March 1940, returning six weeks later on 20 April. The entire crew worked hard collecting and preserving specimens, and though they consumed a great deal of beer and insisted theirs was a leisurely voyage, the amount of work accomplished suggests their pace was anything but leisurely. Back in Monterey, Ricketts completed the difficult task of identifying and cataloguing specimens, and Steinbeck polished the narrative portion.

Critics of Steinbeck's work have long recognized the seminal importance of the log portion of *Sea of Cortez* to any serious study of Steinbeck's worldview, and they have believed that Steinbeck wrote the first part, the narrative of the trip, and Ricketts wrote the second part, a phyletic catalogue. In fact, the book was a joint project, and in several instances Steinbeck even permitted the distortion of his own ideas in order to provide for Ricketts a format for the expression of his worldview. Originally, Ricketts noted, "A journal of the trip was to have been kept by both of us, but this record was found to be a natural expression of only one of us. The journal was subsequently used by the other, chiefly as a reminder of what actually had taken place–this was then passed back to the other for comment, completion of certain chiefly technical details and corrections. . . . The book is a collaboration, but mostly shaped by John."

The record of the Gulf of California expedition was for Ricketts an important one. Out of the trip, he noted, came some "fairly significant contributions to invertebrate zoology, to marine sociology, and even–I wouldn't be surprised–to human thought." Steinbeck understood and appreciated Ricketts's involvement in the work, and in shaping the narrative into a valuable and lasting record of what Ricketts believed was "one of the important expeditions of these times," he commented that this "certainly is the most difficult work I've ever undertaken."

Sea of Cortez: A Leisurely Journal of Travel and Research was published in December 1941. Most literary critics at the time had never heard of Ricketts and considered the volume rather odd. Joseph Henry Jackson, who was at the time the arbiter of literary tastes in San Francisco, thought it suspicious mysticism. Donald Culross Peattie wondered about the disparate sections of the book, which, he claimed, contradicted the idea of shared authorship, and John Lyman wrote in the *American Neptune* that the book was of little interest to the nautical historian as the account of a sea voyage, and that its scientific shortcomings were perhaps even greater.

These opinions notwithstanding, the book is successful in many ways. The phyletic catalogue is a readable and comprehensive account of the marine life of the area and reflects Steinbeck and Ricketts's decision to focus not on rare and unknown forms, but on the common animal, since it, "more than the total of all rare forms, was important in the biological economy." The log portion contains fascinating accounts of the Indians who live in the remote fishing villages of the Gulf regions. In depicting the life of these Indians, Steinbeck and Ricketts note that what we call "progress" may lead to our extinction while the Indians of the Gulf sit in their dugout canoes and remember a "great and godlike race that flew away in four-motored bombers to the accompaniment of exploding bombs, the voice of God calling

them home." The log portion also contains serious discussions of birth and death, navigation, history, and the scientific method. Steinbeck and Ricketts eschew the cultivation of a science divorced from the real concerns of human life, labeling as "dryballs" those scientific specialists who create out of their own crusted minds "a world wrinkled with formaldehyde." And above all, the narrative contains a celebration of a holistic worldview that Ricketts and Steinbeck shared. The best passages in the volume are those in which they depict this worldview in terms more mystical and intuitive than scientific. "It is a strange thing that most of the feeling we call religious," they note, "most of the mystical outcrying, which is one of the most prized and used and desired reactions of our species, is really the understanding and the attempt to say that man is related to the whole thing, related inextricably to all reality, known and unknowable." The book is a unique record of a scientific voyage and of explorations in philosophy, "bright with sun and wet with sea water" and "the whole crusted over with exploring thought."

Work on *Sea of Cortez* had been suspended for a short time during the summer of 1940 while Steinbeck returned to Mexico to work with Herbert Kline on the filming of *The Forgotten Village* (1941), a moving documentary in which Steinbeck depicts the struggle against superstition and disease in rural Mexico. Steinbeck had been interested in the subject of rural health for some time. He was concerned about the failure of the state of California to provide adequate medical facilities for migrant farm workers, and he had discussed with filmmaker Pere Lorentz the possibility of doing some writing about rural health. The film chronicles the life of a peasant boy named Juan Diego, who leaves the traditional way of his people to learn medicine in the Mexican capital so that one day he may return to assist in the fight against disease and superstition.

In the spring of 1941 Steinbeck and Carol Steinbeck separated, and in the fall Steinbeck moved to the East with Gwendolyn Conger (who soon changed the spelling of her first name to *Gwyndolyn*), a professional singer he had met the previous year. They lived for a time in the New York City area until Steinbeck went to Europe as a war correspondent for the *New York Herald Tribune* in 1943. Steinbeck was divorced from his first wife in 1942 and married Gwyndolyn Conger in 1943. They had two sons: Thom, born in August 1944, and John, born in June 1946. During the 1940s they lived at various times in New York and California. Steinbeck and Gwyndolyn Steinbeck separated and were divorced in 1948.

In *The Grapes of Wrath* Steinbeck had expressed his faith that agrarian reform combined with a doctrine of social cooperation could solve the awesome problems of California agriculture caused by a depressed American economy. World War II convinced him not only of the inefficacy of agrarianism as a solution to serious social and economic problems but even led him to doubt the value of the group-man concept. Soon after the bombing of Pearl Harbor, Steinbeck, who had already been writing speeches for government officials, offered his writing talents to the State Department, where they were quickly accepted. In 1942, at the suggestion of Gen. Henry "Hap" Arnold, he wrote *Bombs Away* to tell the American people "of the kind and quality of our air force, of the calibre of its men, and of the excellence of its equipment." Steinbeck takes the issues of the war itself for granted, and he attempts to apply his goal-directed vision of social cooperation to efforts to meet the threat of Nazi Germany. At one point in *Bombs Away*, Steinbeck applies his argument of phalanx to the organization of airmen preparing for raids against the enemy. He notes that "the goal has been set now and we have an aim and a direction, and a kind of fierce joy runs through the country." Unhappily, though, no direction, no fierce joy runs through Steinbeck's narrative. John Ditsky calls *Bombs Away* a slight and even embarrassing book, which, in addition to its more obvious faults, contains "an unintended self-portrait of the artist in the midst of a collapsing theory."

The disintegration of Steinbeck's belief in the phalanx, in group man, is even more apparent throughout the loosely related series of dispatches he wrote in 1943 as a foreign correspondent. These were published in 1958 as *Once There Was a War*. Men, he argues, cannot be treated as individuals in a war effort. Indeed, soldiers in their helmets resemble mushrooms in a bed of mushrooms. And yet, what could have been the central focus in these communiqués about Americans at war—the loss of individuality of men in war—is lost. The majority of Steinbeck's dispatches stress human interest, the hopes, fears, and activities of "GI Joes" under the various conditions of war.

When Steinbeck collected his *Tribune* articles, he admitted "that they were written in haste and telephoned across the sea to appear as imme-

diacies," adding that "perhaps the whole body of work is untrue and warped and one-sided." Many things were not recorded because of "a huge and gassy thing called the War Effort. Anything which interfered with or ran counter to the war effort was automatically bad." Steinbeck's capitulation to political expediency—his commitment to the war effort—however patriotic, prevented him from seeing the whole picture, and the result was two weak nonfiction books.

Steinbeck's one novel about the war reflects his continued interest in holistic thinking, however. *The Moon Is Down* (1942) may have had roots in Steinbeck's dedication to the war effort, but this story of the invasion and occupation of a small Scandinavian village by the army of a highly mechanized collectivist state moves beyond the restricting limits of wartime propaganda. Steinbeck also wrote a dramatic version of *The Moon Is Down*, and both play and novel provoked a great deal of controversy. Efforts to assess Steinbeck's achievement in *The Moon Is Down* were lost amid the objections raised by those critics Steinbeck called "Park Avenue commandoes," who said *The Moon Is Down* was antiwar. Viewed from a distance, however, *The Moon Is Down* is not really a war novel at all, nor is it antiwar. Rather, it is a working out in fictional terms of the philosophical differences between Steinbeck and Ricketts. It is a failure as art not because Steinbeck failed to write a polemic about the horrors of Nazism, but rather because he was unable to relate abstract philosophical visions to concrete reality.

John Ditsky points out that in *The Moon Is Down* Steinbeck attempted to discriminate between the group man he had apotheosized in *The Grapes of Wrath* and elsewhere by scrapping the term and substituting another—*free men*, who are group men with a difference, and who are set apart from those whom Steinbeck calls *herd men*. As Mayor Orden says in *The Moon Is Down*, "Free men cannot start a war, but once it is started, they can fight on in defeat. Herd men, followers of a leader, cannot do that, and so it is always the herd men who win battles and the free men who win wars. . . ." Dr. Winter in *The Moon Is Down*, another of Steinbeck's Ricketts figures, realizes the flaws in the teleology of the "time-minded" invaders who "hurry toward their destiny as though it would not wait" and "push the rolling world along with their shoulders." Winter and his friend, Mayor Orden, discuss the difference between free men and herd men and note that the in-

John and Elaine Steinbeck in Berlin, 1963 (courtesy of the Steinbeck Research Center/San Jose State University)

vading army has taken on "the one impossible job in the world, the one thing that can't be done. . . . To break man's spirit permanently."

In the log portion of *Sea of Cortez*, Steinbeck and Ricketts note that the mutations of a collectivized state and a mechanized army "might well correspond to the thickening armor of the great reptiles–a tendency that can only end in extinction." The invading army in *The Moon Is Down* cannot cope with either the harsh Scandinavian landscape or the ingenious efforts by the townspeople to reject military domination. Gradually the conquerors are themselves conquered by a small group of partisans and by the ever-present Scandinavian snow. "The flies have conquered the flypaper," Dr. Winter prophesies at the end of the novel. "The debt shall be paid."

In 1951 Steinbeck recalled in "About Ed Ricketts" that he and Ricketts often engaged in a game they called "speculative metaphysics": "It was a sport consisting of lopping off a piece of observed reality and letting it move up through the speculative process like a tree growing tall and bushy. We observed with pleasure how the

branches of thought grew away from the trunk of external reality," and, Steinbeck remembered, "Once a theme was established we subjected observable nature to it." As an example of their game, Steinbeck presents their development of the paleontological principle that overarmor or overornamentation leads to decay. This discussion about the effect of overornamentation serves as the philosophical base upon which the novelist builds his distinction between good and bad group men in *The Moon Is Down*. And herein is the chief problem with Steinbeck's story. It is a thinly fictionalized version of Steinbeck and Ricketts's "letting it move up through the speculative process like a tree growing tall and bushy." Watching branches of thought grow apart "from the trunk of external reality" is appropriate to abstract theorizing, but it is catastrophic in fiction. Unlike his California fiction, in which he had been able to supplement abstract philosophical notions with feelings and insights gleaned from personal experience, there was nothing in his background and experience to furnish these feelings for *The Moon Is Down*.

Steinbeck called his first postwar novel, *Cannery Row* (1945), "a mixed-up book" with "a pretty general ribbing in it." It was "a kind of nostalgic thing written for a group of soldiers who had said to me, 'write something funny that isn't about the war. Write something for us to read–we're sick of war.'"

Many critics, disturbed by the suddenness with which Steinbeck cut himself off from social and political concerns, attacked *Cannery Row*, charging that Steinbeck's plot, which deals with the exploits of a group of vagabonds on Monterey's waterfront and their attempts to give a party for Doc, their friend and protector, is sentimental and its philosophy trivial. *Cannery Row* may seem an unrealistic novel, for in it Steinbeck makes heroes out of bums and affectionately describes "a nostalgic thing," a life incompatible with contemporary society, but its philosophy is by no means trivial or superficial. For beneath Steinbeck's casual tone is his clear-visioned evaluation of man's unsuccessful attempt to escape the realities of modern life.

Steinbeck's main theme in the book concerns man's quest to savor the "hot taste of life." The seekers are Doc (Steinbeck's most accurate version of Ed Ricketts) and those to whom he serves as demigod: Mack and the boys, those "no goods" and "blots-on-the-town" whom Steinbeck calls "the Virtues, the Graces, and the Beauties of the hurried mangled craziness of Monterey," beloved children of "Our Father who art in nature."

Steinbeck indicates in *Cannery Row* that man can savor the "hot taste of life" only if he pursues a natural existence within the sheltered confines of a place such as the row itself. Indeed, while the row is an island populated by saints and angels, martyrs and holy men, the behavior of its residents would be inadmissible anywhere else. When Malcolm Cowley suggested that *Cannery Row* might be a "poisoned cream puff" thrown at "respectable society," Steinbeck replied that "if Cowley read the book again, he would have found how very poisoned it was." In *Cannery Row*, Steinbeck indicts the so-called civilized world, and he praises natural life on the row. At the same time, he shows that Doc and Mack and the boys live in a fantasy world, surrounded by a viperous world which will seal their doom. Steinbeck's novel culminates with one of the most celebrated parties in American literature, and the next morning, Doc, immersed in memories, recites part of the Sanskrit poem, *Black Marigolds*:

> Even now
> I know that I have savored the hot taste of life
> Lifting green cups and gold from the great
>   feast.
> Just for a small and forgotten time
> I have had full in my eyes from off my girl
> The whitest pouring of eternal light–

The party is over. Doc has "savored the hot taste of life"; only memories are left. It is not surprising that *Cannery Row* ends with Doc wiping "his eyes with the back of his hand. . . . And behind the glass the rattlesnakes lay still and stared into space with their dusty frowning eyes."

The threat to life on Cannery Row is posed by materialistic self-directed Americans who cannot experience life to the fullest extent, but who, because of their unremitting possessiveness, may ultimately inherit the world. These are the main characters in Steinbeck's next California novel, *The Wayward Bus* (1947), a detailed allegory of modern life in which a diverse group of men and women, thrown together on a bus bound from one California community to another, are forced to reexamine themselves and their relationships with one another. Before the end of their trouble-filled journey, individuals either destroy or redeem themselves, depending upon their willingness to alter their thinking and their patterns of behavior. Following the general outline of the

Everyman allegory, the book tells the story of Juan Chicoy and the eight passengers on his bus (affectionately named Sweetheart), who are bound from Juan's cafe at Rebel Corners to San Juan de la Cruz and who are thoroughly involved in petty struggles, insignificant power plays, and foolish self-deceptions. After Juan allows his bus to swerve into a ditch, the passengers find shelter in three deep, dark caves, where they shed their facades and, almost without exception, arrive at fuller understandings of themselves and of their responsibilities to one another. In the end they work together to dig the bus out of the mud and move on to San Juan de la Cruz. And as the bus resumes its journey, the passengers, repenting their earlier self-centeredness, peer out the windows where they see "a little rim of lighter sky around the edge of a great dark cloud over the western mountains." Finally, the evening star comes into view, shining "clear and washed and steady" on a renewed earth.

Despite Steinbeck's intentions *The Wayward Bus* is unbelievable as a story. Steinbeck's characters are not fully developed, so when they shed their evil ways, their repentances seem insincere, and his portrayal of nature is too symbolic. Additionally, none of the characters adopts a holistic view of life, which gives meaning to the actions of such characters as Jim Casy and Tom Joad. No one breaks through to a knowledge of the deep thing; no one finds the education of the heart philosophically satisfying. Sweetheart lumbers into San Juan de la Cruz, but somehow the reader does not care. In *The Grapes of Wrath*, Steinbeck noted that man is distinguished from all other forms of life by his ability to grow beyond his concepts and "emerge ahead of his accomplishments." Juan Chicoy and his passengers do not grow beyond their concepts because they have none. They do not emerge ahead of their accomplishments because they have accomplished little. Juan and his passengers do no more than the animals Steinbeck and Ricketts observed in the Gulf of California: they exist. And this, the novelist seems to say, is the tragedy of man's wayward pilgrimage through modern life.

Shortly before he began work on *The Wayward Bus*, Steinbeck wrote a short piece based on a story he originally heard during his expedition to the Gulf of California. This was the story about a Mexican boy who found a great pearl which he thought would guarantee him happiness, but which almost destroyed him before he wisely threw it back into the sea. Steinbeck rewrote this fable a number of times, and when it was finally published in 1947 as *The Pearl*, it went largely unnoticed. It was not, in fact, until 1953 that Steinbeck discovered that it was at last "gathering some friends."

In contrast to the raucous bawdiness of *Cannery Row* and the allegorical seriousness of *The Wayward Bus*, *The Pearl* is a simple, lyrical fable which Steinbeck called "a black and white story like a parable." In this story of man's search for happiness and his need to choose between simplicity and complication, between a life in nature and a life in society, Steinbeck shows that the drive for wealth and power ends in tragedy and disappointment. *The Pearl* presents the human dilemma; it is the study of the agony involved in man's recognition of the vanity of human wishes. Kino, Steinbeck's protagonist, finds his pearl and protects it from those who would steal it from him, but he pays dearly. His house and canoe are destroyed, and his child is killed. He comes to see the pearl as a gray, malignant growth and throws it back into the gulf. In doing so, Kino chooses what Ed Ricketts once called "the region of inward adjustments" (characterized by friendship, tolerance, dignity, and love) over "the region of outward possessions."

Steinbeck's early postwar fiction reflects the vision of a man who had returned from a destructive war to a changed America. Trying first to recapture a sense of the past in *Cannery Row*, Steinbeck came to realize that neither the vagrant nor the scientific visionary could survive the onslaught of civilization. Then, in *The Wayward Bus*, he focused directly on the people of that postwar world and attempted with little artistic success to depict their repentance. And finally, in *The Pearl* he employed legend to explain what he regarded as the greatest of human dilemmas. In these books, Steinbeck's organismal view of life, his belief that men can work together to fashion a better, more productive, and more meaningful life, seemed less and less applicable to the world he saw around him. Gradually, John Steinbeck was becoming a novelist without a vision.

Searching for new literary vistas, Steinbeck hired on with the *New York Herald Tribune* for the purpose of visiting the Soviet Union with photographer Robert Capa and sending back essays which would later be the basis of the text for *A Russian Journal* (1948), a volume of essays and photographs. The book is nicely done, particularly those sections in which Steinbeck describes the simple farmers of Georgia and the Ukraine, whom he found to be hospitable people with wonderful senses of humor. He liked them and set down whole conversations with them with a warmth uncharacteristic of his more recent fiction. There are numerous passages in *A Russian Journal* which reflect Steinbeck's distress as to how the Soviet state has stifled individual initiative. There are also long sections which describe the widespread destruction which resulted from World War II, particularly in Kiev and in Stalingrad.

Upon his return from Russia, Steinbeck made preparations to join Ed Ricketts for another collecting trip, this time to the west coast of Vancouver Island and the Queen Charlottes, for the purpose of writing a cold-water *Sea of Cortez*. Steinbeck had never regretted collaborating with Ricketts on the Gulf of California narrative, but he recognized the inherent liabilities of any collaborative endeavor. In 1951 he told his editor, Pascal Covici, that "there are no good collaborations." Yet he had continued to show interest in Ricketts's work by writing the foreword to the second edition (1948) of Ricketts and Jack Calvin's *Between Pacific Tides*, and while he was already making preparations for work on "a giant novel" tentatively titled "Salinas Valley," he looked forward to another collaboration with Ricketts. But the marine biologist was killed in a freakish car/train wreck just weeks before the trip was to begin. Steinbeck was shattered by Ricketts's death. Later, he spoke of having had a kind of conscience removed and of possessing a new fierceness he had not felt for many years. But it is significant that he wrote little of consequence after Ricketts's death. As Jack Calvin has noted so succinctly, "The fountain had been turned off. Obviously, since he went on to write things like *Travels With Charley*, John was not aware that the train that killed Ed had also killed him as a writer." Steinbeck would spend the next several years wrestling in his writing with the fact of his own literary indebtedness to Ricketts. Throughout this period he continued to work on "Salinas Valley," which he finally completed in 1951 and retitled *East of Eden*, but his other writings between Ricketts's death in May of 1948 and the 1954 publication of *Sweet Thursday* reflect a rekindled absorption with Ricketts's person and ideas.

In 1949 the recently divorced Steinbeck met and fell in love with Elaine Scott, then the wife of actor Zachary Scott. She became his third and last wife in December 1950. They lived mostly in and around New York City, and in 1955 when the Steinbecks bought a summer cottage in Sag Harbor, on eastern Long Island, it marked his decision to make the East Coast his permanent home. These changes, as well as his reaction to the death of Ricketts, suggest that the period between 1948 and 1955 was a period of reevaluation for Steinbeck.

In his first works written after Ricketts's death, *Burning Bright* (1950) and "About Ed Ricketts," Steinbeck's depiction of Ricketts was admittedly unrealistic. In "About Ed Ricketts," which he wrote as a preface to *The Log from the Sea of Cortez*, the separate publication of the log portion of *Sea of Cortez*, Steinbeck says, "Maybe some of the events are imagined. And perhaps some very small happenings may have grown out of all proportion in the mind." "About Ed Ricketts" is a warm, personal account of a man who influenced Steinbeck "deeply and permanently" and who, for Steinbeck, will not die because he "is always present even in the moments when we feel his loss the most."

In *Burning Bright*, the only work Steinbeck wrote directly for the stage and his greatest dramatic failure, he attempted to lift a story about what he considered the most interesting aspect of Ricketts's character "to the parable expression of the morality play." The problem with this "play-novelette," as Steinbeck called it, unlike his more successful dramatic ventures (*Of Mice and Men*, *The Moon Is Down*), is that it is less a work of art than an abstract piece of philosophizing. *Burning Bright* deals with the inability of a middle-aged man (Joe Saul) to father a child by his young and beautiful wife (Mordeen). Mordeen is deeply in love with her husband, and she knows of her husband's desire for a child. She therefore commits adultery with Victor, Saul's assistant, and becomes pregnant. When Saul learns of his own sterility and figures out what his wife has done, the narrative turns from the theme of sterility into a parable about man's need to recognize his kinship with the entire human community.

Steinbeck presents in Joe Saul a man who "went away into an insanity" of self-interest and returned to realize, "It is the race, the species that must go staggering on." Learning from his close friend, significantly named Friend Ed (the Ricketts figure in the play), that man's greatest talent is the ability to receive, to receive anything from anyone and to do it gracefully and thankfully, Saul accepts the product of his wife's adultery, an acceptance heralded by his assertion of

the unity of all men. "I had to walk into the black to know—to know that every man is father to all children and every child must have all men as father." In "About Ed Ricketts," Steinbeck noted that Ricketts's greatest talent was his ability to receive. Indeed, says Steinbeck, "Ed's gift for receiving made him a greater teacher."

Steinbeck chose as his epigraph for *Burning Bright* the first stanza of Blake's "The Tyger," which illustrates his celebration of life: despite man's cruelty, violence, weakness, and wickedness, some life force had framed him in "fearful symmetry." Discovering his own symmetry, Joe Saul learns from Friend Ed that "This is not a little piece of private property, registered and fenced and separated. Mordeen! This is *the Child*."

Burning Bright failed as theater and as fiction. The stage production closed after just thirteen performances because audiences and critics found its language unconventional and its archaisms discordant. Steinbeck's abstract character types are even more problematic. For in attempting to universalize his story, Steinbeck, who, as Elaine Steinbeck noted, was too colloquial a writer to write symbolist fiction, abandoned a focus on individuals for philosophical abstraction. Commenting on the failure of *Burning Bright*, Steinbeck pointed out that he hoped his audience would "leap a gulf of unreality" and "join the company in creating a greater reality." But, he conceded, "for some people I suppose we made the jump too long."

The jump is not too long in *Viva Zapata!*, for which Steinbeck wrote the filmscript and which Elia Kazan made into one of the most successful movies of 1952. This script, which in characterization and theme recalls Steinbeck's best work of the 1930s, chronicles the life of the great Mexican revolutionary who occasioned dramatic economic and social reform in that country.

Steinbeck had been interested in the life and work of Emiliano Zapata for some time before he began work on his filmscript. And he treats Zapata and the landless Zapatistas with the kind of understanding and affection that he displayed in portraying his greatest fictional characters. In the course of Steinbeck's script, Zapata becomes corrupted by the misuse of power and so becomes as tyrannical as those he helped to overthrow. But he rectifies his errors and, at the cost of his life, becomes a mythic figure from whom all oppressed people may take strength. In *Viva Zapata!*, Steinbeck warns against the abuse of power, whether exercised by left-wing revolutionaries or right-wing reactionaries. Robert Morsberger observes that for Steinbeck, Zapata was a rebel and a man of individual conscience who could not ignore the hard facts of political and economic oppression. Zapata touched off a mass movement of agrarian reform of which he became the leader and symbol. In so doing, he encountered resistance from Fernando Aguirre, a fervent young man with a typewriter which he calls "the sword of the mind." For Steinbeck, Aguirre is a Mexican version of Mac or Jim of *In Dubious Battle*. In the script Zapata comes to understand the distorted nature of Fernando's principle that successful rule has no opposition. Reminded by his own followers of the corrupting nature of absolute power, Zapata ultimately renounces power, to give it back "where it belongs, to thousands of men." In the end the Zapatistas are strong people who no longer have to be led. "A strong man," says Zapata, "makes a weak people. Strong people don't need a strong man." And finally, when Zapata is himself killed by reactionary Mexican forces, his followers know that the spirit of Zapata, the spirit of reform, can never die: "He's not a river and he's not the wind! He's a man—and they still can't kill him! . . . He's in the mountains. You couldn't find him now, but if we ever need him again—he'll be back." Like Jim Casy in *The Grapes of Wrath*, Zapata is a creative rebel, one of those great personalities of history who stamped his genius upon the society of his period. In his account of Zapata's drive for land reform in Mexico, Steinbeck not only re-creates one of the most turbulent and exciting periods in Mexican history but conveys his belief in man's enduring capacity for greatness of mind and deed.

Even while he was completing work on *Viva Zapata!* and working with Kazan to ensure the success of the film, Steinbeck worked intermittently on what he called "his big novel," in which he wanted "to use every bit of technique I have learned consciously." The bulk of the writing took place during 1951 after he had freed himself from other professional commitments and could work without interruption on *East of Eden*. The record of his writing of this novel is recorded in the posthumously published *Journal of a Novel: The* East of Eden *Letters* (1969). This volume contains a series of letters to Pascal Covici, written from 29 January through 1 November 1951. Written in a notebook that Covici had given him, the letters contain Steinbeck's think-

ing about his novel in progress and chart the book's evolution. On 12 February Steinbeck noted that he had "written each book as an exercise, as practice for the one to come. And this is the one to come: There is nothing beyond this book—nothing follows it." "If *East of Eden* isn't good," Steinbeck said elsewhere, "then I've been wasting my time. It has in it everything I have been able to learn about my art or craft or profession in all these years."

In his first letter to Covici, Steinbeck said that the novel would "be two books—the story of my county and the story of me," and that he was writing the book for his sons, in part as a family history. Not only would the novel provide histories of the Salinas Valley and Steinbeck's mother's family, the Hamiltons, but also, Steinbeck said in the same letter, it would tell "one of the greatest, perhaps the greatest story of all—the story of good and evil, of strength and weakness, of love and hate, of beauty and ugliness." To portray this theme, Steinbeck invented another family, the Trasks, whose story became, over time, Steinbeck's version of the Cain and Abel story, which ends with an affirmation that the individual (in contrast to group man) can assert his moral impulse and, by his own free will, choose good over evil. Eventually the story of the Trasks, who are symbolic characters as opposed to the more realistically drawn Hamiltons, came to dominate Steinbeck's sprawling epic study of three generations in two families.

When Steinbeck submitted the first draft to the Viking Press, his editors felt that he had buried an interesting story in his sprawling epic, and they recommended substantial cuts to bring economy and unity to the book. Steinbeck resisted. He apparently felt that the complexity and psychological density of the manuscript justified its length. He regarded *East of Eden* as his magnum opus, and he forbade his editors to tamper with it. But the book fails, chiefly because it rambles and also because Steinbeck's moralizing badly constricts the range of his vision. In allowing morality to eclipse his earlier biological way of seeing, Steinbeck moved away from a well-conceived and coherent view of group man to platitudes about man's free will. Many of those friendly with Steinbeck during the years when he composed *East of Eden* feel the latter criticism is unfair. His agent Elizabeth Otis believed that *East of Eden* is Steinbeck's greatest and most misunderstood novel. Those who admire the novel assert that Steinbeck's thinking had matured, that he recognized that the individual is capable of achievements impossible among groups.

Yet Steinbeck's individuals (particularly the members of the mythical Trask family) are not quite believable. They are "symbol people" who are so poorly clothed in the trappings of experience that, contrary to Steinbeck's intention, the symbols are not only discernible, but overwhelming. Five years of research, writing, and rewriting went into *East of Eden*. And while it is not a major work in Steinbeck's canon, it is impressive for the largeness of its scope and for the expansive quality of its conception.

Though Steinbeck insisted while writing *East of Eden* that there was "nothing beyond this book," by the time he finished it, he realized that there was something to follow it. *Sweet Thursday* is Steinbeck's effort to recapture the person of Ed Ricketts in fiction for one last time. The novel seems on the surface a sequel to *Cannery Row*, for it is another narrative about Doc and Mack and the boys who live and play on the Monterey waterfront. Unlike *Cannery Row*, however, Steinbeck wrote *Sweet Thursday* with the theater in mind. Rogers and Hammerstein made it into the musical *Pipe Dream*, which opened in New York on 3 November 1955 and ran for a total of 246 performances.

Most reviews of *Sweet Thursday* reflect a misunderstanding of the novel. For many reviewers it was a mediocre repeat of *Cannery Row*. Some called it a "grade-B potboiler" and a "sentimental mish-mash." Even the most sympathetic of reviewers called it simply "good clean fun." The action of the novel centers on the efforts of Mack and his friends to find a suitable spouse for Doc, who, back from World War II, seems lonely and discontented. They match Doc with Suzy, a Monterey prostitute. Finally content, Doc marries Suzy, and together they leave Monterey so that Doc can assume a research position in marine biology at the California Institute of Technology.

On the surface, *Sweet Thursday* is a sentimental novel, and the Doc of the novel seems a weak and ineffectual version of his counterpart in *Cannery Row*. In fact, though, Steinbeck's depiction of Doc in *Sweet Thursday*–as a lonely, dissatisfied man–is for the novelist a statement of the plight of the thinking, feeling man in the wasteland of the modern world. This change in Ricketts is paralleled by a change in Cannery Row itself. In this novel, "the poem, the stink, and the grating noise" of the row are gone. The Cannery Row of *Sweet Thursday* consists of empty streets, silent can-

neries of corrugated iron where "a pacing watchman was their only life. The street that once roared with trucks was quiet and empty." And Doc is a mirror of that change. In *Sweet Thursday* he acts less than he is acted upon; he has become a victim of the aspects of modern society that Steinbeck most disliked. In short, *Sweet Thursday* is Steinbeck's bittersweet lament for the death of an era he loved and for the man who was, for him, its central symbol.

Steinbeck laid down the ghost of Ed Ricketts once and for all in *Sweet Thursday*, but he paid a price for the endeavor. His portrait of the decline of life on Cannery Row signals a similar decline in his writing. That pattern is apparent first in *The Short Reign of Pippin IV: A Fabrication* (1957), a lighthearted tale about "what happens to a retiring middle-aged astronomer suddenly drafted to rule the unruly French." *The Short Reign of Pippin IV* is a sapless and languid novel. Steinbeck's transatlantic leap deprived him of the distinctive idiom which characterizes his best California fiction.

Steinbeck was aware that this novel was a slight book and would have a limited audience. He felt otherwise about his work on a modernized edition of Malory's *Morte D'Arthur*. He began research for this task in 1957 by reading hundreds of books about Malory, and he spent most of 1959 traveling through the English and Welsh countryside with Elaine Steinbeck. He talked extensively with Malory expert Eugene Vinaver and showed him a piece of his work. Vinaver responded positively and offered to aid Steinbeck in any way possible. Buoyed by Vinaver's praise, Steinbeck indicated that this would be his most important work to date. He also believed it would take a decade to complete it.

Over the course of a five-year period, Steinbeck translated a substantial part of the *Morte D'Arthur*. In total, his translations include five of the six parts of the tale of King Arthur, the Gawain, Ewain, and Marhalt sections of the first romance, and all of "The Novel Tale of Sir Launcelot of the Lake." These were published posthumously as *The Acts of King Arthur and His Noble Knights* (1976). The first five sections are a readable and clear translation in modern diction which retains the sense and sensibility of Malory. Steinbeck took more liberties with the Gawain and Launcelot tales by deepening characterization and providing psychological perspectives to his examination of character. Throughout, however, Steinbeck was faithful to the original. His text is readable, and had he completed it, his *Arthur* may well have become a standard edition.

Steinbeck's final novel is *The Winter of Our Discontent* (1961), a book set in the fictional eastern Long Island community of New Baytown, which is above all a vision of the modern wasteland, a piercing study of the moral vacuum in contemporary America. In it Steinbeck chronicles man's fall from grace as a result of his devotion to the all-holy dollar; all codes of individual and group morality have been replaced by a subservience to a fast-buck philosophy. Indeed, the center of the New Baytown community is Mr. Baker's bank with its vault before which a ritual much like a mass is performed each workday morning. As Ethan Allen Hawley, Steinbeck's persona, describes it, he and others "stood at attention as the clock hand crossed nine. There came a click and buzzing from the great steel safe door. Then Joey dialed the mystic numbers and turned the wheel that drew the bolts. The holy of holies swung stately open and Mr. Baker took the salute of the assembled money. I stood outside the rail like a humble communicant waiting for the sacrament."

Hawley, who seeks meaning and purpose in a moral wasteland, spends the novel "taking stock," and, at the end of the volume, after considering suicide, he commits himself to working for a better world. "I had to get back . . . ," says Ethan. "Else another light might go out." But despite his claims of his own salvation, Ethan is unconvincing. His "light" is opaque and reflects Steinbeck's inability to provide a coherent vision for the future.

There is evidence which suggests that by the time Steinbeck finished *The Winter of Our Discontent*, he had lost interest in writing fiction, and in his last years he was more active as a journalist and traveler than as a novelist. His interest in science emerged afresh when he went with scientist Willard Bascom and the "elite and motley crew of Cuss I" to the Mohole drilling site off the coast of lower California. In addition to a lengthy piece he wrote about this expedition for *Life* magazine, Steinbeck authored two volumes of nonfiction during the 1950s as well as a series of columns for *Newsday*, supporting the American military presence in Southeast Asia, a position he later regretted. His two volumes of nonfiction reflect his newly adopted life-style as a journalist and traveler. The first, *Travels with Charley in Search of America* (1962), is the record of Steinbeck's 1960 trip across the United States

with his French poodle, Charley. The latter, *America and Americans* (1966), is a shorter narrative of reflections about this country interspersed with many fine photographs which divert attention from Steinbeck's flat and stylized prose. As in his earlier travel narratives, the log portion of *Sea of Cortez* and *A Russian Journal*, *Travels with Charley* and *America and Americans* reflect both the positive and negative aspects of the American travel experience. Steinbeck's travel writings alternately display a spirit of warmth and open curiosity which enlarges experience as well as the closed belief that the American way of life is best. *Sea of Cortez* is important as a work of travel literature because it contains the kind of curiosity which leads to discovery and thence to knowledge. This is not the case in *A Russian Journal*, for all we really learn about the Russian people is that they are like other people in the world. It does little to help us understand the meaning of either what is observed or the mind of the observer.

Travels with Charley in Search of America is in many ways Steinbeck's most important volume of travel literature. As a whole it is an uneven book. It lacks the unity of the log portion of *Sea of Cortez* and even the steady tone of *A Russian Journal*. Its tone is sentimental, and the writing is, at times, flat and cliché ridden. Still, there are passages in the volume that are as moving as any Steinbeck ever wrote. In the section of the book in which Steinbeck describes his trip across the Mojave Desert, he intuits the great "concepts of oneness and the majestic order" of life in language which recalls the tone of the log portion of *Sea of Cortez*.

Throughout *Travels with Charley*, we learn a good deal about John Steinbeck's vision of America and also about Steinbeck himself. We see the beauty of northern New England, Montana, and the Pacific Northwest. But by and large, the America Steinbeck discovers in *Travels with Charley* is a synthetic land. It is life at the peak of a civilization in which "everything that can be captured and held down is sealed in a clear plastic." "The food we eat," says Steinbeck, "is spotless and tasteless; untouched by human hands." Even the toilet seats have been sterilized for Steinbeck's protection. In the log portion of *Sea of Cortez* Steinbeck and Ricketts questioned the value of some kinds of social change. In *Travels with Charley* he finds that change has destroyed the American landscape. "Why," says Steinbeck, "does progress look so much like destruction." Indeed, the novelist seems to say we have reached a point where progress has become a progression toward strangulation.

Travels with Charley presents Steinbeck's sense of loss. He set out to learn something but returned home not knowing what it was he learned. Late in the volume he remembers that when he and Ricketts went to the Gulf of California, what they found was closely intermeshed with how they felt "so that external reality has a way of not being so external at all." *Travels with Charley* ends with a feeling of great emptiness. Indeed, there is a good deal of irony in Steinbeck's last remark to a New York policeman that "I've driven this thing all over the country–mountains, plains, deserts. And now I'm back in my own town, where I live–and I'm lost."

That sense of loss is also apparent in *America and Americans*, which is about a country Steinbeck finds "complicated, paradoxical, bullheaded, shy, cruel, boisterous, unspeakably clear, and very beautiful." In this volume Steinbeck comments on our government, our concepts of democracy, our pursuit of happiness, and on our loss of principle and purpose. He ends by reaffirming his faith in our people. He hopes for a renewal by noting that "we have failed sometimes, taken wrong paths, paused for renewal, filled our bellies and licked our wounds; but we have never slipped back–never." Somehow, though, one wonders whether Steinbeck really believed that such a renewal could ever take place.

Steinbeck died in December of 1968. At the time of his death he was in critical disrepute, and there were few serious scholars who did not share Harry T. Moore's feeling that in the future Steinbeck's literary status would be that of a Louis Bromfield or a Bess Streeter Aldrich. But the years have proved Moore wrong. Important new books, articles, and conferences about his work have made it clear that Steinbeck was a major American writer who defined well the human experience.

It is impossible to predict the final fate of John Steinbeck's reputation, but it seems likely that his lasting fame will rest largely on his great novels of the American Depression. He was a product of his time and his milieu. As a novelist, short-story writer, journalist, and author of travel literature, he traveled light, unencumbered by the kinds of preconceptions which are impediments to clear vision. As he said in his introduction to the log portion of *Sea of Cortez*, "The design of a book is the pattern of a reality controlled and shaped by the mind of the writer." And the patterns Steinbeck shaped in his fiction and nonfiction are the record of a man who wanted to join in. His works differ widely in scope as well as in quality, but his canon as a whole is the record of a man who in his own time and with his own voice defined and gave meaning to the human experience. The excellence of such volumes as *The Pastures of Heaven, Tortilla Flat, Of Mice and Men,* and chiefly of *In Dubious Battle, The Grapes of Wrath,* and *Sea of Cortez* affirm that he is among the most important writers of our time.

Letters:

Journal of a Novel: The East of Eden *Letters* (New York: Viking, 1969; London: Heinemann, 1970).

Letters from Steinbeck to Viking editor Pascal Covici; written daily as Steinbeck worked on *East of Eden*, the letters trace Steinbeck's changing conception of the novel he was writing.

Steinbeck: A Life in Letters, edited by Elaine Steinbeck and Robert Wallsten (New York: Viking, 1975).

More than eight hundred letters written to and from Steinbeck between 1924 and 1968.

Steinbeck and Covici: The Story of a Friendship, edited by Thomas Fensch (Middlebury, Vermont: Paul S. Eriksson, 1979).

Letters between Steinbeck and Pascal Covici, Steinbeck's early publisher, friend, and editor at Viking Press, with extensive analysis and commentary by Fensch.

Bibliographies:

Tetsumaro Hayashi, *A New Steinbeck Bibliography. 1929-1971* (Metuchen, N.J.: Scarecrow Press, 1973).

A comprehensive bibliography of all primary and secondary materials, including dissertations.

Hayashi, *A New Steinbeck Bibliography: 1971-1981* (Metuchen, N.J.: Scarecrow Press, 1983).

Comprehensive bibliography of all primary and secondary materials, including update for latter to 1981.

Robert DeMott, *Steinbeck's Reading: A Catalogue of Books Owned and Borrowed* (New York: Garland, 1984).

As the title indicates, an impressively researched listing of books influential in Steinbeck's life and work, plus selected bibliography.

Robert B. Harmon, *The Collectible John Steinbeck: A Practical Guide* (Jefferson, N.C.: McFarland, 1986).

The best guide to Steinbeck collecting, thoroughly documented.

Harmon, *Steinbeck Bibliographies: An Annotated Guide* (Metuchen, N.J.: Scarecrow Press, 1987).

An invaluable guide, containing thoroughly and succinctly annotated bibliography by author, title, subject, series, and journal as well as a brief history and introduction to Steinbeck research.

Biographies:

Nelson Valijean, *John Steinbeck: The Errant Knight* (San Francisco: Chronicle Books, 1975).

A somewhat romantic look at Steinbeck's life with emphasis upon boyhood and the Salinas years.

Thomas Kiernan, *The Intricate Music: A Biography of John Steinbeck* (Boston: Atlantic/Little, Brown, 1979).

An unauthorized biography characterized by much speculation by Kiernan as well as a markedly negative view of the subject.

Jackson J. Benson, *The True Adventures of John Steinbeck, Writer* (New York: Viking, 1984).

An impressively thorough, objective, and well-written account of Steinbeck's life, this is the authorized and definitive Steinbeck biography.

Benson, *Looking for Steinbeck's Ghost* (Norman: University of Oklahoma Press, 1988).

Benson's account of experiences during the fourteen years spent writing his biography of Steinbeck.

References:

Richard Astro, *John Steinbeck and Edward F. Ricketts: The Shaping of a Novelist* (Minneapolis: University of Minnesota Press, 1973).

A study of the relationship between Steinbeck and marine biologist Edward F. Ricketts and the influence of this relationship upon Steinbeck's fiction.

Astro and Tetsumaro Hayashi, eds., *Steinbeck: The Man and His Work* (Corvallis: Oregon State University Press, 1971).

Critical essays discussing such Steinbeck works as *Viva Zapata!, In Dubious Battle, Cannery Row,* and *Sweet Thursday,* with attention to Steinbeck's philosophy and the "Steinbeck hero" as well as reminiscence by Steinbeck's lifelong friend, Webster Street.

Jackson J. Benson, "To Tom Who Lived It: John Steinbeck and the Man from Weedpatch," *Journal of Modern Literature,* 5 (April 1976): 151-210.

Examination of Steinbeck's relationship with Tom Collins, director of government migrant camps in California, from whom Steinbeck drew information for *The Grapes of Wrath.*

Benson and Anne Loftis, "John Steinbeck and Farm Labor Unionization: The Background of *In Dubious Battle,*" *American Literature,* 52 (May 1980): 194-223.

An important examination of Steinbeck's preparation for his major strike novel as well as the social and historical context for that novel.

Robert Conn Davis, ed., *Twentieth Century Interpretations of The Grapes of Wrath: A Collection of Critical Essays* (Englewood Cliffs, N.J.: Prentice-Hall, 1982).

Standard reprinted essays on *The Grapes of Wrath*; more recent essays collected here include examinations of the novel's intercalary chapters as well as Ma Joad as archetype. The editor's introduction examines Steinbeck from a contemporary perspective.

Robert M. Davis, ed., *Steinbeck: A Collection of Critical Essays* (Englewood Cliffs, N.J.: Prentice-Hall, 1972).

Twelve essays on selected Steinbeck novels, with introduction by Davis and a negatively subjective overview of Steinbeck's career by R. W. B. Lewis.

Robert DeMott, ed., *Working Days: The Journals of The Grapes of Wrath, 1938-1941* (New York: Viking, 1989).

An annotated edition of the journal kept by Steinbeck as he worked on *The Grapes of Wrath*, with 123 entries from February 1938 through January 1941.

John Ditsky, ed., *Critical Essays on The Grapes of Wrath* (Boston: G. K. Hall, 1988).

Twenty original reviews and essays published here for the first time, including charts and maps of the novel's California setting.

Keith Ferrell, *John Steinbeck: The Voice of the Land* (New York: Evans, 1986).

A critical overview of Steinbeck's life and work, appropriate for younger readers.

Joseph Fontenrose, *John Steinbeck: An Introduction and Interpretation* (New York: Barnes & Noble, 1963).

An important early study of Steinbeck's work, with valuable attention to the role of mythology.

Warren French, *A Filmguide to The Grapes of Wrath* (Bloomington: Indiana University Press, 1973).

A monograph-length discussion of the direction and production of John Ford's film version of the novel, with scene-by-scene analysis, summary critique, and novel-screenplay-film comparison.

French, *John Steinbeck*, revised edition (New York: Twayne, 1975).

Critical overview of Steinbeck's major fiction and nonfiction, published in 1961 in Twayne's United States Authors Series and revised extensively for 1975 publication.

French, *The Social Novel at the End of an Era* (Carbondale: Southern Illinois University Press, 1966).

A close look at the social context of the 1930s, with extensive analysis of *The Grapes of Wrath* as well as works by other writers of the period.

French, ed., *A Companion to The Grapes of Wrath* (New York: Viking, 1963).

A groundwork collection of essays organized according to "Background," "Reception," and "Reputation" of the novel, including Steinbeck's monograph on migrant worker conditions, *Their Blood Is Strong*.

Tetsumaro Hayashi, ed., *John Steinbeck: A Dictionary of His Fictional Characters* (Metuchen, N.J.: Scarecrow Press, 1976).

Introductory guide to characters and roles in Steinbeck's fiction; includes a "Biographical Portrait" by Richard Astro.

Hayashi, ed., *Steinbeck's Literary Dimension* (Metuchen, N.J.: Scarecrow Press, 1973).

Includes essays comparing Steinbeck and such authors as Hemingway, Faulkner, Zola, and others as well as a survey of criticism and bibliography.

Hayashi, ed., *Steinbeck's Women: Essays in Criticism*, Steinbeck Monograph Series, No. 9 (Muncie, Indiana: Steinbeck Society, Ball State University, 1979).

An important (and first) collection of essays focusing upon the sometimes controversial subject of Steinbeck's female characters.

Hayashi, ed., *A Study Guide to Steinbeck: A Handbook to His Major Works* (Metuchen, N.J.: Scarecrow Press, 1974); *A Study Guide to Steinbeck*, Part II (Metuchen, N.J.: Scarecrow Press, 1979).

Valuable introductory works to Steinbeck's fiction.

R. S. Hughes, *John Steinbeck: A Study of the Short Fiction* (Boston: Twayne, 1989).

Valuable background material relating to the composition of Steinbeck's short fiction, including much summary of published criticism.

Howard Levant, *The Novels of John Steinbeck: A Critical Study* (Columbia: University of Missouri Press, 1974).

With an introduction by Warren French, a study of theme and structure in Steinbeck's novels, unique among book-length studies of Steinbeck's work for its strongly negative evaluation of the author's art.

Clifford Lewis and Carroll Britch, *Rediscovering Steinbeck* (Lockport, N.Y.: Edwin Mellen Press, 1989).
A collection of eight original essays on selected Steinbeck works, including nonfiction, Steinbeck's women, and other subjects.

Peter Lisca, *John Steinbeck: Nature and Myth* (New York: Crowell, 1978).
A critical overview of Steinbeck's work updated and revised from Lisca's previous study, *The Wide World of John Steinbeck.*

Lisca, *The Wide World of John Steinbeck* (New Brunswick: Rutgers University Press, 1958).
Contains thorough and very valuable research as well as critical assessment.

Paul McCarthy, *John Steinbeck* (New York: Ungar, 1979).
A critical overview of Steinbeck's life and fiction.

Joseph R. Millichap, *Steinbeck and Film* (New York: Ungar, 1983).
A study of the interrelationship between Steinbeck's fiction and films made from that fiction.

Harry Thornton Moore, *The Novels of John Steinbeck: A First Critical Study* (Chicago: Normandie House, 1939; second edition, with contemporary epilogue, Port Washington, N.Y.: Kennikat Press, 1959).
A pioneering study of Steinbeck's early works.

Louis Owens, *The Grapes of Wrath: Trouble in the Promised Land* (New York: Twayne, 1989).
An introductory study of *The Grapes of Wrath,* including biographical, historical, and critical context, as well as bibliography and new critical analysis of the novel.

Owens, *John Steinbeck's Re-Vision of America* (Athens: University of Georgia Press, 1985).
A critical overview of the major fiction with emphasis upon the significance of the American myth.

E. W. Tedlock and C. V. Wicker, eds., *Steinbeck and His Critics: A Record of Twenty-Five Years* (Albuquerque: University of New Mexico Press, 1957).
A collection of twenty-nine essays and notes, including responses by Steinbeck to his critics.

John H. Timmerman, *John Steinbeck's Fiction: The Aesthetics of the Road Taken* (Norman: University of Oklahoma Press, 1986).
Critical analysis of the major works, including chapters examining Steinbeck as "Literary Artist" and brief overview of the author's career.

F. W. Watt, *John Steinbeck* (New York: Grove, 1962).
Another of the pioneering early studies of Steinbeck's fiction–general critique of major works.

Papers:
Steinbeck's correspondence and manuscript materials are in the libraries of the University of Texas at Austin, the University of Virginia, the University of California at Berkeley, Stanford University, San Jose State University, Ball State University, and the Salinas Public Library.

Wallace Stevens

This entry was updated by Laura Ingram from the entry by Joseph Miller in DLB 54, *American Poets, 1880-1945, Third Series.*

Places	Hartford, Connecticut Key West, Florida	Harvard	New York City
Influences and Relationships	Stéphen Mallarmé T. S. Eliot Harriet Monroe William Wordsworth	E. E. Cummings Marianne Moore Alfred Kreymborg	George Santayana William Carlos Williams
Literary Movements and Forms	Metaphysical Poetry Satire	Haiku Romanticism	Imagism French Symbolism
Major Themes	The Nature of Mankind Reality vs. Imagination	The Need for Belief "Fables of Identity"	Poetry as a Key to the Subconscious
Cultural and Artistic Influences	Avant-garde Theater French Culture	Impressionistic Painting	Orientalism
Social and Economic Influences	World War I	Prosperity of 1920s	Insurance Industry

BIRTH: Reading, Pennsylvania, 2 October 1879, to Garrett Barcalow and Margaretha Catharine Zeller Stevens.

EDUCATION: Harvard College, 1897-1900; LL.B., New York Law School, 1903.

MARRIAGE: 21 September 1909 to Elsie Viola Kachel; daughter: Holly Bright.

AWARDS AND HONORS: Levinson Prize (*Poetry* magazine), 1920; *Nation* Poetry Prize, 1936; elected to the National Institute of Arts and Letters, 1946; Harriet Monroe Poetry Award, 1946; Litt.D., Wesleyan University, 1947; Bollingen Prize in Poetry, 1950; Poetry Society of America Gold Medal, 1951; National Book Award for *The Auroras of Autumn*, 1951; Litt.D., Bard College, 1951; Litt.D., Harvard University, 1951; Litt.D., Mount Holyoke College, 1952; Litt.D., Columbia University, 1952; National Book Award for *The Collected Poems of Wallace Stevens*, 1955; Pulitzer Prize for *The Collected Poems of Wallace Stevens*, 1955; L.H.D., Hartt College of Music (Hartford), 1955; Litt.D., Yale University, 1955.

DEATH: Hartford, Connecticut, 2 August 1955.

BOOKS: *Harmonium* (New York: Knopf, 1923; revised and enlarged, 1931);
Ideas of Order (New York: Alcestis Press, 1935; enlarged edition, New York & London: Knopf, 1936);
Owl's Clover (New York: Alcestis Press, 1936);
The Man with the Blue Guitar & Other Poems (New York & London: Knopf, 1937);
Parts of a World (New York: Knopf, 1942);
Notes toward a Supreme Fiction (Cummington, Mass.: Cummington Press, 1942);
Esthétique du Mal (Cummington, Mass.: Cummington Press, 1945);
Transport to Summer (New York: Knopf, 1947);
Three Academic Pieces: The Realm of Resemblance, Someone Puts a Pineapple Together, Of Ideal Time and Choice (Cummington, Mass.: Cummington Press, 1947);
A Primitive like an Orb (New York: Gotham Book Mart, 1948);
The Auroras of Autumn (New York: Knopf, 1950);
The Relations between Poetry and Painting (New York: Museum of Modern Art, 1951);

Wallace Stevens, 1900 (photo by Bachrach; courtesy of the Henry E. Huntington Library and Art Gallery)

The Necessary Angel: Essays on Reality and the Imagination (New York: Knopf, 1951; London: Faber & Faber, 1960);
Selected Poems (London: Fortune Press, 1952);
Selected Poems (London: Faber & Faber, 1953);
Raoul Dufy: A Note (New York: Pierre Berès, 1953);
Mattino Domenicale, English and Italian, with Italian translations by Renato Poggioli (Turin: Guilio Einaudi, 1954);
Thirteen Ways of Looking at a Blackbird (New York: Knopf, 1954);
The Collected Poems of Wallace Stevens (New York: Knopf, 1954; London: Faber & Faber, 1955);
Opus Posthumous, edited by Samuel French Morse (New York: Knopf, 1957; London: Faber & Faber, 1959);
Poems by Wallace Stevens, edited by Morse (New York: Vintage, 1959);

The Palm at the End of the Mind: Selected Poems and a Play by Wallace Stevens, edited by Holly Stevens (New York: Knopf, 1971).

In "Of Modern Poetry," a poem first published in 1942, Wallace Stevens sets forth the dilemma of the poet in the modern world:

> The poem of the mind in the act of finding
> What will suffice. It has not always had
> To find: the scene was set; it repeated what
> Was in the script.
>   Then the theatre was changed
> To something else. Its past was a souvenir.

Until sometime in the eighteenth century, around the time of the French Revolution perhaps, poets lived in a world where the existence of absolute values and of a providential order in the cosmos was all but universally accepted. It was only with the romantics that the individual imagination was invoked as a sanction for the values and order that men needed to live their lives, when the world had ceased to supply such a sanction. Such is the real distinction between the modern poet and his predecessors. In his own life Stevens himself experienced this loss of faith in a providential order; he took up the challenge of the poet in the modern world; and the success he had in "finding what will suffice," which is considerable, is the measure of his greatness.

Wallace Stevens was born in Reading, Pennsylvania, on 2 October 1879, the second of five children, to Garrett Barcalow Stevens and his wife Margaretha Catharine Zeller, known as Kate. The family was a prominent member of the Dutch Reformed church, and the three Stevens boys attended elementary schools run by the Evangelical Lutheran church. There is a photograph, circa 1893, of Wallace Stevens in a cassock and surplice, but before long, presumably during his years at Harvard, he became an agnostic, and such he remained up to the last days of his life. In lieu of faith in a supreme being and a providential order determined from on high, Stevens sought to discover a transcendent beauty and a transcendent wisdom in the world itself by means of a union of the imagination and external reality, in what he called a "Supreme Fiction," which is to be found in poetry. In his "Adagia," a collection of aphorisms on poetry and imagination that was included in *Opus Posthumous* (1957), he wrote, "The relation of art to life is of the first importance especially in a skeptical age since, in the absence of a belief in God, the mind turns to its own creations and examines them, not alone from the aesthetic point of view, but for what they reveal, for what they validate and invalidate, for the support they give." One of his later poems, "The Bed of Old John Zeller," contrasts the religion of his grandfather ("the habit of wishing") with Stevens's practice of poetry: "It is easy to wish for another structure/ Of ideas and to say as usual that there must be/ Other ghostly sequences and, it would be, luminous/Sequences. . . ./It is difficult to evade/ That habit of wishing and to accept the structure/ Of things as the structure of ideas." This spiritual quest, this difficult, skeptical acceptance of the structure of things as the structure of ideas, is the abiding theme of Wallace Stevens's life and work. It amounts ultimately to nothing less than a rediscovery of a sustaining faith through the imagination.

Garrett Barcalow Stevens was a prominent lawyer in Reading, and the family led a comfortable bourgeois life. Kate Zeller Stevens had been a schoolteacher in Reading before her marriage. Of his home life Wallace Stevens wrote later: "We were all great readers, and the old man used to delight in retiring to the room he called the library on a Sunday afternoon to read a five- or six-hundred page novel. The library was no real institution, you understand; just a room with some books where you could go and be quiet. My mother just kept house and ran the family. When I was younger I always used to think that I got my practical side from my father, and my imagination from my mother." Holly Stevens, the poet's daughter, recalling her childhood in Hartford, says, "As I grew up our house was quiet too, but Sunday afternoons became devoted to listening to the New York Philharmonic orchestra concerts on the radio, and Saturday afternoons to opera, either on the radio or on records. At other times we read, and my mother 'just kept house' and worked in the garden or played the piano. Like his father before him, mine did not entertain business associates at home." Wallace Stevens was all his life an intensely private man, and this quiet, private, daily life is the subject of such poems as "The House was Quiet and the World was Calm," "Large Red Man Reading," and "A Quiet Normal Life" and is implicit in many others. "Poetry is a response to the daily necessity of getting the world right," he wrote in "Adagia"; and also: "Wine and music are not good until afternoon. But poetry is like prayer in that it is most effective in solitude and in the times of solitude as, for example, in the earliest morning."

Shortly before his thirteenth birthday Stevens was enrolled at Reading Boys' High School, where he followed the classical curriculum, which comprised the study of Greek and Latin languages and history, science, and mathematics, as well as English grammar and composition, and the English and American classics. He was an honor-roll student, a reporter for the student newspaper, and a prize-winning orator. One of his high school classmates later said that "at high school Wallace was a whimsical, unpredictable young enthusiast, who lampooned Dido's tear-stained adventures in the cave, or wrote enigmatic couplets to gazelles."

In September 1897 Wallace Stevens went to Harvard, where he studied for three years as a special student, living at 54 Garden Street in Cambridge in a rooming house run by three spinster sisters. One of his fellow inhabitants of this rooming house later wrote of him: "I recall especially his bursting out of his room to recite a new combination of words or a new metaphor that he had just invented, and to share his delight which was infectious." Later Stevens wrote that his "first year away from home, in Cambridge, made an enormous difference in everything." For one thing he was writing poetry, and his first known published poem, "Autumn," appeared that year in the Reading Boys' High School magazine the *Red and Black.* He was also studying diligently, primarily languages and literature, and with instructors of a high caliber, such as Charles Townsend Copeland, whom he later counted among his friends, and Barrett Wendell, whose lecture "Elegance" at the Lowell Institute would certainly have interested the young Stevens. And it was at Harvard that he came to know George Santayana, whose aesthetic philosophy was to have a considerable influence upon his own poetic theory.

In his second year at Harvard Stevens began to keep a journal, which, edited with a commentary by his daughter, is now the principal source of information about his early life and thought. In this journal he recorded daily activities, notes on his reading, poems in various stages of revision, and some extensive observations or meditations upon nature at particular times and places, which read like prose poems and often bear a resemblance to poems he wrote much later in his life. His early poems are more full of echoes of John Keats and Percy Bysshe Shel-

ley than observations of nature, but even when they are sentimental and derivative and sprinkled with archaic poeticisms, they are technically quite accomplished. The first of Stevens's poems to appear in the *Harvard Advocate* was in the 28 November 1898 issue, and it was followed by others over the next two years in that magazine and in the *Harvard Monthly.* In the spring of 1899 he was appointed a staff member and subsequently became a member of the editorial board of the *Harvard Advocate,* for which he wrote stories and sketches as well as poems. A contemporary colleague on the *Advocate* staff has described Stevens the student editor as "a large, handsome, healthy, robust, amiable person, with light curly hair and the most friendly of smiles and dispositions ... frank and amusing ... modest, almost diffident, and very tolerant and kindly towards, alike, his colleagues and contributors of manuscripts." In the second semester of his third year Stevens was elected president of the *Harvard Advocate* and took on the task of writing editorials on a wide range of campus activities. For the first issue under his direction, dated 10 March 1900, he wrote three editorials, a short story, and a poem. "You see," he said years later in an interview, "I was the editor of the magazine, and often one had to furnish much of the material himself." With such experience behind him it is not surprising that the young poet would try his hand at professional journalism.

Because as a special student he had never worked toward a degree and because his father was paying to keep Wallace's two brothers in university at the same time, Wallace Stevens left Cambridge for New York City in the middle of June 1900. There he applied for jobs at the offices of various newspapers and magazines, wrote some sample articles for the *New York Evening Post,* and at the end of the month accepted a position with the *New York Tribune,* to be paid "according to the space I fill." He filled enough space to make a modest living and even took a cut in pay in October when he accepted a regular salary of fifteen dollars a week with a promise of an immediate raise for good work. As a reporter he covered the election campaigns and heard William Jennings Bryan deliver four speeches in three hours. But Stevens seems to have been neither greatly inspired by the work nor ambitious for success in the world of newspapers. "My work on the *Tribune* is dull as dull can be," he wrote in his journal (10 November 1900). "I'm too lazy to attempt anything outside—& the fact that I work two days a week . . . spoils whatever laziness hasn't made on her own." This statement does not mean that he wasted his time. He explored New York from top to bottom and made a special point of seeing the beauties of nature in this urban setting: the trees in Washington Square and the sunset over the Palisades. He studied New York like a text and wrote down his observations and reflections: for example, "West street, along the North River, is the most interesting street in the whole city to me. I like to walk up and down and see the stevedores and longshoremen lounging about in the sun. . . . The street is as cosmopolitan and republican as any in the world. It is the only one that leaves the memory full of pictures, of color and movement. Clattering trucks and drays, tinkling and bouncing horse-cars, hundreds of flags at mast-heads, glimpses of the water between piers, ticket-brokers & restaurant piled on restaurant." And elsewhere: "New York is so big that a battle might go on at one end, and poets meditate sonnets at another. . . . Ate a big, juicy 'bifstek' chez l'Hotel Martin, ce soir. Mais je ne parle pas au garçon; j'eus trop de peur." Often Stevens spent his mornings reading poetry, and from time to time he wrote a poem himself. He attended concerts and plays as often as he could afford. He saw Sarah Bernhardt in Rostand's *L'Aiglon* and in *Hamlet*, and he went several times to see Ethel Barrymore as Mme. Trentoni in Clyde Fitch's *Captain Jinks of the Horse Marines* and was so charmed by her that he hurriedly wrote out a rough draft of a play to be called "Olivia: A Romantic Comedy."

It did not take long for this carefree way of life to pall. Stevens enjoyed New York–"this electric town which I adore"–but he also found himself lonely there, often depressed, and frustrated in his ambitions, which were as yet fairly vague. "I should be content to dream along to the end of my life–and opposing moralists be hanged," he had written in his journal while still at Harvard. "At the same time I should be quite as content to work and be practical–but I hate the conflict whether it 'avails' or not. I want my powers to be put to their fullest use–to be exhausted when I am done with them. On the other hand I do not want to have to make a petty struggle for existence–physical or literary. I must try not to be a dilettante–half dream, half deed. I must be all dream or all deed." The greatest influence in Stevens's life in favor of the deed rather than the dream was clearly his father, who since he had left home had been sending him letters full of fa-

therly advice rather in the style of Lord Chesterfield. In March of 1901, in the middle of writing "Olivia: A Romantic Comedy," Stevens went home to Reading for a brief visit and had "a good long talk with the old man in which he did most of the talking. . . . We talked about the law, which he has been urging me to take up. I hesitated–because this literary life, as it is called, is the one I always had as an ideal & I am not quite ready to give it up because it has not been all that I wanted it to be." A week later he noted in his journal, "I recently wrote to father suggesting that I should resign from the Tribune & spend my time writing. This morning I heard from him &, of course, found my suggestion torn to pieces. If I only had enough money to support myself I am afraid some of his tearing would be in vain. But he seems always to have reason on his side, confound him." He then made inquiries concerning the publishing business as a possible career, only to learn that the positions were chiefly clerical and paid low wages. Wallace Stevens seems to have been a fairly conventional young man, not heedless of his father's prudent advice, without the slightest taste for *la vie de bohème*–that "petty struggle for existence–physical or literary"–and, on 1 October 1901, he entered New York Law School.

Stevens attended New York Law School for the next two academic years, graduating on 10 June 1903. Then he worked for a year as a law clerk for the New York attorney W. G. Peckham, in whose offices he had clerked during his last year in law school and with whom he made an extensive camping trip in the remote Canadian Rockies in the summer of 1903. On 29 June 1904 he was admitted to the bar in New York State and began the long and difficult task of establishing himself as a successful insurance lawyer. After a short-lived law partnership with Lyman Ward, who had been a special student with Stevens at Harvard, he drifted in and out of three New York law firms before joining the New York branch of the American Bonding Company of Baltimore, the first insurance firm for which he worked, in January of 1908. This position gave Stevens the financial security he needed to propose marriage during the following Christmas holidays to Elsie Viola Kachel, whom he had met in Reading four years earlier. They were married in Reading on 21 September 1909, and the Stevenses lived at 441 West Twenty-first Street in New York for the next seven years. Stevens's father died in 1911, and his mother in 1912. In 1913 he was

The poet's parents, Garrett Barcalow and Margaretha Catharine Zeller Stevens (courtesy of the Henry E. Huntington Library and Art Gallery)

named a law officer at the New York office of the Fidelity and Deposit Company of Maryland, which had bought the American Bonding Company. The following year he was hired as a resident vice-president at the New York office of the Equitable Surety Company of St. Louis and remained there after the firm merged with the New England Casualty Company of Boston in 1915 to become the New England Equitable Insurance Company. When that company abolished his position in 1916, he joined the home-office staff of the Hartford Accident and Indemnity Company, where he remained to the end of his life, having become a vice-president in 1934. In May of 1916 Wallace and Elsie Stevens moved permanently to Hartford, Connecticut, where their daughter, Holly Bright Stevens, an only child, was born on 10 August 1924. His new position involved a good deal of travel for Stevens, all over the United States and occasionally to Canada,

and it was on business that he made the first of several trips to Florida, in 1916.

Had Wallace Stevens been a different sort of person, the foregoing summary could easily be the end of the story. Many another young man has gone into the adult world of business and abandoned his halfhearted literary pretensions as so much youthful folly. Stevens himself gave up writing poetry for some ten years when he entered law school. "A good many years ago," he wrote a friend in 1937, "when I really was a poet in the sense that I was all imagination, and so on, I deliberately gave up writing poetry because, much as I love it, there were too many other things I wanted not to make an effort to have them. I wanted to do everything that one wants to do at that age: live in a village in France, in a hut in Morocco, or in a piano box at Key West. But I didn't like the idea of being bedeviled all the time about money and I didn't for a moment like the idea of poverty, so I went to work like anybody else and kept at it for a good many years." He did not write any poems during his years as a struggling young lawyer, but it is apparent from Stevens's journal that he never ceased to be a poet "in the sense that I was all imagination," even while he was all business at the same time. For one thing, on his frequent business trips he made extensive notes on the places and people and views of nature that he saw, many of which are suggestive of details to be found in poems he wrote years later.

Furthermore, Stevens did not cut himself off from the literary and artistic community during those years which saw the arrival of international modernism in America, and nowhere was the atmosphere of revolt and experimentation in painting and literature livelier than in New York. He came to know many of the painters and writers who frequented Greenwich Village, among them William Carlos Williams, Marianne Moore, Alfred Kreymborg, and E. E. Cummings, and he took part in their projects and entertainments from time to time. The famous Armory Show of 1913, which introduced the works of the early modern masters to America, created a whirlwind of enthusiasm for new ideas in all the arts and was doubtless the origin of Stevens's lifelong avocation as a connoisseur and collector of pictures. This period also marks the beginning of Stevens's interest in the arts of China and Japan, in which he found the clarity and freshness that stimulated his imagination and heightened his perceptions of familiar things. He often visited the American Art Galleries, where Chinese and Japanese jades and porcelains were exhibited. He wrote: "The sole object of interest for me in such things is their beauty. Cucumber-green, camellia-leaf-green, apple-green etc. moonlight, blue, etc. ox-blood, chicken-blood, cherry, peach-blow etc. etc. Oh! and mirror-black."

This orientalism was, in fact, a continuation of the same general enthusiasm for the Orient that had been running in and out of the arts of France and England for more than a hundred years: Chippendale chinoiserie, the exoticism of Eugène Delacroix, and the aestheticism of the French impressionists, of James McNeill Whistler, and of many other artists in the late nineteenth century. The litany of colors that Stevens found in the Oriental jades and porcelains signals his long interest in colors, the names of colors, and color symbolism. His reading in Oriental poetry is reflected in the haikulike stanzas of

"Thirteen Ways of Looking at a Blackbird" (first published in the December 1917 issue of *Others*). He responded naturally to the ideas and techniques which the imagists had discovered in Japanese poetry, and the spirit of mild exoticism is never far from Stevens's own poetry, particularly in the early period. He liked the Chinese feeling for landscape–traditional, stylized, symbolic–and one can see, even in the titles, the affinity between many of Stevens's landscape poems–such as "The Evening Bell from a Distant Temple" and "Fine Weather after Storm at a Lonely Mountain Town"–and the seven traditional Chinese landscapes, which are meant to comprehend all landscapes.

Stevens could now see his undergraduate attempts at poetry in perspective, founded as they were upon antiquated English and American poetic models. Suddenly a whole new light was being shed on the art of poetry by the French symbolists, the impressionist painters, and the arts of China and Japan; and Stevens found his interest in writing poetry revitalized. In August of 1913 he wrote his wife: "I have, in fact, been trying to get together a little collection of verses again; and although they are simple to read, when they're done, it's a deuce of a job (for me) to do them. Keep all this a secret. There is something absurd about all this writing of verses; but the truth is, it elates me and satisfies me to do it."

In 1914 two such collections of his verses appeared in little magazines, Stevens's first published poems since his last undergraduate poems had appeared in the *Harvard Advocate* in 1900. The first of these comprises ten poems published in the *Trend,* eight poems in the September 1914 issue under the title "Carnet de Voyage" and "Two Poems" in the November issue. All but four of these poems definitely date from no later than 1909, and none of them can be considered as anything more than juvenilia. But that same November in Harriet Monroe's *Poetry: A Magazine of Verse* Stevens published another four poems, part of a sequence of eleven poems to be entitled "Phases." These poems were all recent work, based on the theme of the European war. None of these poems was ever reprinted during the poet's lifetime, but they are written in the modern idiom, and it is here that Stevens's mature work, leading up to *Harmonium* (1923), properly begins.

The years 1914 and 1915 saw the beginning of a new period of intense creativity for Stevens as a poet, as if the images, influences, and inchoate ideas of fifteen years suddenly merged and came into focus. Two of Stevens's great early poems, the first of any sustained length, were both published in 1915: "Peter Quince at the Clavier" (*Others,* August 1915) and "Sunday Morning" (*Poetry,* November 1915). With remarkable speed he worked through and resolved a number of problems that his new style posed for him. What seemed to his contemporaries as mere affectation and obscurity were for Stevens a way of escaping everything trite and vague that he now saw in the conventional nineteenth-century poetic diction. He sought a position that was both antirationalist and antirhetorical from which to grasp reality, things as they really are, and to put their essence into words. Stevens found inspiration for this effort in Stéphane Mallarmé and the other French symbolists, and company and encouragement in the imagist movement. Early in 1913 Pound published his anthology *Des Imagistes,* with samples of verse by James Joyce, H. D. (Hilda Doolittle), William Carlos Williams, F. S. Flint, Ford Madox Hueffer, and Amy Lowell among others, and in March of that year, in *Poetry,* Ezra Pound (in an article attributed to F. S. Flint) spelled out three rules for imagists: "1. Direct treatment of the 'thing,' whether subjective or objective. 2. To use absolutely no word that did not contribute to the presentation. 3. As regarding rhythm: to compose in sequence of the musical phrase, not in sequence of a metronome." This movement could not fail to have a strong and lasting influence on Stevens, but it did not take long for him to recognize the banality of mere images and to see the possibilities of such images as symbols of larger things. A good example of Stevens's expanded use of imagism is "Six Significant Landscapes" (first published in *Others,* March 1916). Essentially a sequence of six imagist poems, it incorporates as well Stevens's Orientalism, his color symbolism, his anti-rationalist posture, and his idea of the imagination, the image-making faculty, as a means of contact with a reality beneath the surface of things. In "Six Significant Landscapes" "significant" is the operative word.

Imagism appealed to the exotic and aesthetic tastes of Stevens, and nowhere is his subtle play of images over the surface of a profound reality more evident than in "Peter Quince at the Clavier," the aesthete's poem par excellence and one of Stevens's most beguiling creations. As the title suggests, the mood is comic, Peter Quince being, of course, one of the literal-minded mechanicals

in *A Midsummer Night's Dream.* The shape of the poem is that of a piece of baroque music, precisely balanced, decorated with trills and runs and harmonious rhymes, and its images are predominantly those of sound: cymbals, horns, tambourines, sighs, simperings, and other noises. The music of the clavier conjures up the story of Susanna and the Elders, a favorite subject of renaissance and baroque painters, and it is handled with an Oriental refinement of sensuality. The image of Susanna bathing, in her world of innocence and sensuous beauty, is no sooner evoked than it is shattered, when the "simpering Byzantines" shine the lamp of reason on Susanna and reveal her and her shame. The fourth stanza of the poem is a reflection and recapitulation. The poet reflects that "Beauty is momentary in the mind," like music, "But in the flesh it is immortal"–the reverse of conventional wisdom. Beauty in the mind is a sterile abstraction, a mere image, but when it is embodied in the physical, conjured up by the sounds of the clavier, rousing the lust of the Elders, it then partakes of the eternal cycle of things, like the seasons in nature, and "Susanna's music" survives in her memory, and the memory of her, and "makes a constant sacrament of praise," by being a mysterious ritual of the union of permanence and change and of the spiritual in the physical.

"Susanna's music," physical beauty as a sacrament of praise, as a substitute for the sacraments of religion, inspired Stevens's great poem of the *Götterdämmerung,* "Sunday Morning." While this poem is thoroughly archaic and nostalgic in its style, it departs from the nineteenth-century tradition of poems on faith and doubt in that it sees the modern world's loss of faith in Christianity as no different from the loss of faith in Zeus, neither more nor less certain, neither more nor less calamitous. In his "Adagia" Stevens says, "The death of one god is the death of all." This is not to say that the death of God is not calamitous: it is the very calamitousness that gives "Sunday Morning" its profoundly elegiac tone.

The poem opens with a woman in a peignoir in a vivid scene full of color and light, scent and taste, warmth and freedom, and natural beauty: "Coffee and oranges in a sunny chair,/ And the green freedom of a cockatoo/Upon a rug." But the woman cannot accept this beauty, because "she feels the dark/Encroachment of that old catastrophe," which is the old religion, whereby "The pungent oranges and bright, green wings/Seem things in some procession of the dead," because religion posits truth and beauty in the permanence of a supernatural world rather than in the ever-changing, ever-dying natural world where we live.

In stanzas 2 and 3 the meditative voice of the poet takes over. In a tentative, questioning way he develops his idea that the woman could find the same divinity within herself, that the things of earth are to be cherished in their state of constant flux, and that the break with the confinements of supernatural religion would be a liberation to her: "These are the measures destined for her soul." He sets Christianity in the larger context of man's history of mythmaking by comparing it to the worship of Jove, which is certainly dead. In the inevitable evolution of things men will see Christianity in the same light, and then earth shall "Seem all of paradise that we shall know."

Stanzas 4 and 5 each begin with a statement by the woman, followed by a meditation on the part of the poet as an answer to her. "She says, 'But in contentment I still feel/The need of some imperishable bliss.'" The poet replies directly that "Death is the mother of beauty." The only imperishable bliss is in the cycles of nature, in the woman's memory, and in her desire for a profounder contact with nature. This idea is developed further in stanzas 7 and 8: the paradise of religion is seen as a colorless inhuman dream world, where rivers never reach the sea and ripe fruit never falls from the trees. By contrast the earth itself can be a source of bliss to those who recognize its permanence in changefulness, represented by the sun: "Their chant shall be a chant of paradise," and "They shall know well the heavenly fellowship/Of men that perish and of summer morn." Men will find themselves liberated, even glorified, in their new unbelief. As Stevens said in his essay "Two or Three Ideas" (in *The Necessary Angel*, 1951): "in an age of disbelief, when the gods have come to an end, when we think of them as the aesthetic projections of a time that has passed, men turn to a fundamental glory of their own and from that create a style of bearing themselves in reality. They create a new style of a new bearing in a new reality."

In the final stanza of "Sunday Morning" the poet brings the reader back from this tentative myth of an earthly paradise to the uncertain situation of the present. A voice from nowhere enters the poem and tells the woman that "The Tomb in Palestine/Is not the porch of spirits lingering./It is the grave of Jesus, where he lay." This procla-

mation removes Jesus from the realm of spirits, who do not change, and returns him to the realm of men, who do. It does not deny his immortality so much as to deny his transcendence over the world of change. Now he is as immortal as we are, neither more nor less, a member of "the heavenly fellowship/Of men that perish." And so the poem ends as a kind of hymn to Mutability, to Death as the mystical mother of Beauty.

As A. Walton Litz observes in his *Introspective Voyager* (1972), "Sunday Morning" stands alone, different in both language and mood from the poems around it, like "an orphan in the larger context of *Harmonium*, and in the entire canon of Stevens' poetry," and it "belongs not to a personal tradition but to the major line of meditative religious verse, and we learn to read it by reading traditional English poetry, not by reading Wallace Stevens." Furthermore, he adds, "Sunday Morning" differs markedly from Stevens's later long poems in that he does not attempt to substitute any theory of the imagination or of poetry for the lost certainties of religion, and "by remaining skeptical and open the poem connects with the widest range of our personal and cultural experience." "Sunday Morning" has remained one of Stevens's most popular and widely anthologized poems.

In 1916, when the Stevenses moved to Hartford, Wallace Stevens kept up with his Greenwich Village literary friends, visiting them and attending their parties on his frequent trips to New York. They often found him shy, diffident, or aloof, but always agreeable and personally formidable, someone to be reckoned with. Even after the publication of his first book, *Harmonium*, in 1923, many literary people did not see Stevens as an outstanding poet but as merely one of many young modernist poets, most of whom are now totally forgotten. Because he was an insurance lawyer and not a professional man of letters, many people considered him a cultured dilettante and not a dedicated poet at all, but nothing could be further from the truth. Between mid 1916 and the end of 1917 he published about a poem a month in various little magazines, and by 1923 he had published nearly a hundred poems in less than ten years.

One of the New York activities that continued to interest Stevens, even after the move to Hartford, was the theater. A "new theater" had sprung up in New York, radically innovative, modernist, symbolist, and avant-garde, inspired by William Butler Yeats, Gordon Craig, and the Japa-

Cathedrals are not built along the sea;
The tender bells would jangle on the hoar
And iron winds; the graceful turrets roar
With bitter storms the long night angrily;
And through the precious organ pipes would be
A low and constant murmur of the shore
That down these golden shafts would madly pour
A mighty and a lasting melody.

And those who knelt within the gilded stalls
Would have vast outlook for their weary eyes;
There, they would see high shadows on the walls
From passing vessels in their fall and rise.
Through gaudy windows there would come too soon
The low and splendid rising of the moon.

Manuscript for a sonnet that, after its appearance in the May 1899 issue of Harvard Monthly, *provoked Stevens's mentor George Santayana to respond with a sonnet titled "Cathedral by the Sea" (by permission of the Henry E. Huntington Library and Art Gallery)*

nese Nō theater, among others. Stevens wrote three plays for this new theater. His first, *Three Travellers Watch a Sunrise,* was awarded the Players' Producing Company prize in May of 1916 for the best one-act play in verse and was published in *Poetry* in July of the same year, but it was not produced until 1920. His two other plays, written for the Wisconsin Players in New York, were each performed only once, in October of 1917. *Carlos among the Candles* was published in *Poetry* the following December, but *Bowl, Cat and Broomstick* was not published in its entirety until 1969, when it appeared in the *Quarterly Review of Literature.* All three plays, being poetic rather than dramatic, were not successful on the stage, and Stevens soon lost interest in writing for the theater. "I gave up writing plays," he wrote years later, "because I had much less interest in dramatic poetry than elegiac poetry." Yet the plays are of interest. They are virtually without characters or action, but they are rich in ritual and symbol and full of witty language and aesthetic posturing. Carlos, the only figure in *Carlos among the Candles,* is "an eccentric pedant of about forty" and clearly an ironic persona for Stevens himself, who was soon to be forty when the play was written. "He speaks in a lively manner," the stage directions prescribe, "but is over-nice in sounding his words." Carlos pirouettes about the stage, flourishing a taper, lighting candles and blowing them out again, and with each candle he comments in an affected way upon the subtle feelings it inspires in him: "It is like ten green sparks of a rocket, oscillating in air," for example; or "It is like the diverging angles that follow nine leaves drifting in water, and that compose themselves brilliantly on the polished surface." Carlos is a dandy and clearly close kin to the excitable and dandified forty-year-old mock hero of "Le Monocle de Mon Oncle," which Stevens wrote the following year and published in the December 1918 issue of *Others.*

In the framework of *Harmonium,* "Le Monocle de Mon Oncle" is the perfect counterpart to "Sunday Morning." They are of roughly the same length, and both are set off in regular numbered stanzas, but, where "Sunday Morning" is an elegiac meditation, "Le Monocle de Mon Oncle" is high comedy. Witty and urbane, elegant and extravagant, it represents the pinnacle of Stevens's poetic virtuosity in his early manner. It is a monologue in the voice of "an eccentric pedant of about forty," a mercurial Pierrot figure, on the theme of love, language, and the "faith of

forty." As an example of the influence of Jules Laforgue the poem has often been compared to T. S. Eliot's "The Love Song of J. Alfred Prufrock" (1917), and the hero of Stevens's poem is much like Prufrock but more of a dandy and a poet and less anxious, less downcast and disillusioned. Indeed he seems almost gay compared to Prufrock.

"Le Monocle de Mon Oncle" is a kaleidoscope of ironies and reversals, whimsies and mock sentiments. It teeters coyly between youth and old age, spring and autumn, melodrama and farce, the spiritual and the sexual, the sublime and the ridiculous. It is addressed vaguely to Love, which is everything from the "Mother of Heaven" to the "verve of earth," Eve and Venus, a loved-one or a lover, and, in a more extended sense, love as that saving contact with the reality inherent in things, which Stevens always associated with art and language and the power of the imagination. Language as the vehicle of love is as much the subject of this poem as any kind of attachment of one person for another. Hence the verbal fireworks: "Most venerable heart, the lustiest conceit/Is not too lusty for your broadening./I quiz all sounds, all thoughts, all everything/For the music and manner of the paladins/To make oblation fit. Where shall I find/Bravura adequate to this great hymn?" The religious language in this stanza and throughout "Le Monocle de Mon Oncle" is never wholly ironic, and the great love in the poem would in a conventionally religious poet be called the love of God. The witty language is reminiscent of the verbal wrestling with faith and doubt in the religious poetry of the metaphysical poets of the seventeenth century, while the language of "Sunday Morning" is closer to that of William Wordsworth and Matthew Arnold. The poet-voice in "Le Monocle de Mon Oncle" explicitly distinguishes himself from those "fops of fancy" who "in their poems leave/Memorabilia of the mystic spouts,/Spontaneously watering their gritty soils." He says, "I know no magic trees, no balmy boughs,/No silver-ruddy, gold-vermilion fruits." His love, that is, is not to be confused with the mystical madness of William Blake, nor with the fairy supernaturalism of Yeats, nor with the Christianity of Gerard Manley Hopkins. In the final stanza he says he is like a rabbi, a dark rabbi, when young, observing the nature of mankind, and "Like a rose rabbi, later, I pursued,/And still pursue, the origin and course/Of love, but until now I never knew/That fluttering things have so distinct a shade." "The figure of the rabbi," Stevens wrote later, "has always been an exceedingly attractive one to me because it is the figure of a man devoted in the extreme to scholarship and at the same time to making some use of it for human purposes." While the character in the poem is, as Stevens said he had in mind, "simply a man fairly well along in life, looking back and talking in a more or less personal way about life," this "looking back and talking" is no idle reminiscence but an attempt to make some sense of his experience of forty years, of the new perspective on "the origin and course of love" that approaching age offers, and to make "some use of it for human purposes." The "looking back and talking" is nothing less than poetry, its source and substance; "the poet," Stevens wrote in his "Adagia," "is the priest of the invisible," and "God is a symbol for something that can as well take other forms, as, for example, the form of high poetry." The final stanza of "Le Monocle de Mon Oncle," like the final stanza of "Sunday Morning," brings the reader back to the ambiguity and uncertainty of the present situation, and the "fluttering things" which "have so distinct a shade" are not unlike the "casual flocks of pigeons" that "make/Ambiguous undulations as they sink,/Downward to darkness, on extended wings." The stoic resolution of the two poems is the same–that reality is to be found in the changefulness of things–but the tone of the two poems is so different they might almost be seen as mirror images of one another.

If "Sunday Morning" and "Le Monocle de Mon Oncle" are the side panels in the triptych of *Harmonium,* framed by the gilt and gems of the shorter poems, the centerpiece is "The Comedian as the Letter C." This first of Stevens's many long poems he wrote in 1922, at the time he was working with great doubt and dissatisfaction to put together his first volume of poetry, and it is a summary and recapitulation of his poetic career to date, together with a tentative prognosis for the future. He wrote it at about the same time that T. S. Eliot was writing *The Waste Land* (1922), and there are many similarities between the two poems–their autobiographical foundations and their moods of irony, wistfulness, and revulsion–but Stevens's poem is cast in the form of a picaresque narrative in the mock heroic vein, and its hero is himself a comedian.

Crispin as a character had his origins in the commedia dell'arte and made numerous appearances in various guises in the French theater of the seventeenth and eighteenth centuries. He is a

valet, a saint, a jack-of-all-trades, a musician, a pedant, a knave, and a notorious poetaster. "The Comedian as the Letter C" is the story of his odyssey from Bordeaux to the Yucatan and eventually to Carolina, where he settles down and raises a family. Subsumed in this narrative are the story of European poetic traditions transplanted in America, the story of Stevens's poetic development up to 1922, and the story of an introspective Everyman in search of some adequate position vis-à-vis the outside world and the life around him. Stevens wrote later of this poem, "The long and short of it is simply that I deliberately took the sort of life that millions of people live, without embellishing it except by the embellishments in which I was interested at the moment: words and sounds." He also said, "I suppose that I ought to confess that by the letter C I meant the sound of the letter C; what was in my mind was to play on that sound throughout the poem. While the sound of that letter has more or less variety, and includes, for instance, K and S, all its shades may be said to have a comic aspect. Consequently, the letter C is a comedian." Indeed, at a profound level it is language that is the hero of this poem. Much of the comedy of the piece arises from the contrast, as Stevens pointed out, between "the every-day plainness of the central figure and the plush, so to speak, of his stage."

In part 1 Crispin, an ordinary man and a jumble of conflicting identities that he has received from outside himself, like an actor, sets out on a sea voyage in pursuit of an adequate "mythology of self." He leaves behind him the conventional late romantic poetry and thought of the nineteenth century, "that century of wind," "a wordy, watery age," symbolized by the figure of Triton, a myth from which all true belief has vanished, leaving only "memorial gestures." He seeks a substitute myth within himself–"Crispin/became an introspective voyager"–and in the sea he finds a salty, wild, formless, inscrutable reality on which to project his new myth, "the veritable ding an sich, at last." "The last distortion of Romance/Forsook the insatiable egotist," and he finds all his old theatrical ruses "shattered by the large."

In part 2 Crispin arrives in Yucatan, only to be confronted by "the Maya sonneteers" and their poetic conventions, more inflated and more vulgar than those from which he fled. "But Crispin was too destitute to find/In any commonplace the sought-for aid./He was a man made

Elsie Stevens, circa 1916 (courtesy of Holly Stevens and the Henry E. Huntington Library and Art Gallery)

vivid by the sea." What he does find to his liking in Yucatan, however, is a new material for poetry that is rich and ripe and brightly colored, lavish and extravagant. "The fabulous and its intrinsic verse/Came like two spirits parleying, adorned/In radiance from the Atlantic coign,/For Crispin and his quill to catechize." He lets himself go, to the point where he is in danger of turning Dadaist, of finding "a new reality in parrot-squawks," and he is chastened only by a sudden thunderstorm, which is as frightening as the fauna and flora had been seductive. Here is yet another new experience. Perhaps here is "the span/Of force, the quintessential fact, the note/Of Vulcan, that a valet seeks to own." Crispin is "studious of a self possessing him," like a comedian studying a new role.

Crispin leaves the Yucatan, in part 3, to escape the "jostling festival" of the jungle and to seek a new austerity in a northern climate, where "The myrtle, if the myrtle ever bloomed,/Was like a glacial pink upon the air." "How many poems he denied himself/In his observant prog-

ress," like Stevens the young man. First he thinks, "Perhaps the Arctic moonlight really gave/The liaison, the blissful liaison,/Between himself and his environment," but directly that seems "Wrong as a divagation to Peking,/To him that postulated as his theme/The vulgar." Then Crispin thinks perhaps it is in the tension between the two elements, reality and the imagination, that the blissful liaison is to be found, and presently he finds himself going up a river in Carolina–a country somewhere between the arctic and the tropics–surrounded by spring and human activity and "all the arrant stinks/That helped him round his rude aesthetic out."

Beginning with part 4 the poem falls somewhat in intensity, because the autobiographical allegory comes to an end, and Stevens proceeds to speculate about his own, and Crispin's, future. The poem begins with the note: "man is the intelligence of his soil," but Crispin the romantic has become a realist, having "gripped more closely the essential prose/As being, in a world so falsified, /The one integrity for him, . . ./To which all poems were incident," and so now he turns around and states that "his soil is man's intelligence." Crispin settles down and founds a colony. He expands his new philosophy into the social sphere and establishes a reign of realism, celebrating the trivial and quotidian. But, by expanding his ego into an entire colony, Crispin has become an old windbag. Now his "Commingled souvenirs and prophecies," "These bland excursions into time to come,/Related in Romance to backward flights,/However prodigal, however proud,/Contained in their afflatus the reproach/That first drove Crispin to his wandering." He declares that "All dreams are vexing. Let them be expunged."

In part 5 Crispin is discontented and rebellious, but ever contemptuous of "fugal requiems," of "a tragedian's testament," of projecting his own fate upon all men, because "For realist, what is is what should be." Enter "his duenna" to the rescue, who, like a fairy godmother, "brought/Her prismy blonde and clapped her in his hands." Now he is married and content, like Candide, to tend his own garden. Exit poetry. The quotidian, he finds, saps the philosopher out of a man, but "For all it takes it gives a humped return,/Exchequering from piebald fiscs unkeyed." This last line was Stevens's own favorite example of *C* as a comic letter, and it serves equally well as an example of the plush of the stage upstaging Crispin, precisely at the point where he abjures the world of art for the world of facts.

Instead of producing poems Crispin produces daughters, four of them, in part 6, where the comedy takes on a riotous and slightly cruel aspect. Crispin, in his "return to social nature," suddenly finds his house overrun by "children nibbling at the sugared void," these "unbraided femes,/Green crammers of the green fruits of the world." There is a decided decline from the first daughter, "His goldenest demoiselle," who seems like an inhabitant "of a country of the capuchins,/So delicately blushed, so humbly eyed," to the fourth, who is "Mere blusteriness that gewgaws jollified,/All din and gobble, blasphemously pink." When they grow up their love lives look distinctly sordid. Worst of all, one of them becomes "A pearly poetess, peaked for rhapsody." Crispin feels the same ambivalence toward his daughters that he felt toward the tropics. The poem ends at this point, without any resolution, but with a question: considering the daughters as poems, Crispin cannot know whether they are "Seraphic proclamations of the pure/Delivered with a deluging

onwardness," or mere "after-shining flicks,/Illuminating, from a fancy gorged/By apparition, plain and common things,/... proving what he proves/Is nothing." What, then, speaking of the relationship between the poet and his poems, "can all this matter since/The relation comes, benignly, to its end?" Perhaps these are understandable sentiments from a middle-aged businessman about to publish his first volume of poetry. The only answer he has to this question, which is not really an answer, is, "So may the relation of each man be clipped." And with that the poem is clipped.

Harmonium was published by Alfred A. Knopf in September of 1923, in an edition of fifteen hundred copies, and to celebrate the event Stevens took his wife the following month on a cruise to California via Havana and the Panama Canal, returning overland through New Mexico—their first extended vacation since their marriage in 1909. The sea and clouds in the Gulf of Tehuantepec occasioned one of Stevens's most beguiling poems, "Sea Surface Full of Clouds," which was first published in the July 1924 issue of the *Dial*. This poem, lush, meditative, and imagistic, full of color symbolism and ritualized repetition, has an undeniable power of enchantment, but in the final analysis it does not fulfill one's expectations. There is at the heart of the poem a vacuity, as if the poet strove with verbal pyrotechnics to excite an exhausted imagination. After writing it Stevens virtually gave up writing poetry for nearly a decade. His book received very little notice. In 1924 his first and only child was born, and the house grew noisy. "She babbles and plays with her hands and smiles like an angel," he wrote to Harriet Monroe. "Such experiences are a terrible blow to poor literature. And then there's the radio to blame, too." He devoted his energy to his work at the insurance company, and—"haphazard denouement"—he fell out of the habit of writing poetry. He wrote later that "One of the essential conditions to the writing of poetry is impetus. That is the reason for thinking that to be a poet at all one ought to be a poet constantly. . . . Writing poetry is a conscious activity. While poems may very well occur, they had much better be caused." Stevens found himself in the same dilemma where he had left Crispin, unable to reconcile the world of the imagination to the exigencies of reality, and sapped by the quotidian—"now this thing and now that/Confined him, while it cosseted, condoned." When Knopf proposed a new expanded edition of *Harmonium* in 1931, Stevens had only fourteen poems to add, and all of them, with the exception of "Sea Surface Full of Clouds" and possibly three others, had been written before 1923.

"Thought tends to collect in pools," Stevens wrote in his "Adagia," and "It is not every day that the world arranges itself in a poem." When he did return seriously to writing, sometime in 1933, the new poems witness a remarkable advance in thought and feeling. Gone are the coruscating gauds of *Harmonium,* and in their place is a calmer and surer, if barer, diction. "A change of style is a change of subject," as one of the "Adagia" has it, and with this new diction came a new attitude on the part of the poet in his relationship to the world, to the absence of God and the inevitability of death, a new firmness and resolution, as indicated in the title of his next volume of poems, *Ideas of Order,* which was published in a limited edition by the Alcestis Press in 1935 and, with three new poems, by Knopf the following year.

The tone of the new volume is set by the opening poem in the Knopf edition, "Farewell to Florida," which was in fact the last written, too late to appear in the Alcestis Press edition. The poet renounces the tropical moon: "The moon/Is at the mast-head and the past is dead./Her mind will never speak to me again." He renounces the heat and color of the South, the "coraline sea" and "vivid blooms," to return to the North that is "leafless and lies in a wintry slime/Both of men and clouds. . . . To be free again, to return to the violent mind/That is their mind, these men, and that will bind/Me round." It is as if Crispin were once again leaving the squawking parrots and thunderstorms of Yucatan in search of "the blissful liaison,/Between himself and his environment," and "America was always north to him." Wallace Stevens is seeking in the poems of *Ideas of Order* to work beyond the impasse where he left Crispin in Carolina. There is certainly some success in his endeavor, and Stevens's own judgment on the volume was "that *Harmonium* was a better book than *Ideas of Order,* notwithstanding the fact that *Ideas of Order* probably contains a small group of poems better than anything in *Harmonium.*"

The poem in *Ideas of Order* most notable for its coldness and bleakness is "Like Decorations in a Nigger Cemetery." The title, Stevens said, "refers to the litter that one usually finds in a nigger cemetery and is a phrase used by Judge Powell last winter in Key West." He wrote in the

same letter, to Morton Zabel of *Poetry* magazine: "It is very difficult for me to find the time to write poetry, and most of these have been written on the way to and from the office." The fifty separate parts of this poem are more like fifty individual poems, poetic *pensées,* jottings, images, focused on a central theme and arranged very loosely along the variations of that theme, much as Stevens customarily arranged the poems within any one volume. That theme is the autumn of middle age, the prospect of death, the absence of God, and the increasing chaos of the outside world. The poet insists upon these hard realities but stops short of despair in favor of a salvation to be found in the play between the private imagination and the realities of the present moment. There he finds meaning and order. Stanza 3 might be taken as a characteristic statement of the theme: "It was when the trees were leafless first in November/And their blackness became apparent, that one first/Knew the eccentric to be the base of design." Some of the stanzas are more imagistic, more haikulike, than others, but on the whole they are more abstract than similar earlier exercises, such as "Thirteen Ways of Looking at a Blackbird," and some of them are utterly obscure, like the cryptic notes one might write to oneself on the way to the office.

By far the best-known poem in *Ideas of Order* is "The Idea of Order in Key West." It is set once again in Florida, but the tropics now are transformed by a new coolness and clarity. The tone of this poem is elegiac, like that of "Sunday Morning," and the language is simplicity itself. The theme is again the emergence of order out of chaos in the creation of a work of art, as a result of the poetic imagination responding to an outside reality. A girl is walking along the beach, singing of the sea, but she does not express the genius of the sea: "She sang beyond the genius of the sea." The sea is inchoate and inarticulate reality. "It may be that in all her phrases stirred/The grinding water and the gasping wind;/But it was she and not the sea we heard." She masters, orders, and renders meaningful "The meaningless plungings of water and the wind," "And when she sang, the sea,/Whatever self it had, became the self/That was her song, for she was the maker." As a result of hearing the girl's song, the poet and his companion, Ramon Fernandez, are left with a heightened sense of beauty and order in what they see around them. They are inspired by the "Blessed rage for order," which is the impetus behind all art. The poem amounts to no less than an apology for the artifice of art and a justification of Stevens's idea of a romantic realism: an expressiveness not of the physical world but of the imagination in contact with that world, the "blissful liaison." He wrote in his "Adagia" that "Reality is the spirit's true center," and "The ultimate value is reality," while at the same time "Realism is a corruption of reality."

After the publication of *Ideas of Order* Stevens became gradually better known as a poet, but the notices his books received were far from unanimously favorable. Critics such as Stanley Burnshaw and Geoffrey Grigson found much to object to in the dandified virtuosity of *Harmonium* and the serene aestheticism of *Ideas of Order,* in view of the hard realities of a world sunken in depression and threatened by the rise of fascism and the prospects of war. Stevens was shocked and offended by this criticism, feeling that his work spoke as strongly in favor of peace and order in the world as that of the leftist propagandists, and perhaps more eloquently. But the fact cannot be ignored that in the 1930s the Stevenses lived a life that was more than a little remote from poverty and social chaos. In 1932 they bought a very large, new, "colonial" house on a half-acre lot on Westerly Terrace in Hartford, and that same year Stevens could write to a friend that "Generally speaking, there seems to be a feeling in Hartford that things are going to grow better rather than worse." In 1934 he became a vice-president of the Hartford Accident and Indemnity Company, thereby securing firmly his position in the business world. As for his politics very little can be said, as he seems not to have had any strongly held or consistent political views. He was briefly an admirer of Mussolini, as were many other people, and he was by profession a capitalist, but it would be a gross distortion to attribute any fascist sympathies to his life or work. On the contrary, he could only be called a laissez-faire capitalist in the realm of art and the imagination, passionately a champion of individuality, freedom, and spontaneity, and disdainful of ideologies, regimentation, and vulgar materialism. Stevens did not turn a blind eye to the suffering in the world around him, but it cannot be denied that, like many artists, he was more self-absorbed than other men. In his "Adagia" he wrote, "Life is not people and scene but thought and feeling," and "The world is myself. Life is myself." For the Knopf edition of *Ideas of Order* Stevens confronted his critics directly with a little manifesto on the dust jacket, in

which he said, "The book is essentially a book of pure poetry. I believe that, in any society, the poet should be the exponent of the imagination of that society. *Ideas of Order* attempts to illustrate the role of the imagination in life, and particularly the role of the imagination in life at present. The more realistic life may be, the more it needs the stimulus of the imagination." For Stevens pure poetry served a social function by its very purity. In his "Adagia" he wrote: "Poetry is a purging of the world's poverty and change and evil and death. It is a present perfecting, a satisfaction in the irremediable poverty of life." And in "Mozart, 1935" he addressed the poet at the keyboard: "Be thou that wintry sound/As of the great wind howling,/By which sorrow is released,/Dismissed, absolved/In a starry placating."

But Stevens could not comfortably leave the question there. He seems to have been seriously concerned with the true relationship of a private introspective poet and the world of politics and society, and seriously dismayed by the criticism of himself as an irrelevant aesthete. He set about immediately to write a sequence of five poems on this theme, each of them centered around the image of a statue standing in a public place. The statue functions generally as a symbol for art, "but not specifically a symbol for art," he wrote to Ronald Latimer; "its use has been somewhat broadened and, so far as I have defined it at all, it is a symbol for things as they are." Various characters appear in the poems, and each is defined by his particular relationship to the statue. The first of these poems, "The Old Woman and the Statue," was published in the Summer 1935 issue of the *Southern Review,* and the five together were published as *Owl's Clover* by Latimer's Alcestis Press in August of 1936. They are among the weakest of all Stevens's poems, written as they are in long verse paragraphs, full of loose syntax and flaccid rhetoric, utterly unlike the tight little stanzas in which he excelled. Stevens was immediately dissatisfied with *Owl's Clover* and began at once to cut whole sections out of it before including it the following year in *The Man with the Blue Guitar & Other Poems.* He eliminated it altogether from *The Collected Poems of Wallace Stevens* (1954), and the full Alcestis Press version was republished only in *Opus Posthumous* (1957).

The principal interest *Owl's Clover* has for readers today is as a contrast to "The Man with the Blue Guitar." On the dust jacket of *The Man with the Blue Guitar & Other Poems* Stevens once again stated his intentions, this time drawing a dis-

Wallace Stevens, circa 1922 (courtesy of Holly Stevens and the Henry E. Huntington Library and Art Gallery)

tinction between *Owl's Clover* and the new poems: "The effect of *Owl's Clover* is to emphasize the opposition between things as they are and things imagined; in short, to isolate poetry.... This group deals with the incessant conjunctions between things as they are and things imagined. Although the blue guitar is a symbol of the imagination, it is used most often simply as a reference to the individuality of the poet, meaning by the poet any man of imagination."

The contrast in style between *Owl's Clover* and "The Man with the Blue Guitar" is even greater than the contrast in theme. "The Man with the Blue Guitar" consists of thirty-three separate exercises, variations on a central theme, written in tetrameter couplets, varying in length

from four to eight couplets. The couplets are bright and musical, and the poems together move in a rhythm that is more musical than rhetorical. Within the poems there is a remarkable subtlety and playfulness, reflecting the play between reality and the imagination that Stevens is espousing. Both are "fluttering things" with "so distinct a shade," always changing and renewing one another. In poem 32, for example, the poet says, "Nothing must stand/Between you and the shapes you take/When the crust of shape has been destroyed./You as you are? You are yourself./ The blue guitar surprises you." Stevens sought most of all to avoid or to destroy that "crust of shape," whatever makes things static and dull and two-dimensional, be it religious conformity or social engineering or the poetics of literal-minded realism. In his "Adagia" he said, "Life is the elimination of what is dead."

Once Wallace Stevens had returned from the detour of *Owl's Clover* to the central path of his poetry in "The Man with the Blue Guitar," he seems to have discovered anew the "impetus" that is "one of the essential conditions to the writing of poetry," never to lose it again for the rest of his life. Between 1937 and 1942 he wrote all the poems that make up *Parts of a World,* which was published by Knopf in September of 1942, as well as what may be his greatest long poem, *Notes toward a Supreme Fiction,* which was published the following month in a limited edition by the Cummington Press and included five years later in *Transport to Summer* (1947). Many of the poems of this period display an increasing concentration on the theme of Stevens's poetic theory, leading up to the definitive poetic statement of that theory in *Notes toward a Supreme Fiction.* As a prelude to that poem it may be useful first to look briefly at some of Stevens's prose works, in which he develops some of his ideas about poetry. The most important of his essays were written as public lectures and published in *The Necessary Angel* (1951), and the later lectures together with miscellaneous notes and reviews were included in the *Opus Posthumous* (1957).

The seven essays that Stevens collected in *The Necessary Angel,* which bears the subtitle *Essays on Reality and the Imagination,* were intended, he wrote in the introduction, "to disclose definitions of poetry" and "to be contributions to the theory of poetry and it is this and this alone that binds them together." "Obviously, they are not," he added, "the carefully organized notes of systematic study." Neither the book as a whole nor

Wallace Stevens with his daughter, Holly, circa 1925 (photo by Katherine Lee Endero; courtesy of the Henry E. Huntington Library and Art Gallery)

any of its parts can be understood as a philosophical investigation into metaphysics or aesthetics. On the contrary, the essays are more like prose poems or meditations on the theory of poetry. Most of Stevens's central ideas are to be found here, worked and reworked through an exuberance of images, quotations, and allusions, and served up in a form scarcely more straightforward than in the poems themselves. In "The Noble Rider and the Sound of Words," a lecture written during World War II and delivered in spring 1941, when "the pressure of reality"–that is, "the pressure of an external event or events on the consciousness to the exclusion of any power of contemplation"–was burdensome and the ignobility of so many things was painfully evident, Stevens wrote that nobility "is the imagination pressing back against the pressure of reality. It seems, in the last analysis, to have something to do with our self-preservation; and that, no doubt, is why the expression of it, the sound of

its words, helps us to live our lives." "The Figure of the Youth as Virile Poet," a lecture delivered in summer 1943, can be read as a manifesto for the autonomy of the individual imagination as the only saving grace in a world of cold logic and poor facts. In "Three Academic Pieces," published separately in 1947, Stevens argued that the resemblances between things, which are perceived by the imagination, are a significant component of the structure of reality and added, "Poetry is a satisfying of the desire for resemblance. As the mere satisfying of a desire, it is pleasurable. But poetry if it did nothing but satisfy a desire would not rise above the level of many lesser things. Its singularity is that in the act of satisfying the desire for resemblance it touches the sense of reality, it enhances the sense of reality, heightens it, intensifies it. . . . It makes it brilliant." In "Imagination as Value," a lecture delivered in 1948, Stevens wrote: "The imagination is the power of the mind over the possibilities of things; . . . the imagination is the power that enables us to perceive the normal in the abnormal, the opposite of chaos in chaos"; and "the chief problems of any artist, as of any man, are the problems of the normal and . . . he needs, in order to solve them, everything that the imagination has to give." In "The Relations between Poetry and Painting," separately published in 1951, he wrote: "The paramount relation between poetry and painting today, between modern man and modern art is simply this: that in an age in which disbelief is so profoundly prevalent or, if not disbelief, indifference to questions of belief, poetry and painting, and the arts in general, are, in their measure, a compensation for what has been lost." He wrote in his "Adagia," "After one has abandoned a belief in God, poetry is that essence which takes its place as life's redemption." Few poets can ever have taken poetry so seriously. It is this faith in poetry, the embodiment of the imagination, as a means of salvation in a fallen world that informs *Notes toward a Supreme Fiction* and all of Stevens's subsequent poems.

Notes toward a Supreme Fiction is, like most of Stevens's long poems, a sequence of interrelated short poems, a perfect union of his lyric gift and his powers of sustained thought and feeling. It is a philosophical meditation somewhat in the manner of Wordsworth's *The Prelude* (1850), "a philosophical Poem, containing views of Man, Nature, and Society," as Wordsworth put it, and the views that Stevens's poem expresses on the equal and inseparable validity of objective reality and the individual imagination are surprisingly close to those developed originally by Wordsworth and Coleridge, who first established the position of the poet in an unstable and hostile world. In a 1940 letter Stevens wrote: "If one no longer believes in God (as truth), it is not possible merely to disbelieve; it becomes necessary to believe in something else. Logically, I ought to believe in essential imagination, but that has its difficulties. It is easier to believe in a thing created by the imagination." In "Asides on the Oboe," he added, "I say that one's final belief must be in a fiction. I think that the history of belief will show that it has always been in a fiction. Yet the statement seems a negation, or, rather, a paradox." That paradox is summed up in one of his "Adagia": "The final belief is to believe in a fiction, which you know to be a fiction, there being nothing else. The exquisite truth is to know that it is a fiction and that you believe in it willingly." This exquisite truth proceeds from the marriage of reality and the imagination, and such is the central theme of *Notes toward a Supreme Fiction.*

The long poem consists of thirty shorter poems, three sets of ten, plus a short prologue and a coda. The first section, "It Must Be Abstract," emphasizes the poet's belief that the supreme fiction is less a substitution of poetry for religion than a dissolution of the distinction between the two. It is not a new cultus, because it is abstract, that is, utterly mysterious, defying definition. Only a fiction that cannot be contained will continue to satisfy the powers of men's minds. In the second section, "It Must Change," Stevens returns to the theme of "Sunday Morning," that the vision of a changeless reality is insipid, that poetry must "give a sense of the freshness or vividness of life." Poem 8, one of the wedding poems, says: "Then Ozymandias said the spouse, the bride/Is never naked. A fictive covering/Weaves always glistening from the heart and mind." Likewise Stevens takes his readers back to the dazzling language of *Harmonium* in this section to give them a taste of the volatility and playfulness in his philosophical argument, "To compound the imagination's Latin with/The lingua franca et jocundissima." In the third section, "It Must Give Pleasure," Stevens develops one of his deepest convictions, that "the purpose of poetry is to contribute to man's happiness," and be "a present perfecting, a satisfaction in the irremediable poverty of life." Pleasure, peace, order, and beauty are all attributes of the supreme fiction. It is important to remember, as is

clear from the coda, that *Notes toward a Supreme Fiction* is a war poem, perhaps the greatest poem to come out of World War II. The pursuit of a supreme fiction is anything but an exercise in idle aestheticism. "It is a war that never ends," Stevens says; it is the pursuit of a sustaining faith: "How gladly with proper words the soldier dies,/ If he must, or lives on the bread of faithful speech." It is the function of the poet to supply the "proper words" and the "faithful speech."

Although *Notes toward a Supreme Fiction* was published in a limited edition by the Cummington Press in October of 1942, the month after *Parts of a World* appeared, it was not available in a trade volume until it was included in *Transport to Summer* in 1947. There its placement at the end of that volume is somewhat misleading as to the chronology of the writing, but significant in that it emphasizes the absolute centrality of *Notes toward a Supreme Fiction* in the later poetry of Stevens. Stevens himself recognized its crucial place in his poetry and saw in it the governing idea of his life as a poet: the idea of a fiction that takes on the power to compel belief from the power of the poet's words in expressing it. But *Notes toward a Supreme Fiction* was not intended as a definitive statement of that idea. Stevens wrote to Henry Church, to whom the poem is dedicated: "It is only when you try to systematize the poems in *Notes* that you conclude that it is not the statement of a philosophic theory. A philosopher is never at rest unless he is systematizing; constructing a theory. But these are Notes; the nucleus of the matter is contained in the title. It is implicit in the title that there can be such a thing as a supreme fiction." All of Stevens's poems written after 1942 can be seen as further notes toward the same one supreme fiction, which contains diversity in its unity. There were to be no new themes, only new notes. To another friend Stevens wrote: "As I see the subject, it could occupy a school of rabbis for the next few generations. In trying to create something as valid as the idea of God has been, and for that matter remains, the first necessity seems to be breadth." The idea of a supreme fiction has the advantage of breadth, enough breadth that it could embrace every subject and every form of his subsequent poetry. In the same letter to Church Stevens said: "I have no idea of the form that a supreme fiction would take. The *Notes* start out with the idea that it would not take any form: that it would be abstract. Of course, in the long run, poetry would be the supreme fiction; the essence of poetry is change and the essence of change is that it gives pleasure." While Stevens recognized the firm foundation that *Notes toward a Supreme Fiction* provided him, he could not rest upon his achievement in that poem, because it is of the nature of the supreme fiction to require more notes, more poetry, more change, more pleasure. Far from resting on his laurels, Stevens as an old man produced an enormous amount of poetry of the highest quality, with a remarkable energy and consistency, with a new clarity and sense of urgency, at a time of life when most poets have long since concluded their major work.

Always a poet of the weather, Stevens now found new force in the symbolism of the seasons, as the titles of his next two volumes testify: *Transport to Summer* (1947) and *The Auroras of Autumn* (1950). The slow and beautiful transition from the lush ripeness of summer to the cold glory of autumn in New England is an apt description of this late poetry, in which Stevens is more than ever the anti-mythologizing, anti-autobiographical poet of the absolute, of the perfect idea, and of the marriage of the imagination and reality. He embraced the overwhelming movement of nature, which included his own inevitable death. His language was gradually stripped of its finery to a plainness that is virtually transparent. Of "An Ordinary Evening in New Haven," the major long poem in *The Auroras of Autumn,* Stevens wrote to a friend: "Here my interest is to try to get as close to the ordinary, the commonplace and the ugly as it is possible for a poet to get. It is not a question of grim reality but of plain reality. The object is of course to purge oneself of anything false." His purpose was to find in the most ordinary material the possibility of the sublime: section 30 of "An Ordinary Evening in New Haven" says, "The barrenness that appears is an exposing." If the poetry became less ornate, it also became more abstract; yet the mode of this abstraction is not one of flat categorical statement, but one of endless qualification and hesitation. A man of profound intellectual humility, Stevens never abandoned his habit of resolute tentativeness. In section 28 he writes:

> This endlessly elaborating poem
> Displays the theory of poetry,
> As the life of poetry. A more severe,
>
> More harassing master would extemporize
> Subtler, more urgent proof that the theory
> Of poetry is the theory of life,

> As it is, in the intricate evasions of as,
> In things seen and unseen, created from nothingness,
> The heavens, the hells, the worlds, the longed-for lands.

Wallace Stevens is no severe or harassing master. "An Ordinary Evening in New Haven" is also not held up as a definitive statement, but only as further "notes." He renounces any inclination toward finality and remains true to his idea of the changefulness of the supreme fiction, celebrating again the "ambiguous undulations" and the "fluttering things [that] have so distinct a shade." "An Ordinary Evening in New Haven" concludes with these lines:

> These are the edgings and inchings of final form,
> The swarming activities of the formulae
> Of statement, directly and indirectly getting at,
>
> Like an evening evoking the spectrum of violet,
> A philosopher practicing scales on his piano,
> A woman writing a note and tearing it up.
>
> It is not in the premise that reality
> Is a solid. It may be a shade that traverses
> A dust, a force that traverses a shade.

Of his *Notes toward a Supreme Fiction* Stevens wrote to Church: "The truth is that this ought to be one of only a number of books and that, if I had nothing else in the world to do except to sit on a fence and think about things, it would in fact be only one of a number of books. You have only to think about this a moment to see how extensible the idea is." The number of further books Stevens did produce on the theme of *Notes toward a Supreme Fiction* is remarkable, considering that he never came anywhere near having nothing else in the world to do but to sit on a fence and think about things. On the contrary, he was a busy executive in a large insurance company, a position that he clung to jealously, even after he reached the mandatory retirement age of seventy. He welcomed the routine of the office, and he dreaded the isolation from the ordinary world of work that he envisaged in being forced to retire. He refused the invitation from Harvard to occupy the Charles Eliot Norton Chair in 1955 for fear that such a move would "precipitate the retirement that I want so much to put off." That such a prestigious position would be offered to him is indicative of the great esteem that his poetry had won for him in his last years. The literary prizes and honorary degrees flooded in, and yet Stevens walked across Elizabeth Park in Hartford to the office every day up to the time of his final illness, to the office where his colleagues, if they knew he was a poet at all, regarded his poetry as a hobby of no more importance than Winston Churchill's painting. One suspects that Stevens treasured the anonymity. He was a man capable to an unusual degree of enjoying the solitary interior life of the imagination to the exclusion of action and society. One curious fact of his life is that Stevens, the supreme Francophile, never traveled to Europe. When young he was either too busy or too poor, and later, after wars and revolutions in Europe, he preferred the Europe of his imagination. For him France meant books and paintings (which he bought from his Paris bookseller sight unseen) and news from friends abroad and picture postcards and cherished scraps of recherché information. He wrote his bookseller: "I am one of the many people around the world who live from time to time in a Paris that has never existed and that is composed of the things that other people, primarily Parisians themselves, have said about Paris. That particular Paris communicates an interest in life that may be wholly fiction, but, if so, it is a precious fiction." One is reminded of the aesthete and Anglophile Des Esseintes, in Joris Karl Huysmans's *A Rebours* (1884), who says of his decision not to visit England: "I would be mad indeed to go and, by an awkward trip, lose those imperishable sensations." To a friend summering in France Stevens wrote in 1954: "We remain quietly at home, engaged in meditation and prayer and thoughts of Paris."

Only in 1954, on the occasion of his seventy-fifth birthday, did Wallace Stevens agree to the publication of *The Collected Poems of Wallace Stevens*. He included the twenty-five poems he had written since *The Auroras of Autumn* at the end of this book in a section titled "The Rock" because they were not enough to constitute a whole new volume. Among them are some of his most beautiful poems. In "To an Old Philosopher in Rome" Stevens pays his final homage to George Santayana. The figure of Ulysses in "The World as Meditation" is a symbol of the eternal return, Ulysses and not Ulysses, perhaps only the warmth of the sun, and Penelope "would talk a little to herself as she combed her hair,/Repeating his name with its patient syllables,/Never forgetting him that kept coming constantly so near." In

"St. Armorer's Church from the Outside" the poet celebrates in his own "chapel of breath," that element of newness among the ruins, "In an air of freshness, clearness, greenness, blueness,/ That which is always beginning because it is part/ Of that which is always beginning, over and over." In this poem and in "The Planet on the Table" Stevens takes the uncanny stance of looking at his own life as if from the outside. "Prologues to What is Possible" presents the image of a vivid dreamlike voyage in a boat at sea, toward something unknown and mysterious, perhaps frightening, but greatly to be desired. The feeling of all these poems is one of a rare tranquillity, resolution, and fulfillment.

Keeping in mind certain qualifications of the term, the most apt description of Stevens's late poetry is that it is religious. He wrote in a letter of 1951: "I am not an atheist although I do not believe today in the same God in whom I believed when I was a boy"; and to another correspondent the following year he wrote: "At my age it would be nice to be able to read more and think more and be myself more and to make up my mind about God, say, before it is too late, or at least before he makes up his mind about me." In his essay "A Collect of Philosophy" (written in 1951) he wrote: "The number of ways of passing between the traditional two fixed points of man's life, that is to say, of passing from the self to God, is fixed only by the limitations of space, which is limitless. . . . In the one poem that is unimpeachably divine, the poem of the ascent into heaven, it is possible to say that there can be no faults, since it is precisely the faults of life that this poem enables us to leave behind. If the idea of God is the ultimate poetic idea, then the idea of the ascent into heaven is only a little below it . . . . The poets of that theme find things on the way and what they find on the way very often interest as much as what they find in the end." Here Stevens is talking of the true belief in the one supreme fiction, and of true poetry as the many interesting things one finds along the way, expressed with the greatest possible exactness. He concludes that essay by praising the poetry, the fictive imagination, and the existential faith of the most abstract philosophers and theoretical physicists: "It is as if in a study of modern man we predicated the greatness of poetry as the final measure of his stature, as if his willingness to believe beyond belief was what had made him modern and was always certain to keep him so."

Elsie and Wallace Stevens, circa 1938 (courtesy of Holly Stevens)

What Stevens hoped to achieve was "to believe beyond belief." He was a skeptical poet writing in a skeptical age but always with the purpose of finding a release from the bind of skepticism and a deliverance from the poverty and sadness of life. Stevens had come a long way from "Sunday Morning," but there was no sudden reversal or change of mind. It was rather a slow, steady path determined by a steadfastness of purpose and a definite goal. This progress from *Harmonium* to "The Rock," from sensibility to meditation, is charted by Louis L. Martz in his 1958 essay "Wallace Stevens: The World as Meditation." In her book *Wallace Stevens: Imagination and Faith* (1974) Adalaide Kirby Morris argues that "as the Supreme Fiction overthrew the Supreme Being, it assumed many of the accoutrements of traditional religion," and these she traces in Stevens's family heritage, in his language and thought, in his "sacramental symbology," and in his ethics. But to call the "what is possible" of "Prologues to What

is Possible" the God of Christianity would be misleading in the extreme, because it sidesteps the whole problem of belief beyond belief. To the end of his life Stevens trod a fine line between stating a metaphysical position and lapsing into romantic solipsism. He rejected vehemently the materialism and nihilism of the modern world and believed in the existence of an absolute, the rock, the irreducible base of external reality, and in the power of man to know something of that reality through the operation of the creative imagination. What he knows in this way amounts to an intuition of the One, the Good, the True, and the Beautiful, at once immanent and transcendent, and the merest intimations of immortality and of a divine intelligence. In "Long and Sluggish Lines" Stevens says, "The life of the poem in the mind has not yet begun./You were not born yet when the trees were crystal/Nor are you now, in this wakefulness inside a sleep." In "Final Soliloquy of the Interior Paramour," perhaps Stevens's most straightforward statement of his final position, he says, "We feel the obscurity of an order, a whole,/A knowledge, that which arranged the rendezvous./Within its vital boundary, in the mind./We say God and the imagination are one. . . ." In this last line it is important not to ignore the "We say" and the final ellipses, which are Stevens's. For Stevens poetry could never be a vehicle for categorical statement, but always, by the nature of metaphorical language itself, only a vehicle for exploration and approximation. What goes beyond that simply goes beyond poetry, what Stevens finally decided when he came to make up his mind about God, before it was too late, is extraneous to his work as a poet. Although Holly Stevens denies that her father was received into the Roman Catholic church on his deathbed, there is a firsthand witness to that effect in Peter Brazeau's oral biography and several other statements by people who knew Stevens in his last days that serve to mitigate the seeming improbability of such a conversion.

After several months of illness, in and out of the hospital, Wallace Stevens died of cancer on 2 August 1955. He is buried in the Cedar Hill Cemetery in Hartford. Since the time of his death the esteem in which Stevens is held by readers of poetry on both sides of the Atlantic has never ceased to increase. He was introduced late to the British, only with the first *Selected Poems* in 1952, but one of the first books on Stevens, that by British writer Frank Kermode in 1960, did much to redress the balance and remains a useful introduction to Stevens's life and work. Another very fine survey of Stevens's entire career, also from England, is Lucy Beckett's *Wallace Stevens* (1974). There can be little doubt now of the great success Stevens achieved as a poet for the modern world, in "finding what will suffice," to "help us live our lives."

Letters:

Letters of Wallace Stevens, edited by Holly Stevens (New York: Knopf, 1966).
> Selects, from over three thousand letters written between 1895 and 1955, those which best reflect Stevens as an "all-round man"; contains a useful listing of all correspondence reprinted in the volume, noting the date and recipient of each letter.

Bibliographies:

Samuel French Morse, Jackson R. Bryer, and Joseph N. Riddel, *Wallace Stevens Checklist and Bibliography of Stevens Criticism* (Denver: Swallow, 1963).
> Lists works by Stevens, including publications in books and periodicals, and secondary materials, including dedicatory poems, dissertations, foreign reviews, and reviews of books and plays, as well as critical books and articles.

Theodore L. Huguelet, *The Merrill Checklist of Wallace Stevens* (Columbus, Ohio: Merrill, 1970).
> Primary and secondary unannotated bibliography, selective in disregarding outdated and non-English materials; lists only first English and American appearances as well as important collected and individual editions.

J. M. Edelstein, *Wallace Stevens: A Descriptive Bibliography* (Pittsburgh: University of Pittsburgh Press, 1973).
> Lists all primary and selected secondary sources, including some interesting miscellany such as recordings made of Stevens's poetry and musical settings of poems by Stevens.

Biographies:

Samuel French Morse, *Wallace Stevens: Poetry as Life* (New York: Pegasus, 1970).
> Examines Stevens's life through a brief chronological overview of his poetry, letters, and comments by writers such as Marianne Moore, Louis Untermeyer, and William Carlos Williams.

Holly Stevens, *Souvenirs and Prophecies: The Young Wallace Stevens* (New York: Knopf, 1977).
> This account of Stevens by his daughter presents "commingled souvenirs and prophecies" to provide "a 'sense of the world' of Wallace Stevens."

Peter Brazeau, *Parts of A World: Wallace Stevens Remembered: An Oral Biography* (New York: Random House, 1983).
> Records excerpts from interviews with over 150 people who knew Stevens in an attempt to document "the personality, habits, attitudes, sayings and doings of one of our greatest poets."

Milton J. Bates, *Wallace Stevens: A Mythology of Self* (Berkeley: University of California Press, 1985).
> Traces Stevens's development, through the "fables of identity" presented in the poems, into a mature poet.

Joan Richardson, *Wallace Stevens: The Early Years* (New York: Morrow, 1986).
> Using material from his journals and letters, this account of Stevens's life from 1879 to 1923 seeks to explain the eclectic influences which transformed a middle-class American into one of his country's greatest poets despite his "completely un-American aesthetic."

References:

James Baird, *The Dome and the Rock: Structure in the Poetry of Wallace Stevens* (Baltimore: Johns Hopkins University Press, 1968).
> Questions the validity of overly philosophical analysis of Stevens and opts for Stevens's poetry as a guide to and commentary upon itself.

Lucy Beckett, *Wallace Stevens* (Cambridge: Cambridge University Press, 1974).
> Explores the evolution of Stevens's complex ideas about the nature of reality and imagination and relation of poetry to the need for belief and the search for personal fulfillment.

Michel Benamou, *Wallace Stevens and the Symbolist Imagination* (Princeton: Princeton University Press, 1972).
Reprints five periodical essays by Benamou which analyze internal components of Stevens's poetry and attempt to place Stevens in the French symbolist tradition.

Richard Allen Blessing, *Wallace Stevens' "Whole Harmonium"* (Syracuse: Syracuse University Press, 1970).
Sees Stevens's body of work as a single poem attempting to present "a dynamic symbol for the process of life itself."

Harold Bloom, *Wallace Stevens: The Poems of Our Climate* (Ithaca: Cornell University Press, 1977).
Places Stevens in the Romantic tradition of Wordsworth, Shelley, Keats, Emerson, and Whitman and approaches his poetry as a complex and interrelated body of work.

Ashley Brown and Robert S. Haller, eds., *The Achievement of Wallace Stevens* (Philadelphia: Lippincott, 1962).
Collects essays, spanning 1920-1961 and representing Stevens's critical reception, by Harriet Monroe, Marianne Moore, R. P. Blackmur, Randall Jarrell, and others.

Merle E. Brown, *Wallace Stevens: The Poem as Act* (Detroit: Wayne State University Press, 1970).
Argues, in contrast to Blessing's *Wallace Stevens' "Whole Harmonium,"* that "the ocean of Stevens's poetry is real only as it breaks into the emeralds which are his individual poems."

William Burney, *Wallace Stevens* (New York: Twayne, 1968).
Focusing primarily on *The Collected Poems*, this general overview is intended as a guide for readers who are unfamiliar with the poet's work.

Robert Buttel, *Wallace Stevens: The Making of Harmonium* (Princeton: Princeton University Press, 1967).
Views Stevens as an eclectic poet whose main concern was the interaction between imagination and reality and who sought to reconcile the fixed nature of poetry with the mutability of the world it attempts to present.

Joseph Carroll, *Wallace Stevens' Supreme Fiction* (Baton Rouge: Louisiana State University Press, 1987).
Attempts to analyze Stevens's poetic vision to show that he was both a "difficult" poet yet one with an ultimately cohesive sensibility.

Frank Doggett, *Stevens' Poetry of Thought* (Baltimore: Johns Hopkins University Press, 1966).
Sees Stevens as a philosophical poet and explores the form and function of the *concept* in his poetry.

Doggett, *Wallace Stevens: The Making of the Poem* (Baltimore: Johns Hopkins University Press, 1980).
Seeks to use the poet's own explanations of his work and his creative process to illuminate "the 'hidden well' of inventiveness within himself."

Doggett and Robert Buttel, eds., *Wallace Stevens: A Celebration* (Princeton: Princeton University Press, 1980).
An eclectic collection of essays by various Stevens scholars, George S. Lensing, Frank Kermode, and Peter Brazeau among them.

Irvin Ehrenpreis, ed., *Wallace Stevens: A Critical Anthology* (Harmondsworth, U.K.: Penguin, 1973).
Presents Stevens's letters and excerpts from his journals and collects a wide range of critical commentary (1919-1971) by critics such as T. S. Eliot, John Crowe Ransom, John Gould Fletcher, Carl Van Vechten, and John Berryman.

Daniel Fuchs, *The Comic Spirit of Wallace Stevens* (Durham: Duke University Press, 1963).
Analyzes the comic vision in Stevens's works as seen in his use of satire, "dandyism," irony, and wordplay.

Thomas J. Hines, *The Later Poetry of Wallace Stevens: Phenomenological Parallels with Husserl and Heidegger* (Lewisburg: Bucknell University Press, 1976).

Relates the middle and late poetry to phenomenology not so much as a direct influence but as a synchronicity; also explores the mind/reality dichotomy.

Frank Kermode, *Wallace Stevens* (London: Oliver & Boyd, 1960).
Contains a short sketch of Stevens's life, three essays on his major poetry and one on his prose, and a selected primary and secondary bibliography which is superceded by later ones.

Edward Kessler, *Images of Wallace Stevens* (New Brunswick: Rutgers University Press, 1972).
Examines Stevens's works as a series of variations on several "major or controlling images" and asserts that understanding Stevens's poetry requires "no special knowledge from outside the poems, knowledge of history or literature," and "is not dependent upon cultural background."

David M. LaGuardia, *Advance on Chaos: The Sanctifying Imagination of Wallace Stevens* (Hanover, N.H.: University Press of New England, 1983).
A dissection of Stevens's use of the world of Emerson and William James (pragmatism and idealism).

William Van O'Connor, *The Shaping Spirit: A Study of Wallace Stevens* (Chicago: Regnery, 1950).
A general, short overview that provides useful insights into the broader themes in Stevens's work rather than an in-depth analysis.

Robert Pack, *Wallace Stevens: An Approach to His Poetry and Thought* (New Brunswick: Rutgers University Press, 1958).
A sectionalized and fairly brief look at larger themes such as "Secular Mystery" and "The Feeling of Thought."

Roy Harvey Pearce and J. Hillis Miller, eds., *The Act of the Mind: Essays on the Poetry of Wallace Stevens* (Baltimore: Johns Hopkins University Press, 1965).
A collection of varied, and often conflicting, critical essays, useful if supplemented by critical opinion since 1965.

Joseph N. Riddel, *The Clairvoyant Eye: The Poetry and Poetics of Wallace Stevens* (Baton Rouge: Louisiana State University Press, 1965).
Discusses Stevens's poems from philosophical and historical perspectives and sees him as a writer for whom poetry was a way of life and a necessary activity; proceeds from the thesis that "Stevens's total work constitutes metaphysically the act of creating oneself."

Michael Sexson, *The Quest of Self in the Collected Poems of Wallace Stevens* (New York: Edwin Mellen Press, 1981).
A psychological model, based upon the theories of Jung and Erich Neuman, of the religious dimension in Stevens's *Collected Poems*.

Ronald Sukenick, *Wallace Stevens: Musing the Obscure* (New York: New York University Press, 1967).
Useful explication of approximately fifty poems, mostly using the principles of the New Criticism; also includes a chronology listing Stevens's works and life events.

Helen Hennessy Vendler, *On Extended Wings: Wallace Stevens' Longer Poems* (Cambridge: Harvard University Press, 1969).
Argues for a relativistic interpretation of Stevens as humorist, aesthetic hedonist, and epistemologist.

Thomas F. Walsh, *Concordance to the Poetry of Wallace Stevens* (University Park: Pennsylvania State University Press, 1963).
A thorough guide to key words and phrases in Stevens's poetry.

Henry W. Wells, *Introduction to Wallace Stevens* (Bloomington: Indiana University Press, 1964).
A useful, if somewhat glowing, appraisal of Stevens; fair guide for the Stevens novice, but other available sources offer more divergent and in-depth examinations.

Abbie F. Willard, *Wallace Stevens: The Poet and His Critics* (Chicago: American Library Association, 1978).
An overview of criticism arranged by subject, such as "Genre," "World View," and "Lit-

erary Heritage," rather than by schools of criticism.

Leonora Woodman, *Stanza My Stone: Wallace Stevens and the Hermetic Tradition* (West Lafayette, Ind.: Purdue University Press, 1983). Examines dualism in Stevens's work—hermetic man vs. transcendental order; also

argues against atheistic interpretations, especially in later works.

Papers:
The Wallace Stevens archive is at the Henry E. Huntington Library, San Marino, California.

James Thurber

This entry was updated by Peter A. Scholl (Luther College) from his entry in DLB 11,
American Humorists, 1800-1950.

Places	Paris New York City	Connecticut	Columbus, Ohio
Influences and Relationships	E. B. White Mark Twain Harold Ross	Henry James O. Henry Eliot Nugent	George Ade Willa Cather
Literary Movements and Forms	Parody The Humorous Sketch	The Fable Journalism	Children's Literature
Major Themes	The War Between Men and Women The Decline of Language Real and Imagi- nary Animals	The Difficulty of Communication The Threat of Machinery Fantasy vs. Reality	Frustrations of Life Pop Psychology Misanthropy
Cultural and Artistic Influences	The *New Yorker* Cartoons		
Social and Economic Influences	Fascism World War II	The Rise of Technology	McCarthyism

See also the Thurber entries in DLB 4, American Writers in Paris, 1920-1939 *and* DLB 22, American Writers for Children, 1900-1960.

BIRTH: Columbus, Ohio, 8 December 1894, to Charles Lincoln and Mary Agnes Fischer Thurber.

EDUCATION: Ohio State University, 1913-1918.

MARRIAGE: 20 May 1922 to Althea Adams (divorced); child: Rosemary. 25 June 1935 to Helen Muriel Wismer.

AWARDS: Library Association Prize for best juvenile picture book for *Many Moons*, 1943; Ohioana juvenile-book medal for *The White Deer*, 1946; Laughing Lions of Columbia University Award for Humor, 1949; Honorary Doctorate, Kenyon College, 1950; Honorary Doctorate, Williams College, 1951; Honorary Doctorate, Yale University, 1953; Sesquicentennial Career Medal of the Martha Kinney Cooper Ohioana Library Association, 1953; American Cartoonist's Society T-Square Award, 1956; American Library Association's Library and Justice Award for *Further Fables for Our Time*, 1957; Antoinette Perry Special Award, 1960; Certificate of Award from Ohio State University Class of 1916 for "Meritorious Service to Humanity and to Our Alma Mater," 1961.

DEATH: New York, New York, 2 November 1961.

BOOKS: *Is Sex Necessary? Or Why You Feel the Way You Do*, by Thurber and E. B. White (New York & London: Harper, 1929; London: Heinemann, 1930);
The Owl in the Attic and Other Perplexities (New York & London: Harper, 1931);
The Seal in the Bedroom & Other Predicaments (New York & London: Harper, 1932; London: Hamilton, 1951);
My Life and Hard Times (New York & London: Harper, 1933);
The Middle-Aged Man on the Flying Trapeze (New York & London: Harper, 1935; London: Hamilton, 1935);
Let Your Mind Alone! And Other More or Less Inspirational Pieces (New York & London: Harper, 1937; London: Hamilton, 1937);
Cream of Thurber (London: Hamilton, 1939);

James Thurber (Culver Pictures)

The Last Flower (New York & London: Harper, 1939; London: Hamilton, 1939);
The Male Animal, by Thurber and Elliott Nugent (New York: Random House, 1940; London: Hamilton, 1950);
Fables for Our Time and Famous Poems Illustrated (New York & London: Harper, 1940; London: Hamilton, 1940);
My World–and Welcome to It (New York: Harcourt, Brace, 1942; London: Hamilton, 1942);
Many Moons (New York: Harcourt, Brace, 1943; London: Hamilton, 1945);
Thurber's Men, Women, and Dogs (New York: Harcourt, Brace, 1943; London: Hamilton, 1945);
The Great Quillow (New York: Harcourt, Brace, 1944);
The Thurber Carnival (New York & London: Harper, 1945; London: Hamilton, 1945);
The White Deer (New York: Harcourt, Brace, 1945; London: Hamilton, 1946);
The Beast in Me and Other Animals (New York: Harcourt, Brace, 1948; London: Hamilton, 1949);

The 13 Clocks (New York: Simon & Schuster, 1950; London: Hamilton, 1951);

The Thurber Album (New York: Simon & Schuster, 1952; London: Hamilton, 1952);

Thurber Country (New York: Simon & Schuster, 1953; London: Hamilton, 1953);

Thurber's Dogs (New York: Simon & Schuster, 1955; London: Hamilton, 1955);

A Thurber Garland (London: Hamilton, 1955);

Further Fables for Our Time (New York: Simon & Schuster, 1956; London: Hamilton, 1956);

The Wonderful O (New York: Simon & Schuster, 1957; London: Hamilton, 1958);

Alarms and Diversions (London: Hamilton, 1957; New York: Harper, 1957);

The Years with Ross (Boston & Toronto: Atlantic Monthly/Little, Brown, 1959; London: Hamilton, 1959);

Lanterns & Lances (New York: Harper, 1961; London: Hamilton, 1961);

Credos and Curios (London: Hamilton, 1962; New York & Evanston: Harper & Row, 1962);

A Thurber Carnival (New York, Hollywood, London & Toronto: French, 1962);

Vintage Thurber, 2 volumes (London: Hamilton, 1963);

Thurber & Company (New York: Evanston & London: Harper & Row, 1966; London: Hamilton, 1967).

PLAY PRODUCTIONS: *The Male Animal*, by Thurber and Elliott Nugent, New York, Cort Theatre, 9 January 1940;

A Thurber Carnival, Columbus, Ohio, Hartman Theater, 7 January 1960; New York, ANTA Theatre, 26 February 1960.

In a general survey of American humor, James Thurber comes after the traditional horse-sense humorists and before the black humorists of the postatomic era. His most famous and most enduring work developed after he became associated in 1927 with the two-year-old *New Yorker* magazine, a periodical that strove to be sophisticated but not stuffy, urbane but not effete. He never completed a thoroughly unified long work, though he did produce, in collaboration with Elliott Nugent, a successful three-act play, *The Male Animal* (1940). He is best known for his short pieces, especially for his almost conversational yet elegantly crafted "casuals," a word used by *New Yorker* editor Harold Ross "for fiction and humorous pieces of all kinds." Neither Thurber nor his *New Yorker* colleagues created the so-

James Thurber, circa 1906 (Dodd, Mead & Company)

called little man character and the sort of humor with which this well-known twentieth-century type is associated. Still, Thurber's particular elaboration of the type and the near identity of his narrative persona with the personality of the fictional little man became a Thurber trademark, and the phrase "Thurber man" (as well as "Thurber woman"—though she is a different matter altogether) has become commonplace in discussions of American humor. As early as 1919, his friend and collaborator E. B. White wrote that "These 'Thurber men' have come to be recognized as a distinct type in the world of art; they are frustrated, fugitive beings; at times they seem vaguely striving to get out of something without being seen (a room, a situation, a state of mind), at other times they are merely perplexed and too humble, or weak, to move." The characters in his work seem headed toward some final darkness, a tendency symbolized in the title of his last book published in his lifetime, *Lanterns & Lances* (1961). The lances pierce out the eyes that see the light of humor, but it is not all darkness. The lanterns often continue to shine all the way through a Thurber piece, and in his best work the lances serve as poles to raise the lanterns high. Some of the greatest moments in modern American humor are those in which his characters hold both, but use the lanterns instead of lances. For example, in "The Catbird Seat," Mr. Martin plots carefully to "rub out" the domineering Miss Ulgine Barrows, but finds, through Thurber magic in the art of telling tales, a way to comic victory without bloodshed.

James Grover Thurber was born in Columbus, Ohio, the second son of Charles and Mary Thurber. As his secretary told his biographer Burton Bernstein, "all his life, he remained an Ohio boy at heart, with a universal sense of wisdom." Whether it was mainly ambition or his "universal wisdom," he struggled hard to leave the Midwest and ultimately made his way east like many aspiring writers before and after him. Like many of his characters, Thurber became an upper-middle-class Easterner, a self-exiled Midwesterner who restlessly sought, as he put it, "the Great Good Place, which he conceives to be an old Colonial house, surrounded by elms and maples, equipped with all modern conveniences. . . ." He made it to such a place in West Cornwall, Connecticut, but he was not at rest there. He never completely divorced himself from his Ohio roots, as he admitted in 1953: "I am never very far away from Ohio in my thoughts, and . . . the clocks that strike in my dreams are often the clocks of Columbus." His Ohio memories and relatives were fundamental influences on his best work.

Thurber's father, Charles Thurber, was not born in Columbus, but was "A Gentleman from Indiana," as the nostalgic essay about him in *The Thurber Album* (1952) was titled. He dreamed of being an actor, then a lawyer, but he ended up working at various political appointments that were dependent upon his party's fortunes at the polls. Forever miscast and ill at ease, "He wasn't even a politician . . . but, as they say in the theatre of a part in a bad play, it was a job." He was undoubtedly one of the prototypes of the Thurber man, as "he was always mightily plagued by the mechanical. He was also plagued by the manufactured, which takes in a great deal more ground." He was nothing like his wife Mary, or Mame, as she was nicknamed, a daughter of a large, strong-willed, influential Ohio family. After reading the fictionalized description of her in *My Life and Hard Times* (1933) and the more historical portrait of her, "Lavender with a Difference," in *The Thurber Album*, no one can wonder where the original model of the Thurber woman was found. She was a natural actress, a practical joker, a believer in the occult, a strong Methodist, a great cook, and a woman with a memory that rivaled or surpassed Thurber's own much-vaunted "total recall."

If the accident of his birth into a family of loving but eccentric relatives was without parallel for its effect on his work, another accident at a young age had a powerful effect on him. In the summer of 1901, Charles Thurber took his family to live in the Washington, D.C., area where he was to work for an Ohio congressman. The three Thurber boys were playing William Tell in the yard one afternoon when Jamie turned around to see what was taking his older brother William so long–"and the arrow hit Jamie smack in the eye." There was considerable delay in removing the damaged eye, a circumstance that probably led to Thurber's total blindness by 1951. In Columbus, where the Thurbers returned in 1903, the injury set him apart from most other Columbus boys, especially the mixed-race, "laboring-class," pugnacious, and sports-minded schoolboys described in "I Went to Sullivant" (1935). In *My Life and Hard Times* Thurber says that he could never pass biology at the university because he could never see anything through a microscope, and later, he reports that he was ordered to report for an army physical innumerable times, only to be told at the end of every inspection, "Why, you couldn't get into the service with sight like that!"

Glass eye and all, Thurber was still a success in his junior and senior high-school days. Among other honors, he was given the job of writing the eighth grade class prophecy. In this document, critics have found the earliest precursor of the Thurber "Walter Ego" (a punning phrase he used in *Lanterns & Lances*). The young prophet imagines his class on an incredible journey in a "Seairoplane." When the craft catches a piece of rope in its "curobator" and threatens to crash, all are surprised "to see James Thurber walking out on the beam. He reached out and extricated the rope . . . " in the nerveless manner which the most famous of all Thurber characters, the hero of "The Secret Life of Walter Mitty" (1939), attributes to himself in his daydreams. Thurber's early triumphs, unlike Mitty's, were not all imaginary. He graduated from high school with honors, having studied the difficult Latin curriculum, and he was elected president of his senior class. But if he was a somebody in high school, he was a nobody in his first years at Ohio State University, where he enrolled in 1913. He did not receive a bid from a fraternity that year, and he did so badly in many of his classes that he stopped attending altogether during the school year of 1914-1915, without telling anyone at

Thurber (right) with E. B. White, his colleague at the New Yorker *(courtesy of the Department of Rare Books, Cornell University Library)*

home. In the fall of 1916 he met Elliott Nugent, a big man on campus, who was impressed one day with a theme Thurber had written—so impressed that he managed to get him into his own fraternity and helped him become "a regular guy." Thurber and Nugent worked together on the *Ohio State Lantern* and on the *Sundial* (the university's literary and humor magazine), and, following Nugent's example, Thurber joined The Strollers (the university's dramatic group) as well as other groups and clubs. Of his teachers, Thurber was most powerfully affected by English professor Joseph Taylor, from whom he learned to admire the work of Willa Cather, Joseph Conrad, and especially Henry James. But he was also influenced by the comic strips of his day, by melodramas and later by movies, by "nickel novels" and

the stories of O. Henry (who had served over three years in the federal prison in Columbus), and by the humor of Robert O. Ryder, editorialist for the *Ohio State Journal*. Thurber painstakingly imitated Ryder's "paragraphs"—carefully drawn, brief comments on a variety of subjects—in his writing for his high-school paper and the *Sundial*. The restrained humor of "paragraphing" was later to appear in his columns for the *Columbus Dispatch*, and the style anticipates the comments he would write for "The Talk of the Town" at the *New Yorker*.

Thurber left Ohio in 1918 without a degree, but he had distinguished himself sufficiently to be elected to the Sphinx, the senior honorary society. He was anxious "to go with the rest of the boys," and though his eye trouble kept him out of the military, he managed to get to Paris as a code clerk for the United States Embassy, where he served from 1918 to 1920. There he reread *The Ambassadors* several times and even retraced the steps of James's passionate pilgrims, dining at the Tour d'Argent with a former Ohio State coed, reenacting a meeting between Lambert Strether and Mme de Vionnet. Clearly he saw himself as one of James's "supersubtle fry," and in the cultural center of the world, he was trying his best to be "one of those on whom nothing is lost." Yet he was still nine-tenths Ohio boy, and his loss of virginity with a dancer in the Folies Bergères could not rid him of his Midwestern conviction that there are two kinds of women, Mme de Vionnet notwithstanding. In his letters to his brother, the Jamesian sophisticate of infinite delicacy and perception gives way to what a friend described as "the hick in him." "Of all the nations on the earth," he wrote in 1919, "the Yanks easily lead in the matter of pep and enthusiasm, endurance and gogetum stuff...."

When he returned to Columbus in early 1920, his brother Robert recalls, it was evident that he had been "Over There": "He was so independent.... He was jumpy and moody, but he seemed to know what he wanted to be—a writer of some sort." He promptly took a job as a reporter on the *Columbus Dispatch*, working under tough city editor Norman Kuehner. Kuehner, like Harold Ross, was a hard-boiled type who believed that "You get to be a newspaperman by being a newspaperman," and he liked to call college men like Thurber "Phi Beta Kappa." Later on, as Thurber tells this story in *The Thurber Album*, Kuehner began to call him "Author," hav-

Dust jacket for Thurber's 1945 novel which E. B. White called "Exhibit A in the strange case of a writer's switch from eye work to ear work."

ing heard that the young man was writing librettos for Ohio State musicals. This theatrical experience, which included writing, acting, producing, and even going on the road with the Scarlet Mask Club shows, brought him much-needed cash and helped prepare the way for his much later dramatic works *The Male Animal* and *A Thurber Carnival* (a revue that opened in 1960). His renewed contact with the dramatic society also brought Althea Adams into his view. Although she has been described as "aloof, attractive, ambitious, worldly, and very social–all the things Jim wasn't . . . ," the two were married in 1922. The family never warmed to her, especially Thurber's mother, for, as Bernstein sees it, "they were too much alike for comfort–domineering, aggressive, essential females. . . . An amalgam of the two of them became . . . what was later to be known to the world as the Thurber Woman."

Yet it was Althea's drive that helped Thurber leave Columbus to try his luck at free-lance writing. During the summer of 1924 they lived in

a secluded cottage in the Adirondacks, where Thurber wrote and wrote. He managed to turn out "Josephine Has Her Day," the first short story for which he was paid, and had it published in the *Kansas City Star* Sunday magazine in 1926. But the experiment foundered in a tide of rejection slips, and the couple had to return to Columbus. Their ardor for escape was not cooled, however, and in 1925 they sailed for France. There they lived in a musty farmhouse in Normandy. (Their terrifying landlady is described in "Remembrance of Things Past," 1937.) Thurber was trying to write a novel but gave it up after five thousand words. The two fled to Paris to escape the landlady, the threat of poverty, and the agony of novel writing. Though Thurber once told interviewers that he "never wanted to write a long work," this was not the only time he started and failed to finish a novel. In a letter written in 1931 after ending work on another novel after the first chapter, he said that he feared "all of my novels would be complete in one chapter, from force of habit in writing short pieces and also from a natural incapability of what Billy Graves would call 'larger flight.' . . . " In September 1925 Thurber secured a job as rewrite man for the Paris edition of the *Chicago Tribune*, beating out other hopeful expatriates because he was an experienced newspaperman. In December 1925 he became coeditor of the Riviera edition of the *Tribune*.

His friends in France were mainly his fellow reporters and did not include such writers as F. Scott Fitzgerald, Ernest Hemingway, or Gertrude Stein, Thurber says in "The Hiding Generation" (1936). Thurber says in "Scott in Thorns" (1951) that he only met Fitzgerald once, in New York in 1934. Thurber's imagination got good exercise, as the *Tribune* writers had to create eight to ten columns out of news cables that provided only one. It became apparent in 1926, however, that this French interlude was not furthering his career; nor was his marriage faring well, and the money was running low again. Althea stayed on behind when Thurber sailed for New York, hoping to earn money there by free-lancing.

Arriving in New York in June, he began submitting stories and manuscripts to all kinds of magazines, among them the *New Yorker*. His stories came back so fast from the *New Yorker* that he thought they must have a "rejection machine." Near despair, he took a reporting job with the *New York Evening Post*. But he kept writing and submitting humor pieces. Althea Thurber had returned, and, convinced that Thurber was slaving too long over his manuscripts, she told him to time himself with an alarm clock and to send in what he had after forty-five minutes. This method worked, and he sold a piece to the *New Yorker*. "An American Romance" is a short casual about "the flagpole sitting crazes of the day." Following that initial coup in February 1927, he met E. B. White, who in turn introduced him to Harold Ross, and again Thurber's newspaper experience paid off, as Ross hired him as an editor. An editor and organizer Thurber was not, but he could not convince Ross that he would be happier and more effective as a staff writer. Ross was finally convinced when Thurber returned two days late from a visit to Columbus, having overstayed his leave to look for his lost dog. Ross considered that "the act of a sis," as Thurber told the tale in *The Years with Ross* (1959). "I thought you were an editor, goddam it," Ross said, "but I guess you're a writer so write."

"I came to the *New Yorker*," Thurber was later to say, "a writer of journalese and it was my study of White's writing, I think, that helped me to straighten out my prose so that people could see what I meant." The discipline of writing short items for "The Talk of the Town," the punctilious eye of Harold Ross, and the example of White, with whom he shared a tiny office, brought out the artless style of the Thurber casual. It is a style that refuses to call attention to itself, a "played-down" style, as Thurber was later to describe it. And it is evident in *Is Sex Necessary?* (1929), a book for which he and White wrote alternating chapters.

Thurber had long been a compulsive doodler, and some of his drawings had appeared in the Ohio State *Sundial*, but he did not take himself seriously as an artist. His second wife Helen Thurber said that Thurber told her his drawings "sometimes seem to have reached completion by some other route than the common one of intent. They have been described as pre-intentionalist, meaning that they were finished before the ideas for them had occurred to me." It was E. B. White, in the spring of 1929, who first noticed Thurber's drawings and tried to convince Ross to publish some, the first of which was a "thirteen-second sketch Thurber drew on yellow copy paper of a seal on a rock looking at two far-off specks and saying, 'Hm, explorers.'" According to Thurber, Ross asked him, "How the hell did you get the idea you could draw?" White persisted in his role as promoter and persuaded

Thurber's daughter Rosemary on her wedding day (Dodd, Mead & Company)

Harper and Brothers to use Thurber's drawings to illustrate *Is Sex Necessary?* This first book introduced not only Thurber's drawings but many of the major themes that were to dominate this period of his career: the war between men and women, the trouble with marriage, the difficulties raised by easy sex stereotyping, the limitations of genteelism on the one hand and post-Freudian "liberation" on the other. White wrote that the book, published just after the Great Crash, came out of "the turbulence of the late 1920's," a time when there was a great outpouring of books on sex, marriage, and self-analysis. As Wolcott Gibbs remarked, "the heavy writers had got sex down and were breaking its arm." Thurber and White capitalized on this topic; for Thurber, this parodic vein was already quite familiar. In fact, parts of Thurber's contribution to the book are rewritten sections of "Why We Behave Like Microbe Hunters," a long parody he had tried unsuccessfully to have published in 1926. Despite the fact that *Is Sex Necessary?* was not widely advertised, it made the best-seller lists.

John Monroe, the jumpy protagonist in the first eight stories that make up *The Owl in the Attic and Other Perplexities* (1931), a collection of some of Thurber's best *New Yorker* pieces of the period, is Thurber's typical bumbling but humane, illogical but sensitive, sympathetic character. With the publication of this book Thurber's reputation as a writer and an artist was firmly established, and the public was given more reason to associate the author with the man in Thurber's stories after reading E. B. White's introduction. There, Thurber is humorously described as a Conradian hero, a gaunt drifter White had first seen descending from a packet boat in Raritonga, "carrying a volume of Henry James and leading a honey bear by a small chain." "The Monroe stories," Thurber once said, "were transcripts, one or two of them varying less than an inch from the actual happenings." Virtually all the incidents in the battles between Monroe and his wife, between Monroe and a bat, Monroe and hot-water faucets, and so on, were based on events in the troubled married life of the Thurbers. The two other sections of this book included "The Pet Department" and "Ladies and Gentlemen's Guide to Modern English." The first of these demonstrated Thurber's ability to use his drawings in combination with brief writings that revealed his lifelong fascination with animals, real and imaginary. Some of these drawings had first been published in the *New Yorker*'s "Our Pet Department," a parody of the question-and-answer pet columns published in newspapers. In one such column Thurber's drawing of a horse with antlers tied to its head accompanies a letter from a woman who wants to know why her moose's antlers keep slipping around its head. *The Owl in the Attic* is named for another drawing that seems to show a "stuffed cuckatoo" sitting on a "sort of iron dingbat." The final section reveals Thurber's early and lasting fascination with words and language as such and seems more immediately inspired by Harold Ross's fastidiousness and veneration for H. W. Fowler's *Modern English Usage* (1926), which it plays with and parodies. In these pieces he anticipates the concerns for the well-being of the language that mark his late work, but these essays are generally lighter and are not strident or precious like some of the works written after he went blind.

After the success of *Is Sex Necessary?*, Ross asked Thurber for the seal drawing he had rejected. Thurber had thrown it away. He did not get around to drawing another until December 1931 and could not recapture the original: the rock looked more like a headboard, so a headboard it became, complete with a Thurber couple in the bed and the caption "All Right, Have It Your Way—You Heard a Seal Bark!" The cartoon appeared in the *New Yorker* on 30 January 1932, and, according to Bernstein, "it became one of the most celebrated and often-reprinted cartoons of the twentieth century." This cartoon gave the title to a collection of Thurber's cartoons and drawings, *The Seal in the Bedroom &*

Other Predicaments (1932). In her introduction Dorothy Parker said of the "strange people Mr. Thurber has turned loose upon us," that "They seem to fall into three classes—the playful the defeated and the ferocious. All of them have the outer semblance of unbaked cookies. . . ."

Thurber was firmly established as a *New Yorker* artist and writer by 1933, and in that year his series of casuals about growing up in Ohio was published under the title *My Life and Hard Times*. This is Thurber's best single collection of integrated stories, a series that can be read as a well-wrought and unified work of art. Here he exploits for comic effect the distance between the naive Ohio boy, just beginning to be perplexed by the world, and the wiser but still inadequate middle-aged Easterner who is trying to appear worldly and sophisticated, chagrined by the bitter truth that "Nobody from Columbus has ever made a first rate wanderer in the Conradian tradition." Thurber, as he portrays himself in "Preface to a Life," is just a "writer of light pieces running from a thousand to two thousand words," one of those authors who, "afraid of losing themselves in the larger flight of the two-volume novel," have a genius only "for getting into minor difficulties: they walk into the wrong apartments, they drink furniture polish for stomach bitters, they drive their cars into the prize tulip beds of haughty neighbors. . . ."

Though he presents himself in the preface as a nervous person with a tenuous hold on sanity, the narrative voice in the stories themselves is remarkably calm and in clear control of the bizarre events that it relates. The manner of telling recalls the deadpan face and dry delivery of the best oral yarn spinners, who understand that the comedy is heightened by the contrast between the unexcitable delivery and the frenetic events described. The very essence of the *New Yorker*'s studied artlessness—hallmark of the casual—is evident, for example, in the opening line of "The Night the Bed Fell": "I suppose that the high-water mark of my youth in Columbus, Ohio, was the night the bed fell on my father." It is in such plain, deliberate prose as this that he introduces a parade of crazies that would indeed tax our credulity were they not reported with such apparent composure. There is, for example, cousin Briggs Beall, "who believed that he was likely to cease breathing when he was asleep," and so kept waking himself up at intervals with an alarm clock. "Then there was Aunt Sarah Shoaf, who never went to bed at night without the fear that a bur-

Dust jacket for the 1950 book which many critics considered Thurber's parody of the fairy-tale form (Simon & Schuster)

glar was going to get in and blow chloroform under her door through a tube." The chaos that cuts loose in "The Night the Bed Fell" is matched in story after story, with other disasters and close calls such as those that occur in "The Day the Dam Broke," "The Night the Ghost Got In," and "More Alarms at Night." The narrator is himself involved in the action of many of these tales and is the comic protagonist of pieces such as "University Days" and "Draft Board Nights." In this last story, a fictionalized Thurber is called up for a physical examination every week, even though he was exempted from service the first time. He manages to adapt to this insanity by regarding it as comically absurd: "The ninth or tenth time I was called," he tells us, "I happened to pick up one of several stethoscopes that were lying on a table and suddenly, instead of finding myself in the line of draft men, I found myself in the line of examiners." And not surprisingly in this upside-down world, he is accepted by the other physicians as a peer—"A good pulmonary man,"

comments one. While Thurber feels free in this comic autobiography to stray from the facts, inventing cousins and elaborating upon familiar careers, the work displays his characteristic blending of memory and imagination, taking what Henry James called "clumsy life . . . at her stupid work," and painstakingly reshaping life into art. Here we have, as Thurber put it in an interview with Robert van Gelder, "Reality twisted to the right into humor rather than to the left into tragedy." Pathos touches the lives of these eccentrics, but the book is free from the darker shadings of absurdity that sift into his later works. On the other hand, the book is free from nostalgia, sentiment, and the concern for genealogical and historical trivia that mar his later return to many of these scenes in *The Thurber Album*.

Most of the writings and drawings in *The Middle-Aged Man on the Flying Trapeze* (1935) were first published in the *New Yorker*, and some of them continue to use the Columbus material, particularly the essays "I Went to Sullivant," about Thurber's grammar school, and "Snapshot of a Dog," which concerns Rex. A bull terrier, Rex dragged home things like ten-foot rails and small chests of drawers and "lived and died without knowing that twelve-and sixteen-foot walls were too much for him" to jump over. This collection also includes more satiric and parodic pieces, such as "If Grant Had Been Drinking at Appomattox," "The Greatest Man in the World," and "Something to Say," the last of these a takeoff on the work of Henry James. The Thurber man is well represented here, as in "The Remarkable Case of Mr. Bruhl," in which Bruhl discovers that he bears a resemblance to a well-known mobster, high on everyone's hit lists. Badly shaken by his friends' practical jokes, "the mild little man" paradoxically takes to living the role that his friends believe to be so amusingly incongruous with his true personality. His melancholy fix is formally diagnosed by a physician as "a definite psychosis." Bruhl is assassinated, gangland style, and in his last moments, true to his psychosis, he defiantly refuses to talk to the police.

The spiritual relatives of Mr. and Mrs. John Monroe continue their marital skirmishing in this volume, and there is a notable escalation in the level of hostilities. Mr. and Mrs. Bidwell knife each other with their eyes after Bidwell persists in holding his breath for his own amusement, thus exasperating his wife. They are separating as the story ends. Things are not going so well in "Mr. Pendly and the Poindexter" either. The matrimonial warfare in this story is autobiographical, as Pendly, suffering from eye trouble, is chauffeured by his wife: "It gave him a feeling of inferiority to sit mildly beside her while she solved the considerable problems of city traffic." Prefiguring the mental adjustments of Walter Mitty and recalling the young Thurber's adventures in a Seairoplane, Pendly dreams of flying into a garden party in an "autogiro," sweeping his wife away, and zooming fearlessly into the blue. The battle is even grimmer in "The Curb in the Sky," in which Charlie Deshler makes the mistake of marrying a woman who completes sentences for people, driving him over the edge and into an asylum where she corrects and edits even his dreams.

The Thurbers' own marriage was breaking up during the time he wrote these stories (their daughter, Rosemary, was born in 1931 after the Thurbers had briefly reconciled following an earlier separation). They were divorced in 1935. The quarrels, the fights, the infidelities, and the loneliness of these years are animated in the humorous pieces in *The Middle-Aged Man on the Flying Trapeze*; but some of the serious stories in the collection seemed so painfully autobiographical and so bleak that many of the author's friends were openly concerned about his well-being. In "Smashup," the Trinways narrowly avoid death when the nervous husband, Tommy, has to drive in city traffic and involves them in a collision. They are physically unhurt, but their marriage is irrevocably smashed. In "The Evening's at Seven," "One is a Wanderer," and "A Box to Hide In," there is very little that is funny, and the stories all chronicle the wanderings of Prufrockian souls facing forty. The anti-hero of "The Evening's at Seven" visits an old girlfriend only to find that the attraction is gone; he sees it is "eighteen minutes after seven and he had the mingled thoughts that clocks always gave him." Mr. Kirk of "One Is a Wanderer," who seems in better shape, is living alone in a room where his "soiled shirts would be piled on the floors of the closet where he had been flinging them for weeks . . ." (a fitting description of Thurber's own Algonquin Hotel room, according to his biographer). Kirk cannot relax and cannot work, so he drinks one brandy after another, not caring to intrude on friends who have already seen enough of him, because "Two is company, four is a party, three is a crowd. One is a wanderer." Also disturbing is "A Box to Hide In," which concerns a man who is beyond the sort of escape

that brandy can offer and is asking at grocery stores for a box that is big enough for him to hide in: "It's a form of escape . . . hiding in a box. It circumscribes your worries and the range of your anguish," he explains quite lucidly. It is precisely this melancholy light that permeates Thurber's most distinctive work.

The unique Thurber blend of the comic with the dire and the bizarre is found in "Mr. Preble Gets Rid of His Wife." In this story, as in many others in this collection, the Thurber man and woman are frankly fed up with each other. But in this instance their argument is surreal: Mrs. Preble consents to go down into the cellar, even though she knows Preble wants to kill her down there, so that he will shut up and give her a moment's peace. She is not at all unnerved at the prospect of being bludgeoned to death with a shovel, but she is disgusted with his poor choice of murder weapons, and orders him out to look for something more suitable. Dutifully, the exasperated Preble goes out to hunt up "some piece of iron or something," as she demands, promising to hurry and to shut the door behind him, because Mrs. Preble is not about to stand in the cellar all night and freeze.

In *Let Your Mind Alone! And Other More or Less Inspirational Pieces* (1937), Thurber continued to publish stories about husbands and wives who are not getting along well together. Although no blood is spilled in "The Breaking Up of the Winships" and "A Couple of Hamburgers," these "serious" stories hardly deal with marriage optimistically. Yet the book is dedicated to Helen Wismer, the Mount Holyoke graduate and magazine editor to whom Thurber was married just one month after his first marriage officially ended in 1935. The newlyweds sought to escape the frenetic, intolerable pace and style of their New York life by moving to a series of houses in Connecticut. There, in the relative security of a stronger marriage and a greener, more peaceful environment, Thurber developed old and new themes to create a collection that, while not as strong as his previous book, is still one of his half dozen best books.

In the first ten pieces, the "Let Your Mind Alone!" section, Thurber again parodies the writings of mental-efficiency experts, those purveyors of quick, rational, methodical fixes for what ails the human being that he had lampooned in *Is Sex Necessary?* Here he finds that humanity is in deep trouble–doomed, in fact–and he says that "scientists, statisticians, actuaries, all those men who place numbers above hunches, figures above feelings, facts above possibilities . . . ," give advice that is worse than useless in keeping the average Thurber person alive and happy. We do not need to "stream-line" our minds to live more successfully; on the contrary, "The undisciplined mind . . . is far better adapted to the confused world in which we live today than the stream-lined mind." Self-help writer Mrs. Dorothea Brande, author of *Wake Up and Live!* (1936), sanctions daydreaming "only when it is purposeful, only when it is going to lead to realistic action and concrete achievement." This kind of advice would be of little help to the Walter Mittys of this world, and Thurber stands with this yet-to-be-created woolgatherer par excellence in "The Case for the Daydreamer," where he says, "In this insistence on reality I do not see as much profit as these Shapers of Success do." He goes on to give hilarious examples of situations in life where daydreaming presents the most masterful adaptations to the real world. The machine looms large as one of the most ominous forces that threatens human existence, as Thurber presents the case. In "Sex ex Machina," Thurber takes issue with the psychologists, who chalk up fears of speeding automobiles to suppressed sexual urges, to "complexes." Thurber knows a threat when he sees one, and cars are terrifying in their own right. "Every person carries in his consciousness the old scar, or the fresh wound, of some harrowing misadventure with a contraption of some sort," he says, be it with a vending machine or "an old Reo with the spark advanced."

The "Other More or Less Inspirational Pieces" prove to be less, rather than more, encouraging about the prospects for human survival. Animals, the reader is assured in "After the Steppe Cat, What?," will prevail against the combined insanities of fascism and communism and the thousand unnatural shocks of technological life; but man is doomed. Woman, however, may fare better. "Man, as he is now traveling," writes Thurber in "Women Go On Forever," "is headed for extinction. Woman is not going with him. It is, I think, high time to abandon the loose, generic term 'Man,' for it is no longer logically inclusive or scientifically exact. There is Man and there is Woman, and Woman is going her own way." In "The Case Against Women" Thurber elaborates his reasons for "hating women," which include: "they always know where things are," they never have the correct change, and "they never get anything exactly right." Thurber describes his deterio-

rating vision in the last essay in the volume, "The Admiral on the Wheel." Instead of having "only two-fifths vision" with its "peculiar advantages"–like seeing "bridges rise lazily into the air"–the cataract in his eye had grown, and to his ophthalmologist "it was obvious he was going blind." Helen Thurber was driving the car now in the daytime as well as at night, and soon she would have to serve as his "seeing eye wife."

Thurber put off the eye operations he would need to tour Europe with Helen Thurber, to attend the London opening of an art show including his drawings, and to generally "clear his mind." They were out of the country from May 1937 until June 1938, and a record of much of what Thurber saw and thought is in essays such as "You Know How the French Are," "An Afternoon in Paris," and "Journey to the Pyrenees," all collected in *My World–and Welcome to It* (1942). The most significant writing he produced right after returning from Europe, however, was the series gathered from the *New Yorker* and published as *Fables for Our Time and Famous Poems Illustrated* (1940). "Every writer is fascinated by the fable form," he later told Alistair Cooke; "it's short, concise and can say a great deal about life."

In Thurber's fables, there is less reassurance, less sense of a grand consensus of common wisdom and shared values found in the fables of the ancients or even in the *Fables in Slang* (1899) of Midwestern humorist George Ade. Stylistically, Thurber's are Attic, rather than slangy or full of the wordplay and oddities in capitalization which characterize Ade's work. Written at a time when darkness was descending on the world as well as upon the artist, these fables tend toward the sardonic and register twentieth-century wariness and disenchantment. Doom lunges from every corner at unsuspecting chipmunks, humans, turkeys, and flies. Yet some of the mayhem and destruction seem preventable and are caused by ignorance and folly rather than being simply the terrible way things are. Sometimes "He who hesitates is saved." The problem is not that creatures are unredeemable and always corrupt; it is rather that they are credulous and easily swayed by Hitler-like owls and Mussolini-like foxes. The problem is that "You can fool too many of the people too much of the time." As usual, the males seem, more often than not, vulnerable to the perversity of the females. However, in "The Unicorn in the Garden," one of Thurber's best short pieces, a little man gains one of his infrequent victories. One morning, a typical Thurber husband sees the

James Thurber, 1936 (Dodd, Mead & Company)

James and Helen Thurber with Ronald and Jane Williams, Bermuda, 1936 (Dodd, Mead & Company)

"mythical beast" in his own garden. The nagging wife, on hearing of his miraculous discovery, tells him that he is a "booby" and that she is going to have him put "in the booby hatch." When the authorities arrive, he denies ever having mentioned a unicorn, and they grab the wife for going on and on about how her husband swore he saw such a thing. She is carried away screaming and he lives "happily ever after," having sustained another victory for the imagination over the world of dull realities. The moral is "Don't count your boobies until they are hatched." Yet in 1938-1939, for Thurber's barnyard animals in "The Hen and the Heavens," "the heavens actually were falling down." And in the moral he commented, "It wouldn't surprise me a bit if they did."

The year 1939 was probably the most rewarding year in Thurber's creative life. Not only did he produce some of his best writing, he achieved great satisfaction in the summer of 1939 from collaborating with his college friend Elliott Nugent on a play. It was Thurber's idea to write *The Male Animal*, but both men participated fully in the work of writing, revising, and rewriting again during trial performances in San Diego, Santa Barbara, Los Angeles, Princeton, and Baltimore. The play was a financial and critical success and had a run of 243 performances at the Cort Theatre in New York, where it opened 9 January 1940 with Howard Shumlin as producer and Nugent playing the lead of Tommy Turner, an English professor at Midwestern University. Warner Brothers made a film version of the play in 1942, starring Henry Fonda and Olivia de Havilland. The film's March 1942 world premiere in Columbus, the Thurber family in attendance, made it clear to everyone that James Thurber had become one of the city's most celebrated offspring.

Thurber had been interested in the theater for a long time, as his participation in dramatics at Ohio State and his work on musicals for the Scarlet Mask Club between 1921 and 1925 had shown. A Broadway play was a great challenge to this writer of short pieces, who had difficulty writing tightly organized, long, and "serious" works. *The Male Animal*, though it is essentially a romantic comedy, has its serious dimensions. Nevertheless, it portrays the battle between Tommy Turner, a classical liberal and defender of good writing, individualism, and principles in the abstract, fighting against blind conformity, brute force, and the voice of money, power, and vested interests–represented partially by former football

hero Joe Ferguson and chiefly by the villain of the play, university trustee Ed Keller. Tommy Turner, the professorial defender of principle, is married to an atypical Thurber woman, Ellen. Ellen is lovely and rather passive, and functions primarily as the prize to be fought over by the rival men. Tommy, on the one side, represents reason and the old-fashioned liberal ideal of the integrity of the individual; Joe Ferguson, on the other side, represents the values and virtues of animal vigor, football, and dead-level conformity on all matters considered controversial. The trustee, Ed Keller, is an anti-intellectual Red-hunting Babbitt who seeks to have Tommy fired after he learns that Tommy plans to read the last statement of anarchist Bartolomeo Vanzetti. Joe Ferguson, recently divorced, becomes a rival for Ellen's affections, and Tommy appears to play the fool, the defeated Thurber man, as he fantasizes that the "male animal" within him can conquer Ferguson by dint of force. Ferguson knocks him senseless, of course, but he ultimately profits from playing the part of comic victim and butt. For he is a man of principle and of intellect, and can use his experience to gain insight and to adapt. Unlike Walter Mitty, who retreats into fantasy when the world threatens his security, Tommy Turner gains an ironic understanding of himself as a comic figure; at the same time, he can retain a realistic belief in his principles and the virtues of his role as an embattled individualist. In the end, Joe testifies that Tommy is a real "scrapper," and Ellen is convinced that Tommy is "wonderful." The play ends not with a divorce, but with a reaffirmation of the Turners' marriage, as "They are kissing each other very, very hard" when the curtain falls. It is not a very political play, as Thurber was not a very political man. Yet the political dimension was thrown into high relief when the play was revived on Broadway in 1952 as the country labored under the shadow of McCarthyism; it did even better at the box office then than it had originally and subsequently went on a national tour.

The Last Flower (1939) is "a parable in pictures" with a spare written text, yet it can hardly be called a cartoon. Written in the fall of 1939, after Germany had invaded Poland, the book opens with World War XII. Although armies ravage the cities, destroy civilization, and devastate the forests, one last flower remains. The few humans left alive find the flower, and nurture it. The cycle begins again and World War XIII destroys all but one man, one woman, and one flower for them to nurture. *The Last Flower* is said to have been Thurber's favorite of his own books in his later years, and E. B. White, writing in the *New Yorker*'s memorial tribute to Thurber, said that he too liked it best of all Thurber's works. "In it," he contended, "you will find his faith in the renewal of life, his feeling for the beauty and fragility of life on earth." The book was dedicated to Thurber's daughter, Rosemary, "in the wistful hope that her world will be better than mine."

"The Secret Life of Walter Mitty" presents the classic version of the Thurber man. This story is unquestionably Thurber's most famous; published first in March of 1939 in the *New Yorker* and later collected in *My World–and Welcome to It*, the story has been frequently reprinted. The name Walter Mitty, like that of George Babbitt or Don Quixote, can be found in the dictionary, defined as "a commonplace unadventurous person who seeks escape from reality through daydreaming and typically imagines himself leading a glamorous life and becoming famous." Tommy Turner indulges in fantasies of himself as a powerful "male animal," but also sees this indulgence as comical. Such ironic detachment from himself as daydreamer gives him a kind of self-awareness and insight that Mitty does not have. Walter Mitty is a compulsive daydreamer, and in the story he repeatedly retreats from everyday problems by imagining himself as a pulp-fiction hero—the kind of man neither he nor anyone could ever be. "The more he depends on the escape they afford," writes Stephen Black, "the less possibility there is of his confronting his real problems. . . ." Yet Mitty's escapist tactics for surviving in a hostile world of domineering wives, traffic cops, automobiles, and all that goes "ta-pocketa-pocketa" seem more effective than those of even jumpier Thurber men, as other stories in *My World–and Welcome to It* reveal.

If 1939 and 1940 had been years of triumph, 1941 began a period of severe trial. Thurber's eye operation could no longer be postponed, and in fact he underwent five operations that year for cataract, glaucoma, and iritis, problems which were related to his childhood accident and the sympathetic ophthalmia induced by the loss of his left eye in 1901. Other family problems, including the death of Helen Thurber's father and the diagnosis that Mary Thurber had cancer, combined to push Thurber through "the corridors of hell," as he put it in a letter. His operations could not reverse the deterioration of his vi-

sion, and, faced with the prospect of blindness, this intensely visual artist suffered a severe nervous breakdown.

The anxiety, the terror, and the anger of these months were expressed and partially exorcised in some of the darker stories collected in *My World–and Welcome to It*. One of these, possibly the darkest and least amusing little-man story Thurber was ever to write, is "The Whip-Poor-Will," first published in 1941 in the *New Yorker*, just after he had begun to climb out of the mental collapse. Like Thurber, Mr. Kinstrey is an upper-middle-class former Ohioan, and the setting appears to be quite like one of the Thurber retreats in Massachusetts or Connecticut. Kinstrey's mental torment mirrors Thurber's concerns: he is plagued by insomnia and provoked by a "brazen-breasted," persistent, sleep-murdering whippoor-will, that neither his servants nor his wife will admit to having heard. His wife tells him to ignore it, to use his "will power." The pun enters his dreams and blends with the unnerving, rhythmic, intolerable birdcalls. Thurber's concern for his loss of sight, possibly manifest in the dominance of aural effects in the story, is more explicit when Kinstrey objects to his wife's use of the word *spectacle* to describe his furious yelling and cursing at the whippoorwill in the middle of the night. "I never heard such a spectacle," she says the next morning. "You can't hear spectacles," says Kinstrey, "You see them." The image returns on the night he goes completely to pieces, imagining that he can hear his wife chant, "Here are your spectacles, here are your spectacles." There is no magic to save this Thurber man, as there is in "The Unicorn in the Garden" or "The Catbird Seat," and there is no comic resolution: Kinstrey takes out a carving knife and kills his wife, two servants, and himself.

There is a similar dark ending in "A Friend to Alexander," also collected in *My World–and Welcome to It*. Harry Andrews, the troubled husband, shares with Thurber a fascination with Aaron Burr and the song "Bye, Bye, Blackbird." He, too, is in poor physical health, worries about weight loss, and fortifies himself with all kinds of vitamins. He has terrible dreams and suffers a mental breakdown. In his recurrent dreams, Harry is threatened by Aaron Burr, and he takes to practicing, as if for a duel, with a pistol. After he dies mysteriously in his sleep, the doctor comments that his heart "Just stopped as if he had been shot." Mrs. Andrews, like the wife in "The Unicorn in the Garden," blurts out the impossi-

Dust jacket for Thurber's 1957 story of a pirate who hates the letter O *(Simon & Schuster)*

ble truth, that "Aaron Burr killed him the way he killed Hamilton." But when she is pronounced "stark, raving crazy" and is taken away, there is no triumphant humor. There is only grim irony.

There are signs of Thurber's return to mental stability in *My World—and Welcome to It*, however, in several lighter pieces. "You Could Look It Up" is a dialect narrative about a baseball manager who puts in a midget pinch hitter with an infinitesimal strike zone. "A Good Man," expanded and republished as "Adam's Anvil" in *The Thurber Album*, anticipates the nostalgic tone and subject matter of that later volume. Thurber's abiding and deepening interest in the sounds, shapes, and nuances of words is displayed in two other notable pieces, "What Do You Mean It Was Brillig?" and "The Gentleman in 916." Both pieces take off from linguistic anomalies uttered by a "remarkable collection of colored maids," and both reveal his increasingly evident preoccupation with his in-

creasing blindness and the brevity of life. In the first piece, for example, Della perplexes him one day by announcing, "They are here with the reeves." Thurber has a lot of fun with this pronunciation, finally discovering that the "reeves" in question are Yuletide window decorations. In the second, Maisie writes him that she tried to see him in December, "but the timekeeper said you were in Florida." Her reference to "the timekeeper" disturbs him: "Since I have, for the time being, about one-fiftieth vision, I can't actually see him; but I can hear him. It is no illusion that the blind become equipped with the eardrums of an elk hound." Both stories make use of the traditional encounter between the shrewd but uneducated *eiron* with the *alazon*, the word-crazy author who presumes to be smarter than he is. The uneducated Della, for example, says of her employer, "His mind works so fast his body can't keep up with it . . . ," a line which gives Thurber pause. He begins to worry that soon "They will come for me with a reeve and this time it won't be a red-and-green one for the window, it will be a black one for the door."

Many of the themes in Thurber's writing are also found in his drawings. In White's note on the drawings that illustrate *Is Sex Necessary?*, he points out such subjects as "the melancholy of sex," "the implausibility of animals," and the persistent theme of warfare between the sexes. "The War Between Men and Women" is, in fact, the title to a seventeen-part series of drawings, running from the first "Overt Act" (when a man in dinner dress throws a glass of dark liquid in a woman's face) through "The Fight in the Grocery" and "Mrs. Pritchard's Leap," to the ultimate (and baffling) "Surrender" of the women to the men. The series was first collected in *Thurber's Men, Women, and Dogs* (1943), which contains many of Thurber's best and most famous cartoons. Among these is the surrealistic "House and Woman," a drawing that depicts a badly frightened and tiny Thurber man recoiling in astonishment before a three-storied house which somehow has coalesced into an enormous Thurber woman, who glares fiercely at the cowering little man below. Thurber's drawings and cartoons do more than merely illustrate most of his works (they continued to appear in his books even after he had to stop drawing new ones in 1951); they amplify, extend, and open different dimensions of his artistry.

Published in early 1945, after Thurber's five-year struggle with nervous and physical breakdowns including not only the eye operations but a nearly fatal case of appendicitis complicated by pneumonia, *The Thurber Carnival* (1945) signaled his recovery and was proof that Thurber had arrived as an important figure in American letters. In a review for the *New Republic*, Malcolm Cowley approached the book "exactly as if it were the work of any other skillful and serious American writer." The book contains six pieces not previously collected (among them one of his best stories, "The Catbird Seat," and one of his best "dark" tales, "The Cane in the Corridor," a work that clearly alludes to his recent suffering and affliction), a selection of pieces from *My World—and Welcome to It, Let Your Mind Alone!, The Middle-Aged Man on the Flying Trapeze, Fables for Our Time and Famous Poems Illustrated, The Owl in the Attic, The Seal in the Bedroom, Thurber's Men, Women, and Dogs*, and the entire contents of *My Life and Hard Times*. The critical reception was extravagant and wide, and for the first time a Thurber book found a truly mass audience, as the book sold 50,000 copies in the Harper's first edition and 375,000 more with the Book-of-the-Month Club. Cowley found that eight of the pieces "are quite serious in effect and intention, and several of the others balance on the edge between farce and disaster. . . ." Many of them deal with murder, death, or "dreams of killing or being killed, and two with the hero of one and the villainess of the other reduced to raving madness." This latter category includes "The Catbird Seat," which repeats the pattern of "The Unicorn in the Garden" as the put-upon little man, Edwin Martin, manages to have the browbeating Mrs. Barrow fired by behaving outrageously out of character in her presence and then denying his actions after she reports him to the boss. But almost half the selections in the work, Cowley notes, are "largely based on nightmares, hallucinations or elaborate and cruel practical jokes. Entering Thurber's middle-class world is like wandering into a psychiatric ward and not being quite sure whether you are a visitor or an inmate."

Thurber found relief from some of his mental and physical troubles in writing works like the nostalgic *Thurber Album* and in a series of romances for children and adults that included *Many Moons* (1943), *The Great Quillow* (1944), *The White Deer* (1945), *The 13 Clocks* (1950), and *The Wonderful O* (1957). These stories depart from the plain style of the typical Thurber casuals and are characterized by a more poetic density of figures and allusions, and, at times, meter and

rhyme. White called *The White Deer* "Exhibit A in the strange case of a writer's switch from eye work to ear work." Thurber had always written about people who live by virtue of their power to dream, surviving in hostile circumstances with the help of their inner visions. Now this element of fantasy predominates, and these works can be called proper romances, tales of wizards and kings and enchanted forests, of spells and potions and captive princesses. As in the myth of the Fisher King, there is a blight upon the land at the beginning of each of these tales. Thurber's questing heroes manage to break the withering forces of evil and restore order, meaning, and purpose to the world. The heroes are toymakers, sensitive third sons, wandering minstrels, and jesters; in *The Wonderful O* the hero is a poet. They are all men of imagination, shapers who order the meaningless jumble of things and make sense out of them. These fantasists succeed where more practical men—represented by mathematicians, physicians, lawyers, and experts of every type fail. The princess marries the minstrel-prince in *The 13 Clocks* and sails away from the land of the cruel, cold duke, who lives in a land that is so cold that all the clocks have stopped, frozen. They cannot be started again until the princess holds her hand at a certain magical distance from them—at which time they thaw and begin to strike the hours. The minutes of clocks, Thurber seems to be hinting, like the words of stories, create and order the world—they humanize it, they lend it the meaning that it otherwise lacks. It is the inner vision of the artist that creates the bright shapes by which people must live. The poet as the hero of *The Wonderful O* restores the letter *O*s to the land from which they have been banished, and thereby returns to the inhabitants words like hope, love, valor, and freedom.

In the foreword to *The Beast in Me and Other Animals* (1948), Thurber apologized for coming out with "another collection of short pieces and small drawings," when a writer "verging on his middle fifties" "should be engaged on some work dignified by length and of a solemnity suitable to our darkening age. . . ." The darkening was first and most immediately his nearly complete blindness, and the perceptible decline in the quality of this volume compared with earlier collections is apparent. Since 1946 he had been forced to dictate his stories to a secretary and had found this process difficult and complicated further by the need to find a secretary with whom he could be comfortable. It was a troubled time, even though he and Helen Thurber had found a large colonial house that they liked in quiet West Cornwell, Connecticut.

The Beast in Me and Other Animals included "A Sheaf of Drawings," featuring some of his last cartoons and whimsical sketches of Thurber men and women, and also three sets of drawings-with-text under the heading "Less Alarming Creatures" (less alarming than humans, that is). These were some of the last drawings Thurber was able to produce, and all of them were executed with the assistance of technical aids, such as the Zeiss loop–a magnifying helmet used during the war for precision work in defense plants. Some of the creatures are Thurber's versions of real beasts, such as Bosmon's Potto (a species of primate), but other creatures are Thurber's inventions. There are Trochees encountering Spondees, Serenades, and Victuals, for example. Ross was delighted with these pictured puns and asked the artist to continue, but the only addition Thurber could think of would be "a man being generous to a fault–that is, handing a small rodent a nut."

During the mid 1940s and early 1950s, Thurber produced relatively few casuals and stories for the *New Yorker*. His "heart wasn't in it" to write amusingly during this period he said, and Bernstein reveals that in his private life he was often behaving as a tyrannical, temperamental, and sometimes drunken and vengeful "King of Cornwall," given to dyspeptic rages and pronouncements. The pieces he collected in *The Beast in Me and Other Animals* sometimes show "the beast" in him–an opinionated and cantankerous misogynist or an old stick critical of the new, as in "Thix," where he compares the popular-culture radio serials such as "Captain Midnight" with the less harrowing adventures he followed in his own youth through the plays and nickel novels back in Columbus. Such a subject also betrays his dependence on radio for entertainment, as becomes even more evident in his long, five-part investigation "Soapland," which originally ran in the *New Yorker* as a reportorial piece in which "the humor . . . is coincidental." This investigation of radio soap opera and the sex roles and cultural values displayed therein was a popular success in the magazine and demonstrated Thurber's ability as a serious analyst of American culture. *The Beast in Me*–even in its title–also demonstrates Thurber's continued reverence for the work of Henry James, whose "The Beast in the Jungle" he elaborately imitates, more in homage than in parody, in "The Beast in the Dingle."

Ross rejected the piece as too labored and literary, saying that he "understood fifteen percent of the allusions," leaving Thurber to wonder just which fifteen percent those could have been. Ross did print "A Call on Mrs. Forrester," however, Thurber's tribute to Willa Cather and Henry James, told by a sort of Lambert Strether making an imaginary call on Cather's "lost lady" and comparing her to Mme de Vonnet. "It's about a man and two women," Ross said, "and it comes over."

Thurber's love of puns, word games, and puzzles of all sorts had been evident in his work from the beginning and had been further developed in his employment as a code clerk, which led him to read books on cryptography. In this volume, as in the "fairy tales" for adults and children he had been writing, his fascination with the sounds and structures of words is expressed not only in the curious names of whimsical creatures and the loving imitations of Henry James, but with anagrammatic experimentation and wordplay in "Here Come the Tigers." Two friends demonstrate, for example, how they have "discovered a new dimension of meaning," finding "the lips in pistol/And mists in times,/Cats in crystal,/And mice in chimes." Such logomania abounds in Thurber's later work, often amounts to a preponderance of wit over humor, and sometimes becomes excessively private in its significance.

Thurber had never been intensely interested in politics, but as the fever of McCarthyism spread, he became involved in defending the rights of the individual as opposed to the growing enthusiasm for "loyalty" and conformity. In 1946 he supported the staff of the *Sundial*, the Ohio State humor magazine he had edited in his student days, after the university administration had suspended its publication for a year because the magazine had published material they considered offensive. In 1947 he wrote a letter defending E. B. White when the *New York Herald Tribune* referred to White's opinions as potentially dangerous. (White had written a letter to the editor of that newspaper condemning required loyalty oaths as unconstitutional.) And in 1951, after the administration at Ohio State instituted a gag rule for campus speakers, he again took sides and became the first alumnus of that institution to refuse the offer of an honorary degree. In his 1951 letter of refusal, he wrote that acceptance at that time might be construed as approval of Ohio State's recent trespasses against the rights of "free-

James Thurber (Culver Pictures)

and physical afflictions, during 1949 he was grieved over a serious auto accident that injured his daughter, Rosemary; by the nervous breakdown of longtime friend and collaborator Elliott Nugent; and by his wife's surgery for uterine cysts. He was also deeply saddened in 1951 by the death of Harold Ross.

In the face of all these trials, *The Thurber Album* is an impressive achievement and gave Thurber an opportunity to, as his grandfather would have put it, "show his Fisher"—to show the spirit of such ancestors as his maternal great-great-grandfather Jacob Fisher, remembered in "Adam's Anvil" (the story was previously printed as "A Good Man"). This forebear is described as a virtual ring-tailed roarer in the tradition of the humor of the Old Southwest. Jacob Fisher, born in 1808 near Columbus, fought "a thousand fights in his time," including one fight, carefully described, in which he whipped the entire canal-barge crew that had been poaching on his ducks. Fisher used to move horses in his blacksmithing shop by picking them up and carrying them—"it was easier to move 'em that way than to lead 'em sometimes." Not only do these exploits match those told in an earlier age, but the manner of telling also recalls the framework narrative structure as found, for example, in "The Celebrated Jumping Frog of Calaveras County" by Mark Twain. Thurber, as first-person narrator, introduces his uncle Mahlon Taylor, whom he describes and characterizes. Taylor narrates in dialect the inner tale, the yarns about Fisher—stories that seem "mostly true, with some stretchers," as Huck Finn might say. The notable difference from the stories of the horse-sense era is in the character of the first narrator: "A far lesser breed of men," Thurber admits, "has succeeded the old gentleman on the American earth, and I tremble to think what he would have said of a great-grandson who turned out to be a writer."

In *The Thurber Album* Thurber remembers with fondness and wit Margery Albright, the midwife who had delivered him and whom he called "Aunt Margery," though she was not related to him. Aunt Margery was a formidable personage, a homeopath, and a woman of considerable resource and unquestionable resolve; in her and even more in Thurber's portrait of his mother in "Lavender with a Difference," we see the positive side of the Thurber woman. And in "Gentleman from Indiana," about his father, Charles Thurber, we see one of the originals of the Thurber man, the kind of person who, when he tried to

dom of speech and freedom of research." This concern for the rights of the embattled artist and individual is expressed briefly in *The Thurber Album* in "Length and Shadow," the profile of Ohio State English professor and dean Joseph Villiers Denney (the model for Dean Damon in *The Male Animal*). Thurber writes that Denney "must have turned restlessly in his grave" all during the fall of 1951 when "the trustees were qualifying freedom of speech at the university. . . ." But this profile represents a departure from the basic tone and subject matter of *The Thurber Album*, which is mostly nostalgic and sentimental.

He told interviewers that *The Thurber Album* "was written at a time when in America there was a feeling of fear and suspicion. It's quite different from *My Life and Hard Times*," he said, though it treats many of the same times and characters. But the earlier book is "funnier and better. . . . The *Album* was kind of an escape—going back to the Middle West of the last century and the beginning of this, when there wasn't this fear and hysteria." Besides his sense of a general public hysteria and in addition to his personal mental

fix a rabbit pen, could only succeed in locking himself into the cage. The "frankly nostalgic" excursion to friends and faces in the past concludes with a "Photograph Gallery," photographs of nearly all the important figures he had written about in the book, including his eccentric relatives; his Ohio State professors Denney, Taylor, and Graves; football hero Chic Harley; city editor Norman Kuehner of the *Dispatch*; and his early model, journalist Robert O. Ryder.

Despite the strain he was under from 1948 through 1952, Thurber continued to produce casuals for the *New Yorker* and short pieces for other periodicals in addition to the work he was doing on his fairy stories and *The Thurber Album*. The best of these were collected in *Thurber Country* (1953), and while, as Charles S. Holmes points out, there are "no new departures" here, the work is of a high order. A dominant theme that runs through many of the pieces concerns the difficulty of communication and the decay of meaning: the problem of closing the gap between sender and receiver. The telephone, according to "The Case Book of James Thurber," is responsible for the kind of verbal confusion in which a woman whose name seems to be Sherlock Holmes turns out to be Shirley Combs; the maid may think that one's spouse is coming home with a "cockeyed Spaniard," but it is only a new cocker spaniel puppy. The telephone may also tangle the user in the cord, like the one the Thurbers used on one of their trips to France. There, as Thurber says in "The Girls in the Closet," it is possible to have profounder misunderstandings trying to explain in French the problem with the overabundance of *fil* (wire) when it is mispronounced *fille* (girl), indicating that "There are too many girls in the closet," and opening the door to further trouble. Writing letters does not seem to reduce the confusion appreciably, as two epistolary pieces demonstrate. "File and Forget" and "Joyeux Noel, Mr. Durning" are both presented as exchanges of letters between bureaucratic officialdom and the author. In the first, ineradicable confusion persists through a long, complicated exchange between Thurber and a publishing house; and in the second, similar confusion multiplies when a Christmas gift of liqueur sent to Thurber from France is seized by customs and he tries to have it released. Literary talk about T. S. Eliot's play *The Cocktail Party* ends in meaningless doubletalk and endless proliferation of private interpretations. One character wheezes, seemingly beside the point under discus-

sion, but right on the more general intent of these pieces: "Discipline breaking down all over the world." The search in an author's work for what James called "the figure in the carpet" is central to the movement of "A Final Note on Chanda Bell," a story that pays homage to Thurber's old master and also shows the influence of Joyce and possibly Gertrude Stein. The title character is a noted if peculiar novelist given to wordplay that recalls either Joyce's *Finnegans Wake* or Mrs. Malaprop. She draws the narrator into a frenzied search for the secret key to all her work, telling him, "You have found the figure, Thurber . . . but have you found the carpet?" He reads her work backward, upside down, in the mirror, and in the end is trying to read it sideways, but there is reason "to fear that she had perpetrated, in . . . her novels, one of the major literary hoaxes of our time. . . ." It may be that her seemingly meaningless statements are literally meaningless.

Thurber's opinion that the language was decaying and that meaning itself was threatened led to more strident protestations against lax usage in his last works. Accompanying this theme is his fascination with word games, already evident in "Here Come the Tigers" and the verbal wit of the fairy stories. One of his best pieces on word games appears in *Thurber Country* as "Do You Want to Make Something Out of It? (Or, If You Put an 'O' on 'Understo,' You'll Ruin My 'Thunderstorm')," which explains a variation of "ghosts," a word-spelling game. Thurber was a fanatical player of this and other word games during these years, and in this witty and very funny piece he shares some of the linguistic arcana he has discovered both in hours of play and later, while tossing on his sheets, coming up with "bedwords"– words that can't be found in the dictionary (and so cannot be played) but which have the right letters in the middle. "Sgra" bedwords, for example, include such Thurber coinages as "Kissgranny, 1. A man who seeks the company of older women . . . 2. an overaffectionate old woman, a hugmoppet, a bunnytalker"; and "blessgravy. A minister or cleric; . . . *Colloq.* a breakvow, a shrugholy." In a piece that is particularly interesting to the student of American humor, Thurber presents a tale of the confrontation of himself, playing the part of citified wit and *alazon*, against Zeph Leggin, "a character in the classic mold, a lazy rustic philosopher." Thurber cannot stand to be upstaged by this shrewd cracker-barrel philosopher, but in his attempts to duel verbally with the fellow he is soundly defeated. Horse-sense sayings are not to his liking, as his twisted fables reveal; yet he acknowledges their power and makes efficient use of the tradition.

The characteristic attitudes and subjects of Thurber's later work are fully evident in *Further Fables for Our Time* (1956), in which none of the fables is as good as the best in *Fables for Our Time*. Thurber's antipathy to McCarthyism is once again evident in pieces such as "The Peaceful Mongoose," where the deviant animal who tries to use his head is told that "reason is six-sevenths treason." He is condemned to banishment finally, and the moral is: "Ashes to ashes, and clay to clay, if the enemy doesn't get you your own folks may." Thurber's conviction that the lines of communication were fraying is also a prominent theme. "We live, man and worm," says Thurber in "The Weaver and the Worm," "in a time when almost everything can mean almost anything, for this is the age of gobbledygook, doubletalk, and gudda." His pessimism over the state of the language merged with his increasing cynicism and doubts that anything could be done to remedy the world's sorry state. The tools of the humorist apparently are not much use when "the truth is not merry and bright." "The truth is dark and cold," says a squirrel in "The Turtle Who Conquered Time." The sinister truth could be "twisted" in the direction of comedy in Thurber's earlier work, the comic mask providing a mode of adaptation to the darkness, but in *Further Fables for Our Time*, he seems less able to effect the twist of humor and tends to assault the truth head-on. Yet he did not seem to find this method gratifying. "Oh, why should the shattermyth have to be a crumplehope and a dampenglee?" asks the moral of the turtle fable. As "shattermyth" it is impossible to avoid dampening glee. Thurber seemed to be recognizing the change in his work when he described a hen who had been told by her psychiatrist that she had "galloping aggression, inflamed ego, and too much gall."

Alarms and Diversions (1957) is an anthology of selected prose from as far back as 1942 and of drawings from as early as 1931. There is no fiction among the ten new pieces in the volume, none of which is particularly amusing. There are essays on a variety of topics—on child-rearing; on a 1912 gangland murder and scandal (Thurber was fascinated by murders throughout his career); on forgotten American holidays; on the relative durability of men and women (women may

have more of what it takes to survive, he avers); on the relative brevity of life in Thurber's generation of American authors; on the Loch Ness monster—and so on. In "The First Time I Saw Paris" Thurber casts a wistful backward glance on his youth. The subdued tone and the poignant depiction of incidents described contrast strikingly with the exuberant, boyish letters he wrote Elliott Nugent in 1918-1919 when these events were taking place. Thurber's obsession with the decay of language is presented in "The Psychosemanticist Will See You Now, Mr. Thurber," in which he condemns the "carcinomenclature of our times" and links the health of the body politic with that of the body semantic: "Ill fares the land, to galloping fears a prey, whose gobbledygook accumulates, and words decay." This allusive, ornate sentence expresses his thesis and also reveals his late predilection for wordplay, verbal wit, and harangue—at the expense of the humor of character and the comedy of ideas.

The last two years of Thurber's life may have been difficult in many ways, filled as they were with the night fears and drunken scenes described by Bernstein. Yet there was the bright success of his reminiscence, *The Years with Ross*. Thurber had intended to write something about Harold Ross for more than a decade, at one time considering a play. What he finally created was a series of anecdotal essays, published first in the *Atlantic* beginning in 1957 and collected as *The Years with Ross*. The book was an achievement of memory, research, and discipline, and constituted a "strongly autobiographical" but affectionate tribute to his editor and friend, as well as providing an insider's account of the early development of the *New Yorker* and the circle of people that were associated with this important magazine. It proved to be Thurber's longest sustained piece of writing on a single subject, but it was not warmly received by a number of other *New Yorker* "insiders"; most notably, the book was disliked by E. B. and Katharine White, longtime friends of both Thurber and Harold Ross, and people whose opinions mattered very much to the author. Even so, this anecdotal memoir is in a genre at which Thurber excelled, and the book has a lasting power to entertain and move the reader. It was a best-seller and a Book-of-the-Month Club selection and, according to Holmes, "was reviewed more widely, enthusiastically, and in more detail than any of his previous books."

On 7 January 1960 *A Thurber Carnival* premiered at the Hartman Theater in Columbus, the scene of the Scarlet Mask Club productions that Thurber had worked on in the early 1920s. This Columbus homecoming was, Bernstein says, "by far the most spectacular" of all his returns to the hometown. The show opened 26 February 1960 at the ANTA Theatre in New York. Though Thurber wrote a great deal of new material, most of the sketches that were used in this "evening of words and music" consist of tried-and-true pieces, altered and adapted for the stage. The production was the joint creation of a number of people–Haila Stoddard, Don Elliott, and Burgess Meredith–but Thurber worked energetically at all aspects of preparing the show for the stage, and even managed to stimulate the box-office receipts by taking a part, playing himself in the "File and Forget" sketch in September 1960 when the play reopened in New York following a national tour. He appeared in eighty-eight performances and won a special "Tony" award for his distinguished writing. Despite this success, he was restless, often quarrelsome, unable to sleep. His health was failing, and he knew he was losing his ability to write as he had written before.

Lanterns & Lances was the last of his books that Thurber saw in print. In the foreword he defends the "lances" that now appear in his later works, cast "at the people and ideas that have disturbed me, and I make no apology for their seriousness." Though the book has material that was "written in anger" and some pieces that may seem "lugubrious," he wishes that the reader will find in the book a "basic thread of hope." And there is hope to be found, though Thurber writes about the "decline of humor and comedy in our time" in essays such as "The Case for Comedy" and "The Duchess and the Bugs." He also continues to rail about the decline of language in pieces such as "Conversation Piece: Connecticut," "The Tyranny of Trivia," and "The Watchers of the Night." In "The Trouble with Man Is Man" he expands upon his notion, delivered frequently in interviews during these years, that humans as a species are inferior to other creatures. He echoes the sentiments of Mark Twain's satan in *The Mysterious Stranger* when in his own "Here Come the Dolphins" he points out at length that when we humans say the beast in us has been aroused, it would be more accurate to say that the human being in us has been acting up–for animals are far less brutish than people.

Doom lowers on the narrator in this book, and only rarely can he find a way to laugh at his predicament. This is the "Atomic and the Aspirin Age," and the widespread angst he describes is most acute, it would seem, among writers, particularly those in his own generation. In "The Porcupines and the Artichokes" he says, "The literary men roughly in my age group become more articulate, and less coherent, as the years go by, but their age does not keep them away from parties." In *Lanterns & Lances* the narrator is frequently depicted as a distressed, jumpy insomniac. In "The Tyranny of Trivia," for example, he discusses his "preoccupation, compulsive perhaps, but not obsessive, with words and the alphabet. . . ." The purpose of his word games and speculations "is the sidetracking of worrisome trains of thought"; but the image of this worrier is one that seems to evoke in the reader pity and fear rather than laughter. The comic mask does not seem fully in place when he says, "My own habit, in bed at home or in the hospital, of exploring words and the alphabet acts to prevent my talking back to the wallpaper, a practice that, except in the case of the upright figure, may be more alarming than amusing." On the other hand, the narrator of "The Wings of Henry James" appears to be a sensitive and erudite literary critic; and the voice that speaks in so many of the "conversation pieces" is that of the Literatus, the supersophisticated and well-known personality, who jousts idly with half-wits, usually female half-wits, replying to their inanities in his "best Henry James garden-party manner." Only in "My Senegalese Birds and Siamese Cats" do we again hear the voice of the comic and vulnerable Thurber man. This is the only piece that makes extensive use of reminiscence–the familiar Thurber mixture of narrative fact and fiction concerning the fixes he can get into with such things as pets and appliances. In this piece he confesses that he has suffered from "decreasing inventiveness" in his later years, and also makes a remark that crystallizes the Thurber blend of memory and art: "Historicity lies so close to legend in my world that I often walk with one foot in each arena, with side trips, or so may critics declare, into fantasy."

The comic mask had allowed the narrator of *My Life and Hard Times* to make the reader laugh in spite of the awareness of doom. But the narrator in most of the late pieces, whether he is the polished Literatus or the jumpy insomniac, seldom functions as a comedian. "Humor is," as Thurber wrote in 1936, "a kind of emotional chaos told about calmly and quietly in retro- spect." More and more, he seemed to lack the inner quiet and concentrated attention necessary to twist reality into comedy. "I can't hide any- more behind the mask of comedy that I've used all my life," he told Elliott Nugent during his last year. "People are not funny; they are vicious and horrible—and so is life!"

On 3 October 1961 the Thurbers attended the opening of Noel Coward's musical *Sail Away* and a dinner party that followed at Sardi's East. Their evening went badly, and after Coward made a speech, Thurber "stood up and de- manded the microphone, shouting that he had something to say." Undaunted by an appalled au- dience, he sang "Bye, Bye, Blackbird"—a song that held private significance for him. "Suddenly, he staggered and lurched." While many other guests thought he was drunk, the problem was more seri- ous. Later that night, Helen Thurber found him lying in a pool of blood on the bathroom floor of their hotel room; and at the hospital the sur- geons removed a large cerebral hematoma and found "evidence of arteriosclerosis and several small strokes dating back at least a year. He had a senescent brain." He died on 2 November 1961 after developing pneumonia and a blood clot in a lung. His wife reported that near the end "Thur- ber had once seemed to whisper, 'God bless . . . God damn.' "

Helen Thurber in the foreword to the post- humously published *Credos and Curios* (1962) ex- plains that in collecting these pieces she is trying to carry out her husband's plans, as far as she is able to reconstruct them, for another book. Quite a few of the pieces, she notes, "express in some way his credos—his beliefs and feelings about humor and comedy, for example." The most impressive essay of this sort is "The Future, If Any, of Comedy or, Where Do We Non-Go from Here?" As the title would indicate, this piece discusses the decline and fall of humor, lan- guage, and the human species in the same vein that Thurber had been following in many late in- terviews and in *Lanterns & Lances*. Alongside these creedal essays are the "curios"–"Prefaces and short profiles of people he knew and admired"–including a 1938 piece on E. B. White, a 1940 profile of Elliott Nugent, a 1949 piece on Robert Benchley, and "Scott in Thorns," a 1951 essay about a one-night spree with F. Scott Fitzger- ald. There are also three short stories, including two of the last pieces of magazine fiction, "The Other Room" and "Brother Endicott." Both of

the stories are set in Paris and both involve aging centers of consciousness who reckon up the dis- tance they have traveled since youth. The stories seem to comment, if indirectly, on the Jamesian theme of the difference between the European and the American experience. Both stories also represent Thurber's attempt to write "serious" fic- tion, and Helen Thurber draws attention to this di- mension in his life's work by including in the vol- ume "Menaces in May," originally published in 1928. This impressionistic piece, she says, is "inter- esting because it was the first Thurber story in the *New Yorker* to depart from the 'little funny ca- sual' he was writing in those early days." The men- aces that confront the protagonist are quite simi- lar to those that might assault a "funny little man," but here they are not treated humorously. The man wonders over the events of a disturbing day and thinks: "Chaos had threatened a per- fectly directed evening. Maybe his life even. . . ."

Chaos had always threatened Thurber's char- acters; his anti-heroic John Monroes, Walter Mittys, Mr. Martins, and Mr. Kinstreys seem, in fact, to anticipate the spiritual drifters and death- obsessed schlemiels of later *New Yorker* writers Donald Barthelme and Woody Allen. They prefig- ure the characters of "black humor" more often than they recall cracker-barrel philosophers, horse-sense characters, or even the little men of early *New Yorker* writers Clarence Day and Robert Benchley. Benchley's "perfect neurotics" seem well-adjusted to the world when compared with many Thurber men, who frequently wander all the way around the bend to appear as murder- ous psychopaths rather than mildly maladjusted but fundamentally genial human beings. Chaos threatened Thurber personae and characters early and late, and the threat intensified as the years passed and the books accumulated. Yet even at the last, when there were more alarms than diversions, more lances than lanterns, there was that "thread of hope." In "The Case for Com- edy" (originally published in 1960 and reprinted in *Lanterns & Lances*) he mentions that he had heard Walter Lippmann say on the television that he "did not believe the world is coming apart," in spite of all the apparent signs of decay and the growing nuclear stockpiles; "It is high time," Thurber commented, "that we came of age and re- alized that, like Emily Dickinson's hope, humor is a feathered thing that perches in the soul." Intro- ducing the same volume, he had written that it's not just "later than you think" it is also " 'lighter than you think.' In this light, let's not look back in anger, or forward in fear, but around in awareness."

Interviews:

Harvey Breit, "Mr. Thurber Observes a Serene Birthday," *New York Times Magazine*, 4 December 1949, pp. 17, 78-79.
> Talks of Thurber's blindness, his drawings of dogs, the roles of men and women, and his hopes and fears over the future of civilization.

Alistair Cooke, "James Thurber: In Conversation with Alistair Cooke," *Atlantic*, 198 (August 1956): 36-40.
> Tells stories of Thurber's early days in Ohio, and comments on his drawings, the fable form, the decline of humor, and his ability to cope with blindness.

George Plimpton and Max Steele, "James Thurber," in *Writers at Work: The Paris Review Interviews*, edited by Malcolm Cowley (New York: Viking, 1958).
> Discusses Thurber's visual method of writing and the *New Yorker* style of writing and its former editor, Harold Ross. Gives views on Henry James and the place of humor in culture.

Bibliographies:

Edwin T. Bowden, *James Thurber: A Bibliography* (Columbus: Ohio State University Press, 1968).
> Primary bibliography of Thurber's stories, drawings, and volumes as they can be found in periodicals and books and in translations.

Sarah Eleanora Toombs, *James Thurber: An Annotated Bibliography of Criticism* (New York: Garland, 1987).
> Comprehensive catalogue of secondary references with more than eleven hundred entries, representing all books, articles, and reviews determined to be of critical interest. Also lists theses, works in foreign languages, plays, films, and television productions. Introduction authoritatively surveys the history of Thurber's critical reception.

Biographies:

Charles S. Holmes, *The Clocks of Columbus: A Literary Portrait* (New York: Atheneum, 1972).

Literary biography which authoritatively treats Thurber's work in the context of his life, viewed perceptively and sympathetically.

Burton Bernstein, *Thurber: A Biography* (New York: Dodd, Mead, 1975).
> Based on full access to Thurber's papers, replete with detail and lively anecdote, but often mean-spirited and uncharitable.

References:

Stephen A. Black, *James Thurber: His Masquerades* (The Hague: Mouton, 1970).
> Reads Thurber's use of fable and laughter, the comic role inversions, and masquerading characters as devices for coming to terms with a world constantly threatening to destory life and culture; sees Thurber as "the finest comic artist that America has yet produced."

Walter Blair and Hamlin Hill, *America's Humor: From Poor Richard to Doonesbury* (New York: Oxford, 1978).
> Devotes a chapter to "The Secret Life of Walter Mitty" as one of several key texts analyzed in detail to represent major themes and eras in the history of American humor; views Thurber as a bridge between the horse-sense humorists of the nineteenth and the black humorists of the mid-twentieth century.

Max Eastman, *The Enjoyment of Laughter* (New York: Simon & Schuster, 1936).
> Encyclopedic survey of humor which asserts that Thurber's humor, Bergson's theory to the contrary, creates laughter out of pathos; includes Thurber's often-cited theory of humor as "emotional chaos" recollected in tranquility.

Charles S. Holmes, ed., *Thurber: A Collection of Critical Essays* (Englewood Cliffs, N.J.: Prentice-Hall, 1974).
> Collects important interviews, articles, and selections from critical books covering Thurber's varied output.

Catherine McGehee Kenney, *Thurber's Anatomy of Confusion* (Hamden, Conn.: Archon, 1984).
> Treats Thurber as a consummate artist, worthy of comparison with James and Chekov,

whose work anatomizes the confusion of life and the world, subduing it to the grand design of art.

Robert E. Morseberger, *James Thurber* (New York: Twayne, 1964).
First book-length study of Thurber. Attempts to identify Thurber's major themes and techniques and provides a biographical context for critical analyses.

[William Shawn and E. B. White], "James Thurber," *New Yorker*, 37 (11 November 1961): 247.
Obituary by one of Thurber's editors and by his early and longstanding colleague in the magazine for which he worked and in which he grew to fame.

Richard C. Tobias, *The Art of James Thurber* (Athens: Ohio University Press, 1969).

Makes extensive use of myth criticism to treat the body of Thurber's work; finds the fables and fairy stories to be among the richest in the corpus.

Norris W. Yates, *The American Humorist: Conscience of the Twentieth Century* (Ames: Iowa State University Press, 1964).
Authoritative and influential study which discusses Thurber's work in the tradition of American humor; delineates the nature of the "little man" character, showing his differences from earlier and late comic types; distinguishes the "little man" from the persona of the "liberal citizen" found in the late essays.

Papers:
Most of Thurber's papers are in the Thurber Collection at the Ohio State University in Columbus, Ohio.

Nathanael West

This entry was updated by Daniel Walden (Pennsylvania State University) from his entry in DLB 9, American Novelists, 1910-1945.

Places	New York City Hollywood	Brown University	Paris

Influences and Relationships	T. S. Eliot
	William Carlos
	  Williams
	James Joyce
		Sinclair Lewis
		H. L. Mencken
		S. J. Perelman
		Horatio Alger
			Fyodor Dostoyevski
			Gustave Flaubert
			Classical Greek and
			  Roman Writers

Literary Movements and Forms	French Symbolism Satire	Allegory	Surrealism

Major Themes	Violence
	Misogyny
	The Bizarre
	Decay of Society
		The Perversion
		  of Art
		Individualism vs.
		  Conformity
			Degeneration of
			  Morals
			The Predominance
			  of Chaos

Cultural and Artistic Influences	The Movie Industry The Theater	Russian-Jewish Heritage	Freudian Psychology
Social and Economic Influences	The Great Depression	Fascism	

See also the West entries in DLB 4, American Writers in Paris, 1920-1939 *and* DLB 28, Twentieth-Century American-Jewish Fiction Writers.

BIRTH: New York, New York, 17 October 1903, to Max and Anna Wallenstein Weinstein.

EDUCATION: Tufts College, 1921; Ph.B., Brown University, 1924.

MARRIAGE: 19 April 1940 to Eileen McKenney.

DEATH: Near El Centro, California, 22 December 1940.

BOOKS: *The Dream Life of Balso Snell* (Paris & New York: Contact Editions, 1931);
Miss Lonelyhearts (New York: Liveright, 1933; London: Grey Walls, 1949);
A Cool Million: The Dismantling of Lemuel Pitkin (New York: Covici Friede, 1934; London: Spearman, 1954);
The Day of the Locust (New York: Random House, 1939; London: Grey Walls, 1951);
The Complete Works of Nathaniel West (New York: Farrar, Straus & Cudahy, 1957; London: Secker & Warburg, 1957).

PLAY PRODUCTION: *Good Hunting*, by West and Joseph Schrank, New York, Hudson Theatre, 21 November 1938.

MOTION PICTURES: *Ticket to Paradise* (Republic, 1936), screenplay by West and Jack Natteford;
The President's Mystery (Republic, 1936), screenplay by West and Lester Cole;
Follow Your Heart (Republic, 1936), screenplay by West, Cole, and Samuel Ornitz;
Rhythm in the Clouds (Republic, 1937), screenplay adaptation by West;
It Could Happen to You (Republic, 1937), screenplay by West and Ornitz;
Born to be Wild (Republic, 1938), screenplay by West;
I Stole a Million (Universal, 1939), screenplay by West;
Five Came Back (RKO, 1939), screenplay by West, Jerry Cady, and Dalton Trumbo;
Spirit of Culver (Universal, 1939), screenplay by West and Whitney Bolton;
Men Against the Sky (RKO, 1940), screenplay by West;

Nathanael West

Let's Make Music (RKO, 1940), screenplay by West.

PERIODICAL PUBLICATIONS: "Euripedes—A Playwright," *Casements*, 1 (July 1923): 2-4;
"Miss Lonelyhearts and the Lamb," *Contact: An American Quarterly*, 1 (February 1932): 80-85;
"Two Chapters from *Miss Lonelyhearts*: Miss Lonelyhearts and the Dead Pan and Miss Lonelyhearts and the Clean Old Man," *Contact: An American Quarterly*, 1 (May 1932): 13-21, 22-27;
"Miss Lonelyhearts and the Dismal Swamp," *Contempo*, 2 (5 July 1932): 1-2;
"Miss Lonelyhearts on a Field Trip," *Contact: An American Quarterly*, 1 (October 1932): 50-57;
"Some Notes on Violence," *Contact: An American Quarterly*, 1 (October 1932): 132-133;
"Some Notes on Miss L," *Contempo*, 3 (15 May 1933): 1-2;
"The Dear Public," *Americana*, 1 (August 1933): 29;
"Business Deal," *Americana*, 1 (October 1933): 14-15;
"Bird and Bottle," *Pacific Weekly*, 5 (10 November 1936): 329-331.

Nathanael West wrote four novels, *The Dream Life of Balso Snell* (1931), *Miss Lonelyhearts* (1933), *A Cool Million: The Dismantling of Lemuel Pitkin* (1934), and *The Day of the Locust* (1939), a play, *Good Hunting*, with Joseph Schrank, and a smattering of poetry and essays. The dominant theme in West's novels is degeneration of religion, sex, and art in a decaying society. Unlike many other social novelists, West blamed the individuals, not their institutions, for society's decline. All around him he saw hypocrisy, lack of communication, the failure of love to heal. He saw the garish, bizarre, erotic, and grotesque replacing the standard criteria for defining a work of art. The result, he believed, is chaos, a natural concomitant of life and a sure road to the destruction of humankind.

West's friend Isadore Kapstein said that "to be an artist served West in three ways: 1) in fiction he could discharge all the resentment he could not discharge in fact; 2) in fiction he could rise above the world of fact and manipulate it to his will; 3) as an artist in fiction he could prove to the world that had rejected him that it was wrong and that he deserved to be accepted by it." Kapstein concluded that West's writing "was not an end in itself, but a means to an end; the achievement of acceptance, the dream life of Nathanael West come true."

Much of West's feeling of rejection stemmed from his being a Jew, and like other second-generation Jews in America, he changed his name–from Nathan Weinstein to Nathanael West–partly at least in an attempt to gain social acceptance. He did not practice his religion, and Kapstein said that West was not only "unJewish" but also "unmoral," adding, "I find no moral stance whatever in his writing." Another friend, John Sanford (who was born Julian Shapiro), maintained that West "had about as much faith as an ear of corn." Yet despite his lack of religious conviction, West was fascinated by both the Jewish and Catholic religions. Wells Root, a longtime friend, recalled that West read widely about religion, from the earliest church history to the present. West was similarly ambivalent about sex. He went from loose living in his younger days to being disturbed by the lack of morals in Hollywood in his later days. In some ways he seemed to be quite old-fashioned; he held to a double standard, believing that men were free to do what they wished but that women should do what society expected of them. Yet he consciously set out to shock his

readers: Balso Snell in *The Dream Life of Balso Snell* is obsessed with sex; Betty in *Miss Lonelyhearts* is raped and brutalized; another Betty is raped and forced to work as a prostitute in *A Cool Million*. He also had a divided attitude about the role of the artist. He believed that art could impose some order on the world's chaos, but he knew that manipulation of fact was dangerous if it prevented one from facing reality, and he decried the pseudo-artists who substituted fantasy for reality.

There appears to be a relationship among West's ambivalence toward religion, sex, and the role of the artist. Caught between extremes in each case, he seemed to lean on the belief that "The joke of suffering and the joke of comforting killed this world," as he wrote in an early draft of a chapter of *Miss Lonelyhearts*, which appeared in *Contact* magazine in May 1932. He knew that suffering was inevitable, and he knew that comforting could not be a permanent solution. Buffeted between opposites all his life, unable to settle on one or the other, he wrote four novels, one of which, *Miss Lonelyhearts*, is a masterpiece.

Nathan Weinstein was the son of Max and Anna Wallenstein Weinstein, German Jews from Kovno, Lithuania, a Russian province which had a large population of Germans from East Prussia. German Jews had since the Enlightenment considered themselves Germans first, Jews second. In the New World it was natural to continue the same tradition of national pride by teaching their children German and the superiority of German culture, while also trying to become assimilated into American culture. Like any red-blooded child of immigrants, Nathan became a baseball fan, but, although he loved to play, he was not very athletic. At Camp Paradox, a middle-class Jewish summer camp in the Adirondacks, which he attended during his high school years, he was ironically called "Home Run Weinstein" and "Pep" because of his gangling movements and slow speech. His cartoons for the *Paradoxian*, the camp's newspaper, gained him some recognition, however. In elementary school and in high school he was an indifferent student. At DeWitt Clinton High School the future Nathanael West began to emerge. A steady theater and silent-film goer, an omnivorous reader, he became more and more an observer rather than a participant. By 1920, when he left high school without graduating, he already seems to have realized that a gap existed between America's vaunted emphasis on

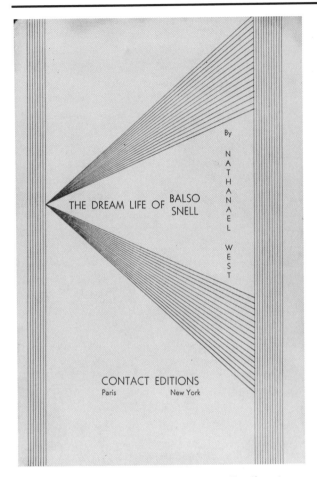

Front wrapper for West's first novel (Lilly Library)

and he was able to graduate with a Ph.B in 1924 only after convincing one of his professors to change a failing grade to a D. During his college years West was creating a new image, first calling himself Nathanael von Wallenstein Weinstein (adding his mother's maiden name preceded by the upper-class *von*). He needed a name consistent with the artistic life he anticipated leading.

From his high school days through college and into his maturity, West read deeply in the Greek and Roman classics, religious literature, the French symbolists, Russian realists, and American and British modernists. Flaubert and his *Madame Bovary* were the author and book he admired most, above all for their style. Drawing on all of these, he learned what it could mean to become a writer.

Despite his literary ambitions, he was critical of those who took literature too seriously. In "Euripedes–A Playwright," a term paper that was later published in the July 1923 issue of Brown's literary magazine, *Casements*, he wrote a serio-comic parody of esoteric scholarship in which he accused Euripedes of constructing his plays from bits and pieces filched from others. Another successful literary hoax was the class-day speech he wrote for his friend Quentin Reynolds in June 1924. According to this speech, a flea named Saint Puce was born under Christ's armpit, fed on his body, and died at the moment of Christ's death. This literary hoax later became a central part of *The Dream Life of Balso Snell*, West's first novel, for which he was beginning to write sketches in June 1924.

During 1924 and 1925, however, progress on the novel was held up while he worked on and off for his father in the building and real estate business. In 1926, shortly before he was to leave for Paris, he changed his name legally to Nathanael West. According to West's cousin Nathan, the change from Nathan to Nathanael came because it looked and sounded better; the name West may have come from his Uncle Sam who had been using the name for some time. At the same time, it is possible that West chose the name to give himself an American identity that would separate him from his Jewish heritage. Yet Edmund Wilson remembered that West, in spite of his attempts to seem American, exhibited a kind of Eastern European suffering and sense of the grotesque, a Russian Jewish soul, a sad, quick Jewish humor, and a Russian Jewish imagination.

In Paris from October 1926 through January 1927 West made the obligatory round of the

individualism and experimentation, and society's demands for conformity and standardization. Like Sinclair Lewis and H. L. Mencken, he perceived the "babbittry" of Mencken's "booboisie" that was reflected in President Harding's call for a "return to normalcy," and he also saw integrity and individualism being left in the past.

In the spring of 1921, with the aid of a falsified high school transcript, Nathan Weinstein was admitted to Tufts College. Asked to withdraw before the end of the first term because he had not attended classes and was failing every course, he applied to Brown University, and on the basis of the transcript of another Nathan Weinstein at Tufts, he was admitted as a second-semester sophomore. According to his roommate, Philip Lukin, West was a typical Joe College dude: he co-owned a Stutz Bearcat and was a snappy dresser. He was a fervent rooter at Brown sporting events, particularly football and baseball, and he could be a good student in the few subjects that interested him. But most of his grades were low,

artists' cafés and occasionally worked on *The Dream Life of Balso Snell*. When he returned to the United States, where most of the economy was still spiraling upward, but where his family was on the brink of disaster because of a recession in the building trade, he had to take a job as night manager at the Kenmore Hall Hotel.

For the next four years West worked on *The Dream Life of Balso Snell*. During this period he was spending time in Greenwich Village with college friends S. J. Perelman (who married West's sister Laura in 1929), I. J. Kapstein, and Quentin Reynolds. In the Village he met and talked with writers such as Michael Gold, Maxwell Bodenheim, Edward Dahlberg, Nathan Asch, Dashiell Hammett, and Philip Wylie. At the nearby offices of the *New Republic* he visited Edmund Wilson and met John Dos Passos and Horace Gregory. He also got together on Sunday afternoons at George Brownoff's Central Park West apartment with a group of young Jewish intellectuals to discuss music, literary criticism, and such writers as Dostoyevski, Chekhov, Ibsen, O'Neill, and Joyce.

During the winter of 1929-1930 he was introduced to and fell in love with Beatrice Mathieu, the Paris fashion writer for the *New Yorker* and a friend of S. J. and Laura Perelman. In May 1930, when he was to have joined her in Paris, where he would live by his writing, he wrote to her that he "was afraid to . . . to try and earn a living writing, hacking, I'd rather work in a hotel, and I'm not sure I could hack out enough. . . ."

By now he had finished *The Dream Life of Balso Snell* and was trying to get it published. After being turned down by commercial houses and several small presses, West's first novel was accepted on the recommendation of William Carlos Williams by Contact Editions, which David Moss and Martin Kamin had taken over from Robert McAlmon. *The Dream Life of Balso Snell* was published in 1931 in an edition of 500 copies. Like other small-press publications, it was not distributed widely, and it was reviewed in only two periodicals. As part of the publishing agreement West had guaranteed the sale of 150 copies, and as late as 1937 he still had a few remaining.

Balso Snell is a Babbitt who gives aphoristic advice freely and explains away chaos just as easily. Searching for identity, he encounters and finds absurd all the major historic events of Western civilization. "Art," Balso Snell concludes, "is a sublime excrement." Yet, in writing a protest against writing, West wrote a professional book, a play on styles, and a lyric novel, at once savage

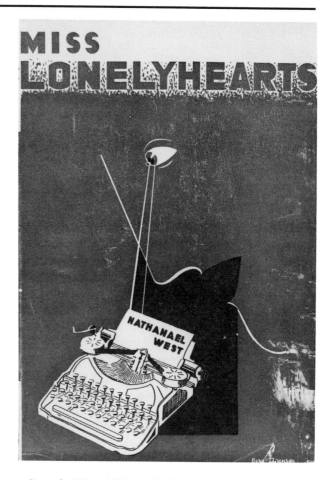

Cover for West's 1933 novel about an advice columnist for a newspaper

and satirical, that represented his strong, even violent, response to sham, intellectualism, poseurs, and the grand myths of our civilization. At base, *The Dream Life of Balso Snell* is a satirical attack against literary games and against the perversion of art. West, lampooning art as escapism, was criticizing the dream makers who divorce art from society. At the beginning, when Balso Snell enters the Trojan wooden horse through its anus, it is clear that West is attempting to shock the reader through scatology and scatological images. He is also portraying what he feared was man's deterioration into a subhuman species. Balso is an effete, impotent poet touring the past of Western civilization. In satirizing the Greek heritage, Catholicism, James Joyce, Dostoyevski, and Freud, West was also satirizing those who perverted them. "O Beer! O Meyerbeer! O Bach! O Offenbach! Stand me now as ever in good stead," Balso's speech before entering the horse's anus, is a parody of Stephen Dedalus's words at the end of Joyce's *A Portrait of the Artist as a Young*

Man: "Old father, old artificer, stand me now and ever in good stead." But West admired Joyce's writing and aimed his parody more at Joyce's imitators than at Joyce himself.

On his travels Balso Snell encounters a Jewish guide, a Catholic mystic named Maloney the Areopagite, a precocious boy named John Raskolnikov Gilson (out of Dostoyevski) and Gilson's eighth-grade teacher, Miss McGeeney. All through his experiences he is confronted with flesh, usually repugnant; John Gilson talks of "a sty on my eyes, a cold sore on my lip, a pimple where the edge of my collar touches my neck, another pimple in the corner of my mouth, and a drop of salt snot on the end of my nose" as reasons for beating his mistress. But Balso is attracted to cripples with "their disarranged hips, their short legs, their humps, their splay feet, their wall-eyes. . . ." Even the body of Christ, as written about by Maloney the Areopagite, is a haven for Saint Puce, a flea who lives in Christ's armpit.

The Dream Life of Balso Snell is a brilliantly conceived comic novel. It is also obsessively scatological, devastatingly anti-Catholic and anti-Jewish as well as misogynistic. Gilson tells Balso: "I need women and because I can't buy or force them, I have to make poems for them. God knows how tired I am of using the insanity of Van Gogh and the adventures of Gauguin as can-openers. . . ." While beating a woman, he cries, "O constipation of desire! O diarrhoea of love!," and the play that he will write is to conclude with the roof opening above the occupants of the theater and the room filling "with tons of loose excrement." The novel, says Stanley Edgar Hyman, is no less than a vision of the world as one vast dung heap.

The Dream Life of Balso Snell was dedicated to West's sister's friend Alice Shepherd, with whom West had fallen in love. When the relationship was terminated in 1933, after he had slept with another woman, it was clear that, as with Beatrice Mathieu, he foresaw a life of failure, a future in which he would have his art and little else.

West had met William Carlos Williams and become friends with him before he knew that Williams had recommended his novel to Moss and Kamin. Shortly after he and Julian Shapiro (John Sanford) had rented a cabin for the summer near Warrensburg, New York, West wrote to Williams to thank him for his support. At the end of September, having been asked by Moss and Kamin to revive *Contact* magazine, which he

and Robert McAlmon had edited during the early 1920s, Williams invited West to be the associate editor of what would now be called *Contact: An American Quarterly*. Only three issues were published, each of which contained parts of the early drafts of chapters for *Miss Lonelyhearts*. The final issue, October 1932, also contains West's "Some Notes on Violence," defending the depiction of violence in American writing on the grounds that "In America violence is idiomatic." He goes on to say that the European writer "often needs three hundreds pages to motivate one little murder. But not so the American writer. His audience has been prepared and is neither surprised nor shocked if he omits artistic excuses for familiar events." A chapter of *Miss Lonelyhearts* also appeared in *Contempo* magazine in 1932, and when the novel was published in 1933, this little magazine published a "symposium on Miss Lonelyhearts," which included comments by Angel Flores, Josephine Herbst, and William Carlos Williams, as well as West's "Some Notes on Miss L," a further defense of his fictional method.

From 1929 on, a friend remembered, West was "very catastrophe oriented. . . . Disaster fascinated him . . . not in a puerile sense, but from the standpoint of human tragedy." In March 1929 West had accompanied Perelman to a Jewish restaurant, Siegel's, where he met a woman who wrote a column for the *Brooklyn Eagle* under the name "Susan Chester." She described the letters she received and suggested that West might be able to use them for comic purpose. Rather than seeing the letters as strictly humorous, however, West saw in them the key to the real character of the time. They formed the basis of *Miss Lonelyhearts*, which Hyman later called one of the three finest novels of the century.

In "Some Notes on Miss L" West described his novel as a "portrait of a priest of our time who has a religious experience." Because violence is a reflection of one of the most common and potent forces in our society, West explained, violent images are used to illustrate commonplace events. *Miss Lonelyhearts* is a story of a lovelorn columnist with a "Christ complex," tormented by his editor Shrike's cynical hedonism and antireligious pronouncements. For Shrike, almost as vicious as the bird whose name he carries, "The church is our only hope, the First Church of Christ Dentist, where He is worshipped as Preventer of Decay. The church whose symbol is the trinity new-style: Father, Son and Wirehaired Fox Terrier." Meanwhile, pierced

2.

A COOL MILLION

The home of Mrs. Sarah Pitkin, a widow well on in
years, was situated on an eminence overlooking the Rat
River, near the town of Ottsville in the state of Vermont. It was a humble dwelling much the worse for wear,
yet exceedingly dear to her and her only child, Lemuel.

While the house had not been painted for some
time, owing to the straitened circumstances of the little
family, it still had a great deal of charm. An antique
collector, had one chanced to pass it by, would have been
greatly interested in ~~the purity of~~ its architecture.
Having been built about the time of General Stark's campaign against the British, its ~~design~~ *lives* reflected the
character of his army in whose ranks several Pitkins had
marched.

One late fall evening, Mrs. Pitkin was sitting
quietly in her parlor, when a knock was heard on her
humble door.

Setting copy for A Cool Million *(courtesy of the University of California Research Library, Los Angeles)*

by the agonies of the miserable people who write him, Miss Lonelyhearts sees his only hope as Betty, who loves him. But the naively optimistic Betty believes that the answer to his malaise is a trip to the country. As Shrike predicts, there is no escape. His bleak world owes a good deal to such modernist writers of the 1920s as Sherwood Anderson, William Faulkner, and William Carlos Williams and to T. S. Eliot's *The Waste Land*. *Miss Lonelyhearts* also owes a good deal to both the symbolists and the surrealists.

Miss Lonelyhearts is a novel of psychological development. That is, though West held that psychology has little relationship to reality, it replaces the myths of religion with new myths by which we try to make some sense out of reality. Reflecting on Freud's influence, West wrote in "Some Notes on Miss L," "The great body of case histories can be used in the way the ancient writers used their myths. Freud is your Bullfinch; you cannot learn from him." It is a story of a deluded innocent in the midst of a corrupt society. Roger Abrahams calls it a tale of an Everyman character whose soul is being fought for by God and Satan, as in *Faust*. Going beyond satire and allegory, Miss Lonelyheart's search for himself, ironically, is futile. Feeling deeply the sufferings of the letter writers, he yearns for a rational and sane life that at first he hopes to find in marriage to Betty. After being hurt time and time again, all that is left is the hope of becoming a rock, impervious to the incursion of the sea. And "What goes on in the sea is of no interest to the rock."

West, in *Miss Lonelyhearts*, wrote that "man has a tropism for order," while "the physical world has a tropism for disorder, entropy," and "every order has within it the germs of destruction." Unable to act, Miss Lonelyhearts can only retreat into himself, or defer to others, or occasionally lash out sadistically. His heart having failed him, he can achieve harmony only in dreams and fantasy. He can never be content with Betty because he cannot accept her simple optimism: "Her world was not the world and could never include the readers of his column. Her sureness was based on the power to limit experience arbitrarily." Nor does Shrike offer a solution to Miss Lonelyhearts's dilemma. His cynicism is a mask for his inability to relate to others, to find love. Shrike is an anti-Christ, a false Messiah, fed by his cynicism and destructiveness. On the other hand, Peter Doyle, a cripple married to Fay Doyle, one of the letter writers who focuses her

sexual desires on Miss Lonelyhearts, is willing to do anything to get love. Ironically, in spite of Miss Lonelyhearts's compassion for Peter Doyle, it is Peter's hand that destroys Miss Lonelyhearts. At the end of the novel Peter is coming to shoot Miss Lonelyhearts because Fay, angry at Miss Lonelyhearts's refusal of her advances, has told Peter that Miss Lonelyhearts has raped her. As Miss Lonelyhearts, perceiving Peter as a symbol of all suffering humanity, embraces him, Peter, struggling to get away and seeing Betty come in at the bottom of the stairs, tries to get rid of the gun he has hidden in a newspaper. In the scuffle he accidently shoots Miss Lonelyhearts.

"I've got a Christ complex," Miss Lonelyhearts has admitted to Betty: "I'm a humanity lover." Unfortunately, as an antidote to the violence that dominates the novel, love is weak medicine. Love can provide motivation and hope, but it cannot impose harmony on discordant forces. Love does not act upon people unless they choose to subordinate individualism, greed, self-actualization to it–which rarely happens. In *Miss Lonelyhearts*, West built a structure in which the myths of love and compassion, so dear to the Judeo-Christian ethic, are swallowed by the reality of a world in which love and feeling are irrelevant and at times destructive. "The attack upon Christian compassion as a delusive myth," says Bruce Olsen, "is made to work by enforcing a quite contrary mythlike view–that the universe is composed of deterministic forces in which feeling has no relevance." *Miss Lonelyhearts* is a masterpiece because it uses an ironic perspective to tell the story of a moral paradox in psychological terms, forcing the reader to sympathize with the suffering and agony of the narrator and laugh at his ways at the same time. *Miss Lonelyhearts* is so masterful that its despair is made absurd by virtue of West's artful irony.

West, although committed to the process of Americanization, early and resolutely rebelled against the American Dream of success. At the height of his powers he told an acquaintance, "I want to interpret. I want to understand. I'm not going to be able to change the course of anything, I just want to know." The fact that America in the 1920s and 1930s seemed to be headed for disaster impelled him to lay bare the corruption of ideals that seemed to be the essential sickness of American society. During the Great Depression, concerned primarily with the exploitation of the individual under unrestrained free enterprise, West reached back to an earlier America to the success myth created by Horatio Alger, for his third novel, *A Cool Million*. As its hero, Lemuel Pitkin, says when summing up his experiences in a lunatic world, "It all seems like a dream to me." For West the central theme of both *A Cool Million* and *The Day of the Locust*, his final novel, was that the American Dream was a monstrous nightmare.

During the 1920s, while West was maturing, he perceived the cruel differences between the myth and the reality of the promise of American life. He considered himself an American, but as a Jew he was treated as an outsider. Having been hurt deeply, he empathized with others who had been scarred emotionally and economically, and he scorned the phony artist who fed on society's belief in the American myth.

Originally entitled "America, America," *A Cool Million* is an inverted fable, a satire with the brutal comedy of American burlesque. Commenting on the threat to foreclose on the mortgage to Lemuel's mother's house, banker Nathan "Shagpoke" Whipple (the ex-president of the United States, who later becomes the leader of an American Fascist party) says to Lemuel, in Alger fashion, "Don't be discouraged. This is the land of opportunity and the world is an oyster." Inspired by such clichés, Lem leaves Ottsville, Vermont, with thirty dollars in his pocket to make his fortune and pay off the mortgage. Progressively "dismantled" by society, he is robbed and arrested, his teeth are pulled out, his right eye is removed, he is scalped, his leg is amputated, and he is killed, all in the name of "the right of every American boy to go into the world and there receive fair play and a chance to make his fortune by industry and probity without being laughed at or conspired against by sophisticated aliens." West, in reversing the Alger myth of success, came up with a truth sufficient for him. In Jay Martin's words, West began in comedy and ended by showing that beneath the comic froth lay "the bitter salt tragedy of betrayed ideals."

In spite of its strengths, *A Cool Million* is possibly the least effective of West's novels. True, the novel's depiction of the latent violence of ordinary but insecure people was a warning that the Nazi madness already begun in Europe could sweep the world in the 1930s and 1940s. This comparatively bland excursion into political satire employs a hero whose efforts to emulate great American success stories are absurd. Devoid of ability, Lemuel is a fool. According to Hyman, *A Cool Million* is "formless, an inorganic stringing together

of comic set-pieces, with the preposterous incidents serving merely to raise the various topics West chooses to satirize." On the other hand, says Alan Ross, "In its awareness of political technique, its devastatingly true analysis of unrestricted capitalistic method, its foreshadowing of Americanism turned into a possible Fascism, *A Cool Million* is brilliantly successful."

A Cool Million seems formless, or possesses a form that follows West's proclivities for introducing the topics he wishes to discuss. At the same time, it is a tour de force in its ability to point up the grotesqueries of the American system, the ways in which the fulfillment of the Alger myth is dependent on chance rather than on the Protestant or Puritan ethic alone, and the pervasiveness of American violence. Yet West's attempts at humor often strain the reader's credulity. It is too much to believe that a deranged warden would pull all Lemuel's teeth, in the belief that teeth are the source of infection; or that Lemuel would be kidnapped by the Communist International for no apparent reason; or that, trying to save the heroine from a "fate worse than death," Lemuel would have his leg caught in a bear trap and be scalped by a Harvard-educated Indian while still in the trap, and then have to have his leg amputated; or that, in order to eat he would be forced to join a vaudeville act in which he is literally beaten up during each performance; or that he would be shot and become a martyr for young American Fascists and the subject of "The Lemuel Pitkin Song." *A Cool Million* seems to be a hastily written attempt to make money on the heels of the good reviews for *Miss Lonelyhearts*. Unfortunately, it got bad reviews, did not sell well, and was soon remaindered.

In 1933 West was hired by Samuel Goldwyn to write screenplays in Hollywood. His first two efforts, "Beauty Parlor" and "Return to the Soil," were not produced, but later in the 1930s, when he returned to Hollywood, West proved himself quite adept at writing the kind of screenplays the studios wanted. In 1935, in Hollywood, West collected material for a new book on the scandals, oddities, and underworld life of the film capital. Living at an apartment hotel close to Hollywood Boulevard, he mixed with bit players, stuntmen, comics, midgets, prostitutes, and the grips on the sets. He went to boxing matches and to cockfights. He hung around Mexican Americans, cops, newspapermen. From 1936 until his death in 1940 he had steady work as a studio writer, first with Republic and then with Columbia,

Drawing of West by David Schorr

RKO, and Universal. Through it all, beginning in 1935, West was fashioning his novel. In the summer of 1938, after many title changes, *The Day of the Locust* was submitted to Bennett Cerf of Random House. Published in the spring of 1939, it got good reviews, but by February 1940 it had sold only 1,464 copies. From his four novels West made a total of $1,280.

The Day of the Locust is about Tod Hackett, a would-be painter who works as a set and costume designer, and his experiences with an assortment of Hollywood grotesques on the fringes of the movie industry. In love with Faye Greener, he befriends her father, Harry, an old vaudeville clown who lives in the past and literally dies laughing. Faye prefers Earle Shoop, the stereotypical cowboy, to Tod until Miguel, Earle's sensual Mexican friend, takes her away. Tod also befriends the dwarf Abe Kusich and tries unsuccessfully to aid Homer Simpson, a simple innocent from the Midwest who out of adoration for Faye provides her with a place to live and buys her clothes. She, of course, has no feeling for him. Homer is reminiscent of Wing Biddlebaum in Sherwood Anderson's *Winesburg, Ohio* (1919) in that he reflects his anxieties and his emotions only through

his hands. They are the hands of a repressed man of violence. At the end of the book Homer, on the verge of madness, stomps on a boy named Adore Loomis and precipitates a riot among the crowd at a movie premiere. Tod is also caught in the riot, and it gives him the final inspiration necessary to complete his apocalyptic masterpiece, "The Burning of Los Angeles," which he has been working on throughout the book. It is significant that Faye is one of the central figures in the painting. Faye, an amoral, sexually precocious seventeen-year-old with the mind of a child, is inviting, but "her invitation wasn't to pleasure, but to struggle, hard and sharp, closer to murder than to love." In spite of her amoral approaches to fulfilling her burning desire for money and success—she even becomes a prostitute briefly to get enough money to pay for her father's funeral—she remains, in Homer's words, "a fine, wholesome child." Nothing can hurt Faye because she is so wrapped up in her fantasies of stardom that she is oblivious to the reality in which she lives.

Early in the novel we meet those who have come to California to die. They seem inoffensive, but, as in *A Cool Million*, the people on the bottom, the lower middle class, are capable of being motivated in one way or another by a strong man or by strong forces and emotions. In the last scene they become a mob. Bored and disappointed, they realize that they've been tricked, cheated, and betrayed. Violence, always simmering just below the surface in America, is the heart of *The Day of the Locust*. Just as Faye triggers acts of violence between men who are attracted to her, so Homer's violent acts toward Adore Loomis encourage the mob. Savage and bitter, they participated in the apocalypse, in the riot. *The Day of the Locust* begins by depicting the artificiality of the movie sets, the people's role playing, and the pseudo-Mexican, Samoan, Mediterranean, Egyptian, Japanese, Swiss, and Tudor facades of the houses, and gradually reveals the primitivism and savagery beneath. Allan Seager, who was doing a radio show in Hollywood and knew West, wrote that the novel "was not fantasy imagined, but fantasy seen." William Carlos Williams wrote that Faye Greener had "a face such as Picasso gives" women, and that West had built Faye "out of such deformity before us." Edmund Wilson said that West "has caught the emptiness of Hollywood; and he is, as far as I know, the first writer to make this emptiness horrible." F. Scott Fitzgerald wrote to Perelman that *The Day of the Locust* "puts Gogol's *The Lower Depth* in the class with *The Tale of Benjamin Bunny*" and "bears an odd lopsided resemblance to Victor Hugo's *Notre Dame de Paris.* . . ." Unfortunately, in spite of its reception, *The Day of the Locust*, repeating past sales performances for West, sold badly in the first year. West–who had been in New York working on an antiwar play, *Good Hunting*, which closed after only two performances–was already back in Hollywood, resigned to the fact that writing screenplays was his only sure source of income.

In a letter to Jack Conroy, West compared Balzac to Eugene Sue and concluded that though Balzac was a royalist and Sue a radical, Balzac was the better writer, in a Marxian sense, because "he kept his eye firmly fixed on the middle class and wrote with great truth and no wish-fulfillment. The superior truth alone in Balzac was sufficient to reveal the structure of middle class society and its defects and even show how it would ultimately be destroyed." This was West's aim, to expose the "superior truth" about the middle class he knew. For the most part, the world he wrote about was repulsive and terrifying, filled with the halt and the lame, emotionally as well as physically. "Fitzgerald saw the mockery" of the American Dream, says James F. Light, and "deep in his bones, Nathanael West felt it. He had written about nothing else."

In his last years West came to understand that the modern tragedy was the loss of soul in modern life. He understood his characters as machines, and he depicted human activity made mechanical. He also realized, as he told Edmund Wilson, that "there is nothing to root for in my books, and no rooters." Yet, sympathetic to the ideals of the Left, he regarded fundamental changes as almost impossible to achieve. By 1939, disillusioned over the state of world politics and unhappy over the apparent failures of his books, West turned more and more to hunting as an escape, and to film scripting as a way of making enough money to take time off to write another novel. On 19 April 1940 he married Eileen McKenney, the model for her sister Ruth's book *My Sister Eileen* (1938). In her, West found a gentleness and love to which he could respond, emotionally and sexually. Meanwhile, with a small list of solo film credits and good reviews for *The Day of the Locust*, West could look forward at last to a promising future in Hollywood and the possbility of more novels to come. Then, on 22 December 1940, returning from a weekend hunting trip in Mexico, Nathanael and Eileen McKenney West

were killed in an automobile accident near El Centro, California. Eileen West died immediately, and Nathanael West died at 4:10 P.M., from a skull fracture and cerebral contusions. He was thirty-seven years old.

In the 1930s when all values were suspect, when the American system was being doubted, when Americans searched for individual and collective identity, West wrote with a quality of "wounded and revived innocence," to use Malcolm Cowley's phrase, about a sick society. His quest, to expose America's myths, was undertaken doggedly. He knew full well that his attempt would bring about little or no change. Yet, compelled to push on, West accomplished what few others have done. Through his carefully controlled ironic despair he dramatized the cancers that eat at the vitals of our society, made us shudder at them in horror while we also laugh from time to time. He left four novels which more and more, says Jay Martin, seem not only to have accurately pictured his time but to be "permanent and true explorations into the Siberia of the human spirit," and he influenced such novelists of the past two decades as Joseph Heller, Thomas Pynchon, and Flannery O'Connor. In Hyman's words, "He was a true pioneer and culture hero, making it possible for the younger symbolists and fantasists who came after him, and who include our best writers, to do with relative ease what he did in defiance of the temper of his time, for so little reward, in isolation and in pain."

Bibliography:

William White, *Nathanael West: A Comprehensive Bibliography* (Kent, Ohio: Kent State University Press, 1975).
> In addition to primary works, including reprints, translations, and paperback editions, provides a thorough, though not exhaustive listing of secondary materials; includes an appendix, "The Uncollected Writings of Nathanael West."

Biography:

Jay Martin, *Nathanael West: The Art of His Life* (New York: Farrar, Straus & Giroux, 1970).
> The most inclusive, major biography of West to date; sees West as a dramatic ironist who uses comedy to reveal "the bitter salt tragedy of betrayed ideals."

References:

Robert M. Coates, "Messiah of the Lonelyhearts," *New Yorker*, 9 (15 April 1933): 59.
Sees *Miss Lonelyhearts* as an allegory of the life of Christ, or, more specifically, of the Stations of the Cross, and credits West with "a verbal agility that Cocteau well might envy."

Victor Comerchero, *Nathanael West: The Ironic Prophet* (Syracuse: Syracuse University Press, 1964).
The second earliest study of West; offers excellent insights on West and his use of irony.

Stanley Edgar Hyman, *Nathanael West* (Minneapolis: University of Minnesota Press, 1962).
This forty-six page pamphlet includes a brief biography of West and treats each of his four novels; claims that "his strength lay in his vulgarity and bad taste, his pessimism, his nastiness."

James F. Light, *Nathanael West: An Interpretive Study* (Evanston: Northwestern University Press, 1961).
The first major study of West and one of the best interpretations of his artistic vision.

Robert Emmet Long, *Nathanael West* (New York: Ungar, 1985).
Equates *Miss Lonelyhearts* with Fitzgerald's *The Great Gatsby* and Hemingway's *The Sun Also Rises*.

Bruce Olsen, "Nathanael West: The Use of Cynicism," in *Minor American Novelists*, edited by Charles A. Hoyt (Carbondale & Edwardsville: Southern Illinois University Press, 1970), pp. 81-94.
Sees West as a cynic whose deterministic view of the universe finds no place for human feelings.

Randall Reid, *The Fiction of Nathanael West: No Redeemer, No Promised Land* (Chicago: University of Chicago Press, 1967).
Claims that West is a minor, but original, artist and a parodist who denounces human self-deception but leaves the reader conscious of his own cynical view of the world.

Alan Ross, "The Dead Centre: An Introduction to Nathanael West," *Horizon*, 18 (October 1948): 284-296; revised and republished in *The Complete Works of Nathanael West* (New York: Farrar, Straus & Cudahy, 1957), pp. vii-xxii.
Views West as a social and political satirist who proceeds from the premise that "life is terrible" and whose fiction reveals "the unreality of the Christian myth."

Kingsley Widmer, *Nathanael West* (Boston: Twayne, 1982).
Claims that as a fiction writer, West is both a masquerader and a masquerade breaker, wildly fantasizing and sardonically attacking fantasies.

Thomas Wolfe

This entry was updated by Carol Johnston from the entry by Leslie Field (Purdue University) in DLB 9, American Novelists, 1910-1945.

Places	Chapel Hill (University of North Carolina)	Asheville, N.C. Paris Berlin	New York City Harvard
Influences and Relationships	J. M. and Margaret Roberts Maxwell Perkins Edward C. Aswell George Pierce Baker	Marcel Proust Sinclair Lewis Mark Twain Frederick H. Koch John Livingston Lowes	Aline Berstein James Joyce Walt Whitman Maxwell Perkins Kenneth Raisbeck
Literary Movements and Forms	Realism Stream-of-Consciousness Narrative	Satire Bildungsroman	Autobiographical Fiction
Major Themes	Education as a Liberating Process Physical and Spiritual Hunger	Alienation of the Artist Coming of Age	The Nature of Time The Buried Life Family Relationships
Cultural and Artistic Influences	The Theater	Humanism	
Social and Economic Influences	World War I Anti-Fascism	Socialism	Racism

See also the Wolfe entries in DLB: Documentary Series 2 *and* DLB Yearbook 1985.

BIRTH: Asheville, North Carolina, 3 October 1900, to William Oliver Wolfe and Julia Elizabeth Westall.

EDUCATION: B.A., University of North Carolina, Chapel Hill, 1920; M.A., Harvard University, 1922; Harvard University, 1923.

AWARDS: Guggenheim Fellowship, 1930; *Scribner's* Magazine Prize, 1932.

DEATH: Baltimore, Maryland, 15 September 1938.

SELECTED BOOKS: *Look Homeward, Angel* (New York: Scribners, 1929; London: Heinemann, 1930);

Of Time and the River (New York: Scribners, 1935; London: Heinemann, 1935);

From Death to Morning (New York: Scribners, 1935; London: Heinemann, 1935);

The Story of a Novel (New York & London: Scribners, 1936; London: Heinemann, 1936);

The Web and the Rock (New York & London: Harper, 1939; London & Toronto: Heinemann, 1947);

The Face of a Nation (New York: Scribners, 1939);

You Can't Go Home Again (New York & London: Harper, 1940; London & Toronto: Heinemann, 1947);

The Hills Beyond (New York & London: Harper, 1941);

A Stone, A Leaf, A Door (New York: Scribners, 1945);

Mannerhouse: A Play Prologue and Three Acts (New York: Harper, 1948; Melbourne, London & Toronto: Heinemann, 1950);

A Western Journal (Pittsburgh: University of Pittsburgh Press, 1951);

The Short Novels of Thomas Wolfe, edited by C. Hugh Holman (New York: Scribners, 1961);

Thomas Wolfe's Purdue Speech, "Writing and Living," edited by William Braswell and Leslie A. Field (Lafayette, Ind.: Purdue University Studies, 1964);

The Mountains, edited by Pat M. Ryan (Chapel Hill: University of North Carolina Press, 1970);

The Notebooks of Thomas Wolfe, 2 volumes, edited by Richard S. Kennedy and Paschal Reeves

Thomas Wolfe, 1938

(Chapel Hill: University of North Carolina Press, 1970);

The Autobiography of An American Novelist, edited by Leslie Field (Cambridge, Mass.: Harvard University Press, 1983);

Mannerhouse: A Play in a Prologue and Four Acts by Thomas Wolfe, edited by Louis D. Rubin, Jr., and John L. Idol, Jr. (Baton Rouge & London: Louisiana State University Press, 1985);

The Complete Short Stories of Thomas Wolfe, edited by Francis Skipp (New York: Scribners, 1987).

"I am . . . a part of all that I have touched and that has touched me . . . ." These words by Thomas Wolfe seem tailor-made for the author. They capsulize his life and art, which often are inseparable. Actually, the brief statement seems tailor-made for this author, who is perhaps the most autobiographical American novelist of our time.

By many objective standards he ranks among the significant practitioners of fiction in the twentieth century, along with William Faulkner, F. Scott Fitzgerald, Ernest Hemingway, and Sinclair Lewis. In their Nobel Award talks, both Faulkner and Lewis praised him effusively, and the reading public soon echoed these voices. Critics, however, have been ambivalent about his fiction, but even they have never indifferently dismissed it.

Wolfe was a romantic who, especially in his early work, moved from a preoccupation with himself to his family, his friends, his town, his America, and finally to the larger, external world outside of himself. In this respect he was much like Walt Whitman, who had sung his own egocentric song as he shouted his "barbaric yawp over the rooftops of the world."

Thomas Clayton Wolfe was born 3 October 1900 in Asheville, North Carolina, a resort community in the Blue Ridge Mountains. His mother, Julia Elizabeth Westall, was a native of the region; his father, William Oliver Wolfe, a tombstone cutter from Pennsylvania, had settled there a few years before he married Wolfe's mother. Tom was the youngest of the eight children born to the Wolfes. Six survived, and they and their parents would be fictionalized by Wolfe in his short life as a would-be dramatist, and later as a novelist.

In 1905 Wolfe enrolled in the Orange Street Public School in Asheville. This was his first breaking away from the family. By 1908 another kind of break occurred. For all practical purposes one could conclude that the Wolfe household then became irrevocably divided, the father living at his establishment behind his stonecutting shop, and the mother a few blocks away at her boardinghouse, My Old Kentucky Home (Dixieland in *Look Homeward, Angel*). Wolfe moved in with his mother and nursed his resentment toward both parents for what he considered to be their aberrant behavior toward him and his siblings. But the boardinghouse experience was not without its rich side effects, which Wolfe subsequently exploited in his fiction.

By 1912 Wolfe transferred to the North State Fitting School, a private institution supervised by Mr. and Mrs. J. M. Roberts. They were to become the Leonards of *Look Homeward, Angel* (1929). He remained under the tutelage of the Robertses for four years, and then at sixteen years of age he entered the University of North Carolina at Chapel Hill.

During his four years at the university, Wolfe studied, wrote, loved, and worked. Home from the university for a visit in the summer of 1917, he had a tempestuous romance with a young boarder, Clara Paul, five years his senior. This first "love affair" would later be apostrophized by Thomas Wolfe/Eugene Gant as the Laura James episode of *Look Homeward, Angel*. It would also foreshadow the Aline Bernstein/Esther Jack love affair which engulfed Thomas

Wolfe's parents, William Oliver and Julia Elizabeth Westall Wolfe (courtesy of the North Carolina Collection, University of North Carolina Library at Chapel Hill)

Wolfe/George Webber. The year of Wolfe's first love was also the year of his earliest published work, a poem, printed in the university magazine.

In the last year of World War I, during the summer of 1918, Tom worked as a civilian at the naval shipyards of Norfolk, Virginia. That fall he enrolled in Professor Koch's folk-playwriting class at Chapel Hill. His writing, however, was disrupted by another traumatic death in the Wolfe family; in October his brother Ben died. They had shared much in life and this death was to have a profound effect on the young Wolfe. It has been said that the fictional version of Ben's death in *Look Homeward, Angel* is equaled in starkness and realism only by Emma Bovary's climactic death some seventy-five years earlier in the last pages of Flaubert's classic novel.

In 1919 Wolfe's play *The Return of Buck Gavin* was presented by the Carolina Playmakers. He played the title role. In March he won the Worth Prize for his essay in philosophy: "The Crisis in Industry." He became editor of the *Tar Heel*, the college newspaper, and his second play, *Third Night*, was offered by the student Playmakers in December.

He graduated from Chapel Hill in 1920 and then entered Harvard Graduate School where he studied playwriting under George Pierce Baker in the famous 47 Workshop. The following year Wolfe's play *The Mountains* was produced by the workshop. Simultaneously, his programmed schooling had come to a close. He received an M.A. in English from Harvard in 1922, the same year that his father died. As always his achievements in life seemed punctuated by periods of great sadness and tragic events. Wolfe stayed on at Harvard, and in the spring of 1923 his play *Welcome to Our City* was presented, but it was rejected by the Theatre Guild of New York, as his plays always had been by New York production companies. Ironically, years later, Ketti Frings would adapt Wolfe's first novel for her Pulitzer Prize-winning Broadway play *Look Homeward, Angel* (1957).

Wolfe had been receiving money from home, but he realized that he needed another source of income. So for the second term of 1924 he signed on as an English instructor at the Washington Square College of New York University. He was to retain that post intermittently for the next few years until he completed his first novel. In the fall of 1924 he sailed for England, his first trip abroad. On New Year's Eve in Paris he met his friend Kenneth Raisbeck, who had been Professor Baker's assistant at Harvard. The kaleidoscope of their Parisian bistro-hopping is depicted fictionally at great length in the Gant/Starwick sequences of *Of Time and the River* (1935).

In the fall of 1925 Wolfe returned by ship to America. Toward the end of his journey he met Aline Bernstein (Esther Jack). She was married, a mother, nineteen years his senior, but for the next five years they would experience an on-again, off-again turbulent love affair, which was immortalized in *The Web and the Rock*.

In America Wolfe resumed his teaching. Then in June of 1926 he took his second trip to Europe, where he joined Mrs. Bernstein in the Lake Country of England. He continued to see himself as a playwright but still had no luck in selling any of his plays. In England he began writing his first novel. When he returned to New York, he shared an apartment with Mrs. Bernstein, who worked as a set designer for the Theatre Guild and used the apartment as her office and home away from home. Wolfe was able to devote full time to his novel. By 1927 he had completed a first draft. Then in the summer he sailed once

again for Europe, returned to the United States, and resumed teaching at New York University.

His novel was completed the following year, and in the spring he made his fourth trip to Europe. It was an eventful sojourn. He was hospitalized as the result of a severe fight at the Munich Oktoberfest, and he received word that Maxwell Perkins, representing Scribners, was interested in his novel. Wolfe had reached a new era in his life.

He returned to New York, and Scribners accepted his novel. Perkins and Wolfe soon began a close editor/author relationship as the manuscript of *Look Homeward, Angel* was being readied for publication. This interaction between the two men was to have far-reaching ramifications for Wolfe's life and art. The book was published on 18 October 1929, a few days before the infamous stock market crash. Because of the novel's autobiographical content, the people in Asheville reacted violently to it and its author. As a result he was frazzled psychologically, but outwardly he resumed the pattern of his New York life. He taught part-time at the university in the spring semester of 1929 and full-time in the fall.

He was awarded a Guggenheim Fellowship in March 1930 and sailed once again for Europe, his fifth trip. Almost simultaneously then he gave up his teaching at the university and severed his relations with Mrs. Bernstein; both activities had become unbearably burdensome. In Europe he often met F. Scott Fitzgerald and later Sinclair Lewis, whom he fictionalized as Hunt Conroy and Lloyd McHarg respectively. In February 1931 Wolfe returned to the United States, moved to Brooklyn, and continued writing. For the next few years he lived in various places in the greater New York area, wrote stories (some of which were published), and continued work on his second novel. Throughout much of 1934 he worked closely with Perkins on the editing of his second book, and finally Perkins insisted that it was ready for publication. Reluctantly, Wolfe surrendered the huge manuscript, which was published as *Of Time and the River* in March 1935.

Although *Look Homeward, Angel* had had a fairly enthusiastic critical and popular reception, Wolfe was nervous about *Of Time and the River*. So just prior to publication he sailed again for Europe (his sixth trip). The book received a mixed critical reception even though initially it had a heavier first printing and distribution than did the earlier novel. He returned to New York on 4 July 1935, shortly before he was to take part as a

The Old Kentucky Home, fictionalized as Dixieland in Look Homeward, Angel. *Julia Wolfe's boardinghouse is now Asheville's Thomas Wolfe Memorial (North Carolina Department of Cultural Resources)*

panelist at the Colorado Writer's Conference on 22 July. With some modifications, the key lecture he delivered there was published the following year as *The Story of a Novel* (1936). In print it became extremely controversial. In it Wolfe recounts his writing theories and reveals the close editor/author relationship he and Perkins had enjoyed. Later, critic Bernard De Voto would attack Wolfe's fiction viciously as he reviewed the little book in an essay entitled "Genius Is Not Enough."

Nevertheless, in 1935 Wolfe was at last a famous writer. He was lionized. His first collection of short stories, *From Death to Morning*, appeared in November. He decided to spend more time traveling in the United States, so he took his first trip to the West Coast, where he visited Hollywood and was even offered a contract to write for the movies, which he turned down.

In 1936 he took other trips: to New Orleans and Raleigh, North Carolina. But the sad experience for him during this period was the quarrel with his longtime editor and friend, Perkins.

That same year Wolfe took his seventh and last trip to Europe. He was in Berlin for the Olympic Games, and later he would write feelingly about his painful final views of the new Germany. His observations of Hitler's Germany as a dark and tragic place first appeared publicly as a three-part essay/story called "I Have a Thing to Tell You" in the *New Republic*. Other versions appeared later in the closing sections of *You Can't Go Home Again* (1940). Old Germany had been the country he grew to love on his many trips to Europe. Now he saw that this land had become corrupt. Moreover, Hitler was for him the "dark Messiah," and Nazism the quintessence of evil.

Back in the United States, Wolfe continued his writing. Then, despite the hostility leveled at him earlier by his hometown, in May of 1937 Wolfe returned for his first visit to Asheville since *Look Homeward, Angel* had appeared. The townspeople now welcomed him, but he needed a quiet place to write, so he spent part of that summer in a cottage not far from his native city. Then he returned to New York where he isolated

Thomas Wolfe at age 16

ful period of writing to a new awareness of life outside of himself, a new social consciousness.

Wolfe enjoyed himself at Purdue. And he continued in a happy vein of camaraderie as he traveled with newfound friends from West Lafayette to Chicago. From there he embarked on his trip to the West and the national parks. But in July he took ill and was hospitalized in Seattle, and then at Johns Hopkins in Baltimore. There his disease spread rapidly, and he soon died of miliary tuberculosis of the brain–on 15 September 1938, a few weeks before his thirty-eighth birthday.

Shortly before his death he had entrusted a packing crate of his manuscripts to Aswell. Within three years of Wolfe's death Aswell had edited much of the material. Under the imprint of Harper's, the following fiction was published posthumously: *The Web and the Rock* (1939), *You Can't Go Home Again* (1940), and *The Hills Beyond* (1941).

More than seventy books about Thomas Wolfe have been published. Many of these, including David Herbert Donald's 1988 Pulitzer Prize-winning *Look Homeward: A Life of Thomas Wolfe*, are well-researched biographical studies of Wolfe. Others are excellent critical and scholarly treatments of Wolfe's writings. In this category at least six should be singled out: Herbert J. Muller, *Thomas Wolfe* (1947); Louis D. Rubin, Jr., *Thomas Wolfe: The Weather of His Youth* (1955); Richard S. Kennedy, *The Window of Memory: The Literary Career of Thomas Wolfe* (1962); C. Hugh Holman, *The Loneliness at the Core: Studies in Thomas Wolfe* (1975); Leo Gurko, *Thomas Wolfe: Beyond the Romantic Ego* (1975); and Leslie Field, *Thomas Wolfe and His Editors: Establishing a True Text for the Posthumous Publications* (1987). *Modern Fiction Studies* devoted a special issue to Wolfe in the autumn of 1965, and since the spring of 1977, a journal called the *Thomas Wolfe Newsletter* (now the *Thomas Wolfe Review*) has been distributed semiannually. The *Thomas Wolfe Review*, a vehicle of the Thomas Wolfe Society, contains a bibliographical update on Wolfe and studies on the author in each issue and prints essays and articles on him by the best of the current Wolfe scholars.

The past decade, which included both the fiftieth anniversary of the publication of *Look Homeward, Angel* (first published in 1929) and the fiftieth anniversary of the publication of *Of Time and the River* (first published in 1935), has been particularly rich in Wolfe scholarship. Of the twenty-four volumes pertaining to Wolfe published in that time, five are either first editions of or new

himself in a hotel. By this time his break with Perkins and Scribners was complete, and he signed a new contract with Harper and Brothers on 31 December, where Edward C. Aswell was his editor.

Throughout the first part of 1938 Wolfe wrote feverishly in seclusion. Then fatigued, ready for a respite from his labors, he accepted invitations to travel to the West, ultimately to tour the national parks. His first stop was at Purdue University, where he delivered a talk at the annual Literary Awards Banquet in May. This turned out to be his last public forum. Years later the talk would be published in *Thomas Wolfe's Purdue Speech, "Writing and Living"* (1964). In it Wolfe expanded his statement about the craft of writing that he began earlier in *The Story of a Novel*. However, now he wanted to reveal his growth since then, his movement away from the romantic egocentrism and narcissism of his youth-

scholarly editions of works by Wolfe; three are limited editions of difficult-to-locate Wolfe items; eleven are books or pamphlets of historical and biographical interest (three volumes of previously unpublished correspondence, a collection of interviews, five volumes dealing with Wolfe's relationships and friendships, a study of Wolfe's relationship to his editors, and one full-dress biography); four are critical works; and one is a bibliography. The proportion of textual and scholarly work to critical work during this period (about two to one) is noteworthy, marking a pivotal moment in Wolfe studies: important attempts by scholars to come to grips with complex textual problems in the Wolfe canon.

Few years between 1979 and 1989 were uneventful: 1980, 1981, 1983, 1985, and 1987, however, were the most productive. The years of "Wolfegate," in 1980-1981, a controversy focusing on John Halberstadt's 1980 *Yale Review* article, "The Making of Thomas Wolfe's Posthumous Novels," were the most turbulent and inglorious. The teapot tempest that found its way into the pages of the *New York Book Review*, the *New York Review of Books*, the *Chronicle of Higher Education*, the *Boston Globe*, and the *San Francisco Chronicle*, among others, centered on Halberstadt's misuse of Wolfe-estate material and on the decision made by the Houghton Library at Harvard (where the materials were housed) that he be barred from the library for a year. Halberstadt did not fabricate the textual problems he saw in the Wolfe canon, and he actually quoted fewer than ten words from previously unpublished Wolfe material, but his charges of literary fraud and his vociferous insistence that Wolfe had really not written his posthumous novels sensationalized and distorted material which had been made public nearly two decades earlier by Richard S. Kennedy in *The Window of Memory* (Chapel Hill: University of North Carolina Press, 1962). What Kennedy perceived to be "creative editing" on the part of Aswell, Wolfe's editor at Harper and Brothers and later his literary executor, made necessary by Wolfe's death in 1938, Halberstadt perceived to be a conspiracy of secrecy designed to disguise the "true author" of Wolfe's posthumous novels. His scenario oversimplified and generalized the complex relationship between editor and writer, presenting sensitive Wolfe-estate material to the general reading public in the worst possible light.

In 1983 and 1985, more responsible Wolfe scholars plumbed a rich vein of archival material.

Aline Bernstein, early 1940s (Aldo P. Magi)

In 1983 Wolfe's unpublished "Last Poem" was discovered by Charles Scribner III in a desk once belonging to Perkins; and John Lane Idol, Jr., convinced a private Wolfe collector to allow him to facsimile the only extant copy of the dummy of the first chapter of Wolfe's abortive second novel, "K-19." That same year, Kennedy included a previously unpublished Wolfe story, "No More Rivers," in his edition of Wolfe's correspondence with Elizabeth Nowell. New versions of previously published Wolfe works, *Welcome To Our City*, *The Story of a Novel*, and "Writing and Living," were published by Kennedy and Leslie Field. In addition, Kennedy, the most indefatigable of Wolfe scholars, edited the correspondence of Wolfe and Nowell, *Beyond Love and Loyalty*, while Suzanne Stutman, who began her work as a dissertation under Kennedy's direction at Temple University, edited the correspondence of Wolfe and Aline Bernstein under the title *My Other Loneliness*. Although 1983 was certainly an important year in Wolfe studies, 1985 came close to rivaling its productivity. In 1985 Louis Rubin and Idol pieced together a jigsaw puzzle of documents to reconstruct Wolfe's play *Mannerhouse*; Richard Walser and Aldo P. Magi tirelessly searched for Wolfe interviews to be published as *Thomas Wolfe Interviewed*; and Suzanne Stutman added to her edition of the Wolfe-Bernstein correspondence in a pamphlet titled *Holding On For Heaven*.

The year 1987, however, was undoubtedly the banner year in Wolfe studies. It brought with it the publication of a major bibliography, an introduction to Wolfe studies, a complete collection of Wolfe's short stories, an intensive study of Wolfe's relationship with his editors, a short biographical study, and a Pulitzer Prize-winning full-length biography. Carol Johnston's *Thomas Wolfe: A Descriptive Bibliography* supplants the George Preston bibliography published in 1943. It focuses entirely on Wolfe's works, distinguishing printings and editions and listing all first book and pamphlet appearances, first-appearance contributions to magazines and newspapers, keepsakes, and putative first appearances of material by Wolfe. This work is primarily of interest to Wolfe scholars and collectors as well as to those involved in advanced study of Wolfe, however. John Idol's *A Thomas Wolfe Companion* is more appropriate to the needs of high-school students. *A Thomas Wolfe Companion* serves as an introduction to Wolfe's life, ideas and attitudes, major themes, editors, and critics. In addition to providing students with a glossary of characters and places, Idol's *Companion* contains genealogical charts of the Gant, Pentland, Hawke, Joyner, and Webber clans.

Francis Skipp's *The Complete Short Stories of Thomas Wolfe* is a collection of Wolfe's often inaccessible short fiction, gathered from various collections, magazines, and newspapers. Another important publication is Leslie Field's *Thomas Wolfe and His Editors: Establishing a True Text for the Posthumous Publications*, which is a detailed historical study of Wolfe's relationship to his editors and focuses largely on complex textual questions in the posthumous novels. It deals with one of the central issues facing Wolfe scholarship today, the establishment of authoritative texts of Wolfe's posthumous publications, and is based on a thorough investigation of the archival material delineating Wolfe's relationship with Perkins and Aswell.

Of two biographical studies, Aldo P. Magi and Richard Walser's *Wolfe and Belinda Jellife* is the most specialized: it is a particularly well-constructed study of Wolfe's friendship with and correspondence with Belinda Jellife; however, David Donald's *Look Homeward: A Life of Thomas Wolfe*, is of more general interest. Donald's some-what controversial biography sparked new interest in Wolfe in the face of the rigorous objection of contemporary critics who would have labeled Wolfe's work "juvenalia." Although not supplanting the work of Elizabeth Nowell and Andrew Turnbull, Donald's biography is a good deal more frank and revealing in its discussion of Wolfe and of the turbulent and sometimes violent nature which served as the substrata for his genius. Less selective in its discussion than Nowell's *Thomas Wolfe: A Biography* (1960) and far more carefully researched and documented than Turnbull's *Thomas Wolfe* (1965), Donald's *Look Homeward* has already become the standard biography.

In his four large novels and two collections of stories, Wolfe was concerned with a few basic themes. In *The Story of a Novel* he pointed out that he had been involved with themes he saw as central to his writing: his various concepts of time, the "Where now?" motif, and man's search for a spiritual father. In the speech he gave at Purdue University in 1938, he said that these earlier themes were no longer crucial. He realized that as a beginning writer he had been too egocentric, too much the sensitive artist divorced from his environment. Late in his short life he saw the need for looking outside of himself, for looking at the political, social, and economic world, and for trying to understand it, assimilate it, and somehow to bring it into his writing. This, in fact, he attempted to do in his last novel, *You Can't Go Home Again*.

In *The Story of a Novel* Wolfe explained briefly the three time elements that he used in his novel: present time; past time, which showed people "as acting and as being acted upon by all the accumulated impact of man's experience"; and time immutable, "the time of rivers, mountains, oceans, and the earth; a kind of eternal and unchanging universe of time against which would be projected the transience of man's life, the bitter briefness of his day." It has been said that the train and the river are for Wolfe two basic symbols communicating to his readers his feelings about time. Time was for Wolfe a perennial, marvelous mystery, and its finest expression is in his second novel, *Of Time and the River*.

Although on its simplest level *Look Homeward, Angel* can be called a chronicle novel describing the first twenty years of Eugene Gant's life, it is also a novel dominated by the passing of time. Old Gant is dying; the family is falling apart; Eugene is growing up. Change is everywhere.

Thomas Wolfe, mid 1930s

The Gants are always in a state of turmoil. Eliza sets up a separate establishment at her boarding-house and busies herself with real estate. Early in the novel Grover dies; much later Ben also dies. Helen marries and leaves. Eugene goes off to college. Stability and certainty in the Gant family are almost nonexistent. The only fixed element is Eugene's own consciousness, and that too changes and expands as he becomes an adolescent and discovers sex, desire, art. Even as a child he had stared at a baby picture of himself and "turned away sick with fear and the effort to touch, retain, grasp himself for only a moment." The novel is a series of episodes strung out in time: almost every chapter of *Look Homeward, Angel* contains in its first paragraph a reference to the flight of time and the coming of the seasons.

Occasionally the characters observe themselves caught in time and can only look with awe and fear at what they see. Old Gant reluctantly sells the stone angel of his youth; he concludes the transaction with Madame Elizabeth, whom he had known quite well in days gone by. In the Madame Elizabeth scenario we have one of Wolfe's most sensitive, perceptive, and complex dramatizations of time, a theme that was to haunt Wolfe

throughout his life. In each phrase of chapter 19 we feel the painful contrasts between youth and age, summer and winter, sex and sterility, then and now, life and death: "one afternoon in the young summer, Gant leaned upon the rail. . . . He was getting on to sixty-five, his erect body had settled, he stooped a little. . . . Life buzzed slowly like a fly." And later, the traumatic and ironic transaction when the angel will find its final resting place–as a tombstone for a whore!

Early in the novel we are introduced to a young Southern boy brought up in a family that does not reflect much formal education. How does Wolfe persuade us to view education as filtered through the sensibilities of Eugene Gant? We start with the infant protagonist imitating a cow: "moo, moo." Later he is sensitized to the classics, to humanities, and a liberal education when he is a student in the private school administered by the Leonards. He is ridiculed by members of his family, but they display ambivalence more than hostility. And Eugene meanwhile learns something of the large world outside of Altamont. He learns of the world of Shakespeare, the poets, and the milieu of writers in general.

Much later we see an iconoclastic Eugene who has built upon his early learning. When Eugene is at the state university, in a few paragraphs one gets a capsule comment on the stultified, pedanticized university and Gene's accommodation to it. He is an eager student and thus prepares his Latin diligently. But the small-minded instructor prefers pony-ridden preparations by the oafs. Then we have the myopic and pretentious English professor whom Eugene satirizes.

Later Gene would satirize the stereotypes of the public university, the big man on campus, the promoters, the nothing creatures who came from small-town North Carolina to the state university and cultivated their future "contacts." They joined, they participated, they paved the way for their futures as state senators or executives in the state's leading industries.

Richard S. Kennedy saw *Look Homeward, Angel* as a bildungsroman: "a series of ordeals and learning experiences through which the hero passes as if going through initiation rites at the brink of manhood." Eugene learns from teachers, school, sex, alcohol, sickness, death. And as Eugene reaches the end of a phase simultaneously with the end of the novel, "he reaches an interpretation of life and finds a way of life that he can follow." In effect, Kennedy concludes, in *Look Homeward, Angel*, Wolfe "has provided a swirl of experience around his hero and made the whole experience of life and of growing up seem exciting and valuable."

In addition to Gene's experiences at school, his reading, romantic fantasies, and sexual awakenings are also important. Early on we have the idyllic Laura James episode and its painful aftermath. Eugene rhapsodizes about Laura. Later, after she rejects him, he goes to Norfolk, Virginia, and on a whirl of conflicting emotions and stratagems, he wants to "get back" at her.

Still another aspect of youthful sex experienced by Eugene is Ella Corpening in funky "Niggertown," where Gene delivers papers. Or even his first "almost" experience with the little waitress Louise. Gene wants and wants, but he cannot focus. He's frightened, insecure, at times even terrified. Much later Gene does have his brothel initiation, but even this is fraught with anxiety and ultimate terror because of fears of venereal disease.

Eugene's sexual education is important, but his relations with his family are no less significant: Eliza and her property, larger-than-life W. O. Grant, salesman Luke, and nondescript Daisy, dissolute Steve, bullying Helen, and finally, secret-sharer Ben. The acquisitive mother, the aspiring and unfulfilled father, the passel of siblings pulling one way or another—all teach Eugene. Turbulence is plentiful, and youth responds.

However, in the midst of the family relationships there is for Eugene a world of introspective romantic fantasy, often mixed with the mystique of religion, heroic bravado, and sexual awareness. For example, young Gene reads of Mainwaring, the melodramatic hero missionary:

> "I am going," he said presently.
> "Going?" she whispered. "Where?"
> The organ music deepened.
> "Out there," he gestured briefly to the West. "Out there—among His people."

There is also Bruce Glendenning, "international vagabond, jack of all trades." And so we have Eugene Mainwaring Glendenning identifying strongly with the fictional figures he reads about, and a bit later he even fantasizes about his fourth-grade teacher.

At the very close of the novel, when Ben has died and Eugene has completed college and is preparing to depart for the North, he stands

Revised galley proof for "The Web of Earth," published in the July 1932 issue of Scribner's *magazine (courtesy of Paul Gitlin, Administrator of the Estate of Thomas Wolfe/ Houghton Library, Harvard University)*

on the porch of the shop exactly as old Gant had done and converses with the ghostly shade of Ben. The fountain in the square is suddenly motionless, frozen in time. The stone animals of the monuments get up and walk. All that he has seen and known parades before Eugene's unbelieving eyes. Then in the climactic moment of the novel, he sees coming along past the fountain carrying his load of newspapers "himself—his son, his boy, his lost and virgin flesh."

It has happened so swiftly, almost without his knowing it; he has grown to manhood, and whatever he once was is lost and unrecapturable. Time, chronology, change–these are the only reality he knows. Then the fountain begins splashing again, and the novel is concluded.

Even though *Look Homeward, Angel* had been rejected initially by several publishers, it was ultimately accepted by Scribners, one of the most prestigious publishing houses in America. This was an unfortunate time for the appearance of a first book by an unknown author because eleven days before the book's publication the stock market crashed. The subsequent economic depression did not help the sales of the novel. However, despite these adverse circumstances, a few weeks after publication it went into a second printing, and although it did not become an American best-seller, it did have a continued and steady sale in the United States and abroad.

Wolfe's second novel, *Of Time and the River*, as the title indicates, is preoccupied with time. In this novel Wolfe probes time's fleetingness, grandeur, pathos, and "the immense and murmurous" sound of time which rises over great railroad sheds and over huge cities. He is also concerned with the nature of time and its properties. Passages that inquire into its nature are more frequent in this novel than in any of his others.

At the opening of the book Eugene thinks, for instance, of the relative qualities of space and time between the little town in North Carolina and New York City. The distance, he says, is more than seven hundred miles. "But so relative are the qualities of space and time. . . . that in that brief passage of this journey one may live a life."

The opening train journey of the novel acts as a transition between Eugene's movement from the South to the North. On the train the present fades, and as Eugene fingers the watch his brother Ben had given him, the image of Ben appears, and the scene changes to Gene's twelfth birthday when he received the watch from his brother. Gene wonders what time is. Then he observes simply that the watch is to keep time with. "What is this dream of time, this strange and bitter miracle of living?" Some have seen this scene as a sharply Proustian one in which there is the recall of the past into the present and the fusion of both into one timeless instant. And once again on the train present and past time fuse when Eugene thinks of his life with his father. Suddenly the thousand images of his father become as "one terrific image."

Of course the novel is much more than a philosophical treatise on time. Wolfe does remove his protagonist from the train and then introduces him to the great Northern city. *Of Time and the River*, since it is a continuation of the story of Eugene Gant, is also a story about continued development or growth of the main character. In the city Wolfe's concern with time seems to be tied to the river, specifically the East River, symbolizing the metropolis of New York. Wolfe was always obsessed by metropolitan areas, and for Eugene Gant, New York becomes the first, the biggest, and the most important city experience. In later novels Wolfe's protagonist will have important experiences with Paris and Berlin, but in a sense these are extensions of his earlier New York experiences. New York, therefore, may be labeled Eugene's urban initiation. But several of Eugene's activities in and reactions to New York and other cities must be explored in order to see Gene, and later George Webber, becoming a whole man and then finally emerging as a creative person, a writer. What is finally seen appears to be the ritual initiation of a hero–so much so, as a matter of fact, that the various labels depicting Gant's New York phase seem like clichés. Of the various phases, four distinct ones emerge in the hero's concern with the city: the boy from the provinces; his disappointment and disillusionment with the city; the provincial accepted; and finally, his realization and acceptance of the realities of the city. By the time we have reached the last phase, the would-be writer has matured, and he is able to see order in the world of his imagination, the world which he has seen and is committing to paper.

Eugene Gant's first impressions of the city are tinged by his entranced vision of golden New York. To Eugene, wealth and fame are desirable and good. His first disillusionment, however, results from his friendship with Joel Pierce. Eugene, visiting Joel's house and family at Rhineskill, is impressed by the wealth and splendor of Joel's life. Eugene realizes that all his dreams of wealth and luxury in the "shining city" were poor replicas of the reality which he now desires even more. As Wolfe puts it, the young Gant could not then see beneath the surface and recognize the sweat, grief, toil, and heartache of innumerable people which had gone into producing this estate, "this fragile image of compacted might."

Of Time and the River was the last "novel" completed by the author himself, albeit with the larger-than-life editorial help of Maxwell Perkins. In the five and a half years that had passed between the publication of *Look Homeward, Angel* and *Of Time and the River*, Wolfe had undergone much turmoil. He wanted desperately to go beyond his first book, but his creativity took many directions until the second book was finally hammered out. Paschal Reeves has pointed out that Wolfe had "set his sights high. His work throbbed to the epic impulse as he sought no less than to capture the essence of American character and the American experience in fiction."

The novel was published 8 March 1935 to mixed reviews. The critics praised its gusto and vitality, but many were dismayed by its incomprehensible form and what was then considered experimental. Nevertheless, it became a best-seller as the public bought copies and while critics argued its merits.

In the posthumous *The Web and the Rock* Wolfe changed his hero's name from Eugene Gant to George Webber. The early part of the book deals with Webber's youth in Libya Hill, his time at Pine Rock College, and his life with other young Southerners in New York. Then George goes to Europe, returns, and meets Esther Jack. The rest of the story is given over to their love affair, a wild and tumultuous phase of Webber's experience. Then we have the rejection of George's novel, a trip abroad, a breakup with Esther, and a reconciliation.

As with *Of Time and the River*, *The Web and the Rock* seems to be an "ode to the city" of New York. Without Esther Jack, however, it could not have been written, because Esther Jack/Aline Bernstein came to epitomize New York and cosmopolitanism for Wolfe. Much in the book is grotesque. He seems to be creating a "state of mind" in this book. We have episodes sharply etched by Wolfe. Two boys are run over by an automobile, a savage and graphically illustrated vignette. Then we have a Dickens-like beast of a butcher and his family, and finally the "Child by Tiger" episode, depicting the Negro Dick Prosser, an ex-soldier who goes berserk, kills several people, and finally is himself killed and mutilated. In *The Web and the Rock* Wolfe attempts to capture the megalopolis for us in a few sharp vignettes.

For many, the Esther Jack/George Webber sections define the book. On one level we have the typically European rather than American initi-

Wolfe with his mother, shortly before his death, in Asheville, 1937 (photo by Elliot Lyman Fisher; courtesy of the North Carolina Collection, University of North Carolina Library at Chapel Hill)

ation theme: a young man initiated into the mysteries of life, love, and sex by the older, more experienced woman. On another we have some of the most powerful, mad scenes of American literature involving graphic descriptions of sex, food, love, prejudice, and the basest and most elevated emotions of man. A typical food/love sequence follows:

> George Webber and his Esther touched the earth and found it tangible, they looked at life and saw it could be seen. They went out in the streets together, and everywhere they went was food and richness.... They bought food with the passionate intensity of poets.... And the grocers would find their finest fruits for them. George, with his out-thrust lip and dark-browed earnestness, would poke at the meat, tweak the legs of the chickens, feel the lettuce, plunk at great melons with his finger, read all the labels on the canned goods with a lustful eye, and breathe all the sharp spicy odors of the shops. And they walked home together with great bags and packages of food.

In many ways *The Web and the Rock* is fictionalized autobiography, as were the first two books, with protagonist George Webber playing Thomas Wolfe. But in *The Web and the Rock* Wolfe seems to be moving outside of himself to a new social awareness, a new social consciousness of people and institutions that are not simply projections of Thomas Wolfe.

In bulk, Wolfe's posthumous work is larger than that which had been published during his lifetime. In the last years of his life he had tried to pull together his massive manuscript for publication, but when he left it in the hands of his new editor, he realized it was still unfinished. He did, however, leave a long outline and summary of his work for Aswell, whose job it ultimately became to edit and organize the material for publication after Wolfe's death.

When *The Web and the Rock* finally emerged, the critics were divided once again. Many noted that the book contained an uncomfortable mixture of brilliance and poor writing. Moreover, to this day, even among Wolfe admirers, the debate continues concerning whether Wolfe's posthumous fiction was well served by the editorial work of Edward C. Aswell.

With his last novel, *You Can't Go Home Again*, Wolfe goes even farther than he did in *The Web and the Rock* in the direction of social consciousness. It is perhaps his most episodic book. Early on George Webber resumes his life with Esther in New York. He awaits the publication of his first novel. He returns home for a visit and has a reunion with a boyhood friend, Nebraska Crane, a professional baseball player. He meets Judge Rumford Bland, a usurer whom he used to know. He ruminates on all that has gone wrong in the town in which he grew up. Then he returns to New York. Wolfe has a chapter on the Jack family in their fashionable New York apartment. A party featuring Piggy Logan and a fire at the Jacks' assume symbolic proportions as Wolfe attempts to contrast the haves and have-nots in depression United States.

As we move to the close of the novel, further episodes involve George's trip to England and Germany. In England he has a wildly kaleidoscopic time with Lloyd McHarg, supposedly fashioned on Sinclair Lewis, and on his last trip to his beloved Germany George sees the face of evil in the Nazis who lionize him, preen for the Olympic Games, and smash in the heads of Jews on the side of the streets of Berlin and Munich. "I Have a Thing to Tell You" is a poignant picture of man's inhumanity to man, the Nazi persecution of the Jews. Finally we have "Ecclesiastes" and the "Credo," on which the book ends. Some of Wolfe's finest expressions of social awareness emerged in *You Can't Go Home Again*. Much of the social awareness or social consciousness involves Wolfe's attitude toward Germany and the Jews. Was Wolfe anti-Semitic? In a very real sense his fiction and especially his letters do reveal bigotry and prejudice. Moreover, in his seven trips to Germany he discovered in himself a strong affinity for the Germans and the Teutonic culture—long before he discovered his America. Yet in the separate piece entitled "I Have a Thing to Tell You," which later appeared as a climactic epiphany in the last part of *You Can't Go Home Again*, Wolfe sees the evil behind the mask of Germany and senses at once that anti-Semitism and humanity are incompatible.

George Webber, having returned to his beloved Germany as a famous author, is now on a train leaving it once more. At Aachen, the last stop before the border, he and other travelers in his compartment are shocked to see that one of their fellow passengers—a nervous little man whom George had privately called Fuss-and-Fidget—had been seized by the authorities. The rumor circulates that he is a Jew caught trying to escape with all of his money. As the terrified little man tries to persuade the officers to let him go since there must be some misunderstanding, he is led past his former traveling companions, his eyes glancing at them for just a moment. But he does not betray them by showing in any way that he knows them, and they board the train, leaving him behind on the platform. "He looked once, directly and steadfastly, at his former companions, and they at him. And in that gaze there was all the unmeasured weight of man's mortal anguish." Wolfe wrote this in 1936, some time before the rest of the world took seriously the plight of the Jew, and well before one heard the terms *final solution, collective guilt,* and *Holocaust.*

Wolfe was gaining in knowledge and sensitivity, but his perception that "you can't go home again" did not break his spirit; indeed, strangely enough, it heartened him. Life is change, he felt, and therefore we can improve it. His final credo, in the last pages of his novel, is no defeated whine or whimper. The loss of false illusions, he said, is only the way to new belief. Here is Wolfe's conclusion:

Wolfe at Yosemite National Park, 1938 (Aldo P. Magi)

I believe we are lost here in America, but I believe we shall be found. And this belief . . . is . . . not only our own hope, but America's everlasting, living dream. I think the life which we have fashioned in America, and which has fashioned us . . . was self-destructive in its nature, and must be destroyed. I think these forms are dying, and must die, just as I know that America and the people in it are deathless, undiscovered, and immortal, and must live.

I think the true discovery of America is before us. I think the true fulfillment of our spirit, of our people, of our mighty and immortal land, is yet to come. I think the true discovery of our democracy is still before us. And I think that all these things are certain as the morning, as inevitable as noon. . . . Our America is Here, is Now, and beckons us, and . . . this glorious assurance is not only our living hope, but our dream to be accomplished.

Thus does Wolfe's long posthumous work end optimistically, as a celebration of the America that he knew and loved. He saw the face of evil all

around him, but he insisted in his fictional letter to Foxhall Edwards/Maxwell Perkins that "we must deny it all along the way."

Wolfe's last full-length novel was generally well received by his readers and the critics although the critical debate concerning his merits as a novelist continues to the present day. His social criticism and more restrained style in *You Can't Go Home Again* have been admired by many. He is still viewed as a flawed writer by some critics. Others continue to single out *Look Homeward, Angel* as his most effective novel and a half-dozen or so separately published magazine pieces as his best stories or novellas.

Even in the short stories and novellas one sees the perennial Wolfe motif—an ongoing love affair with America. Wolfe, as so many before him, had to leave his land to come to know it. True, he criticized the South and indicted the North, but he ultimately came to his own discovery of America—not exactly a Whitmanesque celebration, but his own personal discovery. His exploration of America was an emotional voyage (under-

I suppose the biographical facts about birth, home-town, colleges and so on, are available to the editors of this book, so I shall not bother to give them here. Since almost all the knowledge the world has of me, concerns me as a writer, perhaps it will be better if I try to tell something of the life.

I am thirty-five years old, and although I have written more millions of words than I should like to count— how many I don't know, but perhaps as many as anyone else my age now writing. I have published not more than a tenth of them. Nevertheless, the critics say I write too much - and I don't say that they are wrong. Although I suppose the desire to be a writer has been buried in me for a long time—certainly the itch for it has been there, because I began to scribble when I was not more than fourteen years old. I never dared admit to myself that I might seriously proclaim my intentions until I was about twenty-six.

Before that, I had written a few plays and although I had hoped they might find a producer, I don't think that even then, I had sufficient confidence in my abilities to annouce definitely to my family that I actually intedded to be a playwright and to hope to earn my living that way. I didn't succeed, anyway. And it was not until the twenty-sixth year that I began to write a book, which occupied me for the next two or three years. During this time I was employed at the Washington Square college of the New York University as an instructor in English. I don't think that even then did I consider cretely and reasonably assure myself that I had found my life's

Revised typescript page for Wolfe's "Autobiographical Statement" (courtesy of Paul Gitlin, Administrator of the Estate of Thomas Wolfe/The Humanities Research Center, University of Texas at Austin)

taken not by listing and describing from hearsay and imagination) of the various aspects of a land too broad to be encompassed within the experience and life of one man. Often he chose the little, touching, unnoticed thing–"the sound of a milk wagon as it entered a street just at the first gray of morning"–setting off a stream of recollection into the past too tender for the rough jags of the unreal and made-up. A recollection such as this stirred the affections, not the intellect. It glowed, and it warmed him. In 1930 from London he wrote: "My longing for America amounts to a constant ache." From its tangible substance, Wolfe was able to evoke the emotional personality of his country, bringing it out of memory with all its haunting beauty.

It was filtered through his consciousness, and from it he drew his strength as an artist. Wolfe found, eventually, that America was in himself, and he was trying to echo it in himself. From it he had need to draw his life, his art, his speech. It was no easy discovery, no easy task; but in 1936 he was able to proclaim:

> I have at last discovered my America, I believe I have found my language, I think I know my way. And I shall wreak out my vision of this life, this way, this world and this America, to the top of my bent, to the height of my ability, but with an unswerving devotion, integrity and purity of purpose that shall not be menaced, altered or weakened by any one.

When America was the subject in his fiction, Wolfe was able to exhibit a melody and luxury of speech (often with a pure, clean masculine line) which seemed to capture all the richness and greatness of his large subject:

> I will go up and down the country,
> and back and forth across the country
> on the great trains that thunder over
>   America.
> I will go out West where the States are
>   square;
> Oh, I will go to Boise, and Helena, and
>   Albuquerque.
> I will go to Montana and the two Dakotas
>   and the unknown places.

Toward the end of his life Wolfe launched into ambitious plans to do a great deal more with the America he had discovered. For most students of Wolfe, *The Hills Beyond* is a postscript to his total work. Ironically, the plan for this book appears first as an actual postscript to a letter

which Wolfe wrote his mother in 1934. In the postscript Wolfe asks his mother to "jot down" a brief history of her family. He would like, he says,

> to get a list of the twenty children or more that your grandfather had by his two marriages and what happened to them and where they settled and what parts of the country they moved to, and so forth. . . .
> I'm asking you to do this because some day after I get through with these books I'm working on now, I may wind the whole thing up with a book that will try to tell through the hundreds of members of one family the whole story of America.

Wolfe did go on with his plan, but he died leaving behind only ten chapters of his fragmentary novel.

In the ten chapters of *The Hills Beyond* Wolfe traces the careers of Bear Joyner and those of eight of his children. The children are the offspring of Bear's two marriages. Wolfe does not get around to dealing with the twenty or so children and hundreds of grandchildren and great-grandchildren that his original plan calls for. The children he does develop, in their various occupations–lawyer, politician, teacher businessman–represent the occupational face of America. They stand as prototypes of myriad rural and urban occupations. In the chapter entitled "The Great Schism," Joyner's huge family does split up, some staying on the farm and others going to the city. In effect, these people are the beginnings of the American heritage as Wolfe sees it in his projected series of novels.

In *The Hills Beyond* Wolfe consciously infused in his story various strains of American folklore, especially those stemming from the frontiersman and the Yankee, and it soon becomes apparent that he is out to write a folk novel of America, a novel which would tell the "whole story of America" in addition to his "whole story" of Eugene Gant/George Webber.

An effective way to recapture Wolfe and see him in perspective is to return to his first and best full-length novel, *Look Homeward, Angel*. Does it stand up today for the adult reader, or is it only a novel for the young? True, the initial discovery, and even shock, of recognition are often missing when we return to an old favorite. Mark Twain delineated this succinctly in "Old Times on the Mississippi" as he recounted in semifictional, bittersweet fashion his own life as a riverboat pilot. First was the anticipation, the excite-

Drawing of Wolfe by George Shreiber

the good, which often borders on genius, as well as the bad. From its first appearance *Look Homeward, Angel* had a mixed reception. This has been true of most of Wolfe's fiction. Paschal Reeves in his *Studies in Look Homeward, Angel* reprints about two dozen critical responses to the novel, some contemporary, others that have appeared over the years, to show that in terms of public reception Wolfe's *Look Homeward, Angel* apparently has more than held its own. This has been true of this novel and the rest of the fiction insofar as publication and sales have been concerned.

Wolfe's books are not perfect. Wolfe can be criticized for being excessive and indulgent, and for other shortcomings. But his are rich books and stories which can be read with great and enduring satisfaction.

Letters:

The Letters of Thomas Wolfe, edited by Elizabeth Nowell (New York: Scribners, 1956).

The Letters of Thomas Wolfe to His Mother, edited by C. Hugh Holman and Sue Fields Ross (Chapel Hill: University of North Carolina Press, 1968).

Beyond Love and Loyalty: The Letters of Thomas Wolfe and Elizabeth Nowell Together with "No More Rivers" A Story by Thomas Wolfe, edited by Richard S. Kennedy (Chapel Hill & London: University of North Carolina Press, 1983).

My Other Loneliness: Letters of Thomas Wolfe and Aline Bernstein, edited by Suzanne Stutman (Chapel Hill & London: University of North Carolina Press, 1983).

Interview:

Thomas Wolfe Interviewed: 1929-1938, edited by Aldo P. Magi and Richard Walser (Baton Rouge & London: Louisiana State University Press, 1985).

Bibliographies:

John S. Phillipson, *Thomas Wolfe: A Reference Guide* (Boston: G. K. Hall, 1977).
An annotated secondary bibliography.

ment, the romance; then came education, awareness, experience. Inevitably, the romance and early excitement gave way to another kind of satisfaction, but one not less rich. Yes, Twain talked about riverboating, but he may very well have been discussing one's early and late responses to *Look Homeward, Angel; A Portrait of the Artist as a Young Man; Great Expectations;* or *The Adventures of Augie March.*

We are told that *Romeo and Juliet* is the drama of youth–love in the morning; *Antony and Cleopatra*, the drama of middle age–love in the afternoon. But we return to *Romeo and Juliet* to recapture the fire, excitement, and even the universal verities implicit in the tale of the star-crossed lovers. And so it is with Wolfe's *Look Homeward, Angel.*

Of course, Wolfe is no Shakespeare. Moreover, critics are often correct when they point out adolescent thought and juvenile prose in his fiction. He is fair game for the critics, but he deserves a fair hearing and a fair examination of

Carol Johnston, *Thomas Wolfe: A Descriptive Bibliography* (Pittsburgh: University of Pittsburgh Press, 1987).

A primary bibliography supplanting the George Preston bibliography published in 1943; focuses entirely on Wolfe's works, distinguishing various printings and editions and listing all first book and pamphlet appearances, first-appearance contributions to magazines and newspapers, keepsakes, and putative first appearances of material by Wolfe.

Biographies:

Elizabeth Nowell, *Thomas Wolfe: A Biography* (New York: Doubleday, 1960).

The earliest of Wolfe's major biographies, written by his literary agent; important for its balanced discussion of Wolfe's New York career.

Andrew Turnbull, *Thomas Wolfe* (New York: Scribners, 1965).

Biography containing good discussions of Wolfe's relations with Perkins, Fitzgerald, and Hemingway.

David Herbert Donald, *Look Homeward: A Life of Thomas Wolfe* (Boston: Little, Brown, 1987).

The standard biography; more revealing than Nowell's and more thoroughly researched the Turnbull's.

References:

Leslie Field, *Thomas Wolfe and His Editors: Establishing a True Text for the Posthumous Publications* (Norman & London: University of Oklahoma Press, 1987).

A well-researched discussion of the questions of textual authority in the Wolfe canon that have recently received so much attention; too complex and detailed for many students, but rewarding for those who have a genuine interest in Wolfe's creative processes.

Leo Gurko, *Thomas Wolfe: Beyond the Romantic Ego* (New York: Crowell, 1975).

A critical study that argues for the complexity of Wolfe and his work and suggests that Wolfe's critics oversimplify him.

C. Hugh Holman, *The Loneliness at the Core: Studies in Thomas Wolfe* (New York: Scribners, 1975).

Seven incisive essays commenting on Wolfe's autobiographical methods, attitudes toward the South, literary aspirations, and techniques, many of which originally established Wolfe's importance as a major American writer.

Holman, *Thomas Wolfe* (Minneapolis: University of Minnesota Press, 1960).

An excellent introduction to Wolfe and his work written by a perceptive and important Wolfe critic.

John Lane Idol, Jr., *A Thomas Wolfe Companion* (New York, Westport, Conn. & London: Greenwood Press, 1987).

A series of essays which additionally serves as an introduction to Wolfe's life, ideas and attitudes, major themes, editors, and critics; includes a glossary of characters and places and genealogical charts of the Gant, Pentland, Hawke, Joyner, and Webber clans.

Richard S. Kennedy, *The Window of Memory: The Literary Career of Thomas Wolfe* (Chapel Hill: University of North Carolina Press, 1962).

A well-researched study of Wolfe's development as an artist; traces the process by which each of the major works was crafted. An essential work for those who want to study the creative process of the artist.

Herbert J. Muller, *Thomas Wolfe* (Norfolk: New Directions, 1947).

One of the earliest treatments of Wolfe's writing as an attempt to create an American epic.

Paschal Reeves, *Thomas Wolfe's Albatross: Race and Nationality in America* (Athens: University of Georgia Press, 1968).

Critical study focusing on Wolfe's attempt to overcome his own racial and religious biases.

Louis D. Rubin, Jr., *Thomas Wolfe: The Weather of His Youth* (Baton Rouge: Louisiana State University Press, 1955).

Informative study focusing on the relationship between Wolfe's themes and techniques and the early forces of his youth.

Richard Walser, *Thomas Wolfe: An Introduction and Interpretation* (New York: Barnes & Noble, 1961).

Informed analyses of the major novels.

Floyd C. Watkins, *Thomas Wolfe's Characters* (Norman: University of Oklahoma Press, 1957).

A discussion of Wolfe's use of neighbors and friends as characters in his novels.

Richard Wright

This entry was updated by Edward D. Clark (North Carolina State University) from his entry in DLB 76, Afro-American Writers, 1940-1955.

Places	Mississippi Harlem	Chicago Boston	Paris
Influences and Relationships	H. L. Mencken Ralph Ellison George Padmore James Joyce	Granville Hicks Langston Hughes Arna Bontemps Claude McKay	Gertrude Stein Jean-Paul Sartre Simone de Beauvoir
Literary Movements and Forms	Naturalism Autobiography	Existentialism	Protest Novel

Major Themes	Migration from
	  Rural South to
	  Urban North
		Physical & Spiri-
		  tual Hunger
		The South as Hell
			Relationship between
			  Power and Freedom

Cultural and Artistic Influences	Rejection of Evan-
	  gelical Religion
	Black History
		African Liberation
		  Movement
			Freudian Psychololgy
			African Tribal Culture

Social and Economic Influences	Racism Urban Poverty	The Great Depression Communism	Pan-Africanism Expatriation

See also the Wright entry in DLB: Documentary Series 2.

BIRTH: Natchez, Mississippi, 4 September 1908, to Nathan and Ella Wilson Wright.

MARRIAGES: August 1939 to Dhimah Rosa Meadman (divorced). 12 March 1941 to Ellen Poplar; children: Julia, Rachel.

AWARDS: Guggenheim Fellowship, 1939; Spingarn Medal, 1941.

DEATH: Paris, France, 28 November 1960.

BOOKS: *Uncle Tom's Children: Four Novellas* (New York & London: Harper, 1938; London: Gollancz, 1939); enlarged as *Uncle Tom's Children: Five Long Stories* (New York & London: Harper, 1940);

Native Son (New York & London: Harper, 1940; London: Gollancz, 1940);

How "Bigger" Was Born (New York: Harper, 1940);

Native Son (The Biography of a Young American): A Play in Ten Scenes, by Wright and Paul Green (New York & London: Harper, 1941); revised by Green in *Black Drama, An Anthology,* edited by William Brasmer and Dominick Consola (Columbus, Ohio: Merrill, 1970), pp. 70-178;

Twelve Million Black Voices: A Folk History of the Negro in the United States, photographs selected by Edwin Rosskam (New York: Viking, 1941; London: Drummond, 1947);

Black Boy: A Record of Childhood and Youth (New York & London: Harper, 1945; London: Gollancz, 1945);

The Outsider (New York: Harper, 1953; London & Sydney: Angus & Robertson, 1953);

Black Power: A Record of Reactions in a Land of Pathos (New York: Harper, 1954; London: Dobson, 1956);

Savage Holiday (New York: Avon, 1954);

Bandoeng 1.500.000.000 d'hommes, translated by Hélène Claireau (Paris: Calmann-Lévy, 1955); republished as *The Color Curtain: A Report on the Bandung Conference* (Cleveland & New York: World, 1956; London: Dobson, 1956);

Pagan Spain: A Report of a Journey into the Past (New York: Harper, 1957; London: Bodley Head, 1960);

White Man, Listen! (Garden City, N.Y.: Doubleday, 1957); enlarged edition, translated by Dominique Guillet as *Ecoute, homme blanc* (Paris: Calmann-Lévy, 1959);

The Long Dream (Garden City, N.Y.: Doubleday, 1958; London & Sydney: Angus & Robertson, 1960);

Eight Men (Cleveland & New York: World, 1960);

Lawd Today (New York: Walker, 1963; London: Blond, 1965);

The Man Who Lived Underground: L'homme qui vivait sous terre, translated by Claude-Edmonde Magny, edited, with an introduction, by Michel Fabre (Paris: Aubier-Flammarion, 1971);

American Hunger (New York: Harper & Row, 1977; London: Gollancz, 1978);

Richard Wright Reader, edited by Ellen Wright and Fabre (New York: Harper & Row, 1978).

PLAY PRODUCTIONS: *Native Son,* by Wright and Paul Green, New York, St. James Theatre, 24 March 1941;

Daddy Goodness, by Wright and Louis Sapin, New York, St. Mark's Playhouse, 4 June 1968.

MOTION PICTURE: *Native Son,* screenplay by Wright, Classic Films, 1951.

OTHER: Introduction to J. Saunders Redding's *No Day of Triumph* (New York: Harper, 1942);

Introduction to Nelson Algren's *Never Come Morning* (New York: Harper, 1942);

Introduction to St. Clair Drake and Horace R. Cayton's *Black Metropolis* (New York: Harcourt, Brace, 1945);

Introduction to his *American Hunger,* in *One Hundred Five Greatest Living Authors Present the World's Best Stories,* edited by Whit Burnett (New York: Dial, 1950);

"I Tried to Be a Communist," in *The God That Failed,* edited by Richard Crossman (New York: Harper, 1950), pp. 115-163;

Preface to Chester Himes's *Le Croisade de Lee Gordon* (Paris: Correa, 1952);

Introduction to George Padmore's *Pan-Africanism or Communism* (London: Dobson, 1956);

Richard Wright (photo by Harriet Crowder)

"Five Episodes," in *Soon One Morning,* edited by Herbert Hill (New York: Knopf, 1963), pp. 149-164;

"The American Problem—Its Negro Phase," in *Richard Wright: Impressions and Perspectives,* edited by David Ray and Robert M. Farnsworth (Ann Arbor: University of Michigan Press, 1973), pp. 9-16.

PERIODICAL PUBLICATIONS: "How *Uncle Tom's Children* Grew," *Columbia University Writers' Bulletin,* 2 (May 1938): 15-17;

"What Do I Think of the Theatre?," *New York World-Telegram,* 2 March 1941, p. 20;

"Not My People's War," *New Masses,* 39 (17 June 1941): 8-9;

"US Negroes Greet You," *Daily Worker,* 1 September 1941, p. 7;

"Richard Wright Describes the Birth of *Black Boy,*" *New York Post,* 30 November 1944, p. B6;

"Is America Solving Its Race Problem?," *America's Town Meeting of the Air Bulletin,* 11 (24 May 1945): 6-7;

"A Paris les GI Noirs ont appris à connaître et à aimer la liberté," *Samedi-Soir,* 25 May 1946, p. 2;

"Psychiatry Comes to Harlem," *Free World,* 12 (September 1946): 49-51;

"How Jim Crow Feels," *True: The Man's Magazine* (November 1946): 25-27, 154-156;

"Urban Misery in an American City: Juvenile Delinquency in Harlem," *Twice a Year,* no. 14-15 (Fall 1946-Winter 1947): 339-345;

"A World View of the American Negro," *Twice a Year,* no. 14-15 (Fall 1946-Winter 1947): 346-348;

"Introductory Note to *The Respectful Prostitute* by Jean-Paul Sarte," *Art and Action,* no. 10 (1948): 14-16;

"Comrade Strong, Don't You Remember?," *New York Herald Tribune* (European edition), 4 April 1949, p. 3;

"L'homme du Sud," *France Etats-Unis* (December 1950): 2;

"Richard Wright Explains Ideas about Movie Making," *Ebony,* 6 (January 1951): 84-85;

"American Negroes in France," *Crisis,* 58 (June-July 1951): 381-383;

"The Shame of Chicago," *Ebony*, 7 (December 1951): 24-32;

"Le Noir est une création du Blanc," *Preuves* (Paris), 8 (May 1958): 40-41;

"L'art est mis en question par l'âge atomique," *Arts, Lettres, Spectacles* (Paris), 5 June 1960;

"Harlem," *Les Parisiens*, no. 1 (December 1960): 23.

Any serious discussion of the development of black fiction in modern American literature must include Richard Wright. He was the first black novelist to describe the plight of the urban masses and the first to present this material in the naturalistic tradition. Not only is he the father of the post-World War II black novel, he is also the main precursor of the black arts movement of the 1960s. Ralph Ellison and James Baldwin are but two of many outstanding black writers who profited from his influence. Moreover, he was, as Robert Felgar explains in *Richard Wright* (1980), "perhaps the very first writer to give the white community explanations and themes that cut through its prejudices and forced it to look at the reality of black life in America."

Richard Nathaniel Wright felt victimized by racial discrimination and racial prejudice throughout his life in the United States. He experienced some of the most severe abuses of racial oppression in Mississippi, where he was born on 4 September 1908, on a plantation in Roxie twenty-two miles east of Natchez, to sharecropper Nathan Wright and teacher Ella Wilson Wright. Nathan Wright, like most black sharecroppers, was extremely poor. In 1911 Ella Wright went to Natchez to live with her family while Nathan became an itinerant worker. Later that same year, in an effort to improve their economic status, Nathan Wright loaded his family onto a riverboat at Natchez and migrated to Memphis, Tennessee. Nathan Wright then deserted his family.

Richard Wright lived in Memphis until he was almost eight. As small children he and his younger brother Leon were often hungry and were expected to look out for themselves. The menial jobs that Ella Wright now had to take did not provide adequate income to support the family. Wright's autobiography, *Black Boy* (1945), explains: "I would feel hunger nudging my ribs, twisting my empty guts until they ached. I would grow dizzy and my vision would dim." His mother would send him to beg money from his father, now living with a mistress. In 1914 Ella Wright became ill, and the two brothers were

sent to Settlement House, a Methodist orphanage.

Mrs. Wright and her sons moved to Elaine, Arkansas, to live with her sister, Maggie, and Maggie's husband, Silas Hoskins, in the summer of 1916. In late 1916 or early 1917 Silas Hoskins was murdered by whites who coveted his property, and the family fled to West Helena, Arkansas, where they lived in fear in rented rooms for several weeks. Mrs. Wright took the boys to Jackson, Mississippi, for several months in 1917, but they returned to West Helena by the winter of 1918. Further family disintegration occurred after Mrs. Wright suffered a stroke in 1919. Wright reluctantly chose to live with Uncle Clark and Aunt Jody in Greenwood, Mississippi, where he could be near his mother, but restrictions placed on him by his aunt and uncle made him an emotional wreck. On the verge of a nervous breakdown, he was permitted to return to Jackson, where he lived with Grandmother Wilson from early 1920 until late 1925.

Wright's education was greatly disrupted by family disorganization. The frequent moves and Mrs. Wright's illness made regular school attendance impossible. Wright first entered Howe Institute in Memphis, Tennessee, around 1916. In 1920 he enrolled and remained for a year at the Seventh Day Adventist school in Jackson, Mississippi, with his Aunt Addie, a fanatical Seventh Day Adventist, the only teacher. Wright felt stifled by his aunt and his maternal grandmother, who tried to force him to pray that he might find God. He later threatened to leave home because Grandmother Wilson refused to permit him to work on Saturdays, the Adventist Sabbath. Early strife with his aunt and grandmother left him with a permanent, uncompromising hostility toward religious solutions to mundane problems. Traces of this hostility surface in much of his writing.

Wright's first formal education started in September 1921 when he joined a fifth grade class at Jim Hill Public School, Jackson, Mississippi. Within two weeks he was promoted to the sixth grade. In 1923 he enrolled at the Smith-Robinson School, also in Jackson; because of excellent grades he was made part-time supervisor of the class. Wright also showed special interest in and talent for writing, getting his first story, "The Voodoo of Hell's Half Acre," published in 1924 in the *Southern Register*, a black Jackson newspaper. In 1925 Wright was made class valedictorian. Determined not to be called an Uncle Tom,

Wright's parents, Ellen Wilson Wright and Nathaniel Wright

he refused to deliver the assistant principal's carefully prepared valedictory address that would not offend the white school officials and finally convinced the black administrators to let him read essentially what he had written. In September of the same year Wright registered for mathematics, English, and history courses at the new Lanier High School in Jackson but had to stop attending classes after a few weeks of irregular attendance because he needed to earn money for family expenses.

In November 1925 Wright returned to Memphis with plans to get money to make "the first lap of a journey to a land where [he] could live with a little less fear." The two years he remained in Memphis were especially important, for there he indulged a developing passion for reading. He discovered *Harper's* magazine, the *Atlantic Monthly,* and the *American Mercury.* Through subterfuge he was able to borrow books from the white library. Of special importance to him were H. L. Mencken's *A Book of Prefaces* (1917) and one of his six volumes of *Prejudices* (1919-1927). Wright was particularly impressed

with Mencken's vision of the South as hell.

Late in 1927 Wright arrived in Chicago, where he spent a decade that was as important to his development as his nineteen years in the South were. After finally securing employment as a postal clerk, he read other writers and studied their styles during his time off. His job at the post office eliminated by the Great Depression, he went on relief in 1931. In 1932 he began attending meetings of the Chicago John Reed Club, a Communist literary organization whose supposed purpose was to use art for revolutionary ends. Especially interested in the literary contacts made at the meetings, Wright formally joined the Communist party in late 1933 and as a revolutionary poet wrote numerous proletarian poems ("I Have Seen Black Hands," "We of the Streets," "Red Leaves of Red Books," for example) for *New Masses* and other left-wing periodicals.

By 1935 Wright had completed his first novel, "Cesspool," published as *Lawd Today* (1963), and in January 1936 his story "Big Boy Leaves Home" was accepted for publication in

New Caravan. In February Wright began working with the National Negro Congress, and in April he chaired the South Side Writers' Group, whose membership included Arna Bontemps and Margaret Walker. Wright submitted some of his critical essays and poetry to the group for criticism and read aloud some of his short stories. In 1936 he was also revising "Cesspool."

The year 1937 was a landmark for Wright. After a quarrel with a Communist party leader, he severed ties with the Chicago branch and went to New York in late May to become Harlem editor of the *Daily Worker.* Wright was also upset over repeated rejections of "Cesspool" and other works. He was happy that during his first year in New York all of his activities involved writing of some kind. In the summer and fall he wrote over two hundred articles for the *Daily Worker.* He helped organize *New Challenge,* a quarterly for works of progressive black authors, and wrote for the first issue "Blueprint for Negro Writing," the most complete and profound statement of his theories on Afro-American writing. Wright also wrote articles for *New Masses,* helped with the New York City Writers' Project, and continued revising the stories that would comprise *Uncle Tom's Children* (1938). The year was also a landmark for Wright because he met and developed a friendship with Ellison that would last for years, and he learned that he would receive the *Story* magazine first prize of five hundred dollars for his short story "Fire and Cloud."

Wright completed his final revision of "Cesspool" in 1937, and he was again disappointed that he could not get a publisher. This heavily autobiographical first novel, published posthumously, is in some ways more structurally sophisticated than some of Wright's later works. The dreams, fantasies, and conscious behavior of its protagonist are the roots for later Wright themes: black nationalism, problems associated with mid-twentieth-century migration of blacks from the rural South to the industrial urban areas, and the absurdities of the existentialist hero.

Following the general structure of James Joyce's *Ulysses* (1922), Wright restricts the action of *Lawd Today* to one twenty-four-hour period, 12 February 1937, in the life of his protagonist, black postal worker Jake Jackson, who hates his job, his wife, his race, and himself. Since the date is specific, Wright can deal with more than the activities of one ordinary black man. Wright's greatest technical success in the novel is his ironic use of devices to give the novel additional dimension.

One device is the newspaper Jake reads at breakfast and in the taxi. Jake's comments on what he reads illustrate his acceptance of some of the worst values of white American society. He sounds like a black George F. Babbitt with his empty clichés of money, worship, and even racism directed against "Jews, Dagoes, Hunkies and Mexicans." The central ironic device is the recurrent use of statements from a radio broadcast celebrating Abraham Lincoln's birthday and the northern victory in the Civil War. The continual stream of phrases contains layers of irony. Not only is the contrast between the importance of the events the broadcast relates and the triviality of Jake's life, but also the tragic failure of America to fulfill the promise of the idealism of Lincoln and William Lloyd Garrison.

Wright's unsparing naturalistic technique gives a special strength to *Lawd Today.* Jake Jackson's brutal treatment of his wife Lil, the dreary post office building and monotony of the work in it, the elaborate orgies of drinking, feasting, dancing, and sex—all are described in minute detail. These scenes and others successfully evoke the sights, sounds, and smells of Jake Jackson's Chicago. And Wright makes no overt claims for his protagonist as he does in later works: the implications of Jake's blighted and futile existence speak for themselves.

After Wright received the *Story* magazine prize in early 1938, he shelved his manuscript of *Lawd Today* and dismissed his literary agent, John Troustine. He hired Paul Reynolds, the well-known agent of Paul Laurence Dunbar, to represent him. Meanwhile, the Story Press offered Harper all of Wright's prize-entry stories for a book, and Harper published them under Wright's chosen title, *Uncle Tom's Children,* in 1938.

Uncle Tom's Children, Wright's first book to be published, contains four lengthy short stories whose similarities in themes and method give the work unity. Wright's message is that Uncle Tom is dead, and his children will fight for freedom and survival. In "Big Boy Leaves Home," the first and finest story in the collection, Wright skillfully uses natural setting, varied points of view, and thematic richness to make an apparently simple tale about truancy, murder, lynching, and flight one of high artistic merit. Big Boy Morrison, Bobo, and two fellow truant adolescents are enjoying the idyllic countryside, very much in accord with their natural environment, until a white woman discovers them naked, resting after

Wright and his brother, Leon, in Elaine, Arkansas, 1916

a swim in a creek forbidden to blacks. Black and white fears suddenly translate the Edenic setting into one of violence and murder, terminating with Big Boy killing the white woman's fiancé, after which he hides in a kiln overnight hoping to be ferried away by truck to Chicago the next morning. His hope of safety barely survives the brutal lynching/burning of Bobo by white citizens.

Wright's careful manipulation of viewpoint heightens the intensity of the story. He uses third-person viewpoint in the first two sections, where the narrative focuses upon the four boys and then upon the boys and the two whites. In the third section Big Boy is the major point of interest. The point of view shifts to first person during Big Boy's reveries in the kiln. The reader sees the lynching of Bobo from Big Boy's peculiar vantage point and, as it were, through his eyes.

"Big Boy Leaves Home" examines many of Wright's major themes: fear, initiation into violence, flight, survival, and freedom. Wright uses a setting and action reminiscent of the story of the Fall in Genesis, but here violent white racism drives Big Boy from the southern garden to uncertain freedom in the North; his initiation into violence and flight add poignancy and depth. There

is irony in the title, for Big Boy is not simply leaving home. His survival depends on his flight from home to escape life-threatening racial tensions in his search for justice and freedom. Big Boy Morrison, innocent no longer, and having achieved adulthood through rebellion motivated by fear, is like the protagonists of "Down by the Riverside," "Long Black Song," and "Fire and Cloud," the other stories in the book.

"Down by the Riverside" contains, along with Wright's basic theme of the black man's struggle for survival, the themes of courage and stoic endurance. Brother Mann confronts natural floods and the floods of racial hatred in his futile efforts to save his pregnant wife and son. When the white Heartfield boy whom Mann is able to save from the floods identifies him to the authorities as the murderer of his father, Mann rebels by dashing away from his captors, forcing them to shoot him in the back. A serious weakness in "Down by the Riverside" is that it has too many contrived incidents. Mrs. Heartfield does not report the murder of her husband when she seeks help, and the Heartfields turn in Mann as a murderer after his act of saving the boy.

In "Long Black Song," one of Wright's rare works written from the viewpoint of a female protagonist, he successfully integrates plot, character, and imagery. A white traveling salesman seduces a young black mother while her husband, Silas, is away purchasing supplies. When the salesman returns the next day with a friend, Silas, who has gotten the details from Sarah, horsewhips one of the men and kills the other one. The tragic theme is Silas's oppression and his doomed awareness of himself: " 'The White folks ain never gimme a chance. They ain never give no black man a chance. Their ain nothin in yo whole life yuh kin keep from 'em. They take yo lan! They take yo freedom! They take yo women! N Then they take yo life!' " Silas can assert himself only by fighting to the end, thereby becoming master of his own death. Sarah, in contrast to Silas, is a mother-earth character who sadly watches a lynch mob burn down their house when Silas refuses to come out but not before he has killed one or two additional men. Hers is an inner rhythm that harmonizes with her memories and wishes. Wright fuses images of the seasons, the days and nights, the lush colors, and the earth rhythms to unfold her character. Sarah has a pastoral vision of the world that brings to mind William Faulkner's Lena Grove or Gertrude Stein's Melanctha. The entire story echoes Wright's experiences in Elaine, Arkansas, where his Uncle Silas was killed by white men.

Whereas the first three stories in *Uncle Tom's Children* describe the efforts of the individual black man against the white mob, "Fire and Cloud" deals with the theme of collective resistance to the white oppressor. The story relates the efforts of a black minister, Rev. Dan Taylor, to get food relief for the near-starving community of a southern town. When Taylor does not agree to stop a protest march, he is kidnapped the night before the march by a group of whites and brutally beaten; but the whipping inspires him, and an integrated demonstration takes place with the preacher leading it.

Wright forcefully dramatizes the social issues in the dilemma faced by Taylor, emphasizing themes of freedom and the futility of religion. Taylor, in defying the white power structure, moves from religious resignation to social action. He does not reject God, but he does shift his religious emphasis to accomplish recognizable goals. Under his leadership the group acts and is successful. A major weakness in the work is Wright's reliance on stereotypes. The white villains are all hard, cold, and mean; the blacks are simple, unassuming, driven to their desperate actions only by their hunger. Only Taylor seems an authentic human being. The poor whites joining with the protesting blacks at the end make the conclusion more of a Marxist-desired utopia than an event basically related to the story and undercut Taylor's concluding remark, "Freedom belongs to the strong."

Because of the organization and similarity in theme and method the short stories in the 1938 edition of *Uncle Tom's Children* form a unified work of fiction. The 1940 edition is diluted by the addition of the essay, "The Ethics of Living Jim Crow," and the story, "Bright and Morning Star." The essay is out of place, and "Bright and Morning Star" is very different from the four stories in the 1938 version in that it is a polemic. Wright successfully portrays Big Boy Morrison, Brother Mann, and Silas as individuals fighting oppression and Taylor as a group leader. In "Bright and Morning Star," however, he appears too interested in promoting Marxist themes to delineate a strong character.

The publication and favorable reception of *Uncle Tom's Children* improved Wright's status with the Communist party and enabled him to establish a reasonable degree of financial stability. He was appointed to the editorial board of *New*

Masses, and Granville Hicks, prominent literary critic and Communist sympathizer, introduced him at leftist teas in Boston. By 6 May 1938 excellent sales had provided him with enough money to move to Harlem, where he began writing *Native Son* (1940).

In 1939 Wright met two white women who, he thought, met his criteria for a wife: Dhimah Rose Meadman and Ellen Poplar. He married Dhimah in August 1939 with Ralph Ellison as best man. The honeymoon was delayed until the spring of 1940. During the honeymoon in Cuernavaca, Mexico, Wright discovered how little he and Dhimah had in common, and they left Mexico separately, never to be reconciled. After his divorce from Dhimah, Wright married Ellen Poplar on 12 March 1941. Their first daughter Julia was born on 15 April 1942.

On the strength of *Uncle Tom's Children* and his completion of a section of *Native Son,* in early 1939 Wright was awarded a Guggenheim Fellowship, which made it possible for him to complete *Native Son* for publication by 1 March 1940. The publication of the novel marked the beginning of a black literature that refused to compromise with many white expectations.

Native Son has no chapter divisions but instead consists of three books: "Fear," "Flight," and "Fate," and Wright skillfully uses fear as the controlling motif for the entire work. Three key scenes in book 1 dramatize the theme of fear. The opening, fear-filled scene illustrates the emotional violence manifested by the four members of the Thomas family against one another. All are afraid of a huge rat, and Bigger prolongs the fear (even after he kills it) by swinging the dead rat in front of his sister Vera until she faints. When Bigger joins his street-gang friends until time for a job interview at the residence of the wealthy Daltons, who need a chauffeur, another kind of fear surfaces. The gang plans to rob Blum's Delicatessen, a white man's business, and each gang member becomes afraid. Bigger demonstrates his fear through violence, terrifying Gus with kicks and threats of murder until he thinks the hour set for the robbery has passed. Hired by the Daltons, Bigger's fears mount to hysteria when Mary Dalton's blind mother enters Mary's bedroom, where Bigger has taken her after an evening out drinking with Jan Erlone, her boyfriend, during which she has become drunk. Realizing that he, a black man, is alone in a young white woman's bedroom, in 1940 a crime in most places in America, he places a pillow over Mary's

Wright with Dhimah Rose Meadman, whom he married in 1939

head to prevent her from answering her mother. After his desperate effort results in Mary's accidental death by suffocation, Bigger, still acting out of fear, decapitates her body, stuffs it into the furnace, burns it, and returns home.

In "Flight" Wright emphasizes both Bigger's mental and physical responses to fears initiated in book 1. Bigger begins to rationalize that in killing Mary Dalton he has destroyed symbolically all the oppressive forces that have made his life miserable. He is proud, for "he had murdered and created a new life for himself." Out of fear for his own safety he suggests that Jan Erlone is guilty, a suggestion supported by a ransom note which Bigger sends to the family to lead suspicion from himself. Bigger's fears mount, and he goes to Bessie, his mistress, so that she can comfort him; but she wrings from him a confession of the murder. He instructs her to collect the ransom money. At the Dalton home when the ransom note arrives, and afraid that he might see a vivid image of Mary's face as he had seen it upon the bed, Bigger cannot shake down the furnace ashes. This fear to act leads to the discovery of Mary's charred bones, which makes it necessary for him and Bessie to flee. Deciding that Bessie will become a great liability, Bigger, partially out of fear, brutally murders her. With this premedi-

tated murder Bigger becomes a fearful monster who moves from one tenement to the next, creating fear throughout the black ghetto until the vast police network captures him on a rooftop.

In the first two books point of view is limited to what Bigger sees, feels, and hears. Wright's dramatic dialogue and graphic descriptions of Bigger's actions and surroundings force the reader to take special notice of him. He is not the familiar black victim but the violent attacker and appears to confirm the white man's fantasies of black assault and rape. Bigger is deprived and depraved beyond ordinary humanity.

Book 3, "Fate," mainly an analysis of the action in books 1 and 2, reduces Bigger to a somewhat passive character, thereby eliminating the rapid pacing and extraordinary narrative drive which characterize books 1 and 2. But fear remains the central motif. Wright now focuses not on Bigger's individual fears but on those of other individual blacks and the black and white communities in general. Mrs. Thomas worries over Bigger's fate. She and her minister, the Reverend Hammond, fear for his soul. The prosecution at his trial and the press sensationalize events that arouse public fears, and the Ku Klux Klan burns crosses. Boris A. Max, Bigger's lawyer, explores the causes and effects of fear and racism in his summation, arguing that society is partly to blame for Bigger's crimes. Ironically, what Bigger learns as a result of fear enables him to go to the electric chair declaring in existential terms that what he has done has had value: "It must've been good! When a man kills, it's for something. I didn't know I was really alive in this world until I felt things hard enough to kill for 'em."

Foreshadowing, rich imagery, and symbolism are among the many effective literary devices Wright uses to illuminate his themes. The rat scene is the prime example of foreshadowing. The black rat Bigger fights and kills turns desperately on its enemies when it no longer sees a means of escape. The scene prefigures Bigger's fate. When Bigger leads Bessie to the deserted house to await the ransom money, "something with dry whispering feet flitted across his path, emitting as the rush of its flight died a thin, piping wail of lonely fear." When Bigger is looking for a vacant apartment for a hiding place, he sees a big black rat leap over the snow and looks "wistfully at that gaping black hole through which the rat had darted to safety." Alienated, Bigger himself becomes a trapped rat who futilely fights his pursuers when escape becomes impossible.

Dominant symbols in the novel include the cross, whiteness, and blindness. To emphasize his denial of his mother's Christianity Bigger tears the crucifix from his neck. He later rejects the cross offered him by the Reverend Hammond when the Ku Klux Klan ignites its fiery cross not far from the Dalton residence. The rich religious symbol has been reduced to one level, that of hate and rejection.

Wright consistently uses whiteness to represent Bigger's fear and anxieties. Upon meeting Mrs. Dalton he observes "that her hair and face were completely white; she seemed to him like a ghost." When Bigger returns to the kitchen to get some water, "What he saw made him suck his breath in; Mrs. Dalton in flowing white clothes was standing stone stiff in the middle of the kitchen floor." Later at Mary's bedroom door Mrs. Dalton appears an "awesome blur . . . silent ghost-like." Bigger is never at ease in the presence of Mrs. Dalton and her ubiquitous white cat. Even the weather takes on symbolic overtones. It begins to snow when Bigger flees the Dalton residence. The ice and snowstorms in book 2 are perpetual reminders of the white hostile environment. Bigger, at the end of book 2, is forced on a cross of snow: "Two men stretched his arms

Dust jacket for Wright's 1940 novel, which sold two hundred thousand copies in less than three weeks

out as though about to crucify him; they placed a foot on each of his wrists, making them sink deep down in the snow."

The blindness motif is even more pervasive than that of whiteness. Wright makes all of his characters blind in some way. Mrs. Dalton is physically blind. Racism impairs the moral vision of state prosecutor Buckley. Bigger's limited perception leads him to label all others, especially whites, as blind. Mary Dalton and Jan Erlone believe that the Communist party has all the answers. Mr. Dalton feels that a supply of table-tennis tables in the ghetto recreation rooms is an overwhelming humanitarian act. Mrs. Thomas is certain that her religion will provide all solutions.

Native Son sold two hundred thousand copies in under three weeks, breaking a twenty-year record at Harper. Clifton Fadiman in the *New Yorker* compared Wright to Theodore Dreiser and John Steinbeck and praised his "passion and intelligence" that examined "layers of consciousness only Dostoyevski and a few others have penetrated." Henry S. Canby in *Book of the Month Club News* wrote that, "like *Grapes of Wrath* it is a fully realized story . . . uncompromisingly realistic and quite as human as it is Negro." Ralph Ellison in

New Masses found in it "an artistry, penetration of thought and sheer emotional power that places it in the first rank of American fiction." Jonathan Daniels, Malcolm Cowley, Sterling Brown, and most other eminent black and white critics of the day praised the novel. The few dissenting voices, among them Howard Mumford Jones and David Cohn, had objections that were more personal than literary. While there is yet much critical debate over the place *Native Son* should occupy in the corpus of great literature, there is a consensus that the novel is one of the classic works of American literature.

The period following publication of *Native Son* was a busy time for Wright. In July 1940 he went to Chicago to do research for the text for a folk history of blacks to accompany photographs selected by Edwin Rosskam. While in Chicago he visited the American Negro Exhibition with Langston Hughes, Bontemps, and Claude McKay. He then went to Chapel Hill, North Carolina, where he and Paul Green collaborated on a dramatic version of *Native Son*. In January 1941 Wright received the prestigious Spingarn Medal for noteworthy achievement by a black. *Native Son* opened on Broadway, with Orson Welles as director, to generally favorable reviews in March 1941. *Twelve Million Black Voices: A Folk History of the Negro in the United States* was published in October 1941 to wide critical acclaim.

Twelve Million Black Voices, the outgrowth of a Work Projects Administration assignment, is a sociological study of American black history and the migration from the rural South to the urban North. The text describes the bondage of blacks from slavery and plantation life to sharecropping and to the factories of the North. Wright emphasizes that in the progression from slavery to the industrialized urban cities, blacks have experienced in a few hundred years what whites were exposed to over thousands of years, and blacks should feel proud of their accomplishment. His recurrent themes of freedom, oppression, and survival permeate the work.

Part 1, "Our Strange Birth," traces aspects of black development from 1619 to the Emancipation Proclamation. Wright refers to the slave ships as "floating brothels" and describes the "lecherous crew members as they vented the pent up bestiality of their starved sex lives upon our sisters and wives." He speaks of captivity under Christendom as having "blasted" life, destroying family, traditions, and all the values that had given meaning in Africa before the white man came.

Part 2, "Inheritors of Slavery," covers the period from the Civil War until World War I. Wright discusses the presentness of the racial past, black English, race relations, the importance of books, and the significance of the black church. He explains that the word "Negro," the term by which orally or in print "we black folk in the United States are usually designated is not really a name at all." It is a white man's word–"a psychological island whose objectives form the most unanimous fiat in all American history . . . a fiat which artificially and arbitrarily defines, regulates and limits in scope the vital contours of our lives. . . . " Wright's point was made long before the vast majority of Afro-Americans frowned upon "Negro" and "colored."

In part 3, "Death on the City Pavements," Wright discusses the Great Migration, the movement of southern blacks to northern ghettos. He describes the squalid living quarters, most often old houses converted into kitchenettes, which were "seed bed[s] for scarlet fever, dysentery, typhoid . . . pneumonia and malnutrition" and rented "at rates so high they make fabulous fortunes before the houses are too old for habitation."

In "Men in the Making," the concluding section, Wright stresses that black folk are a mirror of all the manifold experiences of America. "What we want, what we represent, what we endure is what America is. If we black folk perish, America will perish." He emphasizes that black and white workers must unite against the classes that exploit them, the Lords of the Land (those who run the plantations) and the Bosses of the Buildings (those who manage the industries). His Marxist explanations are followed by a description of the march toward freedom that could have been written by Carl Sandburg or Walt Whitman. Wright proclaims: "We are with the new tide. We stand at the crossroads. We watch each new procession. . . . Voices are speaking. Men are moving! And we shall be with them."

In *Twelve Million Black Voices* Wright fully identifies with the black experience and convincingly analyzes the roles of blacks in the total American experience. The beautiful lyrical passages that occasionally creep in tend to mitigate temporarily the severity of the naturalistic details, thereby adding a moderating dimension to the work. Wright's extended prose poem, despite its obvious Marxist orientation, is a forceful, saddening, and encouraging black American epic. Uniformly enthusiastic reviewers, Bontemps among them, hailed Wright as a master of poetic prose, belonging to the fine tradition of the Negro spiritual.

While completing *Twelve Million Black Voices* Wright was also writing two novels–"Black Hope" (unpublished) and "The Man Who Lived Underground," which had only its third section published as a short story in 1944. A visit to Fisk University in April 1943 prompted Wright to start a still unpublished screenplay, "Melody Unlimited," based on the history of the Fisk Jubilee Singers and highlighting the importance of black colleges as a bridge between black and white. The visit also influenced him to begin his autobiography. On 17 December 1943 he sent Paul Reynolds the manuscript of "American Hunger," which chronicled his life up to his departure from Chicago in 1937. The first section of "American Hunger" was published as *Black Boy: A Record of Childhood and Youth* in 1945; the *Atlantic Monthly* published a part of the second section, which described Wright's membership in and eventual rejection of the Communist party, under the title "I Tried to Be a Communist" in August and September 1944. The second section was not published in its entirety until after Wright's death as *American Hunger* (1977).

In *Black Boy* Wright develops the observations recorded in "The Ethics of Living Jim Crow," the introductory section for the 1940 edition of *Uncle Tom's Children*. The entire autobiography is an espisodically structured yet richly thematic work, similar to a movie documentary, with Wright as the narrator. It focuses on significant events in his life from the age of four (1912) through nineteen (1927). With some creative license, according to his biographer Michel Fabre, Wright describes and interprets from an adult perspective the economic, familial, educational, and racial handicaps he faced. The first section helps set the tone for the entire autobiography, for throughout *Black Boy* Wright is showing how boredom and different kinds of sickness unite to form unyielding ties of oppression. It describes the house four-year-old Richard set on fire because he was bored and ordered to stay inside and remain quiet. Young Richard temporarily escapes punishment when, terrified, he hides under the house. Fire as a dominant image and symbol and the underground motif permeate many of his works, but they are particularly signifi-

cant in *Black Boy* because they reinforce its theme, the search for freedom.

Wright relates early familial difficulties. He details how, after a fight with white boys, his mother "lashed so hard and long that I lost consciousness" and " . . . for a long time I was chastened whenever I remembered that my mother had come close to killing me." He remembers hanging a stray kitten to gain triumph over his father: "How could I get back at him? . . . He had said to kill the kitten and I would kill it. I knew that he had not really meant for me to kill the kitten but my deep hate of him urged me toward a literal acceptance of his word."

Wright constantly describes and questions the hunger in his life. He blames his father with a "biological bitterness" for the hunger, "standing at my bedside staring at me." At the foster home, he says, "I was too weak from hunger. . . . " Living with his Uncle Hopkins, at Granny's, nowhere did he feel free from the want of food. One of the more pathetic scenes in the book is near the end of chapter 2, where his only Christmas gift is an orange. He eats it all day long and just before going to bed he tears "the peeling into bits and munched them slowly." Wright laments, "Why did I always have to wait until others were through? I could not understand why some people had enough food and others did not. . . . Hunger was with us always." Midway through *Black Boy* Wright explains, "I vowed that someday I would end this hunger of mine, this apartness, this external difference."

Wright's description of southern whites is totally negative; they are cruel, violent, inhumane persons who will put forth special efforts to debase blacks. Such declarations from Wright are not shocking. What does appear rather unusual is Wright's attitude toward blacks. He explains:

> I used to mull over the strange absence of real kindness in Negroes, how unstable was our tenderness, how lacking in genuine passion we were . . . how lacking we were in those intangible sentiments that bind man to man and how shallow was even our despair. . . . I used to brood upon the unconscious irony of those who felt the Negroes led so passional an existence. I saw that what had been taken for our emotional strength was our negative confusions, our flights, our fears, our frenzy under pressure.

This passage and others like it in *Black Boy* suggest to many that Wright lacked racial pride. He did at times have difficulty expressing individual

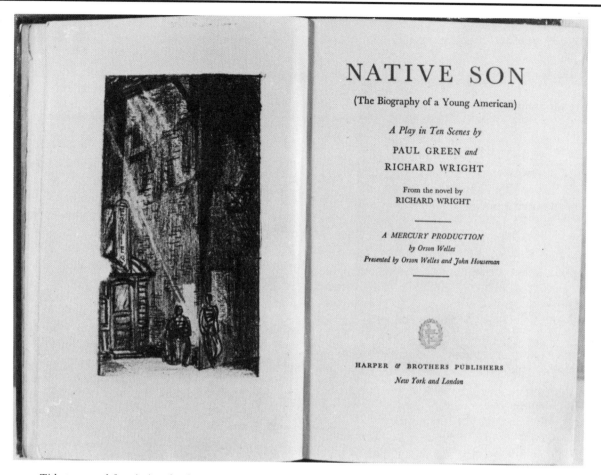

Title page and frontispiece for the 1941 stage adaptation of Native Son *by Wright and playwright Paul Green*

affection for black culture, but he could display admiration for black group achievements as is convincingly shown in *Twelve Million Black Voices.* The fact that Wright is an adult attempting to comprehend almost overwhelming childhood experiences indicates that he is interested in understanding his black culture, not in rejecting it.

Black Boy had phenomenal sales and received tremendous critical praise. By March 1945 it had sold over four hundred thousand copies and was listed at the top of most best-seller lists. Critics from the *New York Times,* the *New York Herald Tribune,* and the *St. Louis Post Dispatch* were among those who wrote glowing reviews. Dorothy Canfield Fisher placed the work on the level with Jean-Jacques Rousseau's *Confessions* and St. Augustine's *Confessions.* Among the thousands of congratulatory letters to Wright was one from William Faulkner, who wrote that "Wright said it well, as well as it could have been in this form." Some blacks expressed mixed acceptance. They felt that Wright spent too much time documenting black despair. A few southern critics made ex-

tremely negative remarks concerning the book's account of race relations in the South. Most critics and the general reader concurred that *Black Boy* merits a place on the shelf next to the autobiographies of Benjamin Franklin, Frederick Douglass, and Henry Adams.

The second part of Wright's autobiography, *American Hunger,* like *Black Boy,* explores many of Wright's recurrent themes: manhood, freedom, flight, oppression. Wright focuses on his experiences in Chicago, and he becomes negatively critical of the entire American system, not just the South, as was the case in *Black Boy,* where he at the end "headed North, full of a hazy notion that life could be lived with dignity."

Perhaps the most significant segments of *American Hunger* deal with Wright's connections with the Communist party and his efforts to retain his integrity despite the party's demands that he sacrifice his artistic aims for the good of the party. After he becomes affiliated with the Chicago John Reed Club, he is upset that he is labeled an intellectual because he reads books

Advertisement for the World Publishing Company reprint of Black Boy

other than those endorsed by the party. When he is threatened by the group and scorned even by black Communists, he asks: "Why was it that I was a suspected man because I wanted to reveal the vast physical and spiritual ravages of Negro life. . . . What was the danger in showing the kinship between the sufferings of the Negro and the sufferings of other people?"

Wright explains, "I wanted to be a Communist but my kind of Communist. I wanted to share people's feelings." After much deliberation he asks that his name be removed from the rolls but continues to work for Communist-affiliated organizations. Because of Communist pressure he loses his job at the Federal Negro Theater, and his position with the Federal Writers' Project is jeopardized. The most humiliating experience, however, comes on May Day when a black Communist invites him to join the parade of marchers, and he reluctantly agrees only to be lifted from the sidewalk by party members and "pitched head-

long through the air . . . the rows of white and black Communists looking at me with cold eyes of nonrecognition." Wright's spirit is crushed, for he had previously seen communism as a viable alternative to the poverty, hunger, and racism in America. Back at his apartment Wright commences reflecting: "Well, what had I got out of living in the city? What had I got out of living in the South? What had I got out of living in America? I paced the floor, knowing that all I possessed were words and a dim knowledge that my country had shown me no examples of how to live a human life . . . I wanted to build a bridge of words between men and that world outside, that world so distant and elusive that it seemed unreal."

Unlike *Black Boy*, whose ending suggests a success story, *American Hunger* represents the culmination of Wright's disappointment with America. Moral, economic, and racial conditions in Chicago and New York City are but additional proof of the country's failures. Wright insists upon an acute awareness of conditions and radical changes including a set of values that will respect the rights of everyone. The special importance of *American Hunger* lies in its vivid presentation of Wright's experiences in the North and its explanation of these wider dimensions of his thought.

The remainder of 1945 and the years 1946 and 1947 were extremely busy and highly critical periods for Wright. He traveled abroad, delivered speeches, engaged in debates, reviewed books, and continued to write. In the fall of 1945 he toured the nation delivering lectures about the racial situation. He gave financial aid to black novelist Chester Himes and secured a grant for James Baldwin. He sailed for Paris on 1 May 1946, where he was lionized by the French press and private citizens. In Paris he became friends with Gertrude Stein and many French intellectuals, including Jean-Paul Sartre and Simone de Beauvoir. Wright and Ellen visited Switzerland in November, where he gave interviews and contacted a publisher for the German edition of *Black Boy*. In late 1946 Wright met George Padmore in London. Padmore, the father of African liberation, introduced him to the progressive, militant leaders of the Third World. This meeting had two significant and long-range effects upon Wright. His friendship with Padmore influenced his political thinking and further increased his interest in Africa. Meeting black leaders from all of the English-speaking African countries indicated to Wright that black America's call for freedom was now being echoed throughout the other nonwhite continents of the world, and he concluded that he must visit nonwhite countries.

By January 1947, when the family returned to Manhattan, Wright had become even more dissatisfied with American racial policies. He constantly contrasted the freedom and acceptance he experienced in Paris against the rampant racism he faced in America. Like James Joyce, he felt that he could not expand his artistic and personal freedom unless he exiled himself from the oppressive soil of his native country. Wright and his family returned to Paris in August 1947 and became permanent citizens. Although Wright traveled extensively, France was his home base until his death in 1960. The last fourteen years of his life are especially notable for a shift in ideological emphases: instead of determinism he explored choice; along with racism he emphasized a more metaphysical isolation; in place of colonialism in the Deep South he focused on global oppression. Existentialism and identification with the people of the Third World are outgrowths of his earlier experiences. Though no longer a card-carrying Communist, his writings still reflect Marxist ideals and sympathies.

In 1948 Wright traveled to Milan with Ellen to celebrate Camillo Pellizi's translation of *Native Son* and attended a reception in Turin, where *Black Boy* was being translated. He met with principal Italian critics. During a five-day stay in Rome in February 1948 he lectured on Afro-American literature. By this time he had started work again on the manuscript of *The Outsider* (1953) and informed his agent that he wanted to rework it completely.

Upon returning to Paris in May 1948 Wright established himself as a model Parisian intellectual. In interviews he praised the poetry of Gwendolyn Brooks, commented on his favorite novels, *Moby-Dick, Ulysses,* and *The Sound and the Fury,* and offered explanations of writers he was currently reading, Franz Kafka, Martin Heidegger, and Søren Kierkegaard among them. Later in the year he stopped working on his new "philosophical" novel, *The Outsider,* and concentrated on acquiring a better understanding of French and German existentialism.

After his second daughter Rachel was born in Paris on 17 January 1949, Wright traveled to Argentina with French director Pierre Cheval to play Bigger Thomas in a film version of *Native Son.* Following his sincere but awkward performance in the 1951 film, an artistic and financial

Wright and his daughter Julia, 1945 (photograph by Studio Gallery, Stockholm)

failure, Wright worked with the French American Fellowship, an organization to combat racism in American businesses abroad. The excessive number of hours he spent working with this group further delayed his completing *The Outsider.* Perhaps a greater impediment to its completion was the unfortunate quarrel with James Baldwin over Baldwin's suggestion in "Everybody's Protest Novel" that *Native Son* was merely Harriet Beecher Stowe's *Uncle Tom's Cabin* (1852) in reverse. Wright felt betrayed, and much of his creative energy was involved in his overt hostility toward Baldwin.

Although Wright published no books between 1947 and 1953, he wrote English articles for *Présence Africaine* and French-language articles for periodicals such as *France-Observateur* and *Les Temps Modernes.* He also wrote short essays for *Encounter* (England), *Twice a Year,* and *Ebony.* The one work of fiction he published was a short story, "The Man Who Killed a Shadow," later collected in *Eight Men* (1960). During this period he enjoyed rich literary exposure, serving on the board of patrons for *Présence Africaine* with Sartre, Albert Camus, and André Gide, all of whom influenced his later works. His purely creative output declined with his move to France, but his political and historical vision certainly deepened.

After almost six years of work Wright finally completed *The Outsider* in London in early 1952. Long and complex, *The Outsider* is perhaps the first consciously existentialist novel written by an American. It is the first Wright novel which does not emphasize racial matters. While the protagonist is black, he is not primarily concerned with his plight as a black; he is a thinking, questioning man in the perplexing twentieth century. Partly autobiographical, *The Outsider* is as much Wright's own spiritual odyssey as it is that of his hero, Cross Damon. Wright's experiences in America, his disaffection with communism, his views on Europe in turmoil based upon his travels during his first year in exile, the long nights spent with Sartre and Beauvoir debating the meaning of freedom, his often deeply felt periods of alienation–all combine to present the picture of a solitary individual intent upon creating the ideal man in the modern world.

Cross Damon feels overwhelmed by tremendous burdens: a wife he no longer loves, a pregnant mistress, and an emotional mother he both loves and hates. When authorities use the overcoat and identification papers he left behind after climbing from a train crash to identify another victim as him, Damon decides to forget his wife and three sons. After assuming a number of aliases he journeys to New York and becomes involved with the Communist party. Damon moves in with Communists Gil and Eva Blount (because the Blounts wish to desegregate their apartment building, managed by the Fascist and racist Langley Herndon) and discovers and reads Eva Blount's diary, from which he learns Gil Blount had deceived her by marrying her not out of love but because the Communist party had ordered it. Alarmed over this cynical violation of individual rights, Damon vows that the party will not destroy his freedom and humanity. That he has violated Eva's privacy never enters his mind. Later, entering a room ostensibly to stop Blount and Herndon from fighting, Damon kills both men and arranges the clues so that it appears they have killed each other. Damon rationalizes that in destroying the Communist and the Fascist he is killing "gods" who would rob him of his freedom. Only much later does he comprehend that in slaying them–exercising his complete freedom–he has himself assumed the role of a god: "Oh, Christ their disease had reached out and claimed him too. He had been subverted by the contagion of the lawless; he had been defeated by that which he had sought to destroy."

In a desperate attempt to conceal his previous crimes Damon murders a high Communist official who has evidence which will convict him.

That Damon has become a demon is further dramatized when district attorney Houston tells him his mother has died, possibly because of his deeds, and then ushers Damon's wife and three sons into the room. Damon (demon) acknowledges no one and nothing. With no positive proof, Houston cannot arrest him. Damon, alone, enters the streets of Harlem and hides in theaters until Communist party members track and shoot him down. In a final scene reminiscent of Bigger Thomas's last scenes with his lawyer, Boris A. Max, Damon explains in existentialist terms: "Don't think I'm so odd and strange . . . I'm not. . . . I'm legion . . . I've lived alone, but I'm everywhere." He warns of a new era when men will stop deceiving themselves about their murderous nature and the meaninglessness of life. Dying, Damon is asked by Houston what he found in life. He responds, "Nothing. . . . Alone a man is nothing."

In *The Outsider* Wright uses existential tenets to expose the myths by which men often irrationally live. Some sections of the novel are little more than existentialist jargon. The novel, however, is an illustration not of Wright's existentialism, but of his rejection of it as an adequate means to cope with the problems of the modern world. Cross Damon equates freedom with power; while exercising his unbridled freedom he murders four human beings and is partially responsible for the deaths of two others. Damon casts aside almost all societal codes of behavior only to realize in the end that human restrictions help humanize man. Neither man nor society can accommodate completely free individuals, for they are threats to human existence.

While thematically rich, *The Outsider* has many obvious flaws. As most contemporary critics noted, there are numerous improbabilities, contrived speeches, and a melodramatic plot. Critics from the *New York Times*, the *New York Herald Tribune*, and *Time* praised some of the detective-story techniques but could not enthusiastically recommend the novel because of its problems. Black writers, the late Lorraine Hansberry among them, called Wright an outsider, outcast from his own people. Only European critics had unqualified praise for the novel, according it a better reception than they did Camus's existential novel *The Stranger* (1942).

The Outsider had scarcely undergone final revision before Wright was back in Paris at work on another book. Wright announced to novelist and fellow expatriate William Gardner Smith

Julia, Ellen, and Rachel Wright, early 1950s (photo by Wright)

that he had completed another novel, one that "like all my future books, I think . . . will take up aspects of the problems broached in *The Outsider.*" Wright managed to generate great enthusiasm among his friends for the completed novel, *Savage Holiday*, but had great difficulty getting the work published. Harper, his regular publisher, rejected the book, and his agent Paul Reynolds agreed that it was an inferior work. Avon Books printed a paperback edition of *Savage Holiday* in 1954. The work is especially notable because it is an important black writer's only novel in which all of the major characters are white, and racial concerns are seldom mentioned.

In *The Outsider* Wright emphasizes tenets of existentialism; in *Savage Holiday* he adds Freud. Retired insurance executive Erskine Fowler, an apparently successful man who lives in a fashionable section of New York and is very much respected by his peers, has locked away his feelings and passions because of his inability to accept the fact that he had incestuous desires for his beautiful, sexually alluring mother. He also feels guilty about his role in the accidental death of the gorgeous and promiscuous Mrs. Blake's five-year-old son Tony. To assuage his dual grief Fowler hopes to redeem Tony's death by redeeming Mrs. Blake through marriage. Fowler courts and proposes to Mrs. Blake, during which time the long-

suppressed Fowler, who wishes to establish a relationship with his mother and possess her sexually, vicariously, through Mrs. Blake, emerges. At the same time he hates Mrs. Blake and vents his sense of outrage against her by killing her: "With machine like motion Erskine lifted the butcher knife and plunged it into her stomach again and again." At this point the novel becomes a Freudian workbook. At the police station where he later reports the murder, Fowler recalls a fantasy he had repressed as a child when his mother scolded him for stabbing a stuffed doll. He decides the stuffed doll represented his mother and concludes that the fantasy arose from an actual occurrence in his childhood when he drew a picture of a dead doll and imagined that he had drawn a picture of his mother. The Freudian movement has been from mother to doll to Mrs. Blake, and the childhood symbolic act has terminated in an adult symbolic act. Fowler feels that he cannot tell the police why he committed the crime because he cannot explain that his real motives originated from a childhood fantasy.

As Edward Margolies points out in *The Art of Richard Wright* (1969), Wright's ending the book as he does makes one feel that he "has somehow made short shrift of all the problems he had been so laboriously posing throughout the novel." Wright is not able to show that Fowler is in control of his passions because of extreme weaknesses of plot and character; and the too obvious Freudian implications further damage the novel's credibility. Wright reworks some of his favorite themes: freedom, religion as an impotent force, the substitution of violence for love, the presentness of the past; he fails, however, to make them unobtrusive parts of the novel. Since *Savage Holiday* was never published in hardcover, it was not reviewed by the American press. Like *The Outsider*, however, it created excitement in Europe, where it was translated into French, Italian, German, and Dutch and received some favorable reviews from the French press.

During 1953, the same year *The Outsider* was published in New York and a few months after completing the first draft of *Savage Holiday*, Wright journeyed through the undeveloped country of the British West African colony of the Gold Coast (later called Ghana) by way of the Canary Islands. *Black Power: A Record of Reactions in a Land of Pathos* (1954), written as a result of that trip, is a very personal book in which Wright draws conclusions about the culture, the people, and the political, social, and economic problems facing the African country. The work has characteristics of a writer's journal of ideas and a travel diary, for Wright includes statistical charts, significant historical data he has gathered from books, dialogue obtained through his questioning of tribal chieftains and British officials, and vivid descriptions of Africans and their country.

In a short introduction, "Apropos Prepossessions," Wright states that the aim of this book is "to pose the problem anew in an area that is proving a decisive example for an entire continent," the problem being whether the West will deal justly with its nonwhite subjects or leave them prey to communism. In doing this Wright reiterates his scorn for religious authority. He reacts to Christian missionary efforts in the same manner that he responded to his Grandmother Wilson's attempts to convert him. Just as his grandmother tried to rob him of his individual freedom for her own satisfaction, so were the missionaries attempting to subjugate and exploit for their own purposes. When he and Nigerian Supreme Court Justice Thomas visit a house of prostitution in Las Palmas, Canary Islands, Wright remarks, "It occurred to me that this shabby whorehouse was perhaps the only calm and human spot in this strongly entrenched Catholic city."

In *Black Power* Wright's recommendation for solving the Gold Coast's problems is simplistic.

He argues that Kwame Nkrumah has to enlist and rechannel the frustrated religious energies of the detribalized masses into the cause of industrialization and nationhood. The people must be subjected to a form of militarization that will give "form, organization, direction, meaning and a sense of justification to those lives. . . : a temporary discipline that will unite the nations, sweep out the tribal cobwebs, atomize the fetish-ridden past, abolish the mystical and nonsensical family relations." Then Nkrumah and his assistants will be able to use people rather than the dollars of Western capitalists to modernize their industrial economy. History has shown that Wright's do-it-yourself formula could never solve Africa's complex political, economic, and psychological problems.

While Wright does some of his best expository writing in *Black Power,* his tendencies to make hasty generalizations and to assume the superiority of Western traditions at the expense of indigenous African culture mitigate the effectiveness of the book. Wright calls the African "an oblique, a hard to know man who seemed to take a childish pride in trying to create a state of bewilderment in the minds of strangers." He asserts that "the African almost invariably underestimated the person with whom he was dealing; he always placed too much confidence in an evasive reply, thinking that if he denied something, then that something ceased to exist. It was childlike." The postscript to *Black Power* concludes, "I found only one intangible but vitally important element in the heritage of tribal culture that militated against cohesiveness of action: African culture has not developed the personalities of the people to a degree that their egos are stout, hard, sharply defined; there is too much cloudiness that makes for lack of confidence, an absence of focus that renders that mentality incapable of grasping the workaday world." A summer tour through a part of one country on the African continent hardly qualifies one to make such judgments. In his introduction Wright states that "the West can meanly lose Africa or the West can nobly save Africa." To follow Wright's plan for African independence, Africa must disband her tribes, industrialize, and become technologically competent in order to assume a position of world leadership, or, as Wright really means, it must become like the West. That native Africans might not wish to replace their entire culture with so-called Western advancements does not seem to occur to Wright. A major theme in the work is

Richard Wright
Dec. 9, 1946.
Paris

He closed the big white door after him, pulled his ragged cap low over his eyes, and headed for the bus line two blocks away. It was Saturday evening; he had just been paid off. A steady breeze from the sea dried his sweaty shirt. Above him red and purple clouds hover above the edges of apartment buildings. He neared a street inter-section, paused, looked at the slender roll of green bills clutched in his right fist. In the deepening gloom he counted his wages:

"Five, ten, fifteen, sixteen, seventeen..."

He walked again, chuckling: Yeah, she never makes a mistake. He was tired and happy. Saturday night. During a sweltering day he had given his bodily strength in exchange for dollars with which to buy bread and pay rent for the coming week. He would spend tomorrow at church, when he returned to work Monday morning, he would feel renewed. Carefully, so that he would run no risk of losing it, he put the tight wad of crisp bills securely into his right trouser-pocket his arms swung free. Street lamps blazed suddenly and there lay before him, two lines of yellow gradually converged in the distance before him.

"Mowing that lawn made my hand sore," he said aloud.

Late revised typescript for The Man Who Lived Underground *(courtesy of Princeton University Library)*

freedom, but one has to consider what kind of freedom at the expense of which freedom or freedoms.

Neither *Time, Newsweek,* nor the daily *New York Times* reviewed the book, and the *New York Times Book Review* called it a caricature of British colonialism "drawn not from life but from the dreary old arsenal of Marxist slogans." The *New York Herald Tribune Weekly Book Review,* the *Boston Globe,* and the *Chicago Tribune* highly praised the book.

In early 1955, with the help of Gunnar Myrdal, Wright attended the Bandung Conference in Indonesia as a representative for the Congress of Cultural Freedom. He finished his report in June 1955 and in the fall began work on a novel tentatively called "Mississippi," later entitled *The Long Dream* (1958). The report on the conference, first published in France in 1955, was circulated in the United States as *The Color Curtain: A Report on the Bandung Conference* in 1956. In this work Wright expands his thesis from *Black Power* that poor and weak Africans are exploited by oppressive whites to include all nonwhites, particularly Asians. His overriding thesis is that race is the central issue in determining the development of the new nations of Africa and Asia. This book, a much shorter volume than *Black Power,* is comprised of excerpts from official speeches and private interviews and Wright's observations and comments.

Wright focuses on Chou En-lai's major speech before the conference, in which Chou concentrated on African-Asian unity rather than East-West political and ideological conflict. As he did in *Black Power,* Wright again offers Western industrialization as the solution to Asia's difficulties: "Is this secular, rational base of thought and feeling in the Western world broad and secure enough to warrant the West's assuming the moral right to interfere sans narrow selfish political motives? My answer is yes."

Reviews of the book were generally favorable. The *New York Times Book Review* praised everything except Wright's tendency "to exaggerate the racial and religious unity in the Third World and the importance of China." The *Saturday Review* called Wright's analysis an "important contribution" to understanding the conference.

Wright visited Spain from August 1954 until mid December and continued his tour in the spring of 1955. He went to the major cities, Barcelona, Madrid, and Seville among them, and traveled to numerous rural villages. In 1956 he

participated in the planning of the First Congress of Negro Artists and Writers, held in Paris. He translated Louis Sapin's play *Papa Bon Dieu* (*Daddy Goodness*), which reflects his great interest in black folk cultures, especially the cults of Father Divine and Daddy Grace. On 22 November 1956 Wright began a tour of Scandinavia, and later the same year he completed *White Man, Listen!* (1957).

Pagan Spain: A Report of a Journey into the Past (1957), is the published result of the excursion to Spain. The five-chapter report contains excellent descriptive scenes of Spain's cities and towns and a rich variety of information about Spanish life collected from interviews Wright conducted and public events he attended. An especially effective structural device is his use of a Franco government-approved handbook which states the aims and principles of the regime. Wright discusses the Spain he sees and at convenient intervals inserts passages from the handbook, thereby providing an excellent contrast between what he actually observes and the propagandistic explanations in the political guide.

Wright issues some severe condemnations of life in Spain. He is convinced that the methods used to persecute and terrorize Protestants correspond to those used in the American South against blacks and other minorities, and he asserts that the church's views toward sex are the reasons sex is the preoccupation among Spaniards and prostitution is a major industry. Poor wages received by women for honest labor force them to prostitution to satisfy the men who do not receive full gratification from the women they love. Wright concludes that Spain is hopelessly mired in an archaic past, that "the prostitution, the corruption, the economics, the politics had about them a sacred aura. All was religion in Spain."

In *Pagan Spain* Wright adds to his gallery of outsiders people who are not persecuted because of color but because of religion and gender. While the work indicates a broader humane concern, it also shows Wright again making too many hasty generalizations in his evaluation of a country and its ways. He again suggests replacing the indigenous culture of a nation with Western technology and ideals. *Pagan Spain* was a financial failure, but it received critical praise. The *New York Times* discussed Wright's great insight into the rituals of Spain. The *Saturday Review* stressed as a strong point of the book Wright's brilliant analysis of the "unconscious sources of religion."

White Man, Listen!, Richard Wright's last book of nonfiction, consists of a series of lectures delivered between 1950 and 1956 in cities in Italy, Germany, France, and Sweden. The order of essays follows the essential pattern of Wright's fiction: movement from bondage to freedom, and the flight to new or changed circumstances. The four essays warn of the catastrophe that can befall the Western world if it continues to deny full freedom to large segments of the world's population. These lectures recapitulate much of what Wright states in earlier essays and books. In "The Psychological Reactions of Oppressed People," the first and longest of the sections, Wright discusses the missionary zeal which instilled in arrogant Europeans the ideas that they could behave paternalistically toward less developed cultures and that they were perfectly justified in overrunning Asia, Africa, and parts of America. He argues that oppressed people must come from behind their masks and confront the oppressor if they expect to keep "the white shadow of the West" from falling across the rest of the world.

In "Tradition and Industrialization" Wright asserts that Christianity can be viewed favorably only in comparison with the mystical Eastern religious philosophies, which are far worse than the Western ones. He is happy that deluded missionaries brought their Christianity to the Third World because the message they brought was so inappropriate for the Eastern world that in attempting to replace their old beliefs with Western dogma, the Easterners completely lost their religious outlook. Easterners can now say, "Thank you Mr. White Man for freeing me from the rot of my irrational customs and traditions." Wright concludes that this newly purged group must be permitted to act free from Western intervention.

"The Literature of the Negro in the United States" is a historical survey of black American writers. Wright begins by pointing out that Alexandre Dumas and Aleksandr Pushkin are black writers who were fully integrated parts of their respective French and Russian cultures, whereas only one black American writer, Phillis Wheatley, has been able to identify fully with the dominant values of her country. Because black writers in this country have not enjoyed full freedom, freedom is a central theme of Afro-American literature. Black literature as such will disappear when blacks are free, for writing by blacks is a kind of barometer of liberty for Afro-Americans. The more freedom blacks enjoy the more muted the cry for it in their literature. After all "the Negro is America's metaphor," Wright asserts.

The concluding discussion in the book, "The Miracle of Nationalism in the African Gold Coast," is really a condensed version of *Black Power*. Wright tells the Africans to overcome their "ancestor worshipping attitudes" and "master the techniques of science." His somewhat paradoxical advice to the continent to throw the West out and then become as Western as possible is another illustration of his failure to see that before man can realize a world larger than race, community, tribe, or state, he must show respectful treatment to all segments of the world's cultures. *White Man, Listen!* is, nevertheless, a very interesting, readable book. It is a provocative exploration of the theme of freedom.

The black press was nearly unanimous in its praise of *White Man, Listen!* J. Saunders Redding wrote in an Associated Press review that Wright "had never written more brilliantly or poignantly." *Time, Newsweek,* and the *Saturday Review* refused to review the work, and the *New York Times* criticized Wright for "treating the white world as a solid block."

By July 1957 Wright had almost finished the second revision of his new novel, which he thought of calling "The Double Hearted" or "American Shadow" until his editor at Harper, Edward Aswell, suggested "The Long Dream." By mid February 1958 Wright had made final revisions for "The Long Dream," and he returned to work on "Island of Hallucinations" until *The Long Dream* was published in New York in mid October 1958.

In *The Long Dream*, the first and only published book of a projected trilogy, Wright returns to the southern world of *Black Boy*. The novel focuses on two major concerns: the relationship between Tyree Tucker, a prominent mortician and owner of a house of prostitution, and his son Fishbelly (called Fish), and the complex relationship symbolized by the father as the economic power of the black community and the white police chief as the legal and political power in the city. In each section of a tripartite structure Wright dramatizes events which develop or alter these relationships.

In part 1, "Daydreams and Nightmares," as Fish watches his father examine the corpse of his friend Chris Sims, a young black murdered and

One winter morning in the long ago, ~~five~~-year-old days
of my life I found myself standing before a fireplace, warming
my hands over a heap of ~~red~~ glowing coals. A wind whistled
outside. ~~The room was cozy, but confining.~~ I was fretful and
impatient, for All morning my mother had been scolding me, ~~telling~~
me to keep still, ~~telling~~ me that I must make no noise, ~~drumming~~
~~it into me that~~ my grandmother was very ill, threatening ~~me with~~
punishment. I crossed restlessly to the window, pushed back
the long fluffy white curtains which I had been forbidden to
touch, and looked out into the empty street. I was dreaming
of running and playing and shouting, but the grim image of my
grandmother's old wrinkled white face, surrounded by a halo of
~~lanky~~ black flowing hair, lying upon the huge pillow in the next
room made me afraid. The house was quiet. Behind me my brother
played placidly upon the floor with some toys. A bird wheeled
past the window and I greeted it with a glad shout.

"You better hush," my brother warned me.

"You shut up," I said.

My mother stepped into the room ~~with an iron face, noiselessly~~
closing the door ~~to my grandmother's room~~ behind her. She came to
me and shook her finger in my face.

"You stop that yelling, you hear?" she ~~said.~~ "Granny's
sick and you better keep quiet!"

She left and I ached with boredom.

"I told you so," my brother said.

Revised typescript for American Hunger *(courtesy of the Beinecke Rare Book and Manuscript Library, Yale University)*

castrated by whites for being attracted to a white woman, he expresses his bitter, angry disillusionment with his father and the black community for their passive reactions. In Fish's mind they also underwent castration, and he decides, in a manner which suggests Wright himself in *Black Boy,* that he can accept neither Southern black attitudes nor white ones. The episode that signals Fish's induction into manhood originates at the Clintonville jail, where Fish and a friend have been arrested for trespassing on a white man's property. When his father comes to get him released, Fish feels humiliated by his subservient behavior before the white officials, but he later realizes that he was released only because of his father's pleas. He then comprehends that Tyree Tucker has been doing all that a black in the South can do and concludes that his secure future is tied in with the acquisition of money and the acceptance of his father's pragmatic philosophy. A central irony is that Fish's maturation is but his accepting his own role as a cheater of other blacks as a way of life, thus denying them freedom.

The main dramatic event in "Days and Nights," part 2, is the Fourth of July fire at the Grove Dance Hall, which takes forty-two lives, including that of Gladys, Fish's mistress. Wright again employs burning, one of his favorite symbols, to bring dramatically to light a corrupt and oppressive business arrangement. The scandal caused by the disaster necessitates a confrontation between Tyree Tucker, who is also the Grove Dance Hall manager, and Gerald Cantley, the white police chief who collects regular payments both to protect prostitution and ignore other violations in the hall. When Tucker attempts to send cancelled checks which show his payments to Chief Cantley to white reformer McWilliams, Tucker is killed in one of Cantley's carefully orchestrated ambushes.

The theme of oppression resurfaces, for Fish now clearly sees that his murdered father followed the same system that the white man uses to oppress and exploit blacks. He retains admiration for his father, however, for he did stand up and strike back at the white oppressor. Ironically enough, Fish will perpetuate his father's oppression and exploitation, for he welcomes the identical corrupt arrangements Tucker had with Cantley and continues to enjoy economic prosperity in Clintonville. Wright creates a mirror effect from one Tucker to the next, symbolizing the continuing fate of the vulnerable southern black.

In "Waking Dream" Fish's long search for his own freedom and dignity evolves into a tragedy. Even though Fish falls on his knees crying that he would not betray a white man, this mirror image of his father's actions does not stop Cantley from having him imprisoned on the false charge of raping a white woman–a terrible irony in that Fish had often imagined raping one. Despite his power in the black community, Fish, like his father, cannot defeat the white power structure. Released after serving two and a half years, Fish, at the first opportunity, leaves for Memphis for a flight to New York and a connecting flight to Paris. An Italian-American on the Paris-bound plane relates to Fish the story of his father's emigration to and successes in America. Fish reflects about himself: "That man's father had come to America and had found a dream; he had been born in America and had found it a nightmare." This last scene clearly shows the particular alienation of the black American and effectively dramatizes Wright's theme of flight from oppression to possible freedom. In "Five Episodes," the only published section of a second part of the planned trilogy, Wright discusses Fish Tucker's life in France.

Two of many noteworthy achievements in *The Long Dream* are Wright's extraordinary portrait of Tyree Tucker and his effective presentation of the black church. Fish Tucker must be labeled the protagonist, but it is Tyree Tucker whom the reader will remember longest. Tyree Tucker is in turn calculating, cunning, loving, pious, predatory, and saccharine, and at each interval he is convincing. He is a respected leader in the black community, a father who obviously loves his son, a black man who knows when to humble himself before whites, one who dares seduce the mother of a boy recently lynched, and one who prospers off the misery of other blacks. Because he is no one type but a composite of types, he is a fascinating antihero.

Wright never expressed faith in religion, but he was aware of the importance of the black church to the black community. His handling of the funeral services for the forty-two fire victims and Tyree Tucker is extraordinary. At one point in the sermon the Reverend Ragland is explaining to the mourners that their miseries are not caused by whites or corrupt economic and political institutions but by God Himself, and His ways are mysterious. He continues:

> Who dares say how many of us'll be here a year from now? Your future's in the hollow of Gawd's Hands now, there's men in this town who say that they run it. . . . The men who run this town can be white as snow, but we know who's the boss! GAWD'S THE BOSS! And He's more powerful than the president, the governor, the mayor, the chief of police.

Reverend Ragland's sermon fully captures in philosophy and color the spirit of the mid-twentieth-century rural black church.

The Long Dream received mostly adverse critical reaction. Granville Hicks in the *Saturday Review* referred to the "crude prose style and weak characterization." Redding in the *New York Times* argued that Wright "had been away too long" and that the work "is sensational and fattened by too much iteration." Other critics such as Ted Poston of the *New York Post* and Nick Aaron Ford writing for *Phylon,* agreed that the novel was bad. Roi Ottley in the *Chicago Sunday Tribune* gave the novel one of a few overwhelmingly favorable reviews. He saw *The Long Dream* as a "superb book balanced by Wright's compassion for his people." Though not a great book, *The Long Dream* has many great moments.

Despite overwhelming negative criticism from his agent, Paul Reynolds, of his four-hundred-page "Island of Hallucinations" manuscript in February 1959, Wright, in March, outlined this third novel, in which Fish was finally to be liberated from his racial conditioning and would become a dominating character. By May 1959 Wright had developed a desire to leave Paris and live in London. He felt French politics had become increasingly submissive to American pressure, and the peaceful Parisian atmosphere he had enjoyed had been shattered by quarrels and attacks instigated by enemies of the expatriate black writers. On 26 June 1959, after a party which marked the French publication of *White Man, Listen!,* Wright became ill, victim of a virulent attack of amoebic dysentery which he had probably contracted during his stay on the Gold Coast. By November 1959 Ellen had found a London apartment, but Wright's illness and "four hassles in twelve days" with British immigration officials made him decide "to abandon any desire to live in England."

On 19 February 1960 Wright learned from Reynolds that the New York premiere of the stage adaptation of *The Long Dream* received such bad reviews that the adapter, Ketti Frings, had decided to cancel other performances. Meanwhile, Wright was running into additional problems trying to get *The Long Dream* published in France. These setbacks prevented his finishing revisions of "Island of Hallucinations," which he needed to get a commitment from Doubleday.

Wright was able to complete two radio scripts and a seventy-page story, "Leader Man," for "Ten Men," a title he had proposed to his editor in 1959 for a new collection. The title became *Eight Men* when his editor convinced him that "Leader Man" and "Man and Boy," a new title Wright suggested for the text of *Savage Holiday,* should not be included. Wright aborted his earlier idea to trace the genesis of each story to give the collection a common theme; hence, the works in *Eight Men* display the variety and development in Wright's literary and thematic skills. After dedicating the collection to the friends he had made in Paris, Wright sold the work to World Publishing Company in March 1960 and eagerly awaited publication, but the collection did not reach the public until two months after his death.

"The Man Who Lived Underground," the most critically acclaimed work in *Eight Men,* brings to mind both Fyodor Dostoyevski's *Notes from Underground* (1864) and Victor Hugo's *Les Misérables* (1862). Wright, however, has gone a step beyond them and included all humanity in his underground community. Fred Daniels, a black man escaping from the police, who have wrongly accused him of murder, takes up residence in a sewer. Following a nightmarish experience during which time he sees images of death and decay around him and views people engaged in deceit and corruption through a crevice, he concludes that the underground where he resides—the sewer—is the actual world of the human heart, and the world above—the metaphysical sewer—is an area where people attempt to conceal the immense darkness of their souls. This emotional experience brings on a sense of guilt, and he rises to the street to announce his guilt to the world. First rejected by a church congregation, he is later mortally wounded by a policeman who exclaims: "You've got to shoot his kind. They'd wreck things."

The work has a black protagonist, but it transcends racial bounds. Its many themes of self-identity, the search for meaning in the world, the need for communication, and alienation are those which concern all mankind. Existentialist tenets—dread, terror, guilt, nausea—are also present, but Wright has successfully made them characteristics of Fred Daniels's personality, not just existentialist clichés, as often is the case in *The Outsider*. The excellent paradoxes, light and dark imagery, and other vivid, concrete details combine to make "The Man Who Lived Underground" a superior work of art. Ralph Ellison's *Invisible Man* (1952) incorporates some of the same structural devices and examines many of the same themes.

The other works in *Eight Men* show great variety. "The Man Who Was Almost a Man" details the struggles of Dave Saunders, who purchases a revolver to assure his manhood will be acknowledged. "Big Black Good Man," one of Wright's few humorous stories, develops the theme of black pride through the adventures of a black sailor. "The Man Who Saw the Flood" is an extended vignette which, like "Down by the Riverside," deals with a black tenant family that returns home after a devastating flood. "The Man Who Killed a Shadow" brings to mind *Native Son* in that its central character is a black man who inadvertently kills a white woman, a major difference being the black protagonist in the story is used as a symbol of libidinal abandon. "Man of All Work" is a delightful unproduced radio script about mistaken identity. "Man, Gawd Ain't Like That," a much more ambitious radio script, illustrates much of what Wright says in *Black Power* and *White Man, Listen!* "The Man Who Went to Chicago" is an autobiographical sketch.

The stories in *Eight Men* are also representative of the different stages of Wright's development. The ones he wrote in the 1930s ("The Man Who Saw the Flood" and "The Man Who Was Almost a Man") deal with southern workers; the stories of the 1940s ("The Man Who Lived Underground," "The Man Who Went to Chicago," and "The Man Who Killed a Shadow") employ an urban setting to depict blackness, invisibility, outsider or underground status; the stories of the 1950s ("Man of All Work," "Man, Gawd Ain't Like That," and "Big Black Good Man") celebrate a new kind of black nationalism, black virility as opposed to white flabbiness, and a proud awareness of African identity.

During 1959 and 1960, the last two years of his life, Wright was fighting amoebic dysentery, and by February 1960 he was constantly ill. On 19 March 1960, after a roundtable discussion on black theater organized by Claude Planson of the Théâtre des Nations, Wright announced to his friend and Dutch translator, Margrit de Sablonière, that he had returned to poetry. He told her, "During my illness I experimented with the Japanese form of poetry called haiku; I wrote some 4,000 of them and am now sifting them out to see if they are any good." Wright had borrowed the four volumes by R. H. Blyth on the art of haiku in order to learn the rules of its composition. He reduced the number of poems to eight hundred by mid April and sent the eighty-page manuscript to his friend and editor William Targ of World Publishing Company.

Targ's company rejected the poems, but the consolation of writing the haiku enabled Wright to live with illness and to endure the attacks he felt were multiplying against him. In February he had received an unfriendly letter from Sartre. The letter turned out to be a forgery, but it had already greatly hurt Wright. Wright concluded that no reply from either St. Clair Drake or Horace Clayton meant they did not want him to write a new preface for *Black Metropolis*. Wright even came to doubt the friendship of Chester Himes and to question his relationship with Dr. Victor Schwarzmann, his personal physician. His illness and his generally suspicious nature caused him to regard any changes in regular procedures or negative responses to his writing as parts of a general plot against him.

In June 1960 Wright recorded a series of discussions for French radio dealing primarily with his books and literary career but also with the racial situation in the United States and the world, specifically denouncing American policy in Africa. In late September, to cover extra expenses brought on by his daughter Julia's move from London to Paris to attend the Sorbonne, Wright wrote blurbs for record jackets for Nicole Barclay, director of the largest record company in Paris. In spite of his financial straits Wright refused to compromise his principles. He declined participation in a series of programs for Canadian radio because he suspected American control over the programs, and he rejected the proposal of the Congress for Cultural Freedom that he go to India to speak at a conference in memory of Leo Tolstoy for the same reason.

Still interested in literature, Wright offered to help Kyle Onstott get *Mandingo* (1957) published in France. His last display of explosive energy occurred on 8 November 1960 in his polemical lecture, "The Situation of the Black Artist and Intellectual in the United States," delivered to students and members of the American Church in Paris. Wright argued that American society reduced the most militant members of the black community to slaves whenever they wanted to question the racial status quo. He offered as proof the subversive attacks of the Communists against *Native Son* and the quarrels which James Baldwin and other authors sought with him.

On 26 November 1960 Wright talked enthusiastically about *Daddy Goodness* with Langston Hughes and gave him the manuscript. Two days later, on 28 November 1960, while waiting in the Eugene Gibez Clinic in Paris for extensive medical examinations, Wright died of a heart attack. He is buried in Pere Lachaise, Paris.

Richard Wright is undeniably one of the most important American writers of the twentieth century. His books have been translated into many languages, and millions throughout Asia, Africa, Europe, and the Middle East have read about the experiences of a Mississippi black boy. Through his "travel" books he brought the oppressed peoples of the Third World countries to the attention of the East and the West. Wright more than any other American author illustrates the premise that America's basic ills are those of racism. His significance as an interpreter of the racial problem in imaginative literature led Irving Howe to assert in "Black Boys and Native Sons" (1963) that after *Native Son* appeared, American culture was changed forever. The claim is perhaps excessive, but no black writer between Frederick Douglass and James Baldwin has offered so moving a testimony and delivered so scathing an indictment of America's racial dilemmas to so large an audience as has Richard Wright. Wright elevated the protest novel to a more highly respected art form that numerous other "native sons" have adopted. While some of his work is weak and unsuccessful–especially that completed within the last three years of his life–his best work will continue to attract readers. His three masterpieces–*Uncle Tom's Children, Native Son,* and *Black Boy*–are a crowning achievement for him and for American literature. They are enduring works of art, each of which transcends any one literary classification.

During the 1970s and 1980s scholars and the general public have shown increasing interest in Richard Wright. Critical essays have been written about his writing in prestigious journals. Richard Wright conferences have been held on university campuses from Mississippi to New Jersey. A new film version of *Native Son,* with a screenplay by Richard Wesley, was released in December 1986. Selected Wright novels are required reading in a growing number of American universities and colleges. *The Outsider, American Hunger,*

The Long Dream, and other long out-of-print Wright books have been reissued by Harper & Row. Several doctoral dissertations have been accepted, and plans are underway to release more of his unpublished work. Today more and more Americans are reading of Wright's life and problems as a sensitive, intelligent, black American. The rising interest in Wright suggests, happily, a wider understanding and acceptance of the literary importance of America's native son.

Bibliographies:

Charles T. Davis and Michel Fabre, *Richard Wright: A Primary Bibliography* (Boston: G. K. Hall, 1982).
　　The most complete, reliable bibliography of Wright's works.

Keneth Kinnamon, et al., *A Richard Wright Bibliography: Fifty Years of Criticism and Commentary: 1933-1982,* (Westport, Conn.: Greenwood Press, 1988).
　　Excellent complement to the above; reliable with extensive listings.

Biographies:

Constance Webb, *Richard Wright: A Biography* (New York: Putnam's, 1968).
　　Complete, solid biography. Contains a primary bibliography, which is useful if Davis and Fabre's is unavailable.

Robert Bone, *Richard Wright* (Minneapolis: University of Minnesota Press, 1969).
　　Defines Wright as a leader of the Chicago Renaissance movement of the 1930s and 1940s.

Michel Fabre, *The Unfinished Quest of Richard Wright* (New York: Morrow, 1973).
　　Considered the definitive Wright biography when it appeared in 1973, this account was later criticized for neglecting the writer's inner life and the importance of his Mississippi background.

Margaret Walker, *Richard Wright: Daemonic Genius: A Portrait of the Man, A Critical Look at His Work* (New York: Warner, 1988).
　　An in-depth, psychological approach, details motivations and influences. Good bibliographical essay.

References:

Houston Baker, ed., *Twentieth Century Interpretations of Native Son* (Englewood Cliffs, N.J.: Prentice Hall, 1972).
A collection of highly significant essays by distinguished international critics.

David Bakish, *Richard Wright* (New York: Ungar, 1973).
Excellent monograph on Wright's life and works. Includes primary bibliography.

Russell Carl Brignano, *Richard Wright: An Introduction to the Man and His Works* (Pittsburgh: University of Pittsburgh Press, 1970).
Examines Wright's career and writings in terms of Marxism, race relations, and non-American criticism.

Edward Berry Burgum, "The Art of Richard Wright's Short Stories," in his *The Novel and the World's Dilemma* (New York: Russell & Russell, 1963), pp. 241-259.
Using "Long Black Song" from *Uncle Tom's Children* as a focal point, Burgum argues that Wright successfully blends details and themes into superior works of art.

Michel Fabre, "Richard Wright: The Man Who Lived Underground," *Studies in the Novel*, 3 (Summer 1971): 165-189.
Rejects Dostoyevski's *Notes from Underground* as one of the sources of Wright's "The Man Who Lived Underground" and explains that the climax of Wright's work is the epiphany of artistic creation.

Donald Gibson, "Wright's Invisible Native Son," *American Quarterly*, 21, no. 4 (1969): 728-738.
Gibson maintains that Bigger Thomas becomes Wright's own invisible native son because too many readers fail to see him as a discrete entity, a particular person who struggles with the burdens of humanity.

Blyden Jackson, "Richard Wright in a Moment of Truth," *Southern University Journal*, 3 (Spring 1971): 3-17.
Discusses the lynching scene in "Big Boy Leaves Home" as a symbolic rite of castration and the complete story as a psychological and anthropological study of American racism.

Esther M. Jackson, "The American Negro and the Image of the Absurd," *Phylon*, 23 (March 1962): 259-260, 364-368.
Brilliantly argues that *Native Son*, like Ellison's *Invisible Man* and Faulkner's *Light in August*, may be read as a record of a dramatic encounter with fate in the climate of the absurd.

George Kent, "Richard Wright: Blackness and the Adventures of Western Culture," *CLA Journal*, 12 (June 1969): 322-343.
Using examples from *Uncle Tom's Children*, *Black Boy*, *Native Son*, and *Lawd Today*, Kent focuses on three sources of Wright's power: his double consciousness, his personal tension, and his dramatic articulation of black and white culture.

Keneth Kinnamon, *The Emergence of Richard Wright* (Urbana: University of Illinois Press, 1972).
A study of the life, literary career, and social milieu of Richard Wright from his birth through the publication of *Native Son*, with a glance in the final chapter at his withdrawal from the Communist party and the beginning of his expatriation.

Edward Margolies, *The Art of Richard Wright* (Carbondale: Southern Illinois University Press, 1969).
Discusses pertinent biographical data and evaluates Wright's nonfiction, short stories, and novels.

Harold T. McCarthy, "Richard Wright: The Expatriate as Native Son," *American Literature*, 44 (March 1972): 97-117.
Forcefully argues that Wright did not learn how to cope as an artist with his experiences of American life until he placed his sense of European life in an American perspective.

John M. Reilly, *Richard Wright: The Critical Reception* (New York: Burt Franklin, 1978).
Well-chosen periodical reviews of Wright's entire output. Introduction is a useful summary of Wright's career.

Kingsley Widmer, "Black Existentialism: Richard Wright," *Wisconsin Studies in Contemporary Literature*, 1, no. 3 (1960): 13-21.

Maintains that Wright's most successful fiction, "The Man Who Lived Underground," is the preoccupying moral drama focusing almost all of Wright's works.

Papers:

The most extensive collection of Wright's papers is in the Richard Wright Archive in the Beinecke Rare Book and Manuscript Library at Yale University. One of the manuscripts of *Black Power* is at Northwestern University. Eighteen letters by Wright are held at Kent State University. Eight of these letters were published (1968) in an unauthorized edition. Rare magazines and newspapers that contain some of Wright's writings are housed in the Schomburg Collection of the New York Public Library, the American Library in Paris, and the Harvard University libraries.

Contributors

Richard Astro...*Northeastern University*
Charles W. Bassett...*Colby College*
William A. Bloodworth...*East Carolina University*
Jewel Spears Brooker ....*Eckerd College*
Edward D. Clark...*North Carolina State University*
Stephen Cummings...*University of Western Ontario*
Leslie Field ....*Purdue University*
Wallace Fowlie ....*Duke University*
George H. Jensen ....*Chicago, Illinois*
Carol Johnston...*Clemson University*
A. S. Knowles, Jr. ....*North Carolina State University*
Richard Layman ....*Columbia, South Carolina*
Joseph Miller ....*Vancouver, British Columbia*
R. Baxter Miller...*University of Tennessee*
Lisa Nanney...*Emory University*
Evelyn Nettles ....*University of Tennessee*
Louis Owens...*University of New Mexico*
Jenny Penberthy...*Simon Frazer University*
Elizabeth Phillips ....*Wake Forest University*
Peter A. Scholl ....*Luther College*
Michael D. Senecal ....*Columbia, South Carolina*
Paul Skenazy ....*University of California*
Linda Wagner-Martin ....*University of North Carolina, Chapel Hill*
Daniel Walden...*Pennsylvania State University*